The World Atlas of Exploration

The
World

Atlas of Exploration

by Eric Newby

Introduction by Sir Vivian Fuchs

CRESCENT BOOKS

New York

Library of Congress Cataloging in Publication Data
Newby, Eric.
    World atlas of exploration.
    Bibliography: p.
    Includes index.
    1. Discoveries (in geography)—History. 2. Explorers.
I. Title.
G80.N43   1985   910.0   84–29201
ISBN 0-517-471523

Publisher Bruce Marshall   **Art director** John Bigg

Project editor Victor Stevenson   **Art editor** Nick Eddison
Deputy editor Daphne Wood   **Design assistant** Malcolm Gipson
Editorial Yvonne McFarlane,   **Picture research** Jackie Webber
Sue Farr, Helen Varley   **Production** Elsie Day

Maps Anthony Nelthorpe, Arka Cartographics Limited

The publishers have received much valuable assistance from a number of
museums and specialist libraries and wish to record their gratitude for this help.
Prominent among them were the National Maritime Museum, Greenwich,
London; Royal Geographical Society, London; Nederlandsch Historisch
Scheepvaart Museum, Amsterdam; Explorers' Club, New York; Smithsonian
Institution, Washington DC; National Geographical Society, Washington DC;
Geografisk Institutt, Oslo; Geographical Society of the USSR, Leningrad; Det
Kongelige Danske Geografiske Selskab, Copenhagen; Real Sociedad Geografica,
Madrid; Geographical Institute of the Academy of Science of the USSR,
Moscow; Institute of Geography of Siberia and the Far East SB AS USSR, Irkutsk;
The American Museum in Britain, Bath; Association de Géographes Français,
Paris; Svenska Sallskapet for Anthropologi och Geografi, Geografiska Institutet,
Stockholm; Museo da Marinha, Lisbon.

Contents

The World Atlas of Exploration
is the story of a 4,000-year odyssey.
It traces chronologically man's exploration
of his world—from the tentative journeys of
the mercenary, inquisitive traders of the eastern
Mediterranean to the maritime adventures of the
Renaissance; from the collisions between old cultures
and new empire builders to the giants of modern discovery,
exploring the continents sketched in outline by their forebears. It is a journey through history in the company of heroes

The secrets of the world

EVERY CHILD is an "explorer" at birth, but as the years pass we are all conditioned by our environment to an appropriate way of life; gradually the early urge "to discover" is channelled and to some extent repressed. Yet despite their circumstances, and sometimes because of them, a few people retain their initial sense of curiosity, which drives them on to a search for satisfaction. Throughout history mankind has benefited from those restless urges of the few, for step by step they have revealed to us the unknown.

At first it was the need for food and the stresses imposed by climate which provided the main driving force; then competition for available resources added pressures, compelling succeeding generations to look farther afield for new hunting grounds, suitable habitats and, as man learnt the use of tools, sources of materials from which to make them. As civilization developed, its needs increased and always it was those with foresight, imagination, determination and curiosity who led— not necessarily as the head men of communities, but by advancing knowledge and showing the way. Yet the essential need for stability in any community produces a resistance to change, and this itself provides a filter which allows only a few to test the product of their imagination in practice. To overcome ob-

struction, inertia, even prejudice, requires determination to persuade and cajole authority into supporting an idea. This itself is a test of the quality of an individual, and his suitability to undertake the difficult, perhaps dangerous, task which he proposes, but which to others may seem both expensive and unprofitable.

Today, when almost every coast or mountain in the world is mapped, exploration has become the perquisite of the scientist, who seeks to discover, in ever greater detail, explanations for the nature of the globe on which we live. This too is curiosity and provides valuable, if abstruse, knowledge to the benefit of our sophisticated society. In days of classical exploration, when men sought new lands and unknown peoples, the reasons were simpler but no less important to the advancement of a nation. For the early explorers their goals were the discovery of new lands to colonize, new sources of gold or spices and, in the case of Christians at least, the propagation of the gospel. There were also, of course, the personal rewards of wealth and position, which success frequently brought to the pioneer.

Yet it was often just the idea that was the mainspring of a venture; gold and the gospel were but selling points with which to gain

the necessary ships and men. Christopher Columbus had such an idea. When a young man, he took to the sea and later wrote, "I went sailing upon the sea and have continued to this day, which very occupation inclines all who follow it to wish to learn the secrets of the world." Certainly he pursued his vocation with great dedication, and once he had conceived the idea of sailing westwards to the Indies across the Atlantic, he spent years in studying the available writings and in seeking support for his venture. He even went so far as to persuade himself that the world was smaller than the philosophers of his day believed, for had he accepted their views, the distance across the ocean would have been palpably too great for the small ships available. He was lucky that in fact America did exist! To his dying day he persisted in saying that he had reached the Indies.

Not many of the great explorers went to these lengths of prevarication, even deceit, but all shared with Columbus curiosity, faith in their ideas and determination to overcome all obstacles. Yet one may ask whether these characteristics were in themselves sufficient to drive men to the feats of daring which were achieved both at sea and on land, usually in the face of expected or known dangers and privations. Surely they were also

conditioned by a sense of achievement in overcoming the difficulties they faced, and of wonder at every new revelation, be it land or mountain range, strange peoples or unknown animals. To overcome the challenge, to prove that it could be done—this was their satisfaction.

Since such men set out of their own free will, it may be inappropriate to have too much sympathy with their misfortunes, but, by the same token, our admiration may be the greater. He who enters knowingly upon a perilous course is not necessarily foolhardy, and may be thought to show courage beyond that of others to whom danger comes without forethought. So we may look back with astonishment at what they accomplished, in small ships with only primitive methods of navigation, or wandering ill-equipped across inhospitable lands where every native was a potential enemy. In the perspective of our present social standards we criticize much in their behaviour. They were often cruel to strangers, and almost without exception they lacked sympathetic understanding of their own men. But their customs fitted the times, it was not possible for them to anticipate by centuries the humane ideas of the present day. For them rigid, ruthless discipline was essential, often for survival and always in

order to control the ignorant waywardness of those who served them. Similarly, the impact of a relatively sophisticated people upon the simple, sometimes treacherous communities they encountered, demanded more understanding than either side had yet acquired. So fear was the weapon used to solve the social problems of the day—it also undoubtedly helped towards success. Had it been otherwise, not many would have returned.

Some nations, some men carried these measures to extremes—this was recognized even then. On the other hand, there were also men like Magellan, who, though he would quell a mutiny decisively enough, was also sympathetic to his men and treated native peoples with unusual consideration and respect. It is ironical that on the one occasion when he departed from this attitude, in trying to impose Christianity by force of arms, he lost his life.

Thus, through the ages, the behaviour of explorers has changed in keeping with the period in which they lived, but their urge "to discover" has remained based on characteristics common to them all. As we learn of their exploits and salute their achievements, we can feel proud that such men have lived.

The explosion of exploration

The focal point of the story of the world's exploration is Europe—or, more precisely, the Mediterranean Sea. What cultures there existed beyond this region, the birthplace of western civilization, had their own "worlds" and, in the course of natural migration, may have put out feelers beyond them; but knowledge of the world as it is, the size of its oceans, the distribution of its land masses and their shapes, owes almost everything to the curiosity and drive of the peoples living along the margins of the Mediterranean. The world projection on this page is unconventional. It shows all the world's land masses, its oceans and both North and South Poles, with what can be called the "epicentre" of the explosion in the central Mediterranean—a calm, landlocked "training ground" for the earliest of the navigators

The colour key at the foot of the page, corresponding with the colours on the map, indicates the stages of exploration achieved across 4,000 years, from the early, pre-Christian examination of neighbouring countries and coastlines by Mediterranean traders, to the 20th century—a century which is not yet complete, yet one in which western man has taken not the least significant stride of all in exploration; into space, and to the Moon
In terms of the time man has existed on Earth, the story of exploration is not much more than a fraction. It has, however, been one of growing momentum, with few checks of any length. At each stage, man's knowledge of the conditions facing him was assisted by a growing technology—particularly the written word, and improved map-making

The late Middle Ages showed a slight shift of the "epicentre" from the central and eastern Mediterranean to the west, as a result of historical pressures. There came to the forefront the Atlantic maritime peoples who, in the space of a few decades in the 15th and 16th centuries proved conclusively what the academics of earlier centuries had deduced —that there was a great continent beyond the western ocean, and that by sailing in one direction it was possible to arrive back at the starting point. The world was indeed round and Magellan and his men had proved it. Within a couple of centuries of that time, knowledge of the world as it really is took shape. There was left only the detailed knowledge of continental interiors, and the one, lost, frozen continent of Antarctica

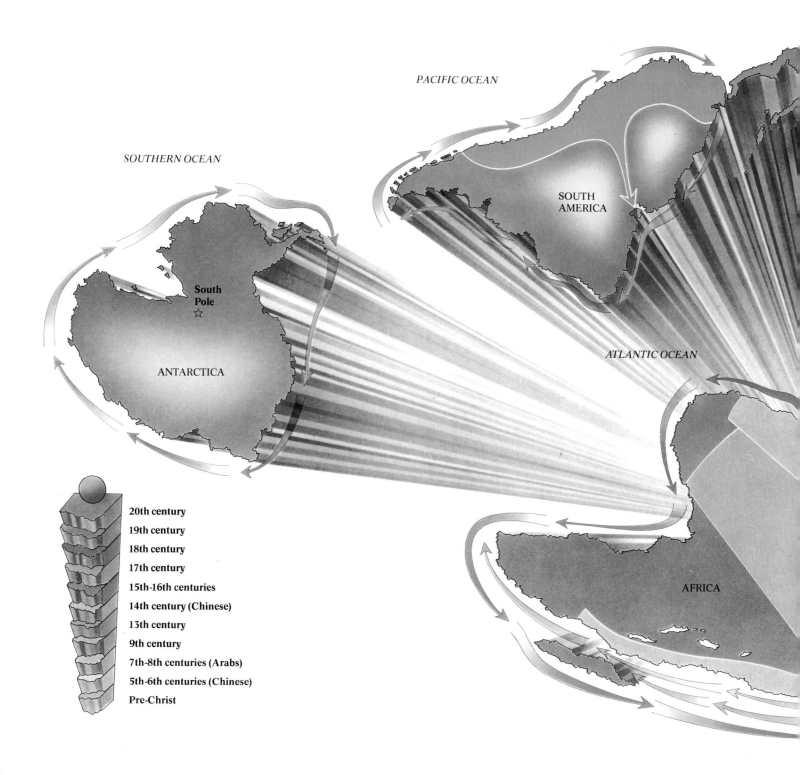

PACIFIC OCEAN

SOUTHERN OCEAN

SOUTH AMERICA

South Pole
☆

ATLANTIC OCEAN

ANTARCTICA

AFRICA

20th century

19th century

18th century

17th century

15th-16th centuries

14th century (Chinese)

13th century

9th century

7th-8th centuries (Arabs)

5th-6th centuries (Chinese)

Pre-Christ

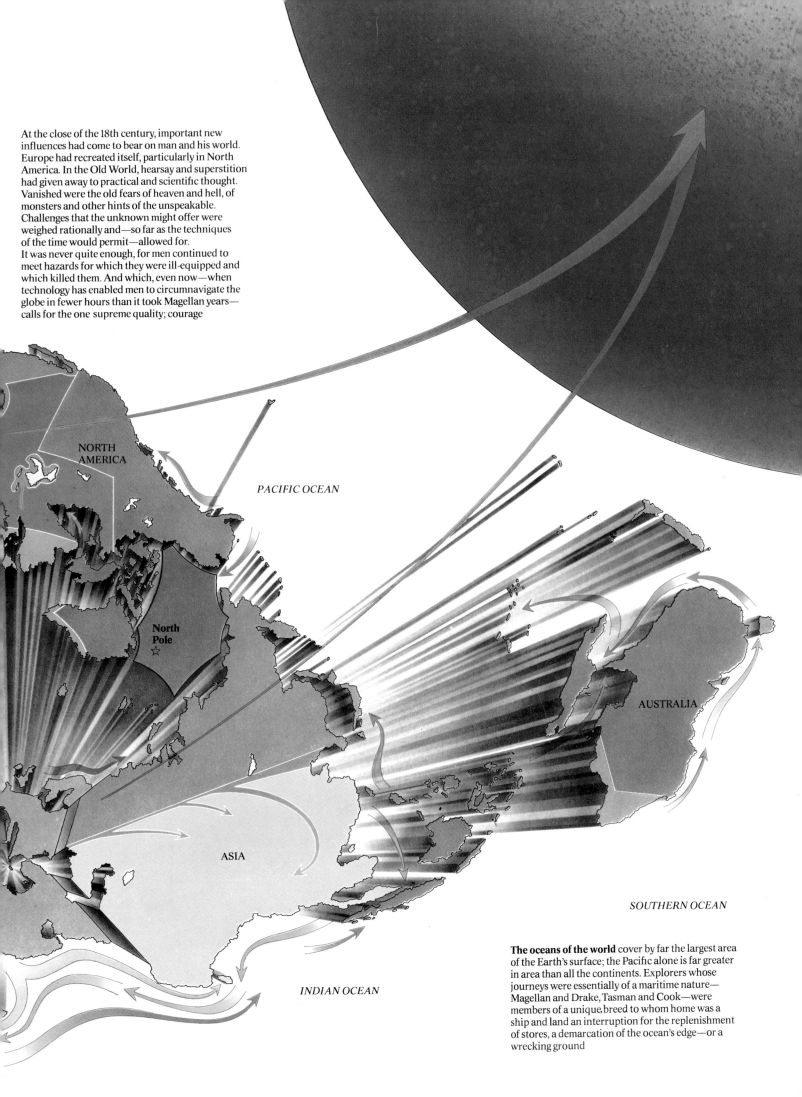

At the close of the 18th century, important new influences had come to bear on man and his world. Europe had recreated itself, particularly in North America. In the Old World, hearsay and superstition had given away to practical and scientific thought. Vanished were the old fears of heaven and hell, of monsters and other hints of the unspeakable. Challenges that the unknown might offer were weighed rationally and—so far as the techniques of the time would permit—allowed for.
It was never quite enough, for men continued to meet hazards for which they were ill-equipped and which killed them. And which, even now—when technology has enabled men to circumnavigate the globe in fewer hours than it took Magellan years—calls for the one supreme quality; courage

NORTH AMERICA

PACIFIC OCEAN

North Pole

ASIA

AUSTRALIA

SOUTHERN OCEAN

INDIAN OCEAN

The oceans of the world cover by far the largest area of the Earth's surface; the Pacific alone is far greater in area than all the continents. Explorers whose journeys were essentially of a maritime nature—Magellan and Drake, Tasman and Cook—were members of a unique breed to whom home was a ship and land an interruption for the replenishment of stores, a demarcation of the ocean's edge—or a wrecking ground

A motive to move

"High up in the North in the land called Svithjod, there stands a rock. It is a hundred miles high and a hundred miles wide. Once every thousand years a little bird comes to this rock to sharpen its beak.

"When the rock is worn away, then a single day of eternity will have gone by."

IN HIS BOOK, *The Story of Mankind*, the Dutch writer Hendrick Van Loon went on to express in visual terms the length of time during which life had existed on Earth by drawing a line four and a half inches long. Below it he drew another line, a dash one-eighth of an inch long, which was the length of time "during which man (or a creature more or less resembling man) has lived upon it".

The book was written for young people; but it is only by such simplifications that human beings of any age can apprehend the immensity of time, the brevity of life on Earth and what a small part of it man's tenure has been.

How much more brief is the period of which we have any record of his activities in the form of rudimentary artefacts, which he made with the aid of his hands—those forefeet which he adapted in such a remarkable fashion once he had learned to stand upright on his hind ones. How much shorter, only about 6,000 years, is the period of which we have any coherent visual or written record of his activities. For the rest only mute bones testify to his existence.

The story of man the hunter is one of continual adaptation to an almost always hostile environment. What impelled him to travel were probably the same reasons that still cause the lesser animals to migrate. The exhaustion of game and other foods due to over-killing, over-cropping and the changing seasons; natural cataclysms and disasters, such as earthquakes and forest fires; and, in the long term, changes in the Earth's climate. When he began to make weapons of stone, about 50,000 years ago, his capacity to kill was vastly increased and the need to find new hunting grounds became urgent. His tenacity of purpose, powers of reasoning and imagination, which continued to increase in the face of difficulty and disaster, enabled him to survive the four great ice ages which, in the space of a million years, covered great tracts of the Northern Hemisphere with enormous sheets of ice, altering its physiognomy. His retreat before them may have been the occasion of the first mass migrations. His crossing of the land bridge between Asia and America about 20,000 years ago, during the last Ice Age, was made possible, it is thought, by the shallowness of the sea. When the ice melted

and the water rose the bridge was submerged and the continents were separated.

Whatever the reasons for man's peregrinations there would soon be few regions of the Earth where a human footprint was unknown: from the west coast of Greenland, high above the Arctic Circle in the Northern Hemisphere, to as far south as Tierra del Fuego, beyond the Magellan Strait. The only continent where no evidence of human occupation has so far been found has been Antarctica; yet even there, on an island close to the Antarctic Peninsula—one of the visible summits of a land bridge that may have linked South America with the southern continent—mysterious spherical stone artefacts were discovered in the 19th century.

It is for this reason—the astonishing ubiquity of man on the face of the Earth (even in the heart of the 250,000-square-mile Rub'al Khali in Arabia, "The Abode of Emptiness", the 20th-century explorers Bertram Thomas and Wilfred Thesiger found that there were men ready to kill them)—that in the entire history of exploration there are comparatively few instances that can be given of man discovering virgin territories which were not already known or inhabited. The assumption, for instance, that the interior of Africa was "discovered" by members of the nations of the West is in a sense as absurd as a claim by an inhabitant of the Congo to have "discovered" New York because he was the first to have travelled there. When Livingstone found what he named the Victoria Falls, "the most wonderful sight I have witnessed in Africa", he learned from the indigenous inhabitants that they already had a name for it, *Mosiottatunya*, "The Smoke that Thunders", by which it is still known to the present inhabitants of Zambia, who consider the name of a foreign and long-dead monarch an affront.

"Westerners", Henri Cordier wrote in his *Histoire Générale de la Chine*, "have singularly narrowed the history of the world in grouping the little that they knew of the human race around the peoples of Israel, Greece and Rome. Thus they have ignored all those travellers and explorers who in their ships ploughed to the China Sea and the Indian Ocean, or rode across the immensities of Central Asia to the Persian Gulf."

Although Western man has tended to see the opening-up of the world as a pre-eminently occidental achievement, in his search for what are to him new lands, he has invariably come across other civilizations already long-established there. When, in 1492 BC, the Egyptian Queen Hatshepsut despatched an expedition to the mysterious land of Punt to obtain myrrh trees to embellish the great mausoleum and temple at Deir el-Bahri, its

members were greeted by people of a high order of civilization who fully appreciated the value of gold, silver, ivory and leopard skins, and very probably of the myrrh tree also. When the Portuguese explorer Vasco da Gama "discovered" the ports on the east coast of Africa in 1498, he found that they were already populated by Arabs, Persians and various mixtures compounded with the blood of the indigenous inhabitants, and that Moorish ships were carrying on a brisk trade with India and beyond, laden with gold and silver, which were exchanged for cloves, peppers and ginger, "as also quantities of pearls, jewels, and rubies, all of which articles are used by the people of this country". When da Gama reached India he found that the Moors had preceded him there and enjoyed a monopoly of trade with the inhabitants. Even the Moors had been anticipated by the Chinese, who had already traded with India and the coast of Africa from Somaliland and Madagascar between the 9th and 12th centuries.

Capital of the Great Khan

The instances are innumerable. When Marco Polo, "the first traveller to trace a route across the whole longitude of Asia, naming and describing kingdom after kingdom which he had seen with his own eyes", reached Khan-balek, the capital of the Great Khan on the site of present-day Peking, he found it to be a city of splendour with walls 24 miles in circumference, which contained eight vast palaces. In one of them there was a banqueting hall that could seat 6,000 persons (the same number that can be accommodated in the banqueting hall of the present Communist Great Hall of the People). When Cortes and his Conquistadors reached Tenochtitlán, the Aztec capital, on the present site of Mexico City, they found a remarkable people whose members had accomplished stupendous works of engineering without the aid of metal tools, beasts of burden or the use of the wheel, and had a civilization even more bloodthirsty than their own. When Pizarro set out to take the great Inca city of Cuzco, which had 250,000 inhabitants, he and his men travelled to it along a magnificent trunk road hundreds of miles long, thousands of feet above the sea in the high sierras, a road which crossed great chasms by means of highly sophisticated suspension bridges. Even that most legendary of legendary cities, Timbuktu, had been flourishing for centuries before the first foreign traveller, the indefatigable Arab Ibn Battuta, set foot in it. The city was to remain a mystery to European man for another 500 years, and it was not until 1826, when it had long been in decline, that the first European, Alexander Laing, succeeded in reaching it. We cannot say that Laing "discovered" Timbuktu, nor for that matter that Ibn Battuta did so.

What, in recorded time, have been the principal motives which inspired men to risk their lives in search of the unknown? Trade, especially to satisfy the demand for luxurious and exotic merchandise; the need to found colonies to relieve overcrowding at home or else to escape from invading peoples; sheer curiosity (evinced at a surprisingly early date); the despatch of missions and embassies to obtain some favourable alliance; the desire to convert the heathen, which often went hand in hand with a policy of national aggrandizement; the study of geography; the desire for gold and silver; the urge to find alternative routes from Europe to the East that engrossed mankind for centuries; the trade in slaves; the belief in the existence of Terra Australis, a great southern continent; scientific enquiry and reconnaissance. In the 20th century a new motive became apparent —exploration for its own sake, sometimes inspired by a desire for personal or national glory, or a mixture of the two. To be the first to reach the Poles; to be the first to climb the highest mountain in the world, "because it is there". This motive, too, inspired to some extent the race to be first in space, first on the Moon.

If it all sounds a little dry, the records left by the explorers themselves are not. They cover the whole range of human experience: of suffering and endurance, exultation, splendour and misery, abominable cruelty to the people they encountered and sometimes self-sacrifice. The temptation was to go on beyond human limits, beyond the possibility of return, which often led them to "the undiscovered country from whose bourne no traveller returns". Many failed to take the advice tendered to Alexander the Great on the banks of the river Jhelum, when he proposed to extend his conquests and explorations to the entire world. "Sir," said Coenus, "if there is one thing above all others that a successful man should know, it is *when to stop*."

Bravery is the thread that binds them. When the monk Rubruck reached the camp of the Tartar Khan, Mangu, after a journey of three and a half months from the Volga in the 13th century, he was told by the great ruler, "Fear not." Rubruck replied: "If I had been afraid I would not have come."

Henry de Tonty, prisoner of the Iroquois on the shore of Lake Michigan, one of whom "plunged a knife into my breast, wounding a rib near the heart . . .", had "a man behind me with a knife in his hand, who every now and then lifted up my hair. They were divided in opinion. Tegantouki, chief of the Isonoutouan desired to have me burnt. Agoasto, chief

of the Onnoutagues wished to have me set at liberty as a friend of M. de la Salle, and he carried his point."

Of another sort was the 19th-century traveller Burckhardt, of whom it was written: "He was of that small company of profoundly wise and foreseeing travellers who go with ease where others may not even go with pain, and knowing no stirring moments in a land wherein to some every hour brings peril. He testifies that he was never more at peace than in Mecca, and nowhere in Arabia suffered any hap more inconvenient than falls to the ordinary lot of wayfarers and pilgrims in the Hijaz."

It is the sea and the reaching of land that have inspired what are perhaps the most memorable descriptions. Coming ashore on an island of the New World after a perilous voyage at the beginning of the 11th century, the Viking crew of Leif, son of Erik the Red, found, to their great delight, "dew on the grass, and the first thing they did was to get some of it on their hands and put it to their lips, and to some of them it seemed the sweetest thing they had ever tasted". Anchored off Tahiti in 1767, Louis Antoine, Comte de Bougainville, wrote of the moment when the inhabitants first came out to the ship in their canoes "crying 'tayo' which means friend. . . . They pressed us to choose a woman and to come on shore with her. . . . It was very difficult to keep at their work four hundred young French sailors who had seen no woman for six months."

Stinking food

Such moments of happiness were rare for the early sailors. On Magellan's voyage to the Pacific in 1609 they were "three months and twenty days without taking in provisions, and we only ate old biscuit reduced to powder, and stinking from the dirt which the rats had made on it . . . and we drank water that was yellow and stinking. We also ate the ox hides which were under the main yard . . . also the sawdust of wood, and rats that cost half a ducat each . . . and the upper and lower gums of most of our men grew so much that they could not eat [due to scurvy] . . . and in this way nineteen died . . . besides twenty-five or thirty fell ill of divers sicknesses, both in the arms and legs and other places."

In such ships the great gales of high latitudes were an awesome experience. Of Drake's ship in the strait between Cape Horn and the South Shetlands it was written that it was driven back again "into 55 deg. towards the pole Antarctic, as a pelican alone in wilderness . . . [with] the most mad seas; the lee shores; the dangerous rocks; the contrary and most intolerable winds; the most impossible passage out. . . ."

John Davis's description, in 1586, of the mouth of the Hudson Strait was equally evocative: ". . . eight or nine great races, currents or overfalls, loathsomely crying like the rage of waters under London Bridge. . . . [The next day] coming close by a foreland or great cape, we fell into a mighty race, where an island of ice was carried by the force of the current as fast as the bark could sail with lum [light] winds . . . where at our great admiration we saw the sea falling down into the gulf with a mighty overfall, and roaring, and with divers circular motions like whirlpools."

The Antarctic explorer Shackleton, sailing with three companions in a 20-foot open boat through the stormiest seas in the world from Elephant Island to South Georgia in search of help for his ship's crew, gives a graphic description. "At midnight I was at the tiller and suddenly noticed a line of clear sky between the south and south-west. I called to the other men that the sky was clearing, and then a moment later I realised that what I had seen was not a rift in the clouds but the white crest of an enormous wave. During twenty-six years' experience of the ocean in all its moods I had not encountered a wave so gigantic. It was a mighty upheaval of the ocean, a thing apart from the big white-capped seas that had been our tireless enemies for many days. I shouted, 'For God's sake hold on! It's got us.' Then came a moment of suspense that seemed drawn out for hours. White surged the foam of the breaking sea around us. We felt our boat lifted and flung forward like a cork in breaking surf. We were in a seething chaos of tortured water; but somehow the boat lived through it, half full of water, sagging to the dead weight and shuddering under the blow. . . ."

Hunger and thirst to the last extremity were a common experience of explorers, whether on land or sea. When the Australian explorer Ernest Giles walked out of the great Gibson Desert in 1873, having lost his companion in the sands, he carried a 45-pound keg of water on his shoulders for 60 miles and, at the end of the stage, finding a small, dying wallaby weighing not more than two pounds, in his own terrible words "the instant I saw it I pounced upon it and ate it, living, raw, dying —fur, skin, bones, skull and all". When Major Egerton Walker attempted to cross the continent from Alice Springs to the Indian Ocean that same year in drought conditions with 17 camels, the animals began to collapse and die one by one. Those that did were either cut up and jerked (dried) or eaten on the spot. "No shred was passed over. Head, feet, hide, tail all went into the boiling pot. . . . The tough, thick hide was cut up and parboiled. The coarse hair was then scraped off with a knife and the leather-like substance replaced in the pot and stewed until it became like the inside

A motive to move

of a carpenter's glue pot, both to the taste and the smell. . . ." In a desperate bid to assuage the tortures of thirst, another Australian explorer, Alexander Forrest, drank the blood of a dead hawk. Not surprisingly, this dire measure failed.

But in spite of all the danger, suffering, trials and tribulations it was worth it, even if individual discoveries, such as that made by the Venetian navigator Cadamosto, were only steps—often accidental—on the long road to knowledge of the world. Cadamosto was striving to find a way to the Indies when he became the first Westerner to observe the Southern Cross, albeit a rather disappointing constellation, off the coast of West Africa in 1455. "During our stay at the mouth of the river we only saw the Pole Star once; and then it sank so low that it seemed to touch the sea, apparently standing only one-third of a spear-shaft above the water. There we also saw six large and wonderfully bright stars. We measured them with the compass. We believed them to be the Great Bear of the Southern Hemisphere." It was a heartening sight, but hardly the longed-for goal. Twenty-seven years passed before Diogo Cão finally succeeded in sailing south of the Equator.

Peary reached the North Pole, realizing his life's ambition, and then pushed on for five miles with two Eskimo companions, from which point he was looking southwards down the other side of the world. "East, west and north had disappeared for us," he wrote. "Only one direction remained, and that was south. Every breeze which could possibly blow upon us, no matter from what point of the horizon, must be a south wind. Where we were, one day and one night constituted a year, a hundred such days and nights constituted a century. Had we stood in that spot during the six months of the Arctic winter night we should have seen every star in the northern hemisphere circling the sky at the same distance from the horizon, with Polaris practically in the zenith."

Beneath the Pole in the Arctic Ocean Peary found no bottom in 1,500 fathoms. The year was 1908. Fifty-two years later Jacques Piccard and Don Walsh sank in the Bathyscaphe *Trieste* to the floor of the world at 35,000 feet in the Marianas Trench. "Like a free balloon on a windless day, indifferent to the almost 200,000 tons of water pressing on the cabin from all sides, balanced to within an ounce or so on its wire guide ropes, slowly, surely, in the name of science and humanity, the *Trieste* took possession of the abyss, the last extreme on our earth that remained to be conquered.

"And to demonstrate well all the significance of this dive, nature would have it that the *Trieste* come down on the bottom a few feet from a fish, a true fish, joined in its unknown world by this monster of steel and gasoline and a powerful beam of light.

"Slowly the fish, a species of sole about a foot and a half long, drifted off through the ooze."

Perhaps the greatest experience reserved for man, apart from Divine revelation, has been to gaze down on the planet that was his birthplace and see it for the first time as a whole. To make this possible more money was expended in one year of interplanetary space exploration than the entire budget of oceanographical exploration since 1900.

Eugene Cernan, one of the three men in Gemini 9, one of the space-craft used to produce the first colour photographic survey of the Earth, described how, "without blinking an eye I could see the high Andes, the Pacific Ocean, the great Altiplano with a jewel-like Lake Titicaca, the rain-forest of the Amazon basin and the Chaco plains on down our orbital path. The broad western bulge of Africa was the most interesting area of the world to see from space. Its dry desolate terrain was nearly always free of clouds, and it was a delight to photograph because there was so little haze to dim its beauty. The tiny Indian subcontinent was especially fascinating, representing the lives of 500 million people whose lives were dependent upon the scattered pre-monsoon cloud cover so clearly visible. Also conspicuous were individual houses in haze-free Nepal, the wake of a ship on the Brahmaputra, an oil refinery near Perth, Australia, and numerous other phenomena such as the Four Corners power plant in New Mexico, whose smoke emission was detectable from 1,000 km out in space, submarines, individual city streets, blast furnaces and a wealth of hurricanes, storms, cyclones, as well as the launch facilities at Cape Kennedy. . . ." In a matter of seconds lands were traversed which took the 14th-century Arab explorer Ibn Battuta (who is estimated to have covered 75,000 miles, without taking into account detours) 30 years of his life.

What were their emotions, these travellers in space? "I saw the brevity of man's lifespan, the insignificance of his problems and an earth so vast, so beautiful, so hospitable even in its most rugged manifestation, so mysterious," said John Young of Apollo 16. "I completely lost my identity as an American astronaut," wrote Rusty Schweickart after his space-walk 125 miles above the Earth. "I felt part of everyone and everything sweeping below me."

Finally the words of cosmonaut Leonov, the first man to walk in space. "When I looked at the capsule", he said, "it appeared to be hanging above the cosmic abyss. The stars appeared motionless, the sun sewn on to

Explorers' worlds: the capital of the Incas (opposite) reached by the Conqistadors in the 16th century. The world from space (above) seen by astronauts

black velvet. The only thing that moved was the Earth."

In one way nothing has changed. Man, with all his efforts, is still poised on the edge of the unknown. We are very dependent on one another and we are not masters of our destiny —a fact of which the early mariners, venturing forth in their fragile vessels, were all too conscious. However great their courage or consummate their skill as pilots and navigators, the early explorers felt themselves at the mercy of a higher power. The Arab captain of a storm-tossed ship could give only the following words of comfort to a terror-stricken passenger: "You must know, that travellers and merchants have to put up with terrible dangers, compared with which these experiences are pleasant and agreeable; but we who are members of the company of pilots are under oath and covenant not to let a vessel perish so long as there is anything left of it and the decree of fate has not fallen upon it; we who belong to the company of ships' pilots never go on board a vessel without linking our own life and fate to it; so long as it is safe, we live; but if it perishes, we die with it; so have patience and commend yourself to the Lord of the wind and of the sea, who disposes of men's lives as He will."

The same fatalistic resignation, the same ultimate trust in a Divine providence, was echoed some 600 years later by the Dutch explorer Willem Barents. Returning in an open boat from the Arctic, where he and his crew had survived a grim winter in high latitudes, the first explorers to do so, the dying Barents asked for a drink.

In the words of one of his men: "He had no sooner drunk but he was taken with so sudden a qualm that he turned his eyes in his head and died presently. The death of William Barents put us in no small discomfort, as being the chief guide and only pilot on whom we reposed ourselves next under God; but we could not strive against God, and therefore we must of force be content."

Monks, myths and magic lands

"THERE ARE THREE STAGES in the popular attitude towards a great discovery: first men doubt its existence, next they deny its importance and finally they give the credit to someone else."

History allows some exceptions to this rule of one of the greatest of explorers, the German Baron Alexander von Humboldt. But the proud claims of a nation for one of its sons is often the cause of the derision of another. New evidence, however much it is supported by scientific research, is greeted with scepticism. Traditional beliefs die hard and it is expensive to change the names of public squares and streets, the more so to celebrate someone else's hero.

In Lisbon—the capital of a country that needs to look to no false heroes to claim its place in the story of discovery and exploration—João Vaz Corte Real is celebrated as the man who discovered America decades before Columbus made his historic landfall in the Bahamas. Now there is conclusive evidence that both men were preceded to the New World by a people who had developed their own way of life thousands of miles away from the main centres of European knowledge and speculation—the Vikings.

Even this is not enough. Claims can be made for many other folk heroes, some with a considerable amount of circumstantial evidence to support them. Belief is suspended at the thought of vessels of the kind still used in Ireland making a passage across the North Atlantic, and returning safely. And yet, to test scientific theories, as well as for fun—in single-handed yacht races—modern man has made similar journeys in vessels little more substantial than the early craft (but, of course, with an up-to-date knowledge of weather conditions and navigational aids).

It is perhaps in the nature of America, a huge continent to which no path (except in prehistory, across the Bering Strait) nor shoreline leads, and reached only in historical times across a trackless ocean, to have created more myths and speculation than any other part of the world, before it was finally found. Africa slept, but was known to be there by the ancients, who had examined much of its coast and, tentatively, parts of its nearer hinterland; and since European civilization had taken form there had been links with another world, the Asiatic Orient, for a land route, however forbidding, does not offer the same barriers to knowledge of what lies beyond it as does the sea.

Man's inability physically to cross the ocean to the west—that "green sea of darkness" of the Arabs—was no bar to his imagination. Tens of centuries before the authenticated journeys of the Middle Ages there existed in the minds of men some belief in a great continent, counterbalancing the world of which they had real knowledge. That there was in fact a real link was far beyond the compass of their knowledge, for the distant continent had been populated, time out of mind, by people from their known, old world. This had happened long before written records; no one remembered the going of the migrants any more than the migrants would have thought of themselves as having left one "world" for another. America, in fact, was populated by distant relatives with whom all contact had been lost.

For almost every nation with a seagoing tradition, particularly those with a seaboard facing the Atlantic ocean, claims have been made for the discovery of America—African, as well as European and Mediterranean. Such are the currents and winds of the Atlantic that, at the right time of the year, anything that floats will make a passage from one continent to the other, and accidental voyages to America cannot be ruled out—just as a migrant wading bird, common to the North American seaboard, will be gusted off course by winds that take it to Europe and into the sight of an ornithologist on the lookout for vagrant species. In this way, it is suggested, Eskimoes in their kayaks may have reached the northern shores of Scotland.

The holy men

Among the earliest of voyages for which scepticism and belief are fairly evenly balanced are those of the Irish monks led by St Brendan, or Brandon, in which, it is suggested, a group of chanting religious found their way from Ireland to the Bahamas and back, in the 6th century. There is no doubt that, sustained by faith as well as by seamanship, they made astonishing passages in waters that for much of the year are as unfriendly as any to be found in the world—the island-studded seas between the north of the British mainland and Iceland, which the seafaring Norsemen were later to reach and settle.

Christianity had come to Ireland some time before in the form of a young Romano–Briton, Succat, or Patrick, who had been captured by Pictish raiders (from what part of Britain, no one is sure; it could have been Scotland or the Welsh coast) and taken to Ireland as a slave. In time he escaped and went to France.

Some years later he returned, this time as a missionary, settled at Armagh and proceeded to convert the inhabitants of Ulster to Christianity. It was a fruitful soil for the faith, for soon Ireland, which had been almost entirely forgotten by western Europe since the withdrawal of the Roman legions from Britain in 409, was entirely Christian.

It was, so far as is known, a conversion achieved without much loss of life on the part of the missionaries and with little opportunity to achieve martyrdom, and with the same impulses that led the early fathers of the Church into the deserts, the holy men of Ireland withdrew to the mountain-tops and to simple chapels and hermitages on the offshore rocks and islands to the west.

They settled on such remote islands as Inishtooskert in the Blaskets off the coast of Kerry where St Brendan—who himself was believed to have discovered an island which was still being sought in the 18th century—built a church; or the Great Skellig, eight miles out in the Atlantic, where the monks built their beehive dwellings and boat-shaped oratories and tended minute gardens made with earth gathered from among the crevices of a pinnacled rock rising more than 700 feet above the Atlantic.

Whenever such places as these became too overcrowded, or seemed to their inhabitants to be insufficiently austere, they made long and dangerous voyages to the north, seeking the equivalent of uninhabited deserts in the sea.

The sort of boat they travelled in probably resembled the currach, a craft in use on the west coast of Ireland to this day, although the early versions may have been larger and would certainly have been equipped with a primitive square sail for running before the wind.

A currach is a rowing boat about 19 feet long, with a square counter (stern) and a turned-up prow to help in launching it through surf, and is simply a light framework of laths covered with tarred canvas. In early times it would have been covered in hide. The oars are tapered, almost bladeless laths and fit over a single thole pin to enable them to be left unshipped while the crew is fishing. Such boats can carry large numbers of people, in good weather up to 12 persons, including a crew of three, or more than a ton of potatoes or other goods.

It is impossible here to follow in its entirety the legendary voyage of St Brendan in such a boat, which is supposed to have taken place in about 525, but whoever recorded it had either seen an iceberg, met someone who had, or heard about icebergs at third hand: "One day they saw a column in the sea, which seemed not far off, yet they could not reach it for three days. When they drew near, Saint Brendan looked towards its summit, but could not see it because of its great height, which seemed to pierce the skies. It was covered over with a rare canopy, the material of which they knew not; but it had the colour of silver, and was hard as marble, while the column itself was of the clearest crystal."

Another description may have been inspired by an eruption on the volcanic coast of

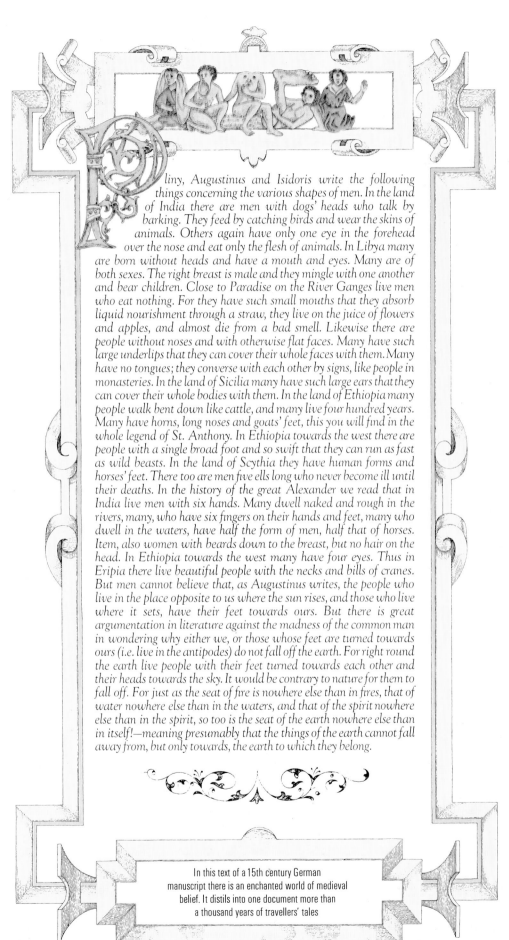

Pliny, Augustinus and Isidoris write the following things concerning the various shapes of men. In the land of India there are men with dogs' heads who talk by barking. They feed by catching birds and wear the skins of animals. Others again have only one eye in the forehead over the nose and eat only the flesh of animals. In Libya many are born without heads and have a mouth and eyes. Many are of both sexes. The right breast is male and they mingle with one another and bear children. Close to Paradise on the River Ganges live men who eat nothing. For they have such small mouths that they absorb liquid nourishment through a straw, they live on the juice of flowers and apples, and almost die from a bad smell. Likewise there are people without noses and with otherwise flat faces. Many have such large underlips that they can cover their whole faces with them. Many have no tongues; they converse with each other by signs, like people in monasteries. In the land of Sicilia many have such large ears that they can cover their whole bodies with them. In the land of Ethiopia many people walk bent down like cattle, and many live four hundred years. Many have horns, long noses and goats' feet, this you will find in the whole legend of St. Anthony. In Ethiopia towards the west there are people with a single broad foot and so swift that they can run as fast as wild beasts. In the land of Scythia they have human forms and horses' feet. There too are men five ells long who never become ill until their deaths. In the history of the great Alexander we read that in India live men with six hands. Many dwell naked and rough in the rivers, many, who have six fingers on their hands and feet, many who dwell in the waters, have half the form of men, half that of horses. Item, also women with beards down to the breast, but no hair on the head. In Ethiopia towards the west many have four eyes. Thus in Eripia there live beautiful people with the necks and bills of cranes. But men cannot believe that, as Augustinus writes, the people who live in the place opposite to us where the sun rises, and those who live where it sets, have their feet towards ours. But there is great argumentation in literature against the madness of the common man in wondering why either we, or those whose feet are turned towards ours (i.e. live in the antipodes) do not fall off the earth. For right round the earth live people with their feet turned towards each other and their heads towards the sky. It would be contrary to nature for them to fall off. For just as the seat of fire is nowhere else than in fires, that of water nowhere else than in the waters, and that of the spirit nowhere else than in the spirit, so too is the seat of the earth nowhere else than in itself!—meaning presumably that the things of the earth cannot fall away from, but only towards, the earth to which they belong.

In this text of a 15th century German manuscript there is an enchanted world of medieval belief. It distils into one document more than a thousand years of travellers' tales

Iceland, where, in the description of the voyage, "a savage man rushed down to the shore bearing in his hand a tongs with a burning mass of the slag, of great size and intense heat, which he flung at once after the servants of Christ. . . . It passed them at a furlong's distance, and where it fell into the sea it fumed up like a heap of burning coals, and a great smoke arose as if from a fiery furnace.

"When they had passed on about a mile beyond the spot where this burning mass had fallen, all the dwellers on the island crowded down to the shore, bearing each one of them a large mass of burning slag, which they flung every one in turn, after the servants of God. And then they returned to their forges, which they blew up into mighty flames, so that the whole island seemed one globe of fire, and the sea on every side boiled up and foamed, like a caldron set on a fire well supplied with fuel.

"All the day the brethren, even when they were no longer within view of the island, heard a loud wailing from the inhabitants thereof, and a noisome stench was perceptible at a great distance."

Nothing is really known about the navigational aids these Christian sailors used or what they knew about the shape of the Earth. It is true that Virgilius, a Scottish bishop of Salzburg, gave as his opinion, towards the end of the 8th century, that the world was a sphere with antipodes, but his views were strongly condemned by the Pope. They undoubtedly reached the Faeroe Islands, between the Shetlands and Iceland, because when the Vikings arrived towards the end of the 8th century, monks were already there.

"There are many other islands in the ocean to the north of Britain which can be reached from the northernmost British Isles in two days' and nights' direct sailing, with full sails and undropping fair wind. A certain holy man informed me that in two summer days and the nights between, sailing in a little boat of two thwarts, he came to land on one of them. Some of these islands are very small; nearly all of them are separated one from the other by narrow sounds. On these islands hermits who have sailed from our Scotia [Ireland] have lived for roughly a hundred years. . . ." So wrote the monk Dicuil, an inhabitant of an Irish monastery school, in 825. In his book *Liber De Mensura Orbis Terrae* he also writes of journeys farther north, to Iceland. "It is now thirty years since priests (clerici) who lived in that island from the first day of February to the first day of August told me that not only at the summer solstice, but in the days on either side of it, the setting sun hides itself at the evening hour as if behind a little hill, so that no darkness occurs during that very brief period of time, but whatever

Monks, myths and magic lands

task a man wishes to perform, even to picking the lice out of his shirt, he can manage it precisely as in broad daylight. . . . They deal in fallacies who have written that the sea round the island is frozen, and there is continuous day without night from the vernal to the autumn equinox, and vice versa . . . for, those sailing at an expected time of great cold have made their way thereto, and dwelling on the island enjoyed always alternate night and day save at the time of the solstice. But after one days sailing from there to the north they found the frozen sea."

There is ample evidence to suggest that the Irish ecclesiastics were extremely skilful as sailors and that in the course of their travels they reached many of the islands scattered in the Atlantic north of the British Isles centuries before the Vikings ventured into these cold and foggy waters. Whether, in their attempts to reach the "land promised to the saints" in the west, they reached the Azores, or the Bahamas, no one will ever be sure.

The stories surrounding St Brendan and his journeys enjoyed a popularity on a par with that of Arthur, the "once and future king" and his knights in the Middle Ages, giving successive generations the opportunity to reinterpret and embroider the first simple facts.

The Irish priests were not the last to sail from Britain in the early Middle Ages and subsequently be honoured as predecessors of Columbus in the New World.

The Welsh prince Madoc is said to have sailed in the 12th century to North America—in what kind of craft is not known, but by now the large, seaworthy ships of the Vikings had appeared frequently in British waters and the Norsemen had certainly raised the coasts of northeast America.

Madoc is supposed to have landed in what is now Alabama and to have taught an Indian tribe to speak Welsh. No evidence has ever been found to support the story (the Mandans, the tribe whose language was said to contain Welsh words, has long since vanished) so Madoc remains one of exploration's enigmas. His arrival, however spectral, in Alabama is celebrated at Mobile, on a plaque placed there by the Daughters of the American Revolution in 1953.

Even the voyages of the Vikings to North America, recounted in their magnificent sagas and substantiated by archaeological finds, are not free from doubt, nor from the suspicion of embroidery many centuries later. The Vinland Map, described as the "most exciting cartographic find of the 20th century", which appeared to confirm everything claimed to support the Viking discovery of North America, looks now to have been a 20th-century forgery; the ink used for it is

Currachs, still used for fishing, are drawn up on a beach in a cove on the west coast of Ireland. Craft similar to these—although probably much larger and covered with hide instead of the tarred canvas of the present day—are said to have carried St Brendan and others to America

such that it could only have been made in the 1920s.

Patriotism and pride in one's forebears being what they are, the Italian Historical Society of America was among the first to congratulate Yale University in 1974, when the University declared the Vinland Map to be, in all likelihood, a forgery, for taking "the moral and legal steps to rectify the harm and injustice that was inflicted upon Columbus".

Scandinavian scholars, on the other hand, took the view that the discrediting of the map did nothing to alter the fact that the Norsemen had reached North America long before Columbus.

If Columbus is obliged to take second place to the Norsemen in terms of time, his voyages were the more important in having rung down the curtain on centuries of mystical belief in a paradise beyond the sea—St Brendan's "land promised to the saints" and the terrestrial paradise of *Mandeville's Travels.*

Mandeville was a fiction, a much-travelled Englishman created by a Liégeois in the 14th century. Mandeville was the distillation of all the travellers' tales that enraptured his time and haunted seafarers and other voyagers into the unknown for centuries afterwards,

an enchanting mixture of fact and fantasy.

On the isle of "Taprobane, toward the east part of Prester John's land" there be "great hills of gold that pissemyres [ants] keep full diligently. And they fine the pured gold and casten away the unpured. And these pissemyres be as great as hounds so that no man dare come to those hills for the pissemyres would assail them and devour them anon, so that no man may get of that gold by of great sleight.

"And therefore when it is great heat the pissemyres resten in the earth from prime of day into noon and then the folk of the country take camayles, dromedaries and horses and other beasts and load them in all haste that they may."

To Mandeville, at least, the world was round. "And beyond the land and the isles and deserts of Prester John's lordship in going straight towards the east, men find nothing but mountains and rocks full great. And here is the dark region where no man may see either by day or by night as they of the country see. And that desert and that place of darkness stretches from this coast unto paradise terrestre where Adam our foremost father and Eve were put that dwelled there for a little while and that is towards the east at the beginning of the earth. But that is not east that we call our east of this half, where the sun rises to us, for when the sun is east in those parts towards paradise terrestre, it is then midnight in our part, for the roundness of the earth." It was a hint of real knowledge.

Mandeville's island was inhabited by other beasts, some recognizable, others with "Alice in Wonderland" qualities. "There be many popengays [parrots] and they speak of their proper nature and salute men that go through the deserts and speak to them as pertly as though it were a man. And they that speak well have a large tongue and have five toes upon a foot. And there be also of other manner, that have but three toes upon a foot and speak not or but a little, for they cannot but cry. In that country and by all Ind be plenty of cockodrilles, that is a manner of a long serpent and in the night they dwell in the water and in the day upon the land in rocks and in caves. And they eat no meat in all winter but they lie as in a dream as do the serpents. These serpents slay men and they eat them weeping. And when they eat they move the overjaw and nought the lower jaw, and they have no tongues.

"There also be many beasts that be called 'orafles', in Araby they be called 'gerfaunts' [giraffes] that is a beast pomely or spotted that is little more high than a steed. But he hath a neck a twenty cubits long. And his crupper and his tail is as of a hart and he may look over a great high house.

"And there be in that country many 'camles' [chameleons] and he liveth by the air and eateth nought at no time. And he changeth his colour oftentime. For men see him often now in one colour and now in another colour and he may change him into all manner colours that him list, save only red and white.

". . . And here be also of other beasts as great or more greater than is a warhorse, and men call them 'loeranez' and some call them 'odenthos'. And they have a black head and three long horns trenchant in the front, sharp as a sword and the body is slender; and he is a full felonous beast, and he chaseth and slayeth the 'oliphant'."

The medieval world populated by Mandeville's heraldic beasts was the world also of Prester John, whose kingdom, described in detail by Mandeville—"a full great land . . . many full noble cities and good towns"—was thought variously to embrace parts of Africa and Asia. As a creation based on half-understood facts and with the usual imaginative embellishments, Prester John and his world were not very much older than Mandeville. The legend gained great circulation after the publication, in about 1165, of a letter purporting to have been sent by him to the Byzantine emperor of the time. Nearly 100 manuscript versions of the letter were still in existence before the First World War.

Prester John's dominions, the letter said, stretched from the Indies to Babylon. His power was so great that 72 kings paid him homage. His wealth was beyond computation as, almost, were the soldiers in his armies—scores of corps, each of 10,000 knights and 100,000 infantry; 30,000 people dined daily at his tables which were hewn from emeralds. At the head of this vast banquet Prester John himself sat, flanked by 12 archbishops on his right and 20 bishops on his left.

This was the land of Mandeville's gold-digging pissemyres, and of the fountain of youth. There, too, was the worm called Salamander, which, living in fire, produced an uninflammable material for the robes of the king. The letter spoke also of the moral purity of Prester John's Christian kingdom which presumably did not extend to his dominions as he had a special mirror (a sort of early warning system) for detecting wrongdoers and conspirators.

The letter, alas, was a forgery, but containing so much of what a European society wanted to believe about the world—an immense wealth, a powerful Christian monarch beyond the barriers thrown up by Islam —that, hundreds of years later, princes of great common sense such as Henry of Portugal sent their men to sea in the hope of making contact with Prester John.

Prester John was one of the last great chimeras sought by men moving away from the superstition-ridden Middle Ages and into the modern age of exploration. There were no gardens of Eden, no lands promised to the saints, no terrestrial paradise or elixirs and fountains of eternal youth. It had become impossible to claim for later explorers achievements hardly separable from fantasy, as with the monkish travellers of the Dark Ages. A real world was there, waiting to be found.

Monument to a myth. The giant figure of a Viking, his shield emblazoned with a bald statement for doubting historians, stands in Alexandria, Minnesota. The Viking celebrates the finding at nearby Kensington, in 1898, of a stone carved with Scandinavian runes and purporting to record a visit to the area by a group of Norsemen in 1362. The stone claims to remember the death of ten Vikings, another ten having been left behind in Vinland, two weeks' journey away. The stone was unearthed from the roots of a tree felled by a Scandinavian farmer and was soon dismissed as a 19th-century fake by scholars; the runic characters were too clean-cut to have weathered for centuries, as they are claimed to have done. Scandinavians had settled the region since the middle of the 19th century and it is suspected that some, proud of their Viking ancestors, may have been guilty of gilding the lily. Other "evidence" that Vikings reached the distant shores of the great lakes from their seaboard settlements are "mooring holes" drilled into rocks. The almost certain likelihood is that the holes were no older than the Kensington Stone — that they were drilled to hold explosive charges to split the rocks for use as house foundations — and were no more than part of the overall myth of Viking penetration to the Middle West of America

An ancient world looks out

FROM APRIL TO OCTOBER the Mediterranean, especially the eastern part, is an almost ideal sea for would-be sailors—the winds are mostly steady from a northern quarter; the skies are limpid; the range of visibility is often enormous and landfalls are easily recognizable. Until far into the 19th century, Mediterranean sailors were accustomed to making passages from one landfall to the next without the aid of either compass or sextant, and this in a sea 2,500 miles long from the shores of Syria to the Strait of Gibraltar and with an area of almost one million square miles. It is not surprising that Homer called its trade routes the "wet lanes".

In it there were none of the terrors of the unknown that were to beset the Atlantic sailor; no ice to come stealing out of the northern fog. Even its storms, though treacherously sudden and violent, are of comparatively short duration—unlike those in the Atlantic, which can whip up the face of its

The world of Ptolemy, geographer, mathematician and astronomer (2nd century AD)—a world in which Africa is shown trending into an unknown southern continent

waters into a howling, hostile wilderness for months at a time.

It has many other advantages; there are good harbours and an abundance of safe anchorages; tidal movement is small and its waters are mostly free from dangerous currents, reefs and shoals. In the Aegean Sea, the northern part of its eastern basin, the islands are so numerous and close together that they form a series of stepping-stones between Asia Minor and Greece, a purpose for which they were actually used by the people of the Ancient World in their early migrations westwards and later in the course of their extensive trading operations.

The Mediterranean was, in short, the ideal sea for the mariner of antiquity. Upon its waters he learned the art of navigation and made the first recorded voyages in the history of exploration.

Among the first to venture out into the Mediterranean were the Egyptians, Minoans and Phoenicians. The Egyptians had an advantage over the other two ancient civilizations: through their country flowed the Nile, the only navigable river that debouched into

the Mediterranean, and it was upon this great river that the Egyptians learned the art of watermanship.

It was the Egyptians, too, who made the earliest recorded sea voyage, although men had, in all probability, been sailing the Mediterranean for at least 4,000 years. The voyage was made during the reign of the Pharaoh Snefru, in *c.* 3200 BC, and was commemorated in a hieroglyphic inscription which recorded the "bringing of forty ships of one hundred cubits with cedar-wood from Byblos", one of the oldest cities in the world.

By the time of the voyage to Byblos, Egyptian civilization was highly developed and sophisticated; but its people used boats for internal communications only. They were not deep-water sailors, depending for their prosperity on intensive farming rather than on external trade. Long ago they had migrated from western Asia to the great river that they called Atur (the Nile), where they settled its banks and mingled their blood with that of the indigenous Africans. By the construction of a primitive yet complex system of irrigation, they succeeded in winning from the great

deserts, which hemmed the river in, a thin, green line of oasis extending from the 1st Cataract at Aswan to the delta. This vast, fan-shaped area of constantly replenished alluvium vied with Mesopotamia, the region between the Tigris and the Euphrates, as the richest farm-land in the Ancient World.

Agriculture flourished, but the Egyptians were dependent on imports for many raw materials. It was the need for timber, for their temples, palaces and ships, that occasioned the voyage to Byblos, the port for timber hewn in the great cedar groves of the Lebanon mountains. Trade also developed in Syrian fir and wheat and, from farther north on the Cilician coast below the Taurus mountains, in pine wood, juniper and resin, an ingredient in the complex embalming process practised by the Egyptians to ensure the immortality of their dead.

As the power and luxury of Egypt increased, so did its need for rare, costly and exotic materials. From the mines on the Sinai peninsula Egyptian ships brought turquoise, malachite and copper. From equatorial Africa, overland, came ebony and other rare woods, ivory, gold and silver. Prized above all were the incenses, frankincense and myrrh, particularly the latter, a gum-resin burned in vast quantities in the temples, and also widely used as an unguent, perfume and embalming agent.

These products became so prodigiously expensive as they travelled slowly up the continent, passing through the hands of one entrepreneur after another, that the Egyptians were eventually impelled to send their own fleets through the Red Sea to what they called The Land of Punt, "The Sacred", in order to trade with the inhabitants direct.

To do so they had to overcome the most appalling natural difficulties. First the materials for building the ships had to be man-handled through 150 miles of desert from the Nile north of Thebes to the shore of the Red Sea, near the present Quseir. Then, with the ships built, their crews faced a 1,500-mile voyage through the Red Sea before entering the less hazardous waters of the Arabian Sea, rowing and sailing under a burning sun through shark-infested waters in which great, jagged reefs of coral rise to within a few feet of the surface, where they are invisible until it is too late. On the way they saw nothing for month after month but an arid, largely unpopulated coast, the outlines of which are often obscured by flying sand or distorted by mirages.

One such large expedition to Punt took place in about 2500 BC in the reign of the Pharaoh Sahure. The prevailing winds at the northern and southern ends of the Red Sea would make it almost imperative for such

Where the story of exploration began; Palestine (top left), the Nile delta (centre) and the Red Sea (top right), photographed from an American satellite

primitive vessels to sail through it southwards sometime between June and September and to make the return voyage between October and December; even so they would meet with calms and variable winds in the middle section of the sea. Such a voyage could scarcely have taken less than a year and may have taken twice as long, depending on the whereabouts of Punt.

Where was this fabled land? Various locations have been suggested from southern Arabia to Dar-es-Salaam and even as far south as the Zambezi, the source of gold, and of antimony—an ingredient of rouge, one of the most highly prized cosmetics of the day. The tree which exudes the myrrh resin, *Commiphora myrrha*, grows extensively inland from the port of Zeila, on the borders of Somalia and Ethiopia, as does the *Boswellia* tree, from which frankincense is derived. The myrrh tree also grows east of Aden and it is from these two coasts that the Egyptians probably drew their supplies. Punt may be the name they gave to all the southern parts of Africa and Arabia that they knew.

A temporary halt
Internal trouble and the invasion of the Hyksos, a soldier people from the east, *c.* 1700 BC, brought a temporary halt to the voyages to Punt. It was not until the reign of the powerful and reputedly beautiful Queen Hatshepsut (1501–1479 BC) that they started up again, inspired by the need for incense and myrrh trees, the latter to adorn the façade of Hatshepsut's newly built mausoleum and temple to the god Amon-Re at Deir el-Bahri, near Thebes. Gold was needed, too, to pay for these costly commodities. The queen was also anxious to enhance her prestige and so,

in the ninth year of her reign (*c.* 1492 BC), she organized the great expedition to Punt that is immortalized in a series of coloured reliefs and hieroglyphic text, the world's first illustrated account of a voyage.

The reliefs show the arrival at Punt; the surprise of the inhabitants who believed that the Egyptians had come to their land by supernatural means—having in the course of the centuries forgotten that their ancestors had met one another before, if, indeed, this is the part of Punt that was visited on earlier voyages.

The presentation of gifts of weapons and ornaments to the king and his amply behinded queen is also recorded; and the departure for Thebes, the ships deep-loaded with ivory, gold, silver, dog-faced baboons, leopard skins, a live panther, dogs, some of the natives and their children, and 31 myrrh trees in tubs from "the mountains of the barbarians" for the adornment of the temple.

"Never", as the inscription says, "was the like brought back to any monarch since the world began."

This voyage to Punt marks the culmination of Egypt's maritime tradition; thereafter interest in sea-going expeditions waned, and was not renewed until some 900 years later.

The first great explorers of the Mediterranean were the Minoans, and it was they who dominated it for 600 years, from 2000 to 1400 BC. It is possible that it was they, rather than the Egyptians, who provided the crews for the first voyage to Byblos. A people of unknown origin, their capital was Knossos,

An ancient world looks out

on the Aegean island of Crete. Strategically placed at the southern end of the Aegean, the Minoans were only three days' sailing from Africa and Egypt and only two from the mainland of Greece.

An able and adventurous people, they had already established trade with Egypt, where they went to load grain in exchange for their own artefacts, sailing there in their own, more seaworthy ships, which are shown on their seal stones; vessels with high sterns and forecastles and with their ribs tied to the keels.

In their home waters, the Aegean, they sailed from island to island in search of obsidian, a much-prized volcanic glass. From Sardinia and Sicily they brought back copper for their currency in the form of plaques of raw metal, and fluorite from the Aeolian Islands (Lipari Islands). Their bronze axeheads have been found as far west as the Balearics, off the coast of Spain.

No one knows the exact cause of their downfall and disappearance. In *c.* 1400 BC the great palace of King Minos at Knossos, a miracle of engineering skill, was destroyed by an earthquake, but it also showed signs, when excavated, of having been plundered and burnt. Perhaps the Minoans were overwhelmed by a tidal wave after the earthquake. Their fate is as mysterious as their origin.

More ambitious merchant explorers than either the Egyptians or the Minoans, and equalled in their colonizing capacity only by the Greeks, were the Phoenicians, otherwise the Kinaahu, the "People of the Purple", so named because they manufactured deep purple dye. The dye was first produced from *Murex brandaris*, a sea shell that existed in vast quantities on the Mediterranean shore of their kingdom. In the 7th century BC, the Phoenicians found two new sources for their dyes in the Canaries and Madeira: "draper's lichen", a litmus, and a deep red resin known as dragon's blood from the dragon tree, *Dracoetia draco*.

About 3000 BC, this dark-skinned, Semitic people had moved westwards from Canaan, later the Holy Land, and occupied a narrow, cultivable strip, no more than 120 miles long and nowhere more than 30 miles broad, between the Lebanon mountains and the Mediterranean. Finding it too small to support them as agriculturists, and being at the nodal point of the caravan routes to Mesopotamia, the Caucasus, the Persian Gulf and farther Asia, they took to the sea.

They built a number of strategically sited ports, the most important of which were Aradus (Ruad), on an island; Byblos, on a cliff, to which Snefru's ships came from Egypt to load timber; Sidon, on a headland; and Tyre, a mainland town that later expanded on to a nearby island.

Tyre was described by the Prophet Isaiah as "the crowning city, whose merchants are princes, whose traffickers are the honourable of the earth", an opinion not shared by all the inhabitants of the Ancient World.

The Phoenicians became the greatest ship builders and carriers of other people's merchandise in the Mediterranean and beyond, cloaking their discoveries in mystery. By 1100 BC they had settled in Gades (Cadiz).

It was in the familiar dual Phoenician role of ruler and merchant that Hiram II, King of Tyre (969–936 BC), entered into a contract on usurious terms with King Solomon of Israel to supply him with fir and cedar wood for the construction of the great temple at Jerusalem. His sailors also played a major part in Solomon's great expedition to Ophir, Solomon's own shipwrights, navigators and seamen being unequal to the task unaided. The voyage lasted three years and is recorded in the sonorous prose of the First Book of Kings: "And they came to Ophir, and fetched from thence gold, four hundred and twenty talents [one talent is the approximate equivalent of £100], and brought it to King Solomon . . ."; they also brought back "gold and silver, ivory and apes and peacocks".

Where was Ophir?
The real whereabouts of Ophir has never been established, but it has been identified with Japan (by Marco Polo), the Spanish Indies (by Columbus) and in more modern times with places as widely separated as the Gold Coast of West Africa, Zimbabwe in Rhodesia, Abyssinia, India and, more wildly, Australia and New Zealand. It was probably on the south coast of Arabia.

Between eight and nine hundred years before Christ, however, disaster overcame the Phoenicians at home: the Assyrians moved westwards to the Mediterranean and took their cities one by one. The inhabitants were driven out to found colonies on the shore of the Gulf of Sirte in Tripolitania, in Sardinia and the Balearics and, on the north coast of Africa, near the present city of Tunis, they founded the city state of Carthage.

In 666 BC, the great island fortress of Tyre fell to the Assyrians, and the Phoenician domination of the eastern Mediterranean was at an end.

But it was not the end of the Phoenicians. Their navigational skill was enlisted yet again by a foreign monarch—the Pharaoh Necho II, who was anxious to expand Egyptian trade. Warned by an oracle not to reopen the canal linking the Nile with the Red Sea (built by Pharaoh Sesostris but subsequently allowed to silt up), he sought an alternative route from the Red Sea to the Mediterranean. In *c.* 600 BC Necho II despatched a Phoe-

nician fleet to find a route round Africa.

Whether the Phoenicians succeeded in circumnavigating the continent is a matter for debate, and one often dismissed as a wild fiction because of the lack of evidence supporting the voyage. The only record is an account written 150 years after the voyage took place by Herodotus, the Greek historian whom Cicero called the "Father of History". "For Libya [Africa]", he wrote, "furnishes proofs about itself that it is surrounded by sea, except so much of it as borders upon Asia; and this fact was shown by Necho, King of the Egyptians, first of all those about whom we have knowledge. He, when he had ceased digging the canal which goes through from the Nile to the Arabian Gulf, sent Phoenicians with ships bidding them sail and come back to Egypt. The Phoenicians therefore set forth from the Erythraean Sea [Red Sea] and sailed through the Southern Sea [Indian Ocean]; and when the autumn came they would put to shore and sow the land wherever in Libya they might happen to be as they sailed, and then they waited for the harvest; and having reaped the corn they would sail on, so that after two years had elapsed in the third year they turned through the Pillars of Heracles [Strait of Gibraltar] and arrived again in Egypt. And they reported a thing which I cannot believe, but another man may, namely that in sailing round Libya they had the sun on their right hand." Although incredible to the Greeks, the report of the position of the Sun offers the most conclusive proof that the voyage took place. South of the Equator a ship sailing west would certainly find that the midday sun was on the right—that is, to the north.

The voyage was a failure in trade terms; no gold or other valuable commodities had been found. If authentic, however, it certainly ranks among the greatest maritime ventures of antiquity and bears testimony to the seamanship of the Phoenicians.

In the western Mediterranean, Carthage perpetuated Phoenicia's long-established tradition of maritime exploration and trade, and by the 3rd century BC ruled an empire stretching from Libya to beyond Gibraltar and encompassing parts of Spain, Sicily and Sardinia.

In *c.* 500 BC Hanno, a chief magistrate of Carthage, set off with a great fleet of 60 ships, each with 50 oarsmen and, according to Hanno's estimate, 30,000 men and women—an impossible number for so few ships. His object was to settle these "Libyphoenicians" (Phoenicians living in Africa) in new colonies along the west coast of Africa and so safeguard Carthaginian access to the Canaries and Madeira, the newly found source of the dye-stuffs to which they were accustomed.

After passing through the Strait of Gibraltar and founding a colony and a temple at modern Mehdiya, he reached the mouth of a river "haunted by elephants and multitudes of other grazing beasts"—the marshes at the mouth of the Tensift River.

From here, sailing south, with the Anti-Atlas on his port hand, he learned of "a freakish race of men, the Troglodytes, who are said . . . to run faster than horses". Then he coasted the Sahara past capes Bojador and Blanco, the two landmarks that were to prove such obstacles to Portuguese explorers 1,500 years later.

On the island of Cerne, possibly Herne Island near the Tropic of Cancer, Hanno founded the last of seven colonies, which was to be the leading trading centre on the West African coast over the next 400 years.

Although he had accomplished his colonizing mission, Hanno, in true exploring spirit, sailed farther south. He saw crocodiles and hippopotamuses at the mouth of a river that may have been the Senegal, north of Cape Verde; great fires on shore that made him think that the earth itself was burning; and "the highest mountains which we ever saw . . . in the centre a leaping flame towered above the others and appeared to reach the stars [identified either as Mount Cameroun, 13,350 feet, in the volcanic range at the eastern end of the Gulf of Guinea or, more probably, as Kakulima, a small mountain, only 2,910 feet high, in Sierra Leone]", which he called "the chariot of the Gods".

Finally he reached some islands, in one of which "by far the greater number were women with hairy bodies. Our interpreters called them Gorillas [more probably, chimpanzees]. We gave chase to the men, but could not catch any, for they all scampered away up steep rocks and pelted us with stones. We secured three women, who bit and scratched and resisted their captors. But we killed and flayed them, and brought the hides to Carthage."

"This", he wrote, "was the end of our journey, owing to lack of provisions."

Hanno's farthest point south is still a matter of dispute; it may have been Sherbro Island off the coast of Sierra Leone or even Cameroon or Gabon. Wherever it was, Hanno had no real successors until the Portuguese in the Middle Ages. Setting out to find a trade route to the East, they were to take over 40 years to accomplish what Hanno had achieved in a single voyage of only a few months.

About the same time that Hanno made his epic voyage, another Carthaginian, Himilco, sailed out of Massalia (Marseille) with instructions to "explore the outer parts of Europe" which faced the still unknown Atlantic. Himilco was probably also in-structed to look for the so-called "Tin Islands", as the yields from the mines in Spain were inadequate to meet the growing demands from the Mediterranean countries.

The details of this expedition were engraved on a bronze tablet, which was subsequently lost, but the gist of it survived in a Roman geography book, the *Ora Maritima* of Avienus written 800 years later (in the 4th century AD).

In his voyage, which lasted four months, Himilco almost certainly succeeded in reaching the coast of Brittany; on the way experiencing flat calms and sighting "sea monsters" and great drifts of weed, probably between Gades and Cape St Vincent. Whether he also reached the "Tin Islands"—variously identified as the Scilly Isles or the coast of Cornwall—is not known, but his voyage firmly established a Phoenician monopoly of the flourishing trade in Cornish tin between Brittany and the Mediterranean.

W ITH THE DECLINE of the Minoans and the westward migration of the Phoenicians, a new civilization emerged in the eastern Mediterranean: the Hellenes or Greeks.

Originally a shepherd people, the Greeks had migrated to the Greek peninsula in about 2000 BC, possibly from the Danube. They found their new home too arid to satisfy their needs and soon turned to the sea for their livelihood, learning the secrets of navigation —and their skill in working metal—from the Minoans.

Imaginative, curious, with an innate appreciation of the beautiful and a genuine love of adventure, very different in character from the secretive Phoenicians, they became fishermen, pirates and merchants and, in the 8th century BC, began the voyages of colonization that changed the face of the Ancient World. Like their counterparts among other ancient peoples, those who made the voyages left the recording of them to their historians and poets.

Their progress was remarkable. By 500 BC, —some 1,500 years after their first appearance in the Mediterranean—they had founded more than 100 colonies from the Black Sea, which was virtually a Greek lake, to Marseille. They controlled the coast of Thrace and the entire littoral of Asia Minor, where they took over the trade previously enjoyed by the Phoenicians. They made Miletus on the Aegean shore the richest of their cities, expeditions going out from there to the Black Sea. They colonized the eastern seaboard of the Adriatic, southern Italy, Sicily, and Cyrene on the coast of Libya.

East of the Black Sea, beyond Colchis (Georgia), where they had established posts for trading with the local tribes, Greek traders

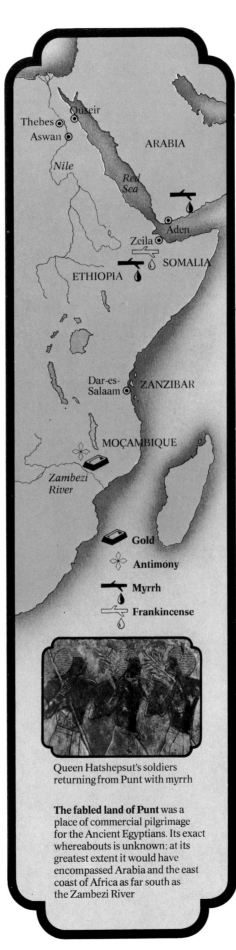

Thebes
Aswan
Quseir
Nile
ARABIA
Red Sea
Aden
Zeila
SOMALIA
ETHIOPIA
Dar-es-Salaam
ZANZIBAR
MOÇAMBIQUE
Zambezi River

Gold
Antimony
Myrrh
Frankincense

Queen Hatshepsut's soldiers returning from Punt with myrrh

The fabled land of Punt was a place of commercial pilgrimage for the Ancient Egyptians. Its exact whereabouts is unknown; at its greatest extent it would have encompassed Arabia and the east coast of Africa as far south as the Zambezi River

Exploration by conquest

crossed the Caspian and may have reached the north of Russia.

In the middle of the 7th century they had established themselves in Egypt, founding the port of Naucratis at one of the now extinct mouths of the Nile (the Canopic Nile). To this port, which later became the city of Alexandria, they brought merchandise, which was paid for by the Egyptians with gold from the Sudan.

By the beginning of the 6th century BC, the Greek colonies in Asia were under Persian rule, and it was at the behest of the Persian king, Darius I, that Scylax, a Greek from Caria in Asia Minor, set out to investigate the course of the Indus.

Probably travelling overland from Caria, Scylax succeeded in reaching the Indus by way of the Kabul River, which rises in Afghanistan. Entering it near the present town of Attock, he sailed down it to its mouth on the Indian Ocean. He then sailed westwards along the wild, barren Makran coast of

Baluchistan, across the Gulf of Oman, along the southern coast of Arabia and up the Red Sea to Egypt.

He was the first known Greek to have sailed in the Red Sea, from which his countrymen had always been denied access by the Egyptians and the Arabians. He also brought back valuable first-hand information about the northeastern part of the Indian Ocean, and less authentic but entertaining reports of the strange people to be seen in India: one-eyed men (Monophthalmi); men who used their feet as sunshades (Sciapodes—shadow-feet men); and men whose ears were fern-shaped and as big as baskets.

In the spring of 401 BC, Cyrus, satrap of Lydia (now nothing more than a village near Izmir in Turkey), set out with an army of about 20,000 Asian and Greek mercenaries on what was to be not only one of the greatest marches in history but also, in its later stages, a journey of exploration through regions unknown to the Persians.

Ostensibly, Cyrus's expedition was against Pisidia, a mountainous area in southern Asia Minor, inhabited by a number of predatory tribes whom the Persians had been unable to subdue. His real objective, however, was to overthrow his elder brother, the recently enthroned king of Persia, Artaxerxes II.

His route took the army across the heart of Anatolia far to the north of Pisidia and then through the Taurus Mountains by the pass known as the Cilician Gates to Tarsus. Here, realizing that they were bound for some more distant destination than they had been led to believe, his soldiers refused to go any farther. Finally, with the assurance from Cyrus that they would not be forced to cross the Euphrates, which was still at least 200 miles to the east, they continued their march, reaching the Euphrates at Thapsacus (Dibse), beyond Aleppo. Here Cyrus was forced to tell the army his real objective: Babylon and the overthrow of the Great King.

Lured on by promises of rich rewards they

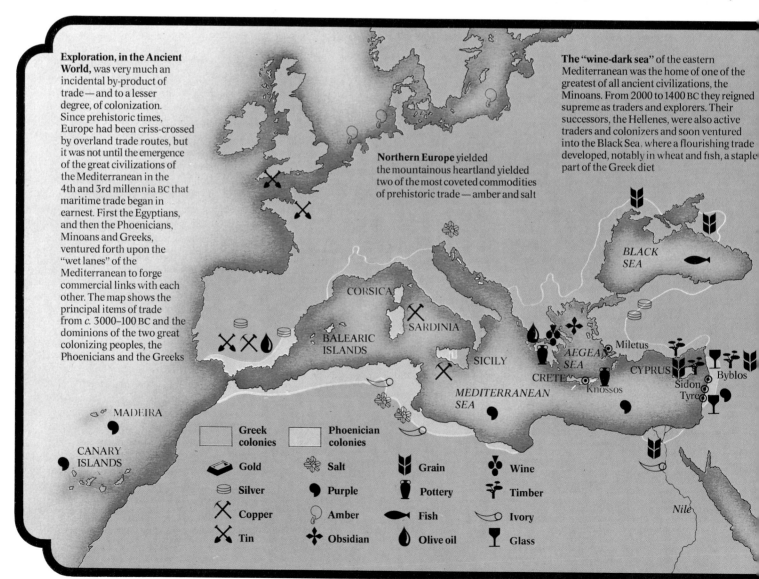

Exploration, in the Ancient World, was very much an incidental by-product of trade—and to a lesser degree, of colonization. Since prehistoric times, Europe had been criss-crossed by overland trade routes, but it was not until the emergence of the great civilizations of the Mediterranean in the 4th and 3rd millennia BC that maritime trade began in earnest. First the Egyptians, and then the Phoenicians, Minoans and Greeks, ventured forth upon the "wet lanes" of the Mediterranean to forge commercial links with each other. The map shows the principal items of trade from c. 3000–100 BC and the dominions of the two great colonizing peoples, the Phoenicians and the Greeks

Northern Europe yielded the mountainous heartland yielded two of the most coveted commodities of prehistoric trade — amber and salt

The "wine-dark sea" of the eastern Mediterranean was the home of one of the greatest of all ancient civilizations, the Minoans. From 2000 to 1400 BC they reigned supreme as traders and explorers. Their successors, the Hellenes, were also active traders and colonizers and soon ventured into the Black Sea, where a flourishing trade developed, notably in wheat and fish, a staple part of the Greek diet

Greek colonies	Phoenician colonies

Symbol	Item	Symbol	Item	Symbol	Item
	Gold		Salt		Grain		Wine
	Silver		Purple		Pottery		Timber
	Copper		Amber		Fish		Ivory
	Tin		Obsidian		Olive oil		Glass

Gold, Silver, Copper, Tin, Salt, Purple, Amber, Obsidian, Grain, Pottery, Fish, Olive oil, Wine, Timber, Ivory, Glass

MADEIRA

CANARY ISLANDS

CORSICA

BALEARIC ISLANDS

SARDINIA

SICILY

MEDITERRANEAN SEA

BLACK SEA

AEGEAN SEA

CRETE

Knossos

Miletus

CYPRUS

Byblos

Sidon

Tyre

Nile

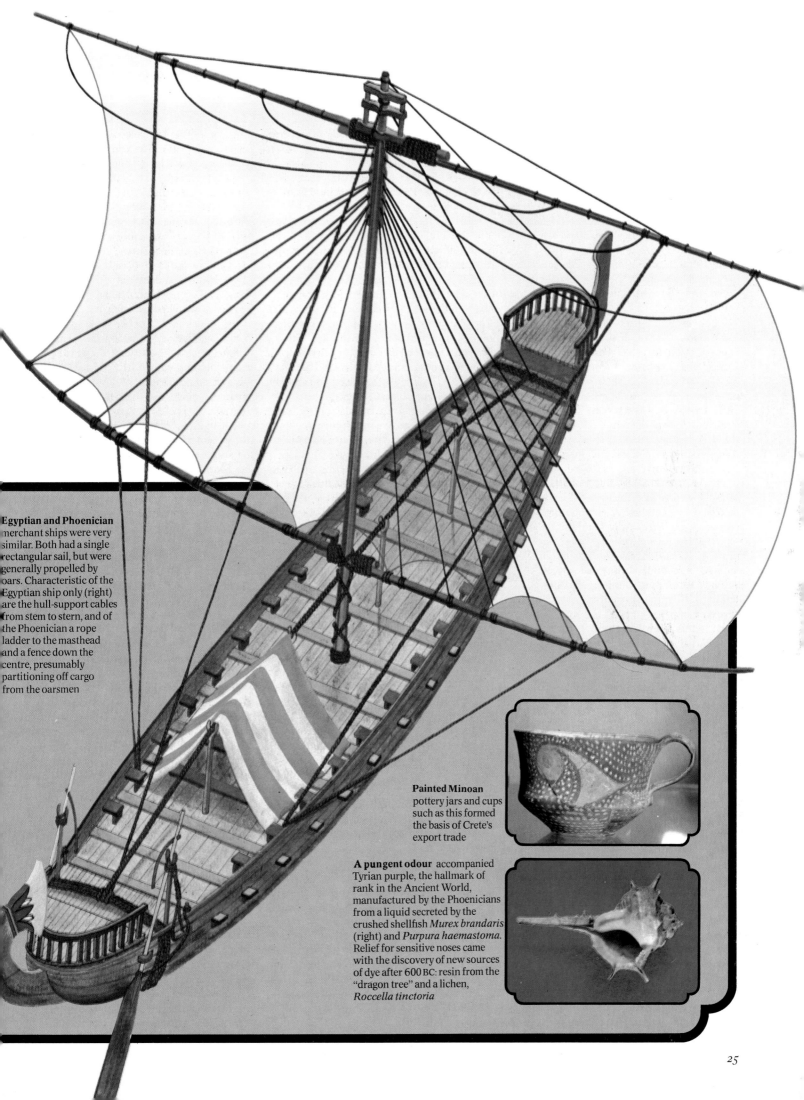

Egyptian and Phoenician merchant ships were very similar. Both had a single rectangular sail, but were generally propelled by oars. Characteristic of the Egyptian ship only (right) are the hull-support cables from stem to stern, and of the Phoenician a rope ladder to the masthead and a fence down the centre, presumably partitioning off cargo from the oarsmen

Painted Minoan pottery jars and cups such as this formed the basis of Crete's export trade

A pungent odour accompanied Tyrian purple, the hallmark of rank in the Ancient World, manufactured by the Phoenicians from a liquid secreted by the crushed shellfish *Murex brandaris* (right) and *Purpura haemastoma*. Relief for sensitive noses came with the discovery of new sources of dye after 600 BC: resin from the "dragon tree" and a lichen, *Roccella tinctoria*

Exploration by conquest

crossed the river and followed it south and east towards Babylon. On the way they passed "five stages through desert country", an unbroken, treeless plain, as level as the sea, and full of wormwood; whatever else there was on the plain by way of shrub or reed was always fragrant, like spices; there were wild animals of all sorts too, including wild asses, ostriches, bustards and gazelles.

At Cunaxa, north of Babylon (near the present Al Fallujah), they met Artaxerxes's army, and Cyrus was killed in the ensuing battle.

The army found itself in a seemingly hopeless situation. It was in completely unknown country, with the river crossings in enemy hands; it was separated from its base by at least 1,500 miles, much of it wild, hostile country; it had no provisions, as the camp had been looted by Artaxerxes. Consequently Clearchus, one of the senior officers, accepted the offer of an escort out of the country for the remaining 10,000 soldiers and camp followers.

Clearchus had not reckoned with the oriental subtlety of Tissaphernes, the Persian satrap who provided the escort. Far from receiving a safe conduct, Clearchus and all his senior officers were trapped and put to death. In the subsequent election of new officers, a civilian, Xenophon, a disciple of Socrates, emerged to command the great retreat.

They set off northwards up the Tigris, intending to turn west after crossing the Jezireh River and pick up the Royal Persian Road, which would have brought them back to Sardis by way of the Gulf of Iskanderun.

Harassed by the Persians, but eventually shaking them off, they passed the great ruined cities of Calah and Nineveh, the Assyrian capital which had been destroyed by the Medes in 612 BC, only to find that the crossings of the Jezireh were held by the extremely warlike Carduchi (Kurds) and that the river was too deep to ford.

After listening to statements "from the men who claimed to know the way in every direction", as Xenophon says in the *Anabasis* (*The Up March*), his account of the retreat, the generals decided to force their way northwards through the mountains of Kurdistan and Armenia on to the high Armenian plateau. This they did, battered by wind and snow storms, passing to the west of Lake Van and crossing the headwaters of the Euphrates, waist deep in its freezing waters. On the roadless way they left behind them "those whose eyes had been blinded by the snow, and those whose toes had been rotted off by the cold".

They were saved from extinction by finding some troglodytic villages cut out of the rock. There they were able to shelter with the cattle and recoup their strength for a month.

From here, without the benefit of the magnetic compass, they had the cruel luck to march eastwards for a whole week along the Araxes River (Aras), believing themselves to be on a river that flowed northwards to the Black Sea.

Realizing their mistake, they turned north, probably following the Araxes into the Valley of Kars, and then west, eventually reaching a city called Gymnias, where they learned that the Greek city of Trapezus (Trebizond) was only a few days' march to the north on the southern shore of the Black Sea. Their moment of supreme joy came when, having reached the summit of Mount Theches, south of the city, they first saw the sea, and with cries of "Thalassa! Thalassa!" (The Sea! The Sea!) embraced one another, generals, junior officers and men alike.

They continued westwards for 100 miles along the coast, took ships from Cotyora to Sinope and Heraclea (Eregli) and marched the last 150 miles triumphantly to Chrysopolis (Scutari), crossing the Bosphorus to Byzantium. The heroic journey home was over and some 2,000 miles of hitherto unknown territory had been added to the maps of the West.

SIGNIFICANT AS Xenophon's achievement was, it was soon to be surpassed by a campaign on a far grander scale—the advance through Asia from west to east, from the shores of the Mediterranean to the easternmost boundaries of the mighty Persian Empire, led by Alexander the Great of Macedonia.

It was Alexander's father, Philip II of Macedonia, who had first dreamed of overthrowing the Persian king, Darius III, and subjugating his vast empire. Before he could put his plans into action, Philip was assassinated, in 336 BC, and in that year Alexander, the newly acceded Macedonian king, was elected Captain-General of the combined Greek forces for the Persian expedition.

As a boy, Alexander had been the pupil of Aristotle, and from him he had learned that the Earth was round, that a great sea, called Ocean, encircled the known world, and that most rivers flowed from north to south, the Nile being a notable exception. This interest in the world about him transcended the simple desire for gain and conquest which animated less complex commanders. Alexander was not merely a brilliant military strategist but an explorer, and it was in the name of curiosity rather than conquest that he attached to his army a number of geographers, astronomers, mathematicians, architects, botanists, an official historian, Callimachus, and *bematistae*, "steppers", to pace out the length of the Asian roads.

In the spring of 334, at the age of 22, he set

out from Pella, his Macedonian capital, with between 30,000 and 40,000 infantry and more than 5,000 cavalry. After crossing the Hellespont (the Dardanelles), Alexander marched through Asia Minor by a circuitous route to the Gulf of Issus (Iskenderun), where he defeated Darius in September or October 333. In January of the following year he began to lay siege to the seemingly impregnable city of Tyre on the Phoenician coast. The fall of Tyre marked the end of the power of the Persian fleet; Alexander had become the master of the Mediterranean.

In November 332 he was crowned as Pharaoh at Memphis, and in the spring of the following year he founded the first of many cities that he named after himself, the sea port of Alexandria in the Nile delta. From there he made the difficult and dangerous journey to the Siwa Oasis to consult the oracle of Zeus-Amon. The substance of what the Oracle told him was never revealed, but he let it be known that "he had been told what his heart desired".

Alexander's first steps into what for him and his men was really unknown Asia began after his decisive defeat of Darius at the battle of Gaugamela, near Nineveh, at the end of September 331.

Now began the pursuit of one great king by another. It took the Greek army to Babylon, the royal winter residence; eastwards across the Tigris to Susa, where Alexander appropriated a great treasure in gold coin and seated himself on the throne of Darius; and, in January 330, southwards to Persepolis. Here the palace was put to the torch and an even vaster treasure taken.

The chase continued by forced marches northwestwards through the mountains to Ecbatana (Hamadan), 6,000 feet up on the Iranian plateau, to which Darius had retreated after Gaugamela. By the time Alexander arrived, Darius had already continued his flight, eastwards to the Caspian Gates, a pass below the Elburz Mountains.

At Ecbatana Alexander dispatched one of his generals, Parmenio, to subdue Cadusia, the region southwest of the Caspian Sea, while he himself set off in pursuit of Darius. Finally, in the second half of July, Alexander caught up with the fugitive king near Hecatompylus (Damghan), only to find him dying from wounds inflicted by the treacherous Bessus, Satrap of Bactria, and others, who had already dispersed. Distressed by the manner of Darius's death, Alexander sent his body to Persepolis for honourable burial. He then took his army through the Elburz Mountains and down the wet, heavily forested northern slopes to the shore of the Hyrcanian (Caspian) Sea.

The Caspian was found to contain no true

sea fish, and this seemed to disprove the theory of the Ancient Greek geographers that it formed the southernmost tip of a bay extending into Asia from Ocean to the north. However, Craterus, one of Alexander's commanders, discovered that seals lived in it and this was taken as evidence that it must once have linked up with Ocean.

Learning that Bessus had retreated towards Bactria and had proclaimed himself Darius's successor, Alexander marched eastwards, founding a chain of Alexandrias, thereby securing the Greek presence in central Asia.

In the spring of 329, believing the Hindu Kush to be the Caucasus, he took the army up the Panjshir valley on the northwestern borders of Kafiristan (Nuristan) and crossed the main mountain range by the 11,640-foot Khawak Pass in March or April. His men were waist deep in snow, suffering from snow-blindness and the effects of altitude; their only food consisted of plants—wild silphium, which exuded a gum, and terebinth (the turpentine tree)—and the raw flesh of mules.

As soon as they reached Bactria, Alexander's Thessalian volunteers mutinied and had to be demobilized, and it was with a depleted force that he occupied the Bactrian cities of Drapsaca (Kunduz), Aornos (Tash-kurgan) and Bactra (Balkh), the capital. His men, who only shortly before had been on the point of freezing to death, now had to march under a flaming June sun through a country laid waste by Bessus on his flight across the Oxus (Amu-Dar'ya) into Sogdiana (now the Uzbek SSR).

Reaching the Oxus at Kelif, the Greeks found that the river was three-quarters of a mile broad and ran so swiftly over a sandy bottom that it was impossible to bridge; the crossing was eventually made on rafts constructed from leather tent covers stuffed with hay. On the far side of the river, Bessus, betrayed by his own generals, one of whom, Spitamenes, was to become an even more formidable opponent, was finally delivered into the hands of Alexander.

His fate was a dreadful one. In accordance with Alexander's command he was exposed naked to the army at the roadside, except for a wooden collar, which he wore as a sign of servitude. He was then flogged, sent to Bactra, where his nose and the tops of his ears were cut off, and subsequently, in lingering agony, taken to Ecbatana, where he was executed before an assembly of Medes and Persians.

From the Oxus, Alexander marched via Maracanda (Samarkand), the summer residence of the Sogdian rulers, to the southern bend of the Jaxartes River (the Syr-Dar'ya).

Here, where a series of Sogdian forts protected the river line on the northeastern border of the Persian Empire, with the great

Asian steppes beyond, he founded Alexandria Eschate, the "Farthest". From here he crossed the Jaxartes to attack the Scythians, the wild inhabitants of the Asian steppes, reaching the northernmost point of his entire campaign and contracting gastro-enteritis in the process, no novelty in this part of the world. That year, too, he reached Bukhara.

The winter of 329–328 was spent at Bactra and most of 328 in complex and fruitless campaigning against Spitamenes, who was like a will-o'-the-wisp. In the course of one of these expeditions an oil well was discovered while the foundations were being dug for Alexander's tent, near the Oxus, but the discovery was not developed, the Greeks foregoing the opportunity to become the great oil magnates of the Ancient World.

In the autumn of 328, one of Alexander's

Ruins at Pella in Macedonia, the birthplace of Alexander

characteristic bacchanalian excesses ended in the murder of Cleitus, the distinguished Macedonian cavalry commander who had saved his life in battle five years earlier. Alexander had begun to assume Persian dress and manners. Angered by Cleitus's taunts that he had forgotten his Macedonian birthright and grown arrogant, Alexander hurled a spear at his friend, killing him outright.

In January 327, Alexander launched a campaign in the Paraetacene country, probably Badakhshan, north of the Hindu Kush and west of the Pamirs, where, in the course of operations, 2,000 of his men froze to death. None the less, the campaign was another decisive military victory and a tribute to Alexander's skilful deployment of his men. Using iron pitons, specially chosen Greek mountain troops scaled the sheer face of the "Sogdian Rock"—the crag on which the Sogdian ruler, Oxyartes, had his stronghold. Among the prisoners was Oxyartes's daughter Roxane, whom, perhaps out of political expediency, Alexander married. It was an adroit move:

Oxyartes became a valuable ally.

With this victory Alexander had finally subjugated the whole of central Asia, if only temporarily, and was now ready to set off for India. With his army, which may have numbered more than 60,000 but was probably less than half this figure, he recrossed the Hindu Kush, possibly by the 14,340-foot Kaoshan Pass, in ten days—a remarkable feat with such a force—and marched to Alexandria ad Caucasum, where he spent the winter of 327–326, and made final preparations for his descent on India.

He and his advisers knew little about the sub-continent beyond the Indus. They believed that what is now Pakistan was a part of Egypt, though a distant one, where the headwaters of the Nile might be discovered and that Ocean, the Great Sea, lapped its southern shores to the foot of the Imaus Mountains (the Himalayas), and then encircled the whole world to the north and west. The Persian satraps in the Punjab must have known much more about the real size and nature of India, but by the 4th century their satrapies had ceased to exist.

Early in 326 Alexander despatched Hephaestion, one of his generals, through the Khyber Pass with the main body of his army to secure the Indus crossing. He himself, with Craterus as second-in-command, set off with a lighter force via the Kabul River and the valleys of the Kunar and Swat rivers.

Seventy miles up the Indus from Attock, Alexander attacked the seemingly impregnable Rock of Aornos on the Pir-Sar Ridge, which looms thousands of feet above the river. Eventually, he succeeded in taking it, but only after the construction, with immense expenditure of labour, of a causeway, which enabled him to bring his siege engines within effective range.

In April, Taxila, the most important city in the Punjab, yielded without a shot being fired, on condition that Alexander would destroy the power of Porus, the neighbouring rajah, who ruled the country beyond the Jhelum, then known as the Hydaspes.

Unwisely, Alexander allowed his army to remain at Taxila until June, by which time the monsoon had broken. The Jhelum was in full flood and more than 800 yards wide. On the far bank Porus was awaiting Alexander, together with his entire army, which included large numbers of chariots and war elephants —a relative novelty to the Greeks—whose formidable appearance and stentorian trumpetings filled the Greek cavalry horses with terror.

By employing various ruses Alexander succeeded in making a swift crossing upstream in the middle of a violent electric storm with a force of 15,000 men, which in-

Exploration by conquest

cluded such souvenirs of his travels as Scythian horse-archers and cavalry from Bactria and Turkestan. In one of the most brilliantly executed battles of his entire career, he defeated the gallant rajah, who afterwards became his loyal ally.

Here, his famous war horse, Bucephalus, died of wounds and old age and gave his name to Bucephala, one of the cities which rose near the site of the battle.

This was not the end of Alexander's ambition, however. Crossing the Hydraotis (Ravi) and defeating the Cathaeans (Hindus who practised suttee, the burning of widows), he finally reached the Hyphasis (Beas) near Gurdaspur, at the foot of the Himalayas. Here he announced to his exhausted and thoroughly apprehensive army that he now proposed to march to the Ganges, which lay 300 miles to the southeast, across the grain of difficult country, and sail down it to Ocean. His speech summarized his geographical knowledge. "If any of you wish to know", he said, "what limit may be set to this particular campaign, let me tell you that the area of country ahead of us, from here to the Ganges is comparatively small. You will undoubtedly find that this ocean is connected with the Hyrcanian Sea [Caspian Sea], for the great Stream of Ocean encircles the earth. Moreover I shall prove to you my friends [at which point he sounds a little like a professional conjuror] that the Indian and Persian Gulfs and the Hyrcanian Sea are all three connected and continuous. Our ships will sail round from the Persian Gulf to Libya as far as the Pillars of Hercules [Strait of Gibraltar], whence all Libya to the eastward will soon be ours, and all Asia too, and to this empire there will be no boundaries but what God Himself has made for the whole world. . . ."

After a long silence, inspired by this dangerous nonsense, he was answered by Coenus, one of his generals, the gist of whose reply was contained in a single sentence. "Sir, if there is one thing above all others that a successful man should know, it is *when to stop*." And he was forced to.

With the aid of Egyptian, Carian, Cypriot and Phoenician sailors and shipwrights a fleet of ships was built on the Jhelum. Sailing down it with his army Alexander saw crocodiles, which reinforced his belief that he was on one of the headwaters of the Nile; and on the Acesines (Chenab), which they descended to the Indus, he saw the "Indian Lotus", a bean which reminded him of one that he had seen growing in Egypt. Only when he reached Patala, on the delta of the Indus, near the present city of Hyderabad, in July 325, did he finally realize that neither river was a tributary of the Nile.

Downstream, in the western arm of the delta, they encountered a strange new phenomenon—a tidal bore. The ebb tide left the ships aground, the rising tide later refloating them—a marvel to sailors from a nearly tideless sea.

Finally Alexander reached the mouth of the river and the Arabian Sea, where, according to Arrian, who wrote five and a half centuries later, "leaving the estuaries of the Indus behind him, he set sail for the open ocean, with the professed object of finding out if there was any other land near by—though I dare say his chief object was the mere achievement of having sailed in the Great Sea Beyond India. There on the ocean he slaughtered bulls as a sacrifice to Poseidon and flung their bodies overboard, and poured a libation from a golden cup, and flung the cup, too, and golden bowls into the water for a thanks-offering, and prayed that Poseidon might grant safe conduct to the fleet which he proposed to send under Nearchus's command to the Persian Gulf and the Euphrates."

Later, he also explored the eastern arm of the Indus downstream to its mouth at modern Lakhpat, in the salt marshes of the Great Rann of Kutch, and this became the forward base for a great voyage by Nearchus, Alexander's admiral.

The army was divided into three. One part was to travel to the head of the Persian Gulf in Nearchus's fleet. According to Arrian, it originally numbered 1,800 transports and war galleys, but was probably between 100 and 150 ships, with a complement of between

To the easternmost limits. To the Ancients, the East started on the eastern shores of the Mediterranean and stretched across Asia Minor to some nebulous frontier abutting "Ocean", the vast sea encircling the world. Exploration was essentially a story of conquest first by the Persians and then the Greeks. Darius I, the Persian king, sent out the first real reconnaissance expedition, led by Scylax, to determine the course of the Indus. A combined Greek–Persian foray led by Cyrus and, later, Xenophon, added some 2,000 miles of new territory to the Greek map. The most outstanding campaign of all was that of Alexander the Great, who advanced to the easternmost limits of the known world and set up one of the biggest empires of antiquity

Sardis

MEDITERRANEAN SEA

Alexandria

Siwa

RED SEA

The first Greek to venture as far east as the Indus, Scylax was also the first to sail in the Red Sea — the province of the Arabians and Egyptians

Alexander the Great and his horse Bucephalus

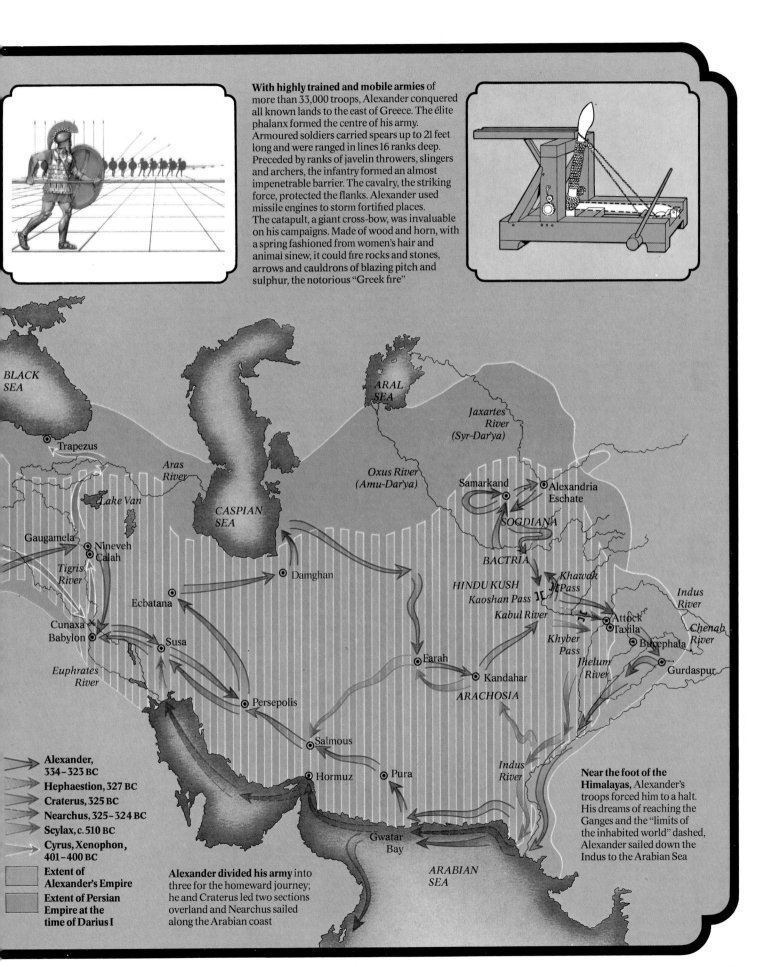

With highly trained and mobile armies of more than 33,000 troops, Alexander conquered all known lands to the east of Greece. The élite phalanx formed the centre of his army. Armoured soldiers carried spears up to 21 feet long and were ranged in lines 16 ranks deep. Preceded by ranks of javelin throwers, slingers and archers, the infantry formed an almost impenetrable barrier. The cavalry, the striking force, protected the flanks. Alexander used missile engines to storm fortified places. The catapult, a giant cross-bow, was invaluable on his campaigns. Made of wood and horn, with a spring fashioned from women's hair and animal sinew, it could fire rocks and stones, arrows and cauldrons of blazing pitch and sulphur, the notorious "Greek fire"

BLACK SEA

Trapezus

ARAL SEA

Aras River

Jaxartes River (Syr-Dar'ya)

Lake Van

Oxus River (Amu-Dar'ya)

Samarkand

Alexandria Eschate

CASPIAN SEA

SOGDIANA

Gaugamela

Nineveh Calah

BACTRIA

Tigris River

Damghan

HINDU KUSH

Khawak Pass

Indus River

Ecbatana

Kaoshan Pass

Kabul River

Attock

Cunaxa

Babylon

Susa

Khyber Pass

Taxila

Chenab River

Euphrates River

Farah

Bucephala

Kandahar

Jhelum River

Gurdaspur

Persepolis

ARACHOSIA

Salmous

Indus River

Hormuz

Pura

Near the foot of the Himalayas, Alexander's troops forced him to a halt. His dreams of reaching the Ganges and the "limits of the inhabited world" dashed, Alexander sailed down the Indus to the Arabian Sea

Gwatar Bay

ARABIAN SEA

Alexander,
334–323 BC

Hephaestion, 327 BC

Craterus, 325 BC

Nearchus, 325–324 BC

Scylax, c. 510 BC

Cyrus, Xenophon,
401–400 BC

Extent of Alexander's Empire

Extent of Persian Empire at the time of Darius I

Alexander divided his army into three for the homeward journey; he and Craterus led two sections overland and Nearchus sailed along the Arabian coast

Exploration by conquest

3,000 and 5,000 men. One of Nearchus's jobs was to survey the coast and find water-points on what Alexander intended to be a regular shipping route from the Euphrates to the Indus. The second section, under Alexander, which has been estimated at as many as 85,000 and which included all the non-combatant men, women and children, must have had the appearance of a migrant people rather than an army. This section was to march overland and explore the shore of the Arabian Sea and the Persian Gulf. The third, under Craterus, was to proceed with three battalions, the sick, wounded and all the elephants by way of Baluchistan, Arachosia and Carmania (Kerman) to the city of Salmous (Golashkerd), about 70 miles inland from the Strait of Hormuz.

In September, Alexander began his march through the desert regions of South Gedrosia, along the Makran coast of Baluchistan, where his army and women and children alike were soon forced to make long detours inland of the mountain range where it ran close to the sea, all the time suffering agonies of thirst, encountering quicksands and tormented by sandstorms. After some 200 miles, in the course of which they killed all their animals and burned all their wagons for fuel, they reached the sea at Pasni, more than 100 miles east of the present Iranian frontier. Here, at last, they found good water by digging wells in the gravel. Then, after following the coast for a week, always finding good water, they struck inland to Pura, the capital of Gedrosia, 150 miles north of the Arabian Sea.

They were safe at last; but at what cost. Alexander estimated that the 60 days on the Makran coast had cost the lives of 60,000 people and all their animals and baggage. The only cheerful news he received was from Craterus, who had crushed a revolt in Arachosia. Now they set off again, on a march

of more than 200 miles to Salmous, where they were finally joined by Craterus and his army towards the end of 325 BC.

Nearchus had had better luck. Forced to wait at the mouth of the Indus for the north-east monsoon, he sailed in October or November 325, following the same route as Scylax in 508, landing every day in search of food and water. On the Makran coast he saw hairy, primitive men who used their finger nails as if they were iron tools, and wore the skins of animals, and also the Ichthyophagi, fish-eaters, who made flour from fish meal, fed their flocks on dried fish because there was no pasture and lived in huts made from the bones of stranded whales.

Soon, he and the crew saw whales for themselves, spouting; and, according to the Greek geographer Strabo: "Nearchus . . . signalled them to turn the ship's prow on towards the whales as if to give them battle. . . . But when they actually were nearing the monsters, they shouted with all the power of their throats, and the bugles blared and the rowers made the utmost splashings with their oars. So the whales, now visible at the bows of the ships, were scared, and dived into the depths."

To Hormuz

From Gwatar Bay, on the Pakistan–Iran border, they sailed westwards. Entering the Strait of Hormuz they came to the mouth of the Anamis (Minab) River in the district of Armazia, from which the port of Hormuz derived its name (the port was later moved to a nearby island and became a flourishing commercial centre in the Middle Ages). Here, they met a Greek, one of a search party sent out by Alexander, who conducted Nearchus and a companion to Salmous, five days' march into the interior. Alexander failed to recognize them at first because of their ragged clothes and long, brine-filled hair.

Nearchus then sailed eastwards to the head of the Persian Gulf, and Alexander set off overland to Susa through the mountains, the main body of the army following the easier but longer route along the coast.

Sometime towards the end of February 324, the two men met again at the junction of the Tigris and Pasitigris to discuss plans for the future use of the fleet, one of which may have included the circumnavigation of Africa, and the establishment of trading posts on the Arabian coast of the Persian Gulf.

Alexander's immediate plan was to re-habilitate Babylon and make it into a great port; and this required the deepening of the Euphrates. It never happened. He died there on June 10, 323 BC, at the age of 32. He may have been poisoned, and it has been suggested that his tutor, Aristotle, prepared the draught and his cup-bearer handed it to him. It is equally likely that he died from a combination of the ills which explorers in Asia are heir to, aggravated by debauchery, a wound that he received in India and sheer fatigue.

Since he first crossed the Hellespont into Asia Minor only ten years had elapsed, in the course of which he and his armies had travelled more than 20,000 miles and more than 70 cities had been founded. Although many of the regions they marched through were known, if somewhat sketchily, to the

The Roman Empire

A T A TIME WHEN Alexander the Great had carved himself an empire as big as the United States—territory stretching from the eastern Mediterranean to the banks of the Indus—the Greeks astonishingly had given no more than a passing glance to the north and west. It was not until some years after Alexander's death in 323 BC that a Greek first ventured into the chill waters of the northern Atlantic and beyond to the Arctic Circle. This was Pytheas of Marseille, not only the first Greek but also the first southern European to visit the northern seas.

Geographer, navigator and accomplished astronomer, Pytheas was the first person to work out the position of true north. Besides linking the alternation of the tides with phases of the Moon, he also invented an accurate method of determining latitude with a calibrated sundial.

Some time towards the end of the 4th century BC, Pytheas set out from Marseille on reconnaissance, on which his first objective was to establish whether Britain was an island or a spur of some misty, darkly timbered northern mainland.

His first view of Albion (Britain) was of Land's End (Belerium), in Cornwall, where the Phoenicians and Carthaginians had long enjoyed a monopoly of the tin trade. "The natives of Britain by the headland of Belerium are unusually hospitable," he found, "and thanks to their intercourse with foreign traders have grown gentle in their manner."

From here Pytheas sailed round Britain, which he described as triangular in shape with three unequal sides. Its perimeter he reckoned at 4,670 miles—only some 900 miles out. On the way he may have visited the interior or spoken to people on the coast who had. "The inhabitants of Britain", he wrote, "are said to be sprung from the soil and to preserve a primitive style of life. . . . They are simple in their habits, and far removed from the cunning and knavishness of modern man. Their diet is inexpensive and quite different from the luxury that is born of wealth. The island is thickly populated, and has an extremely chilly climate. . . ."

"Above Britain" (probably in the notorious Pentland Firth, south of the Orkneys), Pytheas reported sea running "eighty cubits high" (an exaggerated 120 feet). Undaunted, he went on to make a six-day crossing of the North Sea to "Thule", where "there is neither sea nor air, but a mixture like sea-lung, in which earth and air are suspended; the sea-lung binds everything together . . . at night the sun retires to its resting place for two or three hours."

Pytheas's report of Thule, which caused more of a stir than all his other findings put together, still leaves room for speculation.

Fired by ambition and by an unquenchable thirst for knowledge, Alexander the Great was a brilliant general and indefatigable explorer. With an imagination kindled by Homer's tales of glorious deeds, of prowess on the battlefield as well as indulgence at the banqueting table, and an ambition heightened by a sense of personal divinity, Alexander accomplished his father's unfulfilled dream—the conquest of the Persians. The outcome of his consummate military ability was the establishment of one of the biggest empires of the ancient world. On this page is a detail from a mosaic (above left) depicting Alexander at the Battle of Issus—his first successful encounter with the Persian king, Darius III

Persians, to the Greeks they were largely unknown territory. Through his records, through the information collected by his scientists about the geography, plant life and peoples of the countries they passed through, Alexander added immeasurably to the geographical knowledge of the Greeks, and corrected many misconceptions about the East.

He left behind him a vast empire, stretching from the shores of the Mediterranean to the Syr-Dar'ya river and the foothills of the Himalayas. Although this empire was split up soon after Alexander's death, first by his generals and later by invading tribes, the enclaves of Greek subjects dotted across its vast territory ensured that the spirit of Hellenism persisted in the East for centuries.

The Roman Empire

Where was Thule? Iceland? Fair Isle? Or—now thought most likely—Norway, somewhere in the region of the Trondheim Fjord? Also, what was "sea-lung"? A swarm of jellyfish or ice-sludge? Perhaps an eery blanket of fog and ice?

Leaving the strange, unearthly gleam of the Arctic ice fields, Pytheas turned back to a further commercial objective, a reconnaissance of the amber lands. Sailing along the coast of Europe, "beyond the Rhine to Scythia", he saw or heard of an island called Abalus, where so much amber was cast up on the shore that it was burnt as fuel. Abalus could be Bornholm in the Baltic, the estuary of the Oder or Vistula on the Baltic coast, where this fossil resin has always been abundant, or Heligoland in the Friesian Bight at the mouth of the Elbe.

Sadly the original account of the voyage has been lost, and so Pytheas's story—like that of other ancient explorers—has suffered in the retelling, distorted by the blunders of copyists and translators. Also, since to some extent Pytheas was acting in the role of a commercial spy, his mission was no doubt cloaked in a certain amount of secrecy. For these reasons perhaps, his services to world exploration were never fully acknowledged.

But, although the Greeks may be said to have turned geography into a science, the contributions of Eudoxus of Cyzicus were mostly accidental. In a series of flirtations with the unknown—the last of which presumably took him to a watery grave—Eudoxus proved himself one of the most enterprising explorers of antiquity.

Eudoxus came to Egypt some time after 146 BC when Euergetes II was on the throne. This ruler commissioned the Greek to undertake a voyage to India, guided by an Indian pilot who had been cast ashore in the Gulf of Aden. The Indian introduced the explorer to the monsoon route to India and Eudoxus returned with a cargo of aromatics and precious stones which was promptly seized by the king under Ptolemaic law.

Cape of spices

A second voyage was commissioned by Cleopatra. This time, returning from India on the Northeast Monsoon, Eudoxus's ship was driven ashore south of Cape Guardafui (the "Cape of Spices") in Somalia, the easternmost spur of Africa. He was well received by the inhabitants, and it was here that he found, floating in the sea, the prow of a wooden ship with a horse carved on it. When he got back, this was identified as the figurehead of a ship from Cadiz. Someone, he realized, had succeeded in rounding Africa and had sailed into the Indian Ocean.

Prompted no doubt by this chance discovery, Eudoxus (who had been forced to surrender his second cargo as well) now decided to find his own route round Africa to India to avoid the exactions of the Ptolemies. Returning to Cadiz, the Greek built his own ship, stocked it with minstrel boys and girls (gifts for the Indian harems), physicians and carpenters, and finally set off for India "favoured by constant western breezes".

In spite of these the ship ran aground on the coast of Morocco. Another vessel was built with salvaged timber and Eudoxus set sail again, moving south until, he thought, he had reached the same coast where he had found the figurehead. Now he turned back to Morocco, where he tried unsuccessfully to persuade the ruler to sponsor a further expedition.

Undeterred, Eudoxus returned to Cadiz and built two more vessels. He put on board agricultural implements, seeds and carpenters, and again set out with a view to the same circumnavigation. If the voyage were delayed, his plan was to spend the winter on the island he had seen, to sow seed and reap a crop before continuing. But somehow, possibly in a cyclone off the African coast, this enterprising Greek must have perished, for he was never seen again.

Whereas a Greek would set out on some hazardous journey partly out of curiosity, Roman motives for exploration were more mundane. With them science counted for little. When Romans explored, they did so mostly with the express purpose of enriching in some way the mighty Roman Empire, which, even before the birth of Christ,

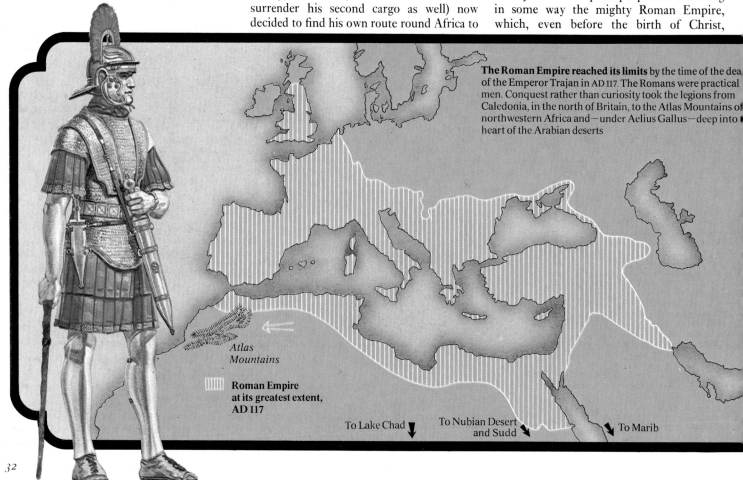

The Roman Empire reached its limits by the time of the death of the Emperor Trajan in AD 117. The Romans were practical men. Conquest rather than curiosity took the legions from Caledonia, in the north of Britain, to the Atlas Mountains of northwestern Africa and—under Aelius Gallus—deep into heart of the Arabian deserts

Atlas
Mountains

Roman Empire
at its greatest extent,
AD 117

To Lake Chad   To Nubian Desert   To Marib
and Sudd

extended east and south to the frontiers of Arabia.

As well as military conquest and exploration, the Romans were motivated by what one historian describes as "an unmixed love of gain". Rapid growth of wealth in Rome itself and in the western provinces led to a demand for exotic luxuries on a scale previously unknown. This is why, although the Romans were no strangers in the north, much more effort was turned towards the south and east. After the fall of Egypt in 30 BC, a new sense of security marked the reign of Augustus, and this sparked a fresh spirit of enterprise. Although the Romans did not engage directly in the eastern trade, they were ready to back the Greek traders in their long voyages to the unknown East.

These men were the first to bring back any real information about India since Megasthenes, an Ionian, went as ambassador to Patna, on the Lower Ganges, in 302 BC (he had travelled widely, passing through territory in the Indo–Gangetic Plain which few, if any, other Europeans had seen). But traffic to India was still painfully slow: unlike the vanished Eudoxus, no one knew how to utilize the monsoons, and Greek skippers were limited to hugging the coastline all the way.

The breakthrough came early in the reign of Augustus's successor, Tiberius (AD 14–37), when the Greek merchant Hippalus came on the scene. With an uncanny knowledge of the geography of the area and of the action of the

winds, Hippalus sailed boldly away from the Arabian coast and out to sea. Making use of the Southwest Monsoon—the prevailing summer wind in the Arabian Sea—he made a landfall somewhere near the Indus, returning on the Northeast Monsoon.

By AD 50 Roman ships were leaving the Arabian mainland on what became known as the "Hippalus Wind" and reaching ports south of Bombay, the most important of which was Cannanore on the Malabar Coast.

By the reign of Hadrian (AD 117–38), Roman ships were sailing in the Bay of Bengal (Ptolemy describes the coastline from the Indus to the Ganges delta in detail), and by 166 they had reached Cochin-China. Thanks partly to Hippalus, trade and exploration flourished until after the 2nd century, when, due to economic decay and loss of purchasing power, Roman subjects ceased to ply to India and the Far East.

Meanwhile, Arabia remained largely unknown. The main initiative against this territory was ordered by Augustus in 25 BC. Led by Aelius Gallus, an expeditionary force of 10,000 men set out on the sweltering journey from the Red Sea coast over desert tracks to Arabia Felix, at that time a fertile country on the coast of Yemen. But six months later Gallus had to turn back from the interior with the remnants of an army depleted by hunger and thirst.

Military expeditions to the African interior were less ruinous. Also in 25 BC, Petronius led a foray against Candace, Queen of Ethiopia, which yielded much new information. Instead of following the great bend of the Nile upstream from Korosko, he took the short cut to Abu Hamed by marching more than 200 miles through the Nubian Desert, then turned downstream to capture Candace's capital, Napata, near the Fourth Cataract, where the Nile swings north and east.

The White Nile
Nero (AD 37–68), planning a full-scale expedition up the Nile, sent a small advance party to attempt to discover its source. They reached Meroe on the White Nile, where there were woods, green grass and traces of elephant and rhinoceros. They went on more than 600 miles upstream to a region, according to Seneca, of "immense marshes, the outcome of which neither the inhabitants know nor can anyone hope to know, in such a way are the plants entangled with the waters, not to be struggled through on foot or in a boat, because the marsh, muddy and blocked up, does not admit any unless it is small and holding one person" They had reached the Sudd—vast swamps of papyrus and rotting vegetation on the Upper Nile, which no European was to see again until the 19th century.

A Roman coin bearing the head of Trajan (c. 53–117), the Spanish-born Emperor of Rome, during whose rule the empire reached its greatest extent, from Britain in the west to the Black Sea in the east, and south into Africa and Arabia

In North Africa the cultivatable fringe was vulnerable to raids by desert tribes, and Roman policing of this territory often became something of a ticket into the unknown. In 19 BC Cornelius Balbus, Governor of Tunisia, crossed the Libyan Desert to occupy Jerma, capital of the Garamantes, a desert tribe in the Fezzan region of the Sahara. Later another Roman officer, Julius Maternus, joined the Garamantes on a four-month raid into the interior, to the region of Agisymba "where the rhinoceroses foregather". It is not certain whether Maternus got as far as Lake Chad, 1,000 miles to the south, but he undoubtedly emerged from the Sahara on to the Sudanese plain.

Some years later, in AD 42, Suetonius Paulinus broke new ground when he set out to quash a revolt among the Moors. Paulinus —the future victor over Boadicea—pressed the chase right across the Atlas Mountains and beyond to the unidentified River Ger. Probably the first European to cross the Atlas, he reported dense growths of scented timber, which was most likely larch and juniper.

Admittedly these episodes added little to the explicit geography of Africa. But then the Ancient World buzzed with some pretty bizarre notions of geography (Caesar, for instance, had Britain facing "westward towards Spain"). Explorers of the time were handicapped by lack of equipment. In overcast conditions, with no Sun or stars in view, they had no way of taking bearings. Similarly there was no formula for measuring speed since no one had yet delineated a precise unit of time. The concept of an hour was unknown to the ancients: their day began when the Sun rose and ended when it slipped beneath the horizon. Given these conditions, the exploits of Pytheas, Eudoxus, Hippalus and the rest assume the proportions of great exploration.

Ultima Thule. Pytheas, the first Greek to venture into the northern Atlantic, reached Thule —perhaps Iceland or Norway— by way of the British Isles. (Below) The limits of Roman expeditions, the routes of Hippalus and Eudoxus to India, and Eudoxus's route round Africa

Atlas Mountains

Alexandria

Indus

Nile

Marib

Lake Chad

Sudd

The silken link

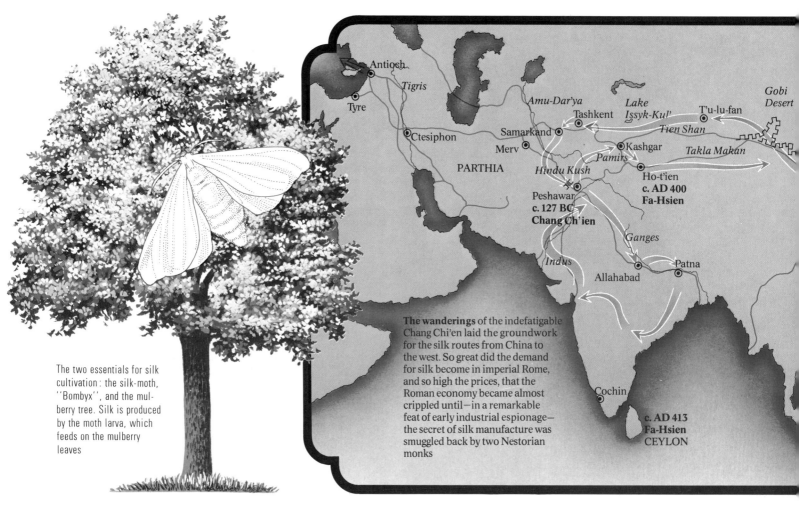

The two essentials for silk cultivation: the silk-moth, "Bombyx", and the mulberry tree. Silk is produced by the moth larva, which feeds on the mulberry leaves

The wanderings of the indefatigable Chang Chi'en laid the groundwork for the silk routes from China to the west. So great did the demand for silk become in imperial Rome, and so high the prices, that the Roman economy became almost crippled until—in a remarkable feat of early industrial espionage—the secret of silk manufacture was smuggled back by two Nestorian monks

TO CONQUEST, CURIOSITY and conversion there has always been added commerce as one of the underlying factors in the outward movement of men from their settled, civilized bases into worlds of hearsay. Such contacts as there were between the ancient realms of East and West grew as the result of the need of the Mediterranean civilizations for a luxury commodity, silk.

The silk came into Parthia (Persia) from beyond the Pamirs and the Tien Shan, the Celestial Mountains, which swing in a huge crescent north from the western Himalayas to separate Sinkiang and western China from the old world of Greek and Roman. The silk was produced by the mysterious "Seres", a people whose name derives from the Chinese word for silk. The silkmakers remained beyond the reach of the Romans, whose ambassadors could go no farther than Parthia, but in their turn the Chinese were endeavouring to send missions to the West. In AD 97 an ambassador named Kan Ying set out from China to Rome, but he too was halted in Parthia.

Nobody in the West knew how silk was made. Virgil recorded how "the Chinese comb off trees their delicate down". At all events it was costly to buy and eventually became a drain on the financial resources of Rome. Pliny estimated: "Our imports from China and Arabia cost a hundred million sesterces per annum." As early as 100 BC, 12 caravans a year, each with 100 men, were leaving China for the West.

Agents to Kashgar

In about AD 120, Maës Titanius, a Greek merchant, sent out agents along the silk road as far as Kashgar and the information they brought back enabled Ptolemy to give a fairly accurate description of the mountain ranges on the western borders of the land of the Seres. The silk, with which the women—and later the men—of the Roman Empire became enamoured, furs, cast-iron work, essences of cinnamon and cinnamon bark (the best of which cost a fortune) came to the Mediterranean from northwestern China by the road which ran along the north side of the Nan Shan Mountains, south of the Great Wall in the province of Kansu.

Where the wall ended, on the borders of Sinkiang, there was a choice of roads, either to the north or south of the great Takla Makan Desert, the shifting sands of which rendered it uninhabitable, to Kashgar, the important staging post at the foot of the Pamirs and to the Tien Shan, a journey of

seven months from Ch'ang-an, the metropolis in the later Han dynasty.

At Kashgar the road divided again, the northern route crossing the Tien Shan range by the Torugat Pass into the Fergana Basin and continuing by way of Samarkand to Bukhara and Merv.

The southern route, one of the wildest roads in the world, led over the Pamirs southwards by the Taun-murun Pass, crossed the upper waters of the Oxus and entered Badakhshan, eventually reaching Merv by what was called the Stone Tower and Bactria.

The man principally responsible for the opening-up of these routes through the Tien Shan and the Pamirs was Chang Ch'ien, an emissary of the Han Emperor Wu Ti, who, in 138 BC, was sent to make contact with the Yuechi, a Chinese tribe which had been displaced by the Huns and forced to migrate westwards from Kashgaria, over the Hindu Kush, eventually settling in northern India around Peshawar.

Chang Ch'ien's journey was protracted. Captured by Huns, presumably while on the way to Kashgar, he spent ten years in captivity, then escaped into Fergana and eventually reached the Yuechi capital, Heyuchi, near Peshawar, close to the Khyber Pass.

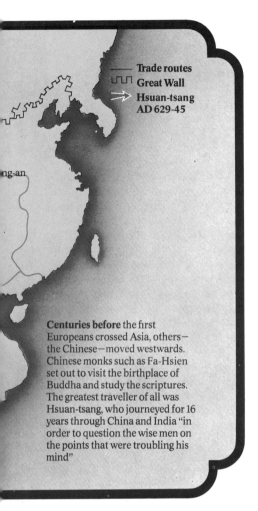

Centuries before the first Europeans crossed Asia, others— the Chinese—moved westwards. Chinese monks such as Fa-Hsien set out to visit the birthplace of Buddha and study the scriptures. The greatest traveller of all was Hsuan-tsang, who journeyed for 16 years through China and India "in order to question the wise men on the points that were troubling his mind"

On his way back to China, in Tibet he was again captured by Huns, spent 12 more years as a prisoner, and eventually reached China in 116. The following year he was sent to Fergana to establish a forward base for the trade in silk with the West.

From Merv the road ran west through northern Iran to Ecbatana; then, from Seleucia-Ctesiphon (two cities, one Seleucid, the other Parthian, which occupied opposite banks of the Tigris below the present Baghdad) it followed the "royal road" used by the Achaemenidian and Seleucid kings, through northern Mesopotamia and Syria to Antioch, more than 6,000 miles from its beginnings in China.

From Antioch the silk was either shipped to Italy or else sent south to be dyed and woven at Beirut, Tyre, Sidon, Gaza or other places on what had previously been the Phoenician coast. To serve these places, a more direct route was opened to the Mediterranean across the Syrian Desert by way of Palmyra.

In the 6th century, two monks, probably Nestorian Christians, succeeded in smuggling to Byzantium the eggs of the silk-moth, *Bombyx mori*. It was an early example of industrial espionage—they had been bribed

by the Emperor Justinian to break the monopoly which the Persians had established over the trade. They brought them "from a country where there were many nations of the Indians and which was called Serinda" (possibly Cambodia, Champa, or even Kashgaria). When the eggs hatched successfully, Europe eventually became independent of the East for its supplies of raw silk.

From the 4th century on, Chinese monks began to make long journeys beyond the frontiers, setting out from their Buddhist monasteries to study the sacred books of their religion at their sources (some Chinese versions had become obscure in the process of translation from the Sanskrit). One of the greatest of these travelling monks, Fa-Hsien, known as "the Manifestation of the Faith", accompanied by three others, reached Khotan in Tartary on the southern side of the Takla Makan Desert in 399, finding there large communities of monks who practised the form of asceticism known as The Great Vehicle.

Spitting dragons

Fa-Hsien then crossed into India through "mountains covered with snow both in winter and summer . . . they shelter also dragons which, if once provoked, spit out their poison" and passed through Dardistan (modern Gilgit).

Reaching the valley of the Ganges, Fa-Hsien eventually reached Ceylon and embarked for China, arriving there in 414, after an absence of 15 years. On his return he wrote the *Fo-Kwe-Ki* (Memoirs of the Buddha Realms), an account of his travels.

The 15-year journey in search of knowledge by Fa-Hsien was equalled some 200 years later by another Chinese, Hsuan-tsang, known to his contemporaries as the "Master of the law". He left China in 629 to "travel to the countries of the west in order to question the wise men on the points that were troubling his mind".

After evading the authorities, who forbade his departure, riding an old horse that was reputed to have crossed the Gobi Desert 15 times, Hsuan-tsang made his lonely way to the southern slopes of the Barkol Tagh Mountains. On the way, he narrowly escaped being killed by an arrow while passing the Chinese forts on the western borders of Sinkiang and in the desert had visions of mounted warriors—probably the effect of mirage.

The following spring he crossed the Tien Shan range by a glacial pass, a journey on which a dozen fellow travellers lost their lives, descending from it to the Issy-kul Lake, where he met the Khan of the West Tartars. Passing through the Khan's capital, Tashkent, and Samarkand he reached

Bamian, where he saw the two great standing Buddhas cut in the cliff face and another, recumbent and 1,000 feet long, which (if it ever existed) has now disappeared. Crossing the Hindu Kush by the Shibar Pass, where he was rescued in a blizzard by hunters, he spent some time in a monastery near Kabul before moving on to Nagarahara (Nagara, near Jalalabad), where he contemplated relics and visited a cave in which Buddha had left his shadow after an encounter with a dragon.

Travelling east through the Khyber Pass he set off for the Upper Indus, and in Dardistan found that, just as they are today, "perilous were the roads, and dark the gorges. Sometimes the pilgrim had to pass by loose cords, sometimes by light stretched iron chains. Here there were ledges hanging in mid-air; there flying bridges across abysses; elsewhere paths cut with the chisel, or footings to climb by." Returning to Peshawar he crossed the Indus and stayed for two years in the neighbourhood of the by then decayed city of Taxila, studying in its monasteries, after which he made a protracted descent of the Ganges, visiting among other places Allahabad, where he saw the sacred banyan, Banaras and Patalipura (Patna). By now Patalipura was nothing more than a small town surrounded by the deserted city of stone built by King Asoka. It had probably been sacked by the Huns about half a century before his arrival. He also visited Assam, southern India, Ceylon, the Deccan and many other parts of India.

By about 643 he was back at the Indus, and, in crossing it, lost many manuscripts and a collection of rare seeds before once again setting off northwards across the mountains with an elephant, which had been given to him. The elephant was drowned after it had rushed into a river in panic when the caravan in which it was travelling was attacked.

In spite of these perils Hsuan-tsang succeeded in reaching Kashgar and then Khotan, where he stayed for eight months at the invitation of the king, lecturing to 5,000 monks. Finally he arrived at Ch'ang-an in the spring of 645, where he was given a great welcome after an absence of 15 years. He arrived back, according to accounts and pictures that have survived, with a great chariot drawn by 20 horses and loaded with more than 700 religious books, statues of Buddha and relics.

He spent the rest of his life, until his death in 649, supervising the compilation of the *Ta-T'ang-Si Yu-Ki* (Memoirs on Western Countries) issued by the T'ang dynasty, which the Emperor Tai-T'sung ordered him to produce. It has been estimated that the wordage translated in the last five years of his life was 84 times that of the Bible.

North and west to a New World

T HE RAGGED COAST of Scandinavia offers little in the way of a living to a society whose culture and way of life are based on tillage or pasture. Such a society was that of the Germanic migrants who moved out northwards from central Europe at the time of the "Folk Wanderings", the dispersal of the Indo–European peoples 1,000 years and more before the birth of Christ.

The slender resources of the Scandinavian shores may well have been sufficient, at first, to sustain these migrants, the forebears of those men who enter history's pages as the Vikings. There was the sea, and its inshore harvest of fish, at hand to help feed them and to teach them the seafaring skills that they were to put to such good use in later centuries. But, in the course of time, the pressures of population growth outran the ability of the land to support them. The sea beckoned, and they responded, for there was nowhere else to go. The Viking age had begun.

In the course of the centuries during which they forged their place in history, the Norsemen (which more accurately describes them: *Viking* means warrior, and the men on whom the real achievement was based were traders and settlers, albeit brave ones) were the first

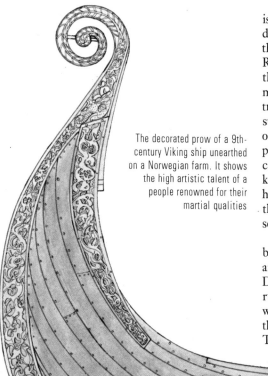

The decorated prow of a 9th-century Viking ship unearthed on a Norwegian farm. It shows the high artistic talent of a people renowned for their martial qualities

Europeans to reach the New World, the home in future centuries of one of the superpowers of the 20th century, the United States. But these Scandinavians also fanned out to the east, and with their trading centres on the great waterways of Russia, laid the foundations of the other superpower, Russia.

Portage points

Hauling their vessels at portage points between one riverhead and the next through regions that are frozen for much of the year, the Scandinavians—known as Varangians to the Slavic people with whom they came in contact, or Rus (possibly derived from a Finnish word describing men from the Baltic)—made their way swiftly south. At first engaged in pillage and slaving like their counterparts in the west, the Rus soon realized that they had a firm grip on a natural trade route, there to be exploited commercially. The wandering bands of raiders came together under one leader, Rurik (862), and, establishing their headquarters at Novgorod, looked south for further conquest. Smolensk gave them a base on the great River Dnieper and this, in turn, led them to Kiev, mother city of medieval Russia.

Before it reaches the Black Sea, the Dnieper is broken by fierce rapids. A contemporary description of them, and the way in which they were overcome by the Rus, says "the Russes do not dare to pass through them; they put in at the bank, landing some of the men and leaving the goods in the boats; they try out the way with their bare feet lest they strike a rock. While some at the prow and others at the middle do this, those in the stern propel with poles and so, with the greatest care, they get past this first obstruction, keeping in close to the river bank. When they have got through, they take on those whom they had set down and come down to the second obstruction."

There were seven such rapids to be passed before the travellers reached smoother waters and a four-day journey to the mouth of the Dnieper. Here they added masts, sails and rudders and, coasting Bulgaria, made their way to the city they knew as Micklegirth—the great Byzantine capital of Constantinople. The first visit by the Norsemen to this city,

in 860, was a raid of the kind with which western Europe was growing familiar. It was as Russians, with Novgorod and Kiev united under Prince Oleg, that they replaced raiding with trading—but not before Viking ships had passed through the Bosphorus and the Aegean into the Mediterranean as far as Sicily. Together, the Norsemen from Norway, Denmark and Sweden had encircled Europe in less than a century.

South and east from the frayed coasts of their homelands, the Norsemen had little difficulty in leeching on to the prosperous, settled communities of Europe. A natural energy and drive, superior leadership and weaponry were enough to send their prey into the churches to appeal for divine protection against the Norseman's wrath. Few of these military qualities were of use to the Scandinavians, who set another course—westwards from the fjords and skerries of Norway into the North Atlantic. Hardiness and courage were needed in plenty, but to these qualities was added a maritime expertise of a kind hitherto unknown—and one which was to vanish again with the decline of the Vikings, for hundreds of years.

The vessels the Norsemen used for

The Folk Wanderings. The people who were to spawn the Vikings and their great maritime tradition reached Scandinavia more than 1,000 years BC with the break-up of the Indo-European community, a vast conglomerate of pastoral people who inhabited central Europe (map below). When they reached the fjord-frayed northeastern coasts of Europe and social presssures once again forced movement upon them, there was only one way to go—to sea. There then grew the great sea-warrior tradition which was to strike fear into the heart of any nation with a seaboard community in Europe—and added a new prayer to the litany of the early Christians: "May God free us from the fury of the Norsemen." But there was more to the Vikings than violence. They were also colonizers, traders and explorers who developed skills in shipbuilding and of seamanship and navigation which took them to an unknown New World

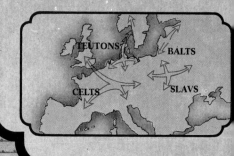

trading and long voyages were not the warships that figure in films—many-oared with low, shield-hung freeboards and prows decorated with the drakkar, the snake emblem, to strike terror into the hearts of their enemies. The voyaging ship was the *knorr*; shorter, with a deeper draught and with more freeboard than the fighting ship, it was clinker-built with pine planks caulked and tarred and frames and keel of oak.

Tackle and anchor cable were of walrus hide and the square sail, made of wadmal (a sort of coarse woollen cloth), was bent to a yard that was raised and lowered by a halliard. There were few oars in such a ship, which was steered by a rudder over the starboard quarter by a helmsman using a right-angled tiller.

In the early days it was only possible to sail with the wind abaft the beam; but later, by running out a boom to brace up the yard it was possible to sail with the wind on the beam. With a good wind it was possible to make about ten knots.

The larger ships could carry two or three dozen people, as well as cattle, sometimes horses, fodder, farming gear, a couple of pulling boats and cargo, which, stowed amid-

ships, was lashed down under oxhide covers. Up forward there was a half-deck, a sort of fo'c'sle head, under which it was possible to get some shelter from sea, rain and snow.

Smaller ships, the sort that made some of the longest early voyages of reconnaissance, with a crew of not more than six, had no half-deck and only one pulling boat.

The only protection against the elements for the crew were hooded, ankle-length smocks made of similar material to that used for the sail, and sleeping bags made from sheepskin or cowhide.

How they steered

Navigation out of sight of land was by estimate of distance run either in *dogr sigling*, a day's run of approximately 120 nautical miles under sail, or *vikar sjafar*, a four-to-five-mile turn at the oars, possibly calculated with a sand glass or a water clock. Speed through the water was estimated by watching drifting objects and bubbles.

At night the North Star was used as a guide and by day the Sun, although in the high northern latitudes they were often invisible for long periods.

The Vikings almost certainly employed

the hollow sundial of the sort invented by Eratosthenes, a later version of which consisted of a wooden disc, marked out with concentric circles, which floated in a tub of water. At the centre of the disc a gnomon, adjustable according to the declination of the Sun at various seasons, cast a shadow across the rings, each of which was marked with destinations from north to south. By turning the ship's head at noon until the shadow began to coincide with the circle of destination it was possible to make an approximate determination of the latitude along which it was desired to sail.

The Vikings were adept at drawing conclusions from natural phenomena that would help them in their navigation. They observed the difference between the run of the sea and the direction of the wind due to currents, the onset of fog, the presence of ice, the change in colour and temperature of the water—particularly helpful when approaching the coast of Greenland, where the cold East Greenland and Polar currents were encountered, and they observed too the habits of coastal and oceanic birds, such as eider ducks and fulmar petrels.

According to the *Landnamabok*, the "Book

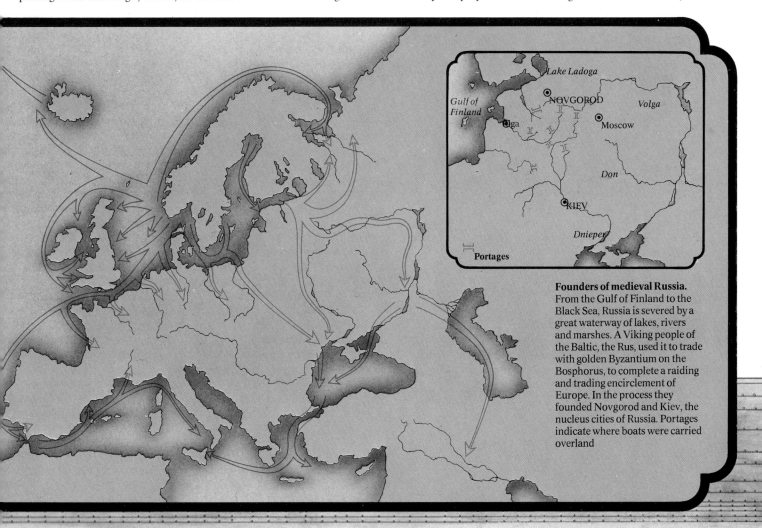

Founders of medieval Russia.
From the Gulf of Finland to the Black Sea, Russia is severed by a great waterway of lakes, rivers and marshes. A Viking people of the Baltic, the Rus, used it to trade with golden Byzantium on the Bosphorus, to complete a raiding and trading encirclement of Europe. In the process they founded Novgorod and Kiev, the nucleus cities of Russia. Portages indicate where boats were carried overland

North and west to a New World

of Landtakings", which records the settlement of Iceland and the bloodthirsty proclivities of the early settlers (few died a natural death, but instead destroyed one another in a variety of gruesome ways), an early voyager from the Faeroes to Iceland, Floki Vilggerdarson, released three ravens on three consecutive days to help him estimate his course and position. The first returned to the Faeroes, the second to the ship and the third flew west, giving him his direction. From this time on he was known as Raven-Floki.

The Orkneys, Shetlands and Faeroes were the first islands to be settled, followed by Iceland, which was already occupied by what the Norsemen called "papar"—monks and anchorites—about 860. The first to reach it, of whom any record exists, was a Swedish Viking, called Gardar, who made a landfall on the southeast coast at Austürhorn (Eastern Horn), a headland that was to become a familiar landfall on what, in normal conditions, was a week's sailing from Norway.

From here he sailed westwards about, doubling the Austürhorn, the North Cape of Iceland, to reach Skjalfandi, a bay on the north coast, where he built a house at Husavik (House Bay). The following spring he continued his circumnavigation of the island, but left three of his party behind.

He was followed by Naddod, a West Viking, who reached Reydarfjord on the east coast, saw the haven obliterated by snow when sailing off shore and named the island "Snaeland".

The third was Floki, who made his landfall with the help of his ravens and built a house on the Breidafjord (Borgarfjördur), on the east coast, among what were green pastures when he arrived in the summer. Improvidently, he and his companions did not make any hay because the fishing was so good and as a result, when winter came, they lost all their livestock and spent a miserable winter followed by a second when contrary winds prevented them from sailing home. Floki named it "Island", the island of ice, after seeing a fjord surface covered with it.

Growing population

By about 920 the country was so extensively settled that all the good land had been taken. By this time the population numbered about 30,000. By 1100 it was about 80,000 and the Icelanders had become Christian with their own rather unusual sort of Christianity.

The first recorded sighting of the coast of Greenland, the largest island in the world, was by an Icelander, Gunnbjörn Ulfsson (Ulf-Krakason is another version), at the end of the 9th century. On a passage from Norway to Iceland he was driven past the island in a storm and into what he described as skerries on the east coast of Greenland. They have been identified as the islands near the modern settlement of Angmagssalik on the east coast, 60 miles south of the Arctic Circle, though some believe that what Ulfsson saw were icebergs.

In 978, a shipload of colonists led by Snaebjord Galti arrived from Iceland on this bitter, exposed coast, where they spent a winter of horror, and murder was committed.

In 982, Erik the Red (so-called because of his flaming hair and beard) was outlawed and exiled from Iceland for manslaughter and sailed for Greenland, following the route supposedly taken by Gunnbjörn Ulfsson nearly a century before. Erik and his people sailed west from Iceland, using the Snaefellsjökull, a great cone-shaped mountain and its glacier, as a landmark and sailed westwards for 450 miles—a simple enough voyage for Vikings with the easterly winds of early summer behind them. They made their awe-inspiring landfall on the east coast of Greenland near the glacier they called "Blaserk" (Blueshirt), near Angmagssalik, not far south of the Arctic Circle.

From here they sailed south, probably rounding the southern point not by doubling the dangerous Cap Farvel (Cape Farewell) but by passing through Prins Christian Sund to the north of it. Here a spectacular wall of glacial ice hems in the northern shore for a distance of 50 miles.

Now they entered warmer waters on a more friendly coast, from which the ice-cap was invisible, with long sheltered fjords running into the land and where there were rich, well-watered pastures that had never known sheep or cattle. Here, in what was to be the "Eastern Settlement" of Erik's and other Icelandic sagas, in the Julienhåb Bight, they passed the winter on an island and, in the following spring, entered a fjord to which Erik gave his name, where he built a homestead of turf and stone.

The next two years of exile were spent in exploring the west coast, on which they saw the remains of boats and the ruins of houses of former inhabitants; they may have crossed

The "knorr", like the "drakkar", was guided by a long oar, the steerboard, on the side of the ship to which it gave its name—starboard

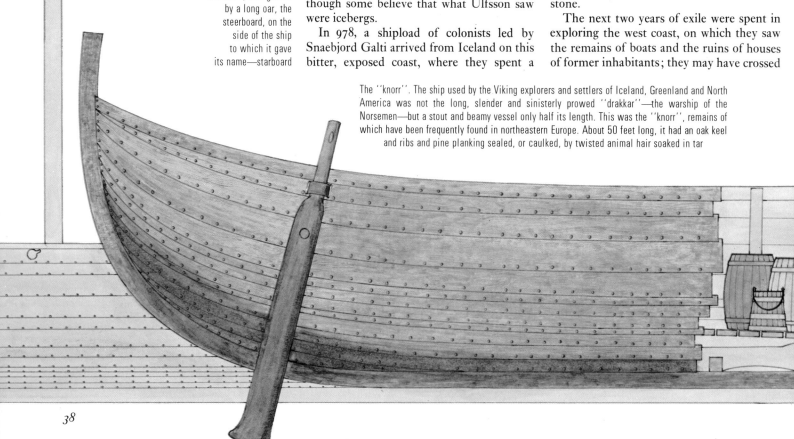

The "knorr". The ship used by the Viking explorers and settlers of Iceland, Greenland and North America was not the long, slender and sinisterly prowed "drakkar"—the warship of the Norsemen—but a stout and beamy vessel only half its length. This was the "knorr", remains of which have been frequently found in northeastern Europe. About 50 feet long, it had an oak keel and ribs and pine planking sealed, or caulked, by twisted animal hair soaked in tar

A typical Viking warship, the Oseberg ship, c. 800, was found preserved in clay and can be seen in an Oslo museum

the Davis Strait to the Cumberland Peninsula on Baffin Island, only 200 miles to the west, although there is no record of their having done so.

Returning to Iceland, Erik, who named the new country Greenland because "people would be much more tempted to go there if it had an attractive name", had no difficulty in persuading people to settle. In about 986 a fleet of 25 ships set out for the new land. Only 14 ships reached their destination, although some of the others succeeded in returning to Iceland.

There, on the southwest coast, in the Eastern Settlement, 190 farmsteads were built around Erik's house at Brattahlid on the shore of the fjord and another, the Middle Settlement, grew up in the Ivigtut Bight, 30 miles to the north. Two hundred miles up the coast, near what is now Godthåb, the Western Settlement was founded with 90 farms.

They flourished. Although there were no useful minerals and no wood, except driftwood, fit for anything but fuel, it was much warmer then, though not warm enough to grow cereals. It was the period of what is known as the "Little Climatic Optimum", which lasted from about 1000 to 1200, when the coast was largely ice-free; drift ice was rare south of 70N and permanent ice started only at 80N. Both sea and land teemed with fish, bird and animal life.

Soon missionaries arrived, a bishop was appointed and a cathedral built. From the settlements, adventurous explorers and hunters reached 72.55N, north of Umanak, where Erling Sighvatsson, Bjarni Thordarson and Eindridi left cairns and a runic inscription to prove it. The Prologue to the 12th-century *Landnamabok* stated that: "According to learned men, it is seven days' sail from Stad in Norway to Horn in the east of Iceland; and from Snaefellsness it is four days' sail to Cape Farewell in Greenland. From Hern Island, off Norway, one can sail due west to Cape Farewell, passing north of Shetland close enough to see it clearly in good visibility, and south of the Faeroes half-sunk below the horizon, and a day's sail to the South of Iceland.

"From Reykjaness in the south of Iceland it is five days' sail to Slyne Head in Ireland. From Langaness in the north of Iceland it is four days' sail to Jan Mayen Island, at the end of the ocean, and a day's sail from Kolbeins Island to the uninhabited regions of Greenland."

At the greatest period of their prosperity the Greenlanders numbered about 3,000, but in the 13th century things began to go badly when they lost their independence to Norway

and were forbidden to own sea-going ships. Economic troubles and the outbreak of the Black Death meant that ships did not come either to Iceland or Greenland, sometimes for years at a time. From 1200 onwards the temperature began to fall and drift ice borne south to Cape Farewell and the northwest hemmed the settlements in. In these conditions the Eskimoes moved south and there was fighting between natives and settlers. By 1430 the northern hemisphere was in the grip of a little Ice Age and temperatures in Greenland were between 3° and 7°C less than they had been in Erik's time, and soon the Western Settlement collapsed. The increasingly debilitated inhabitants of the Eastern Settlement lingered on until about 1500 when they too perished. By this time Greenland had been almost entirely forgotten by the outside world; when in 1540 a man called Jon Greenlander was blown into a fjord there while on a voyage from Hamburg to Iceland he said that he and his companions found houses and "a dead man lying face downwards on the ground. On his head he wore a well-made hood, and in addition clothes both

The simple upswept prow and stern of the "knorr" lacked the carvings and ornamentation of the forbidding "drakkar"

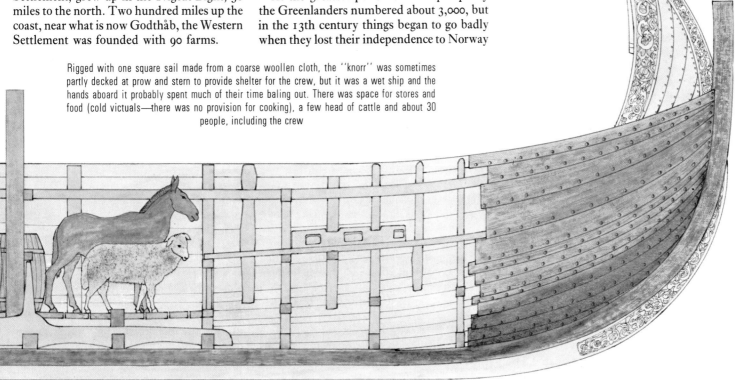

Rigged with one square sail made from a coarse woollen cloth, the "knorr" was sometimes partly decked at prow and stern to provide shelter for the crew, but it was a wet ship and the hands aboard it probably spent much of their time baling out. There was space for stores and food (cold victuals—there was no provision for cooking), a few head of cattle and about 30 people, including the crew

North and west to a New World

of frieze and of sealskin. Near him was a sheath-knife, bent and much worn and wasted away. This knife they took with them as a keepsake."

According to the Icelandic Sagas it is a matter of doubt who first discovered America; that the Norsemen did discover it there seems no reason to doubt. In fact it would be strange if, during their period of settlement in Greenland, one of their ships had not come upon at least its northeastern coasts, either by accident or design. The lack of timber alone would have provided an incentive for exploratory voyages westwards.

The Groenlendinga Saga relates that in about 986 Bjarni Herjolfsson, on a voyage from Iceland to visit his family in Greenland (which he himself considered foolhardy), was blown off course and reached the continent at two separate points; the first "not mountainous, but well wooded and with low hills", was certainly no part of Greenland; the second, reached after "leaving the land on the port quarter and . . . sailing for two days", was "flat and wooded".

The next sighting was of another land, which they saw after sailing before a southwest wind for three days. "This one was high and mountainous and topped by a glacier" and they found that it was an island. Then, as it began to blow a gale, they ran to the east for four days, finally reaching Greenland.

There have been numerous theories as to where these sightings took place. Sandwich Bay on the coast of Labrador in 53.30N, 57.15W has been suggested for the first, South Bay, 200 miles to the north, for the second and somewhere in the region of Frobisher Bay, 63.30N, 66W, at the southern end of Baffin Island, for the third.

In the words of the same saga "there was now great talk of discovering new countries. Leif, the son of Erik the Red of Brattahlid, went to see Bjarni Herjolfsson and bought his ship from him, and engaged a crew of thirty-five . . . among them was a Southerner called Tyrkir [probably a German]. . . . They made their ship ready and put out to sea. The first landfall they made was the country that Bjarni had sighted last. They sailed right up to the shore and cast anchor, then lowered a boat and landed. There was no grass to be seen, and the hinterland was covered with great glaciers, and between glaciers and shore the land was like one great slab of rock. It seemed to them [as it had to Bjarni] a worthless country."

Leif, whom the saga describes as "tall and strong and very impressive in appearance . . . a shrewd man and always moderate in his behaviour", named it Helluland, "The Land of Flat Stone". Putting to sea again they sighted a second land and again they went

ashore. "This country was flat and wooded, with white sandy beaches wherever they went; and the land sloped gently down to the sea. Leif said, 'This country shall be named after its natural resources: it shall be called Markland [Forest Land].'"

This was probably Labrador, the first land that Bjarni had sighted. After two more days sailing before a northeast wind they again made a landfall, coming in to an island which lay to the north of it.

"There was dew on the grass, and the first thing they did was to get some of it on their hands and put it to their lips, and to them it seemed the sweetest thing they had ever tasted."

Now they sailed through the sound between the island and a headland on what they took to be the mainland. Beyond it to the west the tide was running out and their ship was left high and dry.

Here, they were at the mouth of a river that flowed from a lake and when the tide made sufficiently they took their ship up into the river.

They passed that winter on its shore, living in huts made of stone and turf, which they probably covered with cloth or hides. "There was no lack of salmon in the river or the lake, bigger salmon than they had ever seen. The country seemed to them so kind that no winter fodder would be needed for livestock: there was never any frost all winter and the grass hardly withered at all.

"In this country, night and day were of more even length than in either Greenland or Iceland: on the shortest day of the year, the sun was already up by 9 am, and did not set until after 3 pm"—no doubt a welcome contrast to the almost permanent dusk of a Greenland winter.

An odd German
During this time Leif sent out reconnaissance parties, on one of which Tyrkir, who is described as having "a prominent forehead and shifty eyes, and not much more of a face besides . . . short and puny-looking but very clever with his hands", having been separated from the others, made an historic discovery which it was difficult for him to communicate to the others as he was so excited that for some time he spoke only in German. He had found vines with grapes growing on them.

They made a great harvest. "It is said that the tow-boat was filled with grapes." Then, in the spring, with a cargo of timber, they sailed for Greenland. Leif named this happy place Vinland or Wine-land.

Some time later—possibly about 1004—Leif's brother Thorvald set off in the same ship with 30 men to find out more of Vinland.

The first winter was spent in Leif's en-

Although shaky in coastal delineation, the Skólholt map, c. 1600, pinpoints Helluland, Markland and Skraelingsland, and shows Greenland joined to North America

campment, and in the spring a small party sailed westwards in one of the ship's boats along the coast, where they found "woods stretching almost down to the shore and white sandy beaches. There were numerous islands there, and extensive shallows. They found no trace of human habitation or animals except on one westerly island, where they found a wooden stack cover. That was the only man-made thing they found; and in the autumn they returned to Leif's Houses."

The following summer Thorvald sailed first to the east and then north along the coast, where the keel of his ship was so badly damaged that it had to be replaced and Thorvald erected the old one on a headland, which he named Kjalarness (Keelness), to the northeast of Vinland.

Then, still sailing east, they came to a point between two fjords where they had their first sight of the inhabitants of America, nine men living under three skin boats. Not being anthropologically inclined, the Norsemen killed eight, the other escaping.

Not surprisingly they were attacked by more "Skraelings"—a derogatory name used by the Greenlanders to describe the Eskimoes, in this case Red Indians—who paddled up to their ship in a whole fleet of skin boats and began to shoot at them.

In the course of the action Thorvald was mortally wounded by an arrow, which struck him in the armpit. He told his men to bury him on a headland that he had thought of as a good site for a settlement. "'I said that I would settle there for a while,' he said. 'Bury me there and put crosses at my head and feet, and let the place be called Krossaness for ever afterwards.'"

War and craftsmanship went hand in hand for the Vikings, as this sword with its elaborately worked silver hilt testifies

A 16th-century woodcut of a "portage" point on the Russian waterways, where the Scandinavian Rus carried their boats from one riverhead to another. In this way they traversed the largest country in Europe

Having buried him the rest returned to their camp, where they spent the winter and gathered grapes and vines as cargo for the ship (how they kept the grapes unless in the form of wine or grape juice is not clear). In the spring they set off on the voyage to Greenland: "They made land at Eiriksfjord, and had plenty to tell Leif."

In about 1010, according to Erik's Saga, Thorfinn Karlsefni set off from the Western Settlement on a larger expedition for Vinland with three ships and 160 people, visiting Helluland and Markland, finding the keel of Thorvald's ship on Kjalarness and naming the coast Furdustrands, "Wonder Strands". After passing these enormous beaches Thorfinn put ashore a Scotsman and a Scotswoman, who were part of the crew and both of whom "could run faster than deer", to carry out a reconnaissance. Naked except for the *bjafal*, a sort of hooded shirt, they returned in three days with grapes and wild wheat.

From here Thorfinn sailed into what he named Straumfjord, where there was tall grass on the shore and mountains behind. He and his men spent a terrible winter there having been incredibly slack about providing fodder. At one time they thought themselves saved by the almost miraculous stranding of a whale; but the meat made them ill.

There was now a split in the party—Thorhall the Hunter, taking one ship and heading north in search of Vinland, departing with the bilious words: "Let us head back to our countrymen at home; let our ocean-striding ship explore the broad tracts of the sea while these eager swordsmen who laud these lands settle in Furdustrands and boil up whales."

They were never seen by their companions again. According to the saga "Thorhall and his crew sailed northwards past Furdustrands and Kjalarness, and tried to beat westward from there. But they ran into fierce head-winds and were driven right across to Ireland [where Norsemen were not appreciated]. There they were brutally beaten and enslaved; and there Thorhall died." The remainder sailed south along the coast and entered the estuary of a river which, because of sandbars, they could only enter at high tide.

It was good country with an abundance of fish and with wild wheat and vines. While they were there they encountered the first Skraelings, "small and evil-looking, and their hair was coarse; they had large eyes and broad cheekbones".

Here, they spent the winter. There was no snow and no need of fodder for their cattle; and in the spring they began to trade with the Skraelings, who arrived in skin boats.

Terrified by the sudden appearance of a bull brought by the Norsemen, which came bellowing from the woods, the Skraelings fled. Three weeks later they reappeared and put in such a savage attack that the day was only saved by the sudden irruption of Erik's illegitimate daughter Freydis, pregnant and armed with a sword with which she slapped one of her naked breasts in such a fearsome manner that once more the Skraelings fled.

Leaving this fertile but dangerous country to its inhabitants they sailed north, finding on the way five skin-clad Skraelings asleep beside a loathsome concoction of deer-marrow mixed with blood, a sort of pemmican in

Baffin
Bay

GREENLAND

Cape Austurhorn
ICELAND

Snæfellsjökull

HELLULAND

Ûmanak

Arctic Circle

Angmagssalik

Davis
Strait

Godthåb

Julianehåb

Ivigtut

Cape Farewell

Frobisher
Bay

MARKLAND

Sandwich Bay

Lake
Melville

L'Anse aux
Meadows

NEWFOUND-
LAND

?

VINLAND

——— **Northern limit
of wild vine**

----- **Southern limit
of salmon**

Viking America. Evidence of Norse exploration and settlement in the New World is largely based on the old Scandinavian sagas and their references to wild vine and salmon, but in 1961 a substantial settlement was excavated at L'Anse aux Meadows, in Newfoundland. Scepticism greets most claims that they may also have reached the Great Lakes and Minnesota

Bleak abodes: the Greenland ice sheet (top) limited the Norse settlements to a narrow coastal strip. Thingvellir (above), the site of the old Icelandic parliament

which they had presumably been over-indulging. The Norsemen killed them.

Later that year, while searching for Thorhall the Hunter, north and west of Kjalarness, Thorvald had an encounter with a "Uniped", on the edge of a wild and gloomy forest. One of the more improbable inhabitants, but possibly a witch doctor in full dress "it came bounding down towards where the ship lay. Thorvald, Erik the Red's son, was sitting at the helm. The Uniped shot an arrow into his groin.

"Thorvald pulled out the arrow and said 'This is a rich country we have found; there is plenty of fat around my entrails.' Soon afterwards he died of the wound."

After spending a third winter on the coast at Straumfjord, they sailed for Markland, where they captured two Skraeling boys whom they taught their language and later baptised, and in the summer returned to Greenland.

The Vinland sagas date from the 12th and 13th centuries, long after the events that they describe; but a far earlier account of Vinland was written by a priest, Adam of Bremen, about 1075, about 60 years after the expedition of Thorfinn Karlsefni.

He had visited King Svein Ulfsson at his court in Denmark, who had told him "that there was another island in that ocean which had been discovered by many and was called Vinland, because vines grow wild there and yield excellent wine, and, moreover, self-sown grain grows there in abundance; it is not from any fanciful imaginings that we have learned this, but from the reliable reports of the Danes."

Where was Vinland? Newfoundland, Nova Scotia, the mouth of the St Lawrence, the coast of New England, the United States seaboard as far south as Florida have all been suggested. If what the Groenlendinga Saga says about Leif's men finding that the Sun was already risen by 9 am on the shortest day of the year, and did not set until after 3 pm, then it must have been somewhere between latitude 50N and 40N. It would include much of Newfoundland and the Gulf of St Lawrence and the coast as far south as New Jersey.

Whatever doubt surrounds the magnitude of Norse achievement in North America—whether or not they scattered the eastern seaboard with conveniently placed relics, or penetrated the Middle West—the old sagas in which their journeys were described display enough knowledge of seamanship to leave without doubt the fact that the *Vester-vegen*—the western route to Iceland and Greenland—took the seafarers of Norway to North America more than 1,000 years ago; and that on sparsely searched shores more clues to Atlantic history lie hidden.

IT WAS MEN with the reputation of barbarians who raised the curtain between East and West, bringing together the two halves of the medieval world. Before the Mongols swept across Asia, the great civilizations of India and China on the one hand and Christendom on the other had barely met. For centuries East and West, though conscious of each other's existence, stood apart.

The warehouses of Europe had long been enriched with the treasures of the East—spices from Java, Persian carpets, silks from China, chessmen hand-carved from Siamese ebony—but the only points of contact with Eastern trade were the ports of the Levant. Westerners could venture no farther along the caravan routes, for the Turks were entrenched throughout Central Asia, cutting off the road to the East.

Trade routes

At this time there were two established trade routes from the Orient to the West: overland from Central Asia to the shores of the Black Sea or southwards to Baghdad; and the sea route, which stopped short of the Mediterranean, blocked by the great land mass of Arabia. So, although Western merchants—Greeks and Italians mostly—thronged the Black Sea ports and the thriving Mediterranean termini, they were confined to trading at Asia's back door. Islam, the bitter foe of Christendom, stood as an impenetrable barrier between the West and all possible routes to the East.

In the mid-13th century all this changed. Incredibly, in the wake of the Mongol conquests, East and West were to be free to mingle as never before. Freed from Turkish domination, Central Asia was to be opened up to exploration, its forbidding terrain mapped and charted by a succession of travellers—missionaries and merchants—who were to spend their lives forging the first-ever real contact with the East.

The prelude to this time of enlightenment and freedom was a bloodbath. In 1206, the Mongols, known in the West by the medieval name of Tartars, came together under a 44-year-old chieftain, Temuchin, who created a powerful and loyal army to exact tribute from neighbouring civilizations. Summoning a *kuriltai*, a great assembly of tribal chieftains, Temuchin assumed the name and title that were to fill both Europe and Asia with terror: Genghis Khan.

What followed—a campaign of conquest lasting more than 50 years—had never been seen in history before. Alongside the eventual Tartar domain, the Roman Empire would have seemed like an undersized weakling. Even the adventures of Alexander, who had fought his way to India and back, paled into

God and commerce

insignificance. By the time Genghis died in 1227, his cavalry, the toughest the world had ever seen and deadly with bow and arrow, had carved out an empire which stretched from the Dnieper to the China Sea.

After Genghis Khan's death this empire was divided up into four khanates. The Great Khan himself—Genghis's third son, Ogadei, succeeded him—held court in Khan-balek (Peking), which had fallen in 1214; his territory included the whole of China, Korea, Mongolia, Manchuria and Tibet. The Chagatai Khanate, based at Almalik (Kulja), governed Central Asia, Turkestan and Afghanistan. The Kipchak Khanate (the Golden Horde), with its capital at Sarai on the Volga, held the country north of the Caucasus, Russia and part of Siberia. And the whole of Persia, Georgia, Armenia and part of Asia Minor formed the Persian Ilkhanate, which had its headquarters at Tauris (Tabriz). The Mongols, however, continued to regard themselves as one nation, remaining loyal to the Great Khan at Peking.

Meanwhile, at the mere thought of the wild Mongol horsemen—barbaric, it was said, beyond description—Europe became paralysed with fear. Contemporary accounts of the invaders' brutality included the rape of Ryazan, a settlement southeast of Moscow: ". . . the inhabitants, without regard to age or sex, were slaughtered with the savage cruelty of Mongol revenge; some were impaled, some shot at with arrows for sport, others were flayed or had nails or splinters driven under their nails. Priests were roasted alive, and nuns and maidens ravished in the churches before their relatives. No eye remained open to weep for the dead."

Moscow and Vladimir suffered the same fate, and when it was the turn of Kozel'sk, near Kaluga, the Mongol excesses were so terrible that they themselves renamed it Mobalig, City of Woe. In 1240, when the Mongols stormed Kiev on the Dnieper (the first home of the Greek Church in Russia), so many people took refuge on the roof of the metropolitan church that it collapsed, turning the building into one vast, terrible tomb.

Already, two years earlier, fear of the Mongols had reached such a pitch in western Europe that merchants from Scandinavia and Friesland had refused to set sail for England to trade at the Yarmouth herring fishery, in case they met the barbarians on the way. By 1241 it seemed as if the invading hordes would engulf the entire known world, trampling Christendom into the dust. With the defeat of Christian forces in Poland, Silesia and Hungary, Emperor Frederick II appealed to Henry III of England and other princes for a united effort against this new "Scourge of God".

But the course of history now took one of its most curious turns: in December 1241 Ogadei, the Great Khan, died. The Mongol high command withdrew to Karakorum, 200 miles from Ulan-Bator (the present capital of Mongolia), to await the *kuriltai* that would determine who would be the next Great Khan. Fate had handed Christendom a reprieve.

Inevitably there were fears that the Mongols would be back: in 1245 Pope Innocent IV convened a council at Lyons to discuss measures for halting the next invasion. This council "advised, besought and entreated all Christian people to block every road or passage by which the enemy could pass, either by means of ditches, walls, buildings and other contrivances".

Fortunately for the Christians concerned, this naïve little directive was never put to the test, for the dreaded invaders never rode back into Europe. When the Mongol war machine began to roll westwards again, it moved not against Christendom but against the caliphates of Baghdad and Syria. By 1258, Tartar rule had been established in the heart of Islam, and much of the Middle East was theirs.

Gradually Europe's view of the Mongols was beginning to change. Now they came to be seen less as enemies than as possible allies against the common enemy, Islam. Also, it became obvious that the Mongols, with no strong religious beliefs of their own, were tolerant of most creeds. Some were even said to have embraced Christianity. By midcentury, therefore, Western rulers were eyeing the barbarians as potential allies and converts.

Now, too, the barrier between East and West was raised. In undermining Muslim influence throughout Asia, the Mongols paved the way for a brilliant era of exploration and trade and cultural exchanges with the Orient such as had never been possible before. It was to last for a century—roughly from 1245 to 1345—a unique period in the history of medieval travel.

At first, however, Innocent IV was still uneasy enough to despatch legates to carry letters to "the King and People of the Tartars" exhorting them to "avert their onslaughts on Christendom through fear of divine wraths". Paradoxically, besides trying to discover what the Great Khan's future invasion plans might be, the legates were also to establish whether there were any Christian tribes among the Mongols who might be enlisted to fight against Islam.

The first of the great travellers to set out was an Italian, John of Pian de Carpini, Provincial of the Franciscan Order at Cologne. He left Lyons in April 1245, travelling by a northern route through Bohemia, Poland and the snow-bound Ukraine, where he became so ill that he had to be transported in a cart. Reaching Kiev, which was just beginning to recover from its sacking by the Mongols five years previously, Carpini and his companions were advised that only with Tartar horses would they succeed in getting through to the East, "for they alone could find grass under the snow, or live, as

A group of European merchants on their journey to the lands of the Great Khan, from the 14th-century "Catalan Atlas." According to the Florentine banker, Peglotti, the route was perfectly safe, both by day and night. Travelling with imperial posts, and using a variety of transport, from horses to camels and pack asses, merchants crossed the continent in five to six months; caravans took longer. Trade goods ranged from the "fruits, muscadel wines and dainty biscuits", with which Friar Rubruck rather naïvely stocked up his oxcarts, to fine linens and silver

In the name of God and commerce

animals must in Tartary, without hay or straw".

Early in February 1246 Carpini came upon a Mongol encampment on the right bank of the frozen Dnieper, where 60,000 men were guarding the western frontiers of the empire. Nobody here was able to translate the Papal letters, but the party was provided with guides and relays of horses.

The next stop, on April 4, was made at the camp on the Lower Volga, where they were made to submit to the Mongol purification ceremony, which involved passing between fires. Here, while the Papal letters were being translated into Russian, Arabic and Mongol, they nearly starved to death, having fasted during the 40 days of Lent, apart from a thin porridge made with millet mixed with water melted down from snow.

Towards Mongolia

Four days later, changing horses now as many as seven times a day, they set off on the last stage of the journey towards the arid plateau of Mongolia. Of this and similar steppe regions Carpini wrote: "In certain places thereof are small store of trees growing but otherwise it is altogether destitute of woods. Therefore all warm themselves and dress their meat with fires made of dung. The air also in that country is very intemperate. For in the midst of the summer there be great thunders and lightnings, and at the same time there falleth great abundance of snow. There be also such mighty tempests of cold winds that sometimes men are not able to sit on horseback. . . . There is never any rain in winter but only in summer albeit in so little quantity that sometimes it scarcely sufficeth to allay the dust or to moisten the roots of the grass."

In northwestern Mongolia, although it was by then midsummer, the travellers endured heavy falls of snow. Finally, after a series of forced marches, they reached the imperial encampment near Karakorum on July 22, 1246. Here, after a 15-month journey of over 3,000 miles, they arrived to find the camp bristling with activity in preparation for the long-awaited Mongol *kuriltai* to elect a new Great Khan.

On August 24 the enthronement of Guyuk (son of Ogadei, who had died four and a half years previously), took place in the Golden Horde, a tent of silk brocade supported by gold-plated pillars. The ceremony, attended by a gathering of 4,000 noblemen and envoys from all corners of the Tartar Empire, was followed by a seven-day orgy of eating and drinking, in which wagonloads of meat and salted broth sauce were consumed, washed down with kumiss (fermented mares' milk) and mead.

Even so, in the midst of this lavish spread Carpini's party again suffered from lack of food, the daily ration allowed them by the Mongols being barely sufficient for one man. They were saved from starvation only by the kindness of a Russian goldsmith.

The Mongol overlords meanwhile were distinguished by the lavishness of their apparel and the gold-plated body armour of their horses. Carpini noted, too, loot snatched from subjugated states as far west as Hungary and an array of gifts which included an awning covered with precious stones, caravans of camels, 500 carts loaded with gold, silver and silk, and a red velvet tent containing an ebony throne embellished with gold, precious stones and pearls.

The festivities over, the Christian envoys had two audiences with Guyuk, after first being searched for hidden weapons. Carpini described this new Great Khan as being over 40, a man "of a mean stature, very wise and polite, and passing serious and grave in all his demeanour. . . . Certain Christians of his family earnestly and strongly affirmed unto us that he himself was about to become a Christian. . . . He had likewise a chapel of Christians, near unto his great Tent. . . ."

At length, on November 13, Carpini took his leave of the Mongol ruler, carrying with him Guyuk's reply to the Pope. With the whole of Central Asia snowbound, the return journey was even worse than the outward one, and it took them until the following June to reach Kiev.

In November 1247, Carpini delivered the Great Khan's reply to the Pope. It was, to say the least, discouraging: ". . . you must come yourself at the head of all your kings and prove to Us your fealty and allegiance, And if you disregard the command of God and disobey Our instructions, We shall look up on you as Our enemy. Whoever recognizes and submits to the Son of God and Lord of the World, the Great Khan, will be saved, whoever refuses submission will be wiped out."

Though not yielding an immediate panacea for the medieval world's ills, Carpini's trail-breaking journey—undertaken when the friar was already turned 60 years of age—had opened up the first real dialogue with the East. Moreover, Carpini was an astute observer, and his account of his travels, *Historia Mongolorum*, furnished Europe with the first glimmer of insight into Tartar customs and beliefs.

The following year Louis IX of France was

While the Europeans were setting out across the seas, the Mongols were striking out across the vast steppes of Asia by the fastest means available, the horse. Probably the first to tame the horse, they also invented the saddle.

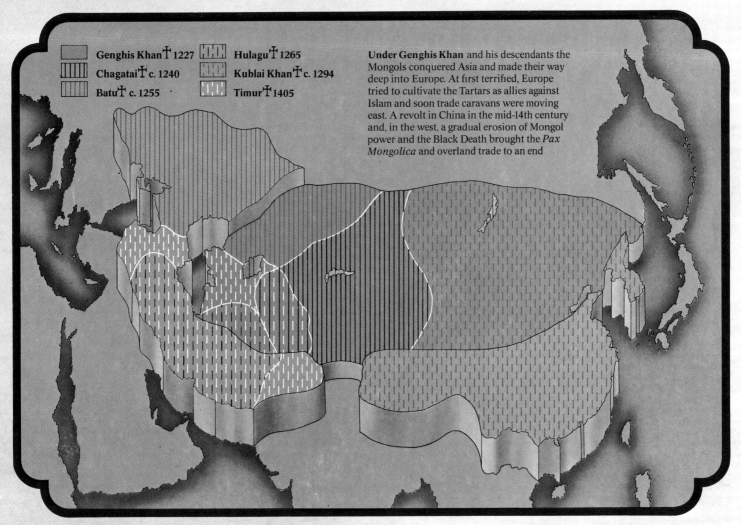

Genghis Khan✝ 1227　Hulagu✝ 1265
Chagatai✝ c. 1240　Kublai Khan✝ c. 1294
Batu✝ c. 1255　Timur✝ 1405

Under Genghis Khan and his descendants the Mongols conquered Asia and made their way deep into Europe. At first terrified, Europe tried to cultivate the Tartars as allies against Islam and soon trade caravans were moving east. A revolt in China in the mid-14th century and, in the west, a gradual erosion of Mongol power and the Black Death brought the *Pax Mongolica* and overland trade to an end

in Cyprus organizing the disastrous Sixth Crusade against the Saracens (Mamelukes) in Egypt, when he received an envoy from the Mongol commanding general at Tabriz in Persia. This messenger brought news that the Great Khan and his nobles had been converted to Christianity three years previously, and there was a hint, too, of the possibility of the Mongols helping Louis to fight the Saracens.

This welcome overture prompted the immediate despatch of a second mission to the court of Guyuk, this time headed by a Dominican, Andrew of Longjumeau. Travelling at ten leagues a day, he and his companions reached Mongolia only to find that Guyuk had died two years previously without becoming a Christian, and that no further *kuriltai* had taken place. In the absence of a Great Khan, the Regent-Mother sent the mission home with an arrogant message to the effect that unless Louis sent a yearly tribute to her court he and his subjects would be destroyed.

In 1249, during Longjumeau's absence, Louis was defeated by the Saracens. Undeterred by the Regent-Mother's threat, he now sent a further delegation to Karakorum. This was headed by the second of the great friar travellers of the Middle Ages, a 30-year-old Flemish Franciscan named William of Rubruck. He was to travel as a missionary rather

than an ambassador, to save the French king from further humiliation if the Mongols chose to hand out another snub.

After a year at Constantinople preparing for the journey, Rubruck went by sea to the Crimea, landing in May 1253. From there he set off with four carts, which greatly increased the time the trip would have taken on horseback. With him went another Franciscan, Bartholomew of Cremona, a dragoman/interpreter, a slave boy bought in Constantinople and some drivers for the carts.

Mongol tents

Three days from the coast they reached the first Mongol encampment, where they saw the *yurts*, domed tents of felt, which had an opening in the top to serve as a chimney. These tents were either black or whitened with chalk, clay or powdered bones, and the interiors were embroidered with trees, vines, birds and beasts. Up to 30 feet in diameter, the tents of the Mongols could only be transported on immense wagons drawn by as many as 22 oxen. Bedding and valuables, packed in huge chests made from plaited osiers, were carried on tall carts drawn by camels.

The women lived on the eastern side of the tent, men on the western side. Felt images in the shape of human beings (which Christian missionaries later took pleasure in destroying) were suspended above the heads of the

husband and his chief wife. At either side of the entrance, which was closed with a carpet, hung the teat of a mare and a cow's udder (mares were milked exclusively by men, cows by women).

Both men and women of the ruling class wore rich clothing, and, in winter, furs next to the skin. The men shaved a square patch on top of their heads, leaving a tuft to fall over their eyebrows, with longer hair at the back and sides. The women smeared their faces in a manner quite grotesque to Western taste. Rubruck found that the men had wives "as many as they would", and that any of their female slaves could be their concubines. Marriageable girls were often taken by force, with the connivance of their fathers, the union being consummated by what was pretty well an act of rape.

In mid-July the little party crossed the Don —then regarded as forming the frontier between Europe and Asia—using punts lashed together to ferry the carts across. At the beginning of August they reached the court of Sartakh, west of the Volga, where King Louis's letters were read.

Although Sartakh employed a Nestorian as his master of ceremonies and asked Rubruck and Bartholomew to give a blessing, rumours that Sartakh had become a Christian were seen to be without foundation. "I don't know whether he believes in Christ or not,"

In the name of God and commerce

Rubruck wrote, "but this I do know, that he will not be called a Christian, and it even seemed to me that he mocked Christians."

From here they pushed onwards through country infested with brigand bands of runaway slaves, spending the nights underneath their carts and seeing no habitation. In mid-September they were at a Tartar camp on the Volga when a messenger arrived with orders to take them to Inner Asia, to Mangu (another of Ogadei's sons), who had succeeded Guyuk as Great Khan. The guide warned it would be a four-month journey "and the cold so intense that it splits stones and trees".

Equipped with sheepskin clothing, hoods and felt stockings, they reached the Ural River, which flows into the Caspian Sea, at this time still thought to be an inlet of the northern ocean. Rubruck later wrote of the Caspian: "This sea is compassed on three sides with the mountains but on the north side with plain ground. A man may travel round it for four months. And it is not true, which Isidore reported [St Isidore, Bishop of Seville, leading medieval authority on many branches of positive science and writer of encyclopaedic works, died 636], namely that this sea is a bay or gulf coming forth of the ocean; for it doth in no part thereof join with the ocean but is environed in all sides with land."

The next month was spent crossing the great steppes of Kazakhstan, and somewhere in this part of Asia they saw *kulan*, wild asses. Later, Rubruck was to become the first European to mention the *arghai*, the long-horned mountain sheep of the Pamirs, which he and his party encountered on the way into Inner Asia.

Then they turned southeast and climbed for seven days through the Tara Tau range, a part of what is now called the Kirgizskiy Khrebet, in the Kirgizskaya SSR, itself a western extension of the Tien Shan, which Rubruck believed to be part of the Caucasus.

All this time their guides gave them food only at night, and what they did get was often semi-raw because the only fuel was dung and scrub, both of which were in short supply. During the day they had to content themselves with millet gruel or water—barely sustenance for men who each day were covering "about the distance from Paris to Orleans".

On November 8 they reached Kenchat, a Muslim town in the cultivated valley of the River Talas, where they were kindly treated by the Mongol governor—a rare experience for Western travellers.

They now crossed the northern spurs of the Kirgizskiy Khrebet, and entered "a most beautiful plain ... with on the left a sea or lake twenty-five days' journey in circumference. The whole of this plain fertilised by streams that flowed from the adjoining mountains into the lake." This was Lake Balkhash, the large, shallow salt-lake in southeastern Kazakhstan.

At long last, on December 27, having crossed a plain "as vast as a sea", they reached the Horde of the Great Khan, where the Mongols regarded the two monks, who had resumed the dress of their order and went barefoot to an audience, with amazement.

A week later they had their long-awaited audience with Mangu, having shaved their beards for the occasion. The Great Khan's tent was "all covered inside with cloth of gold, and there was a fire of briers and wormwood roots ... and cattle dung, in a grate in the centre of the dwelling. Mangu was seated on a couch, dressed in a skin spotted and glossy like a sealskin. He is a little man, of medium height, aged forty-five years, and a young wife sat beside him...." The two monks were given *terracina*, rice-wine, to drink. "Mangu himself appeared to be tipsy."

The black capital

They remained at the encampment until March, suffering terribly from the cold. Then, when Mangu transferred to his still bitterly cold summer capital at Karakorum (the Black Capital), they went there, too. Rubruck found Karakorum small, "excluding the Khan's palace, not as big as the village of St Denis" (now a suburb of Paris). "It has two quarters," he wrote. "In that of the Saracens are the markets, and here a great many Tartars gather on account of the court.... The other is the quarter of the Cathayans, all of whom are artisans.... There are twelve idol temples of different nations; two mosques ... and one Christian church at the very end of the city, which is surrounded by a mud wall and has four gates."

Outside the palace there was a wine fountain, constructed in the form of a great silver tree by a Parisian goldsmith who had been taken prisoner in Hungary. From the branches flowed wine, *caracosmos* (clarified mares' milk), boal (made with honey) and *terracina*. On top of the tree was an angel holding a trumpet, which was sounded by a man concealed in a compartment below the trunk. "When a drink is wanted, the head butler calls to the angel to blow his trumpet. Then the man concealed in the vault blows with all his might in the pipe ... and the angel places the trumpet to his lips and blows it right loudly. The servants who are in the cellar, hearing this pour the different liquors into the proper conduits ... and the butlers draw them and carry them into the palace."

At a further audience with the Great Khan at the end of May, Rubruck received permission to return to Europe. Mangu, "with a not infrequent consultation of the flagon at his side", embarked on a homily on the failings of Christians before handing over his letter in reply to King Louis. "This, by the virtue of the Eternal, throughout the great world of the Mongols, is the message of Mangu Khan to the Lord of the French," it read. "Wherever ears can hear, wherever horses can travel, there let it be heard and known: these who do not believe, but resist Our Commandments, shall not be able to see with their eyes, or hold with their hands, or walk with their feet.... If you will obey Us, send your ambassadors, that We may know whether you wish for peace or war...."

The Franciscan had to leave behind his companion, Bartholomew, who was not fit enough to make the journey (although the wretched monk had defiled the Khan's threshold by stepping on it while backing out of his presence, normally a capital offence, Mangu agreed to keep him at court and look after him). By the following May, King Louis had already returned to France, and Rubruck, sent to Acre by the Provincial of the Franciscans, was never able to deliver the Great Khan's letter in person.

Fortunately for Louis and his Christian allies, the tipsy Mangu was succeeded as Great Khan in 1259 by 43-year-old Kublai, grandson of Genghis. Although as much a nomad by nature as any Mongol, he was to prove, in the course of a 35-year reign, the most civilized and humane ruler of the entire dynasty, and, with his grandfather, the most able. The omens for East–West relations were beginning to look rosier.

A S THE FIRST EUROPEANS to make the formidable overland journey to Mongolia and back, Carpini and Rubruck had pioneered the field. There now came the second wave of great medieval travellers. These were not monks or ambassadors but merchants—men of a class which was to provide the main spur to further travel in this adventurous era. By land and sea they were to circle the whole of the known world. The best known of them, Marco Polo, was to go down in history as the greatest traveller of the Middle Ages.

No doubt these distinctions were far from the minds of the brothers Nicolo and Maffeo Polo, Venetian jewel merchants, when they set sail for the Crimea in 1260. They planned simply to do business and sell jewels—principally at the Golden Horde, capital of the Kipchak Khanate, on the Volga. In the event, they were to be away half a lifetime.

The Polo brothers were well received on the Volga and stayed there for a year, during which time war broke out between this khanate and the Persian Ilkhanate. With the road back to the Crimea cut off, they decided to continue eastwards to visit the Khan of Central Asia. Making their way across the great steppes, they reached Bukhara, an important town on the silk route, in 1263.

Clearly adaptable souls, the Polos remained in Bukhara for three years, learning the Tartar tongue, until one day they were persuaded to join a party of envoys travelling back from Persia to Peking. The Great Khan, they were told, would be pleased to welcome "Latins" from the West.

A year later, after a journey of 3,000 miles, the Italians were well received in the Great Khan's capital, Khan-balek. Although not a Christian himself, Kublai recognized the value of contact with the West. Having absorbed as much as the Polos could tell him about Europe, he sent them on their way with a letter addressed to Pope Clement IV asking for 100 priests and men of learning to educate his Tartars and for a supply of oil from the lamp at the Holy Sepulchre in Jerusalem.

To make sure the brothers would be given every assistance on their travels, he presented them with a golden tablet a foot long and three inches wide and inscribed with the words: "By the strength of the eternal Heaven, holy be the Khan's name. Let him that pays him not reverence be killed."

With this safe conduct, they retraced their steps across Asia—a slow and hazardous journey lasting three years. They reached Acre in 1269, only to find that Clement IV had died the previous year and that the Cardinals had not yet elected a successor. And so they returned to Venice, where Nicolo's wife had died in his absence, leaving a son, Marco, who was now 15 years old.

Two more years passed, and, as there was still no sign of a new Pope being elected, the intrepid brothers decided to return to China, taking young Marco with them. At Acre the Papal Vice-Regent of the Levant, Tedaldo Visconti of Vicenza, wrote letters for them to the Emperor, explaining the situation. Having obtained a supply of sacred oil from Jerusalem, they set off in November 1271 for Ayas on the coast of Cilicia in Little Armenia, terminus of the trade route from Tabriz and the more distant parts of Asia. Here they heard the news that Tedaldo himself had been elected Pope (Gregory X), and so they hurried back to Acre, where the new Pope made them his ambassadors to the Great Khan and assigned them two Dominican brothers, who deserted as soon as they reached Ayas.

Amid some confusion, then, Marco Polo began a career of adventure and exploration that lasted for 20 years. Many years later he set down his experiences in *The Book of Ser Marco Polo, the Venetian,* which has been described as the greatest work of its kind to emerge from 13th-century Europe.

It is an encyclopaedia rather than a travel book. At the time, however, his misfortune was that, having on the whole written an accurate book (apart from such common medieval faults as grossly overestimating the size of cities and the number of their inhabitants), his contemporaries found the contents incredible and indeed much of what he wrote was regarded with suspicion until it was confirmed by travellers of the 18th and 19th centuries.

But although Marco Polo received little recognition from the geographers of his time, some of the information in his book was incorporated in some important maps of the later Middle Ages, such as the Catalan World Map of 1375, and in the next century it was read with great interest by Henry the Navigator and by Columbus.

According to the great geographer Sir Henry Yule, who edited the standard English edition: "He was the first traveller to trace a route across the whole longitude of Asia, naming and describing kingdom after kingdom which he had seen with his own eyes; the Desert of Persia, the flowering plateaux and wild gorges of Badakhshan, the jade-bearing rivers of Khotan, the Mongolian Steppes, cradle of the power that had so lately threatened to swallow up Christendom, the new and brilliant Court that had been established at Cambaluc: the First Traveller to reveal China in all its wealth and vastness, its mighty rivers, its huge cities, its rich manufactures, its swarming population, the inconceivably vast fleets that quickened its seas and its inland waters; to tell us of the nations on its borders with all their eccentricities of manners and worship, of Tibet with its sordid devotees, of Burma with its golden pagodas and their tinkling crowns, of Laos, of Siam, of Cochin China, of Japan, the Eastern Thule, with its rosy pearls and golden-roofed palaces; the first to speak of the Museum of Beauty and Wonder, still so imperfectly ransacked, the Indian Archipelago, source of those aromatics then so highly prized and whose origin was so dark; of Java the Pearl of Islands; of Sumatra with its many kings, its strange costly products, and its cannibal races; of the naked savages of Nicobar and Andaman; of Ceylon and the Isle of Gems with its Sacred Mountain and its Tomb of Adam; of India the Great, not as a dreamland of Alexandrian fables but as a country seen and partially explored, with its virtuous Brahmans, its obscene ascetics, its

High up on the Pamir plateau, Friar Rubruck and, later, Marco Polo saw ''a wild sheep of great size, whose horns are good six palms in length''. Polo's statement was no exaggeration. Old rams can grow horns over four and a half feet long, curving outwards in a wide sweep. The species is now called ''Ovis poli''

In the name of God and commerce

diamonds and the strange tale of their acquisition, its sea bed of pearl, and its powerful sun; the first in mediaeval times to give any distinct account of the secluded Christian Empire of Abyssinia, and the semi-Christian Island of Socotra; to speak, though indeed dimly, of Zanzibar with its negroes and its ivory, and the vast and distant Madagascar, bordering on the dark Ocean of the South, with its Ruc and other monstrosities; and, in a remotely opposite region, of Siberia and the Arctic Ocean, of dog-sledges, white bears, and reindeer-riding Tunguses."

Meanwhile, still only a boy of 17, Marco Polo, again with his father and uncle, found himself on the threshold of Asia, travelling north from Ayas to Erzincan, then east by way of Erzurum through "greater Hermenia", where "the Ark of Noah exists on the top of a certain great mountain [Ararat], on the summit of which snow is so constant that no one can ascend".

Reaching Tabriz they made their way south to Hormuz on the Persian Gulf—perhaps intending to take ship for the long sea journey to one of the Chinese ports. The young Marco was fascinated by the activity at Hormuz: "Merchants come thither from India, with ships loaded with spicery and precious stones, pearls, cloth of silk and gold, elephant's teeth, and many other wares, which they sell to the merchants . . . and which these in turn carry all over the world."

From Hormuz, however, finding the ships "wretched affairs . . . only stitched together with twine made from the husk of the Indian nut", they decided to go overland to China and rode north by way of Kerman and then through deserts in which the water was saline to Herat, seeing, near Tabas, the solitary "Arbre Sec", probably a chinar or oriental plane, believed by local people to be a descendant of the tree of which Alexander the Great was supposed to have asked, "Shall I become King of the World?" To which the tree replied: "You will; but you will never see Macedon again."

From Herat they went to Balkh and then up into Badakhshan, where the Balas rubies were mined, and here Marco Polo convalesced from an illness which delayed them for a year. On the move again, they found themselves on the "Plain called Pamier", the 15,600-foot Pamir Plateau, "said to be the highest place in the world" (this is the first time in history that the name appears).

Here they saw, as William of Rubruck had, "wild sheep of great size, whose horns are good six palms in length. From these horns the shepherds make great bowls to eat from; and they use the horns also to enclose folds for their cattle at night." These were the beasts

which, in 1840, the English zoologist Edward Blyth named *Ovis poli* in honour of the travellers.

There were no birds here and it was cold, and "because of this great cold," Marco said, confusing cold with the effects of altitude, "fire does not burn so brightly, nor give out so much heat as usual, nor does it cook food so effectually".

After travelling for 40 days over the Pamirs they reached Kashgar, where there were gardens and vineyards and cotton grew—a place which must have seemed a paradise after the hardship they had endured, although the natives were "a wretched niggardly set of people". From here they headed southeast for 150 miles across a level plain to Yarkand, where a large proportion of the inhabitants suffered from goitre—"Swoln legs, and great crops at the throat"—which Marco correctly diagnosed as being caused by "some quality in their drinking water".

Rigours of the Gobi

There were more rigours to be endured crossing the Gobi Desert: ". . . where its breadth is least, it takes a month to cross it. It is all composed of hills and valleys of sand, and not a thing to eat is to be found in it. But after riding for a day and a night you find fresh water, enough mayhap for some 50 or 100 persons with their beasts and no more."

Marco Polo also described the phenomena of the Gobi—the mirages and the sounds made by the shifting sands. "Sometimes", he wrote, "stray travellers will hear as it were the tramp and hum of a great cavalcade of people away from the real line of a road, and taking this to be their own company they will follow the sound; and when day breaks they find that a cheat has been put upon them and that they are in an ill plight. . . . And sometimes you shall hear the sound of a variety of musical instruments, and still more commonly the sound of drums. Hence in making this journey it is customary for travellers to keep close together. . . ."

On the edge of the steppes, in what is now the province of Ningsia in Inner Mongolia, Marco, his father and his uncle were met by messengers from Kublai. They were escorted to the Mongol court, where they arrived in May 1275. The journey had taken three and a half years.

They were well received by the Great Khan, prostrating themselves before him, touching the floor with their foreheads, and he was extremely pleased with the sacred oil. Marco, to whom Kublai became a hero (his high opinion of Kublai was shared by contemporaries and by future Chinese historians), described him as "of a middle height. He has a becoming amount of flesh and is

very shapely in all his limbs. His complexion is white and red, the eyes black and fine, the nose well formed and well set on.

"He has four wives," Marco continues, "whom he retains permanently as his legitimate consorts. . . . He has also a great number of concubines, and I will tell you how he obtains them. You must know that there is a tribe of Tartars called Ungrat, who are noted for their beauty. Now every year a hundred of the most beautiful maidens of this tribe are sent to the Great Khan, who commits them to the charge of certain elderly ladies dwelling in his place. And these old ladies make the girls sleep with them, in order to ascertain if they have sweet breath (and do not snore), and are sound in all their limbs. . . . Thus six of these damsels take their turn for three days and nights, and wait on him when he is in the chamber and when he is in bed, to serve him in any way. . . . At the end of three days and nights they are relieved by another six. And so throughout the year."

The young Marco was intrigued to find that Khan-balek was arranged in squares like a chess-board: "Inside it were his palaces . . . enclosed all round by a great wall . . . the whole compass thereof is four miles. . . . At each angle of the wall there is a very fine and rich palace in which the war-harness of the Emperor is kept, such as bows and quivers, saddles and bridles, and bowstrings, and everything needful for an army. Also midway between every two of these corner palaces there is another of the like; so that taking the whole compass of the enclosure you find eight vast palaces stored with the Great Lord's harness of war. . . . Inside of this wall is a second. . . . This enclosure also has eight palaces corresponding to those of the outer wall . . . in the middle . . . is the Lord's Great Palace."

This, Marco decided, was "the greatest palace that ever was". The walls were covered with gold and silver and the Hall was "so large that it could easily dine 6,000 people". At the feast of the Great Khan the "Barons" who waited on him had "the mouth and nose muffled with fine napkins of silk and gold, so that no breath nor odour from their persons should taint the dish or goblet presented to the Lord".

On New Year's Day, he noted: "Among the customary presents there shall be offered to the Khan from various quarters more than 100,000 white horses . . . on that day also, the whole of the Khan's elephants, amounting fully to 5,000 in number, are exhibited, all covered with rich and gay housing of inlaid cloth representing beasts and birds, and each of them carries on his back two splendid coffers; all of these being filled with the Emperor's plate and other costly furniture

The East seen through western eyes: this series of pictures from the 15th-century illuminated manuscript "Les Livres du Graunt Caam" illustrates some of the highlights of Marco Polo's journey to the East. (Right) Marco Polo's home port of Venice, showing the travellers embarking. The Palace of the Doges and St Mark's Cathedral are recognizable in the background. (Below) A merchant leading his beast of burden across the bridge to Sindufu, one of the towns in Tibet through which Marco Polo travelled

required for the Court on the occasion of the White feast."

The Italian travellers saw, too, Xanadu (inspiration for Coleridge's *Kubla Khan*), the summer residence in the north. Here there was a palace made of cane supported by 200 silk cords, which could be taken to pieces and transported when the Emperor moved. Here, too, he kept a stud of 10,000 speckless white horses, whose milk was reserved for his family and for a tribe which had won a victory for Genghis Khan.

Impressed with Marco Polo's powers of observation, Kublai Khan soon took the young Italian into his service, employing him on various missions which gave him scope to explore the fabulous empire which he was the first European to see. The distances covered were immense—he went to the farthest frontiers of the empire and beyond, through the provinces of Shansi, Shensi and Szechwan, along the borders of Tibet and into Yunnan and northern Burma, territory which otherwise remained unknown until the middle of the 19th century.

For three years he was governor of Yangchow, a city on the Grand Canal, northeast of Nanking. He also visited Karakorum and the country towards Siberia. Meanwhile his father and uncle took part in the assault on the town of Siang Yang Fou, for which they

(Above left) A strange combination of activities: a butcher's shop and, in the foreground, snake-catching. (Above right) A Chinese Venice, the city of Quinsay, rose up out of the water, the canals spanned—according to Polo's impossibly exaggerated calculation—by some 12,000 bridges "so lofty that a great fleet could pass beneath them". (Left) Pearl fishing off the Malabar Coast of India, one of the many sights of the East that Polo recorded on his voyage home

In the name of God and commerce

designed and constructed siege engines.

The cities that impressed him most were Kinsai (Hangchow), capital of South China, and the great port of Zaiton—probably the haven of Amoy—facing the Formosa Strait, in the province of Fukien. Of the two, Kinsai, "The City of Heaven", was the most beautiful. Standing on the shores of the Western Lake, this was like some splendid Venice of the East with its waterways crossed by 12,000 bridges "for the most part so lofty that a great fleet could pass beneath them".

Perhaps it was here that Marco Polo gazed in awe at the great ocean-going junks: "These ships . . . are of fir timber. They have one deck, though each of them contains some 50 or 60 cabins, wherein the merchants abide greatly at their ease, every man having one to himself. . . . The ship hath but one rudder, but it hath four masts; and sometimes they have two additional masts, which they ship and unship at pleasure. . . . Each of their great ships requires at least 200 mariners (some of them 300). They are indeed of great size, for one ship will carry 5,000 or 6,000 baskets of pepper. . . . When there is no wind they use sweeps, and these sweeps are so big that to pull them requires four marines to each."

Marco Polo became the first European to speak of Burma, Siam, Java, Sumatra and Ceylon. In Sumatra ("Java the Less") he saw the unicorn, "a passing ugly beast to look upon, and is not in the least like that which our stories tell of as being caught in the lap of a virgin", and the Sumatra rhinoceros, which had a tongue "covered all over with long and strong prickles (and when savage with any-one they crush him under their knees and then rasp him with their tongue)". Java he found to be "of surpassing wealth, producing black pepper, nutmegs, spikenhard, gallin-gale, cubebs, and cloves and all other kinds of spices". The Great Khan's business carried him, too, to India and to the Andaman and Nicobar islands, the former being inhabited by men with "heads like dogs, and teeth and eyes likewise . . . they are a most cruel genera-tion, and eat everybody they can catch, if not of their own race".

In the low latitudes of the East Indies, near the Equator, he noticed that the "north pole, which is vulgarly called the tramontaine star, is not seen at all . . . the stars of the Greater Bear, that is those which vulgar people call the plough-beam, are not seen neither little nor much".

Eventually the old Khan reluctantly agreed to allow the Polos to return to Europe after 16 years in China. They were anxious to be on the move, since, as wily Venetians, they feared that if Kublai—now in his late seven-ties—were to die, they might not be able to

get their considerable fortune out of the country. They set sail from Zaiton in January 1292, taking with them a Tartar princess who was betrothed to Arghun, Ilkhan of Persia.

The voyage, involving a fleet of 14 ships, was a two-year ordeal during which 600 passengers and crew died—presumably from scurvy or cholera or by drowning. Finally they docked at Hormuz, on the Persian Gulf, only to learn that Arghun had died two years previously (the princess married his son instead).

In Persia they learned, too, of the death of Kublai, an enlightened ruler and their patron for so many years. His protection, however, outlived him, for it was only by showing his tablet of authority that they were able to secure safe conduct through the bandit-ridden interior. From Trebizond on the Black Sea coast they went by sea, by way of Constantinople, to Venice, arriving home in 1295.

The mass of information that Marco Polo brought home in his head proved of in-calculable value to the West, both to the world of commerce and to church leaders who still cherished hopes of converting the Tartars. At the conclusion of his book someone—perhaps

an inspired translator—has written: "There never was a man, be he Christian or Saracen or Tartar or Heathen, who ever travelled over so much of the world as did that noble and illustrious citizen of Venice, Messer Marco Polo. Thanks be to God! Amen! Amen!" In his enthusiasm he has perhaps overlooked the fact that arguably the greatest feat of all was that performed by Nicolo and Maffeo in reaching Peking in the first place.

Now, from the 1290s onwards for about 50 years, a steady stream of travellers followed in the pioneers' footsteps. No longer limited, as their forebears had been, to trading with middlemen at the Mediterranean termini, European merchants crowded the caravan routes to carry their wares into the heart of Asia themselves. In fact the unification of Asia by the Mongols—and with it direct access to the East—was probably the single most important development for commerce in the Middle Ages.

But although the most numerous travellers were the merchants, who for the most part were men who left no record of their adven-tures—Marco Polo was a brilliant exception. Instead, history relies for its account of the East on the writings of the Christian mission-

The existence in ancient China of an advanced civilization had made itself known to Europe long before recorded contact had been made with it by medieval travellers from the West. Quite apart from those outcrops of military technology which the Chinese are known to have possessed —including incendiary and explosive devices and the crossbow—they were using the simple but important mould-board plough, horse harness, and even the humble wheelbarrow. They had also harnessed their waterways to feed an advanced system of irrigation and canals. The greatest of China's many artificial waterways, the Grand Canal, was begun in the 5th century BC to form a channel of communication between the Yangtse and Huai rivers. By the time of the Manchus in the 13th century it had become an important transport system, carrying grain from Hangchow in the fertile lower Yangtse valley to the empire's political centre at Peking. Rising to a summit level of 138 feet above the mean level of the Yangtse, the Grand Canal had a system of locks almost 1,000 years before the method was used in the West. Flash locks (right) were controlled by a single gate. Boats were hauled through against the upstream current by winches, while those travelling downstream shot through with the "flash" of water as the gate was opened. In the more efficient double slipway (below), ropes and capstans hauled the boats up or down an incline to the next level

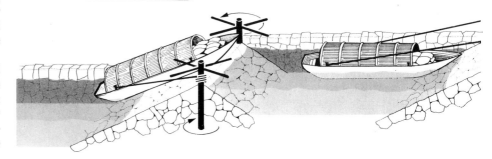

aries, especially the Franciscans. One of the most dedicated of these was John of Monte Corvino, at first papal legate to and later Archbishop of Peking, who, in the space of a few letters, drew a vivid picture of the Far East and his life and work there.

Already in his forties, Corvino set out to take the gospel to the heathen in 1289. Over the next 40 years he was to become the first Latin Christian to leave us a picture of India. He is remembered, too, as the true founder of the Latin Church in China.

Corvino's route took him first to Tabriz, where he met Peter of Lucolongo, "a faithful Christian man and a great merchant", and together they set off for India, probably sailing from Hormuz, embarking there in one of the ships to which Corvino reacted in much the same way as the Polos had done. It was, he recalled, "flimsy and uncouth, without nails or iron of any sort, sewn together with twine like clothes, without caulking, having but one mast, one sail of matting, and some ropes of husk". Nevertheless, it succeeded in carrying them, by Corvino's reckoning, some 2,000 miles to the Malabar Coast and from there to the Bay of Bengal, where they spent a year near the shrine of St Thomas.

In a long letter to Europe two or three years after leaving, Corvino wrote of the monsoon winds—the first writer to mention them since ancient times—describing how, because they blew from the west from March to October and from the east for the rest of the year, it was not possible in these seas to make more than one voyage every 12 months.

His second letter, dated January 8, 1305, and carried overland to Persia by an important Mongol official, was written from Peking 12 years after he arrived in China. It told how, in all this time, he had received no news from Europe and had worked alone until a German friar from Cologne had joined him a year or two previously.

Soon after his arrival in Peking in 1293, Corvino had been granted an audience by Kublai to whom he had delivered the papal letters. But he had failed to convert the emperor, who died the following year at the age of 80. He also drew a blank with his successor, Timur Oljaitu, who was more inclined to Buddhism, but had won over a Nestorian, King George of Tendhuc, "of the family of the Great King Prester John of India", who, to mark the occasion, built a church 20 days' ride from the capital. The King's conversion inspired many of his followers, but after his death they all lapsed.

According to Corvino, the best route to China—though at that time closed by wars—was through the lands of the Goths and Northern Tartars, the Crimea and Kipchak regions, across the Don, the Volga and the steppes. This was a journey which, with an imperial messenger to lead the way, might be accomplished in five or six months, whereas the sea route by which he had come might take two years.

In a postscript to his second letter from the capital (where he was still receiving assistance from Peter of Lucolongo), written on February 13, 1306, the Franciscan announced that he had baptized 400 persons on the previous All Saints' Day, and had received a deputation of Ethiopians, who had begged him either to come to their country himself, or else to send "other preachers".

In 1307, Clement V nominated Corvino Archbishop of Peking and seven bishops were sent to aid him in his work. However, three died on entering "Lower India" and a fourth failed to make the journey. Still, by the time the Archbishop died in 1328, at the age of 81, several thousand people had been baptized in China.

Although the Mongol rulers were liberal to the religious cause and Corvino's mission had been given a great deal of material assistance, it had not been easy. In 1305 he wrote to Rome: "I myself have grown grey and look like an old man, although I am no more than

fifty-nine. I speak and write Tartar with perfect fluency. I have translated into this tongue both the New Testament and the Psalter, and I have seen to it that they were translated as beautifully as possible."

There was to be no great successor to Corvino and it would not have been of much avail if there had been. Most of what he and his bishops had created was swept away after 1368 when the Chinese rose against the Mongols, brought down the dynasty and drove them north of the Great Wall. Under the Ming dynasty China resumed her traditional isolationist policy, becoming once again, so far as European travellers were concerned, a forbidden land.

But some years before the curtain finally came down on this brilliant age of exploration another of the great missionary travellers set course for the Far East. This was Odoric of Pordenone, also a Franciscan, who made the long sea voyage from Hormuz to Canton, stopping *en route* at Tana, north of Bombay.

Martyrs' bones
Here Odoric collected the bones of four recently martyred missionaries for burial at some later date. Continuing by junk, he came to the Malabar Coast, where he saw the great pepper and ginger markets at Quilon and the so-called Black and White Jews. He then visited Ceylon, where he saw what he described as a two-headed bird, probably a hornbill.

Following Marco Polo's route in reverse, Odoric visited Sumatra, where the inhabitants went naked, the women were common property and human flesh formed part of the normal diet. In Java he found there was a great trade in spices and the king ruled over seven lesser monarchs from a palace with gold and silver pavements and with rooms where the walls and ceilings were of gold plate.

In "Talmasin", possibly some part of Borneo, there were trees which produced flour (the sago-palm), honey and the poison used by the inhabitants in the *sumpit*, the great blowpipe, from which they discharged an "iron poison bodkin". After an excursion possibly to the Andaman and Nicobar islands in the Indian Ocean, the next certain port of call was Canton, "three times as large as Venice", where he saw edible snakes and strange-shaped geese.

From here Odoric travelled overland to Zaiton by way of "many lands and cities", leaving no description of a region that was to remain unknown to Europeans for centuries. In this great port, "twice the size of Bologna", he at last laid the bones of his martyrs to rest in one of the religious houses that had been established there.

Odoric's lively account of his travels

Asian tracks of trader and missioner

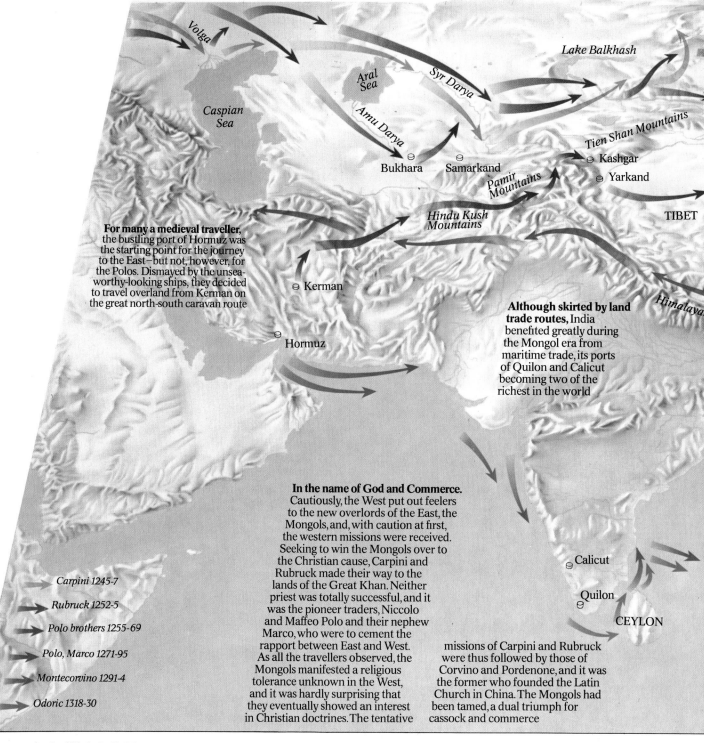

Volga

Caspian Sea

Aral Sea

Syr Darya

Lake Balkhash

Amu Darya

Bukhara

Samarkand

Tien Shan Mountains

Kashgar

Yarkand

Pamir Mountains

TIBET

Hindu Kush Mountains

Himalayas

For many a medieval traveller, the bustling port of Hormuz was the starting point for the journey to the East – but not, however, for the Polos. Dismayed by the unseaworthy-looking ships, they decided to travel overland from Kerman on the great north-south caravan route

Kerman

Hormuz

Although skirted by land trade routes, India benefited greatly during the Mongol era from maritime trade, its ports of Quilon and Calicut becoming two of the richest in the world

Calicut

Quilon

CEYLON

Carpini 1245-7

Rubruck 1252-5

Polo brothers 1255-69

Polo, Marco 1271-95

Montecorvino 1291-4

Odoric 1318-30

In the name of God and Commerce. Cautiously, the West put out feelers to the new overlords of the East, the Mongols, and, with caution at first, the western missions were received. Seeking to win the Mongols over to the Christian cause, Carpini and Rubruck made their way to the lands of the Great Khan. Neither priest was totally successful, and it was the pioneer traders, Niccolo and Maffeo Polo and their nephew Marco, who were to cement the rapport between East and West. As all the travellers observed, the Mongols manifested a religious tolerance unknown in the West, and it was hardly surprising that they eventually showed an interest in Christian doctrines. The tentative missions of Carpini and Rubruck were thus followed by those of Corvino and Pordenone, and it was the former who founded the Latin Church in China. The Mongols had been tamed, a dual triumph for cassock and commerce

The pace and style of life in the "wild gorges of Badakhshan" have seemingly altered little since the Polos journeyed through the country. Here a traveller leads his horse over one of the glacier-fed rivers with the snow-clad wall of the Hindu Kush towering up in the background. Now the northeastern corner of Afghanistan, Badakhshan is bounded to the north by the Amu-Dar'ya River and to the south by the main chain of the Hindu Kush, where some of the peaks rise to 24,000 feet. Here, the Polos interrupted their journey for a year, while Marco recovered from illness

The wind plays its tricks in the Gobi Desert and has eroded the pillar of sand (right), creating a curious "sliced loaf" effect. To Marco Polo, the Gobi seemed to be "all composed of hills and valleys of sand", but in fact only small parts of its vast expanse are covered with sand or dunes. Much of it is bare rock. Little water is to be found either in the form of rainfall—mainly in spring and autumn—or in rivers. Travellers are also subject to extremes of temperature. During the summer, it falls after dark by as much as 70 degrees Fahrenheit from its daytime peak

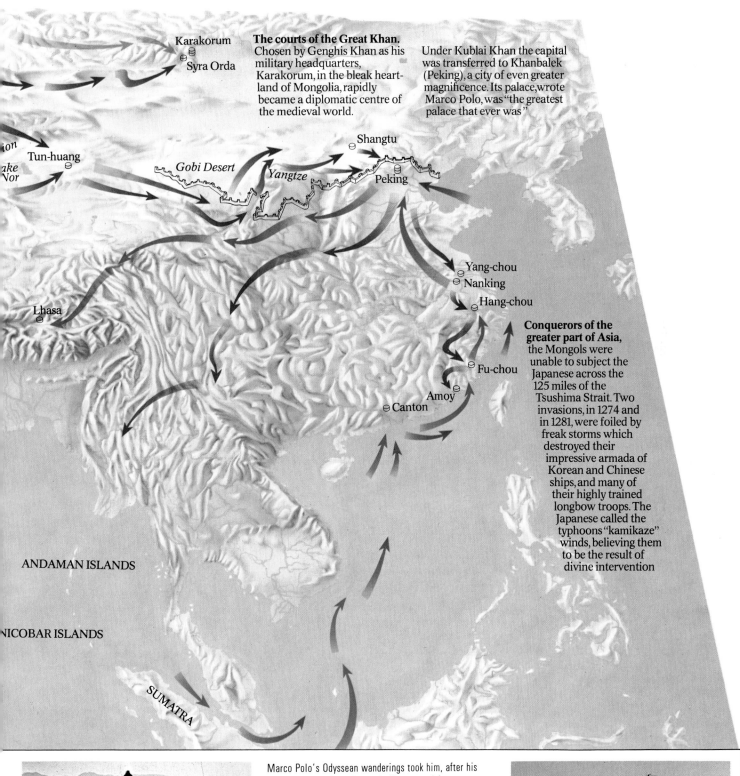

Karakorum

Syra Orda

The courts of the Great Khan.
Chosen by Genghis Khan as his
military headquarters,
Karakorum, in the bleak heartland of Mongolia, rapidly
became a diplomatic centre of
the medieval world.

Under Kublai Khan the capital
was transferred to Khanbalek
(Peking), a city of even greater
magnificence. Its palace, wrote
Marco Polo, was "the greatest
palace that ever was"

Shangtu

Gobi Desert

Yangtze

Peking

Tun-huang

ion

*ake
Nor*

Lhasa

Yang-chou

Nanking

Hang-chou

**Conquerors of the
greater part of Asia,**
the Mongols were
unable to subject the
Japanese across the
125 miles of the
Tsushima Strait. Two
invasions, in 1274 and
in 1281, were foiled by
freak storms which
destroyed their
impressive armada of
Korean and Chinese
ships, and many of
their highly trained
longbow troops. The
Japanese called the
typhoons "kamikaze"
winds, believing them
to be the result of
divine intervention

Fu-chou

Amoy

Canton

ANDAMAN ISLANDS

NICOBAR ISLANDS

SUMATRA

Marco Polo's Odyssean wanderings took him, after his
arrival in China from the south, Yunnan and Amoy, up to
the northernmost provinces, which were bordered by one of
the greatest of human artefacts, the Great Wall of China, a
defensive fortification. Walled frontiers already existed
in the 4th century BC, but in the 3rd century they were
joined together and new sections added to form a
continuous wall, to keep out raiding Asian tribesmen. Built
of earth and stone, its eastern part faced with bricks, it
snakes across some 1,500 miles, much of it mountainous,
from the Yellow Sea to the deep frontiers of Mongolia

includes a number of firsts. He was, for example, the first European to describe how the Chinese make use of cormorants for fishing, which he saw somewhere *en route* from Fukien to Chekiang. Also he gave the first description of the long finger-nails of the Chinese men (some of whom had thumb-nails which curved right round their hands), of the women's bound feet and their immensely tall head-dresses.

His is altogether a more personalized narrative than the somewhat colder print, say, of Marco Polo. Odoric shows us the people of China: "Indeed in that country the number of people is so great that among us here it would be deemed incredible; and in many parts I have seen the population more dense than the crowds you see at Venice on Ascension Day. . . .

"And all the people of this country are traders and artificers, and no man ever seeketh alms, however poor he be, as long as he can do anything with his own hands to help himself; but those who are fallen into indigence and infirmity are well looked after and provided with necessities. The men, as to their bodily aspect, are comely enough, but colourless, having beards of long straggling hairs like mousers. And as for the women, they are the most beautiful in the world."

After a three-year sojourn with Corvino and other fellow Franciscans in Peking, Odoric set off on the long journey back to Italy in 1328. He seems to have made his way north of the Great Wall in Inner Mongolia and, by an unspecified route, to have reached Lhasa, capital of Tibet and abode of "the Chief of all Idolators", the Grand Lama. Here he found that the walls of the city were black and white and the buildings were adorned with the horns of sheep. The Tibetans lived in black felt tents, practised cannibalism, and drank from the skulls of their ancestors. Those who died were left in the open to be eaten by birds of prey, which the Tibetans regarded as angels who carried the dead to Paradise.

The rest of Odoric's route is difficult to trace, but, some time in 1330, after an absence of 16 years, he reached Padua, where he wrote his memoirs. The following year, while planning a new assault on the heathen of Asia with the aid of 50 friars, he died at the age of 45, having baptized some 10,000 people.

Five years later the death-knell was already sounding for East–West relations when the last of the Mongol emperors, Toghan Timur Ukhagatu (Shunti), whose empire was now disintegrating, sent an embassy under Andrew the Frank with 16 Mongol princes in its train to Pope Benedict at Avignon—"the Christian Lord in the Land of the Franks, where the sun sets" as the emperor styled

him. His purpose was "to make a way, so that We may be able to send embassies to the Pope and the Pope send embassies to Us more frequently than before, so that the Pope's blessing may be over us, and so that he may commend Us and Our Servants the Alans, his own Christian sons, in his prayers. Also from the setting sun let there be sent to Us horses and other things of value."

The Alans were a people from the Central Caucasus, who provided some of the best troops in the Tartar army, had been converted to Christianity by Corvino and now called themselves The Slaves of the Pope. It was they who had sent news of Corvino's death (eight years before) and asked for a new Archbishop to be appointed.

In response to this last desperate bid for a closer *entente*, an important papal embassy was despatched to Peking in 1338 under a Florentine aristocrat, John Marignolli, yet another Franciscan. He took the overland route, reaching Peking in June 1342.

Marignolli and his party were extremely well treated by the emperor, who was delighted with the carefully worded letter of Pope Benedict and gifts which included splendid horses. He humbly and willingly, according to the monk, accepted the blessing that Marignolli bestowed on him. In fact it was only after four years or more that he and his companions were able to persuade the emperor to allow them to depart, to return by sea from Zaiton with a stop in South India.

An era closes

After an absence of 14 years, Marignolli bequeathed to posterity the last European account of the Far East at this period. For the Emperor's initiative had come too late: in the struggle for the soul of Tartary, Christendom had lost. Gradually the whole of Kipchak and Central Asia went over to Islam, cutting off the land route which, for a little while, European travellers had been free to traverse. Similarly, the Ilkhans of Persia, having for years tried in vain to nudge the West into a common crusade against the Saracens, had finally turned to Islam in 1316. This territory, too, was virtually closed to the Infidel by the middle of the 14th century.

The fact that the long-hoped-for Tartar–Christian alliance did not materialize was due less to the barbarians than to the niggardly bickering of rival Christian factions. As it was, towards the end of the century fanaticism ruled in Persia, Central Asia was in a state of anarchy and China was in the grip of an anti-foreign dynasty. Once again the frontiers of Asia were sealed. Condensed in a few rich volumes of travellers' tales, a whole era of brilliant and courageous exploration now seemed little more than a legend.

A HUNDRED YEARS after the death of Mohammed in 632 the Muslim Empire extended from Persia through the Levant and Egypt, along the North African coast, where the Moors were converted to Islam, and northwards into Spain, where Abdurrahman en-Nasir founded the Caliphate of Cordova. It would have been even greater if the Moors, under Tariq Ibn Ziad, had not been defeated by Charles Martel near Tours in France, while on their way to take Paris, in what was one of the decisive battles of the world.

The Arabs were by nature great seekers after scientific knowledge and they were now in a position to indulge their passion, for they had occupied all the ancient centres of learning in Asia and Africa.

Arab geography of this period has certain defects. It is, as one 20th-century geographer wrote dryly, "vitiated by tendencies to rambling and to story-telling and has an altogether inadequate conception of the sea". Influential Arab scientists and theologians believed that what they called "The Sea of Darkness", the Encircling Ocean, was impassable; that "whirlpools always destroyed any adventurer" and that it was "boundless, so that ships dared not venture out of sight of land; for even if the sailors knew the direction of the winds, they would not know whither those winds would carry them and, as there was no inhabited country beyond, they would run the risk of being lost in mists of fogs".

Such beliefs were to inhibit later explorers, particularly the Portuguese, and they were widely held in spite of the fact that the roundness of the Earth was known and taught by Arab geographers. They also believed, as did Ptolemy, that it was the centre of the universe, the stars and planets revolving round it.

This is not to denigrate the very real contribution that Arab geographers, mathematicians and astronomers made to the knowledge of the world during what, in Europe, were dark ages, nor the part they played in preserving and amplifying the knowledge, accumulated in the Ancient World, which might otherwise have disappeared.

The need to trade and the desire to visit the holy places of Islam made the Arabs great travellers, and—because they were a people who had emerged from the great, sterile emptiness of the desert and were accustomed to the contemplation of an infinitely vaster heaven above—they were unafraid. The need to orientate themselves in the direction of Mecca three times a day and to know the time of day with accuracy, encouraged them to study the problem of latitude and longitude.

In the 10th century Al Maqdisi found the

Earth to be a globe consisting of a northern and southern hemisphere, dividing its circumference into 360 degrees of longitude and 180 degrees of latitude. Arab scientists, working at the famous academy of the Caliph Al Maamoun at Baghdad, calculated the length of a degree of latitude by making men walk due north and south until the pole star had risen or set one degree, the distances being marked on a rope.

Another scientist, Al Bairouni, calculated the difference in longitude between two points by taking the latitude and the shortest distance between them. Using this method he found that the length of the Mediterranean was 17 degrees less than Ptolemy had calculated it to be.

The Arabs, and those they converted to Islam, founded large numbers of observatories. They employed the astrolabe, the compass—which the Chinese were the first to use at sea—water clocks, a form of theodolite and an instrument known as a parallactic ruler, with which the apparent change in the position of a star to an observer who has himself moved could be measured.

Mohammed himself initiated this new era of enquiry and discovery when he sent messages explaining the Faith to various foreign rulers, one of whom was the Emperor of China, who gave permission to Muslim preachers to go to China and expound it.

"The Merchant" writes

Of the large numbers of geographers and travellers who, from the 9th century onwards, left records of what they accomplished, it is only possible to mention a few.

In the 9th century, Sulaiman el Tagir, "The Merchant", born at Siraf on the Persian Gulf, sailed to India and China, and the book he wrote about his voyage in 851 called *Sequence of Historical Events* was amplified in the next century. It described the routes used by the Chinese trading junks between Khanfu (Canton) and Siraf in what was then called the Chinese Gulf, where cargoes were transhipped into smaller vessels for onward shipment to Basra, or taken to Jiddah on the Red Sea and from there to Qolzom, the Arabic name for a port at the head of the Gulf of Suez.

In 846, Ibn Khurdathabah of Baghdad compiled his *Book of Routes and Kingdoms.* He described the great caravan route from western to Central Asia, which linked up with the Silk Road on the borders of China, and the maritime trade—much of it in the hands of polyglot Jewish merchants—between western Europe and China, where such goods as furs and weapons were exchanged for silk, spices and Chinese iron.

In 921, Ibn Fadlan was sent by the Abbasid Khalif as religious adviser on a mission to the King of the Bulgars on the east bank of the Volga, where the people had recently been converted to Islam.

Here, he met the Rus-folk, Vikings from the Baltic, who had trading posts on the river. They were pagans, worshipped idols, sacrificed animals and were dirty and primitive in their habits. Ibn Fadlan gives a vivid des-

A miniature from an old manuscript depicting the Islamic astronomer Taqi al Din and the observatory at Istanbul. Greek, Persian and Indian learning contributed to the rise of astronomy in Islam

cription of a Viking ship burial, in the course of which the dead chief's property was divided into three parts, one being retained by his family, the other two being sold to finance a loathsome ceremony. In it, a female slave, who had "volunteered" for the honour, was intoxicated with a liquor which Fadlan calls "nabid" and dragged into the dead chief's tent, where, after a sexual orgy in which six lesser chieftains took part, she was ritually murdered by two of their number who strangled her, and by a hag who stabbed her repeatedly. Her body was then placed next to that of the chief inside the ship, which was then burned.

In the 10th century, Al Mas'udi of Baghdad, who died in 956, was the first to visit the Aral Sea. It was Mas'udi who believed that the Atlantic, "The Green Sea of Darkness", was unnavigable. He was the author of *Meadows of Gold and Mines of Precious Stones,* and also produced a map of the world which shows the Atlantic and Indian oceans connected to the south of Africa, the Nile Valley in its correct position, India with the Indus and Ganges, "Sarandeeb" (Ceylon) and the Caspian and Aral seas, both as inland waters.

In 943, Ibn Haukal of Baghdad, a geographer and cartographer who produced a diagrammatic map of the world, set out on an immense journey of 25 to 30 years' duration, in the course of which he visited the entire Muslim world. His book, *Of Ways and Provinces,* gives the first account of the western Sudan, where he visited Kumbi, the capital of the old kingdom of Ghana, on the edge of the Sahara. He also saw the Niger, which, flowing to the east at that point, led him to believe that it was the Nile. "I have not described the country of the African blacks", he wrote, "and the other people of the torrid zone: because naturally loving wisdom, ingenuity, religion, justice and regular government, how could I notice such people as these, or magnify them by inserting an account of their countries."

In the 12th century Il Idrisi of Ceuta travelled widely in northwestern Europe, probably visiting Denmark and England, and Asia Minor. He also stayed at the court of the Norman ruler Roger II, in Sicily, where he produced for him a famous globe and map of the world engraved on silver and wrote an encyclopaedic work, *The Would-be Travellers Promenade,* which supplemented it.

The most indefatigable traveller in the Muslim world, or in any world for that matter, the man whose journeys far exceed those of the Polos in scope and distance covered, was the Berber, Ibn Battuta, born at Tangier in Morocco in 1304, "the traveller not of an age but of Islam". It has been estimated that, at the very least, he travelled 75,000 miles, not counting detours.

A Muslim of the most devoted sort, he left his birthplace at the age of 22 on what he originally intended to be a pilgrimage to Mecca and Medina, with "neither companion", as he wrote in his memoirs, "to delight in nor caravan to accompany, my sole inspiration coming from an uncontrollable desire and long-cradled fancy in my breast to visit these holy places".

The learned Arabs set out

What follows is the despair of anyone wishing to give even the barest outline of where he went and what he saw and experienced; even a list of the regions and cities he visited resembled the gazetteer of an atlas. Like Polo the only thing to do with Ibn Battuta is to read him.

Leaving Tangier in 1325 he travelled along the North African coast to Egypt, where he saw the Pharos at Alexandria, one of the Seven Wonders of the Ancient World, and from Cairo ascended the Nile to Syene (Aswan), following the caravan route to Aidhab on the Red Sea, where a tribal war in Arabia prevented him crossing to Jiddah, the pilgrim port of Mecca. Retracing his route through Egypt he reached the Levant, visiting Jerusalem and Damascus, and then journeyed south through Arabia by the Derb el Haj, the pilgrim road to Medina and Mecca on what was to be the first of four visits. From Medina he went through the heart of northern Arabia to Basra, attaching himself to a caravan (later he travelled with his own considerable retinue), and from there to Shiraz, birthplace of the two great 13th- and 14th-century poets, Sadi and Hafiz, which he thought extremely beautiful; then to Baghdad (still in ruins after its sacking by Timur), Mosul on the Tigris and to the walled city of Diyarbakir in southeastern Anatolia.

About this time he was impelled to return to Mecca, where he spent three years studying law, his knowledge of which was to help him finance his future travels.

From Jiddah again, he travelled by sea to Yemen, noting that summer was the season of rain and the Southwest Monsoon, seeing the great reservoirs at Aden and the large numbers of merchants gathered there and, when the Northwest Monsoon began to blow, sailing as a trader across the Gulf of Aden to Zeila in Somalia, the dirtiest place he had visited. From here he sailed eastwards, doubled Cape Guardafui, the extreme eastern point of Africa, thence for 1,200 miles down the east coast to Mombasa, finally reaching

Kilwa, on the coast of Tanzania, 350 miles to the south, a fine town of wooden houses, inhabited by "very dark skinned Africans".

Back at Jiddah he failed to find a ship bound for India and crossed over into Egypt and, after enduring great hardships on the road to Syene, reached Syria. He now sailed eastwards to the predominantly Genoese port of Kaffa in the Crimea, where he made one of his rare contacts with Christian civilization.

Land of darkness

His steps now took him through Caucasia to the land of the Tartars, where he stayed at the camp of the Kipchak Khan, Muhammad Uzbek, whose name was later given to the Uzbek peoples, and from there travelled northwards up the river to Bolgar (54.54N), visited by Ibn Fadlan 400 years previously. From here he wanted to set off into the northern ice-clad deserts of "The Land of Darkness"—Siberia—by dog sledge, but if he did so he soon turned back. It was extremely cold and he had insufficient provisions for the 44-day journey.

He then returned to Constantinople where he was given an audience with the Byzantine emperor, Andronicus, and from there returned east again, this time as far as Bukhara, Herat and Kabul. During this journey he passed through the Hindu Kush mountains, being first to record their name. He reached the Indus in September 1333.

Visiting Multan, he eventually arrived at the court of the mad Sultan, Mohammed Tuglaq, the Indian Caligula, at Delhi, of whom he wrote: "There was no day that the gate of his palace failed to witness alike the elevation of some object to affluence and the torture and murder of some living soul." To name only one of his follies, Tuglaq despatched an expedition of 100,000 men to the Himalayas of whom, reputedly, there were only ten survivors. He was, however, also a patron of scholars and here Ibn Battuta remained for eight years in the capacity of judge with a great salary; nevertheless he

succeeded in falling into debt and out of favour with Tuglaq. Recalled from retirement to travel with 15 Chinese ambassadors to China on an embassy to the last Mongol emperor, he saw the junk carrying the envoys and gifts wrecked at Calicut.

Afraid, and with some reason, of returning to Tuglaq with such a story, he eventually reached the Maldive Islands in the Indian Ocean, 400 miles southwest of Ceylon, where he gained an official office and took four wives, remaining there for some time until, in August 1344, after quarrelling with various important persons, he left, taking one wife with him, for Ceylon.

Ibn Battuta's incredible voyages did not stop there. Reaching Bengal, he travelled in a Chinese junk to Sumatra, where the Muslim ruler lent him another to take him to Zaiton in China, from where he went on to Sin-Kalan, the Arabic name for Canton.

He eventually returned to the West by way of Sumatra, India, Arabia, Persia and Damascus, where he saw the ghastly ravages of the Black Death, which killed 2,400 persons in one day. After yet another pilgrimage to Mecca he finally reached Fez in Morocco in November 1349 at the age of 45, after an absence of 24 years.

On his return the Sultan of Morocco, Abu Ainan, provided him with a secretary, who transcribed and corrected his manuscripts, a work which took more than 30 years.

Ibn Battuta's journeys were not yet done. Although he had seen more of the known world than any man before him—and much more than the most indefatigable travellers since his time—he set out once again in 1352 and, heading southwards through the Atlas Mountains, reached the Niger, visited Timbuktu and travelled across the silent reaches of the Sahara with the gold caravans.

Ibn Battuta arrived back at Fez in September 1353, his travels at an end. Throughout the remainder of his life he declared the superiority of his native Morocco to every other land that he had seen. He died in 1377.

Under a cloudy sky navigators could set a course by the "shore sighting" birds. Fulmars (2) fly landwards to roost at night; flocks of eider ducks (3) are a sure sign of land

within 100 miles; great auks (4) once fished the northern coasts. If released from a ship out at sea a raven (5) or a dove (6) will head for land as far as one day's sail away

Flocks of migrating geese (1) led Irish monks to Iceland in the 9th century

Norse pilots crossing from Norway to Greenland would keep in sight the vast shoals of herring (7), cod (8) and haddock (9), which feed on the rich marine life bordering the continental shelf

Tides, currents and changes in colour, temperature and depth of the ocean were indications of position

Navigation without a compass

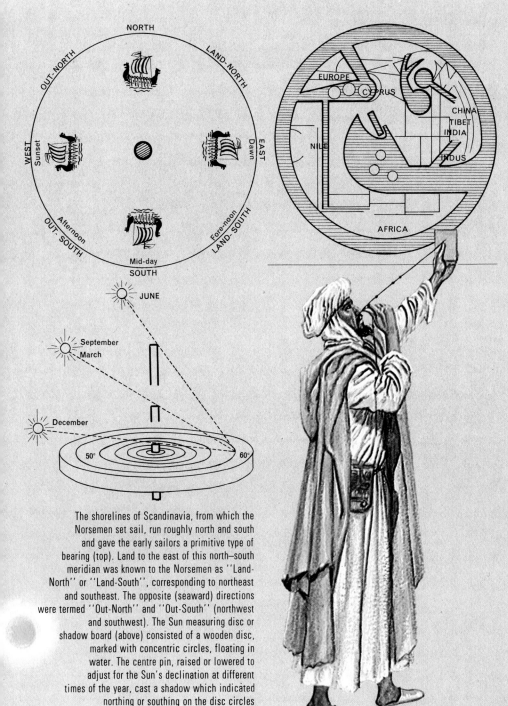

The shorelines of Scandinavia, from which the Norsemen set sail, run roughly north and south and gave the early sailors a primitive type of bearing (top). Land to the east of this north–south meridian was known to the Norsemen as ''Land-North'' or ''Land-South'', corresponding to northeast and southeast. The opposite (seaward) directions were termed ''Out-North'' and ''Out-South'' (northwest and southwest). The Sun measuring disc or shadow board (above) consisted of a wooden disc, marked with concentric circles, floating in water. The centre pin, raised or lowered to adjust for the Sun's declination at different times of the year, cast a shadow which indicated northing or southing on the disc circles

Remote in their Scandinavian fastnesses, the Norsemen had no contact with the mainstream of scientific thought—that of the Arabs—at the time they began to emerge from their fjords to raid, trade and explore. On long journeys across deserts without landmarks, the problems of Arab travellers were akin to those of mariners out of sight of land, and it was probably in the darkness of the desert night, with its clear skies, that the Arabs first came to be aware of the shifting patterns of heavenly bodies and their importance in navigation. As a result, astronomy was one of the first of the sciences to be developed by the people of the Near East. The astrolabe, a means of fixing the altitude of heavenly bodies, was invented by the Arabs c. 700 AD but, needing a stable base to be used properly it was not of much use at sea. A simple device which the Arab mariner used in place of the astrolabe was the Al-Kemal, Arabic for ''the consummation'' or guiding line (left). A rectangle of horn was held at arm's length with its base on the horizon, then moved towards the user until the Pole Star rested on the top. A cord from the centre of the rectangle was then placed on the user's nose and knots—indicating observed latitudes—were counted. The compass, the knowledge of which, from their journeys in the Indian Ocean, the Arabs first brought from its origins in China, was probably not much used by them as the clear tropical skies made it possible to observe celestial bodies. The Arab map (top left) bears little resemblance to modern cartography—it is rather more like the back of a watch—but it gives an accurate indication of the landmasses and seas with which the Arabs were familiar.

Thousands of miles away, beneath the lowering skies of the North Atlantic, the Norsemen solved their problems of navigation by observation of natural phenomena, some examples of which are shown across the foot of these pages. They are known to have possessed a few simple instruments of navigation, such as the Sun measuring disc. A claim that they used a sunstone a crystal by which the Sun's rays could be detected through cloud, is now regarded as dubious. The difficulties of the Norsemen were compounded by the change during the seasons of the Sun's course, and its rising and setting points—a problem that did not exist for sailors in lower latitudes. The Norsemen were therefore thrown back on the nature of the sea and its changes, on the wildlife they observed, and by ''rule-of-thumb'' estimation of a day's sailing and an estimation of speed through the water. It was enough to take them to a new continent

Above snow-covered land or ice fields the sky appears luminous white in colour. A sea channel through pack-ice is detectable by a sky-coloured break in this ''ice-blink''

Norse hunters studied the seasonal movements and extent of the sea ice and the habits of sea creatures living around it. Seals (10), trapped for skins and meat, and walruses (11), their hides used for ships' cordage and their tusks a source of ivory, followed the melting edges of the ice. The Greenland whale (12) lived off the abundant krill of the continental shelves

Voyages of the Three-Jewel Eunuch

"WESTERNERS", HENRI CORDIER wrote, in his *Histoire Générale de la Chine*, "have singularly narrowed the history of the world in grouping the little that they knew of the human race around the peoples of Israel, Greece and Rome. Thus they have ignored all those travellers and explorers who in their ships ploughed to the China Sea and the Indian Ocean, or rode across the immensities of Central Asia to the Persian Gulf."

The European "discovery" of the Indian Ocean in the 15th and 16th centuries was not even the rediscovery of a part of the world that had been found and then forgotten. It was only new to them as western Europeans. The Ancient Egyptians had traded on the African shores of the Indian Ocean. The Arabs began to settle it in the 8th century AD—Mogadishu, in Somalia, in about 720, Sofala, about 780, and Madagascar in the 9th century. These were the bases from which their subsequent explorations began. Chinese junks were in the harbour at Malacca when Albuquerque arrived there.

It is not known how many Chinese sailors and merchants visited the east coast of Africa between the 8th and 14th centuries. Chinese texts as early as AD 860 described the south coast of the Gulf of Aden and the Somali Coast. Malindi (Mo-Lin) was known about 1060 and the Zanzibar Coast (Tsheng-Pa) and Madagascar (Khun Lun Tsheng-Chhi) about 1178.

Coins and porcelain

The physical evidence that the Chinese were on the east coast of Africa is provided by the quantity of their hardware that has been discovered there—coins dating from the 7th century onwards (the majority from the Sung dynasty 960–1279) and in such numbers that it seems that they must have been used in payment for goods, as well as an immense quantity of porcelain, dating from the 10th century onwards.

In the early 15th century the great Chinese voyages to the Indian Ocean began and they are as well documented as any in the West. The first was in 1405, described in a contemporary Chinese account. "In the third year of the Yung-Lo reign the Imperial Palace Eunuch Cheng Ho (the Three-Jewel Eunuch) was sent on a mission to the Western Oceans. The Emperor Chheng Tsu, under the suspicion that the previous Chien-Wen Emperor might have fled beyond the seas, commissioned Cheng Ho, Wang Ching-Hung and others to pursue his traces. Bearing vast amounts of gold and other treasures, and with a force of more than 37,000 officers and men under their command, they built great ships sixty-two in number, and set sail from Liu-chia Kang in the prefecture of Suchow,

whence they proceeded . . . to Chang-Chhen [Champa, Indo-China], and thence on voyages throughout the western seas.

"Every country became obedient to the imperial commands, and when Cheng Ho turned homewards, sent envoys in his train to offer tribute. The emperor was highly gladdened . . . and Cheng Ho was commissioned on no less than seven diplomatic expeditions. . . ."

The seven expeditions are described by Dr Joseph Needham in the chapter on Voyages and Discoveries in his monumental *Science and Civilisation in China*.

The first (1405–7) reached Indo-China, Java, Sumatra, Ceylon and Calicut; the second (1407–9) Siam, Cochin and other ports on the west coast of India; the third, based on Malacca, voyaged in the East Indies and some ships were on the southwest coast of India and Ceylon when another leader, the eunuch Hou Hsien, appeared.

On the fourth voyage the squadrons divided, some continuing to sail in the East Indies, while others, based on Ceylon, explored the Bengal coast and the Maldive Islands and yet others reached Hormuz.

On the fifth voyage, or voyages (1417–19), Java, the Ryukyu Islands (the great 700-mile-long archipelago southwest of Japan between Kyushu and Formosa) and Brunei in northwest Borneo, were some of the places to which the Pacific squadrons went. The coasts between Hormuz and Aden, Mogadishu in Somalia, Malindi and the coast farther south were explored by the squadrons in the Indian Ocean.

The sixth expedition (1421–2) was an amplification of the previous one. This time 36 states were visited, between Brunei and Zanzibar. In 1431, the seventh and last Grand Treasure Ship Fleet set out.

By the time it returned to China, in 1433, it had increased the Chinese knowledge of the world north and west of Java by 20 realms, as far north as Jiddah in the Red Sea.

It was the last great venture of the Ming Navy. From now on the inward-looking Confucian faction was in the ascendant. It regarded the things brought from beyond the seas as superfluous. Among them were the tusks of elephants, rhinoceros horns (still prized among expatriate Chinese), pearls and aromatics from Africa and, above all else, spices—the same merchandise that the Arabs and later the Portuguese prized so highly.

It is more than possible that they got as far as the southern Atlantic and some of their captains may have doubled the Cape and seen the West African shore.

This was at a time when the most informed European cartographer had but the vaguest notion of Africa's true shape.

First round the Cape. According to 15th-century mapmaker Fra Mauro, Chinese junks doubled the Cape of Good Hope in 1420—some 60 years before the Portuguese captain Bartolomeu Dias

That acute observer Marco Polo never let astonishment and wonder cloud his eye for detail. Impressed by the size and strength of the great junks, he noted also the ways in which they were clearly in advance of Western technology in their construction—the great centre rudder (unlike the steerboards of the Mediterranean) and the bulkheads

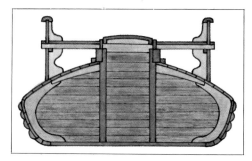

The bulkheads of a Chinese junk. These made it possible to seal off leaking or holed sections. It was centuries before Europe followed suit

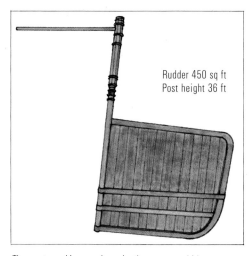

Rudder 450 sq ft
Post height 36 ft

The centre rudder, overhung by the poop, could be used as a centreboard—drop keel—when a junk was being sailed to windward

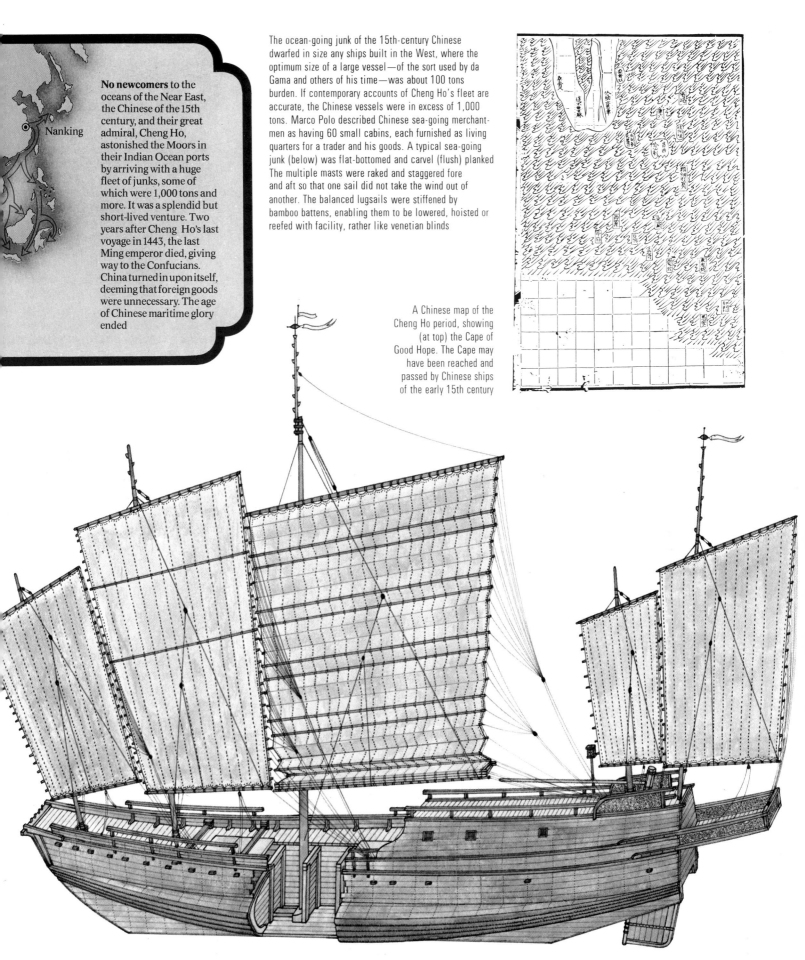

No newcomers to the oceans of the Near East, the Chinese of the 15th century, and their great admiral, Cheng Ho, astonished the Moors in their Indian Ocean ports by arriving with a huge fleet of junks, some of which were 1,000 tons and more. It was a splendid but short-lived venture. Two years after Cheng Ho's last voyage in 1443, the last Ming emperor died, giving way to the Confucians. China turned in upon itself, deeming that foreign goods were unnecessary. The age of Chinese maritime glory ended

Nanking

The ocean-going junk of the 15th-century Chinese dwarfed in size any ships built in the West, where the optimum size of a large vessel—of the sort used by da Gama and others of his time—was about 100 tons burden. If contemporary accounts of Cheng Ho's fleet are accurate, the Chinese vessels were in excess of 1,000 tons. Marco Polo described Chinese sea-going merchant-men as having 60 small cabins, each furnished as living quarters for a trader and his goods. A typical sea-going junk (below) was flat-bottomed and carvel (flush) planked The multiple masts were raked and staggered fore and aft so that one sail did not take the wind out of another. The balanced lugsails were stiffened by bamboo battens, enabling them to be lowered, hoisted or reefed with facility, rather like venetian blinds

A Chinese map of the Cheng Ho period, showing (at top) the Cape of Good Hope. The Cape may have been reached and passed by Chinese ships of the early 15th century

Europe: the plague and the scimitar

THE OVERSEAS EXPANSION by which Europe was to assert itself powerfully upon the pattern of world history began in the 15th century, with the departure of the first Portuguese maritime explorers from their Atlantic havens.

They put out from an embattled Christian continent which had for centuries been denied access to much of the known world by the hostile forces of Islam—an Islam whose threat to the western part of Europe had only lately been diminished to a foothold in Granada, in the south of Spain. Two other vital events had helped create and complete this isolation and the new, outward-looking spirit that it engendered.

One was the advance into the Balkans of the Ottoman Turks, and the fall of Constantinople in 1453. The Byzantine capital had been a gateway to trade with the east for the Venetians and others, for whose mercantile power the success of the Islamic Turks had sounded the death knell. The other, far more dreadful, event had occurred a century before. This was the Black Death. In the course of its march from China to the westernmost lands of Europe, it brought to a standstill the new, exciting commerce along the "golden road to Samarkand" and beyond, which had been pioneered by the Polos and others.

A new society emerges

The awful plague, in which unknown millions died (more than a million, a third of the population, in England alone), had far-reaching social effects. Labour was in short supply; the old, cosmopolitan feudal system began to break down. A new class of merchants and bankers emerged who were later to provide finance for overseas exploration. A Europe—at least in the west—of independent nations started to take shape and with it, national ambitions and rivalries.

From 1400 to 1700, first one and then another of the western seaboard nations came to the fore. From their Atlantic outpost, the Portuguese led the way, and on their heels the Spanish, seeking wealth for their country whose agriculture, so carefully nurtured during the Moorish occupation, had been destroyed by a system of sheep farming (the *Mesta*); the Spaniards despised tilling the soil as a menial task. England and France, locked in combat between the mid-14th and mid-15th centuries, took up the challenge of the distant horizons followed by the Dutch, after they had shaken off the yoke of Spain. The flags of these five maritime nations broke out across the world, clashing in one sphere of influence, reaching an accommodation in another. Between them they were to assert the tongues and customs of European civilization on to the better part of the world.

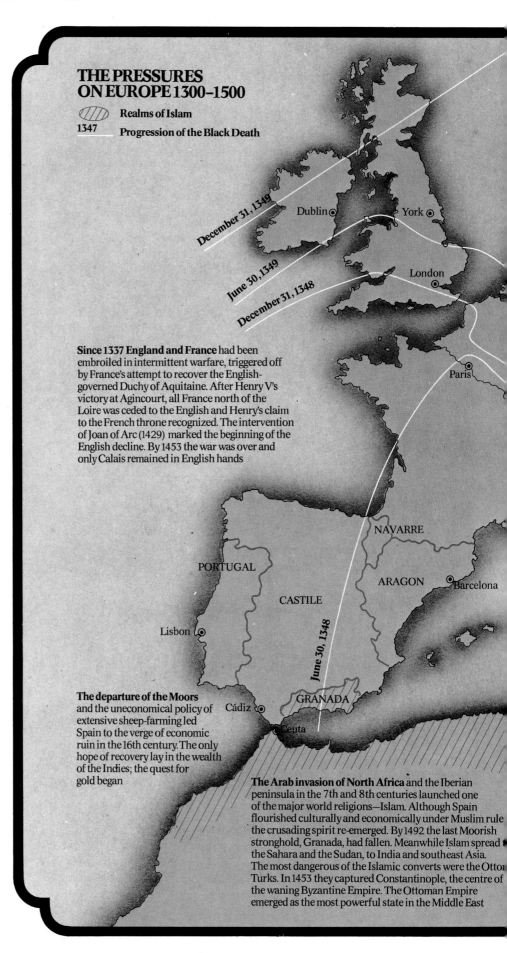

THE PRESSURES ON EUROPE 1300–1500

- Realms of Islam
- 1347 — Progression of the Black Death

December 31, 1349
June 30, 1349
December 31, 1348
June 30, 1348

Dublin
York
London
Paris
NAVARRE
PORTUGAL
ARAGON
Barcelona
CASTILE
Lisbon
Cádiz
GRANADA
Ceuta

Since 1337 England and France had been embroiled in intermittent warfare, triggered off by France's attempt to recover the English-governed Duchy of Aquitaine. After Henry V's victory at Agincourt, all France north of the Loire was ceded to the English and Henry's claim to the French throne recognized. The intervention of Joan of Arc (1429) marked the beginning of the English decline. By 1453 the war was over and only Calais remained in English hands

The departure of the Moors and the uneconomical policy of extensive sheep-farming led Spain to the verge of economic ruin in the 16th century. The only hope of recovery lay in the wealth of the Indies; the quest for gold began

The Arab invasion of North Africa and the Iberian peninsula in the 7th and 8th centuries launched one of the major world religions—Islam. Although Spain flourished culturally and economically under Muslim rule the crusading spirit re-emerged. By 1492 the last Moorish stronghold, Granada, had fallen. Meanwhile Islam spread the Sahara and the Sudan, to India and southeast Asia. The most dangerous of the Islamic converts were the Ottoman Turks. In 1453 they captured Constantinople, the centre of the waning Byzantine Empire. The Ottoman Empire emerged as the most powerful state in the Middle East

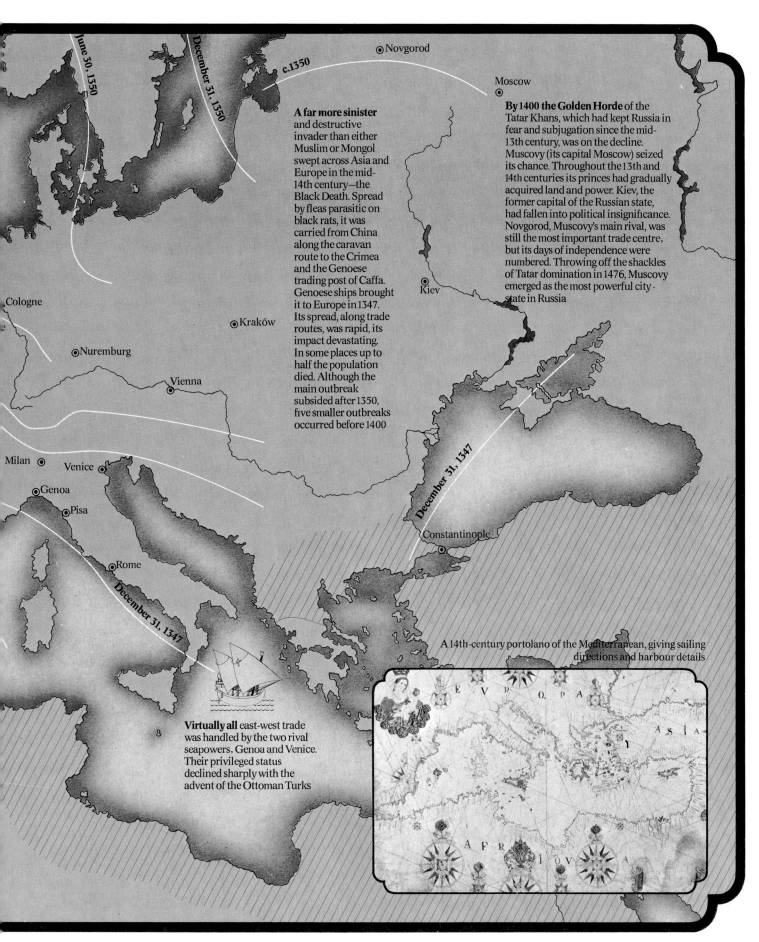

Novgorod

Moscow ⊙

c.1350

June 30, 1350

December 31, 1350

A far more sinister and destructive invader than either Muslim or Mongol swept across Asia and Europe in the mid-14th century—the Black Death. Spread by fleas parasitic on black rats, it was carried from China along the caravan route to the Crimea and the Genoese trading post of Caffa. Genoese ships brought it to Europe in 1347. Its spread, along trade routes, was rapid, its impact devastating. In some places up to half the population died. Although the main outbreak subsided after 1350, five smaller outbreaks occurred before 1400

By 1400 the Golden Horde of the Tatar Khans, which had kept Russia in fear and subjugation since the mid-13th century, was on the decline. Muscovy (its capital Moscow) seized its chance. Throughout the 13th and 14th centuries its princes had gradually acquired land and power. Kiev, the former capital of the Russian state, had fallen into political insignificance. Novgorod, Muscovy's main rival, was still the most important trade centre, but its days of independence were numbered. Throwing off the shackles of Tatar domination in 1476, Muscovy emerged as the most powerful city-state in Russia

Cologne

⊙ Kraków

Kiev ⊙

⊙ Nuremburg

Vienna ⊙

Milan ⊙

Venice ⊙

Genoa ⊙

Pisa ⊙

December 31, 1347

Rome ⊙

Constantinople ⊙

December 31, 1347

A 14th-century portolano of the Mediterranean, giving sailing directions and harbour details

Virtually all east-west trade was handled by the two rival seapowers, Genoa and Venice. Their privileged status declined sharply with the advent of the Ottoman Turks

Beyond the barrier of fear

"To discover what lay beyond the Canaries and Cape Bojador; to trade with any Christians who might dwell in the lands beyond; to discover the extent of the Mohammedan dominions; to find a Christian king who would help him to fight the infidel; to spread the Christian faith; to fulfil the predictions of his horoscope, which bound him to engage in great and noble conquests and attempt the discovery of things that were hidden from other men; to find Guinea."

THESE, ACCORDING to Gomez Eannes de Azurara, his chronicler and contemporary, were the aims of Prince Henry of Portugal, known as The Navigator, younger son of King João (John) I.

He made them known not long after the successful Portuguese expedition in 1415 to capture the Moorish seaport of Ceuta. The expedition was ostensibly a crusade—and Henry was a crusader in the real sense of the word—but there was also the pressing need to put down the Moorish pirates who infested the entrance to the Mediterranean and who were a nuisance to every Christian nation that traded in the inland sea. With the pirates under control there was a real possibility that the Portuguese might be able to take over the caravan trade—an important part of which was in gold dust—that Ceuta enjoyed with the African interior. In the event, the attempt to capture this trade failed, the caravans thereafter travelling to other cities in Moorish territory.

And so there emerged another purpose. This was to discover from which parts of Africa the merchandise, particularly the gold dust, emanated and, having done so, to contrive to have it rerouted so that, instead of ending up on the southern shores of the Mediterranean in the realms of the infidel, it would be carried to stations on the Atlantic coast in which the inhabitants would already have been converted to Christianity and of which the King of Portugal would be the ruler.

Standing on the edge of the cliffs at Cape St Vincent, at the southwestern extremity of Europe, with the Atlantic working restlessly more than 170 feet below, one begins to have some inkling of the measure of Henry's achievement, the power of his imagination, his tenacity of purpose.

And here, too, one begins to understand the nature of the terrors to which his captains, and their crews, were subject when, at his direction, they set off southwards into the unknown.

Cape St Vincent lies in latitude 37N and only eight degrees of latitude (little more than

600 miles) of ocean separate it from Cape Non on the edge of the Sahara, in the arid country of Ifni, where the mountains of the Anti-Atlas finally expire. This was the point beyond which few sailors of whom any records exist had penetrated, apart from Hanno the Phoenician, and the details of his voyage were so far back in the mists of time that they must have seemed apocryphal.

In 1415 and for some years to come, European man (except for a few unorthodox persons who remembered the writings of Herodotus and some other writers who referred to men passing unscathed through the tropics) still believed himself to be enclosed in the Northern Temperate Zone, one of five which encircled a spherical world, the invention of Mediterranean philosophers between the 5th and 2nd centuries BC.

In this zone, they imagined themselves prisoners in a sort of sandwich between the eternal ice of the Northern Frigid Zone and the fires of the middle, Torrid Zone, an uninhabited, uninhabitable Hell where the Sun passed so close to the sea and the land that the former boiled and the latter was on fire. It was known that the Northern Frigid Zone could be entered but not deeply penetrated; but south of the Torrid Zone were the impenetrable South Temperate and South Frigid Zones, and no one knew whether or not human, animal or plant life existed in the first of these.

But it was not even necessary to have a real conviction of the impassability of the Zone of Fire to make the journey to its outer limits seem impossible. Even to reach its confines it was necessary to pass through what the Arabic geographers called the "Green Sea of Darkness", a fearful area of perpetual fog and contrary currents from which, once it was entered, there was no return.

Fogs and contrary currents

The "Green Sea of Darkness" was thought to begin somewhere to the south of Cape Non, and when Cape Bojador was first sighted in latitude 27N, it had all the attributes of fogs and contrary currents needed to convince the early navigators that they were on the very edge of it.

At the time of the capture of Ceuta, Henry was 21 years of age. About three years later, in 1418, he abandoned the Court and began to turn his attention to promoting the voyages that were to engross him for the rest of his life. Surprisingly little is really known about him. Physically strong, an immensely hard worker, not particularly learned and perhaps not even a great patron of learning, pious, chivalrous, generous to those he employed in his ventures, he was a Medieval Man, not a Renaissance Humanist, and it was medieval

thinking that was to continue to influence him and those who followed him, as it influenced Columbus, until the very end of the century.

He had his critics. His own elder brother, Dom Duarte, who later became king, considered him unmethodical (which seems strange), hasty, too lavish with money (as Governor of the Order of Christ he was able to devote their large revenues to his designs; they were never enough, however, and he left great debts) and not too scrupulous about the methods he employed to obtain it. Transcending all was his militant Christianity.

On the desolate and lonely promontory at Sagres, between Cape St Vincent and the bay of Lagos, he established a school of navigation and pilotage, built a church and a chapel, an observatory and a modest palace, the nucleus of what was to become a small town, Villa do Infante, and a shipyard. What is left of the great windrose that he had set up here can still be seen.

Little is known about what actually went on at Sagres. The extreme secrecy enveloping the whole history of Portuguese discovery, enforced for reasons of state security, involved the obliteration from the records of entire voyages. The death penalty was instituted for the misappropriation of charts, and the deliberate falsification of log books by the substitution of different latitudes and longitudes for the real ones extended also to the planning side.

How wide was Henry's knowledge—and

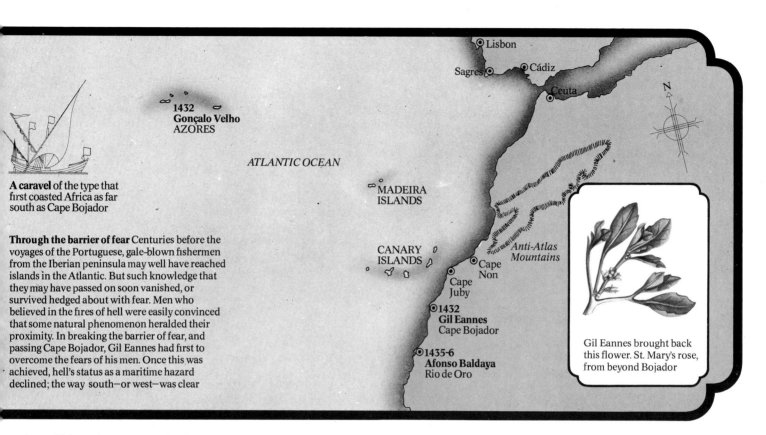

1432 Gonçalo Velho AZORES

ATLANTIC OCEAN

Lisbon

Sagres

Cádiz

Ceuta

N

MADEIRA ISLANDS

CANARY ISLANDS

Cape Non

Cape Juby

Anti-Atlas Mountains

1432 Gil Eannes Cape Bojador

1435-6 Afonso Baldaya Rio de Oro

A caravel of the type that first coasted Africa as far south as Cape Bojador

Through the barrier of fear Centuries before the voyages of the Portuguese, gale-blown fishermen from the Iberian peninsula may well have reached islands in the Atlantic. But such knowledge that they may have passed on soon vanished, or survived hedged about with fear. Men who believed in the fires of hell were easily convinced that some natural phenomenon heralded their proximity. In breaking the barrier of fear, and passing Cape Bojador, Gil Eannes had first to overcome the fears of his men. Once this was achieved, hell's status as a maritime hazard declined; the way south—or west—was clear

Gil Eannes brought back this flower, St. Mary's rose, from beyond Bojador

that of his assistants—at this time? Did he know of the *Mappae Mundi*, the work of the Jewish, Catalan and Italian cartographers? Some, such as the *Catalan Atlas*, produced for the French King Charles V in 1375 by Abraham Cresques at Palma di Mallorca, showed caravan routes across the Sahara and Sudan from the gold-producing regions on the Upper Niger and Senegal rivers. The information about these routes was supplied by Jewish merchants, who were able to travel more or less safely among the Muslims. Even farther afield such maps delineated some countries of the East, including India.

It seems likely that Henry saw a copy of the *Catalan Atlas*, at least in outline. The son of its compiler was Yahuda Cresques, also a cartographer and instrument maker, also from Mallorca. So, too, was Master Jacome, whom Henry hired at great cost to work for him at Sagres. It has been suggested that Jacome and Yahuda are one and the same person.

This, the second decade of the 15th century, was a good time for Portugal to begin its voyages of discovery. The war with Castile had ended in 1411, leaving Castile riddled with conspiracy and in a state of ferment. Portugal had long since expelled the Moors; in Spain they were to hang on, in Granada, for another 70 years. In France the Hundred Years' War was to continue to rage for more than 30 years (until 1453). In eastern Europe and the Near East the Turks were menacing Constantinople and the Levant. As a base Portugal was, for the time being, secure.

The prospects were excellent. In order to foster the growth of a small but efficient merchant marine in what was basically a nation of agriculturists, King Fernando I, by a letter of privilege in 1377, offered unprecedented inducement to the new mercantile class to build ships and trade with them.

Inducements

Anyone building a vessel of more than 100 tons burden was allowed free timber from the royal forests. Gear for fitting out could be imported without tax from other countries, and there was an extremely generous relaxation of import and export duties on goods carried in the ships themselves. This was to encourage trade with France and Flanders, principally in cloth and timber. Fernando also set up a form of marine insurance that was far ahead of its time. The only ingredient lacking was an adequate number of deep-water seamen and this was to plague the Portuguese throughout the period of their maritime expansion until, in the 17th century, they actually began to lose the possessions on which they had expended so much energy in finding and acquiring. (Flemings and Italians were among the crews on the early voyages.)

For 12 years or more Henry sent out specially chosen men, who had already distinguished themselves elsewhere, in the charge of vessels which he hoped would pass Cape Bojador; none succeeded. According to Afonso V, writing in 1443, he sent them out some 14 times before the rounding was

accomplished, and there were probably many more attempts than this, rather than fewer.

Anchoring at night, coasting by day, both masters and men were full of fears which Henry himself, who must have been extremely irritated by what he probably secretly regarded as craven procrastination, endeavoured to assuage. "Why," Henry's men are supposed to have said, "should we attempt to pass the limits which our forefathers set up, and what profit can result to the Infant from the loss of our bodies and souls?"

Today we are less afraid of being thought to be afraid than our ancestors, and to anyone who has any knowledge of the African coast between capes Non and Bojador their apprehensions seem reasonable. It is a sinister coast; off Cape Non itself the sea is red, discoloured by the sands blown offshore from the deserts which here approach the coast. Not only is it coloured, but so densely that the track of a vessel passing through it is visible for a considerable time afterwards. And even the ships themselves become red, tinged with the red sand.

As far south as the cape the currents follow the lines of the coast, but beyond it, and as far to the southwest as Cape Juby, they strike it obliquely. This is the most dangerous coast between the Strait of Gibraltar and Bojador, as the wrecks of numerous vessels that have been embayed on it testify. And in the narrow funnel between Juby and Fuerteventura, the innermost of the Canaries, there are frequent heavy swells from the northwest, and the

Beyond the barrier of fear

current runs at six knots. Off the cape itself the sea is dark green. In winter there is a lot of fog on the entire coast.

Southwards to Cape Bojador the coast is exceptionally inhospitable—sandstone cliffs with desolate tablelands behind, interminable dune-fringed beaches on which the surf crashes endlessly, a coast on which everything is indistinct behind a screen of spray and flying sand. No wonder the Portuguese loathed and feared it.

In 1433, having spent a great deal of money with little result, apart from the discovery, or rediscovery, of Sta Maria, one of the southeastern group of the Azores, by Gonçalo Velho in 1432, Henry sent out his Shield Bearer, Gil Eannes, with instructions to pass Cape Bojador at all costs, but he got no farther than the Canaries.

Impetus

His subsequent interview with Henry, in the course of which he was given a dressing down for listening to hearsay (in this case the pessimistic talk of some Flemings who had never been near the cape and knew nothing of the use of the compass or charts), gave him impetus and the following year he succeeded in doubling the cape. A strand of red sand with a gradual descent towards the sea, the western extremity of Cape Bojador formed a small bay with a chain of rocks offshore, on the heads of which the dark green sea broke heavily. Behind it there were cliffs which extended for about four miles to the south, with small bushes and creepers growing on

them—a weird and desolate place, but with few of the other terrors attributed to it. The current, which in theory would allow no ship to return, ran sedately at about half a knot.

Eannes brought back with him from the shore flowers of a kind known in Portugal as St Mary's rose, but saw no signs of human life. At this distance of time what he accomplished may seem little, but it required great courage and was an important moment in the history of exploration as an almost tangible barrier had been broken through.

Immediately after his return to Portugal he was sent out again in company with Afonso Gonçalves, Henry's Cup Bearer. They reached a point between 30 and 50 leagues beyond the cape, where there was a bay which they named Angra dos Rivos. There were no habitations or people, but they saw footprints of men and camels.

Believing that some settlement or port must be close by, Henry ordered Afonso Baldaya to sea in 1435–6, and he reached a point about 120 leagues beyond Bojador, where he found an arm of the sea which he thought might be a river. Here Baldaya put ashore two young noblemen to reconnoitre. They met a party of spear-carrying natives and in the ensuing fracas one of the Portuguese was wounded. Baldaya's men withdrew and, continuing south, he passed the mouth of the Rio de Oro, reaching a point just north of Cape Blanco in latitude 20.46N.

Baldaya's journey brought to an end a period of successful reconnaissance. There were to be no more expeditions sponsored by Henry for six years, but Bojador, the first important hurdle, had been cleared and the way opened to a Portuguese empire, which is only now drawing to its close in Africa.

FROM NOW ON the dread of the unknown began to diminish, for Eannes and Baldaya and their men had overcome their first fears. The number of men willing to engage in voyages of this kind increased, and the combination of greed and religious fervour that was the driving force of the 15th-century explorers was ever more in evidence. Africa and its riches now lay at hand, for the first time, to the European.

In 1441, Antão Gonçalves, Henry's youthful chamberlain, and Nuno Tristão, another member of his household, made history, however deplorable it may seem to us now, with hindsight, by bringing back a number of captive Negroes (probably Senegalese) and what were described as Azenegues, non-Moorish Muslims from the fringes of the Sahara, whom they had taken in the vicinity of Rio de Oro. One of them was a chief called Adahu, who spoke Moorish.

Gonçalves sailed for home, but Tristão went on and reached Cape Blanco, a barren headland which terminates in a sheer white cliff with two very dangerous shoals offshore.

Thus began a new time of tribulation for the indigenous people of the seaboard and the interior—new, because the Muslim trade in human beings was already long established.

Papal approval

Henry was pleased and in 1443, with the possibility of being able to engage in the conversion of pagans and Muslims on an extensive scale, he obtained from Pope Eugenius IV a bull of plenary indulgence for those who might die in the course of the work. At the same time Pedro, the Regent of Portugal, bestowed on him a proportion of the royal profits from voyages to help him with his own huge disbursements and, also, the sole right to grant licences to sail beyond Cape Bojador.

On Gonçalves's next voyage, Adahu was put ashore with the intention of allowing him to ransom himself for half a dozen Negroes who would be more tractable to conversion than Muslims, but—not unnaturally—he was not seen again. However, two of his followers whom the Portuguese had prudently kept on board were successfully exchanged for ten men and women, selected from more than a hundred unwilling candidates by the official ransomer, sent by Henry for the purpose.

Gonçalves brought back a shield, some gold dust and a number of ostrich eggs, which were subsequently consumed at the Prince's table with no ill effects. The voyage was regarded as a great success—God and Mammon being almost equally served—and it marks the beginning of European trade with the Sahara, although a network of Arab trading routes

Native fishing boats drawn up on the beach in West Africa. Small fleets of them appeared ''like giant birds'' to the Portuguese explorers

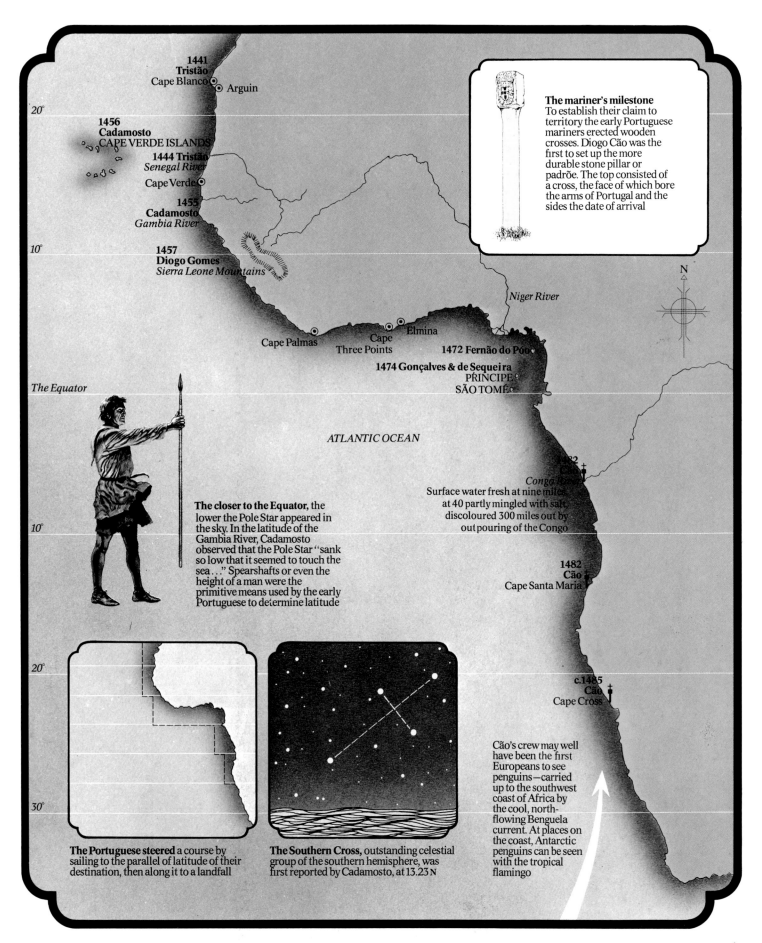

1441
Tristão
Cape Blanco ⊙ ● Arguin

20°

1456
Cadamosto
CAPE VERDE ISLANDS
1444 Tristão
Senegal River
Cape Verde ⊙

1455
Cadamosto
Gambia River

10°

1457
Diogo Gomes
Sierra Leone Mountains

Niger River

N

Cape Palmas   Cape   Elmina
          Three Points
                    1472 Fernão do Póo
          1474 Gonçalves & de Sequeira
                    PRÍNCIPE
                    SÃO TOMÉ

The Equator

ATLANTIC OCEAN

The mariner's milestone
To establish their claim to territory the early Portuguese mariners erected wooden crosses. Diogo Cão was the first to set up the more durable stone pillar or padrõe. The top consisted of a cross, the face of which bore the arms of Portugal and the sides the date of arrival

1482
Cão
Congo River
Surface water fresh at nine miles, at 40 partly mingled with salt, discoloured 300 miles out by outpouring of the Congo

The closer to the Equator, the lower the Pole Star appeared in the sky. In the latitude of the Gambia River, Cadamosto observed that the Pole Star "sank so low that it seemed to touch the sea…" Spearshafts or even the height of a man were the primitive means used by the early Portuguese to determine latitude

10°

1482
Cão
Cape Santa Maria

20°

c.1485
Cão
Cape Cross

30°

Cão's crew may well have been the first Europeans to see penguins—carried up to the southwest coast of Africa by the cool, north-flowing Benguela current. At places on the coast, Antarctic penguins can be seen with the tropical flamingo

The Portuguese steered a course by sailing to the parallel of latitude of their destination, then along it to a landfall

The Southern Cross, outstanding celestial group of the southern hemisphere, was first reported by Cadamosto, at 13.23 N

Evolution of the oceanic sailing ship

The oceanic sailing ship, on which the prosperity of the great maritime empires was based, had a clear genealogy. Until the beginning of the great age of discovery in the 15th century, European sailing experience had been almost entirely coastwise. The vessels that were to chart the world, often out of sight of land for many weeks, were the result of a growing technology, which drew its inspiration from a number of sources. Southern Europe learned its trade by sailing an enclosed lake, the Mediterranean, making largely coastwise passages in often calm conditions. From the Baltic to Biscay, the journeys were still largely coastwise, but in far rougher, murkier conditions. The result was, in the north, a tubby, bouncy little ''holk'' and—in the Mediterranean—the slender butterfly-winged lateener. The maritime cultures met in the waters off the Iberian Peninsula, and from the parentage there sprang the three-masted, decked square-rigger of which Columbus's ''Santa Maria'' was a typical example. Ships used for oceanic voyages in subsequent decades, first to reach India then to circumnavigate the world, were similar in general appearance though refined in detail

Characteristic of the early northern ships was ''clinker'' construction (overlapping planks, left). A centre rudder (right) was another feature used by northern shipwrights, and which later became standard to all oceanic ships

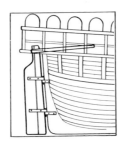

The square sail of the northern ships (above) had reefpoints to furl the sail. They went out of use for centuries, then re-emerged. Northern mast-shrouds had ladder-like rat-lines for climbing

The longship of the Viking was the parent of the northern ships. Clinker-built and long-keeled (for grounding on beaches), it made great journeys from its home in the Scandinavian fjords

A Hansa cog of the 13th century. The cog, a northern ship, was often depicted on seals of maritime towns

Three-masted herring buss of northern waters, square-rigged on all masts

In caravel, or carvel, planking (left), the planks are flush against each other, presenting a smooth hull surface to the sea

As the ships of the north looked to the longship of the Viking for their ancestry, Mediterranean vessels had their parentage in the Arab craft of the Middle East. Sailing vessels which would be immediately recognizable to medieval man in the ports of the eastern Mediterranean are still to be seen working the Nile and the Red Sea coasts

The caravel, in which the Portuguese made their first journeys along the coast of Africa, used a centre rudder instead of the steerboards of the Arab ''baghlas''. In other respects they were similar, with triangular lateen sails, which were excellent for inshore working. They had the flush, edge-to-edge carvel planking

The carrack was the prototype galleon. The square rig of its sails was far more suitable for running before the oceanic trade winds than the lateen of the caravel. The lateen remained on the third—mizzen—mast to aid steerage in light winds. The high stern, which provided living quarters, protected the ship from being ''pooped'' by following seas

had for centuries criss-crossed the desert.

Voyages now began to take place with increasing frequency. In 1443, Tristão sailed along the low-lying coast of Mauritania, which is almost devoid of fresh water, and reached Arguin Island, an arid rock only three miles long and two wide, lying in a bay backed by white dunes. Five years later a fort, the remains of which still exist, was built on it and it became the first Portuguese slaving station. Here, Tristão saw large numbers of canoes filled with naked men and on first sight thought they were giant birds. He and his men captured some, and, indeed, the account reads more like that of a hunt than the kidnapping of primitive human beings for the good of their immortal souls.

Slavery begins

The following year Lançarote, the Revenue Officer of Lagos, captained a large raiding party—for it was nothing more—of six caravels, capturing 233 natives. The best were offered to the Church (one became a Franciscan friar at Cape St Vincent), and the heart-rending scenes when the captives were taken ashore at Lagos are described by the chronicler, Azurara: "And these, placed together in that field, were a marvellous sight, for amongst them were some white enough, fair to look upon and well proportioned, others were less white like mulattoes; others again were as black as Ethiops, and so ugly,

The Dutch East Indiaman was an end and a beginning in the development of sailing ships. It embodied the lessons learned by men like Columbus, da Gama, Magellan and Drake, and incorporated inherited features from northern waters and from the Mediterranean. It was built not only for oceanic voyages but also to carry cargo in its deep hull, for trade was the motive power behind the 17th-century expansion. Its canvas was broken up into a greater number of sails to allow ease of handling by smaller crews. Two hundred years later, the "Cutty Sark" (right) was to show how far these refinements could be taken. Its crew was often less than 20 men

both in features and in body, as almost to appear the images of a lower hemisphere. But what heart could be so hard as not to be pierced with piteous feeling to see that company? . . . and then it was needful to part fathers from sons, husbands from wives, brothers from brothers. No respect was shewn either to friends or relations, but each fell where his lot took him. . . .

"The Infant was there, mounted upon a powerful steed, and accompanied by his retinue, making distribution of his favours, as a man who sought to gain but small treasure from his share; for he made a very speedy partition of the 46 souls that fell to him as his fifth. His chief riches lay in his purpose, and he reflected with great pleasure upon the salvation of those souls that before were lost. And certainly his expectation was not in vain, since, as we said before, as soon as they understood our language, they turned Christians with very little ado. . . ."

In 1444, Tristão reached the north side of the delta of the Senegal River and saw green country with palm trees growing in it. It was the Africa of the popular imagination, the Land of the Negroes, the first greenery after 600 miles of desert coastline. Tristão was followed by Dinis Dias, who passed the mouth of the Senegal which, in the rainy season, produces a prodigious breaking sea where the outflood meets the Atlantic.

The Senegal separated the land of the

The green and gold of Africa

Azenegue Moors from that of the Jaloff Negroes, but it was not by any means the place where Muslim influence ceased, as future explorers were to discover. What was important to the Portuguese was that they believed the Senegal to be the Nile, or at least a tributary of it.

Dias sailed along a coast backed by sandhills until he reached a low cape with two prominent hills on it at the end of a green, wooded peninsula. He named it Cape Verde. Although he could not know it he was at the westernmost point of Africa; what he must have known was that he was 2,000 miles from home.

The following year Antão Gonçalves managed to bring back from the desolate but inhabited shores of the Bay of Arguin the squire João Fernandes, who at his own request had been left there in the course of an expedition by Gonçal de Sintra, seven years before. Fernandes, who had learned the language of the Azenegues from a slave, told a remarkable story. Guided by men who used the wind and stars as navigating aids, he had visited the interior of northwestern Africa and seen Arabs, Azenegues and Berbers living in their tents, herding their flocks and selling slaves to the Moors for bread (on which they set a great price) and other commodities.

In 1445, a large fleet of 26 vessels from Lagos, Lisbon and Madeira was sent out to reduce the island of Tider, whose Moorish inhabitants were a nuisance to the Portuguese. One ship of this fleet went on to engage in a voyage of discovery—the caravel commanded by Alvaro Fernandes.

New landmark

Sailing along a low, wooded coast on which the surf breaks violently, Fernandes reached what he called the Cape of Masts because of the tall, mast-like palms which grew on it, near the estuary of the Gambia River. It was to become a well-known landmark for explorers. On his next voyage, in 1466, he may have reached a point 110 leagues beyond Cape Verde. Fernandes and his men had some fierce encounters with the Negroes, who were armed with bows and poisoned arrows, and some of them were wounded; but their most

memorable discovery was "some elephant's dung of the bigness of a man, according to the judgement of those that saw it; and because it seemed not a place to make booty they returned to their caravel". One can hardly blame them.

That same year, poisoned arrows also accounted for the death of 20 of a ship's company, including its leader Nuño Tristão, which occurred while they were exploring one of the rivers of the Gambia delta. There were only five persons left, most of them boys, fit enough to work the ship, and after a terrible voyage of two months, always out of sight of land, they finally made landfall at Sines, south of Lisbon.

By now, 51 caravels had sailed 450 leagues beyond Cape Bojador and everything that had been discovered was recorded meticulously on the Portuguese charts. Nine hundred and twenty-seven infidels had been taken to Portugal, most of them being successfully converted to Christianity. Trading had not been up to expectations owing to the intractability of the people—which was not surprising, considering the treatment the natives had met with at the hands of the Portuguese. Most important of all, Portugal had been confirmed in her unique position in relation to Africa by a number of papal bulls, the three most important of which were *Dum Diversas*, 1452, *Romanus Pontifex*, 1455 and the *Inter Caetera*, 1456.

They first authorized the Portuguese king to attack Saracens, pagans and all unbelievers, capture and keep their possessions and reduce their owners to perpetual slavery. The second, which was very long, summarized Henry's achievements since 1419, confirmed the absolute monopoly in all matters in every

One of the early maps of West Africa, which was prepared on the basis of information brought back by the early Portuguese explorers and by trading Jews, who, unlike Christians, were free to wander through the domains of the Muslim. It was drawn by Lazaro Luis in 1563 and is now in the Lisbon Academy of Sciences. The map depicts camel trains laden with salt, the Sierra Leone Mountains (where the rumble of thunder reminded travellers of the roar of a lion), and the wealthy and ancient kingdom of Benin in southern Guinea

place to which Portuguese conquest had extended and might extend in the future, even as far as the Indies, and prohibited any other nation from infringing their monopoly in the realms of discovery, conquest and commerce. They were even given permission to trade with the Saracens.

Most of the accounts of voyages up to 1448 that have survived are of those sponsored by Henry and set down by Gomez Azurara, the official chronicler, in his *History of Guinea*, but these come to an end with the journey of Vallarte (the name is probably a Portuguese version of his real one). A courtier of King Christopher of Denmark, Vallarte set out in a Portuguese ship with the intention of making contact with the ruler of the Cape Verde Negroes, who was thought to be a Christian and might possibly be a vassal of Prester John, the legendary ruler of a great Christian empire in Africa, whose existence was the subject of constant speculation among the explorers and their patrons. Vallarte was either killed or taken prisoner.

The first eye-witness
It is fortunate for posterity that, in 1455, Alvise da Cadamosto, a Venetian trader, nobly born but short of money, accepted the terms laid down by Henry for his participation in a Portuguese expedition—Henry was to equip a vessel and receive an equal share of any proceeds. For Cadamosto had an observant eye, a retentive mind and the ability to write; and his story is the first of the eye-witness accounts that have come down to us.

He set off in a caravel captained by Vincent Dias to seek for spices, a commodity about which the Venetians had more knowledge than the Portuguese. By the middle of the 1450s raiding had been largely superseded by more conventional forms of trading. They sailed by way of Madeira and the Canaries and finally raised Cape Blanco after a voyage of 870 miles, most of it out of sight of land.

Cadamosto describes the inhabitants of the interior of Mauritania and the articles of trade—copper, silver and wheat from Barbary —which were exchanged for slaves, gold and pepper; and the camel routes—from Blanco to Ouadane, 300 miles and six days' march inland and another six days to Terhazza, where rock salt was hewn in large blocks. The salt was taken by the Azenegues and Arabs to Timbuktu in 40 days and from there for another 30 days, through terrible country in which men and animals frequently died in large numbers because of the aridity and the heat.

Over the last stage the blocks were carried on the heads of porters to an unnamed place where there was water and where a strange, anonymous barter took place. First the blocks

of salt were deposited and the porters withdrew half a day's journey. When they were gone the tribe which was buying the salt arrived by boat and left a quantity of gold by each block. If the vendors took it then the buyers took the salt; if it was not enough they added more gold or else left the salt. Neither side ever saw the other, neither group knew what the other looked like.

The gold itself was sent on its journey from Melli by three routes: one to Cairo and Syria, another via Timbuktu to Tunis, and the third via Ouadane bound for the north coast of Africa and, ultimately, for Italy and the Mediterranean countries.

From Cape Blanco, Cadamosto sailed to the Senegal River, where he met Budomel, a Negro Muslim and an autocratic ruler. Cadamosto offered him horses and was invited to the king's capital of reed huts 25 miles inland, where he stayed 28 days and was well treated.

Two other caravels now joined Cadamosto, one captained by Antoniotto Usodimare, a Genoese, the other by one of Henry's squires. Together they worked their way down the coast, passed Cape Verde and, anchoring well offshore at night, arrived in the territory of the Serreri and the Barbacini, whose predilection for poisoned arrows had been noted by Alvaro Fernandes. Cadamosto marked the Barbacini River on his chart.

The Gambia, which rises in the same highlands as the Senegal, was two miles wide at the mouth and wider still once the entrance was passed, allowing Cadamosto to sail his caravels upstream, where they encountered a fleet of canoes, manned by about 150 Negroes whose greeting took the form of showers of arrows. The Christians retaliated by firing off four cannon, but the natives were only momentarily taken aback. They were finally repulsed by crossbow fire, which killed a number of them.

There was no question of having friendly relations with such people who, as they contrived to make known to the expedition's two surviving interpreters, believed the white men to be cannibals who bought Negroes for the purpose of eating them. Cadamosto and his men withdrew.

It was now that the Venetian made an important discovery. "During our stay at the mouth of the river," Cadamosto wrote, "we only saw the Pole Star once; and then it sank so low that it seemed to touch the sea, apparently standing only one-third of a spear-shaft above the water.

"There we also saw six large and wonderfully bright stars. We measured them with the compass. We believed them to be the Great Bear of the Southern Hemisphere. It is not contrary to reason that we saw this

constellation before we lost the Pole Star. . . ."

What they were in fact the first to see was the Southern Cross, which begins to be visible over the southern horizon in 30N and can be seen in its entirety in about 15N. The mouth of the Gambia lies in 13.23N. That they were equipped with neither astrolabe nor quadrant is proved by the reference to the use of the spear-shaft.

Cadamosto set out again in 1456, once more in company with Usodimare, with three caravels, and found the Cape Verde Islands, 320 miles west of Cape Verde. The islands were uninhabited and beautifully wooded, their seas teemed with fish, some of them giant, and there was an abundance of salt.

Two years after Cadamosto, Diogo Gomes sailed up the Gambia and obtained a quantity of gold. He also learned of the gold mines behind the Sierra Leone range, mountains not destined to be seen or named until Pedro de Sintra sailed south in 1462 and called them this because, it was said, the thunder that rumbled about the peaks and ridges sounded like the roaring of lions.

Mud and mangrove
In the course of this journey up the river, on the banks of which it is very difficult to land because of the mud and the dense growth of mangroves, a number of Portuguese were killed. But Gomes did not withdraw until he had made contact with a previously hostile king called Nomi-Mansa, who was so won over by the Portuguese that he dismissed his Muslim priests and asked to be baptized. And this was done, sometime about 1458, when Henry sent out a young priest, João Delgado, who took up temporary residence in Nomi-Mansa's domain.

The guiding star of Portugal's pioneering navigators was now to vanish. "In the year 1460," Gomes records, "the lord Infant Henry fell ill in his town at Cape St Vincent and died of the illness on the 13th November . . . and on the night of his death, he was taken to the Church of St Mary at Lagos and there honourably buried. And the King Afonso . . . was very saddened, both he and his people, by the death of so great a lord, because he spent all his revenues and all he got from Guinea in war and in continual fleets at sea against the Saracens for the faith of Christ . . ."

The following year, Gomes continues, "the Infant's body was buried in a great and most beautiful chapel (in the monastery of St Mary of Batalha) . . . and there the King himself [Henry's father] lies and his wife D. Philippa, mother of the Infant and his five brothers . . ."

Prince Henry was 66 when he died. Two years before, he had taken part in the expedition to capture the Moorish fortress of Alcacer,

The green and gold of Africa

an enormous amphibious operation which set off with the blessing of Pope Calixtus III, and this—and the debts he left—effectively brought a halt to fresh voyages of discovery (as opposed to those for the purpose of trade) for some years.

In 1469, King Afonso leased the trading rights on the Guinea Coast to Fernão Gomes for five years, on condition that 100 leagues of fresh coastline should be explored every year. Only two places were exempt from the arrangement, Arguin Island and the Cape Verdes, both of which already had "captains" in charge of them. In the Cape Verde Islands the captain was Antonio da Noli, who had sailed with Diogo Gomes on a voyage in 1462 (of particular interest because of the recorded use of the quadrant to find the altitude of the Pole Star).

In the course of this voyage they had "discovered" the island of São Tiago, which was a matter of dispute, for Cadamosto claimed the distinction. Whatever the truth Noli, with his brother, settled the island and founded the town of Ribeira Grande.

Fever coast

What lay between the River Gambia and the easternmost part of the Gulf of Guinea, where the land finally turned south towards the Cape of Good Hope, was more than 2,000 miles of coast, most of it fever ridden, almost all of it subject to tornadoes and sudden fogs. Violent winds, the Harmattans, swept out from the interior. It took nearly the whole of the five years for Gomes's explorers to work their way along it and across the Equator.

South of the Gambia, for more than 600 miles, the coasts of what was later Portuguese Guinea, the Republic of Guinea and Sierra Leone as far as Cape St Ann south of Freetown were infested with reefs, shoals and small islands, and further complicated by river estuaries and swamps choked with mangroves. To the southeast, the Grain Coast, the coast of modern Liberia (so called because of the coarse malagueta pepper produced there), is flat, swampy, with some inlets but many reefs and rocks, as far as Cape Palmas. The cape is an unimpressive peninsula, but the place where for the first time the shoreline trends to the east along the lagoon-locked almost harbourless Ivory Coast.

Three hundred miles to the east, beyond Cape Three Points, is the Gold Coast, now the coast of Ghana, the Minho d'Ouro (Gold Mine) of the Portuguese, with its alluvial gold in the inland rivers. It is sandy for 200 miles as far as the River Volta, but the surf is so heavy that landing is difficult.

Still farther east is the Slave Coast of Dahomey and Togo on the Bight of Benin,

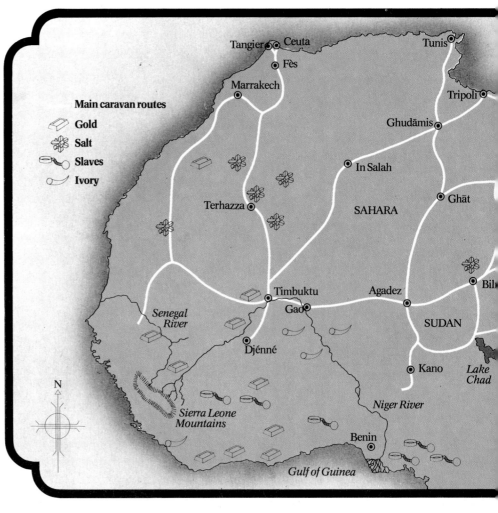

which for more than 400 miles is so low-lying that, from an offing of 12 miles and an elevation of 13 feet, the whole shore dips below the horizon and even when it is visible from closer in is often obscured by exhalations known as "smokes".

Here the Benin River enters the sea. It is one of 18 that discharge themselves through the Niger delta, the biggest mangrove swamp in the world. Benin itself was a highly civilized kingdom, and later the Portuguese established a trading station up the river at Gato, which was to become an important place in the trade in slaves and fine pepper.

Gomes's men sailed almost as far as Cape Three Points and in the succeeding years reached the Benin. In 1472, Fernão do Poo discovered the island that now bears a corruption of his proper name and title, an island occupied by aboriginals, the Ediyas or Bubis, which culminates in a remarkable volcanic cone over 10,000 feet high. To the east, on the mainland, loom the Cameroon Mountains, rising to over 13,000 feet.

In 1474, Lopo Gonçalves and Ruy de Sequeira, sailing southwards, once more crossed the Equator off the coast of Gabon, and reached 2s, discovering the islands of

Principe and São Tomé off of the mainland.

With the outbreak of the War of Succession between Portugal and Castile in 1475 the Portuguese possessions in the islands and on the African coast were soon involved in the power struggle. Ignoring claims of monopoly and papal bulls, Spaniards (and also Flemings) had already been engaged for some time in clandestine trade with Guinea, and the Spanish privateers' right to do so was formally confirmed by Queen Isabella in 1475. In the next three years they set out in large numbers to harry homeward-bound Portuguese ships.

The war ended in 1479 with the Treaty of Alcaçovas. Beaten in their homeland, the Portuguese succeeded in making the Castilians agree to accept their monopoly of West Africa, while acknowledging their right to the Canaries. It was a brilliant piece of diplomatic bargaining.

Fortress

To reinforce their ability to hold on to what they already had, the Portuguese constructed a fortress and factory at Elmina Point, 60 miles east of Cape Three Points, and all the coast from Liberia to the Niger delta became known as Elmina, "The Mine". The fortress—

The timeless trade routes of the desert. Featureless, barren and friendless in contrast both to Europe to the north, and the savannas and rich rain-forests to the south, the Sahara has been criss-crossed by trade routes since time out of mind. Much of the trade was in goods which added to the quality of life of those who bartered in them; but salt, the most important of all, was needed to sustain life and health in the desiccating atmosphere of the desert and subdesert. And Cadamosto, the Venetian, maintained that the gold miners of Guinea needed salt to prevent their "huge and red" pendulous lower lips from putrefying. All this tremendous commerce was closed to Europeans by Muslim antipathy, until, sweeping round the coast in their caravels, the Portuguese by-passed both the maritime "barrier of fear" at Bojador, and the blockade of Islam

Trade in salt still plays an important part in the commerce—and in the survival—of desert peoples. The photograph (below) shows salt being crystallized in the sun in Mauritania, in the western Sahara

In the desert fringes, where sand gives way to savanna, then forest, donkeys are used for transport; only camels have the strength and staying power for the great desert journeys

factory soon began to yield a great profit in trade with ivory, palm oil, wax gum, among other goods, in exchange for cloth and hardware and, of course, pure gold at a profit ratio of five to one in favour of the Portuguese. In spite of the tremendous profits the place was fearfully unhealthy and the Portuguese died like flies. It was the first "white man's grave".

As soon as the fortress was more or less finished—it was built with extreme speed, the central tower being completed in 20 days —Diogo Cão, who had been sent out expressly for the purpose of further exploration, sailed south in a caravel. Cão was not a nobleman, but he was of a family of distinguished sailors.

Among his stores was a number of padrões, stone columns each surmounted by a cube and a cross with the arms of Portugal, a text either in Latin or Portuguese and the name of the king with provision for the names of the explorers and the date of the discovery to be added, as appropriate. These replaced the impermanent wooden crosses that had been used up to this time.

On this, the first of two great voyages in the course of which he discovered more new land than any other Portuguese had done before, Cão reached the mouth of the Congo,

known to those who lived beside it as the Zaire, or Great River, and set up a padrõe.

Three hundred and fifty miles to the south of Cape St Catherine, after skirting a coast with little but lagoons and mangroves visible on it, he entered Loanga Bay and then sailed across the mouth of the Congo (finding fresh water five leagues out at sea) to the south side, where he erected a padrõe.

The farthest point Cão reached on this voyage was Cape Santa Maria in 13.26s, sailing down to it along a granite coast in which mica and quartz reflect the sun's rays like a great mirror. Here, 800 miles south of the Congo, he set up a padrõe named after St Augustine, which until recently was still visible from the seaward side and is now in Lisbon with the inscription: "In the year 6681 from the Creation of the world and 1482 from the birth of Our Lord Jesus Christ, the most high, most excellent and powerful prince King João, second of Portugal, ordered this land to be discovered and pillars to be put up by Diogo Cão, squire of his household."

On the return voyage, hearing from the "Black Ethiops" in the Congo that companions he had put ashore (in the hope that they might contact Prester John) had not

returned, he took four natives back to Portugal as hostages and to be converted.

On his next voyage, about 1485, he was accompanied by two astronomers, who were to find out whether there was a southern equivalent of the Pole Star. Failing to find one, they employed themselves in measuring the altitude of the sun, using the *Almanach Perpetuum* of the Jew, Abraham Zacuto.

Cão returned the Negroes to their homes, took off the men he had left behind on his previous voyage (no record of what they accomplished remains) and sailed 750 miles farther south as far as Cape Cross, a low, red-coloured truncated pyramid on the shore of the Namib Desert in 21.47s, and there he erected a padrõe.

The rest of his life is a mystery. Some say he died here, others think he may have reascended the Congo, for, on a rock, 80 miles up the river above rapids that run at ten knots, there is an undated inscription with his name on it and those of some of his companions. The inscription reads: "To this place came ships sent by João II King of Portugal; Do Cão, Po Annes, Po da Costa." Another records the death of "Jo de Santyago ✱ of disease, Jo Alvez. . . ."

The lonely spy sets out...

FROM THE Strait of Gibraltar to the mist-shrouded, gem-rich (although the Portuguese were not aware of it) littoral deserts of southwestern Africa, the western coast of the continent was now clear. What lay deep in the heart of this mysterious land remained conjectural.

The great financial returns from the Guinea coast enabled João II to give more attention to these mysteries. João, much more in the Machiavellian mould than his predecessors, was a man who suffered fools less patiently than Henry, punishing incompetence, but rewarding generously those who served him well. And he was a man with good servants.

Christian ruler

He listened with considerable interest to João Afonso de Aveiro, who had founded a factory at Benin. De Aveiro spoke of a ruler called Ogané, probably a Christian, whose kingdom lay 20 moons' march eastwards from Benin. This king, whose people venerated him as Catholics venerated the pope, conferred his authority on many rulers, including those of Benin, by the bestowal of regalia and crosses, which they wore on their chests. He was never seen, conducting his audiences with envoys while hidden from view behind a silk curtain.

King João and his advisers thought that Ogané and Prester John might be one and the same, and their constant hope was that Prester John, whose kingdom lay astride it, might show them the way to India, rather than that they might gain great wealth in the land of the Priest King.

The legend of Prester John gained its greatest circulation with the publication, about 1165, of a letter purporting to have been sent by him to the Byzantine Emperor Manuel, of which almost 100 versions exist—or did before the First World War.

His kingdom was variously located; first in Asia, then in Africa on the Nile, or in eastern or southeastern Africa, where it might be arrived at, according to the map drawn for the Portuguese Crown by Fra Mauro in 1449, by sailing round Africa. It was known to exist. In Abyssinia (or Ethiopia) Coptic Christians had lived isolated from the West by the Arab Empire since the 7th century, visited only rarely from the 14th century onwards by friars who were sufficiently fortunate to get permission to pass through the Muslim lands.

By the later part of the 15th century, however, the Portuguese could scarcely have still believed the early embellishments. In 1452, eight years before Prince Henry's death, an ambassador from Abyssinia visited Lisbon, although the fact did not come to light until the 20th century. Two years later King Afonso, for some reason perhaps related to this visit, gave Henry's Order of Christ spiritual jurisdiction over Nubia and Abyssinia.

It was now decided to send out two expeditions: one to travel to the east side of Africa by way of the Middle East, with the intention of making contact with Prester John and also finding out as much as possible about India and the way to it; the other to attempt to circumnavigate Africa from the west.

So began, in May 1487, the almost unbelievable journey of Pedro de Covilhão and, in August of the same year, the great voyage of Bartolomeu Dias.

Covilhão was a member of the king's bodyguard and had acted as a spy in Spain. He spoke fluent Spanish as a result of having spent seven years in the household of the Duke of Medina Sidonia in Andalusia, and fluent Arabic, for he had carried out various missions in North Africa.

His companion was Afonso de Paiva, a man of the Canary Islands, who also spoke Arabic, and the details of the journey were worked out with the same Jose Vizinho and Master Rodrigo (the latter also being the king's physician) who had been present at the abortive interview with Columbus, and also with Diogo Ortiz, the royal chaplain.

Covilhão was to visit all the ports of importance on the route to India, India itself and the east coast of Africa, while de Paiva was to make contact with Prester John.

On May 7 they received their final instructions from the king and 400 gold cruzados. The cruzado, which was a pure gold coin, was one of the fruits of the African trade, first minted in 1457 and the first gold coin to be circulated in Portugal for nearly 200 years. It is unlikely, however, that the two men carried such a sum on their persons and they probably made use of letters of credit in the early stages.

Reaching Rhodes, they disguised themselves as Moorish merchants and bought a quantity of honey to sell in Egypt, but in Alexandria they both fell ill and the governor impounded it.

When they recovered they bought more merchandise, having received some reimbursement for the honey, and went on to Cairo. Here they met numbers of Muslim merchants who traded with India, and, in 1488, together with some of them, sailed down the Red Sea to Aden in a small Arab vessel, stopping at El Tor in Sinai (until recently a quarantine station for Mecca pilgrims) and Suakin, then the chief port in the Sudan, a voyage of about two months.

Here they separated, de Paiva setting off for Abyssinia, Covilhão across the Indian Ocean on the southwest monsoon in a pilgrim ship to Cannanore, one of the ports on the low-lying Malabar Coast of southwest India.

From here he visited Calicut (now Kozhikode), the richest port in India, where Arab ships with goods from the West arrived in August and September and traded for local products—pepper and cinnamon and precious stones, as well as cloves, pearls, silk, rhubarb and porcelain from the Far East—with the local merchants, who were Muslim. Loaded with these priceless cargoes the ships sailed home in the winter, around February, on the northeast monsoon.

At Goa (Panjim), 300 miles to the north, where splendid Arab horses were sold to the Indian rulers for their cavalry, Covilhão took ship to Hormuz on the Persian side of the narrow strait that separates it from Arabia. It was the principal port of the Persian Gulf at that time, and the place from which Marco Polo had continued his journey to China by land. The next part of Covilhão's journey was an immensely long voyage on the monsoon to Sofala, an important Arab gold port on the coast of Africa, opposite Madagascar.

The task completed

It was here, speaking with the merchants, that he became convinced that Africa could be circumnavigated, and in 1490, with all the essential information that he had amassed, he arrived in Cairo for an arranged rendezvous with de Paiva, having visited Moçambique and the east coast ports of Kilwa, Mombasa and Malindi.

De Paiva was not at Cairo. Instead, there were two Jewish agents of King João, Joseph de Lamego and Abraham de Beja, one a shoemaker who had visited Baghdad, the other a rabbi. They told him that de Paiva had died

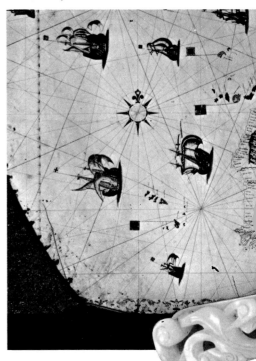

...and the great cape is doubled

before completing his mission and that if he himself felt that his mission was ended then he should return home, otherwise he was to take the rabbi to Hormuz and himself complete de Paiva's mission.

What his feelings were, nobody can say, but after writing a report to João (which the king probably received; Vasco da Gama's instructions for his voyage to India in 1497 contained information which would not otherwise have been available), he delivered the rabbi to Hormuz.

Instead of going straight to Abyssinia—perhaps he had premonitions of what would happen there—Covilhão sailed to Jiddah, the port of Mecca on the Red Sea, and, disguised as a pilgrim, dressed in white and with shaven head, successfully visited the Holy City, one of the most dangerous ventures imaginable. He then went to Sinai, where he heard mass chanted by the Orthodox monks in the Monastery of St Catherine at the foot of the holy mountain.

Sometime in 1493 he finally reached Abyssinia and from that moment was never seen again in the outside world. The first Portuguese to set eyes on Prester John, personified by a black Negus, neither very rich nor particularly cultivated, with followers, some of whom could only be described as barbarous, Covilhão was not allowed to leave. Perhaps he had seen too much.

A Portuguese ambassador met him in 1520 while on a visit. He enjoyed the confidence of the ruler, was well off and married to an Ethiopian. He lived in the country for 30 years and was undoubtedly responsible for the influence that Portugal was to enjoy there for a whole century.

WITHIN MONTHS of Covilhão's departure from the Portuguese court in 1487, two caravels and a store ship headed south, commanded by Bartolomeu Dias. They were to double the great cape which marks the southernmost tip of Africa.

Dias took with him two Negroes who had been captured on Cão's expedition, and four Negresses, all of whom were put ashore on the way south, well clothed and equipped, with samples of spices and precious metals which it was hoped—somewhat optimistically—they would contrive to carry to the court of Prester John, eastwards from Guinea.

About Christmas-time, they reached Angra do Pequena (Lüderitz Bay in South-West Africa) in 26.38s, where there is a fairly good anchorage, and here they set up a padrõe on the west point. Here, also, they left the store ship with a small party in charge.

From now on they had both southeast winds and the cold northwest-running Benguela Current to contend with as far south as Cape Voltas, near the mouth of the Orange River; and at this point, after five days of fruitless attempts to weather it, they stood off the land to sail southwest or south-southwest, for many days meeting with terrible storms. In about 40s, they picked up the world-circling westerlies and ran before them, expecting to make the west coast.

Failing to do so, they shaped a course to the north, finally made landfall and entered a bay with a sandy beach which they named

Enthroned in splendour, Prester John, the legendary Christian potentate. Rich beyond dreams, he was supposed to dominate Africa. The truth was different, as Covilhão, sent to find him, found out

Angra dos Vaqueiros (Cowherd's Bay, because of the cattle that were grazing there. It is now Mossel Bay). They were in fact in 34s, 22E, had doubled the Cape of Good Hope without realizing it and were four degrees to the east, in the Indian Ocean.

They were lucky. If they had raised the Cape close to the current, which sets strongly northwest, it might have embayed them on the rocky, mountainous coast between it and Cape Agulhas, the true southernmost point of Africa.

Unable to make contact with the natives, they sailed east—excited because they were doing so—to Algoa Bay, the site of the present city of Port Elizabeth, and here, on Cape Padrone, they erected a padrõe.

By now the crew were worn out and afraid that if they sailed farther east they might not have sufficient food to return to their store ship at Angra do Pequena.

Most of them wished to return, but they agreed to go on for two more days on condition that they then turned back. And this they did, reaching a river about 25 miles farther on with bushy hills on either side faced with sand. Here the current sets southwest and the water is warm.

They named it Rio do Iffante (now the Great Fish River), after Prince Henry. They were in longitude 27E, the farthest point that they were to reach on the way to India, the time probably midsummer of 1488. On the return voyage they finally saw the famous Cape, which is really two points about a mile and a quarter apart, one with sheer cliffs, both surmounted by peaks 800 feet high.

Here, Dias set up a padrõe which he called after St Philip and named the cape Tormentoso, the Cape of Storms, subsequently it is said, changed to da Boa Esperança, or Good Hope, by King João. At Angra dos Aldeas, after an absence of nine months, they found only three of the nine men they had left with their store ship still alive, the remainder having died either in fights with the natives, or of fever, although one, very ill, is supposed to have died of joy at their return. They burned the ship, which was damaged and worm-eaten, and set sail for home, on the way rescuing Duarte Pacheco, future author of the chronicle *Esmeraldo de Situ Orbis* (a book of navigation and sailing directions in Indian waters), from the island of Principe, on which Pacheco, with some others of his crew, had been shipwrecked. Dias arrived back in Lisbon in December 1488 after an absence of 16 months and 17 days, after a journey in which another milestone had been added on the odyssey to the East. Dias was to die on a later journey to India when his ship, part of Cabral's fleet, was one of several which sank during an Atlantic storm.

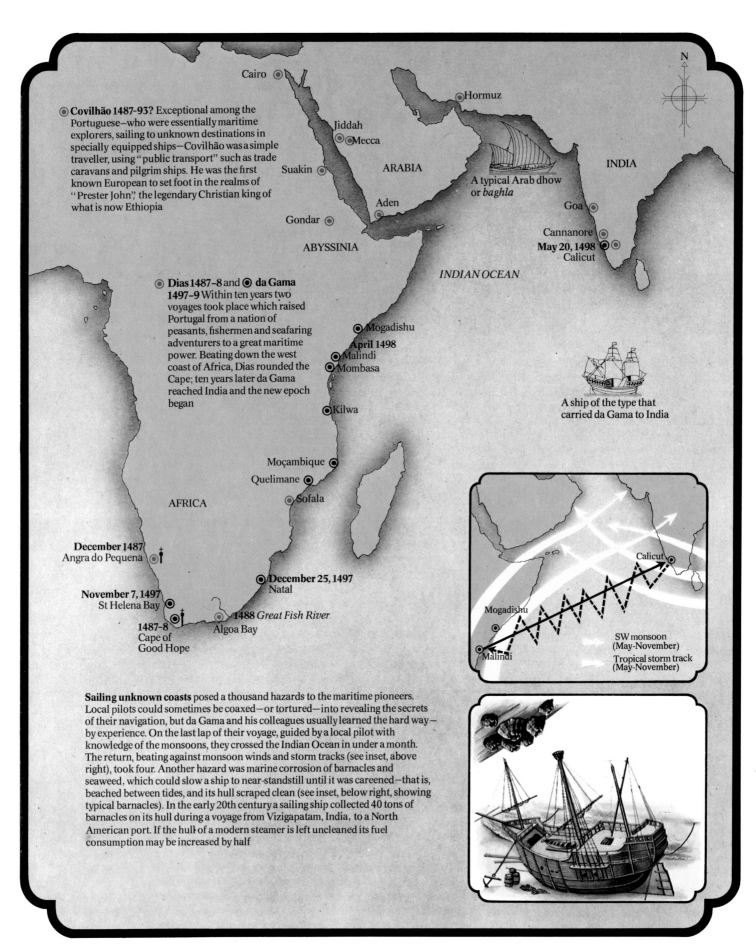

Covilhão 1487-93? Exceptional among the Portuguese—who were essentially maritime explorers, sailing to unknown destinations in specially equipped ships—Covilhão was a simple traveller, using "public transport" such as trade caravans and pilgrim ships. He was the first known European to set foot in the realms of "Prester John", the legendary Christian king of what is now Ethiopia

Dias 1487–8 and **da Gama 1497–9** Within ten years two voyages took place which raised Portugal from a nation of peasants, fishermen and seafaring adventurers to a great maritime power. Beating down the west coast of Africa, Dias rounded the Cape; ten years later da Gama reached India and the new epoch began

Cairo

Hormuz

Jiddah
Mecca

Suakin

ARABIA

INDIA

Aden

A typical Arab dhow
or *baghla*

Goa

Gondar

Cannanore

May 20, 1498
Calicut

ABYSSINIA

INDIAN OCEAN

Mogadishu

April 1498
Malindi
Mombasa

A ship of the type that
carried da Gama to India

Kilwa

Moçambique

Quelimane

AFRICA

Sofala

December 1487
Angra do Pequena

December 25, 1497
Natal

November 7, 1497
St Helena Bay

1488 *Great Fish River*

1487–8
Cape of
Good Hope

Algoa Bay

Mogadishu

Calicut

Malindi

SW monsoon
(May-November)

Tropical storm track
(May-November)

Sailing unknown coasts posed a thousand hazards to the maritime pioneers. Local pilots could sometimes be coaxed—or tortured—into revealing the secrets of their navigation, but da Gama and his colleagues usually learned the hard way— by experience. On the last lap of their voyage, guided by a local pilot with knowledge of the monsoons, they crossed the Indian Ocean in under a month. The return, beating against monsoon winds and storm tracks (see inset, above right), took four. Another hazard was marine corrosion of barnacles and seaweed, which could slow a ship to near-standstill until it was careened—that is, beached between tides, and its hull scraped clean (see inset, below right, showing typical barnacles). In the early 20th century a sailing ship collected 40 tons of barnacles on its hull during a voyage from Vizigapatam, India, to a North American port. If the hull of a modern steamer is left uncleaned its fuel consumption may be increased by half

The passage to India

DIAS HAD ESTABLISHED beyond doubt that there was a sea lane to the east around the southernmost tip of Africa, and the wandering Covilhão had made contact with the strange—albeit disappointing—Christian kingdom in East Africa. Together, the mariner and the overlander had provided the knowledge that would open the east to European influence. The stage was set for the entrance of one of history's great travellers, Vasco da Gama. Ten years were to pass before the curtain was finally raised on his journey.

There is no single reason for the delay; rather it was the sum of a number of reasons, not all of which are known with any degree of certainty.

In 1493, Columbus returned from his first westward voyage to the Americas under the flag of Castile and Aragon, and anchored in the Tagus off Lisbon.

In audience King João heard him speak of the countries of Cipangu and Antilia and generously acknowledged his mistake in not giving him a more sympathetic hearing, although it would have been impossible for him to support Columbus on his terms. Listening to Columbus, it was reasonable for the king and his advisers to suppose that he had reached the easternmost coasts of Asia, if not India itself, and João began immediately to fit out an expedition to be commanded by Admiral Francisco de Almeida, in order to lay claim to the new lands, under the provisions of the Treaty of Alcaçovas.

Almeida's ships never sailed. This was a time of great tension between Portugal and Castile and Aragon, verging on war. The two Spanish kingdoms had become one in 1479 and the strength of the union had been enhanced by the conquest of Moorish Granada in 1492. And it was now that Pope Alexander VI (who was himself Aragonese and had dynastic ambitions for his own son which could be furthered by supporting the Spanish interest) issued, on the advice of Columbus, a series of bulls in favour of Spain—but without consulting the Portuguese.

Spheres of interest

The first two gave to Ferdinand and Isabella, by his apostolic authority, all lands discovered or to be discovered in the regions towards the Indies, westwards in the ocean, providing that they were not already under Christian rule; the third, *Inter Caetera*, drew an imaginary line of demarcation from north to south 100 leagues west of the Azores and the Cape Verde Islands, to the west of which everything would belong to Spain. The fourth, *Dudus Siquidem*, resembled the sting of the scorpion. In addition to what had been given to the rulers by the previous bulls it granted them: "All islands and mainlands

whatever, found or to be found . . . in sailing or travelling towards the west and south, whether they be in regions occidental or meridional and oriental and of India." The interpretation of leagues and their length was left vague in Alexander's pronouncement—which was fortunate for the Portuguese. After a great deal of diplomatic exchange the Treaty of Tordesillas, signed in 1494 between João and Ferdinand and Isabella, confirmed a demarcation line 270 leagues west, which not only gave the Portuguese the real route to India but also the southern Atlantic and Brazil, of which neither party knew the existence. It was yet another great diplomatic triumph for the Portuguese.

The following year João died and was succeeded by Manoel I, "The Fortunate", a young man of 26, who was eager to see the Portuguese established in India. The project was debated in Royal Council, but there was such a lack of unanimity that Manoel decided to go on with it without further discussion. The leader of the voyage to India was to be Vasco da Gama, a gentleman of the king's household, aged about 35, who had served in the royal fleets but whose chief role was to be that of an ambassador in charge of a commercial embassy. His job was to establish good relations with local potentates and further the cause of Christianity, rather than regard himself as a discoverer. This being his brief, it seems all the more probable that the information sent by Covilhão had reached the Portuguese.

The operation was meticulously planned. The ten years that had elapsed since Dias's expedition, years in which voyages into the southern Atlantic had become a matter of routine, must have led to a great increase in the knowledge of winds and currents and, certainly, to an improvement in charts and navigating instruments.

And in ships. Dias's experience had shown that the ordinary caravel was not sufficiently robust for doubling the cape in high latitudes, neither did it have sufficient cargo capacity or give adequate protection for the crew

Lateen-rigged sailing ships still ply the coasts of the Indian Ocean, much the same as in da Gama's day

on a prolonged voyage. Four vessels were provided. Two, the *St Gabriel*, the flagship commanded by da Gama, and the *St Raphael*, commanded by his brother Paul, were nãos, square-rigged ships of shallow draught of about 200 tons by modern computation; the *Berrio*, commanded by Nicolau Coelho, was a lateen-rigged caravel of about 100 tons; and the fourth was a store ship.

Firepower

Each of the three principal ships had pilots whose names are as important to posterity as those of the captains, as without their presence on board the expedition would not have arrived. They were Pero de Alemquer, João de Coimbra and Pero de Escolar. Altogether the ships had a fire power of 20 guns, bombards and some breech-loading weapons of smaller bore. The men were armed with crossbows, axes and pikes and wore leather jerkins and breastplates for protection; the officers wore armour and carried swords—but, presumably, only when action was imminent.

Abraham Zacuto had charge of the provision of navigating instruments and tables and Diogo Ortiz, Bishop of Tangier, of maps and sailing directions. The fitting out was under the direction of Bartolomeu Dias and he accompanied the expedition in a caravel on the first part of the voyage. Fortified by a plenary indulgence, da Gama was given a silk banner by the king, on which the cross of the Order of Christ was emblazoned, and which he swore to hold high against every adversity and in the face of the infidels. After a night of vigil in the Chapel of Our Lady of Bethlehem on the bank of the Tagus, the little company sailed out on July 8, 1497, with its complement of 170 men, some veterans of Dias's voyage, some convicts who were to be employed in hazardous circumstances, together with several priests. Half of them were to die before the round trip was completed.

A week later they passed between the Canaries and the African shore, making a landfall on the mainland at Terra Alta, north of the Rio de Oro. Separated by thick fog they made harbour at São Tiago in the Cape Verde Islands on July 27, and stayed there for a week provisioning and repairing their ships.

Then they stood out to the southeast for 200 leagues, in the course of which the flagship's mainyard broke in a squall, forcing da Gama to heave-to for two days and a night while the yard was sent down and replaced. Now, to avoid the doldrums and the Guinea Current, they shaped a circular course southwest, crossing the Equator well out to sea, in about the longitude of Cape Verde (a course that presupposes some previous knowledge and one which was to be used by outward-

The passage to India

bound East Indiamen in following centuries).

During this time, working their way southwest across the southeast trades, they saw nothing but whales and birds; then sailing east, finally, on November 4 they made a landfall. It appeared unsuitable and, standing off again from the coast, the tiny fleet closed with it once more three days later and entered the 30-mile-wide St Helena Bay, 96 days out from the Cape Verde Islands, the longest voyage that had ever been made by a European crew out of sight of land. Overjoyed, they shot off cannon and dressed their ships with flags.

Here they spent eight days cleaning the ships' bottoms and collecting wood, and here they saw their first Hottentots. This first meeting is recorded by an unknown author, who took part in the voyage: "The inhabitants of this country are tawny-coloured. Their food is confined to the flesh of seals, whales and gazelles and the roots of herbs. They are dressed in skins, and wear sheaths over their virile members. They are armed with poles of olive wood to which a horn, browned in the fire, is attached. Their numerous dogs resemble those of Portugal and bark like them. . . . The climate is healthy and temperate, and produces good herbage."

They took one native on board, gave him a good meal which he ate with pleasure, and then set him free, comprehensively clothed, and on succeeding days traded seitls—copper coins—with the Hottentots, receiving in return shells and one of the sheaths.

It all ended badly as most such encounters seemed doomed to. When one of the crew, put ashore at his own request to consume a meal of seal and roots, sought to return to the ship the natives became hostile, throwing their horn-tipped assegais and injuring the Captain Major, who had gone ashore with a landing party.

Mossel Bay

Estimating that they were only 30 leagues from the cape (they were only two leagues out) they set sail on November 16, sighted it on the 18th, doubled it on the 22nd and on the 25th anchored in Mossel Bay.

Here they broke up their store ship, remaining 13 days at anchor, and found the natives (who had been hostile to Dias and his men, pelting them with stones) friendly when offered little round bells and red caps for which they gave in exchange ivory bracelets.

"On Saturday [December 2], about two hundred Negroes came, both young and old. They brought with them about a dozen oxen and cows and four or five sheep. As soon as we saw them we went ashore. They forthwith began to play on four or five flutes, some producing high notes and others low ones, thus making a pretty harmony for Negroes, who are not expected to be musicians; and they danced in the style of Negroes. The Captain Major then ordered the trumpets to be sounded, and we in the boats danced, and the Captain Major did so likewise when he rejoined us. This festivity ended, we landed where we had landed before, and bought a black ox for three bracelets. This ox we dined off on Sunday. We found him very fat and toothsome as the beef of Portugal. . . . The oxen of this country are as large as those of Alemtejo, wonderfully fat and very tame . . . upon the fattest among them the Negroes place a pack saddle made of reeds, as is done is Castile, and upon this saddle they place a kind of litter of sticks, upon which they ride." These Arcadian pleasures, like a scene in a painting by Poussin, were spoiled when a quarrel broke out, this time about access to drinking water, and the Captain Major had to put ashore a landing party and fire off a couple of bombards. Before leaving they set up a high cross made from a mizzen mast and a pillar, both of which the natives destroyed.

Here, for the first time, they saw sea lions.

Setting sail once more on December 8, the Feast of the Immaculate Conception, they endured a fierce storm from the west and southwest, losing sight of Nicolau Coelho's ship. Eventually he came up with them and they passed the Great Fish River, the farthest point reached by Dias, sailing along a beautifully wooded coast.

On November 20, the current setting down the coast was so strong (it was the warm Moçambique Current) that it carried them back to the Ilha da Cruz (Cross Island), which they had passed five days before; but on Christmas Day they reached a coast which they named Natal. They had been reduced to cooking their food in sea water.

On January 11, 1498, 23 days' sailing beyond the Great Fish River, they reached a coast they named the Terra da Boa Gente, because of the kindness which they encountered. "They [the landing party] were received hospitably. The Captain Major in consequence sent the chief a jacket, a pair of red pantaloons, a Moorish cap and a bracelet. The chief said we were welcome to anything in his country of which we stood in need—at least that is how Martin Afonso understood. This country seemed to us densely peopled. There are many chiefs and the number of women seems to be greater than that of the men, for among those who came to see us there were forty women to every twenty men."

The river which entered the sea here they called Rio do Cobre, because of the profusion of copper ornaments with which the local people, who were very tall, adorned themselves. After five days they continued their voyage, passing Cape Corrientes at the mouth of the Moçambique Channel, where the current runs strongly, and passing, but not sighting, the gold port of Sofala, visited by Covilhão almost eight years previously.

They were now in the Arab sphere of influence, a coast inhabited by people of mixed blood—Arabs, Persians and various mixtures of these compounded with the indigenous peoples. It was a rich coast, where the inadequate merchandise that they had brought with them would be appraised with eyes that were disenchanted by the goods that Europeans had to offer.

Friendly people

But this had yet to happen. On the night of January 25 the two bigger ships entered the mouth of the Kiliman (Quelimane) River, where Coelho's caravel was already anchored. This was another of the Arab trading places, but this time the people were friendly: "These people are black and well made. They go naked, merely wearing a piece of cotton stuff around their loins, that worn by women being larger than that worn by the men. The young women are good-looking. Their lips are pierced in three places and they wear in them bits of twisted tin. These people took much delight in us. They brought us in their almadias [bark canoes] what they had, while we went into their village to procure water. . . ."

They remained 32 days, careening their ships and repairing the mast of the St Raphael.

Now scurvy broke out. The unknown chronicler records: "Many of our men fell ill here, their feet and hands swelling, and their gums growing over their teeth, so that they could not eat." But, on the whole, they were cheered by their stay. While there, they met a young man who ". . . so we understand from their signs, had come from a distant country, and had already seen big ships like ours. These tokens gladdened our hearts, for it appeared as if we were really approaching the bourne of our desires. . . . And we erected here a pillar which we called the Pillar of Saint Raphael, because it had been brought in the ship bearing that name. The river we called Rio dos Bons Signaes [River of Good Omens]."

On February 24 they put out to sea once more, and after six days of sailing by day and lying-to at night, seeing nothing but three small islands—one of which was covered with tall trees, probably casuarines—the little fleet entered the harbour of Moncobiquy, otherwise Moçambique. At the entrance the Berrio ran aground on a sandbank and then, having got off, it struck the point of the island and shattered its helm.

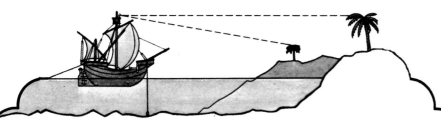

Sailing and navigation 1400–1600

Once land slips below the horizon, a sailor is faced with navigational problems that do not exist inshore, where he can see and feel—from the depth of water under his keel—where he is. The oceanic pioneer had to develop means of finding his position and so there grew the new science of navigation, which took into account the movements of celestial bodies and the settled paths of winds and tides

Simple navigation close to the coastline (above) was based on the three ''L''s of lookout, lead-line and log. The leadline had a hollow weight to sample the seabed; the log, flung over the side, helped the sailor estimate his speed through the water

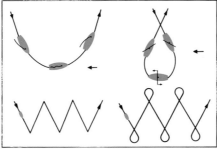

Sailing ships made good their course by different means depending on their rig, when sailing into the wind. Fore-and-aft rigged ships such as caravels (above left) tacked like a modern yacht; the square rigger—carrack and galleon—often ''wore about'' in a series of loops when working to windward (above right)

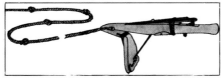

The simple cross-staff (above) enabled the mariner to gauge the height of a celestial body— such as the North Star—above the horizon, and thus to establish how far north or south he was; the lower the North Star was in the sky, the farther south was his ship

Wind direction

Sailing efficiency into wind —old and new (above); 1 modern yacht; 2 lateen ship; 3 modern full-rigger; 4 Renaissance square-rigger; 5 & 6 Ancient Egyptian ship

An early log and line (above). The knots were counted as the line was paid out, and the ship's speed reckoned in knots—a term still used at sea, and on aircraft air speed indicators (left). The traverse board (below, left), used in conjunction with a compass, enabled the helmsman to keep track of the course he was sailing. Every half-hour, by the hour glass, the pegs were moved along the course bearing. Later a bell was rung at that moment by the ship's boy, making eight bells to each of the four-hour watches

The mariner's astrolabe, an instrument for measuring Sun and star altitudes, was developed from that used by the early astronomers

A simple quadrant (right) was another means of observing the Sun's altitude

Here, they were in a world which must have seemed unbelievable: "Their language is the same as that of the Moors. They all wear toucas, with borders of silk embroidered in gold. They are merchants, and have transactions with white Moors, four of whose vessels were at the time in port, laden with gold, silver, cloves, pepper, ginger and silver rings, as also quantities of pearls, jewels, and rubies, all of which articles are used by the people of this country . . . all these things, with the exception of the gold, were brought thither by these Moors; and we were told that further on, where we were going to, they abounded, and that precious stones, pearls and spices were so plentiful that there was no need to purchase them, as they could be collected in baskets. . . . We were told, moreover, that Prester John . . . held many cities along the coast, and that the inhabitants of those cities were great merchants.

"The residence of Prester John was said to be far in the interior, and could be reached only on the backs of camels. These Moors had also brought hither two Christian captives from India. This information, and many other things which we heard, rendered us so happy that we cried with joy, and prayed God to grant us health, so that we might behold what we so much desired." Their rapture was to be short lived. Here, at Moçambique, it suited the sultan to keep up a pretence that he thought them to be Turks or Moors; but only until such times as he had satisfied his curiosity about them. Coming on board, where he was dined, he treated the Portuguese merchandise and the things they had brought from the other coast of Africa with contempt, asking for scarlet cloth, of which they had none.

Pilots provided

On Sunday, March 10, they said mass, well away from the infidel, under a tall tree on the island of São Jorge, set up a pillar and sailed immediately, taking with them two pilots provided by the sultan.

The winds and currents were now against them. Becalmed for two days, they were then carried back four leagues down the coast beyond Moçambique by the current.

Forced to return to the town, they found that the water they sought was surrounded by newly erected palisades and defended. The Portuguese were forced to open fire with their bombards, and having taken water they retired to São Jorge. There was only one pilot (the other having escaped) and he, having tried to lure the Portuguese into danger, was flogged and an island which he had represented as being part of the mainland was named after him Ilha do Asoutado (The Island of the Flogged One).

The passage to India

Having by mistake passed the entrance to Kilwa in 8.56s, which they wished to visit—they had heard that Christians lived there—they arrived at Mombasa on April 7, with many of the crew ill with scurvy.

It had been difficult for them at Moçambique; here, they were in real peril. Attempts were made to lure them ashore to meet non-existent communities of Christians; Muslim envoys appeared, feigning Christianity; Muslim merchants showed the Captain Major's envoys drawings of the Holy Ghost in order to convince them of their Christian piety (any genuine Christians in Mombasa were kept in subjection); armed men attempted to board their ships in the harbour and swimmers were sent to cut the cables.

To find out what the Muslims' plans were, "The Captain Major questioned two Moors [from Moçambique] whom he had on board, by dropping boiling oil upon their skin, so that they might confess any treachery intended against us. They said that orders had been given to capture us as soon as we entered the port, and thus to avenge what we had done at Moçambique. And when this torture was being applied a second time, one of the Moors, although his hands were tied, threw himself into the sea, while the other did so during the morning watch."

Da Gama stayed two days more "after the malice and treachery planned by these dogs had been discovered" in the hope of getting a pilot, although it is difficult to imagine anyone volunteering for the post. Finally he sailed on April 13 and, desperate for a pilot, literally picked out of the sea a party of Moors who had thrown themselves overboard from their vessel in an attempt to escape.

On Easter Eve, April 14, they reached Malindi (on the present-day coast of Kenya), only three degrees south of the Equator.

Here, one of the prisoners was put ashore as an emissary and friendly relations were established; the king came out in a boat and spoke with the Captain Major, who lay alongside in one of his own pinnaces. The Captain Major then released the prisoners.

Outrigger fishing craft on the Malabar coast of southern India, where da Gama made his historic landfall in 1498

78

"This gave much satisfaction to the King, who said that he valued this act more highly than if he had been presented with a town. And the King, much pleased, made the circuit of our ships, the bombards of which fired a salute. . . .

"The King wore a robe of damask trimmed with green satin and a rich touca. He was seated on two cushioned chairs of bronze, beneath a round sunshade of crimson satin attached to a pole. An old man who attended him as page carried a short sword in a silver sheath. There were many players on anafils, and two trumpets of ivory, richly carved and of the size of a man, which were blown from a hole in the side, and made sweet harmony with the anafils."

Strange "Christians"

They stayed here for nine days, being entertained to fêtes, sham fights on the shore (the Captain Major refused to land in spite of the king pressing him to do so and offering hostages for his safety) and the loosing-off of bombards and rockets—these by what were described as "Indian Christians", actually Hindus from four ships in the harbour who, when they went aboard Paulo da Gama's vessel and saw an altarpiece which showed Our Lady holding Christ in her arms at the foot of the Cross, prostrated themselves before it, and continued to visit it, bringing spices and other gifts.

These same Christians gladdened the Captain Major by calling out what the Portuguese took to be "Christ! Christ!" but was almost certainly "Krishna!"

"These Indians are tawny men. They wear but little clothing, and have long beards and long hair, which they braid. They told us they eat no beef. Their language differs from that of the Arabs, but some of them know a little of it, as they hold much intercourse with them."

On April 24, between the monsoons, they sailed for Calicut with a Gujarati pilot named Ibn Majid provided by the king (Malindi, with its whitewashed houses, reminded the author of the chronicle of Alcochete on the Tagus), and after following the coast for some days, they set a course across the Indian Ocean, running before the wind.

On April 29 they saw the North Star for the first time since leaving the Atlantic and finally, on May 18, "after seeing no land for twenty-three days, we sighted lofty mountains, at a distance of 8 leagues". They had raised the Western Ghats of the Indian subcontinent, having sailed, by their own computation, 600 leagues.

They found bottom in 45 fathoms and that night stood south-southwest, keeping a good offing. Heavy rain and thunderstorms made

The curiosity—and the economic pressures—which drove Europe to maritime exploration in the 15th century, was part of one of the great periods in the history of the continent, the Renaissance. Print propagated words, painting gave knowledge of man and his world a new depth and dimension. As a result, the journeys of the Portuguese pioneers were documented in detail as no others had been, up until that time.
The illustration is part of the "Livro dos Armadas", now in Lisbon. It is more than an account of the adventures of da Gama and his captains; the artist was clearly a man of seafaring experience and knowledgeable in the rig of the caravels and nãos (carracks) which made the journey east

it difficult for the pilot to know precisely on which part of the coast he was, but at last, on May 20, he was able to identify some mountains as being above Calicut and that night they anchored two leagues from the city. The great journey to India had been made, after a voyage of ten months.

The ruler was the Samuri, a Hindu with whom da Gama had a friendly audience soon after his arrival. In the course of the interview he told the ruler that the efforts that he and his predecessors had made to reach India were not for gold and silver, but because they knew that Christian rulers existed there.

Da Gama and his men remained on the coast of India for three months, but his embassy was not a success. The Arab merchants were on close terms with the Samuri and other rulers elsewhere on the coast, and they did everything in their power to make things as difficult as possible for the Portuguese, who failed to establish a trading post. Besides, the gifts da Gama had brought with him were too few and too mean for those used to oriental magnificence and the trade goods were worse– good enough for the Guinea Coast but unsuitable for the sophisticated Indian market. It was only with perseverance that he managed to acquire some pepper, cinnamon, ginger, cloves, nutmeg and some precious stones.

Nevertheless, it was a remarkable exploit, the greatest piece of sailing in the history of European seamanship up to that time, certainly greater than Columbus's, because of the far greater difficulties that had to be overcome, not least of which were the contrary monsoon winds of the Indian Ocean.

They sailed for home at the end of August, taking with them half a dozen Indians and a letter from the Samuri to King Manoel, asking for gold, silver, coral and scarlet cloth in exchange for spices and precious stones.

It took four months to cross the Indian Ocean in the teeth of unfriendly monsoons, and 30 of the crew died of scurvy. They raised the African coast near Mogadishu on January 3, 1499, and four days later, Malindi, where they burned the *St Raphael.*

Landfall in Brazil

As they made their way home they erected Padrões and on March 20 the *St Gabriel* and the *Berrio* rounded the cape together. Parted by a storm, they ran independently up to the Equator before the southeast trades and then by way of the Cape Verde Islands to the Azores. The voyage had taken two years and they had been 300 days at sea. Vasco's brother Paulo died on the homeward voyage and when he himself reached port on September 9 he mourned for nine days before entering the capital, a triumphant homecoming marred by bereavement.

After his long oceanic passage to the cape, da Gama's journey had been along peopled coastlines. As a feat of navigation, however, in the light of the knowledge of the times, his was a journey to rank with the greatest.

He had been able to establish the truth or otherwise of what, until that time, had been no more than hearsay knowledge in Europe, and to extend the knowledge of maritime techniques—both oceanic and coastwise—which were later to enable his fellow countrymen to build an empire undreamed of before Henry the Navigator.

SIX MONTHS AFTER da Gama's sad arrival back in the Tagus, Pedro Álvares Cabral, a man in the Captain Major's mould, sailed for India. Early in the voyage, he made a landfall of singular importance, one which was to impose the Portuguese tongue and culture on a hitherto unmapped part of the world. Thirty days out from the Cape Verde Islands, he reached Brazil, at a point on the coast near Mount Pascoal, about 16.53S.

Cabral's discovery may have been by design or by accident, but his claim of the new land for Portugal was upheld by the Pope and confirmed the following year (1501) by a second trip (the command of an unrecorded captain). On this 15-month journey more than 2,000 miles of the South American coastline were explored.

The discovery of Brazil by Cabral was an adventitious by-product of a new, more powerful essay to India. Cabral had sailed at the head of a fleet of 13 ships equipped for an 18-month voyage, carrying merchants as supercargo, and Franciscan monks. Among his captains was the veteran Bartolomeu Dias, the first to round the cape.

After a month ashore, in which the Portuguese met their first South American Indians—a gentle, vegetarian people—Cabral's fleet put to sea in early May.

Great storm

On May 23 there was a great storm and four of the ships, including that of Bartolomeu Dias, the first captain to round the cape, were lost; and for 20 days the rest of the fleet ran before the storm under bare poles.

Sailing well to the south of the Cape of Good Hope they at last made Sofala, after 76 days at sea, "more fit to return to the kingdom, if it had been near, than to conquer others".

On July 20 they reached Moçambique, where they had a similar reception to that experienced by da Gama, and on the 26th, Kilwa, where they were treated as pirates; but at Malindi they received the same good treatment as da Gama, being able to engage in trade, repair their ships and obtain the services of a Gujerati pilot for the crossing of the Indian Ocean.

On August 22 they reached Anjediva Island, about three miles west of the north Kanara coast on the Indian mainland, in 14.45N, 74E—little more than a rock, three-quarters of a mile long with coconut trees growing on the summit.

Here they passed 15 days, in the course of which they received holy communion and confessed their sins; and on September 16 they anchored off Calicut on the Indian mainland after a voyage of six months, the first known men to sail by way of South America and the Cape of Good Hope to Southeast Asia.

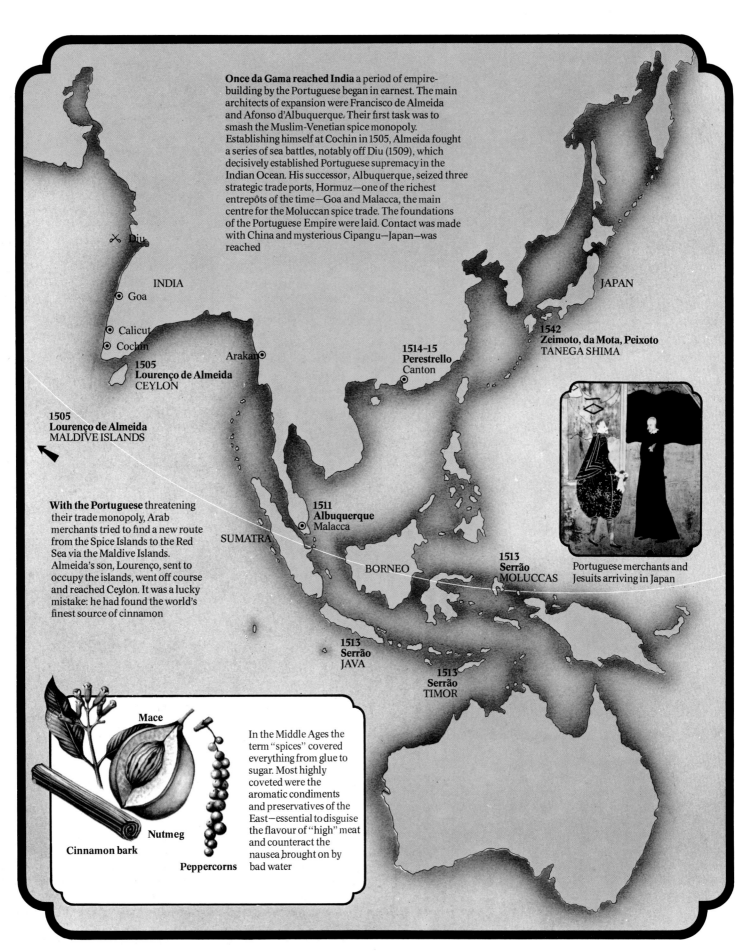

Once da Gama reached India a period of empire-building by the Portuguese began in earnest. The main architects of expansion were Francisco de Almeida and Afonso d'Albuquerque. Their first task was to smash the Muslim-Venetian spice monopoly. Establishing himself at Cochin in 1505, Almeida fought a series of sea battles, notably off Diu (1509), which decisively established Portuguese supremacy in the Indian Ocean. His successor, Albuquerque, seized three strategic trade ports, Hormuz—one of the richest entrepôts of the time—Goa and Malacca, the main centre for the Moluccan spice trade. The foundations of the Portuguese Empire were laid. Contact was made with China and mysterious Cipangu—Japan—was reached

Diu

INDIA

⊙ Goa

⊙ Calicut
⊙ Cochin

Arakan ⊙

1505
Lourenço de Almeida
CEYLON

1505
Lourenço de Almeida
MALDIVE ISLANDS

JAPAN

1542
Zeimoto, da Mota, Peixoto
TANEGA SHIMA

1514-15
Perestrello
Canton
⊙

With the Portuguese threatening their trade monopoly, Arab merchants tried to find a new route from the Spice Islands to the Red Sea via the Maldive Islands. Almeida's son, Lourenço, sent to occupy the islands, went off course and reached Ceylon. It was a lucky mistake: he had found the world's finest source of cinnamon

SUMATRA

1511
Albuquerque
⊙ Malacca

BORNEO

1513
Serrão
MOLUCCAS

Portuguese merchants and Jesuits arriving in Japan

1513
Serrão
JAVA

1513
Serrão
TIMOR

Mace

Nutmeg

Cinnamon bark

Peppercorns

In the Middle Ages the term "spices" covered everything from glue to sugar. Most highly coveted were the aromatic condiments and preservatives of the East—essential to disguise the flavour of "high" meat and counteract the nausea brought on by bad water

An empire reaches its limits

ONCE THE PORTUGUESE had overcome the natural hazards of the sea journey from Europe to India, they moved purposefully to establish a commercial dominance in Southeast Asia. King Manoel sent a permanent force to India, led by Francisco de Almeida, in 1505. On the way, Almeida took Kilwa and razed Mombasa, before setting himself up as Governor-General of India, based at Cochin. His son Lourenço reached Ceylon, an important source of spices, and the Maldives, an island chain in the Indian Ocean.

Arab supremacy is ended

There then began the great fleet actions between the Portuguese and the Muslims in which the superior fire power of the Europeans was to oust Arab influence from the Indian Ocean, culminating in one of the decisive battles of the world, off Diu Island in 1509. In command of a small force of perhaps only 19 ships, Almeida totally vanquished the combined Muslim fleets of 100 vessels. It was the end of Arab power east of Aden.

Almeida was succeeded as Governor-General of India by one of the great empire-builders of Portuguese history, Afonso do Albuquerque, in 1509. During his years of command—they could hardly be described as years of exploration—Albuquerque seized Goa, on the Indian mainland (it remained in Portuguese hands until 1961, when Indian forces occupied it), captured Malacca at the gateway to the strait to which it gives its name, and secured Hormuz for Portugal. Hormuz, at the entrance to the Persian Gulf, was a huge entrepôt, described by a 15th-century Russian traveller as a "vast emporium of the world", and it was regularly visited by merchants from all parts of Asia, including Chinese, in their great junks.

The seizure of Malacca was perhaps the most important of Albuquerque's feats, for it gave to the Portuguese access and control of the routes to the Spice Islands—the Moluccas—and to China and Japan.

Albuquerque, known to his countrymen as "The Great" and "The Portuguese Mars", died after capturing Hormuz in 1515. A brilliant strategist, he understood, as well as any man before or since, the great design and the value of sea power. In accomplishing what he did, at no time was he able to call upon the services of more than 4,000 Europeans. For the most part he had to be content with half that number; and it was this chronic shortage, and the need to colonize the territory of Goa, that made him encourage mixed marriages between his own men and local women, a very successful policy which finds its echo today in the number of Portuguese names among eastern Eurasians.

He was not only short of manpower. He was chronically short of capital to further his plans, instead of being surrounded, as one might imagine, by an embarrassment of riches. He was buried in the Church of Our Lady at Goa and it speaks for the respect, if not love, that he inspired, not only in his own countrymen but in Hindus and Muslims, that for a long time large numbers of members of these mutually antagonistic religions visited his tomb. This was in spite of his revolting cruelty, though it was no greater than that of most of the other great Portuguese sailors and little better or worse than that shown by the Arabs and Indian warriors. Only the Chinese explorers seem more or less free of the taint.

"Cruelties", wrote the historian R. S. Whiteway, "were not confined to the baser sort, but were deliberately adopted as a line of terrorizing policy by Vasco da Gama, Almeida and Albuquerque, to take no mean examples. Da Gama tortured helpless fisher-

The Portuguese arrive in Japan. Their stay there was to be shorter than elsewhere in the East. The Japanese expelled all westerners in the 17th century and withdrew from contact with the outside world until the mid-19th century.

men; Almeida tore out the eyes of a Nair who had come in with a safe-conduct because he suspected a design on his own life; Albuquerque cut off the noses of the women, and the hands of the men who fell into his power on the Arabian coast. To follow the example of Almeida and sail into an Indian harbour with the corpses of unfortunates, often not fighting men, dangling from the yards was to proclaim oneself a determined fellow."

In 1513, Francisco Serrão, sailing in a junk, visited Java, reached Amboina Island and Banda Island in the Moluccas—the Spice Islands, which were the great producers of nutmegs and cloves—and annexed Timor Island, only about 400 miles from the nearest part of the Australian continent. Shipwrecked off Ternate he had managed to reach the island, where he made a treaty with the sultan which enabled the Portuguese to trade in cloves in exchange for military assistance against the sultan of the neighbouring island of Tidore, another important spice centre.

Serrão built a fortified warehouse on Ternate and remained there for the rest of his life. He was a friend of Magellan and at some time wrote a letter to him describing the Spice Islands.

Both Serrão and Abreu, who was with him on the first part of the voyage, were helped by the acquisition of a large-scale chart of Java, which was locally made.

In 1514, the first Portuguese mission reached Canton (Kwangchow) and, although not allowed to land, it was well received by the Chinese. Two Italians, Andrea Corsali and Giovanni di Empoli, went with it.

The following year Rafaello Perestrello, another Italian in the Portuguese service, also reached Canton in a junk and returned with a good cargo and a high opinion of the Chinese who, he said, regarded the Portuguese as "good people" with whom they desired to trade.

These early visits to China, the first Europeans for 150 years, were followed by an official embassy, carried in the fleet of Fernão Peres d'Andrade, which arrived at the mouth of the Canton (Pearl) River in 1517.

Japan was reached in 1542 by chance, rather than design, when Francisco Zeimoto, Antonio da Mota and Antonio Peixoto, sailing for China with a cargo of skins, were shipwrecked on Tanega Shima Island, south of Kyushu.

The reaction of the Japanese on first seeing Europeans, and vice versa, was one of undisguised incredulity. The Portuguese saw men whiter than Chinese, but with small eyes and scanty hair; the Japanese, as recorded by a chronicler, were astounded at seeing a "ship's company, of strange aspect, their speech incomprehensible, their dwelling place unknown". And it was not until seven years later, when the Jesuit Francis Xavier and his companions reached Japan by way of the spice island, Ternate, and China that a more coherent account of the place and its inhabitants emerged.

In 1557, in recognition of the assistance that they had rendered to the Chinese in exterminating Chinese pirates, the Portuguese were granted a lease of a piece of territory on the peninsula of Macao (to this day a Portuguese colony) at the mouth of the Canton River. And from here they carried on trade under close surveillance, exporting silk and spices, and later in the 16th century lacquered objects, porcelain and tea. They also engaged in a profitable trade as entrepreneurs between China and Japan (the Chinese being forbidden during the Ming dynasty to trade with those they called the "dwarf robbers"), exchanging on their behalf raw and woven silk and gold for silver bullion.

A land to be desired

VAIN, ARROGANT, BOASTFUL, ambitious for wealth and power, deceitful; a man of towering imagination (sometimes to excess), with a faith in the Almighty and his own powers that enabled him to encourage his crews, who were not the best, to accomplish what they believed to be impossible.

This was Christopher Columbus, born about 1451 in Genoa, son of a wool-comber, educated at Pavia University in mathematics, natural science and, possibly, astronomy.

He had settled in Lisbon about 1479, marrying the daughter of Bartolomeo Perestrello, the first governor of Porto Santo in Madeira Island.

At Porto Santo he spent some time studying his late father-in-law's collection of navigational works, talking to sailors about their voyages and making charts.

His ambition was "to penetrate the mysteries of the universe"—in practical terms, to reach Asia by sailing westwards into the setting sun across the Atlantic.

There was undoubtedly land beyond the western horizon, but how far away no one knew. West of the Azores, Martinho Vicente, a Portuguese pilot, had found an intricately carved piece of wood; Columbus's brother-in-law had seen great pieces of cane (bamboo), so thick that they were capable of holding four quarts of wine between joint and joint; two men washed up dead on the shore at Flores, the westernmost of the Azores, were "very broad-faced and differing in aspect from Christians", fir trees of a sort hitherto unknown were also thrown up, coming from the west—all carried by the currents of the Gulf of Mexico.

Like Aristotle and Eratosthenes, who had successfully calculated the circumference of the Earth more than 1,600 years earlier, Columbus knew the world was a sphere. Most of his reading seems to have been medieval—Mandeville, Marco Polo or books based on medieval assumptions. And it was Marco Polo's overestimation of the east–west extent of Asia and the distance of Japan from the Asian mainland, that led him to believe that the voyage westwards from Europe to Japan would be less than 3,000 nautical miles. In fact (had it then been possible) it would have been several times greater, sailing on the great circle.

Columbus sought patrons for many years, but all rejected him—the Senate of Genoa, Henry VII of England, and João II of Portugal. After this last setback, in 1484, he went to Spain, where his diligent lobbying met with success. Support for the great quest was gained from Ferdinand and Isabella, and preparations were soon under way.

The expedition sailed on August 3, 1492, from Palos, a port on the Rio Tinto in Huelva province. It is now silted up. There were three ships: the *Santa Maria*, the Admiral's flagship, a three-masted, square-rigged, decked ship of about 280 (modern) tons with a crew of 50; and two caravels, the *Pinta*, lateen-rigged with a crew of 30, under Martin Alonzo Pinzón, and the *Niña*, with 24 men, under Martin's brother Vicente Yanez.

Sabotage

Three days later, the abstract from the Admiral's journal records, the rudder of the *Pinta* "jumped out of gear", and sabotage was suspected. It was temporarily repaired.

On August 9 they reached the Canaries, repaired the *Pinta*'s rudder properly and square-rigged her, met men who "swore that every year they saw land to the westward beyond the setting sun" and took in water, meat, wood and other stores. They sailed on September 6, narrowly escaping interception by the Portuguese, experienced two days of calm, followed by a strong gale from the northeast, after which Columbus held course to the west. On September 11 they saw a piece of a ship's mast and on the 14th, nine days out, the *Niña*'s crew saw a tern and a tropic bird "and these birds", recorded Columbus, inaccurately, "never go more than twenty-five leagues from land".

At sunset on September 25, after sailing through the seaweed-thick Sargasso Sea, Martin Alonzo declared that he saw land, a sighting that was confirmed by many others, but it was a collective hallucination. There was another false sighting from the *Niña* on October 7 when, about longitude 48w, the admiral altered course to sail southwest instead of west.

Trouble brewed, not for the first time, among the crews, who said that they could bear no more; but the admiral "heartened them as best he could . . . and [said] that it was vain for them to complain, since he was going to the Indies and must pursue his course until, with the help of Our Lord, he found it". At last, at two in the morning, on October 12, 36 days out from the Canaries, Juan Rodriguez Bermeo, a sailor in the *Pinta*, sighted land and the little fleet reduced sail "and kept jogging, waiting for day!"

When it came they could see naked people on shore and here Columbus and the Pinzón brothers, together with a large part of the crew, landed, taking with them two banners of the Green Cross, the admiral's personal flags. All gave thanks to God (those of the crew who had doubted the admiral begged his pardon) and Columbus took possession of the land in the name of the Sovereigns of Spain.

They had reached what is now called Watling Island, one of the outer cays of the Bahamas in 24N, 74.30W, about 250 miles northeast of Cuba. The island was called Guananhui by the natives and named San Salvador by Columbus. Only 12 miles long and five miles wide, its interior a place of salt-water lagoons separated by low wooded hills, it bore little resemblance either to the India or Japan of the European imagination.

The people were friendly, as they were

"I saw another island, distant about eighteen leagues from the first [San Salvador], to the east and to it I at once gave the name 'Espanola'. It is a land to be desired. . . ." —Columbus's verdict on the island of Hispaniola, which he discovered on his first epic voyage across the Atlantic. The island was, so he wrote to his royal patrons Ferdinand and Isabella, "in the best position for the mines of gold" and for trade with the mainland of Asia. Columbus's over-optimistic assertion was based on the fact that he had found some alluvial gold on the island. The friendly natives also gave him some gold bracelets and nose-plugs in exchange for Spanish trinkets. Columbus left Spain with three ships, from left to right, the "Santa Maria" (his flagship), "Niña", "Pinta". The "Santa Maria" was wrecked off Hispaniola and Columbus transferred his flag to the "Niña". The "Pinta" was re-rigged with a square sail in the Canaries, after leaving Spain as a lateen-rigged caravel; the square rig was more suitable for running before the trade winds

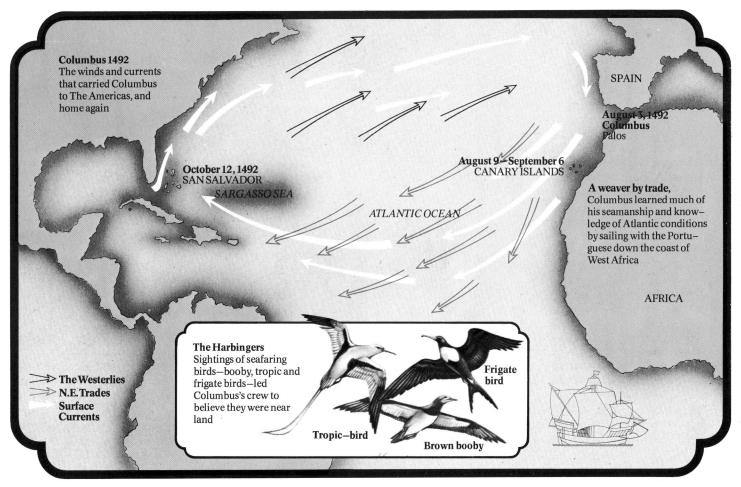

Columbus 1492
The winds and currents that carried Columbus to The Americas, and home again

SPAIN

August 3, 1492
Columbus
Palos

August 9 – September 6
CANARY ISLANDS

October 12, 1492
SAN SALVADOR

SARGASSO SEA

ATLANTIC OCEAN

A weaver by trade, Columbus learned much of his seamanship and knowledge of Atlantic conditions by sailing with the Portuguese down the coast of West Africa

AFRICA

↠ **The Westerlies**
↠ **N.E. Trades**
↠ **Surface Currents**

The Harbingers
Sightings of seafaring birds—booby, tropic and frigate birds—led Columbus's crew to believe they were near land

Frigate bird

Tropic—bird

Brown booby

---

with few exceptions in all the islands Columbus was to visit on this voyage. They swam out to the ships with parrots, cotton thread, spears made from reeds, some with points made from fishes' teeth, and were given in exchange red caps, glass beads and hawks' bells, of which they were exceedingly fond. They were naked, handsome people with long black hair as coarse as that of a horse's tail, their skin neither black nor white; Columbus called them Indians, certain that he had arrived in Asia, in the Great Khan's realms.

After discovering other islands, Santa Maria del Concepción (Rum Cay) and Fernandina and Isabella (Long and Crooked Islands), he wrote to his patrons: "I wish to leave for another very large island, which I believe must be Cipangu [Japan] according to the signs which these Indians whom I have with me make; they call it 'Colba' . . . but I am still determined to proceed to the mainland and to the city of Quinsay [according to Marco Polo, the city of the Great Khan] and to give the letters of Your Highnesses to the

Grand Khan, and to request a reply and return with it." On October 28 he reached the island he thought was Cipangu, sailing south-southwest into a river mouth, very green with trees. His men were on the north coast of Cuba, in 76w.

The inhabitants cultivated sweet potatoes and lived in tent-shaped houses made from palm branches. They were more shy than the people he had first met, but they told Columbus that there was gold in the interior and pearls in the sea. He named the island Juana after the Crown Prince Don Juan.

Early in December, Columbus sailed east and entered a harbour on a rocky coast which he named Puerto de San Nicholas (the present Haitian shore of the Windward Passage between Cuba and Haiti). He called the island Española (Hispaniola).

On this coast the people—they were Arawaks—were timid and there was evidence of Carib cannibalism among them. On December 25, the *Santa Maria*, with a boy at the helm (perhaps on account of Christmas revelry), went aground on a reef bordering the Borde de Mer de Limonade, east of the present Port Haiti. The crew were unable to kedge off, but with the help of a friendly chief, Guacanagari, who sent his canoes to unload the ship, everything was brought to shore.

A land to be desired

Here they built a fort, La Navidad, which the admiral garrisoned with 43 officers and men, using the timber from the wreck. He himself transferred his flag to the *Niña*.

On January 16, 1493, after losing touch with Martin Pinzón in the *Pinta*, he set sail for home, meeting the *Pinta* again eastwards off El Morro de Monte Cristi, an immense, truncated rock. After initial difficulty beating against the northeast trades, he picked up the westerlies somewhere off Bermuda, finally reaching Santa Maria in the Azores on February 18. Here, the Portuguese governor threatened to seize his ships and imprison him and it was not until March 4 that he reached the Tagus, where he was received by the King of Portugal.

At Barcelona, which he entered in triumph, he was received by Ferdinand and Isabella, who heaped further honours on him and confirmed those already bestowed.

The second voyage

The main object of his second journey—although he continued to try to find a passage through the island to the mainland—was the colonization of Hispaniola (Haiti and the Dominican Republic).

On September 25, 1493, he set out with three great carracks, 14 caravels and 1,200 men—soldiers, farmers and missionaries—and everything necessary to establish a colony, including domestic animals and seed.

On November 3 he reached Dominica, the mountainous island between Guadeloupe and Martinique in the Windward Islands, which was populated by wild Caribs (cannibal is a corruption of their name). Sailing north he discovered Maria Galante and Guadeloupe and some of the Leeward Islands, including Montserrat and Antigua, Santa Cruz (St Croix) in the Virgin Islands, and Puerto Rico, reaching La Navidad, his settlement in Haiti, in November 1493 to find that it was no more and all its inhabitants were dead.

Forty miles east of Cape Haiti he established a new settlement at Isabella and sent parties into the Sierra Cibao to look for gold. The new colony was not a success. There was not enough food and there was indiscipline and a bad relationship with the natives, whom the colonists regarded as potential slaves (Columbus himself can be said to have initiated the trade by a letter sent to the king and queen in 1494 and five ship-loads were sent to Seville in 1495).

From Haiti Columbus sailed along the south coast of Cuba (which he still considered to be part of the Asian mainland) and visited the north coast of Jamaica. He sailed for home on March 10, 1495, under a cloud, for a commissioner had been sent out to enquire into his ability to rule. He went by way of

Arawak Indians panning alluvial gold in Cuba (above). Sugar-cane (left) was introduced there by the Spanish

Columbus's great journey to the New World overshadows his later voyages around the islands of the Antilles. His second, to colonize the island of Hispaniola, was his least successful. The original settlement he established, at La Navidad, was wiped out by natives and the one he built to replace it fared little better. Columbus was a far better sailor than he was a colonizer. A replacement, Juan de Aguado, was sent to the colony and Columbus returned to Spain in disgrace

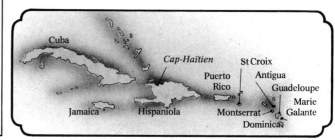

Slavery of the native Arawak people of the islands became commonplace, but in captivity they pined and died, unlike the fiercer Caribs, who fought on and—albeit in few numbers—survived

Columbus reached Trinidad on his third trip to the Indies in 1498. He found pearls and mistook the mainland of South America for an island. He noted the strong currents of fresh water from the Orinoco and believed himself to be at the mouth of one of the four rivers of Paradise, at the top of a pear-shaped Earth

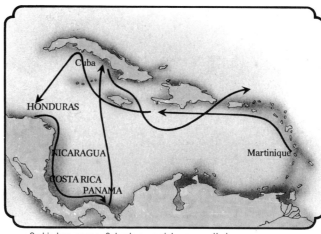

On his last voyage, Columbus—a sick man—sailed along the mainland at what is now Honduras and there, optimistically, wrote that "from there to the river Ganges there are ten days"

The sweet potato of the Arawaks (above) was popular in Spain. The pineapple (below) came also from the Antilles

The man called America

Guadeloupe, arriving at Cadiz on June 11, 1496, gloomy and dressed as a Franciscan, after 62 days at sea.

He was not, as he thought, in disgrace. His power, in fact, was greatly increased and he was sent out again on May 30, 1498, with six ships crewed by pressed men and released criminals, the only men who could be found. This time, sailing south as far as the Cape Verde Islands, and then westwards, hoping to follow the parallel of 8.30N, he reached and named the island of Trinidad in 10N. Here he found pearls, and the following day saw, for the first time—although at the time he did not know it—the mainland of South America, naming it the Island of Zeta.

Then, at great risk to his ships—because it was the meeting place of vast quantities of fresh water from the Orinoco River with the tides of the open sea—he sailed southeast along the coast of what is now Venezuela, convinced that what he had reached was greater than an island.

By now he was ill, suffering from gout and ophthalmia, and his ships were in terrible condition. He gave up, altered course to the northeast and after a remarkably navigated voyage arrived at Santo Domingo on August 30, to find the colonists in revolt.

Meanwhile, in Spain, Queen Isabella (her husband had been less enthusiastic about Columbus from the beginning) had been horrified at the news that the Indians, her new subjects, were being turned into slaves. She decided to remove Columbus from his position and despatched Francisco de Bobadilla out to the colony, where Columbus was arrested and sent home in chains, at a moment when things were going better and the gold mines were beginning to show a profit.

His arrival in this condition provoked great indignation and the Queen herself felt bound to reinstate him in her favour. Bobadilla was recalled, but was drowned on the way home.

After this Columbus made one last voyage, sailing on May 9, 1502, once more presumably in search of a way to Asia and on the way discovering Martinique and the mainland of Honduras. He had no means of knowing that the Pacific was not more than 300 miles to the west, and (without any idea of who they were) he captured a canoe-load of Mayans—mainlanders.

He then sailed south along a low-lying coast, backed by impenetrable forests, which he named Costa Rica because of its abundance of gold. His crew were by now semi-mutinous, and his ships in an appalling state; nevertheless, he attempted to found a colony.

He failed. After a protracted voyage attended by every sort of misfortune, he reached Seville on September 7, 1504, dying two years later, a disillusioned and broken man.

IT FELL TO AN Italian, neither the first nor the most important of the explorers of the Western Hemisphere, to be accorded the most singular honour of all—that of having an entire continent named after him. His name was Amerigo Vespucci.

It was an act of recognition adopted at the suggestion of the geographer Martin Waldseemüller, whose great map of 1507 describes the work as having been made "according to the tradition of Ptolemy and the voyages of Amerigo Vespucci" and, in another context, "a fourth part of the world, which, since Amerigo found it, we may call Amerige or America" (*Cosmographiae Introductio* 1507).

What Vespucci actually accomplished is not certain; the accounts of his voyages are not well documented and those documents that exist are the subject of great controversy.

An Italian, and the son of a notary, he was born at Florence, where he studied astronomy, natural philosophy and geography, in which he was encouraged by his uncle, a Dominican and a friend of Savonarola. But these interests were to be subordinated for the first part of his life when he became a clerk working for the Medici and later as their representative, working on supply contracts in Spain, where they sent him in 1492. He undoubtedly knew Columbus, as he worked for a merchant who was in charge of fitting out some of the Admiral's ships for his second, colonizing expedition of 1493, and he may have sailed with the fleet in his capacity as a victualler. There is no proof either way of his participation.

Four separate voyages are credited to Vespucci on the basis of letters by him, the contents of which, garbled and sometimes completely altered, appeared in a famous book of discoveries, *Paesi novamente retrovati*, published by Francanzano da Montalboddo at Vicenza in 1507. More dependable are three letters Vespucci wrote to Lorenzo di Piero Francesco de Medici which deal with two of his supposed four voyages, those of 1499 and 1501, although they are not very detailed—probably for reasons of security.

Expert navigator

All this is a bit unfair to Vespucci. He was not a charlatan, neither did he seek fame or publicity. He was well off, knew navigation, a subject in which he was an expert, and undoubtedly he was an explorer, but he has been ill-served by his contemporaries, some of whom may have been trying to lionize him.

On the first of the suspect voyages, he is supposed to have sailed from Cadiz on May 10, 1497, reaching the Canaries, and then, after 27 days, "a coast that we thought to be that of a continent" which may have been the shore of Campeche Bay, the innermost part

of the Gulf of Mexico. From here he may have followed the southern seaboard of North America, doubled Cape Sable, the extreme southwestern tip of Florida and reached Cape Hatteras on the coast of North Carolina. On the first of the two "real" voyages that are now thought to have taken place, Vespucci sailed out of Cadiz with Alonzo de Ojeda and three ships on May 16, 1499, exploring at first separately and later together. Vespucci arrived on the coast of Brazil about the latitude of Cape da São Roque—in which case he may have been the first to discover Brazil—then sailed northwest along the coast, across the mouth of the Amazon. Ojeda began somewhere on the coast of Guiana, perhaps on that part of it which is now Surinam (Dutch Guiana), visited Margarita Island, off the coast of Venezuela (discovered by Columbus on his third voyage in 1498), and realized the enormous potential of the pearl-fishery there, in which so many slaves of the Spanish were later to die while acting as divers.

From this point it is possible that they went on together to the Gulf of Maracaibo, from there sailing to Santo Domingo and arriving back at Cadiz on September 8, 1500.

It is on his next journey, however, another "real" voyage, that Vespucci's fame depends. Having transferred his services to King Manoel of Portugal he sailed from Lisbon on May 10, 1501, arriving at Cape de São Roque on August 16. He then sailed down the Brazilian coast, reaching Rio de Janeiro Bay on New Year's Day 1502, and, going on beyond the mouth of the River Plate in 35s, may have passed Puerto San Julian on the coast of Patagonia in 49.15s. He may even have reached South Georgia, 800 miles east of the Falkland Islands in 54s, 38w—within the extreme northern limits of pack-ice and just over ten degrees north of the Antarctic Circle.

If he did, and it seems improbable, he had been farther south than any man of his times, and had revealed to the European world the immense extent of the continent. He returned to Lisbon on September 7, 1502, and made three other unsubstantiated voyages before his death in 1512.

The next important recorded voyage on the east coast of South America was made in 1515 by Juan Diaz de Solis, who discovered the estuary of the Rio de la Plata, which had already been passed to seaward. De Solis, his eyes set like all others on a route to the Orient, was seeking a westward passage around the southern continent. On their return, members of the de Solis expedition told Ferdinand Magellan of the southwesterly trend of the coast to the south—convincing him that it was in Spain's sphere of influence. The first circumnavigation was soon to follow.

Magellan's vanishing fleet

"First you are to go with good luck to discover the part of the ocean within Our Limits and Demarcation. . . . Also you may discover in any of those parts what has not yet been discovered, so that you do not discover nor do anything in the demarcation and limits of the most serene King of Portugal . . . nor to his prejudice but only within the limits of our demarcation."

THESE WERE THE diplomatically worded instructions given by the young Hapsburg king, Charles (later the Emperor Charles V), who had only recently ascended the throne of Spain, to Ferdinand Magellan (Fernão de Magalhaes in Portuguese) just before he sailed on the greatest single voyage in the entire history of discovery. Magellan died long before it ended, but such was his determination and spirit that the first circumnavigation is his perpetual honour.

Magellan was Portuguese, born about 1480. An hidalgo—one of the lower nobility—he had spent his childhood in the house of Queen Leonora, wife of Henry II. He had fought with distinction in the Indies, been at Malacca, and may have taken part in Abreu's expedition to the Spice Islands. In Morocco, fighting against the Sultan of Azmor, he received a wound which left him lame for life.

After this campaign, in about 1513, feeling that his services to the crown were undervalued, he asked King Manoel II, who disliked him, for an increase in pay. The request was refused and the king told him, bluntly, that he could seek service elsewhere if he wished; and in 1517, at the age of 37, Magellan renounced his nationality and left Portugal for Spain and service with the Spanish Crown.

The right time

At Seville he frequented the famous Casa de Contretacion (where Amerigo Vespucci had been Pilot-Major), the great clearinghouse for information on pilotage, navigation and the geography of the Spanish Indies. It was the right moment for Magellan to be there. Spain had not only been beaten by Portugal in her attempts to acquire spices; she had not even begun to acquire any, and the knowledge that great cargoes of the stuff were arriving at Lisbon from the Moluccas created an atmosphere in which her rulers were ready to listen to a well-considered scheme for reaching the island by way of a passage to the West.

Magellan was granted interviews with the king's counsellors and eventually with Charles himself, to whom he stated his belief that a passage could be made at the extremity of South America westward to the Moluccas, the latitude of which he had learned from

September 1519: Ferdinand Magellan, Portuguese Captain-General, stood to sea from the Guadalquivir in southern Spain, with five ships: the *Trinidad*, his flagship; the *San Antonio* (captain Juan de Cartagena); the *Concepción* (Gaspar de Quesada); the *Vittoria* (Luis de Mendoza); and the *Santiago* (João Serrão). Two months later he raised the coast of Brazil. He spent several months coasting towards the southern tip of the continent, during which time two captains (Quesada and Mendoza) died in mutinies, and the *Santiago* was wrecked on a reconnaissance trip; all but one of her crew survived

September 1522: Three years after Magellan's fleet of five ships had set out from the Guadalquivir with a complement of 237 men, del Cano arrived back in the *Vittoria* with a crew of 18, the world's first circumnavigators. The pumps were working and the ship was leaking in every seam, but one of the greatest voyages of discovery had been made. Del Cano made his first landfall from the Moluccas at the Cape Verde Islands, one of the longest open-sea passages up to that time. Even so close to home, troubles still beset him. He ran foul of the Portuguese when his men went ashore and 13 were taken prisoner. Happily for posterity, the survivors of the epic journey included the Italian chronicler Pigafetta, whose account of it survives

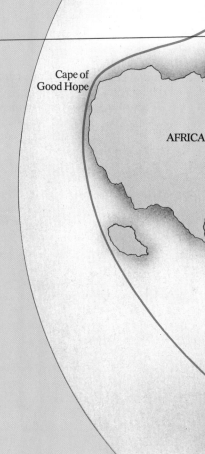

Cape of Good Hope

AFRICA

September 1519
September 1522

February 1522: The *Trinidad* ran into difficulty straight away. Her hold literally bursting with the enormous cargo, she ran aground in the estuary off Tidore. Repairs would take months and the two ships decided to separate, so that one at least could take advantage of the monsoons in the Indian Ocean. With the Basque del Cano as captain and a crew of 60, the *Vittoria* set a course across the Banda Sea and past Timor. Several months later Magellan's old flagship set out across the Pacific, hoping to reach Panama, but was forced to turn back. She was captured by the Portuguese and few of her crew ever saw home again

January-February 1522: The two ships loaded their precious cargo – cloves, ginger, silk, precious jewels, and even talking parrots. Neither ship was really seaworthy but they embarked on the long haul home

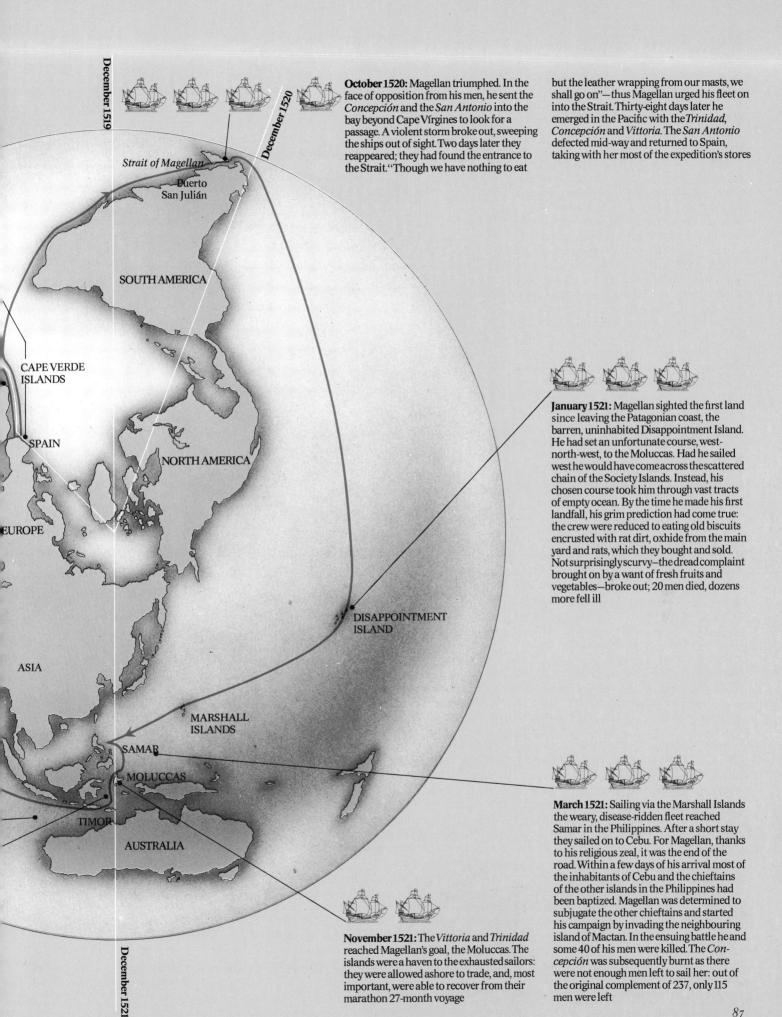

December 1519

December 1520

Strait of Magellan

Puerto
San Julián

SOUTH AMERICA

CAPE VERDE
ISLANDS

SPAIN

NORTH AMERICA

EUROPE

ASIA

MARSHALL
ISLANDS

SAMAR

MOLUCCAS

TIMOR

AUSTRALIA

DISAPPOINTMENT
ISLAND

December 1521

October 1520: Magellan triumphed. In the face of opposition from his men, he sent the *Concepción* and the *San Antonio* into the bay beyond Cape Vírgines to look for a passage. A violent storm broke out, sweeping the ships out of sight. Two days later they reappeared; they had found the entrance to the Strait. "Though we have nothing to eat but the leather wrapping from our masts, we shall go on"—thus Magellan urged his fleet on into the Strait. Thirty-eight days later he emerged in the Pacific with the *Trinidad*, *Concepción* and *Vittoria*. The *San Antonio* defected mid-way and returned to Spain, taking with her most of the expedition's stores

January 1521: Magellan sighted the first land since leaving the Patagonian coast, the barren, uninhabited Disappointment Island. He had set an unfortunate course, west-north-west, to the Moluccas. Had he sailed west he would have come across the scattered chain of the Society Islands. Instead, his chosen course took him through vast tracts of empty ocean. By the time he made his first landfall, his grim prediction had come true: the crew were reduced to eating old biscuits encrusted with rat dirt, oxhide from the main yard and rats, which they bought and sold. Not surprisingly scurvy—the dread complaint brought on by a want of fresh fruits and vegetables—broke out; 20 men died, dozens more fell ill

March 1521: Sailing via the Marshall Islands the weary, disease-ridden fleet reached Samar in the Philippines. After a short stay they sailed on to Cebu. For Magellan, thanks to his religious zeal, it was the end of the road. Within a few days of his arrival most of the inhabitants of Cebu and the chieftains of the other islands in the Philippines had been baptized. Magellan was determined to subjugate the other chieftains and started his campaign by invading the neighbouring island of Mactan. In the ensuing battle he and some 40 of his men were killed. The *Concepción* was subsequently burnt as there were not enough men left to sail her: out of the original complement of 237, only 115 men were left

November 1521: The *Vittoria* and *Trinidad* reached Magellan's goal, the Moluccas. The islands were a haven to the exhausted sailors: they were allowed ashore to trade, and, most important, were able to recover from their marathon 27-month voyage

Magellan's vanishing fleet

Serrão, and that their probable position was close to South America in the Spanish hemisphere. Of equal importance, he would be able to discover where the Line of Demarcation actually lay.

At first the Council was divided, but with the support of one of its members, Fonseca, Bishop of Burgos, the opposition collapsed. An agreement was made on March 22, 1518, between the king and Magellan by which the king promised to fit out five ships for a voyage of two years (Magellan's calculation of how long it might last, based on what must have been a deliberate overestimate, shows how much closer to America he believed the Moluccas to be than they actually were).

The king took a great interest in the fitting-out of the expedition, drawing up an almost too comprehensive manual of instructions covering every possible contingency, and before the fleet sailed he addressed a final letter to Magellan as Captain-General. In it, he wrote less vaguely than he had in his original instructions, perhaps fearing that they might fall into the hands of the Portuguese. "Inasmuch as I know for certain . . . that there are spices in the islands of Maluco, and chiefly you are going to seek them . . . my will is that you should straight way follow to the said islands."

The five ships were the *Trinidad* (110 tons), the Captain-General's flagship, the best though not the largest; the *Santo Antonio* (120 though not the largest; the *San Antonio* (120 *ción* (90 tons) under Gaspar de Quesada; and the *Vittoria* (85 tons) under Luis de Mendoza, treasurer of the fleet. All these men were Spaniards. The smallest ship, the *Santiago*, was commanded by João Serrão, a Portuguese, said to have been brother to the Francisco Serrão who wrote to Magellan from the Moluccas. Most of the ships were in poor condition, even before they sailed. The crew was an extraordinary collection of Spaniards, Portuguese, Basques, Genoese, Sicilians, French, Flemings, Germans, Greeks, Malays (Magellan's personal slave was from the Moluccas), Neapolitans, Corfiotes, Negroes and one Englishman, Master Andrew of Bristol, a gunner who died on the voyage. Altogether, officers and men, they numbered 237 according to Antonio Pigafetta, an Italian gentleman volunteer from Vicenza who was one of the company and wrote a first-hand account of the voyage.

The trade goods, which were provided by the Fuggers, the South German mercantile house that had also sent ships and representatives on da Gama's voyage to India, were specially chosen as a result of the experience they had gained in the Portuguese trade. The goods included looking-glasses, knives, beads, fish-hooks, red caps, materials, ivory, quick-

The End of the World
Magellan's discovery of the strait that now bears his name proved that there was a way to the east, to the south of the newly-discovered Americas. But was it merely a lane from one ocean to another, between two giant land masses? Was Tierra del Fuego part of a giant continent to the south? The map **below**, post-Magellan and pre-Drake, indicated the doubt that existed. It took Drake's accidental race before the westerlies, to the south of the uttermost cape, to prove truly that there was open water below Tierra del Fuego. And it took the Dutch, in the footsteps of the English privateer, to give the cape its name—Hoorn, or Horn, after their home port

Right Ferdinand Magellan, Portuguese hidalgo in the service of Spain, was the greatest navigator and the most determined of men in a period of history punctuated by giants. To him falls the honour of the greatest of journeys—the circumnavigation of the world —although he died long before its completion

Right Francis Drake, Devon-born folk hero of the English. He led the second circumnavigation of the world, but the twin objects of his journey were different. He was to have found Beach (Australia), in which he failed, and to cause as much trouble as he could to England's arch-rivals, the Spanish —which he did

silver, brass bracelets and 20,000 hawks' bells.

For navigation they took 23 parchment charts, six pairs of compasses, 21 wooden quadrants, seven astrolabes, 37 compass needles and 18 hour glasses.

The story of the great journey, which began on September 20, 1519, at Sanlucar de Barrameda, in the estuary of the Guadalquivir in Spain, is one of the best known in history. It is shown graphically, with its highlights, on a unique world projection on the preceding pages.

Mutiny and disease

Mutiny, the loss of ships and men and valuable stores, unspeakable diseases such as scurvy, for which there were only the most ineffectual remedies, haunted Magellan and later his surviving captain, the Biscayan del Cano. And all these were in addition to the maritime hazards of long sea passages and the first journey through one of the most tempestuous of the world's waterways, the strait that now bears Magellan's name. It lies, twisting tortuously, between the mainland of South America and the bleak and friendless Tierra del Fuego, a stormy watery valley, literally, in the Andes Mountains which there tumble into the sea.

The navigational difficulties that Magellan

had to overcome in making the passage in 1520 were no less for sailing ships until the advent of steam, and they are summed up in the *South American Pilot, Part 3, 1916*. It is not given to exaggeration. "At no season of the year is it advisable for a square-rigged vessel of any size, with sails only, to attempt the passage from east to west, even should good fortune enable the strait to be made, and both narrows passed with an easterly wind; for it is highly improbable this would continue through the whole strait, and the vessel would be working through channels, ranging from 10 miles to 2 miles wide, in thick, wet weather, with furious squalls or williwaws, so variable in their direction as to prevent a straight course being made, and with most of the harbours difficult both of ingress and egress. The passages of the old voyagers, some of which were more than 80 days between Port Famine (70.55W) and Cape Pillar (74.41W, the northernmost point of Desolation Island at the Pacific end), sufficiently attest the inadvisability of the attempt for sailing ships . . . while . . . westward of Cape Froward in 71.18W (the southernmost point of the South American continent and nearly midway in the strait) . . . it is probable that no portion of the globe frequented by man, experiences the whole year round, worse

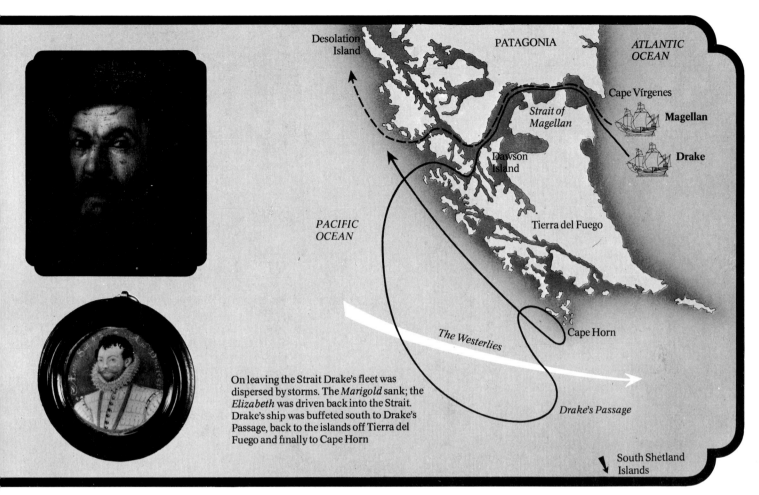

On leaving the Strait Drake's fleet was dispersed by storms. The *Marigold* sank; the *Elizabeth* was driven back into the Strait. Drake's ship was buffeted south to Drake's Passage, back to the islands off Tierra del Fuego and finally to Cape Horn

weather. Winter and summer alike, rain, snow, hail and wind are absent for only very brief periods."

With none of the knowledge available to his successors, Magellan made his way to the Pacific. First to the west, through the first and second narrows, with grassy treeless land on either hand; then, where the narrows opened out, to the south, with a wooded coast to starboard and the great mountains on Dawson Island and Monte San Felipe looming up ahead without any apparent passage through them. Then west-northwest from Cape Froward, beech trees among peat hags and great growths of moss on the shore, and behind them mountains covered with snow and ice, through which great glaciers poured down almost to the water's edge or hung on the lips of precipices; the dark sea with long streamers of kelp on its surface, growing up from the reefs below; and on the port hand the glow from the fires of the Onas Indians burning on the coast of what Magellan named for this reason Tierra del Fuego, the Land of Fire.

Once through the forbidding passage, Magellan's tiny fleet now challenged, for the first time, the greatest ocean in the world. They crossed it, but in what must have been unimaginably harrowing circumstances, mak-ing as great a sea passage as any man has ever made. Within a month of its completion, Magellan died in a pointless fracas with natives in the Philippines.

Magellan's brother-in-law, Duarte Barbosa, and João Serrão succeeded him as commanders, but both were killed by natives. The survivors, now under the command of one of the original mutineers, Sebastian del Cano, burnt the *Concepción*, there not being enough survivors to man her, and sailed the *Vittoria* and the *Trinidad* across the Sulu Sea and through the South Balabac Strait off northern Borneo, to the city of what is now Brunei, a sort of Eastern Venice nine miles up river on the west coast of the island.

City on stilts
"The city is entirely built on foundations in the salt water, except the houses of the king and some of the princes: it contains twenty-five thousand fires of families. The houses are all of wood, placed on great piles to raise them high up. When the tide rises the women go in boats through the city selling provisions and necessaries."

At last, on November 8, 1521, they reached Magellan's goal, Tidore, in the Moluccas, after 27 months in search of it. At Ternate, Magellan's friend Serrão was already dead; but in spite of this they spent five weeks at Tidore loading cloves. They were well received by the sultan and established a rival warehouse to the Portuguese.

The two ships were now in such terrible condition that not even the bravest could contemplate returning by way of the strait through which they had come, and it was decided that the *Vittoria* should continue westwards across the Indian Ocean, while the *Trinidad*, Magellan's old flagship, should attempt to reach the Isthmus of Panama. It was subsequently captured by the Portuguese.

Del Cano with the *Vittoria* succeeded. At first with a crew of 60, dodging the Portuguese all the way, he sailed south into the Indian Ocean by way of the Banda Sea, passing Timor. He then crossed the Indian Ocean on a course west-southwest, making his call at the Cape Verde Islands, "and then only constrained by extreme necessity", as Pigafetta, who was with him, says.

His reluctance was justified, for the Portuguese took 13 of his men when they went ashore and it was with a crew that numbered 18 men that he finally arrived in the bay of Sanlucar on September 6, 1522, with the pumps working and the ship leaking in every seam. Somewhere, in a sailor's heaven, Magellan would have smiled—and relaxed.

'Once, in an English ship'

BY THE TIME Elizabeth I of England ascended the throne in 1558, Portugal's seafaring warriors had laid claim to the rich trade routes from Europe to the east, as far as Japan. To the west, the wealth of Central and much of South America was in the cruel grip of Spain.

It was the lumbering, bullion-loaded galleons of the Spanish—ripe plums for the picking of the privateer—that took the first of England's great sailors, Francis Drake, west to the Americas. Drake was a regular privateer, holding the commission of Queen Elizabeth, in which capacity he did great injury to the Spaniards in the West Indies and on the Spanish Main. During one foray across the Isthmus of Panama he saw the Pacific for the first time. He was said to have "besought Almighty God of his goodness to give him life and leave to sail once in an English ship in that sea".

His opportunity came in 1577, when he set out on what was to be the second successful circumnavigation of the globe. If, on his departure, he was intent on achieving the great feat, his official instructions did not say as much. They stated that he was to enter the Pacific by the Strait of Magellan and discover Terra Australis, otherwise Beach, the continent shown in the atlas of Ortelius as extending northwest to 30S beyond its western end.

Once there, he was to spend five months ingratiating himself with the rulers, finding suitable sites for warehouses in which trade in English cloth could be carried on, and investigating the potential of what was hoped to be got in exchange: gold, silver, drugs and spices.

He was then to return home by the way he had come or, if this was impossible, he was to sail to about 40N, where it was believed that the so-called Strait of Anian led eastwards into the Atlantic. Before he sailed, however, these instructions were amended to allow him to sail northwest as far as the Moluccas, and from there return across the Pacific to the coast of North America.

The five ships were the *Pelican*, of about 100 tons, Drake's flagship; the *Elizabeth*, 80 tons, Captain John Winter, Vice Admiral; the *Marigold*, a bark of 30 tons, Captain John Thomas; the *Swan*, a flyboat of 50 tons, Captain John Chester; and the *Christopher*, a pinnace of 15 tons, commanded by Captain Thomas Moone. The crews numbered 164 and the stores and trade goods, which are not enumerated, included "divers shows of all sorts of curious workmanship, whereby the civility and magnificence of his native country might, amongst all nations withersoever he should come, be the more admired".

All this was provided with the assistance of the Virgin Queen, who had engaged in a more private briefing of the admiral from which greater profit than the official instructions could be hoped for. Sailing officially for Alexandria (and not without opposition from his men when Drake made known his intention), they reached the Brazilian coast in 31N on April 5, just north of Rio Grande do Sul, where the inhabitants kindled enormous fires when they were sighted. At the River Plate, the *Christopher*, which had become separated from the rest of the fleet in a gale, again appeared. (This was a new *Christopher*, the original having been exchanged for a vessel Drake had captured near Cape Blanco on the North African coast, but retaining the name.)

On May 29 they reached Puerto San Julian, where they were confronted by the inhabitants, not as giant as Pigafetta, on Magellan's voyage, had made out, though still enormous: "Peradventure the Spaniards did not think that ever any Englishman would come thither to reprove them, and thereupon might presume the more boldly to lie; the name Pentagones, Five cubits, viz., 7 foot and a half, describing the full height (if not somewhat more) of the highest of them." They were no more friendly than their ancestors when they had been captured by Magellan's men 58 years previously: ". . . This is certain that the Spanish cruelties . . . have made them more monstrous in mind and manners than they are in body . . . for the loss of their friends (the remembrance whereof is assigned and conveyed over from one generation to another . . .) breedeth an old grudge."

"Conjuror" executed

By this time Drake had cannibalized a prize, and two of his ships, the *Swan* and the *Christopher*, and the *Pelican* was renamed *Golden Hind*. Here, too, just as Magellan did, he extinguished a mutiny by beheading its ringleader, his former friend, Thomas Doughty. Doughty was charged with "conjuring" (conspiracy) and given the alternatives of being marooned or being taken back to England. Instead, he chose instant death. Here, in this unhappy place where the bones of Magellan's mutineers were still lying on the shore, Drake remained for two months.

On August 20, the three remaining ships entered the strait, finding "it is true which Magellan reporteth of this passage: that there be many fair harbours and store of fresh water; but some ships need to be freighted with nothing else besides anchors and cables, to find ground in most of them to come to anchor, which when any extreme gusts of contrary winds do come, is a great hindrance to the passage, and carrieth with it no small danger".

In the Sea Reach, where Drake had himself "rowed in a boat to descry the passage", a canoe-load of natives was met with. It was "made of the bark of divers trees . . . bearing in it most comely proportion and excellent workmanship . . . not for the use of so rude and barbarous a people, but for the pleasure of some great and noble personage, yea of some Prince . . . with no other closing up or caulking in the seams, but the stitching with thongs, made of seal-skins, or other such beast, and yet so close that it received very little or no water at all". The people were "of a mean stature, but well set in all their parts and limbs; they have great pleasure in painting their faces". Their houses were like tents, a framework of poles covered with skins; their only tools "knives made of most huge and monstrous mussel shells".

On September 6 they cleared the strait, 17 days after entering it, and on the seventh they were struck by the first of a succession of great westerly gales which raged for 52 days, scattering the fleet, driving the flagship to 57S, "and something better", south of the latitude of Cape Horn, in 55.59S, into the passage between it and the South Shetlands which now bears his name. The *Marigold* sank with all hands, after being last seen "spooming along before the sea"; and the *Elizabeth*, commanded by John Winter, was driven back into the mouth of the Magellan Strait, where the shipmaster insisted on turning back "and so coasting Brazil, they arrived in England June 2 the year following".

Driven back again, "into 55 deg. towards the pole Antarctic, as a pelican alone in wilderness . . . [with] the most mad seas; the lee shores; the dangerous rocks; the contrary and most intolerable winds; the most impossible passage out . . ." they ran in among the innumerable islands off the southwestern side of Tierra del Fuego, where they anchored and had two days' respite. They found "divers good and wholesome herbs" and "the waters there to have their indraught or narrow and free passage, and that through no small guts or narrow channels, but indeed through as large frets or straits as it hath at the supposed straits of Magellan. . . ."

Yet even this howling desolation supported human life. A few leagues to the south, also among the islands, "we found the people of the country travelling for their living from one island to another, in their canoes, both

men, women, and young infants wrapped in skins, and hanging at their mothers' backs; with whom we had traffic for such things as they had, as chains of certain shells and such trifles".

Finally, forced to run still farther to the southeast, they reached "the uttermost cape or headland of all these islands. It stands near in 56 deg, without which there is no main nor island to be seen to the Southwards, but that the Atlantic Ocean and the South Sea meet in a most large and free scope. . . ."

Geographically, Drake had made two important discoveries: that there was open water to the south of Cape Horn; and that there was no truth in the widely held belief that once reached from the Atlantic it was impossible to return to it from the Mar del Zur (the Pacific) because of a supposed easterly current and a prevailing Levanter (east wind).

It was not, however, until the 19th century that sailing ships began to make regular passages into the Pacific from the Atlantic, beating against the westerlies round Cape Horn, instead of using the strait.

Now realizing that it was impossible, because of the prevailing west winds, to carry out his instructions to find Beach, Drake sailed the *Golden Hind* along the labyrinthine western shores of Patagonia and along the desiccated coast to the north, a coast on which the anchorages are exposed to violent winds called northers and to tidal waves—the aftermath of the earthquakes which frequently convulse this part of the Chilean littoral.

Here, and on the Peruvian coast, he and his men plundered to their hearts' content (relieving one Spaniard whom they found asleep on the shore of 13 bars of silver, without waking him), and, with the capture near the Equator of the *Cacafuego*, a treasure ship carrying a hoard valued at 360,000 pesos, amply fulfilling the Queen's more secret instructions, at a time when England and Spain were not officially at war.

Searching for the passage eastwards to the Atlantic through the non-existent Strait of Anian, Drake sailed as far as 48N, approximately where the United States and Canada are now joined; then he returned south to the coast of California, where he spent a month refitting and careening his ship. He named the place New Albion, because of the resemblance of its white cliffs to those on the south coast of England.

Here, the local people were very friendly "of a tractable, free and loving nature, without guile or treachery".

They finally sailed on July 25 westwards for the Moluccas, Drake having committed himself to a circumnavigation. They passed south of the Marshall Islands, along the whole length of the Caroline Islands, through the Palao Archipelago at the western end and on November 4 reached Ternate, in the Moluccas, where they were well received by the sultan. The *Golden Hind* went on a reef in the Celebes but Drake got off with difficulty and reached Java on March 16, 1580; doubled the Cape of Good Hope; watered the ship on the coast of Guinea and reached Plymouth on November 3, having been away for "two years, ten months, and some few odd days besides, in seeing the wonders of the Lord in the deep, in discovering so many admirable things, in going through with so many strange adventures, in escaping out of so many dangers and overcoming so many difficulties in this our encompassing of this nether globe, and passing round the world".

A short time later a delighted queen went aboard the *Golden Hind* at Deptford in the London river and after banqueting with Drake, dubbed him knight and commanded that the ship should be preserved as a monument—which it was for 100 years until it became so decayed that it was broken up in the reign of Charles II.

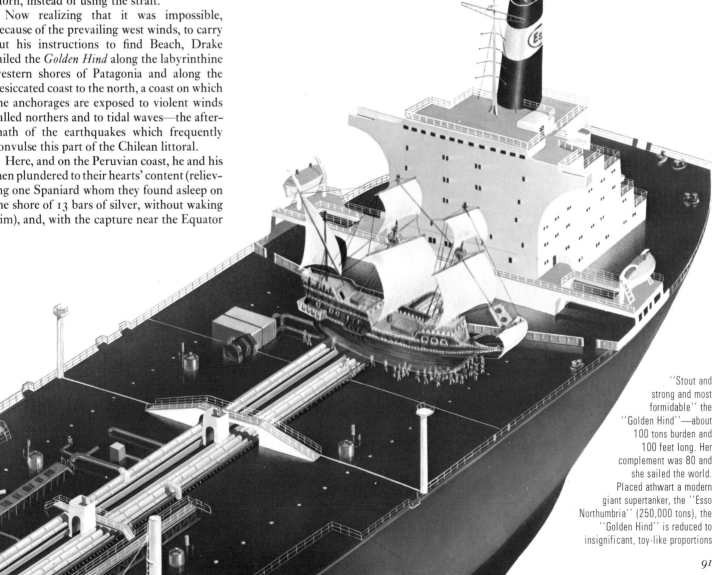

"Stout and strong and most formidable" the "Golden Hind"—about 100 tons burden and 100 feet long. Her complement was 80 and she sailed the world. Placed athwart a modern giant supertanker, the "Esso Northumbria" (250,000 tons), the "Golden Hind" is reduced to insignificant, toy-like proportions

A collision of cultures

THE DEATH OF Columbus in 1506, his dream of a westward passage to Asia unrealized, more or less marked the end of the professional navigator-discoverer working under the patronage of rulers. It was followed by a period of colonization in which many islands in the Spanish Indies, notably Cuba, were settled. Cuba, thought by Columbus to have been part of the Asian continent, was found to be an island in about 1508 and was settled within three years.

The settlers (the word is inappropriate, as many of them had no intention of settling anywhere for long) were men of similar character to those who had sailed with Columbus and who had been such a problem to him. Few were sailors, but many were soldiers, veterans of Spain's campaigns in Europe and Africa. Some were minor nobility or younger sons of nobles; few were farmers either by occupation or by temperament.

They had not come to the Spanish Indies to earn a living by toil. Work was for their Indian and—later, when the indigenous supplies dried up—their West African slaves. They had come west to make a fortune and they were dazzled by the prospect of the seemingly unlimited gold that would be theirs when they eventually conquered the mainland (in Hispaniola the mines were already running short). These were the sort of men who filled the ranks of the Spanish Conquistadors.

The first of these brave, greedy adventurers was Vasco Nuñes de Balboa. Born in 1475, like Magellan, he too was an hidalgo but less well connected, with fewer means and fewer scruples, though no less brave or determined.

In 1501, he sailed from Spain on an expedition fitted out by a merchant, Rodrigo de Bastidas. The party completed the exploration of the northern coast of South America by sailing from the Gulf of Maracaibo along the coast of Colombia as far as the Gulf of Darien. During the trip, a rich haul of gold and pearls was acquired in exchange for a modest outlay in cloth and beads.

Left penniless when the expedition's ships had to be abandoned on the coast of Hispaniola because they were unseaworthy, and receiving nothing from the proceeds of the voyage because the cargo was seized by the governor of the island, Balboa, in the best Conquistador tradition, spent a number of years there farming without any apparent success.

Escape in a barrel

In 1510, being heavily in debt and also being pressed by his creditors, he had himself, so the story goes, conveyed on board a ship in Santo Domingo harbour, hidden in a barrel. This was one of two ships commanded by Martin Fernandez de Enciso, a lawyer of the town, which were taking supplies to Alonzo de Ojeda, who had sailed the previous year to found the settlement of San Sebastian in Colombia. (At the same time Diego de Nicuesa set out to found a similar colony at Veragua in Panama.) Both were equally disastrous. Within a year of their arrival there were only a few survivors out of 1,000 men.

When Balboa arrived he found San Sebastian abandoned and in ruins and that Ojeda had already sailed for Hispaniola. He sailed southwest into the Gulf of Uraba at the head of the Gulf of Darien and, at the mouth of a small river, established the settlement of Santa Maria de la Antigua, after first beating off a force of hostile natives.

Balboa now led an expedition to the interior, and, in what was to become standard Conquistador practice, coming "first to the lands of the Cacique (Chief) Ponea, and not finding him at home, he destroyed them". Subsequently he met a King Comagre with seven sons, one of whom gave the Spaniards "a regalo of near 4,000 pesos of fine gold", about the division of which a quarrel broke out between two of the soldiers. The fight was stopped by the pagan, who threw the balance on which it was being weighed to the ground, in horror at the Spanish behaviour.

On September 1, 1513, Balboa set off from Coiba with a force of about 190 (some reports say he left half to guard his ships) to cross the Isthmus of Darien, making his way through the land of the chief whose villages he had destroyed, this time with an exchange of presents; and through that of another chief with a display of force.

On September 26, led by guides produced by the previously hostile Cacique Ponea, and having forced its way through marsh and dense jungle, the expedition reached the watershed on the Serrania del Darien, the dividing range between east and west, where Balboa went forward alone "desiring to have the glory of having himself been the first man that ever saw the South Sea", and looked down on the Gulf of San Miguel—an inlet from the great ocean which covers more than a quarter of the Earth's surface.

Descending on the Pacific side they entered the territory of the Cacique Chiapas who "opposed them with his people who were stout and clumsy, yet by setting the dogs [they were bloodhounds] at them, and beginning to fire their muskets, they were routed".

Afterwards, peace was made, and there was an exchange of presents; and three of Balboa's captains, one of whom was Francisco Pizarro, went down to the shore to reconnoitre, followed later by Balboa, who "going into the sea up to the mid-leg with a naked sword in his hand ... took possession of it,

and all the coasts and bays of it, for the crowns of Castile and Leon. ...."

In the course of the next four years Balboa made a number of journeys across the Isthmus to the Pacific, where he built four ships with enormous difficulty, for much of the material for them had to be carried over the mountains. The ships were intended for a voyage southwards towards Peru; but it never took place, the only discovery being the Archipelago de las Perlas, offshore in the Gulf of Panama.

In spite of the fact that the emperor had named him Adelantado (Captain-General) of the South Sea and Governor of Panama and Coiba he was not appointed Governor of Darien. This task was given to the fearful Pedro Arias de Avila, who was to turn the Isthmus into a land of misery. An alleged conspiracy was made the excuse for getting rid of Balboa and he was condemned to death for treason and beheaded in 1519.

An expedition which had far-reaching effects was that of Hernandes de Cordova when he discovered Yucatán, landing on the northwestern point of the peninsula in February 1517. Here he saw "thickly peopled countries, with masonry houses, and people who covered their persons and went about clothed in cotton garments, and who possessed gold and who cultivated maize fields"; people who were descendants of the Mayans, whose civilization had come to an end only about 200 years before.

Of warlike character, wearing beautifully wrought gold ornaments, they still bore signs of civilization far higher than anything the Spaniards had so far encountered.

The Conquistadors have left accounts of the dazzling white cities of the Maya, such as Chichen Itza and Uxmal (actually there were more than 1,000), when they had scarcely begun to decay. The more accessible parts of Yucatán were taken possession of by the Conquistador de Montego in 1528.

As more than half of Cordova's force died in the course of this expedition and the leader himself as a result of it, the expedition of the following year was led by Juan de Grijalva.

He was given an equally hostile reception in Yucatán, but suffered fewer losses and eventually established friendly relations with some native chiefs on the rivers which flow into Campeche Bay to the west.

From them he obtained solid gold armour plates and magnificent gold and jewelled artifacts, as well as information about a great king, whose capital was high in the interior, thus becoming, with his men, the first Europeans (with the exception of some Spanish castaways) to land in Mexico and set eyes on the Aztecs.

The Aztec nation had been found and the stage set for the greatest of the Conquistadors, Hernando Cortes. A native of Estremadura and the son of a well-born soldier, Cortes was 33 or 34 years old and wealthy as a result of his support of Velasquez during the expedition to take Cuba. He sailed from the island in 1519 to seek the mysterious capital city of which Grijalva had heard. With him he had about 600 volunteers—he was a man capable of inspiring great loyalty—about 15 horses and some cannon.

Landing in Campeche Bay he repudiated the commission he had from Velasquez and drew up a new one, making himself the direct representative of the emperor. Boldly he wrote to Spain asking for confirmation, describing the new land as having "as many riches as that from which Solomon is said to have obtained gold for the temple".

Now, having founded Vera Cruz on this unhealthy coast, the "terra caliente" (hot land), and having learned that the Aztec

Continued on page 96

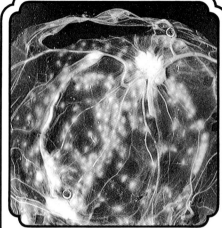

"Variola", the smallpox virus. It dealt a fatal blow to an ancient people.

The Aztec nation and its golden, bloodthirsty culture came to an end with a dreadful suddenness. The vectors of extinction were not the lances of the Conquistadors, for all the Spanish skill at arms. By far the deadliest of the invaders from the Old World was one to whom the Spanish probably attached the least importance—a Negro slave who had been captured in West Africa.

The Negro was a carrier of *Variola*, the virus of smallpox, a disease which until that time had been unknown in the New World and to which the Amerindian people had no resistance.

Ironically, the Negro was one of a troop of men sent from Hispaniola to arrest Cortes for flouting its Governor's orders. Cortes was not arrested, but his task of subduing the Aztecs was made horrifyingly easy. Smallpox is the most highly contagious of infectious fevers and within six months of its introduction into Mexico it killed three and a half million people, more than half the total population of the empire.

The streets of the capital, Tenochtitlán, were choked with bodies. "A man could not set his foot down," said Cortes, "unless on the corpse of an Indian." A city which, at the beginning of the 16th century was healthy and clean, and had never known an epidemic, was reduced to "a vast charnel house, in which all was hastening to decay and decomposition".

The worst of the plague lasted only two months. A contemporary chronicler wrote: "The time that this plague was active was 60 days, 60 deathly days. It began at Cuatlan; when it was realized, it was too late."

The Spanish sword in Middle America

"Is it possible you should value so much a thing that so little deserves your esteem? And that you should leave the repose of your houses, and pass so many seas, exposed to such dangers, to trouble those who live quiet in their own country? Have some shame, Christians—do not value these things; but, if you are resolved to search for gold, I will show you a country where you may satisfy yourselves. . . ."

IT WAS TO the soldiers of Balboa, the first of the great Conquistadors, that these words were delivered, by an American Indian, as they quarrelled over their share of booty. The pioneering journeys westwards of skilled European sailors and navigators had, in less than 20 years, degenerated into a frenzied scramble for riches. Hardy and savagely ruthless (a manner deemed perfectly proper at the time, when dealing with pagans), the Conquistadors were few in number compared with the peoples with whom they came into contact. But their drive and their fervour enabled them to confront and subdue an area greater in size than the continent they had left behind.

The New World of the European adventurers and geographers was no new world to millions of people whose forebears had migrated to America 15,000 to 20,000 years before. They had crossed from Asia by an ancient land bridge where the Bering Strait now provides a seaway, and spread, in subsequent generations, to people both North and South America. Certainly by 10,000 years ago there were migrant hunters in South America. At the time the Spanish arrived, it is estimated that 16 million people lived in the Western Hemisphere, with the heaviest concentration in what is now Mexico. Only about one million lived in North America, made up of tribes whose names are part of modern North American lore. The Indians with whom the Europeans came first into collision were those of the high civilizations of Maya (the first to flower) and Aztec, whose city culture was based on the cultivation of maize. As they moved north, the Spanish met a scattering of tribes, some of them sedentary and living in villages (picture above) like the Pueblo Indians, others following the timeless life of the hunter-gatherer on the plains and in the forests. And to the south, they found the Inca, the artists and the engineers of the high Andes

Colorado River

Grand Canyon

1539
Ulloa

1539
de Niza

1529-36
de Vaca

Decked in the feathers of the quetzal, a bird native to the forests of Central America, Montezuma, the king of the Aztecs, is borne on the shoulders of his subjects

Ecological upset: Like the wandering tribes who were to people America, the bison migrated there from its birthplace, Asia, across an ancient land bridge, now the Bering Strait. The horse, which originated in North America, migrated to Asia and vanished from its homeland until reintroduced by the Spanish. The North American Indians took to the horse with alacrity and the partnership of man and one beast began the decline, almost to extinction, of another beast, the bison, on the great plains

1540-41
Coronado

Arkansas River

Mississippi River

Savannah River

1539-42
de Soto†
Moscoso

1528
Narvaez

The moist lands of the southeast were home to about one-tenth of the North American Indian population at the time of the European invader

1542
Moscoso

CUBA

HISPANIOLA

1517
de Cordova

Campeche Bay

YUCATÁN

Tenochtitlán
(Mexico City)

Vera
Cruz

1521
Cortes

1523
Alvarado

1513
Balboa

*Bering
Strait*

AMERICA

ASIA

ALEUTIAN
ISLANDS

Isthmus of Darien

A collision of cultures

capital of Tenochtitlán was in the middle of a vast lagoon, he set off for the high plateau of central Mexico, having scuttled all but one of his ships. With him were 500 men, the horses which inspired such terror in the inhabitants, six cannons and his mistress, Marina, daughter of a chief, who also acted as his adviser and interpreter. It was a remarkable march, over high passes, through territory in some parts hostile, where he had to fight, in others where he was welcomed by people who were held in subjection by the Aztecs and whose chiefs he baptized. On the way he met Spanish castaways, who went with him as interpreters, and sent a party up the snow-covered 17,887-foot Popocatepetl, "the steaming mountain" of the Aztecs, from which the great lagoon was first seen. Arriving at it with his new allies he found a number of cities, one surrounded entirely by water, another reached by a causeway and a third, Iztapalapa, which contained more than 12,000 stone houses, part of it on land, part in the lagoon.

The following day, crossing a causeway "that extends two leagues . . . and well constructed so that eight horsemen can ride on it abreast", he and his men reached the capital, where "there came to meet me at this place nearly a thousand of the principal inhabitants of the great city, all uniformly dressed according to their custom in very rich costumes and . . . each one as he approached me, performed a salutation in much use among them, by placing his hand upon the ground and kissing it; and thus I was kept waiting an hour, until all had performed the ceremony".

Now, crossing a drawbridge, Cortes had his first meeting with Montezuma: "I advanced alone to salute him; but the two attendant lords stopped me to prevent me touching him, and they and he performed the ceremony of kissing the ground."

Montezuma was a warrior and a brave one and to some who served him he was generous. But he was also intolerably arrogant and despotic, and the punitive taxation which his humbler subjects endured had made him extremely unpopular with them. This was to bring about his death at the hands of his own people.

Now, however, in the presence of Cortes, he pretended a humility that he can scarcely have felt, in spite of the widespread rumour that Cortes and the rest of the Spaniards were indestructible white gods returning to their ancient home. "'These people I know,' he said, 'have informed you that I possessed houses with walls of gold . . . and that I was a god, or made myself one, and many other such things. The houses you see are of stone and lime and earth.' And then he opened his

robes and showed his person to me saying, 'You see that I am composed of flesh and bone like yourselves, and that I am mortal and palpable to the touch,' at the same time pinching his arm and body with his hands."

All these protestations were useless in dealing with Cortes, who had already received rich presents from the hands of Montezuma's envoys long before entering the city.

Soon Montezuma was seized and loaded with chains, which were only removed on payment of an immense ransom in gold, and even then he was still kept a prisoner.

About this time Cortes was forced to return to Vera Cruz to deal with Panfilo de Narvaez, whom Velasquez had sent to take him prisoner; and when he returned, having managed to win over a number of the new arrivals to his cause, he found that the behaviour of his men had been so atrocious that fighting was imminent. When the Aztecs rose at last they set fire to the Axayacatl Palace in which Montezuma was kept prisoner, and in an attempt to stop the fighting Cortes forced him to appear before his people. They stoned him to death.

The situation was now hopeless for the Spaniards and Cortes, having lost a quarter of his entire force, retreated across the causeway and took refuge at Tlaxcala, where the inhabitants were allies.

It was not until August 13, 1521, that Tenochtitlán finally fell to Cortes in the course of an amphibious attack, and then only after very heavy fighting. Later in the day he received the surrender of Montezuma's successor, the young King Quauhtemoc, surrounded by nobles in full ceremonial dress and regalia.

Tortured

He was a gallant man. Dissatisfied with the amount of treasure that was found within the city Cortes had him put to the torture and "when his companion, who was put to the torture with him, testified his anguish by his groans, Quauhtemoc coldly rebuked him by exclaiming, 'And do you think I, then, am taking my pleasure in my bath?'"

With the fall of the capital (later to be rebuilt as Mexico City on the same site in the now-drained lagoon) the whole ordered civilization of the Aztecs came to an end. The secrets and skills that accomplished stupendous engineering works, without the aid of metal tools, beasts of burden or the use of the wheel, were lost for ever.

The passing of the priestly hierarchy can be mourned by nobody, however. For the first time in their search for colonies the Spaniards had encountered a race that was more bloodthirsty than they were. As the historian W. H. Prescott writes in the *History*

A species of camel, the llama is widely used by the montane people of South America. The Inca used the llama as a beast of burden, for its wool, and its meat in religious rites.

of the Conquest of Brazil: "Human sacrifices have been practised by many nations, not excepting the most polished nations of antiquity; but never by any, on a scale to be compared with those in Anahuac. The amount of victims immolated on its accursed altars would stagger the faith of the least scrupulous believer. Scarcely any author pretends to estimate the yearly sacrifices throughout the empire at less than twenty thousand and some carry the number as high as fifty thousand. . . . It was customary to preserve the skulls of the sacrificed, in buildings appropriated to the purpose. The companions of Cortes counted one hundred and thirty-six thousand in one of these edifices."

From now on Cortes, as Governor and Captain-General of Mexico, was responsible for despatching expeditions, the aim of which was either to search for a strait linking the Atlantic with the Pacific; or failing that to find sites for seaports, and also for cities, and in this way the inland cities of Oaxaca and Colima and the ports of Acapulco and Zacatula on the Pacific were established.

In 1523, Pedro de Alvarado led an overland expedition into Guatemala by way of the Isthmus of Tehuantepec; and between 1524 and 1526 Cortes himself made a fearful march from Mexico City to the Gulf of Honduras, crossing mountain ranges and swamps and forcing his way through the dense forests of southwestern Yucatán, for the purpose not of discovery but putting down Cristobal de Olid, one of his captains whom he had sent with ships into the Gulf of Honduras to search for an east–west strait, and who had usurped his authority.

His last expedition was in 1536, when he sailed up the west coast of Mexico and some way into the Gulf of California. Francisco de Ulloa finally reached the northern end in 1539, sailed down the coast of Lower California, doubled Cape S Lucas at the southern end and sailed up the Pacific side to about 30N.

Cortes died, loaded with honours, but prudently deprived by the emperor of over-much power, near Seville in 1547.

Death of the Inca

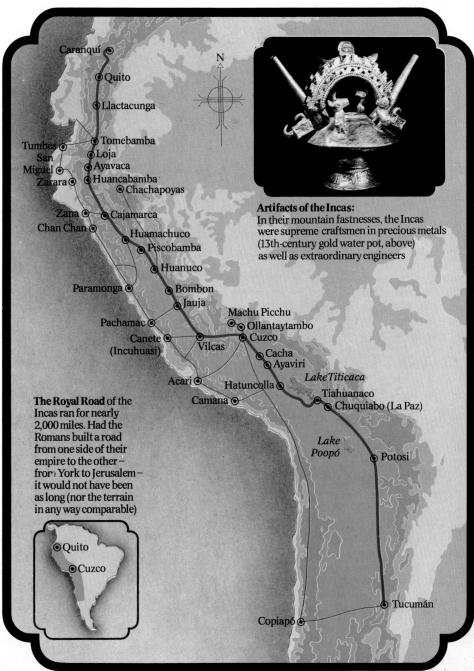

Artifacts of the Incas:
In their mountain fastnesses, the Incas were supreme craftsmen in precious metals (13th-century gold water pot, above) as well as extraordinary engineers

The Royal Road of the Incas ran for nearly 2,000 miles. Had the Romans built a road from one side of their empire to the other – from York to Jerusalem – it would not have been as long (nor the terrain in any way comparable)

"**B**ELOW THE ADVENTURERS, its white houses glittering in the sun, lay the little city of Caxamalca, like a sparkling gem on the dark skirts of the sierra. At the distance of about a league farther, across the valley, might be seen columns of vapour rising up towards the heavens, indicating the place of the famous hot baths much frequented by the Peruvians. And here, too, was a spectacle less grateful to the eyes of the Spaniards. Along the slopes of the hills a white cloud of pavilions was seen covering the ground, as thick as snowflakes, for the space, apparently, of several miles.

'It filled us all with amazement,' exclaimed one of the conquerors, 'to behold the Indians occupying so proud a position! So many tents, so well appointed, as were never seen in the Indies till now! The spectacle caused something like confusion and even fear in the stoutest bosom. But it was too late to turn back, or to betray the least sign of weakness, since the natives in our own company would, in such case, have been the first to rise upon us. So, with as bold a countenance as we could, after coolly surveying the ground, we prepared for our entrance into Caxamalca.'"

It was the end of an infinitely toilsome search for the kingdom of the Incas, the last of the great American Indian civilizations; a search founded on rumours of a great kingdom in the south that had begun to circulate among the Spaniards after the foundation of Darien on the mainland 20 years before.

Its fate, and ultimate downfall, was decided that afternoon when the Conquistador Francisco Pizarro and his followers captured the reigning Inca, Atahualpa, who himself had just dethroned his half-brother, Huascar, after defeating him in battle.

Pizarro was born about 1471 in Estremadura, as Balboa and Cortes had been. His background was markedly different. He was

Death of the Inca

an experienced soldier, who had fought in Italy and Navarre. He was the illegitimate son of a soldier, brought up totally illiterate in the most humble circumstances. His character was also very different. Balboa and Cortes were cruel, as were all the Conquistadors, and in the manner of the age. Pizarro not only far excelled them in insensate cruelty, he was also extremely perfidious, though their equal in courage and determination.

Pizarro's first voyage southwards along the west coast was made with Diego de Almagro, a Conquistador with a somewhat similar background to his own, being a foundling.

They set off from Panama in two small vessels in November 1524, sailing southeast across the gulf, passing Puerto de Piñas and along a coast in which in this, the rainy season, the land itself was under water, a coast of gloomy, impenetrable forests and hostile inhabitants, some of whom were addicted to cannibalism.

Farther south they encountered more friendly Indians who were wearing gold ornaments and heard from them of the existence of a rich kingdom far to the south. On this expedition de Almagro reached the mouth of the San Juan River in the Bay of Buenaventura in 5N and, after suffering every kind of privation and misfortune (they lost a number of men and de Almagro was badly wounded) they returned to Panama.

They were not put off, however. In 1526, at Darien, where he had been with Balboa and had received a "repartimento" of land which had made him a man of substance, Pizarro entered into a contract with de Almagro, and Hernando de Luque, a priest who produced most of the capital. The contract was for nothing less than the conquest of Brazil.

On the second voyage, which took place in 1526–7, they sailed with 160 men whom it had been difficult to recruit after the ghastly appearance of the survivors of the previous expedition had been seen.

This time, once they reached the San Juan River, the pilot, Bartolomé Ruiz, was sent on ahead, and, crossing the Equator, came to "places very rich in gold and silver, and inhabited by more intelligent people than they had previously met with", returning with specimens of all three. To Ruiz should probably go the credit for the discovery of Peru.

Sailing on they reached Tumbes, on the southern shore of the Bay of Guayaquil in Ecuador, which they found to be a beautiful and civilized town, from which the inhabitants came out to their ship in boats made of balsa wood. The natives brought with them all sorts of game, fish, vegetables and fruits,

and llamas (of which Pizarro had only seen a sketch, made by Balboa), the "Peruvian sheep", which supplied the Inca people with wool for weaving their materials and provided their only beast of burden.

Here, an Inca nobleman came on board to whom Pizarro proceeded to give the reasons why he had come, which were to convert the inhabitants and to assert the supremacy of the Spanish king, both of which were received without comment.

Subsequently, two Spanish envoys were sent ashore, one of whom, a Greek knight, was dressed in a suit of shining armour with which he dazzled the inhabitants, and an arquebuse, which he shot off to their great alarm. While on shore they noted the strength of the fortress and the abundance of gold—in one temple, fruit and vegetables were reproduced in solid gold and silver.

Place of the dead

From here Pizarro sailed some 200 miles to the south where he doubled Cape Aguja, with the Andes looming up—as they had done ever since he entered the Gulf of Guayaquil—on his port hand, and still farther until he reached the town of Santa near where the Incas burned their dead.

Here he heard, yet again, of a great city in the interior, the capital of a powerful monarch. And here, on this first trip, he turned back for Panama, leaving at Tumbes some of his men who had succumbed to the charms of the women and the place, taking with him some of the natives, and arriving home after an absence of 18 months.

In 1529, Pizarro went to Seville where he secured from the emperor the title and emoluments of Governor and Captain-General of the kingdom, which he had scarcely seen. He returned, now 50 years old, to South America with his four half-brothers, together with Almagro, 180 men and 27 horses, and, in January 1531, set out to conquer Peru.

From Tumbes, which they found mysteriously destroyed and abandoned, they struck inland *en route* for Caxamalca, which the Inca, the monarch, had made his capital, by way of the Piura Valley, where they established the first settlement, San Miguel, skirting the Sechura Desert and crossing fearful passes to reach the crest of the Andes.

From it they began the descent of the eastern side through a series of defiles, in one of which they met an envoy sent by the Inca, who was told by Pizarro that Caxamalca was surrounded by a Spanish army which was only a league from the city; he was in fact the best part of a week's journey from it.

What followed belongs more to military history than to a history of discovery.

On November 15, 1532, the city was taken. In it and the surroundings between 5,000 and 10,000 Incas were put to the sword; the city was looted, enormous quantities of gold, as well as large emeralds, being found. The Inca was imprisoned and a ransom demanded from him of a quantity of gold sufficient to fill a room 22 feet long and 17 feet broad to a height of nine feet, while two smaller rooms were to be filled with silver.

Immediately, emissaries were sent to distant parts of the kingdom to arrange for its collection and after a few weeks it began to arrive; but too slowly for the Spaniards. Impatient, Pizarro set off on the 600-mile journey (as the crow flies) southwards to Cuzco, a city of 200,000 inhabitants high up in the Peruvian Andes. After an astonishing march along the even more astonishing trunk road which the Incas had built thousands of feet above the sea along the high sierras, they arrived at the city, which they entered and sacked in November 1533.

Atahualpa, the Inca, was already dead, and so was his half-brother, whom he had caused to be drowned in a river. Atahualpa had been sentenced to death by burning at a trial by the Spanish that was a travesty of any kind of justice; but this was subsequently commuted to death by the garotte (a form of strangulation), the sentence being carried out by some Negro slaves belonging to Pizarro. The Inca refused to be converted to Christianity before he died.

So vanished the power of the Incas, whose kingdom extended from Ecuador in the north for 2,000 miles, as far as latitude 35S in present-day Chile, although the Manco Inca, last of his line, lived for another ten years, a ruler on the run. With them vanished their great skill in engineering and architectural works, which they accomplished without the aid of iron tools, the wheel, the keystone arch or the written word to help them in their plans and calculations (instead they used the quipu, a cord made up of different coloured threads, which acted as a superior form of abacus). To vanish also was their skill in working precious metals; their worship, which was directed at the Sun, unaccompanied, as was that of the Aztecs, by human sacrifice and ritual cannibalism; and their system of education, which was based on the aristocratic assumption that, in the words of the great Tupac Inca Yupanqui: "Science was not intended for the people; but for those of generous blood. Persons of low degree are only puffed up by it, and rendered vain and arrogant. Neither should such meddle with the affairs of government; for this would bring high offices into disrepute, and cause detriment to the state". Now all this vanished, as if it had never been.

Amazon odyssey

ONCE THE SPANISH had the wealth of the Inca Empire in their grip, Peru became the base for expeditions that branched out in several directions from the new capital, Lima, which Pizarro had founded in 1535. In that year Diego de Almagro set off along the "royal road" of the Incas, south from Cuzco through the altiplano, the bleak, high plain lying trapped between the eastern and western cordillera of the Andes.

This was no happy journey for the hot-blooded Spanish, for all their well-earned reputation for hardiness. Not only were temperatures savagely low, at these altitudes the air is rarified, making the simple drawing of breath a painful exercise for the lowlander. The natives of the region suffered no such trouble. Their hearts and lungs were adapted to the demands made upon them.

Almagro and his men reached the great lake of Titicaca, which now separates the southern marches of Peru from northern Bolivia, moved on into the northwest corner of what is now Argentina, then traversed,

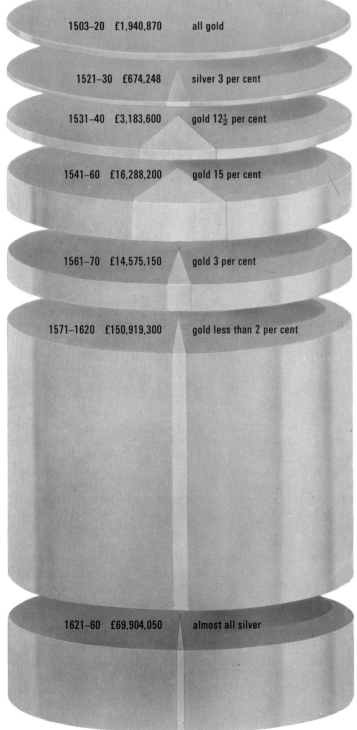

1503–20	£1,940,870	all gold
1521–30	£674,248	silver 3 per cent
1531–40	£3,183,600	gold 12½ per cent
1541–60	£16,288,200	gold 15 per cent
1561–70	£14,575,150	gold 3 per cent
1571–1620	£150,919,300	gold less than 2 per cent
1621–60	£69,904,050	almost all silver

Bullion imports to Spain in the 16th and 17th centuries. The flood of gold and silver from the Americas in the 16th century began as a mere trickle—less than a quarter of a million pounds, in modern terms, in the two years that followed the death of Queen Isabella in 1503. In the last decade of the century, during the reign of Philip II, it had swelled to a torrent of four to five million pounds annually. At first, bullion imports consisted entirely of gold, but by 1531 had become, for the most part, silver. The wealth was to add a gleaming lustre to the crown of Spain, but in the outcome the lustre dimmed as imports fell away. Wars abroad (the Spanish army was the most efficient of its time) against the French, English and Netherlanders ate into reserves. Philip II's foreign policy has been described as the most expensive and ambitious since Ancient Rome. Without America's gold, that policy would have been unthinkable. Spanish industry was allowed to decline by the ruling Hidalgos, who had a contempt for it, foreign debts mounted up, claiming what spare bullion there was, and inflation became rampant. Steadily, the currency became debased. Gold coinage was rare in 1600: by 1624, both gold and silver coinage were out of circulation. All payments in Spain had to be made in copper, with the result that wagon loads were needed for quite small deals. A golden age, in its most precise sense, had come to an end

once again, the high passes of the Andes into northern Chile, about 37s. Spaniards died in their scores, their native bearers in hundreds.

Before turning back—he had reached the southernmost limits of the Inca Empire—Almagro searched for gold, but found none. The fact that he had reached a green and gentle land did not impress him at all. He probably thought about it longingly on his return journey north, for it took him through one of the most barren regions in the world, the coastal Atacama Desert. Rainless, but perpetually shrouded in a cloudbank of mist and studded with weird, xerophytic (drought-resistant) plants, it was as inhospitable as any region through which the Conquistadors marched.

Almagro was followed into Chile some years later by Pedro de Valdivia. In the fertile regions which Almagro had treated with disdain, Valdivia laid the basis of modern Chile and founded its capital, Santiago.

This was in 1541, a year in which Pizarro sent out another expedition, one which was to earn an important place in the history of exploration. It began when Pizarro sent his brother Gonzalo north from Cuzco to Quito, and from there across the Andes, in search for more gold, and large forests of cinnamon trees which were held to exist beyond the cordilleras. The journey began in February 1541, with Gonzalo leading a force of 220 Spaniards (some with horses), dogs (a mobile source of food), about 4,000 Indian slaves, and llamas ("Peruvian sheep") as pack animals. Large numbers of slaves died of exposure as they passed through the mountains, although their route was only about 40 miles south of the Equator. On the way, Gonzalo was overtaken by Francisco de Orellana, a 30-year-old kinsman whom he made his lieutenant-general. It was Orellana who was to achieve the historical fame at the end of the journey.

Gonzalo pressed on ahead with about 80 men to reconnoitre the country on the eastern watershed of the mountains, forcing his way through forest that was so dense that "in many parts they had to open a road by main force, and with blows of hatchets".

Reunited with Orellana, Gonzalo pushed on under a deluge of rain that continued for six weeks without intermission. They eventually reached the place where the cinnamon trees grew. It was so remote that the trees could never be of commercial value.

Now they came upon a broad reach of the Napo River, a tributary of the Amazon, which has its source on the flanks of a group of Andean volcanoes.

Before them, on either hand, was the Amazon basin, more than two and a half

Amazon odyssey

million square miles of completely unknown territory making up one-third of the whole of South America. Although they did not know it, they were nearly 3,000 miles from the Atlantic.

Gloomy reports were coming in from advance parties about the state of the country ahead of them. It was, they were told, nothing but a vast morass (during the rainy season the Amazon floods out from its banks to merge with the surrounding rain-forest). When he encountered a party of natives who were unable—probably out of ignorance—to enlighten him about what lay beyond it, Gonzalo had them either burned alive or torn to pieces by those dogs that still remained with him.

Finally they reached the Napo River, a tributary of the Amazon, where, using nails from the shoes of the horses that had died and been eaten on the journey, gum from the trees as pitch and their own rags for oakum, they built a boat large enough to take the weaker half of the company. It was a task that took them two months.

As the stronger members of the company forced their way along the bank, the boat's crew descended the river for 43 days, finding little food, except "toads and serpents". They even ate the leather of their belts and saddles.

Now, hearing from an Indian guide that the Napo entered another, greater river, a few days' journey downstream and that one day's journey up it from the junction "there was an inhabited land well supplied with provisions and rich in gold, and in all other things which they wanted", Gonzalo sent Orellana ahead in the boat to find it. With him went 50 men, one of whom was Friar Gaspar de Carvajal, a Dominican, who recorded the rest of Orellana's remarkable voyage, for Orellana and the men with him never returned—he had sailed on down the great river with the intention of reaching Spain and claiming the credit for its discovery. (Orellana's version was that the current in the Napo—which runs at about five knots—made it impossible for him to return and that he went on to seek help. His story was corroborated by the Dominican.)

It is difficult to imagine the feelings of Gonzalo and his men on receiving this news, but as a true Conquistador—whatever his other failings—Gonzalo was undoubtedly courageous. He rallied his men, turned them round and set off for Quito, this time taking a more northerly route and reaching the city in June 1542.

Orellana, having reached the Amazon, embarked on its main stream, and arrived at a village inhabited by friendly Indians. Here, in 35 days, using materials provided by the

Rare spices were as valuable as silver and gold in 16th-century Europe. Lured by fables of forests rich in cinnamon trees on the far side of the Andes, Pizarro and Orellana crossed the cordillera in the heavy snows of mid-winter

At the confluence of the Amazon and the Negro and for many miles, the "black" waters of the Negro run without mingling with the pale Amazon waters. The colouring is caused by differing sedimentary influences

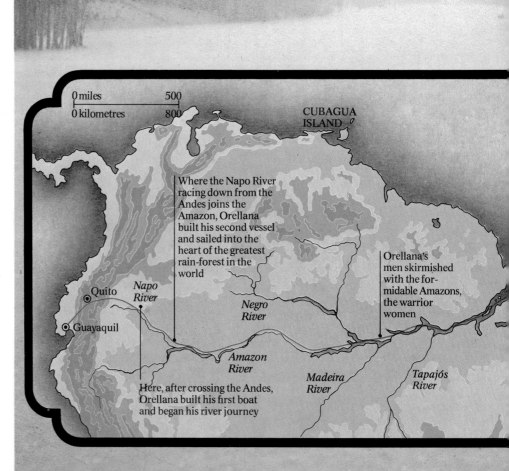

0 miles 500
0 kilometres 800

CUBAGUA ISLAND

Where the Napo River racing down from the Andes joins the Amazon, Orellana built his second vessel and sailed into the heart of the greatest rain-forest in the world

Quito

Napo River

Negro River

Orellana's men skirmished with the formidable Amazons, the warrior women

Guayaquil

Amazon River

Madeira River

Tapajós River

Here, after crossing the Andes, Orellana built his first boat and began his river journey

Into North America

Timeless scene at the Amazon delta, where Orellana, approaching the end of his river journey, rigged his ships with blanket sails before heading for the open sea, Cubagua Island—and Spain

The greatest of river journeys, down the greatest river of all, the Amazon, was made by Francisco Orellana, a Conquistador who had already crossed the Andean cordilleras before he began his river odyssey in 1541. It lasted 17 months. In two boats, built from what materials there were to hand after crossing the Andes, he and his men drifted on the sluggish current of the river which, in the rainy season, is almost indivisible from the immense forest which lines its banks. To a modern explorer, the feat would pose an epic challenge. To Orellana it was, no doubt, no more than a natural hazard similar to others the Conquistadors had encountered and overcome

The great delta of the Amazon. Orellana beached his craft, rigged them with sails made from blankets and sailed for Cubagua Island. On his arrival back in Spain he was given a hero's welcome

Indians, the Spanish built a second vessel, a "brigantine", and sailed downstream.

On May 12 they entered the domains of the overlord Machiparo. His people included turtles in their diet and the starving Spaniards put a party ashore that collected from a store "enough to feed . . . 1,000 men for a year".

This provoked a battle in which a number of Spaniards were seriously wounded. The rest of the voyage down the Amazon was marked by running fights with hostile natives armed with bows and poisoned arrows, in the course of which Orellana lost an eye. Among their fiercest fights were those with Amazon warrior women, who were "acting as captains over men", a spectacle that gave great stimulus to the friar's already abundant imagination. "These women are very white and tall, and have hair very long, and braided and wound about the head, and they go about naked but with their privy parts covered, with their bows and arrows in their hands, doing as much fighting as ten Indian men. Indeed there was one woman among these who shot an arrow a span deep into one of the brigantines, and others less deep, so that our brigantines looked like porcupines."

Tidal bore

About 400 miles from the mouth, somewhere near the confluence with the Tapajos River, the Spaniards encountered the tide for the first time and, leaving "the good country and the savannas and the high land", entered reaches full of islands and so wide that they never saw the mainland again; the tide that now came up with "great fury" was possibly the proroca, the tidal bore of the Amazon.

On July 28, Holy Saviour's Day, they put their vessels ashore on a beach where "both brigantines were entirely repaired, and rigging was made for them out of vines, as well as the cordage for the sea [voyage], and sails out of the blankets in which we had been sleeping and their masts set up."

Here they remained for 14 days, living on snails and crabs, until on August 26, after having been continually set back upstream on the flood tide (being without anchors), they reached the mouth of the great river, where the main channel is 50 miles wide. Sailing northwest along the coast of Guiana and present-day Venezuela for more than 1,000 miles, they finally reached Nueva Cadiz on Cubagua Island on September 11, 1542, after a journey of 17 months, the first known men to cross the South American continent.

In Spain, Orellana was well received. Given a commission by the king to exploit the land he had passed through, he died in the ship that was taking him back to it. Eventually, the vast land through which he travelled fell within the Portuguese sphere of influence.

THOUSANDS OF MILES from Spain, the Conquistadors carried into the heartlands of the New World those characteristics that had been shaped by the turbulent history of their homeland. Bravery, for they had fought, and ultimately overcome, the bravest, the warriors of Islam. A hunger for wealth, because Spain had become impoverished. A brutal disregard for life—their own as well as those of the natives with whom they came into contact. And little concern for the natural potential—apart from precious minerals—of the lands into which they marched, for they had developed an historic contempt for anyone who tilled the soil.

The looping explorations of the Spanish in North America began in 1528, seven years after Tenochtitlán had fallen to Cortes and three years before Pizarro set out from Spain to devastate the mountain empire of the Inca.

In 1528, Panfilo de Narvaez, the governor of Mexico who had been sent to Vera Cruz to arrest Cortes, was given the right to conquer and colonize the unknown country between the coast of Florida and the eastern borders of Mexico. He landed near Tampa Bay on the west coast of Florida and marched north until he reached the shores of Apalachee Bay, where the coast begins to trend to the west.

He was as inept a leader of explorers as he had been in his efforts to arrest Cortes. His intention was that the ships should follow, but they failed to make contact and Narvaez decided to build five boats and carry on.

This was done, but in the course of the voyage westwards past the Mississippi delta, and along the shores of Texas, they were separated by winds and currents, the survivors coming together in November near where Galveston now stands, and where they wintered.

At the end of the winter there were only 15 left of the 80 men who had arrived in November and of an expedition that had set out with 600 soldiers and colonists. They had been reduced to cannibalism, using the dried flesh of their dead companions as a food reserve.

One of those who managed to survive this dreadful trip was a young man of 21, Alvar Núñez de Vaca. With his small party of men he moved inland from the coastal regions of Texas and he and his men were not to meet any of their fellow countrymen again for many years.

De Vaca set himself up as an itinerant trader in goods among the nomadic Indian tribes of the area, although the trade he conducted cannot have been very fruitful, since the tribes were among the poorest met in the New World. He never abandoned hope of moving west from this "country, so remote and malign, so destitute of all resource".

To gain a safe conduct through the tribal

Into North America

lands of the people they met, de Vaca and his men posed as healers—probably not the first and certainly not the last time Europeans have gained the confidence of simple, remote communities in this way. Eventually, de Vaca, with three other survivors, made an amazing journey of at least 1,200 miles on foot to the Gulf of California, crossing the lower reaches of the Brazos and Colorado rivers, then west to the Pecos River across the Rio Grande and through the Sierra Madre in Mexico to the Sonora River, which flows into the Gulf of California.

The next expedition, that of Hernando de Soto, was of far greater importance. He landed, probably in Tampa Bay, Florida, in May 1539 with 600 men, 200 horses and the usual horde of dogs, in search of regions that would yield gold and silver; and here the Indians told them that to the west there was a place called Cale in which "the inhabitants did wear hats of gold, in manner of head pieces".

From Apalachee Bay they moved west, never meeting with the gold-hatted Indians and more or less following the route of Narvaez; then, listening to the talk of the Indians of gold, pursued the chimera northeast into modern Georgia, crossing the grain of the country and the rivers flowing into the Atlantic, through good country with an abundance of long-needled pine and wild turkeys to the banks of the Savannah River, where, at a settlement of the Creek Indians called Cufitachique, one of the women (either a chief or the wife of a chief) invested de Soto with great ropes of pearls. Now, always well received by the Indians, they followed the Savannah northwest to the Great Smoky Mountains in the Appalachians and then, with winter coming on, marched south to a walled or stockaded settlement of the Creek Indians, Mauvilla, north of Mobile.

At first they were welcomed by the Indians, who came out to them singing and playing flutes; and the chief gave them presents of mantles made with the fur of martens. But soon fighting broke out which resulted in the slaughter of 2,500 Indians to the loss of 18 Spaniards killed and 150 wounded. The town was destroyed. Now, driving a great herd of dogs before them which bred *en route*, they marched north and then northwest, crossing the Mississippi near its junction with the Arkansas, below the present city of Memphis, hoping to discover "a path to the northward whereby to come out on the South Sea", from which they were separated by some 1,800 miles of unknown territory. Then, returning south, they crossed the Arkansas and forced their way on to the difficult, dissected plateau of the Ozark Mountains, from which de Soto's men found it impossible

to make a passage in a westward direction.

From here they retreated to the bayous of the Mississippi and, farther south, while trying yet again to move through the swamps to the west—perhaps somewhere between the Arkansas and the Red River—de Soto died.

He was succeeded as commander by Luis de Moscoso, who, realizing that they could go no farther, ordered seven "brigantines" to be built on the bank of the Arkansas with nails forged on the site, henequen (sisal) as caulking, and with the help of a Genoese "whom it pleased God to preserve, for without him they would never have come out of the country".

They descended the Arkansas and the Mississippi for 17 days, pursued by hostile Indians in canoes and, reaching the river mouth on July 18, made a remarkable journey of 52 days to the Panuco River on the east

The Grand Canyon: Coronado was the first European to see it, during his 1540 expedition

coast of Mexico, arriving there on September 10, 1542, after an absence of more than three years.

In about 1539, Marco de Niza, a Franciscan monk, made a journey northwards into New Mexico and Arizona in company with the Moroccan-born Negro slave, Estebánico. The slave had been, with de Vaca, one of the four survivors of Narvaez's expedition and gave a Rabelaisian air to the venture, travelling with a sort of harem, and acting as a scout until he was killed by the Zuni Indians on the way. De Niza returned, with reports of one of the fabulous "Seven Cities of Cibola", which were "large and powerful villages, four and five stories high". They were the pueblos of the Indians; and they inspired the expedition of the following year, led by Francisco Vasquez de Coronado, the 30-year-old son of an aristocratic family who had married an heiress in Mexico.

The overland part of the expedition seems to have started from Culiacan, near the

mouth of the Gulf of California, up which its ships, under Pedro de Alascon, sailed into the Colorado River. Marching northwards up the valley of the San Pedro River, the Spanish reached an almost entirely uninhabited region of Arizona, where they saw "grey lions and leopards" (possibly cougars and wild cats). Then, passing through the more fertile country of the hostile Zunis, they defeated them in battle (Coronado was one of the principal targets for their stones and arrows, as he was dressed in glittering, gilded armour) and sacked their pueblo.

From here Coronado's forward scouts reached the Grand Canyon, from the edge of which, desperate for water, they looked down the best part of a sheer mile at the Colorado River, which they were unable to reach. They were the last Europeans to see it until a missionary, Father Francisco Garces, tottered on a mule along its edge in 1776, after which it was again lost to western eyes until Lieutenant J. C. Ives of the US Army reached it in 1857–8.

Coronado turned east, crossed the upper waters of the Rio Grande and its tributary, the Pecos, and then southeast into Texas. Here he saw, for the first time, the Great Plains, teeming with animals—antelopes, deer, elk and wolves. He saw, too, the plains Indians, who followed the immense herds of buffalo, which supported their entire economy and who moved from place to place carrying the lodge poles of their tepees on travois drawn by large dogs (the horse being a Spanish importation).

Of the buffalo Coronado said: "At first there was not a horse that did not run away on seeing them. . . . Their eyes bulge at the sides so that when they run, they can see those who follow them. They are bearded like very large she-goats. . . ."

Now they travelled northwards, across the panhandle of Oklahoma into Kansas. The magnitude of the Great Plains astonished them. "The country is like a bowl, so that when a man sits down, the horizon surrounds him all around at the distance of a musket shot."

The graphic imagery of Coronado and his men could not hide their disappointment at the almost complete lack of loot. The rich and black soil which they had noted could in no way compare with the smooth gleam of gold. They turned back.

The Indians whose lands they passed through were now wary of the white man who had placed intolerable demands upon their slender subsistence economies. Coronado had to fight much of the way to his arrival back in Mexico and a cool reception from the viceroy. There were to be no more inland journeys into North America for many years.

'To the spicerie, by our seas...'

"With a small number of ships there may be discovered divers new lands and kingdoms . . . to which places there is left one way to discover, which is into the North. . . ."

MERCHANT AND GEOGRAPHER Robert Thorn wrote these words in 1527, pleading a new trade route to the east. The search for the Northwest and Northeast passages had begun. The Venetian in English service, John Cabot, the Portuguese Corte Real brothers and the Italian Verrazano (paid by the French) had already examined the prospects.

Few great explorers have left less trace of their background and what they accomplished than John Cabot, "a lower-class Venetian, of a fine mind, very expert in navigation", as he was described by a contemporary. He was born, probably at Genoa, between 1450 and 1453 and ten years later his father took him to Venice, where he became a naturalized citizen of the Republic in 1476. From about 1490 he lived in Valencia in Spain, where he failed to arouse interest in a voyage to the Indies by a route shorter than that of Columbus; and in about 1495 he settled in Bristol, then England's second most important seaport. He was able to interest Henry VII (who was probably regretting having turned down Columbus) in a voyage to Asia in search of spices.

He left about May 20, 1496, in the *Matthew*, a vessel of about the same tonnage as Columbus's *Niña*, with a crew of 18, including a Genoese barber, and simple navigational instruments—compass, quadrant and traverse table.

Their last sight of land was Dursey Head, northwest of Bantry Bay on the coast of Cork about May 22; their first American landfall on June 24, either on Cape Breton Island, Nova Scotia or more probably on the east coast of Newfoundland between Cape Degrat in 51.37N and Cape Bonavista, the former being in about the same latitude as Dursey Head. Wherever it was, they landed, made a procession, set up the standards of St George of England and St Mark of Venice and Cabot took possession in the name of the English king. He believed himself to be on the mainland of Asia in the realm of the Great Cham, but saw nobody—only what looked like cultivated fields, some snares, fishing nets and animal dung.

They remained on the American coast until about July 20, fishing for cod among the seething shoals of the Grand Banks with weighted baskets, arriving back at Bristol about August 6. Henry VII gave him £10 and an annuity of £20.

The last we hear of Cabot is setting out in May 1498 for "Cipango, situated in the equinoctial region", with five ships loaded with trade goods, of which one returned quite shortly, the others simply disappearing. He may have sailed south along the eastern seaboard of America; there is no certainty.

In 1500, Gaspar Corte Real, a Portuguese whose father had been connected with the court and whose mother was Spanish, set off, also to the northwest, with three ships that he had equipped at his own expense. He sailed north up the east coast of Greenland into the Denmark Strait, from which he was forced to turn back by the ice, then doubled Cape Farewell and sailed up the west coast. He may have reached the Arctic Circle.

In these high latitudes he and his men are said to have met people who were "very wild and barbarous, almost to the extent of the

Henry VII, the English monarch who supported John Cabot's search for a westward route to the East

natives of Brazil, except that these are white". Who they were is an enigma. Corte Real himself believed that he had been on the coast of northeastern Asia.

The next year he sailed again, this time reaching the coast of Labrador in about 58N, a coast with high cliffs, indented with fjords and with innumerable offshore islands. Turning south, he sailed into Hamilton Inlet in 54N, where he saw caribou and, in another inlet near the mouth of the Belle Isle Strait, trees taller than the biggest ships afloat.

On the coast of Newfoundland, which he named Terra Verde, he captured 50 Beothuk Indians, a gentle and beautiful tribe whose goodness and beauty were of no help to them. Two of the three ships sailed for Portugal with Beothuks under hatches, and when they arrived the king was delighted at the prospect of a new hunting ground in which slaves could so easily be picked up—in contrast to Africa, where the Negroes were now wary and more difficult to take.

Corte Real himself sailed on in his ship to the southwest, in search of regions more likely to yield spices. He and his men were never seen again, although various search parties were sent out after him.

The French now entered the field of discovery, one in which the Portuguese had had more than 70 years' experience and the Spanish more than 50.

In 1524, Francis I, patron of all things Italian, accepted a plan put forward by Giovanni da Verrazano, a 36-year-old Florentine gentleman-navigator with an excellent record, to search out a passage in the north to the land of Cathay.

Verrazano left Madeira in January 1524 in *La Dauphine*, a naval vessel of 100 tons with a crew of 50 and provisions for eight months. After sailing west for 49 days (and a distance of 4,900 miles by his own computation), on about March 1 he reached a shore with great fires burning on it, in 34N. It was Cape Fear, North Carolina.

Finding no safe anchorage he sailed south, but fearing to encounter Spanish ships he turned north again somewhere short of Charleston and anchored somewhere near his original landfall off a low, sandy coast with dunes on it. The inhabitants were friendly "black, not much different from the Ethiopians . . . entirely naked, except that about their loins they wear skins of small animals, like martens".

On April 17 he anchored in the Narrows now spanned by the Verrazano Bridge at the entrance to New York Harbour, "a very pleasant place, situated amongst certain steep little hills, from . . . which there ran down into the sea a great stream of water, which within the mouth was very deep, and from the sea to the mouth . . . any great vessel may pass up". And here at the mouth of the Hudson River, the Indians appeared "dressed out in the feathers of birds of various colours".

After a stay of 15 days, he sailed north across Massachusetts Bay to Maine and found the Abnaki Indians, "of such crudity and evil manners, so barbarous, that despite all the signs we could make, we could never converse with them. . . . Clothed in peltry of bear, lynx, 'sea-wolves' and other beasts" they reciprocated his feelings by showering his crew with arrows.

From Maine, missing the Bay of Fundy, he sailed northeast off Nova Scotia, up the eastern side of Newfoundland, taking his departure for Europe, probably in 49.50N, off Fogo Island and arriving at Dieppe on July 8, 1524, after an Atlantic crossing of only two weeks. Verrazano met a culinary doom four years later when he reached the coast of Brazil and was captured and eaten by Indians.

Frobisher and fool's gold

SIR HUMPHREY GILBERT, who was later drowned when his ship was pooped off the Azores, published in 1576 *A Discourse to prove a Passage by the North-west to Cathaia and the East Indies*. Gilbert, an Etonian and step-brother to Raleigh, was a soldier, navigator and first governor of Newfoundland (Britain's first colony, which he founded in August 1583). He argued in his book that America was the mythical island of Atlantis and that it was possible to sail round it to the north by a strait (the Strait of Anian) similar to the Strait of Magellan in the south.

The first Englishman to test Gilbert's theories was Martin Frobisher, an experienced and tough navigator of 37, born near Wakefield in Yorkshire. He had made his first voyage to Guinea in 1554 (in 1562 he was a prisoner in El Mina, the Portuguese fortress on the Gold Coast) and had been examined by the English authorities on suspicion of piracy at one stage of his career.

He had powerful sponsors, among them Gilbert and the Earl of Warwick who persuaded Burghley, Elizabeth's Lord High Treasurer, to bring pressure to bear on the Muscovy Company to give up the monopoly over exploration to the Northwest, of which they had never made practical use.

He sailed from Ratcliffe on the Thames in June 1576 with three vessels: two barks, the *Gabriel* of between 15 and 30 tons, with a crew of 18 including one George Best, who wrote the account of the voyage, and the *Michael* 20 to 25 tons, with a crew of 17; and a small pinnace with a crew of four.

A complete list of what they took with them has come down to us. It includes two works on cosmography and the Antarctic by the Frenchman André Thevet; the book of Sir John Mandeville; a cross-staff and a special instrument for taking celestial altitudes; two sorts of astrolabe; an *armilla tolemei* (an armillary sphere); 20 different sorts of compass; a "carta of navigation . . . ruled plain", a quantity of sea coal; and three hogsheads of aqua-vitae to keep the cold out.

On June 26 they were off "St Tronions"— St Ninian's in the Shetlands—and on July 11, having sailed slightly north of west, sighted under a full moon the east coast of Greenland, hemmed in by pack-ice. At this point the master and crew of the *Michael* "mistrusting the matter, conveyed themselves privily away from him and returned home where they said that the *Gabriel* had been cast away. . . ."

Resolution Island

Off Cape Farewell, the southernmost point of Greenland, a 2,000-foot-high promontory on Egger Island, notorious for its evil weather, the *Gabriel* was laid on its beam ends and the mizzen mast had to be cut away. Frobisher himself worked on the topsides of the hull with his men.

They ran south before the gale until they could pump the ship dry and rig a new mizzen mast; they then altered course to the west, and on July 20 sighted a new land of "marvellous great height . . . with a great store of ice". It was Resolution Island in 60w off Baffin Island, on the north side of the entrance to the Hudson Strait. Although it is only about 500 feet high, its hills rise abruptly from the sea and, seen by the light of a moon in its last quarter, it must have looked impressive.

Now sailing northwards, he saw "another foreland, with a great gut, bay, or passage, dividing as it were two mainlands or continents asunder".

It was an exciting moment for Frobisher. He believed that he was in the western approaches to the Strait of Anian with the coast of Asia to starboard and the American continent to port. Three years later Drake, sailing round the world, vainly sought its eastern entrance in the Pacific.

In fact Frobisher was at the mouth of an inlet, 150 miles long, which runs northwest into Baffin Island, and one that was still thought to be a strait as late as 1860.

He sailed into it on July 21, naming the point on an island off the northern side of the entrance Queen Elizabeth's Promontory and the inlet "Frobisher's Straits, like as Magellanus at the southwest end of the World, having discovered the passage to the South Sea . . . called the same Magellan's Straits".

"They be like Tartars, with long black hair, broad faces, and flat noses." That was Frobisher's description of the Eskimoes, first seen by him in their kayaks "fleeting in the sea a far off"

Now he sailed his ship into it between bare, snow-covered mountains, passing the great Grinnell Glacier on the southwestern shore, before turning back not far from its end.

Back at the mouth, he saw from the top of a hill "a number of small things fleeting in the sea a far off", which he supposed to be "Porposes or Ceales, or some kind of strange fish". They were Eskimoes in kayaks.

Soon he was surrounded by them and some came on board to trade furs, seal flesh and salmon, and to swing in the rigging.

They were cunning as well as agile. Five men who went off in a boat, disregarding Frobisher's instructions not to land, were never seen again, and the ship's company was reduced to 13. When Frobisher made some show of force and tried to take hostages to secure the release of his own men the Eskimoes struck their sealskin tents and disappeared.

Later, a fleet of kayaks gathered round the ship, crewed by Eskimoes who had a hostile air. Frobisher cleared his ship for action and managed to lure one of them alongside by ringing bells, of which the Eskimoes were fond. Having lured one of them alongside, he "caught the man fast, and plucked him with his main force, boat and all, into his bark out of the sea".

Now, having tried in vain to exchange the Eskimo for his five men, and having acquired some heavy, glittering minerals that he took to be gold, but were in fact pyrites or "fool's

Glistening but worthless pyrites, the "fool's gold" brought back in tons from the Northwest Passage by Frobisher

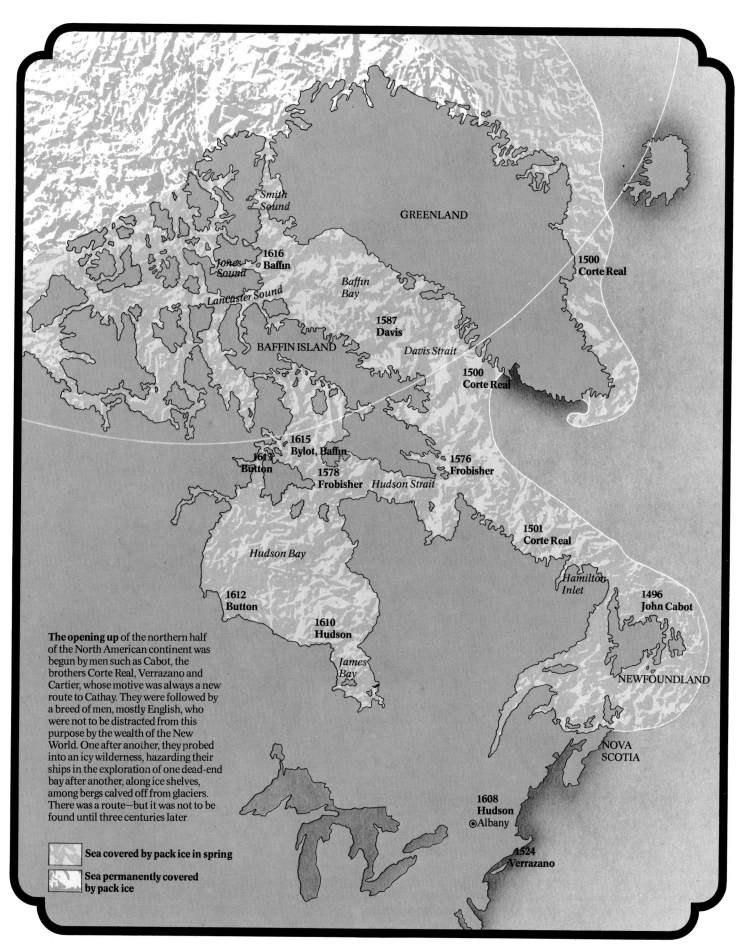

GREENLAND

Smith
Sound

1616
Baffin

Jones
Sound

Baffin
Bay

Lancaster Sound

1587
Davis

Davis Strait

1500
Corte Real

1500
Corte Real

BAFFIN ISLAND

1615
Bylot, Baffin

1613
Button

1578
Frobisher

1576
Frobisher

Hudson Strait

1501
Corte Real

Hudson Bay

Hamilton
Inlet

1612
Button

1610
Hudson

1496
John Cabot

James
Bay

NEWFOUNDLAND

The opening up of the northern half of the North American continent was begun by men such as Cabot, the brothers Corte Real, Verrazano and Cartier, whose motive was always a new route to Cathay. They were followed by a breed of men, mostly English, who were not to be distracted from this purpose by the wealth of the New World. One after another, they probed into an icy wilderness, hazarding their ships in the exploration of one dead-end bay after another, along ice shelves, among bergs calved off from glaciers. There was a route—but it was not to be found until three centuries later

NOVA
SCOTIA

1608
Hudson
⊙Albany

1524
Verrazano

☐ **Sea covered by pack ice in spring**

☒ **Sea permanently covered
by pack ice**

Frobisher and fool's gold

gold", he sailed home, arriving at London on October 9 where "he and his crew were joyfully received with the great admiration of the people, bringing with them their strange man and his boat, which was such a wonder unto the whole city and to the rest of the realm that heard of it". The Eskimo died soon after, of pneumonia.

The pyrites that Frobisher brought back was assessed in such a way that he was appointed High Admiral of all seas and waters, countries, lands and isles, as well as of Cathay as of all other countries and places of new discovery. No such expensive jurisdiction had been conferred on an explorer since Columbus.

"The hope of the same gold ore to be found, kindles a greater opinion in the hearts of many to advance the voyage again", and it was with gold rather than the Northwest Passage in mind, that Frobisher's second expedition sailed from Blackwall on May 25, 1577.

This time he had a large ship, the *Aid*, of 200 tons, two smaller vessels and a company that included gentlemen of good family, soldiers, sappers and miners and some criminals whom someone, not Frobisher, had put aboard. They were to be set ashore in Friesland (Greenland) to "civilize" the inhabitants. And there was a young man named John White who painted in watercolours the first European pictures of the Eskimo and who later became one of the first

settlers in Virginia, where he also recorded his vivid impressions of the country and the people.

After putting ashore at Harwich the six criminals and other "proper men, which with unwilling minds departed", Frobisher attempted to land in Greenland, which he reached on July 4, in 60.30N. On the way there he met some English fishermen on their way home who took letters for him, and saw "many monstrous fish and strange fowls". On July 17 he anchored in a sound which he named after the Countess of Warwick, the wife of one of his patrons.

Hostile Eskimoes

Here, in order to have some hostages to exchange for his five missing men, he tried to seize some Eskimoes who, at first friendly, had become hostile.

Apart from collecting "about two hundred tun" of worthless ore which two German assayers in London somehow came to the conclusion contained sufficient gold and silver to make further mining a worthwhile proposition, the expedition accomplished little. It took with it to England three Eskimoes and a "sea unicorn's tusk, two yards long, growing out of the snout or nostrils wreathed and straight, like in fashion to a taper made of wax", which Frobisher presented to the Queen. It was a narwhal's tusk.

Nothing more was heard of the five men (although some of their clothes were found

in the Eskimo tents) until 1861, when an American explorer, Charles Hall, who stayed with the Baffin Island Eskimoes for two years, heard from an old woman that long ago "Kodlunas" (white men) had come there in three successive years—and that five of them, captured by her tribe, had tried to build a boat with timber left behind by the white men, and had frozen to death.

In Bristol, when Frobisher eventually arrived, the assessment of the ore showed that a profit of five pounds a ton might be expected and this inspired the Cathay Company to send him out again, this time with 15 ships carrying a prefabricated house and sufficient miners and soldiers to colonize the *Meta Incognita*.

He sailed from Harwich at the end of May 1578 and on July 3 arrived at the entrance to the "Strait", but was unable to enter it because it was choked with ice. Then fog closed down over his fleet, followed by a violent southeasterly gale which rose when they were "compassed on every side by ice". By a miracle they escaped destruction and when the sun came out on July 7 a meridional altitude showed that they were in 62.10N; but by the evidence of their eyes, no longer in the strait, but another.

Two ships had taken shelter in Countess of Warwick Sound before the onset of the gale and another, with the portable house on board, had been lost, although its crew was saved. Frobisher with the remaining 12 men

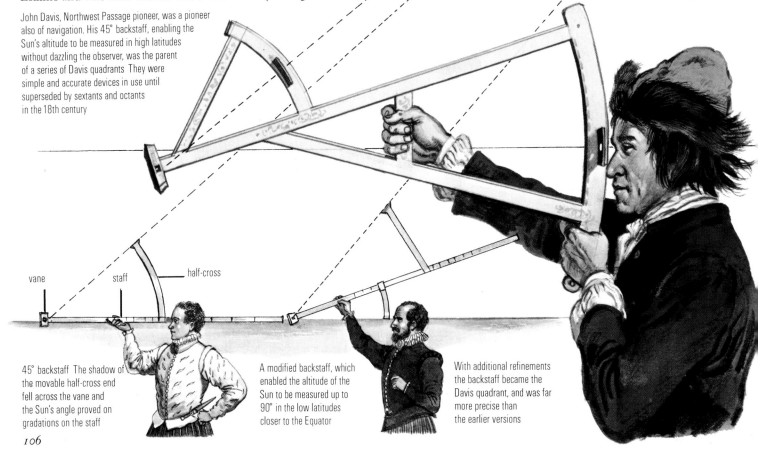

John Davis, Northwest Passage pioneer, was a pioneer also of navigation. His 45° backstaff, enabling the Sun's altitude to be measured in high latitudes without dazzling the observer, was the parent of a series of Davis quadrants They were simple and accurate devices in use until superseded by sextants and octants in the 18th century

vane   staff   half-cross

45° backstaff The shadow of the movable half-cross end fell across the vane and the Sun's angle proved on gradations on the staff

A modified backstaff, which enabled the altitude of the Sun to be measured up to 90° in the low latitudes closer to the Equator

With additional refinements the backstaff became the Davis quadrant, and was far more precise than the earlier versions

sailed up what he called "The Mistaken Strait" for 20 days, most of the time in fog, before turning back.

In it they encountered "a swifter course of flood than before time they had observed. And truly it was wonderful to hear and see the rushing and noise that the tides do make in this place, with so violent a force that our ships lying a hull, were turned sometimes round about . . . after the manner of a whirl-pool."

Frobisher and his ships were in the Hudson Strait, the 430-mile-long channel separating Labrador on the Canadian mainland from Baffin Island in which, as the *Arctic Pilot* says, "the tidal streams . . . attain a great velocity, especially at the eastern . . . and at the western end . . . and the ice is whirled about them in every direction, making it dangerous for a vessel becoming entangled by it". The sequel of this expedition was disastrous: the 1,350 tons of stone Frobisher brought back, which defied even the most indefatigable smelter to extract anything resembling precious metal, led to much recrimination and the winding up of the Cathay Company, which lost £20,000 of shareholders' money. Frobisher, however, emerged unscathed to become vice-admiral in Drake's expedition to the Spanish West Indies in 1586. He covered himself with glory in the Channel against the Spanish Armada in 1588 and was knighted for it. Finally, after a life of action, he died of a wound received in an expedition against Brest in 1594.

I N 1585, JOHN DAVIS, son of a yeoman farmer near Dartmouth and a neighbour of the Gilbert brothers and their half brother Sir Walter Raleigh, sailed from Dartmouth with two ships for the Northwest Passage. They were the *Sunshine*, 50 tons, and the *Moonshine*, a smaller vessel, the total complement being 27 men, including four musicians.

Davis had the powerful backing of the Gilbert brothers; Sir Francis Walsingham, who had been chief of the secret service and was now Secretary to Queen Elizabeth's Privy Council; John Dee, mathematician, necromancer and traveller (one of whose multifarious activities was the drawing up of hydrographical and geographical descriptions of newly discovered countries for the Queen) and William Sanderson, a London merchant, who provided the money.

Sailing from Dartmouth on June 7, he was held up in the Scilly Isles until June 28 and raised the east coast of Greenland just north of Cape Farewell (which he named) and the coast in the same latitudes on the west coast which he called, with reason, The Land of Desolation, "the most deformed

rocky and mountainous land we ever saw".

Doubling Cape Farewell, which is over 2,000 feet high and often hemmed in by drift ice encircling it up to 160 miles out to sea, he found land in 64.15N a complex of fjords, islands and skerries, the abode of eider duck and full of driftwood brought there by the polar current. He named the fjord in which the present town of Godthåb stands Gilbert Sound.

Davis now sailed across the strait which bears his name, finding the eastern extremity of Baffin Island in 66.40N, naming Cape Dyer and Exeter Sound and entering Cumberland Sound, which has mountains rising to 8,000 feet on its north side. "We had great hopes of a very fair entrance or passage . . . altogether void of any pester of ice, and the water of the very colour, nature, and quality of the main ocean, which gave us the greater hope of our passage."

Bad weather and the lateness of the season stopped further exploration and he returned to Dartmouth on September 30, believing that Exeter Sound was the entrance to the Northwest Passage.

He sailed again the following spring financed by the merchants of Exeter, with two extra vessels, the *Mermaid* and a pinnace, the *North Star*. The *Sunshine* and *North Star* were sent under Captain Pope to try and force a passage to 80N between Greenland and Iceland, but failed. Davis with the other two ships again reached Gilbert Sound, where they put on a show of English country dancing for the Eskimoes and played them at football, "and our men did cast them down as soon as they did come to strike the ball". They examined the coast "finding ten miles within the snowy mountains, a plain champion country, with earth and grass such as our moory and waste grounds of England are".

The stinging "muskyto"

With a kidnapped Eskimo on board, they now sailed to Sukkert in 66.33N, along a coast behind which a seemingly endless chain of snow peaks hemmed in the great ice cap, and found a harbour ". . . very hot . . . and were very much troubled by a fly which is called muskyto, for they did sting grievously".

This was an Eskimo settlement, Kangamuit (Old Sukkertoppen), where the coast is entirely obliterated by ice which, on reaching the shore, breaks off and forms icebergs. Here the *Mermaid*, which had a sick crew, was sent home and Davis went on alone in the *Moonshine* "as God should direct me", making Baffin Island to the westward near Exeter Sound, then sailing south passing the Cape of God's Mercy (now Cape Mercy) on the southern extremity of the north coast of Cumberland Sound. For some reason he did

not enter it. He then sailed to the coast of Labrador, where he took on a great quantity of salted cod and sealskins and arrived at Ratcliffe on the Thames on October 6, all the other ships having already arrived except the pinnace, which was lost.

The Exeter merchants failed to support the third voyage, which set off on May 19, 1587, with three ships, the *Sunshine* belonging to Sanderson, the *Elizabeth* and the *Ellen*, a clinker-built pinnace. To ensure some tangible return two of the ships were to fish while Davis was to do the exploring in the other.

On June 16 they again came to anchorage in 64N—probably in Gilbert Sound—where the Eskimoes were angered by the captain of the *Sunshine*, who was stupid enough to kidnap one of them. Here, on June 21, the ships separated; two making for the west side of Davis Strait, where they were supposed to fish and wait for Davis but did not. Davis himself in the *Ellen*, the pinnace, sailed north in a "free and open sea", the weather very warm, seeing land on either side of the strait in 67N, which made him think that he was in a gulf, bartering with Eskimoes at Disco Island in 69N lying off the most magnificent coast in western Greenland. He reached his highest latitude on July 30 beyond 72N, "the sea all open to the westwards and northwards".

With the wind shifting to the north Davis was forced to sail west, encountering a lot of ice and making landfall on Baffin Island, where he sighted Mount Raleigh, a high, pyramidal mountain on the north side of Exeter Sound. Sailing south, touching the coast at various points, according to his traverse book for that day, "we crossed over the mouth of a great inlet or passage, being twenty leagues broad, and situated between 62 and 63 degrees. In which place we had eight or nine great races, currents or overfalls, loathsomely crying like the rage of waters under London Bridge, and bending their course into the said gulf." The next day, "at noon, coming close by a foreland or great cape, we fell into a mighty race, where an island of ice was carried by the force of the current as fast as the bark could sail with lum winds, all sails bearing . . . this cape . . . the most Southerly limit of the gulf . . . where at our great admiration we saw the sea falling down into the gulf with a mighty overfall, and roaring, and the divers circular motions like whirlpools". This was the mouth of the Hudson Strait and after naming Cape Chidley, the northernmost point of Labrador, he set a course for England, on the way being chased by a Biscayan ship on the Grand Banks, arriving at Dartmouth on September 15. On his return he wrote: "I have been in 73 degrees, finding the sea all open, and fifty leagues between land and land. The passage most

Hudson, Bylot and Baffin

probable, the execution easy, as at my coming you shall fully know."

He was a great navigator whose discoveries were incorporated in the Molyneux globes, and the author of two books, one on the Northwest Passage, *The Worldes Hydrographical Discription*, the other a navigational manual, *The Seaman's Secrets*. He was the originator, too, of the Davis quadrant, a backstaff used for observing the altitude of the Sun. This worthy seaman took part in later voyages of exploration, one of which found the Falkland Islands. He was killed off Singapore by Japanese pirates in 1605.

THE TRAGIC END of Henry Hudson, cast adrift, like Bligh, by his men in the icy waters of the great bay which now bears his name, is perhaps the best-known story of the early search for the Northwest Passage. His story is that of a man whose courage was undoubted and whose skill as a navigator was unquestioned. But it is the story, too, of a man of human frailties. The poignancy of his legend owes much to an oft-reproduced painting which shows him, with his small son's head in his lap, cast adrift in a longboat.

An Englishman who had earned his reputation in the service of his country's Muscovy Company, Hudson had already carried out a number of northerly voyages on behalf of the Dutch and—for them, also—reached the site of what is now New York and sailed into the river which, like the northern bay, now bears his name. This journey led to the establishment by the Dutch of a fur trading post at Albany, and the founding by them of New Amsterdam in 1625. His last expedition in 1610, the one for which he is principally remembered, was once again in the interests of his native country. His purpose in sailing northwest was: "To try if, through any of those inlets which Davis saw but durst not enter, any passage which might be found to the other ocean called the South Sea." With him was Robert Bylot, who eventually brought Hudson's ship, the *Discovery*, safely back to England.

On the outward passage they saw Mount Hecla in eruption, the 5,579-foot-high volcano near the southern point of Iceland, "which cast out fire, a sign of foul weather to come in short time"; raised the east coast of Greenland on June 4, in 64N, "... very mountainous, and full of round hills, like to sugar loaves, covered with snow"; doubled Cape Farewell; passed Desolation Land on June 15; and nine days later entered the strait that now bears his name.

Sailing into it, Hudson sighted and named Cape Hope's Advance on the western point of Ungarva Bay in north Labrador, the Islands of God's Mercy (the Savage Islands)

and, on August 2, the Foreland on Salisbury's Island, an island with cliffs from 500 to 1,000 feet high, at the northwestern end of the strait, in 63N, 77W.

"We ran from them west-southwest fourteen leagues", Hudson wrote in his *Journal*, "in the midway of which we were suddenly come into a great and whirling sea. . . . Thence sailing west and by south seven leagues farther we were in the mouth of a straight and sounded, and no ground at one hundred fathoms." Now they sailed south and entered the 480,000 square miles of Hudson Bay, calling it "the Bay of God's great mercies" and following its eastern side as far south as James Bay, about 500 miles from the entrance.

Hudson's *Journal* ends abruptly on August 3 when his ship was in 61.20N. Thereafter one of the few records is that of Abacuck Prickett, who was one of the company.

They seem to have passed the winter in the southeastern corner of James Bay, where their ship was frozen in on November 10, supplementing their slender rations with partridge and, when the weather improved, swans, geese and duck as the birds moved northwards.

Mutiny

As the ice began to break up the ship was freed. It was now that the crew mutinied. They believed, with some reason, that Hudson had been helping himself to the stores and they put him, his son John and seven others away in a shallop (a rowing boat, possibly with a lug sail) with "a piece, and powder, and shot, and some pikes, an iron pot, with some meal, and some other things". Then with the shallop in tow, they stood out of the ice "and so (when they were nigh out, for I cannot say they were clean out) they cut her head fast from the stern of our ship, then out with their top-sails, and towards the east they stood in a clear sea" leaving Hudson and his companions to a miserable death.

In Hudson's cabin, according to Prickett, "we found two hundred of biscuit cakes, a peck of meal, of beer to the quantity of a butt, one with another". It was a bad business. The survivors, after suffering great privation, arrived in Bere Haven, on the southwest coast of Ireland.

IN 1612, the Company of Merchants of London Discoverers of the Northwest Passage was formed for it was believed that Hudson had actually discovered the Passage.

The Company sent out Sir Thomas Button, a naval captain who was later to become an admiral, and Captain Ingram with two ships, the *Resolution* and Hudson's *Discovery*. Button succeeded in reaching the mouth of Nelson's River on the west side of the bay in

57.10N, naming it after the master of his ship, who died there, and there he and his crews spent a long, hard winter.

In 1615, Robert Bylot—he who had sailed with Hudson—Button and Gibbons left the Thames on April 16 in the now veteran *Discovery*. With him, as chief pilot, was William Baffin, an experienced navigator of the calibre of Davis.

They entered Hudson Strait where Baffin meticulously delineated the coasts, taking sights (he tried for the first time to establish longitude by means of lunar distance) and noting the set of the currents. The excellent map he made is still in existence. At the end of June they raised Salisbury Island (first sighted by Hudson in 1610) and reached Cape Comfort on the northwestern coast of Southampton Island in 65.5N, 83W, so naming it because of the renewed hope that they now had of finding the Passage.

It was not fulfilled, "the further we proceeded the more ice and shoaler water, with small show of any tide". They concluded correctly that they were in a cul-de-sac and turned back.

In 1616, Baffin, having expressed his opinion to the Company that the Passage would not be attained by way of Hudson Strait, the two men set off again in the *Discovery*, this time to try to reach it by the Davis Strait, which Davis himself had believed to be the way to it.

They sailed on May 26, reaching Davis's extreme northerly point, Sanderson's Hope, on the west coast of Greenland, at the end of June, and their northernmost point on an ice-bound coast, the entrance to Smith Sound, in 78N. This in fact turned out to be the way to the Polar Sea, but it was not explored until 1852. At Smith Sound they had to run to the west before a heavy gale and then, turning south, passed the entrances to Jones and Lancaster sounds. Both lead out to the Polar Sea and the Bering Strait, and the Lancaster Sound was finally navigated by Parry in 1819.

They were disappointed in what they found. None of these three sounds seemed to allow enough sea room for sailing ships engaged in regular trading, and there was a lot of ice in them. Bylot and Baffin were looking for something which did not exist—a much larger strait—and Baffin reported to the Company that in his opinion it was useless to continue the search. This was Baffin's last voyage to the Arctic, but the search for a northwest passage continued—in vain.

What the later expeditions did find, however, by their exploration of Hudson Bay and its approaches, was a way into Canada other than by the French-controlled St Lawrence River, giving the English access to the fur-producing regions of the north and west.

The Northeast Passage

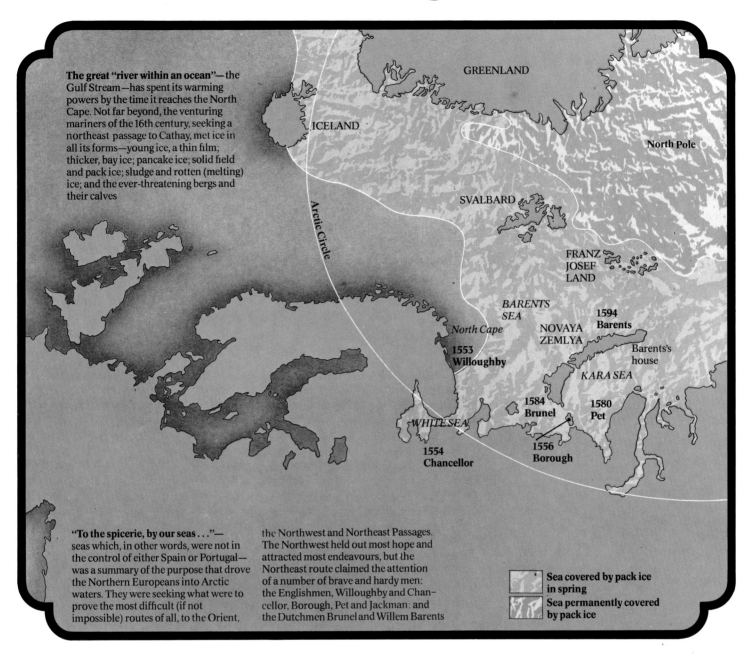

The great "river within an ocean"—the Gulf Stream—has spent its warming powers by the time it reaches the North Cape. Not far beyond, the venturing mariners of the 16th century, seeking a northeast passage to Cathay, met ice in all its forms—young ice, a thin film; thicker, bay ice; pancake ice; solid field and pack ice; sludge and rotten (melting) ice; and the ever-threatening bergs and their calves

GREENLAND

ICELAND

North Pole

SVALBARD

FRANZ JOSEF LAND

BARENTS SEA

1594 Barents

Arctic Circle

North Cape

NOVAYA ZEMLYA

Barents's house

1553 Willoughby

KARA SEA

1584 Brunel

1580 Pet

WHITE SEA

1556 Borough

1554 Chancellor

"To the spicerie, by our seas…"—seas which, in other words, were not in the control of either Spain or Portugal—was a summary of the purpose that drove the Northern Europeans into Arctic waters. They were seeking what were to prove the most difficult (if not impossible) routes of all, to the Orient,

the Northwest and Northeast Passages. The Northwest held out most hope and attracted most endeavours, but the Northeast route claimed the attention of a number of brave and hardy men: the Englishmen, Willoughby and Chancellor, Borough, Pet and Jackman: and the Dutchmen Brunel and Willem Barents

☐ Sea covered by pack ice in spring
☐ Sea permanently covered by pack ice

A S COMPETENT AND BRAVE explorers sailed into one icy dead-end after another in vain attempts to find a northwest passage, so there were others, seeking the other northerly route, around Norway's North Cape. Little was known of this, the Arctic northeast; but perhaps a little more was known about it than the northwest. In 1496, two Russians, Gregory Istoma and an envoy named David, had sailed round the north of Norway using light boats that could be carried overland and by this time Russians, Karelians and Norwegians were probably making fairly regular voyages into the White Sea.

On May 10, 1533, three ships—the *Bona Esperanza*, *Bona Confidentia* and *Edward Bonaventure*—sailed from the Thames under the command of Sir Hugh Willoughby, with Richard Chancellor as "pilot-major", for

"Cathay, and divers other regions, dominions, Islands and places unknown".

A violent storm having separated Chancellor's *Edward Bonaventure* from the other two off the Varanger Fjord on the north coast of Norway, Chancellor was driven eastwards in the Barents Sea, sighting land in 72N—probably Goose Land, the southwestern part of the Novaya Zemlya islands.

Encountering ice, Willoughby's ships took refuge in the mouth of the Varzina River on the barren, rugged Murman coast of the Kola Peninsula, about 150 miles east of Murmansk.

In October the following year some Russian fishermen found the two ships frozen in the ice. On board there were some corpses, and in the *Bona Esperanza*, Willoughby's flagship, they found the commander's journal.

Apparently, intending to spend the winter there, he first sent out three expeditions in search of help, but they found no living thing and he and his crews died a slow death from cold and starvation.

Chancellor, in the *Edward Bonaventure*, was luckier. He succeeded in sailing southwest from the Barents Sea into the White Sea, reached the site of Archangel, which was established as a trading place as a result of his visit, and set off for Moscow with some of his officers by horse sledge. He met Emperor Ivan IV (The Terrible) and succeeded in arranging for trading to begin between England and Russia. He sailed for home in 1554, and, as a result of his voyages, in 1555, Sebastian Cabot formed the "Mystery and Company of Merchant Venturers for the discovery of Regions, Dominions, Islands

The Northeast Passage

and places unknown", otherwise the Muscovy Company. The following year Chancellor was drowned while returning from Russia.

In April 1556 the Company, with its sights set on the East, sent out Richard Borough, who had been master of the *Edward Bonaventure* on the 1553 voyage. In a small vessel, the *Searchthrift*, he reached the North Cape at the end of May, followed the coast to the Kola River and from there, in company with some Russian fishermen, reached the Pechora River on the Barents Sea in 52.20E and on July 31 was "at an anker among the Islands of Vaigats" (Vaygach Island, between Novaya Zemlya and the mainland).

Now, "because of the continual Northeast and Northerly winds . . . great and terrible abundance of ice . . . [and] because the nights waxed dark, and the winter began to draw on with his storms", he decided to turn back.

Nearly 25 years passed after Borough's voyage before another English attempt was made to force a sea passage. Then, in 1580, the Muscovy Company commissioned Arthur Pet of Ratcliffe and Charles Jackman of Poplar, both captains from Thameside districts of London, to sail to the northeast.

They left Harwich on June 1, lost contact with one another after passing the North Cape and after sailing separate courses on which Pet discovered the Proliv Yugorskiy Shar (strait) between Vaygach Island and the mainland, which was to be the scene of desperate efforts by the Dutch to pass through it 15 years later, they came together again and entered the Kara Sea, either by it or through the Kara Strait which separates Vaygach from Novaya Zemlya and is often blocked with ice throughout the summer. Whichever strait they used they met impassable ice in the Kara Sea and were forced to return.

THE DUTCH TOO took an active interest in opening up a northeast route to the East, a route unencumbered by Portuguese and Spaniards. The man chiefly responsible for developing trade between Holland and the White Sea was Olivier Brunel. He also made voyages eastwards, reaching the Kostin Shar, a strait on the southwest coast of Novaya Zemlya.

His last recorded voyage was in 1584 from Enkhuizen, a port in Holland as famous in the history of discovery as Sagres in Portugal, in the course of which he lost his ship with a cargo of furs on the shoals at the mouth of the Pechora River.

In 1594, inspired by Peter Plancius, a brilliant geographer who was also a churchman, three ships and a Terschelling fishing boat were fitted out with the financial help of Dutch merchants, eager to channel their wealth into the northeast venture.

With them sailed Willem Barents, Cornelis Nai, Brant Tergales and Jan Huyghen van Linschoeten, who had lived in the Indies and was a great authority on eastern trade.

The fleet split up on reaching the Murman coast, according to Plancius's plan: Barents, who was to earn undying fame, to sail to the west coast of Novaya Zemlya and attempt to enter the Kara Sea through the Yugorskiy Shar, which is only 20 miles long and from one and a half to seven miles wide and in places not more than seven fathoms deep.

A little-known coast

Barents sailed on June 29 and on July 4 reached the 600-mile-long coastline of the Novaya Zemlya islands at Sukhoi Nos (point) in 76.15N, then sailing north along the coast that the *Arctic Pilot* of 1918 was still able to refer to as "little known", with high, snow-covered mountains looming on his starboard hand, above glacier-filled valleys— a land where even lichens find difficulty in existing, shunned by even the mosquitoes which in summer made the tundra of the mainland a hell.

On July 10 he reached Cape Nassau, in 75.15N, and on the night of July 15 the ship ran into the ice, "a great store of ice, as much as they could descry out of the top, that lay as if it had been a plain field . . ."

On July 24 he was off the northern point of the island in 77N, where the land is low-lying and covered by an immense ice sheet, and this he called Great Ice Cape.

On August 3 he discovered the Orange Islands off the northwest tip, but was able to go no farther, his men being reluctant to continue.

Sailing south he passed the entrance to the Matochkin Shar, the tortuous strait little more than a mile wide, hemmed in by snow peaks and glaciers, that divides Novaya Zemlya into two and links the Barents with the Kara Sea, 56 miles to the east. On August 15 Barents met the other captains off Vaygach Island. They had managed to pass through the Yugorskiy Shar, naming it Nassau Strait, and into the Kara Sea; and had then sailed about 200 miles to the east-southeast reaching the mouth of a river, perhaps the Kara, in 65E, which they believed to be the Ob and near the extreme north of Asia at the end of the Northeast Passage. They reached Holland in September.

Barents had shown himself the most determined member of the 1595 expedition, and when a second (not led by him) failed, another was despatched in May 1596 from Vlieland near Amsterdam, Barents sailing as chief pilot in the ship commanded by Jacob van Heemskerck, the other ship being captained by Jan Corneliszoon Rijp.

This time they sailed farther to the west and on June 9 discovered Bear Island, between North Cape and Spitzbergen, the cliffs of which teem with sea-birds and on the south side plunge 1,300 feet sheer to the sea.

Sailing north, they reached the ice pack on June 16 and, journeying along the edge of it, raised the ice-bound northwest coast of Spitzbergen in 80.10N, coasting the mouths of its western fjords—which are free from ice in the summer because of the warm Atlantic currents—reached Bear Island on July 1, where the ships separated, their captains differing about the proper course to take: Rijp sailing to the north of Spitzbergen, which he failed to round to the eastwards; Heemskerck and Barents to Novaya Zemlya, passing the Great Ice Cape and doubling Mys Zelanija (Cape Mauritius), the extreme northeast point of the island.

From here they attempted to sail down the east coast of Vaygach Island, but were unable to do so because of the ice. On August 26 they entered Ice Inlet, in 76.10N, 68.15E where their ship was beset, the pressure of the ice on the hull "most fearful both to see and hear, and made all the hair of our heads to rise upright with fear".

The Golden Age of Dutch maritime power had lowly origins—the herring trade of the North Sea. As herring became an increasingly popular food and valuable export commodity, more salt for pickling and timber for casks and ships were needed from abroad. Thus Dutch merchant trade expanded, and the longer trips and need to process fish on board called for a new type of ship with more deck and storage space—the herring buss with its characteristic square rig and "double-ended" hull

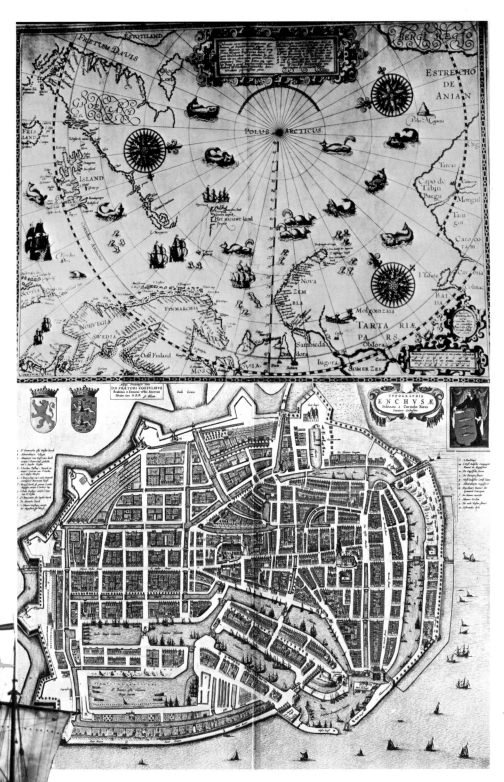

On September 11 they found driftwood on the coast of this treeless land. With it, wrote the chronicler of their stay, Gerrit de Veer, they built a house in which "we were forced in great cold, poverty, misery, and grief, to stay the winter".

A contemporary illustration shows the interior: a sick man lies close to the fire; a great barrel serves as a bath tub against vermin; the lamps are fed with polar bear fat (the liver made them sick when the men ate it); there is a Dutch clock on the wall and an hour-glass on the table; the men sleep in bunks. Another shows the outdoors, where they trapped foxes and shot bear until, with the approach of the polar night, the bears moved southwards. The men suffered terribly from scurvy, one being Barents himself.

On January 24, 1597, they saw the Sun again for the first time and in April played golf "thereby to stretch our joints", finally sailing on June 13 in two open ship's boats, bound for Holland by way of the Great Ice Cape, through the still abundant drift ice.

The house was not seen again until three centuries later, in 1871, when Elling Carlsen, a Norwegian fisherman, found it still standing, and a number of relics, including the clock and a powder horn with Barents's report of the expedition's experiences inside it. Seven days after setting out, while the boats were hauled out on the ice, Barents announced that he was about to die: "'Gerrit, give me some drink', he said, and he had no sooner drunk but he was taken with so sudden a qualm that he turned his eyes in his head and died presently.... The death of Willem Barents put us in no small discomfort, as being the chief guide and only pilot on whom we reposed ourselves next under God; but we could not strive against God, and therefore we must of force be content."

The survivors kept alive by taking seabirds and their eggs. On July 28 they met two Russian ships at the south end of the island and then they found "lepel leaves" (scurvy grass), which restored them to health.

From here they made their way to Kola, on the Lapland coast, where they found three Dutch ships, one of them under the command of Jan Rijp; after being fed and given good strong Swedish beer the 13 survivors arrived in Amsterdam in November 1597.

Barents was perhaps the greatest and most indomitable of all the Dutch explorers. He and his company were the first Europeans to survive a winter in such high latitudes. Like so many other explorers they did not reach their goal, but what they learned about the waters in which they sailed gave their countrymen encouragement to trade with Russia on a large scale and to send their fishing and whaling fleets to the far north.

A 17th-century view of Enkhuizen, one of the leading and most prosperous fishing ports of the time, by the Dutch cartographer Joan Blaeu. The important part played in the town's economy by herring is symbolized by its coat of arms—a fisherwoman with three fish. The wealth derived from the herring trade was soon channelled into greater ventures—the quest for a northeast route to China. One of the town's most famous citizens was the traveller van Linschoeten, who had served in the east with the Portuguese and who did much to encourage Dutch competition. It was in his great atlas of 1596 that the map (top) first appeared. Drawn by Willem Barents, it shows the coasts bordering the icy northern waters where he and his men were marooned for a long, cruel winter and where Barents was to die. It is the first map to incorporate all the regions newly discovered by the English and Dutch in their search for a northeast passage. It is also the first map of the Arctic regions to dispense with the mythical Arctic continent which had appeared in earlier maps.

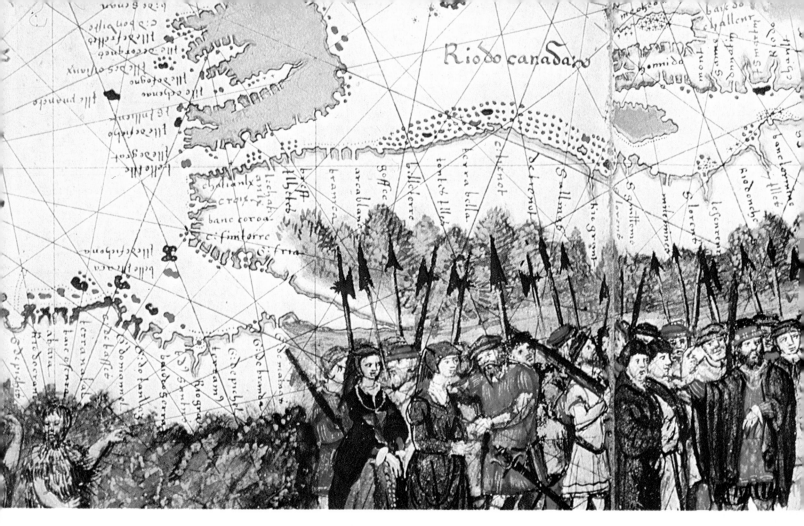

The French find their 'Terres Neufves'

THE EXPLORATION AND conquest of Middle America during the first half of the 16th century was the province entirely of men from the Iberian Peninsula sailing from ports at the southwestern extremity of Europe. Once the search had begun for more northerly routes to wealth, new breeds of men, standing out from new home ports, entered the story. The search for northwest and northeast passages, described in earlier pages, only marginally involved the Iberians—the Corte Real brothers were Portuguese. For the rest, the exploration of the chill and foggy waters was carried out by northern men in northern ships, sailing from northern ports and backed by northern money. Cabot and Verrazano were, admittedly, Italians, but they were hired by the crowns of England and France.

In the course of his voyage in 1498, John Cabot had struck upon the first hint of the riches that were waiting to be exploited by those whose eyes were not dazzled by the riches of the east. He found the Grand Banks, off the Newfoundland coast, where fish swam in shoals almost as dense as the weed of the Sargasso Sea. Within a few years English and French fishing boats were reaping the harvest of these, the richest of maritime pastures. It was soon found that the catch of cod survived the long journey

back to the markets of Europe if it was dried and lightly salted, instead of being taken "green" and heavily salted. Fishing stations sprang up along the Newfoundland shores, where the fish were dried on racks and stored. At these small "factories", or processing plants, English and French fishermen came into increasing contact with the native population of Indians—and with a second, equally important commodity that in subsequent centuries was to be, with fish, one of the two staples of the Canadian economy; this was fur, mostly the fur of the beaver, which the Indians, who had little else to offer, were prepared to trade for the metal edge-tools and weapons of the white man.

Difficult to settle

If the stony, fir-clad countryside was unwelcoming to settlement on a permanent basis, there were ample reasons for hardy adventurers to seek a fortune and they were to be found mostly among the French, during the next two centuries. One by one, small groups of them moved inland, almost always using the lakes and waterways that abound in northern North America, adopting the techniques of the natives for survival, hunting and transport. Champlain, one of the most famous names in French–Canadian history, was one of the first to advocate the use

of the spruce and birch-bark Indian canoes with which, he said "one may travel freely and quickly throughout the country", adding, optimistically, "a man may see all that there is to be seen, good and bad, within the space of a year or two".

Just as it was the anonymous fishermen of the Grand Banks who—as it were—opened the door to the storehouse of furs in their trade with the Indians, so it was largely anonymous individuals who provided the basic knowledge of the interior of North America. These were the hardy *coureurs de bois*—literally wood-runners—whose grasp of the ways of the Indian and knowledge of lake and forest travel paved the way for the men whose names now stud any gazetteer of North American towns—Duluth, Joliet, La Salle, Marquette.

At the heart of all French achievement in North America in the 16th and 17th centuries lay the fur trade. In the long term it was one of the fundamental causes of France losing all it had gained in North America—where settlement takes place, forests and forest animals are diminished. The fur monopolists preferred to build trading posts and forts rather than to settle communities which would eat into their monopolies. The result was that west of the St Lawrence the French Empire was little more than a series of trading

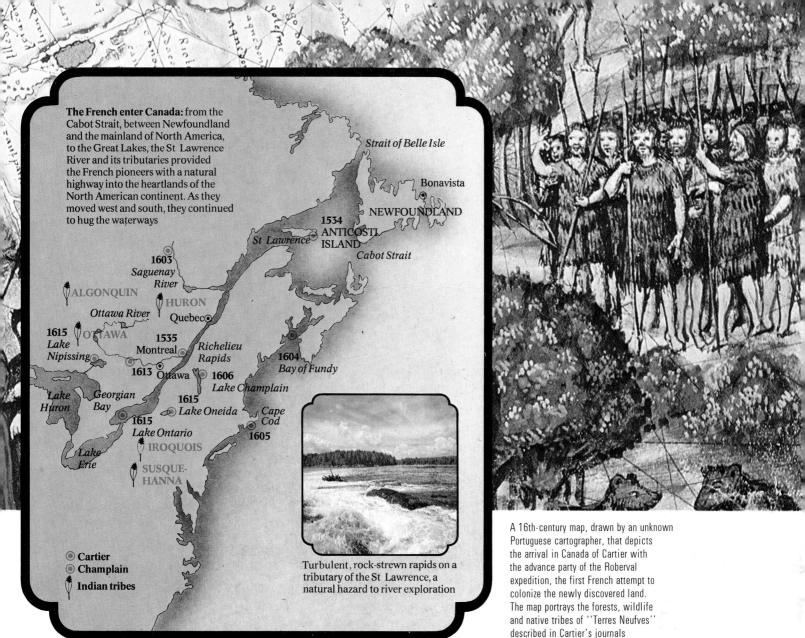

The French enter Canada: from the Cabot Strait, between Newfoundland and the mainland of North America, to the Great Lakes, the St Lawrence River and its tributaries provided the French pioneers with a natural highway into the heartlands of the North American continent. As they moved west and south, they continued to hug the waterways

Strait of Belle Isle

Bonavista

NEWFOUNDLAND

1534
ANTICOSTI
ISLAND

St Lawrence

Cabot Strait

1603
Saguenay
River

ALGONQUIN

HURON

Ottawa River

Quebec

1615
OTTAWA

1535
Montreal

Richelieu
Rapids

Lake
Nipissing

1604
Bay of Fundy

1613 Ottawa

1606
Lake Champlain

Lake
Huron

Georgian
Bay

1615
Lake Oneida

Cape
Cod

1615
Lake Ontario

1605

Lake
Erie

IROQUOIS

SUSQUE-
HANNA

◉ Cartier
◉ Champlain
♟ Indian tribes

Turbulent, rock-strewn rapids on a tributary of the St Lawrence, a natural hazard to river exploration

A 16th-century map, drawn by an unknown Portuguese cartographer, that depicts the arrival in Canada of Cartier with the advance party of the Roberval expedition, the first French attempt to colonize the newly discovered land. The map portrays the forests, wildlife and native tribes of "Terres Neufves" described in Cartier's journals

stations and forts to protect the trade; while to the south and east, along the Atlantic seaboard, the English settlements were developing into successful colonies—and forming the embryo of a new nation.

All this lay ahead of France and its empire in North America when Jacques Cartier, a *maître-pilote* of St Malo—a grim-looking man but a first-class navigator—was given a brief by the French king, the knightly and powerful Francis I, to discover and explore "Terres Neufves". He sailed from St Malo, a citadel-walled Breton port that had already despatched its fishing fleets to the cod fisheries of the Grand Banks. "Terres Neufves" was outside the experience of the rude fishermen on whose knowledge Cartier undoubtedly drew; but his crew of 60 or more, in two ships, probably contained many of these tough Bretons.

Cartier sailed in April 1534 and raised Cape Bonavista, Newfoundland, on May 10. At first held up by the last of the winter ice, he sailed to the north end of the Belle Isle Strait between Newfoundland and Labrador, entering it when the ice cleared, and passed right through it to the south. Examining the coast on either hand, he wrote "if the soil were as good as the harbours, it would be a blessing; but the land should not be called the New Land, being composed of stones and horrible rugged rocks; for along the whole of the north shore [of the Gulf] I did not see one cart-load of earth and yet I landed in many places".

The first Indians

Cartier now crossed the mouth of the Cabot Strait to Prince Edward Island, off the western side of New Brunswick, where he was unable to find a landing place, and entered what he named La Baye de Chaleur, because of the warm climate, on the mainland in which "we had hopes of discovering a strait". North of it, in Gaspé Bay, he saw Indians—"more than 300 persons with some forty canoes . . . we gave them knives, glass beads, combs and other trinkets . . . at which they showed many signs of joy, lifting up their hands to heaven and singing and dancing in their canoes. . . . This people may well be called savages for they are the sorriest folk in the world. . . ."

From here he sailed three-quarters of the way eastwards around the Isle de l'Assumption (Anticosti Island) in the Gulf of St Lawrence, mistaking the southern approaches to the river for a bay. Finding it impossible to overcome the current and headwinds beyond the narrows on the north side of the island "we assembled all the captains, pilots, masters and sailors to have their opinion and advice as to what was best to be done. . . . When these opinions had been heard, we decided by a large majority to return home."

Sailing the same day for the Belle Isle Strait with a strong favourable wind—which became a heavy gale from the east-northeast before they reached it—Cartier put into a bay on the north side of the entrance and remained there for six days, sailing for home on August 15 and reaching St Malo on September 5. Cartier and his men were the first known Europeans to see the great river that for at least two centuries was to be the principal way into the great heartland of Canada and the United States.

His second voyage (1535-6) was undertaken "for the completion of the discovery of

The French find their 'Terres Neufves'

the western lands, lying under the same climate and parallels as the territories and kingdom of that prince [Francis I], and by his orders already begun to be explored". He sailed from St Malo on May 16 with three ships—the *Grande Hermyne* (100–120 tons), *Petite Hermyne* (60 tons) and the *Emerillon*. On the crossing the ships were separated but were reunited at Blanc Sablon, his safe anchorage at the southwestern end of the Belle Isle Strait, on July 26.

They then sailed along the coast through the islands and along what were hereabouts the sterile shores of Quebec province, examining them and not arriving at the mouth of the St Lawrence until August 24.

With two young Huron Indians as their only pilots they set off from Bic Harbour on the south bank, where the river is still 25 miles wide, "to make our way towards Canada"; a name which Cartier reserved for the reaches of the river above Grosse Island, 130 miles upstream. On September 1 they passed the cliffs at the mouth of the Saguenay River, which flows through an amazing fjord-like reach from the west, and encountered shoals and currents which run up to seven knots on the ebb; and on September 10, working the ships up with sweeps, reached "a great island" which he named Ile de Bacchus, because of the great number of vines growing on it (later, he prudently renamed it Ile d'Orléans after Charles, the monarch's son).

Here they were well received by the Hurons who, "made good cheer" and brought them eels, maize (their staple food) and melons, and met Donnaconna, "the Seigneur of Canada", the Huron chief.

Rowing upstream the next day they came to a great rocky promontory more than 300 feet high with a squalid Indian village, Stadacona, huddled at the foot of it. It was to be the site of the future city of Quebec.

On September 19 Cartier with the *Emerillon*, towing two longboats, pressed on upstream. Nine days later, having negotiated the Richelieu Rapids (where the river is only a quarter of a mile wide and runs at five and a half knots) and five other narrow channels—and making only about eight miles a day—he reached Lac St Pierre, about 60 miles downstream from the city of Hochelaga, of which Cartier had heard from the Hurons.

The lake had such a variety of channels flowing into it that Cartier decided to continue the voyage in the longboats, and on September 29, with two of his shipmasters, four gentleman volunteers and 28 sailors, set off towards Hochelaga, which they reached four days later.

Hochelaga, on the site where Montreal was to rise, was a stockaded citadel containing about 50 dwellings of wood and bark and the

house of Donnaconna, the chief, about three miles from the left bank of the river. Here, the French were given a splendid reception by more than a thousand Huron Indians and the following day Cartier climbed a hill, which he named Mont Royal, above the citadel. From its summit he could see the Laurentians and the Adirondacks to the south and the river itself to the west, rendered impassable to anything but canoes by the Lachine Rapids.

From here he returned 140 miles downstream to Quebec, where the whole party spent the winter of 1535-6, from mid-November to mid-April, with their ships frozen deep in the ice, suffering intensely from the cold and ravaged by scurvy, which afflicted Indians and Frenchmen alike. They eventually cured the scurvy with the juice of a tree known as the annedda (*Thuja occidentalis*)—some of the sailors even alleging that it cured the syphilis from which some of them had been suffering for years.

On May 6, 1536, Cartier sailed, taking only the *Grande Hermyne* and the *Emerillon*. His last—and worst—act was the kidnapping of the chief, Donnaconna, whose tales of vast quantities of gold and precious stones to be found in a non-existent region called Saguenay had excited his cupidity. He took with him also a number of other Indians and a small boy and girl, who had been given him as a gift. Reaching the gulf he sailed south of Anticosti Island to Cape Breton Island, across the Cabot Strait to Cape Race in Newfoundland, reaching St Malo on July 16, 1536.

Unsuccessful expedition

It was an important voyage. Not only had Cartier found sites for two extremely important French settlements, but he had discovered that the St Lawrence was not a strait, as he had hoped, but a river.

His third and last expedition, which was a colonizing one, was not a success. It sailed in 1541 with several hundred emigrants, including convicts, of both sexes, and the settlement of Charlebourg-Royal was founded about nine miles upstream from the present site of Quebec. Here, the winter was passed, but the place was untenable and in June 1542 Cartier abandoned it.

After Cartier's last voyage to the St Lawrence in 1541 French exploration in North America had come to a halt, although French fishermen still continued to frequent the offshore waters. The great war between Francis I and Charles V, the Holy Roman Emperor, and the civil wars between the Protestants and the Catholic League, created a situation in which it was impossible to contemplate any sort of overseas expansion.

Through la Salle's voyage down the Mississippi, France added Louisiana to its empire. It became a valuable base for trade

It was not until 1603 that Samuel de Champlain, a member of a seafaring family, set off on the first of the series of expeditions that were to initiate a fresh and intensive phase of colonizing operations.

If Cartier was France's most important pioneer in the New World, Champlain was to be the father of New France, the consolidator of settlements and the architect of the great fur trade. Champlain was to give 30 years of his life to the French dominions in North America, which were firmly established by the time of his death. The blot on his record was the support he gave to the Huron Indians against their enemies, the Iroquois. The outcome was the ultimate slaughter of the Hurons and the siding with the British and Dutch of the powerful Iroquois. Champlain was born in 1567. In 1599 he had sailed to the West Indies and Mexico with a Spanish fleet, writing a very interesting account of his experiences. His voyage from Honfleur in Normandy, in March 1603, was undertaken at the wish of Aymar de Chastes, who had obtained a patent for a colonizing enterprise from King Henry IV. Like James I of England, the French king had found that the most effective way of exploiting the potential of newly discovered lands was to grant monopolies, in which the holders ran the risk of losses.

Champlain reached Hochelaga, the Indian settlement on the St Lawrence visited by Cartier almost 70 years previously, but found only a few Algonquin Indians, failed

A pioneer of inland exploration in North America and an ardent colonizer, Samuel de Champlain firmly established French influence in the New World

to penetrate beyond the St Louis Falls rapids upstream, went some way up the Saguenay River—and returned to France to find that his sponsor, de Chastes, had died.

In April 1604, with the Sieur de Monts, a Calvinist who had secured a monopoly in the trade in furs, Baron de Poutrincourt and a number of Calvinist ministers and Catholic priests, Champlain once again sailed for North America. He reached the coast of Nova Scotia, doubled Cape Sable at the southern end of the peninsula and explored the Bay of Fundy, where de Monts founded a colony, St Croix, on an inlet which now forms part of the border between New Brunswick and Maine. The colony was destroyed by an outbreak of scurvy in 1605. De Poutrincourt founded a similar settlement of small farmers, which was named Port Royal, in the Annapolis basin, an arm of the Bay of Fundy.

After a barren exploration of the coast southwest beyond Cape Cod in 1605, Champlain was sent out from France to the St Lawrence in 1608, where he founded Quebec, building a fort, which commanded the river (here only a mile wide), and three huts, where the lower town now stands. The city was to become the great fur-trading centre of New France (French Canada).

Here he spent the winter establishing good relations with the Indians before setting off with a raiding party of Hurons and Algonquins in the hope of finding a passage to the Pacific. They journeyed up the St Lawrence as far as the head of Lake St Pierre, from which point they paddled 80 miles up the Richelieu River, reaching the long, narrow lake which now bears his name, between the Green Mountains of Vermont and the Adirondacks in New York State.

Here, following the western shore, the Indians reached the stockaded camp of their enemies, the Iroquois, and defeated them with the help of Champlain's firearms (the first the Iroquois had seen or heard). In spite of the assistance given to him by the aristocratic Hurons, Champlain's verdict was that they were "a band of dirty fellows . . . vain men who treated affairs of state with as much sang-froid and gravity as the Junta in Spain, the Council of Sages in Venice or the old men of Sparta" of whom, presumably, he held no high opinion.

In 1611, Champlain established the trading post of Mont Royal near the site of the Indian town of Hochelaga, the farthest point reached by Cartier on his second voyage up the St Lawrence in 1535. Hochelaga had by that time disappeared and Champlain went on to reach the Lachine Rapids, which Cartier had seen from the summit of Mont Royal, the extinct volcano on the slopes of which the city of Montreal now stands and from which it takes its name. On yet another pioneering venture he set off on an extremely difficult journey up the rapids of the Ottawa River in search of a route to the northern sea that had been reported by an imaginative adventurer named Vignan. He got as far as Allumette Island beyond the Chaudière Falls, about 100 miles west-northwest of Ottawa, before he realized that this was not a route to the sea.

In 1615, he again went up the Ottawa, this time taking with him Etienne Brûlé as an interpreter. Brûlé, a young man of 23, had come out from France with Champlain in 1608 and had spent the best part of three years living with the Huron and Algonquin Indians. He had already been to Lake Huron and its huge inlet, Georgian Bay, 400 miles west of Montreal.

First evangelists

Their destination was the Huron territory on the eastern shore of the lake, where Champlain hoped to meet the Huron chiefs and discuss an alliance with them against the Iroquois. Travelling ahead of them was a Recollet Friar, Joseph le Caron, one of the first of many brave evangelists who helped further the cause of France and Catholicism in the New World.

Reaching the Mattawa, a tributary of the Ottawa, they followed it westwards to its source near Lake Nipissing, crossed the lake and followed the French River from its source at the southwestern end to Georgian Bay, reaching the Huron tribal settlements, where le Caron had already started teaching.

From here, in September, Champlain and Brûlé set off with the Hurons on a long-planned raid into the Iroquois country, pushing southwards through a labyrinthine region of lakes and streams to the north shore of Lake Ontario. They followed the shoreline to its eastern end, crossing the St Lawrence where it enters the lake, and then marched 100 miles south to Lake Oneida, north of the present town of Syracuse in New York State, where one of the Iroquois tribes, the Oneida, had a stronghold. The Hurons attempted to fire the stockade but the Oneidas beat them off. Champlain was wounded and had to be carried by the Hurons; the winter was spent retreating and hunting for food. Champlain, who on one occasion was lost for some days in the wilderness, returned to Quebec the following year.

The result of Champlain's alliances with the Algonquins and the Hurons was the alignment of the Iroquois with the Dutch and the English: with the Dutch in 1617, when they made a treaty with Corlear of the Amsterdam Company near Albany in 1617; and with the English in 1664 at what was then called Fort Orange (Albany). Both treaties were scrupulously observed and because of the great power of the Iroquois, French colonial expansion in North America was eventually halted and New France lost to the English.

After his expedition against the Iroquois Champlain devoted himself to the administration of the colony. In 1629 an English fleet sailed up the St Lawrence and captured Quebec, and Champlain was taken as a prisoner to England. He returned to his beloved Canada in 1633 and died in 1635, aged 65. He was a great man, very different in nature to a Conquistador, believing—as he wrote—that only those who would plight themselves body and soul to the country, settle down in it and learn from its first inhabitants, were destined to open up its unknown regions.

Brûlé did not accompany Champlain to Lake Oneida. He went to the Erie country, south of Lake Ontario, wintered there with the Indians and in the spring travelled with them down the Susquehanna River from its source in Lake Otsego in New York State 440 miles to the sea at Chesapeake Bay, passing through the territory of the Seneca Indians.

This was not the end of his astonishing career. In 1616 he was captured and tortured by the Iroquois while travelling northeast from Lake Ontario along the south side of the St Lawrence; and in 1621 he went west to Lake Huron and followed the north side of it to the rapids on St Mary River, which links Huron with Lake Superior. From this point

The French find their 'Terres Neufves'

he may have followed its southern shore from Sault Sainte Marie in Michigan to the site of the present city of Duluth in Minnesota, 1,200 miles from the Atlantic and 1,500 from the Pacific. About 1633 he was boiled and eaten by his friends, the Hurons, at Touanche. He had learned their language, but not enough to read the menu.

Jesuit missionaries began to make their appearance in New France, where the Franciscans had already been long in the field, and shortly before the death of Champlain two of them, Brebeuf and Daniel, travelled westwards to establish a mission among the Hurons.

That same year Jean Nicolet, who had lived among the Algonquins and the Nipissing Indians (from whom he heard of a hairless, beardless people whom he presumed to be Japanese or Chinese living to the west), was sent out by Champlain to find a passage to the "Sea of the West".

Following the Ottawa River route to Lake Huron he set off by canoe with Indian guides and reached the outlet of Lake Superior but, instead of crossing over to it, paddled through the Mackinac Strait into Lake Michigan, round the northern shore and then south to the head of Green Bay, a 100-mile-long inlet on the west side, in modern Wisconsin.

There he met the Winnebago Indians, of whom one of Nicolet's chroniclers wrote: "A sedentary people who are very numerous, whom some of the French call the nation of stinkers because the Algonquin word *ouinipeg* signifies stinking water and they give this name to the water of the salt sea, so that these people are called *Ouinipigou* because they come from the shores of a sea of which we have no knowledge."

Stinkers or not, the Winnebagos must have been vastly impressed by Nicollet's appearance, for he carried with him a ceremonial robe of damask, embroidered with flowers and birds in many colours.

The "Great Water"
Now following the Fox River, which enters the bay at this point, Nicolet went beyond Lake Winnebago where only a short portage separates the headwaters of the Fox from the Wisconsin River on the divide between the St Lawrence and Mississippi river systems. He may have gone even farther. Hearing from the Indians of what they called "The Great Water" (the Mississippi), Nicolet concluded that he was close to the Pacific and had found the route to Japan and China. He returned by way of the south shore of Lake Michigan, passing close to the site of Chicago.

In 1641, two Jesuits, Raymbault and Jogues, travelling west to Sault Sainte Marie,

heard from the Indians there of the existence of the Mississippi River and of the Sioux Indians of the prairies who lived by it. The following year Jogues was captured by Iroquois and taken into their territory by way of the then unknown Lake George, south of Lake Champlain, which the Iroquois called Andiatarocte, "Place where the Lake Narrows". They later released him.

In 1648, warfare broke out between the tribes of the Five Nations (Iroquois) and their neighbours to the north, the Hurons and Algonquins, and until peace was signed in 1653 travel of any kind, whether for commerce in beaver skins or the purpose of evangelization, was equally hazardous. When it was slightly safer to do so, missionaries and

A peaceful stretch of the Mississippi in Iowa. The name comes from the Indian "missi" (great) and "sippi" (river)

the *coureurs de bois* (fur traders with an intimate knowledge of the wilderness and the Indians, whose principal business was collecting parties of them together and guiding them to Montreal) became active; and about that time Father Poncet explored the southern side of Lake Ontario in the Iroquois country, and another Jesuit, Le Moyne went farther south to the Oswego River.

In 1658, the *coureurs de bois* Groseilliers and Pierre Radisson, reached Green Bay, wintered there, and made the portage from the Fox River to the Wisconsin. According to Radisson's journal they reached "a great river", presumably the Mississippi; but this may have been later, when they penetrated westwards along the southern side of Lake Superior and struck southwards through Wisconsin towards the tributaries of the Mississippi.

It was these two men who subsequently persuaded the English (after first approaching their own compatriots, who showed little enthusiasm) to interest themselves in the Hudson Bay region; and two years later one of their comrades called Peré succeeded in

crossing the watershed between it and Lake Superior. The lack of interest by the French in the northern regions around Hudson Bay, and the interest shown by the English in Groseillier and Radisson's suggestions were to play an important part in the diminution and final extinguishing of French power in Canada.

Between 1665 and 1669 a Jesuit, Father Allouez, established missions at Ashland on the southwestern shore of Lake Superior and at Green Bay on Lake Michigan and these became valuable advance bases for further exploration towards the Mississippi.

In 1669, Robert Cavelier Sieur de la Salle, later known as "the Canadian Vauban" because of his skill as a military engineer, set off with two priests, Dollier and Gallivée, sailed along the south shore of Lake Ontario and reached the Niagara River. He heard the roar of the falls, but did not see them. (Champlain had heard of them from the Indians and must take credit for one of the greatest understatements of all time. The falls, he said, were "somewhat high, and where little water flows over".)

Near where Hamilton now stands at the western end of Lake Ontario they met Louis Joliet, who had been sent to find a copper mine near Lake Superior and had come by a new route—by way of Lake Huron, entering Lake Erie by the St Clair and Detroit rivers, and of Lake St Clair at the southern end, then following its north shore eastwards to the mouth of the Grand River, going up it for some distance and then reaching Hamilton overland. After exchanging information with Joliet, la Salle left the two priests and travelled south of Lake Erie, where he may have discovered the Ohio River, the principal eastern tributary of the Mississippi.

In 1671, the energetic Intendant (Governor) Talon, who had sent out Joliet on his original expedition, was replaced by the Comte de Frontenac, and that summer Joliet and Père Marquette went up the Fox River from Green Bay, crossed the divide at the head of it with guides from the Miami tribe, floated down the Wisconsin and after a week emerged from it on to the Mississippi, the great river of North America and the goal that so many explorers had dreamed of reaching; but it was still not the Northwest Passage.

Continuing downstream they saw for the first time the great prairies with their huge herds of buffalo in the territory of the Illinois Indians. They passed the mouths of the Illinois and the Missouri near the present-day city of St Louis and where they were still 1,270 miles from the Gulf of Mexico. Finally, they turned back, near the confluence of the Arkansas and the Mississippi rivers.

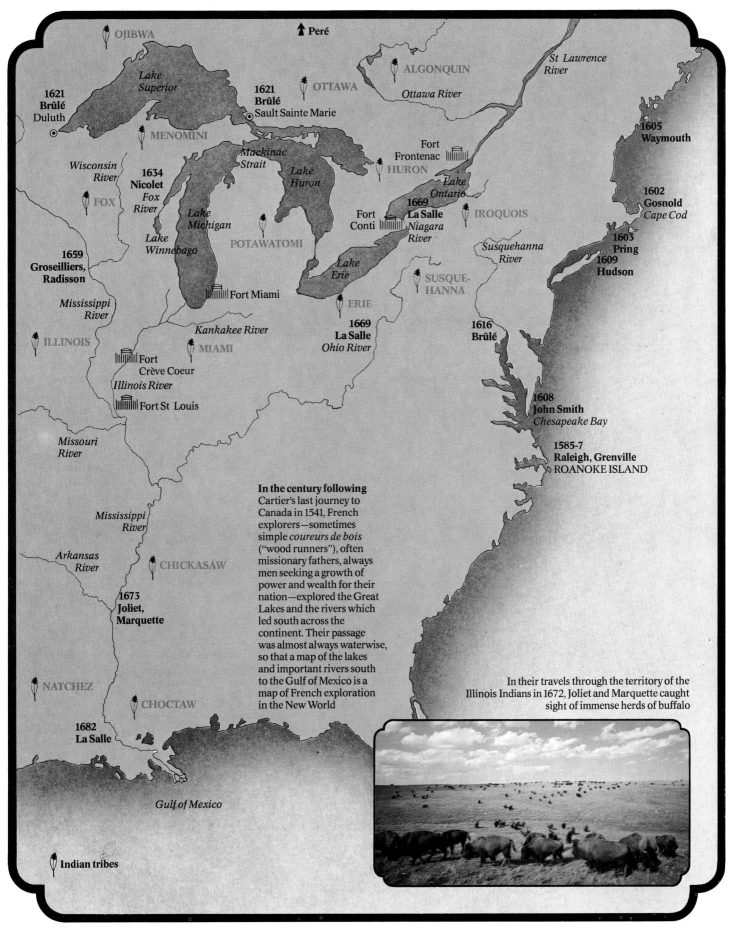

↑ Peré

OJIBWA

Lake Superior

1621
Brûlé
Duluth

MENOMINI

Wisconsin River

1634
Nicolet
Fox River

FOX

1621
Brûlé
Sault Sainte Marie

Mackinac Strait

Lake Huron

Lake Michigan

Lake Winnebago

POTAWATOMI

ALGONQUIN

St Lawrence River

Ottawa River

OTTAWA

HURON

Fort Frontenac

Lake Ontario

1669
La Salle
Niagara River

Fort Conti

IROQUOIS

Susquehanna River

1605
Waymouth

1602
Gosnold
Cape Cod

1603
Pring
1609
Hudson

1659
Groseilliers,
Radisson

Mississippi River

ILLINOIS

Kankakee River

Fort Miami

MIAMI

Lake Erie

ERIE

1669
La Salle
Ohio River

SUSQUE-
HANNA

1616
Brûlé

Fort Crève Coeur

Illinois River

Fort St Louis

Missouri River

Mississippi River

Arkansas River

CHICKASAW

1673
Joliet,
Marquette

1608
John Smith
Chesapeake Bay

1585-7
Raleigh, Grenville
ROANOKE ISLAND

In the century following Cartier's last journey to Canada in 1541, French explorers—sometimes simple *coureurs de bois* ("wood runners"), often missionary fathers, always men seeking a growth of power and wealth for their nation—explored the Great Lakes and the rivers which led south across the continent. Their passage was almost always waterwise, so that a map of the lakes and important rivers south to the Gulf of Mexico is a map of French exploration in the New World

NATCHEZ

CHOCTAW

1682
La Salle

Gulf of Mexico

♠ Indian tribes

In their travels through the territory of the Illinois Indians in 1672, Joliet and Marquette caught sight of immense herds of buffalo

The French find their 'Terres Neufves'

Reaching the mouth of the Illinois on the east bank they followed it for 500 miles to its source southwest of Lake Michigan, crossed the divide and went north up the lake to Green Bay, which they reached at the end of September 1673 after a journey of 3,000 miles, having proved—without much doubt but without quite reaching it—that the mouth of the Mississippi was on the Gulf of Mexico.

Marquette died two years later while returning from another expedition to the Illinois, where he had gone to establish a mission. Six years later Joliet was appointed Royal Pilot and Hydrographer because of the excellent work he had done on the Labrador coast and in the St Lawrence, work connected with the fisheries. He had also visited Hudson Bay.

In 1678, Louis XIV gave la Salle the task of building a line of forts across New France which would serve as bases for trade and exploration, and from Fort Frontenac in Ontario he set off in the autumn of 1678 to establish Fort Conti, on a bank of the Niagara River linking Lake Ontario and Lake Erie.

Here a small vessel, the *Griffon*, was built and la Salle was joined by a rather unusual Belgian priest, Father Louis de Hennepin. The Belgian was the first to write an account, and illustrate it, of the Niagara Falls.

With Henri de Tonty, his Italian-born lieutenant, Hennepin, two other Recollet friars and his crew, la Salle sailed west through Lake Erie, north through Lake Huron, west through the Mackinac Strait, into Lake Michigan and down its eastern shore to the mouth of the St Joseph River, where they built Fort Miami, sending back the *Griffon* with a cargo of furs.

It was December 1679 before they could continue their journey up the St Joseph to a point where a portage could be made to the Kankakee, a river which rises near South Bend, Indiana, and which, because it flowed into the Illinois, was to be an important link between the Great Lakes and the Mississippi for future settlers.

At an Indian settlement on the Illinois, la Salle built a fort which he named Crèvecoeur (Heartbreak) and, leaving Tonty to build another vessel, made a terrible journey overland to Detroit in midwinter and from there to Montreal in order to raise more funds.

Returning to the Illinois he found that most of Tonty's men had deserted and Tonty himself had become involved in a tribal war between the Iroquois and the Illinois Indians and had fled to the west side of Lake Michigan. Tonty had been exposed to great privation and danger, living on wild garlic which he dug down through the snow to reach. He had a spine-chilling encounter with the

Iroquois when they captured him, one of whom "plunged a knife into my breast, wounding a rib near the heart. . . . There was a man behind me with a knife in his hand, who every now and then lifted up my hair. They were divided in opinion, Tegantouki, chief of the Isonoutouan [Senecas] desired to have me burnt. Agoasto, chief of the Onnoutagues [Onandagas], wished to have me set at liberty as a friend of M de la Salle, and he carried his point." La Salle now descended the Illinois as far as the Mississippi in search of his men. He was unsuccessful and returned to Fort Miami where he wintered and made preparations to set out again the following year.

In the meanwhile Hennepin, with two companions, Accault and du Gay, had been sent off from Fort Crèvecoeur down the Illinois to the Mississippi, where they were captured by Sioux who took them to their tribal grounds on the upper reaches of the river, in Minnesota. The Sioux stole Hennepin's religious vestments but were overawed by a chalice that glittered in the sunlight. They thought it was inhabited by a spirit. While in this region Hennepin met a pioneer named du Lhut (after whom the city of Duluth was named) who had been exploring the headwaters of the Mississippi for two years, and together they travelled east to Green Bay and through the Mackinac Strait to Montreal.

In December 1681, la Salle set off with his men on his greatest journey, descending the Illinois in canoes and reaching the Mississippi the following February.

On March 13, when they were near the mouth of the Arkansas River, they heard through the fog "the sound of the tambour". It was the drums of the Arkansas tribe. La Salle and his men were well received in the villages of cedar-bark cabins and the Indians "danced the calumet" for their benefit.

The Gulf of Mexico

Now, reaching the great delta, they began to see and kill large alligators with which the river was infested, and at long last emerged from it into the Gulf of Mexico, where la Salle, in a ceremony on the shore, took formal possession of the whole Mississippi valley in the king's name, calling the whole vast territory Louisiana in honour of Louis XIV the *Roi Soleil*; and, on his return upstream, building Fort St Louis near the mouth of the Illinois, before returning with infinite difficulty to Montreal.

With the intention of founding a settlement at the mouth of the Mississippi, he sailed from France for the last time in June 1684, but failed to find the delta. It is an indication of the patchy navigational knowledge of the time that he and his captains could not find so

large a natural feature despite the advances in equipment available. But while, at that time, a latitudinal position was relatively easy to prove, the longitudinal, or east–west, position had to await the arrival of the chronometer to be established with any precision. This did not take place until the following century.

La Salle landed with his men 400 miles away in the lagoons on the northwest side of the gulf, losing his only store ship in the process. An attempt to reach the Mississippi overland across Texas failed and now, without boats of any kind, la Salle proposed to cross the continent from north to south on foot. On the way a mutiny broke out and la Salle was murdered. The loyal survivors—two priests and three others, under the capable command of one Joutel, a gardener's son—reached the Arkansas River, where they were rescued by a search party.

The death of la Salle brought to a close the great epoch of French exploration in North America just as Coronado's journey had closed that of the Spanish. Individual journeys by others were still to take place, but politics and imperial design, echoing Old World rivalries, were to govern the following decades.

NATURE'S OWN BARRIERS—mountains, rivers, deserts and oceans—have filled important roles in shaping the political histories of nations and empires. In North America, the Appalachian Mountains played their part in the rise and fall of the French and the emergence and consolidation of Anglo-Saxon influence.

The Appalachian system begins at the mouth of the St Lawrence River and runs southwestwards for more than 1,000 miles to Alabama, providing an effective natural barrier between the Atlantic seaboard and the heartlands of the continent.

Almost all French endeavour in North America took place to the north and west of this mountain wall. Champlain and a few others made some small penetration of its forested, near trackless hills, but in the early colonial days it was as effective as the English Channel—an Old World barrier—in keeping apart the interests of the old adversaries, England and France.

In the years during which Champlain and his successors charted their way by river and lake from the St Lawrence to the Mississippi, the English and Dutch were examining the potential of the seaboard, and establishing colonies there. These, too, found the Appalachians to be an almost insuperable barrier and the English particularly concentrated their efforts on exploiting and developing the seaboard regions. From this there grew an independent, commercially and politically

English foothold strengthened

solid community with an industrial life of its own—in complete contrast to the scattered, tenuously linked French interests beyond the mountains. The strength of the one was eventually to oust the fragile structure of the other.

The first attempts to settle and explore the seaboard were made in 1585 and 1587 by Sir Walter Raleigh, soldier, sailor, explorer, author and for some years favourite of Queen Elizabeth. They took place on Roanoke Island, an island only about ten miles long and two broad, heavily wooded and inaccessible except to small boats along the dunes of Pamlico Sound, north of Cape Hatteras on the coast of North Carolina.

The actual operation of transporting and supplying the colony was in the hands of Sir Richard Grenville, Raleigh's cousin. The scheme was a failure. There was not enough food, the English colonists like their Spanish counterparts in the Caribbean being obsessed by the search for precious minerals, rather than the pursuit of agriculture. There was not enough livestock, not enough capital and Grenville himself, with the threat of the Armada hanging over England, was not able to return. When help finally arrived in 1590, the inhabitants of the second colony, founded in 1587, had completely disappeared, leaving behind them the word "CROATOAN" (the name of a nearby island) carved on a post; but the rescuers failed to reach it and nothing more was ever heard of the second settlers.

In 1602, Bartholomew Gosnold, a navigator, later one of the founders of Jamestown, made the first direct transatlantic voyage to Massachusetts Bay and traded with the Indians, bringing back a cargo of sassafras bark, in demand in Europe for making medicinal infusions. He discovered also the rich fishing grounds around Cape Cod and the nearby islands.

Raleigh was in the Tower of London accused of conspiring against King James I when, in 1603, Captain Martin Pring, sailing for the merchants of Bristol and encouraged by Richard Hakluyt (the great geographer and author of *Principall Navigations, Voiages, and Discoveries of the English Nation*, 1589) explored the coast of Maine and that of New Hampshire and Massachusetts, as far as Martha's Vineyard. He again visited Maine in 1606.

In 1605, Captain George Waymouth explored the Penobscot River, the largest in Maine. Waymouth had followed Frobisher and Davis in search of the Northwest

A satchel with a difference. Made of wood, not leather, it served as a desk in schools in 17th-century Holland. Engraved on it is a picture of New Amsterdam (later New York), the capital of the Dutch colony in the New World

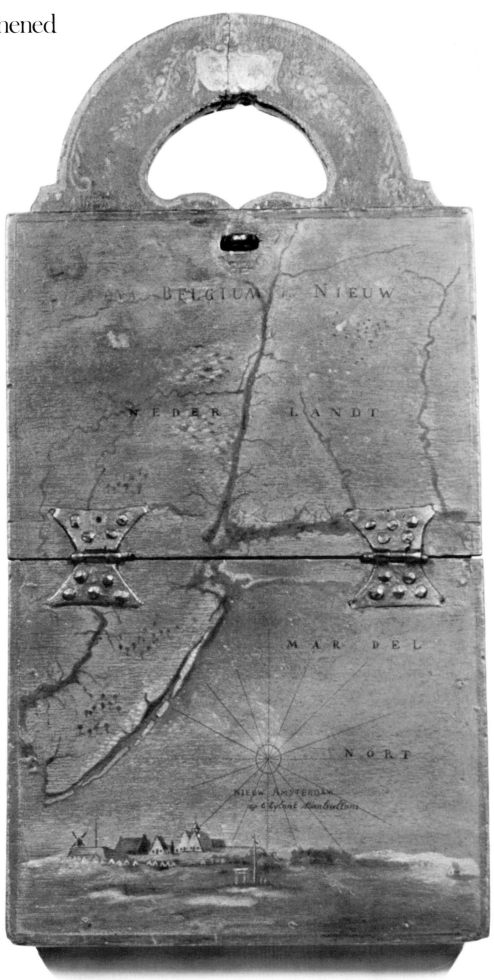

English foothold strengthened

Passage in 1602 and, having penetrated some way into the Hudson Strait, believed that it was a "passage of more probability than Davis his Straits".

On May 13, 1607, Jamestown, the first permanent English colony, was established in the present state of Virginia on the James River, under the auspices of the London Company, one of two formed under charter from James I (the other was less successful in its attempt to settle on the Kennebec River in Maine).

The Jamestown colony barely survived its early years. During the first three months, dozens of the colonists died from disease. The survivors were to find a strong man in John Smith, a native of Willoughby in Lincolnshire, who was asked by the colonists' council to seek food from the Indian tribes in the area.

Smith had the martial qualities of the Conquistador. He had travelled extensively in Europe and the Near East and had been captured at the Battle of the Rotenthurn Pass in Transylvania in 1602, while fighting against the Crimean Tartars. He was sold into slavery in Constantinople, where a young woman fell in love with him and had him sent to the Don River region in order to save his life. From there he escaped and returned to England.

The way with women which had saved his life once saved it again when he left Jamestown to make contact with the Indians. Travelling by way of the Chickahominy River, a tributary of the York, he was captured by Powhatan warriors. Although at first he impressed them as something of a magician, he was due to be executed when the daughter of the chief stepped in and saved his life.

On his return to the colony, Smith became its leader, and proved to be a hard taskmaster. His behaviour was nothing less than was needed, for when he left for England in 1609 the colony once again approached the point of collapse. Only the timely arrival of a fleet with stores saved it from extinction.

Tobacco

From now on the Virginia colony grew, but not without setbacks. After Smith returned to England, a colonist, John Rolfe, began the development of tobacco as a cash crop and this—with the arrival, later, of Negro slaves to work the plantations—laid the foundations of the colony's prosperity. Rolfe married Pocahontas, the Indian girl who had saved John Smith's life. Fêted on her arrival with her husband in England, Pocahontas contracted smallpox and died.

The second important English settlement sprang up in the north, on the coast of what was to be known as New England. It was something of an accident, for the migrants—since known as the founding fathers—had intended to land in southern Virginia. Storms hindered their passage and they made their landfall in Plymouth Bay, Massachusetts, in December 1620. The two colonies, Virginia and New England, were to become the nucleus of a nation, a settled, industrial society that was to exert a terminological pressure on the French holdings in America.

The other swing of the pincer movement on the French was the growth of English interests in the regions around Hudson Bay. The French *coureurs de bois* Groseilliers and Radisson, failed to gain the interest of their compatriots in the bleaker regions to the north of the Great Lakes with the result that the English gained a permanent foothold with ready access to the fur-rich west.

Soon after the restoration of the monarchy in England, a successful trading mission to Hudson Bay led to the formation of the Hudson's Bay Company in 1670. It was incorporated under a charter granted by Charles II to Prince Rupert and 17 others—a charter which gave them complete overlordship of an immense, vague territory.

The Company's first posts were established by 1682 in James Bay, at the mouth of the Moose River (Moose Factory), and on the west coast farther north at the mouth of the

The world's largest fresh-water lake, Lake Superior (below) was discovered by Radisson and Groseilliers, who in 1660 transported the first cargo of valuable furs for sale in the east. The region rapidly became the centre of a flourishing fur trade. The otter (above) was one of the animals to provide pelts

Hayes River (York Factory) and on the Nelson and Churchill rivers. From this moment a struggle for supremacy between France and England was inevitable.

By the second half of the 17th century explorers from the seaboard colonies had crossed the Blue Ridge Mountains (part of the Appalachians), but an ignorance of what the French had achieved still led them to believe that the Pacific might be at hand, once the mountains were crossed. A German, Dr John Lederer, was the first to reach the crest, where he hoped he might catch a glimpse of a great sea to the west. He was still 2,500 miles from it. The seaboard settlers, by 1700, had achieved nothing significant in the way of geographical knowledge, but they had pointed the way to the future political structure of the continent. The rainbow's end of early North American exploration—a route to the great ocean in the west and, beyond that, the Orient—was as far away as ever.

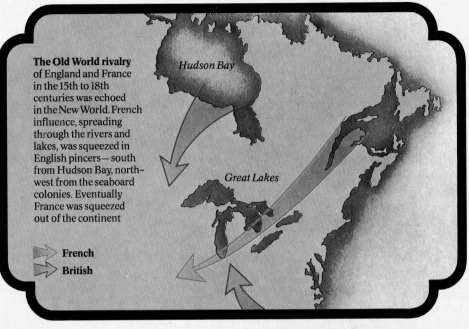

The Old World rivalry of England and France in the 15th to 18th centuries was echoed in the New World. French influence, spreading through the rivers and lakes, was squeezed in English pincers—south from Hudson Bay, north-west from the seaboard colonies. Eventually France was squeezed out of the continent

Hudson Bay

Great Lakes

➤➤ French
➤➤ British

The remarkable dams and lodges which the beaver builds across a small river are easy to spot, but the animal is difficult to catch. North American fur trappers of the 19th century learned to bait their steel traps with castoreum, a substance secreted by the beaver to attract the opposite sex. Within a few years of the discovery of castoreum by the white trapper, the North American beaver was sharply reduced in numbers

Just as beaver pelts were made into hats for Europe's fashionable heads, the skin of the elk was prized as shoe leather. By the beginning of the 18th century the elk (American red deer) had been hunted to extinction in areas of white settlement. Still rare today, the marten, inhabitant of the northern forests, was trapped more than any other Canadian animal. Its rich winter fur was used for trimmings and linings

Pioneers in the Pacific

THE EASE WITH WHICH the Spanish found the Pacific, once they had found Central America, probably disguised for the French in Canada, and for the English (in their search for the elusive Strait of Anian), the sheer magnitude of northern North America and the distance which lay between its eastern and western seaboards. And while these two nations edged their way westwards, diverted by one and then another colonial enterprise, the Spanish were sailing back and forth on that great sea, the northern Pacific.

The first to cross it from west to east was a sailor-monk, Andres de Urdaneta. His journey, in 1565, followed the start of colonization of the Philippines by the Spanish. Avoiding the northeast trades as much as he could (which are adverse winds when sailing the northern Pacific in this direction), he stood north through an area in which variable winds and typhoons are equally likely—a cemetery, in fact, for sailing ships—going as high as 42N, where westerlies predominate. It was the route that Spanish galleons, commuting out of Manila to the west coast of America, were to follow, giving them a landfall in California, from where they coasted south to Acapulco.

Two years later, Alvaro de Mendaña set out on an enormous triangulation of the Pacific, sailing from Callao, in Peru, to discover "certain islands and a continent, because many men well versed in mathematics had deduced that they existed for certain in these positions".

One of these well-versed men was Pedro Sarmiento de Gamboa, who believed that a great continent existed in the south, extending from the latitude of Tierra del Fuego to about 15S and lying about 600 leagues to the west of it. He sailed with the expedition, too, a cruel and disagreeable man.

Mendaña failed to find the continent, reaching 15.30S in the appropriate longitude, but he did sight the Ellice Islands and, 82 days out from Callao, the Solomon Islands.

From here Mendaña sailed for home on August 11, 1568, passed through the Marshall Islands, where they failed to find water, and after a fearful passage of 4,000 miles or more and 131 days from the Solomons, reached Colima, near Acapulco on the coast of Mexico.

In April 1595, Mendaña sailed again from Peru with four ships, and a mandate from the Viceroy "to go and subject and people the western islands of the South Sea" and, specifically, to revisit the Solomon Islands.

The expedition was doomed to disaster by the nature of the persons who sailed with it. They included Mendaña's wife (an impossible woman) and her three brothers —one of whom commanded a ship—and a motley collection of soldiers, sailors and their wives and children.

Islanders murdered

The most able person was the chief pilot, Pedro Fernandes de Quiros, a Portuguese who had become a Spanish subject in 1580 and was now 30 years old.

On July 28 they reached a group of islands that Mendaña named the Marquesas. Here 200 of the inhabitants, whose only vice was a natural curiosity, were murdered by his men.

They sailed on from this now blighted paradise and reached an island, which loomed before them when the thick fog in which they had been navigating suddenly lifted at midnight on September 7.

The island, which Mendaña subsequently named Santa Cruz, was one of the Solomons, a vast archipelago which covers an area of 15,600 square miles of the southwestern Pacific.

Its people were friendly when the Spaniards arrived, paddling out to their ships in outrigger canoes. They had very dark skins, frizzled hair dyed red and white, red teeth and they wore red flowers in their hair and nostrils. Their friendliness was of no help to them. Here, to the accompaniment of the

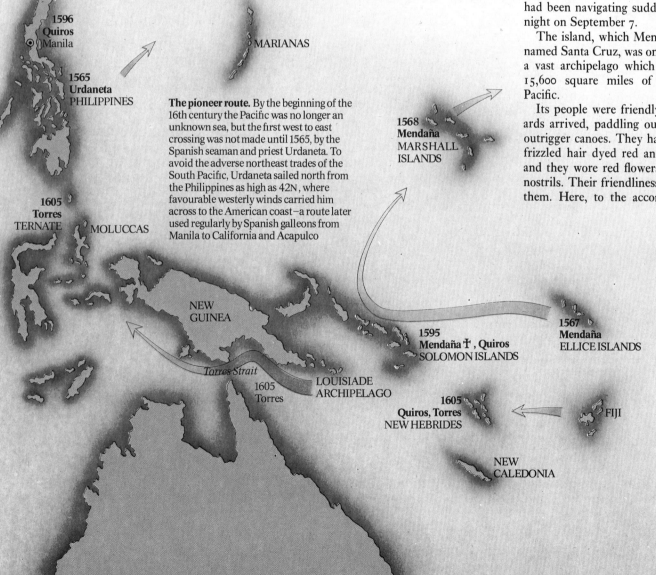

1596 Quiros Manila

1565 Urdaneta PHILIPPINES

MARIANAS

The pioneer route. By the beginning of the 16th century the Pacific was no longer an unknown sea, but the first west to east crossing was not made until 1565, by the Spanish seaman and priest Urdaneta. To avoid the adverse northeast trades of the South Pacific, Urdaneta sailed north from the Philippines as high as 42N, where favourable westerly winds carried him across to the American coast–a route later used regularly by Spanish galleons from Manila to California and Acapulco

1605 Torres TERNATE   MOLUCCAS

NEW GUINEA

Torres Strait

1605 Torres

LOUISIADE ARCHIPELAGO

1568 Mendaña MARSHALL ISLANDS

1595 Mendaña ✝ , Quiros SOLOMON ISLANDS

1567 Mendaña ELLICE ISLANDS

1605 Quiros, Torres NEW HEBRIDES

FIJI

NEW CALEDONIA

insensate massacres and burnings (of which Quiros was a bitter but powerless opponent) that characterized this loathsome expedition, a colony of sorts was established and, ironically, with slaughter going on daily, a church was built.

The Spaniards now began to murder one another, having already killed the native chief. Mendaña himself sickened and died, on his death bed nominating his wife as governess of the expedition.

On November 18, with Quiros in command of the ships, the surviving Spaniards left the island. Now began a terrible voyage. With a starving company of men, women and children and with a mounting death roll, Quiros sailed first west-southwest and then, when no land was encountered, northwest to try to reach Manila in his leaking, rotten ships.

Largely exempt from the sufferings of their people were Doña Isabela, Mendaña's widow, and her three brothers, who had a store of oil, vinegar and wine which they refused to share with the others, who lived (if they did not die) on a ration of half a pound of bread and half a pint of dirty water a day.

They finally reached Manila on February 11, 1596. Of the entire company 60 died in Quiros's ship alone. At Manila Doña Isabela buried her husband with pomp and soon afterwards married again, the survivors, still under Quiros, sailing for home in August, 1597, arriving at Acapulco four months later.

It was the Portuguese navigator, Quiros, a man of quite exceptional religious zeal, who now set off in search of the fifth great continent, which he believed to lie somewhere to the east of the islands that he had reached on his previous voyage.

With him, as one of the pilots, went Luiz

Vaez de Torres, of whose antecedents little is known; his sailing directions from Quiros were "to be very diligent both by day and night, in following the Capitana ship which will shape a west-southwest course until the latitude of 30 degrees is reached; and when that is reached and no land has been seen, the course will be altered to northwest until the latitude of 10.15, and if no land has yet been found, a course will be followed on that parallel to the west, in search of the Island of Vera Cruz".

If the original course had been sailed they would have reached the Australian continent on the coast of New South Wales.

Quiros sailed from Callao on December 21, 1605, his departure being witnessed by a vast throng.

He had three ships: the *Capitana*, 60 tons; the *Almiranta*, 40 tons; and a launch, with 300 Spanish, Portuguese and Flemish soldiers and sailors, some Franciscan monks and four nursing brothers.

No gambling

Quiros did not endear himself to the more ungodly members of the crew when he had their gambling tables thrown overboard early in the voyage and bombarded them with a series of orders of the day filled with exhortations on how to comport themselves.

The agreed course was held until January 22, 1606, when "with a squall and showers from the southeast and with a great swell from the south", which "brought out the timidity in some, saying: 'Whither are they taking us, in this great gulf, in the winter season?'" Quiros sickened and, although strongly opposed by Torres, decided to stand on a west-northwest course, which put them

Colima
Acapulco

among the mountainous islands and coral-fringed atolls of the Tuamotu Archipelago, where they were unable to find an anchorage. At last, on February 10, they reached Anau Island, 200 miles east of Tahiti.

Still making a northing they discovered a number of islands, probably in the Society group, and with the crew near to mutiny passed north of Samoa and the Fiji Islands, reaching Taumaka, near Santa Cruz Island (now part of the Solomon Islands).

Here they were told by the chief of the existence of a large number of small islands and a larger one, which he called Manicolo, to the south and Quiros set a course for it, reaching it on May 1, 1606.

The island, which was mountainous, and with a population that was implacably hostile, was the biggest in the New Hebrides, a volcanic group with three active volcanoes, about 500 miles west of the Fiji Islands. Quiros was convinced that the island, Espiritu Santo, was part of the fifth, southern continent and, in a state bordering on ecstasy, took possession of them in the king's name "and of the site on which is to be founded the city of New Jerusalem, in latitude 15.10S, and of all the lands which I sighted and am going to sight, and of this region of the south as far as the Pole, which from this time shall be called Austrialia [*sic*] del Espiritu Santo, with all its dependencies and belongings". "Austrialia" was an allusion to the Spanish king, who was also Archduke of Austria.

To Quiros it was a paradise which would soon become a thriving colony, and what his feelings were when he and his company were blown to leeward of the island, in the *Capitana*, on June 8, and were never able to regain it, can only be imagined.

Eleven days later he sailed away to the

Callao

1595
Mendaña, Quiros
MARQUESAS

SOCIETY ISLANDS

1605
Quiros, Torres
TUAMOTU ARCHIPELAGO

COOK ISLANDS

The elusive continent. From their American colonies the Spaniards set out eagerly—as the Dutch were to, from their eastern spice empire—in search of the great southern continent. Although the first attempts led by Alvaro de Mendaña failed, several new groups of islands were put on the map, including the Solomons. After Mendaña's death, the quest was taken up with almost fanatical zeal by his chief pilot, Quiros. Lighting on Espiritu Santo, a volcanic island

in the New Hebrides, Quiros believed he had found part of the continent and returned jubilantly to Acapulco, recommending that it should be colonized. The commander of the other ship, Luis Vaez de Torres, reached New Guinea. "I could not weather the east point," he wrote, "so I coasted along to the westward on the south side." Torres had discovered the strait that now bears his name, narrowly missing Australia itself

Netherlanders sail east

north and, in the latitude of Guam, set a course to the west, reaching Acapulco on November 23, 1606.

What induced him to leave without making greater efforts to get back is a mystery. Possibly he was forced to sail away by his men. He was very sick at the time, as were many of the others, from eating poisonous fish.

Torres himself, in the *Almiranta*, having waited 15 days for Quiros to return, and having searched the coast in vain for wreckage, caused the sealed orders from the Viceroy of Peru to be opened. These gave the command to Don Diego de Prado, as senior officer, which he seems largely to have relinquished to Torres. The sailing directions were to proceed to 20s in search of land (New Guinea), follow its coast northwards and then make for Manila.

Unable to sail round the island because of the currents, Torres sailed southwest, but finding no land altered course and found the islands of the Louisiade Archipelago, off the southeastern end of New Guinea.

Here, he was among the reefs for five days before sailing up the south coast of New Guinea, naming it and holding a course to 9s, where he encountered shoals and changed course to southwest. In 11s he saw "some very large islands and more were seen to the south", which must have been those off Cape York on the Australian mainland. He had reached the 90-mile-wide strait which now bears his name between it and New Guinea, the meeting place of the Coral and Arafura seas.

He reached Ternate in the Moluccas, and on May 22, 1607, Manila, having lost only one man on this amazing and most hazardous voyage, which proved, beyond reasonable doubt, that New Guinea was an island (although the Dutch, in the absence of any published information about the voyage, still believed until after the time of Tasman that New Guinea was joined to Australia).

Torres never returned from Manila. His ship was requisitioned and he stayed there to write his report, which remained entombed in secret archives until the capture of Manila by an English force in 1762, when it fell into the hands of the hydrographer Alexander Dalrymple, who gave details to the world.

As for Quiros, the rest of his life was devoted to preparing and sending 50 memorials and 200 maps to King Philip III, begging to be allowed to continue his exploration of "Austrialia". Nothing came of his efforts. He was a fine navigator, a man of unalterable piety, and one of almost Quixotic eccentricity, who believed that the indigenous inhabitants of the countries he discovered should be kindly treated. He died at Panama in 1615, preparing a new voyage.

THE EMERGENCE OF THE DUTCH as a power on the seven seas must have come as a severe shock to the pride of Castile and Leon. In half a century, during which the Spanish were at the peak of their power and wealth, the Netherlanders rose from the subjection of Spanish suzerainty to a position of pre-eminence among the maritime powers.

The Dutch, more than most, knew what the sea was all about; they had, after all, wrested their country from it. Throughout their history it had always been at their shoulder, ready to seize back the fertile polders. They had traded in their characteristic round-hulled ships along the Atlantic seaboard and stood out into the stormy North Sea in their busses, to the rich herring grounds of the Dogger Bank and north. Their skill as seamen was to play an important part in their struggle for freedom, no less than in later years it was to take them to and around the "lost continent" of Australia before anyone else. The legendary "Sea Beggars" with "rusting cannon, nailed to splitting decks" snapped at the high-pooped galleons of Spain and drove them from Dutch waters. A leader, William of Orange, "The Silent", was found and by 1584 the northern United Provinces declared their independence from Spain. Their success had the effect of closing all Iberian ports, particularly Lisbon, to the Dutch. Lisbon was the great port of arrival for spices from the Portuguese Indies; the Dutch now had to make their own way to the east.

If they needed any encouragement to flout the Portuguese and Spanish monopolies, the defeat by the English of the Spanish Armada in the English Channel in 1588 provided it and from now on Dutch ships sailed wherever it was expedient—the English were already doing so, as privateers.

The first Dutch expedition to the east sailed from the Texel in February 1594 with four ships under Cornelius Houtman. It reached Bantam in Java and returned home by sailing eastwards along the north coast of Java as far as the Bali Strait; then along the south coast of the island—something that the Portuguese, apparently, had never done. By 1605 they had taken Amboina, a key spice island in the Moluccas, from the Portuguese.

Strait of Magellan

In June 1599 (the year that the English founded the East India Company), Admiral James Mahu set off with a small fleet from Rotterdam to sail westwards across the Pacific. He died off the Cape Verde Islands, but his ships succeeded in passing through the Strait of Magellan in very bad weather. After one was forced back and returned home, another, under Dirck Gerritz, may (for it is not certain) have been driven as far as

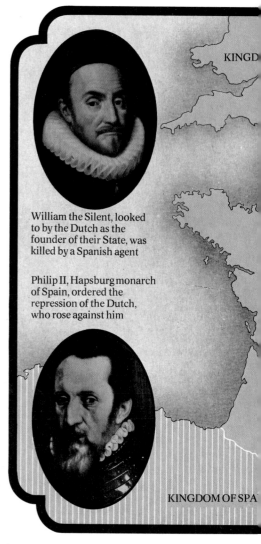

William the Silent, looked to by the Dutch as the founder of their State, was killed by a Spanish agent

Philip II, Hapsburg monarch of Spain, ordered the repression of the Dutch, who rose against him

KINGD

KINGDOM OF SPA

62s and seen the South Shetlands (which were formally discovered and claimed for Britain by Captain William Smith in 1819).

The remaining ships, under Simon de Cordes, who had with him an English pilot, William Adams, sailed up the coast of Chile to the Mocha Islands off the Chilean coast, where Cordes and some of his men were killed by the inhabitants. The survivors decided to sail for Japan, intending to trade the cargo of woollen cloth there. Here the ships were separated in a storm, but Adams's ship eventually reached Bungo (Oita) on the northeastern coast of Kyushu Island, with its crew on the point of death.

Adams was kept a prisoner in Japan and never allowed to return, but he succeeded in gaining the Imperial favour and was influential in making trade possible between Holland and Japan.

The year before Mahu's expedition Olivier van Noort had set off on what was to be the first Dutch circumnavigation of the world. It took him first through the Strait of Magellan then up the coast of Chile, where he engaged and captured a Spanish merchant ship.

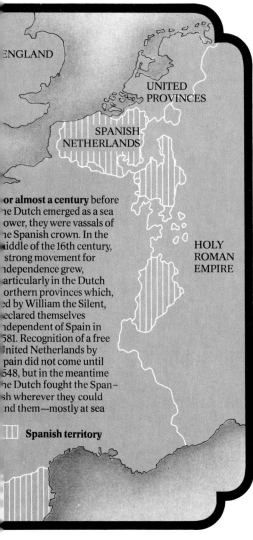

ENGLAND

UNITED PROVINCES

SPANISH NETHERLANDS

HOLY ROMAN EMPIRE

or almost a century before he Dutch emerged as a sea power, they were vassals of he Spanish crown. In the middle of the 16th century, a strong movement for independence grew, particularly in the Dutch northern provinces which, led by William the Silent, declared themselves independent of Spain in 1581. Recognition of a free United Netherlands by Spain did not come until 1648, but in the meantime the Dutch fought the Spanish wherever they could find them—mostly at sea

Spanish territory

From there he sailed to the Ladrones and then the Philippines, roughly following Magellan's course, and he fought a successful action with another Spanish ship. From Brunei in Borneo he sailed between Java and Sumatra, crossed the Indian Ocean and rounded the Cape of Good Hope, reaching Holland with one ship almost three years after his departure.

The Dutch East India Company, which was formed in 1602, soon took upon itself monopolistic powers. No captain, unless he was a member of the Company, was allowed to sail to the east by way of the Cape of Good Hope (later to be known to the Dutch, because of its victualling station, as the "tavern of the Indian Ocean") or by the Strait of Magellan.

In the state of knowledge at that time, it meant effectively that nobody could sail to the Indies from Europe without the Company's blessing. It caused trouble in Amsterdam, where a well-known Jewish merchant, Isaac le Maire, addressed a remonstrance to the States-General which questioned the power of the Company, then formed one of

his own, in 1610, which was to find a means by which the monopoly could be circumvented. It was given permission to trade in Tartary, China, Japan, Terra Australis and all the islands of the South Sea and the expedition of 1615 mounted by le Maire and an experienced navigator, Willem Corneliszoon Schouten, discovered a route which did not include either the Magellan Strait or the Cape of Good Hope.

Schouten believed that there must be a passage south of Tierra del Fuego, a belief that was based on what he had learned from Drake's account of his experiences and on a study of Dutch and English charts, which showed the existence of an archipelago. He was made a director of le Maire's Australian Company together with some burghers of the town of Hoorn on the Texel.

Secret destination

Schouten and Jacob le Maire, son of Isaac, sailed from the river for a secret destination with the *Eendracht*, a ship of 220 tons and a crew of 65, and the *Hoorn*, a jacht of 110 tons and a crew of 22, which was captained by Schouten's brother, Jan.

With scurvy breaking out among the crews, they put in at Sierra Leone and took on 25,000 lemons as an anti-scorbutic, which they exchanged for "a few beads and some poor Nuremberg knives".

After a long-drawn-out voyage through the South Atlantic, on December 4 they reached Puerto Deseado (Port Desire) on the coast of Patagonia in 47.40S, where both the ships dragged their anchors and were set so high on the rocks that when the tide ebbed it was possible for a man to walk underneath them.

Luckily both ships floated off, but a fresh disaster occurred when the *Hoorn* caught fire and was burned to the waterline.

After transferring anything of value that they had saved from the *Hoorn* to the *Eendracht* they sailed south in January 1616. Eleven days later they sighted the eight-mile-wide strait (Le Maire Strait) between Tierra del Fuego and Staten Island, seeing penguins, seals and "whales by thousands". They called the island Staten Landt, thinking that it might be part of the great southern continent.

With the wind from the north they sailed through the strait, seeing high, snow-covered mountains on the starboard hand and sand beaches with seals hauled out on them. "In the evening the wind veered to the southwest and we then ran southward that night with a heavy roll from the southwest and very blue water, from which we opined and were certain . . . that it was the great South Sea, whereat we were very glad, holding that a way had been discovered by us which had

until then been unknown to man, as we afterwards discovered to be the truth. . . . Towards the evening we again saw land to the northwest. . . . It consisted entirely of high mountains covered with snow, and ends in a sharp corner, which we called the Cape of Hoorn." One of the greatest of landmarks was thus pinpointed and named.

Two and a half months later the expedition was among the islands of the Tuamotu Archipelago (French Polynesia), in 15.12S and about three weeks later reached two islands, midway between Fiji, Tonga and Samoa, which they named Cocos and Verraders (now Boscawen and Keppel's islands), Verraders (Traitors) being so named because a visit to the ships by a chief bearing a pig as a welcoming gift suddenly turned into an attack which the Dutch repulsed by firing off cannon loaded with a mixture of musket balls and old nails. Wherever it went in the Pacific the Schouten–le Maire expedition was attended by the loosing-off of guns and much slaughter.

So far they had not found "Austrialia", Quito's Southern Continent; but after passing to the south of Samoa, they were rewarded by a landfall on the coast of New Ireland, an island only a few miles wide but 200 miles long, which they thought must be a part of Terra Australis. They had not noticed the strait between it and New Britain, the next island to the west.

Sailing from here they closed with the north coast of New Guinea, reduced to a basic diet of bread, oil and wine and one glass of brandy a day. They might have done worse. Thanks probably to the 25,000 lemons they had taken on board (and because Dutch ships were less crowded than those of their Portuguese and Spanish predecessors) they were almost entirely free from scurvy, and suffered little from other diseases. In the course of the entire voyage of $16\frac{1}{2}$ months only three men died.

On September 17 they reached Ternate, where they were kindly treated by their fellow countrymen, but a different fate awaited them when they reached Jakarta on October 28.

There, Jan Pieterzoon Coen, the Governor, who was such an ardent supporter of the Company's monopoly that he had declared its coasts out of bounds even to his compatriots, seized the *Eendracht* and its cargo and sent Schouten and le Maire home, virtually as prisoners, in one of the ships of a large fleet under the command of Admiral Joris van Speilbergen, who was himself on the last lap of a voyage round the world by way of the Strait of Magellan. In the course of the ignominious voyage le Maire died.

It is inconceivable that the mainland of Australia was unknown to all but the native

Netherlanders sail east

aboriginal people before the Dutch made the first landfall there by westerners. Indonesians certainly, quite possibly the Chinese, had touched upon its shores at some stage, but there is no evidence. The formal credit, therefore, goes to the Dutch and to a captain from Amsterdam, Willem Jantszoon, who sailed into the Gulf of Carpentaria, between Arnhem Land and the Cape York Peninsula, in 1606.

His landfall had fatal results for some members of his crew, who were killed by the first aboriginals ever seen by Europeans.

Over the next two decades, Dutch sailors were to make one landfall after another on the western seaboard of Australia. An important factor in these voyages was the discovery by the Dutch East Indiamen of the westerly winds which blow constantly and strongly in the latitudes of 40 to 50s—the Roaring Forties. By shaping south of the conventional

route to the Indies they reduced the sailing time from Holland to Java from 16 months to six and pioneered a shipping route which eastbound sailors in the tea and wool clippers of the 19th century were customarily to use.

In 1616, the Dutch East India Company instructed their captains to take this more southerly route and that year Dirck Hartogszoon of Amsterdam, sailing in the *Eendracht* in these higher latitudes, made a landfall off the coast of Western Australia at an island with light-brown sandstone cliffs and drifts of white sand on it in 26s. It was named Dirk Hartog Island and a pewter plaque was set up on the shore recording the visit. From there he sailed north along the coast, which he named Eendrachtsland, and then to Bantam.

The plaque remained on Cape Inscription until February 25, 1697, when Captain Willem de Vlamingh in the ship *Geelvinck* from Amsterdam reached the Cape and

replaced the plaque with another, which recorded not only Hartogszoon's original inscription, but the details of the *Geelvinck's* arrival and that of the two other ships with him.

There it remained until 1801, when the French explorer Louis-Claude de Freycinet found it still nailed to the original oak post, half buried in the sand. It is now in an Amsterdam museum.

Sightings of the west coast now followed in rapid succession. In 1617, Haevick Claeszoon in the *Zeewolf*, having sailed east in the Indian Ocean in 39s, turned north and found land in 21.20s on the northwest coast, which he rightly thought to be part of the mainland; and the following year Lenaert Jacobszoon in the *Mauritius* reached the same coast in about 22s near the Northwest Cape. In 1619, Frederik Houtman, sailing with the *Dordrecht* and the *Amsterdam*, raised the coast in the latitude of the present city of Perth, naming it Dedelsland. He then sailed north, discovering the rocks known as Houtman's Abrolhos, 50 miles offshore in 28.30s.

Two years later the unknown master of the ship *Leeuwin* discovered the cape at the southwest corner of the continent, from which point the coast begins to trend to the eastwards; and in 1628 Gerrit de Witt, inward bound from Java, was carried far to the south of his course, making landfall on the northwest coast around 21s (near the present town of Roebourne) which was subsequently known as De Witt's Land.

In 1627, an immense stretch of the south

"...**Setting dogs to spring the game,** which as soon as they had done, was seized by others." This, in the view of a 17th-century writer, was the fate of the Portuguese in the East Indies. The game was the spice "emporium" and the main beneficiaries were the Dutch. Spanish embargoes prevented Dutch trade with the Iberian Peninsula, the point of arrival of eastern goods. Dutch attempts to find a northeast passage to the east had foundered. The only

remaining solution was for them to oust the Portuguese from their eastern strongholds. Backed by a growing mercantile class at home, the Dutch sailed east round the Cape of Good Hope. In 1602 the United East Indies Company was set up. Within three years the Company had captured the main spice islands and Portuguese influence came to an end. The Dutch were masters

For centuries the belief in a great southern continent had persisted, but it was the Dutch, sailing from their spice empire in the East Indies, who finally shed some light on the nature of this fabled continent. In 1606 came the first recorded sighting of Australia.
Over the next 30 years Dutch sailors gradually pieced together the jigsaw, exploring the north, west and south coasts. The last great piece of the Australian jigsaw, the entire east coast, was not added until the next century—by Captain Cook

Tasman's first voyage
Tasman's second voyage
Dampier's voyage

TIMOR

1636
Pieterszoon
MELVILLE
ISLAND

WESSEL
ISLAND

1623
Carstenszoon,
Van Colster

Cape York
Peninsula

1605-6
Jantszoon
Cape
Keer-weer

ARNHEM
LAND

Staaten
River

1636
Pool ✝, Pieterszoon
NEW GUINEA

NEW
IRELAND

NEW
BRITAIN

Arafura Sea

1617
Claeszoon
1618
Jacobszoon
North West
Cape

1616
Hartogszoon
DIRK HARTOG
ISLAND

Shark
Bay

1619
Houtman

1629
Pelsaert
1696
Vlamingh

Swan
River

1627
Thijszoon,
Nuyts
NUYTS ARCHIPELAGO

VANUA LEVU
FIJI ISLANDS
TONGATAPU

NEW
ZEALAND

TASMANIA

Cape Leeuwin
1627
Thijszoon, Nuyts
Point Nuyts

coast was discovered beyond Cape Leeuwin when François Thijszoon in the *Zeepard*, with Pieter Nuyts, a high official of the Dutch East India Company, was separated from an outward-bound fleet of East Indiamen and sailed along 1,000 miles of it to Nuyt's Archipelago, off Ceduna at the eastern end of the Great Australian Bight. At the end of this voyage, which lasted from January to April 1627, they arrived safely at Batavia.

The first landing proper on the west coast of Australia was made by François Pelsaert, a native of Antwerp, in 1629.

After his ship, the *Batavia*, was wrecked on Houtman's Abrolhos, Pelsaert set out with a party of 30 in open boats with the intention of finding water on the mainland.

Aborigines

When he did succeed in putting a party ashore the immediate interior was found to be a wasteland, inhabited by aborigines, whom they saw but with whom they were unable to make contact.

There was a pause in the Dutch exploration of the north coast of Australia between Jantszoon's voyage of 1606 and the next, by Jan Carstenszoon, in 1623. His brief, on sailing from Amboina, was to further examine the Gulf of Carpentaria.

Carstenszoon kept an excellent journal of his voyage. Like Jantszoon, he thought that the western entrance to the Torres Strait was "a dry bight" in a continuous coast of which the south coast of New Guinea was also a part.

After reaching the coast of New Guinea,

The man chosen to dispel much of the mystery enveloping Australia and its connection with the hypothetical southern continent was Abel Janszoon Tasman (portrayed with his wife and daughter). Tasman discovered Tasmania, New Zealand, the Tonga and Fiji Islands, and proved that Australia was entirely separate from the supposed polar continent

where his men suffered casualties in a battle with natives, he sighted the western side of the Cape York Peninsula. A party landed near Cape Keer-weer, where they had their first real encounter with the aboriginals: "These blacks showed no fear and were so bold as to touch the muskets of our men and try to take the same off their shoulders, while they wanted to have whatever they could make use of. Our men accordingly diverted their attention by showing them some iron and beads, and espying vantage, seized one of the blacks by a string which he wore round his neck and carried him off to the pinnace. The blacks who remained on the beach set up dreadful howls and made violent gestures, but the others who kept concealed in the wood remained there. These natives are coal-black with lean bodies and stark-naked, having twisted baskets or nets around their heads. In hair and figure they are like the blacks of the Coromandel coast, but they seem to be less cunning, bold, and evil-natured than the blacks at the western extremity of Nova Guinea. . . ."

Carstenszoon coasted south for a month as far as the mouth of what they named the Staaten River in 17.08s, where he erected a wooden column with an inscription, and then after naming rivers on the Cape York Peninsula, sailed to the Aru Islands in the South Moluccas.

In 1636, Gerrit Thomaszoon Pool and Pieter Pieterszoon sailed from Banda, explored part of the western peninsula of New Guinea and had a similar encounter with the natives to that of Carstenszoon's men, in the course of which Pool was killed. Pieterszoon took command and the expedition sailed south across the Arafura Sea to Melville Island and the mainland at the extreme northeastern tip of Arnhem Land, naming the island Van Diemen's Land (after the great Governor-General of the Dutch East Indies, Anthony van Diemen, who did so much to further Dutch exploration) and the mainland Maria's Land. On these wild shores they did not see a single human being, only the smoke of the aboriginals' fires rising in the even more forbidding interior.

Tasman

It was Abel Janszoon Tasman who was now to find the answers to some of the questions which the rather disjointed explorations of the north, south and west coasts had been unable to provide.

Tasman was born in a small village in Groningen in Holland about 1603. In 1634 he entered the service of the Dutch East India Company in Batavia; and in June 1639 he was sent on a voyage which took him, and the commander of the other ship, Matthijs

Quast, from Batavia to the coasts of Korea and Japan and far west into the Pacific, Tasman acting as second-in-command.

The objects of Tasman's great voyage in 1642, the most important in the whole history of Dutch exploration, although it was not so regarded at the time, were to sail in the Indian Ocean far to the south of any route that had been used up to that time, as far south as latitude 54; to discover whether the South Land (Australia) reached to the south polar regions, by attempting to circumnavigate it; and to explore the north and south coast of New Guinea, which the Dutch still believed to be part of the Australian continent.

In planning his voyage Tasman had the backing of van Diemen, the Governor-General, and the help of the exceptionally able Jacobszoon Visscher, one of the greatest Dutch pilots, whose *Memoir concerning the Discovery of the South-Land* incorporated most of the sailing instructions which he gave to Tasman.

Tasman, with Visscher as Pilot-Major and chief adviser, sailed from Batavia on August 14, 1642, with two ships, the *Heemskerck*, a jacht, and the *Zeehaen*, a fluyt—a warship carrying only part of her armament—to act as a transport.

Each ship had a crew of 60, provisions for 12 months—but enough rice to last 18—and "divers commodities and minerals", which the East India Company provided for trade.

Passing through the Strait of Sunda they reached Mauritius, a volcanic island in 20s, 57E, about 550 miles east of Madagascar, which had been discovered by the Portuguese in 1505. Here they carried out some work on the ships—the *Zeehaen* being particularly decrepit—and took on firewood and water in accordance with the detailed directions already laid down by Visscher.

Sailing south on October 8 they reached latitude 40s and then sailed southeast into the Roaring Forties across the Southern Indian Ocean until they reached 69.40E, the longitude of the Kerguelen Islands, a group with one large island more than 6,000 feet high and about 300 others, famous for a sort of cabbage. It lies between 40 and 50s.

On October 27 they saw floating branches of trees, seaweed and leaves and men were sent to the mastheads with the promise of a reward of three pieces of eight and a can of arrack for the first to sight land.

The next day they saw more floating debris, but the weather was so dark and foggy that during the next night they had to fire guns and muskets to avoid the ships losing touch with one another. A week later they were in 49.4s, 97E, their highest latitude, and about ten degrees farther south than any ship had previously managed in this longitude.

Netherlanders sail east

By now they were running before a strong gale from the west in a heavy sea, and the weather was bitterly cold for men who had spent so much time in the tropics.

A council of officers was called in the flagship and on Visscher's advice it was decided to sail north to latitude 44S, run on this parallel until they were in 150E, and then to go north to latitude 40 and east to 160E.

On November 17 they calculated that they were in the longitude of the farthest point reached by Nuyts on his unpremeditated voyage in 1627, but on the parallel they were sailing they were about 650 miles to the south of Australia, in the Great Southern Ocean.

On November 24, Tasman noted in his journal, "at noon found latitude 42.25S and longitude 163.31E [from Tenerife—the Dutch still reckoned from a meridian in the Canaries nearly 19 degrees west of Greenwich]. Course held east by north and sailed 120 miles; the wind out of the southwest and then south with a light topsail breeze. Afternoon, about 4 o'clock we saw land, had it east by north of us by our estimation 40 miles. Towards the evening we saw in the east-southeast three high mountains and in the northeast saw also two mountains, not so high as that in the south."

They were off the southwest coast of Tasmania. The next day Tasman wrote: "This land is the first land in the South Sea that we have encountered, and is still known to no european people, so we have given this land the name of Anthoonij van Diemens Land in honour of the Hon. Governor General our high superior who sent us to make this discovery, the Islands lying round it as many as are known to us we have named after the Hon. Councillors of India. . . ."

On December 1, after sailing round the southern coast, a party was put ashore in Frederick Henry Bay, west of the present city of Hobart, where they found a country covered with vegetation and trees, some of which had notches cut in them to allow the natives, who remained invisible (though audible) to climb them. It was thought that the natives must be giants because the notches were five feet apart.

Memorial

The following day Tasman took formal possession of the country on behalf of the Dutch States-General, but the surf was so heavy that the ship's carpenter had to swim through it and plant a pole with a flag on the shore "as a memorial to those who shall come after, and for the natives of this country who did not show themselves".

They then sailed north along the coast and then because of head winds, eastwards, without discovering the existence of the Bass Strait, which separates Tasmania from the Australian mainland.

On December 13 they sighted the west coast of the South Island of New Zealand with a great mountain range looming behind it—the crests of the Southern Alps.

Thinking that this must be part of the Great South Land connected with the Staten Landt of Schouten and le Maire, Tasman named this and their subsequent discoveries Staten Landt; and the sea they had crossed from Van Diemen's Land, Abel Tasman's Passage (now the Tasman Sea).

Rounding Cape Farewell, the extreme northern point of the South Island, they sailed into the 100-mile-wide bight between it and the North Island—the northwestern approach to the Cook Strait.

Here they had their first encounter with the native Maoris, whose skins were yellowish-brown. Their bodies were bare to the waist; their black hair, which was done up in tufts, was adorned with white feathers; their voices were harsh; and they had double-hulled canoes of unusual construction, of which Tasman made a sketch.

The Maoris were also extremely warlike, killing four members of Tasman's crews after ramming one of the Dutch ship's boats with a large canoe.

Hoping that there might be a passage to the South Sea at the end of the bight they now tried to work their way through it, but the tides ran so strongly that they had to abandon the attempt. It was left to Cook to discover the strait that bears his name.

On December 26 they sailed northwards along the west coast of the North Island, sighting the northwest point, which they

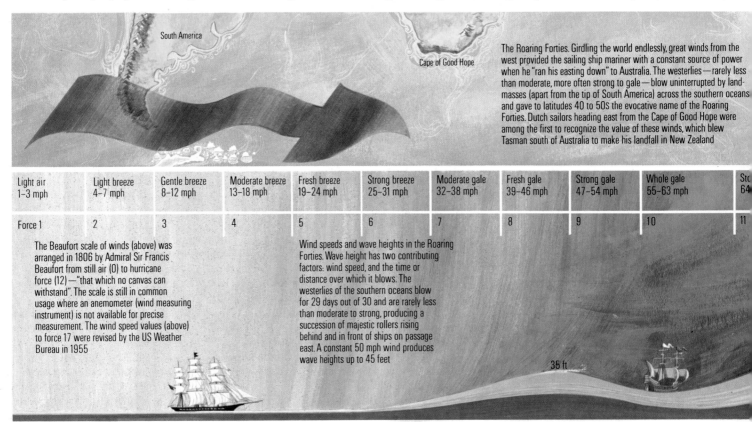

South America

Cape of Good Hope

The Roaring Forties. Girdling the world endlessly, great winds from the west provided the sailing ship mariner with a constant source of power when he "ran his easting down" to Australia. The westerlies—rarely less than moderate, more often strong to gale—blow uninterrupted by land-masses (apart from the tip of South America) across the southern oceans and gave to latitudes 40 to 50S the evocative name of the Roaring Forties. Dutch sailors heading east from the Cape of Good Hope were among the first to recognize the value of these winds, which blew Tasman south of Australia to make his landfall in New Zealand

Light air 1–3 mph	Light breeze 4–7 mph	Gentle breeze 8–12 mph	Moderate breeze 13–18 mph	Fresh breeze 19–24 mph	Strong breeze 25–31 mph	Moderate gale 32–38 mph	Fresh gale 39–46 mph	Strong gale 47–54 mph	Whole gale 55–63 mph	Sto 64
Force 1	2	3	4	5	6	7	8	9	10	11

The Beaufort scale of winds (above) was arranged in 1806 by Admiral Sir Francis Beaufort from still air (0) to hurricane force (12)—"that which no canvas can withstand". The scale is still in common usage where an anemometer (wind measuring instrument) is not available for precise measurement. The wind speed values (above) to force 17 were revised by the US Weather Bureau in 1955

Wind speeds and wave heights in the Roaring Forties. Wave height has two contributing factors: wind speed, and the time or distance over which it blows. The westerlies of the southern oceans blow for 29 days out of 30 and are rarely less than moderate to strong, producing a succession of majestic rollers rising behind and in front of ships on passage east. A constant 50 mph wind produces wave heights up to 45 feet

35 ft

named Cape Maria van Diemen in honour of the Governor's wife, a week later.

At the Three Kings Islands, 30 miles northwest of the cape (so named because it was reached on the Epiphany), they saw running water, of which they were in great need, but the heavy surf—and the sight of a crowd of enormously tall people moving about on the hills behind, all bellowing and waving great clubs—decided them that a landing here would not be a good thing. Another attempt to get water on January 6 was also frustrated because of the difficulty of making a landing.

The wind now forced them to take a north-easterly course instead of the easterly one they had planned, and on January 21, after sighting a small island, which they named Hooge Piljstaert (High Tropic-Bird Island), they reached Tonga-tabu, the largest of the 150 coral and volcanic islands of the Tonga Islands, southeast of Fiji.

Here, they were able to obtain an abundance of food, including pigs, fowls and fruit, in exchange for white linen, old iron nails, a Chinese looking-glass, beads and so on. The people were friendly, as they were on the neighbouring island of Eua.

On February 1 they sailed to the northeast, and in about 17N entered waters filled with small islands and reefs, sailing through them in thick weather at a time of year when the southeast trades meet the monsoon from the north. At another council of officers it was

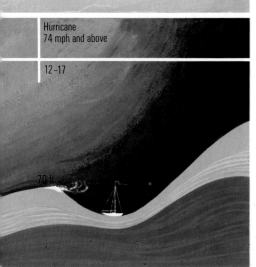

decided to sail to latitude 4N and then west to New Guinea, instead of heading due west immediately—which would have put them among the islands at the southeastern end of New Guinea, where they would have been in danger in such weather.

With rain falling almost every day during which they were unable to take a sight, they sailed northwest of Vanua Levu Island in the Fijis, mistaking its densely wooded windward shores for part of a very much larger body of land. On April 1 they were off the northern end of New Ireland, in 3S, the second largest island in the Bismarck Archipelago, which they thought to be a part of the mainland of New Guinea, as Schouten had done.

From here they sailed along the north coast of New Guinea, bartering for food on the way and looking for a strait by which they could reach Cape Keer-weer on the Cape York Peninsula to the south; and after reaching Pulao Waigeo, an island off the western extremity of New Guinea, discovered Djai-lolo, now Halmahera, the large island in the Moluccas east of the Celebes.

Sailing south through the strait between it and Waigeo Island to the east (it being too late to attempt to reach Cape Keer-weer) they sighted Ceram on May 26 and reached Batavia on June 14, 1643, after a voyage of more than 5,000 miles. They had proved that Australia was a great continent surrounded by water and was unattached to any land mass to the south; but they had still not discovered that it was possible to sail between New Guinea and Australia by way of the Torres Strait.

Cool reception

The great voyage was over. Although they had accomplished much, Tasman and Visscher were given a cool reception. "A remarkable voyage", it was conceded, but they "had been to some extent remiss in investigating the situation, conformation and nature of the lands and peoples discovered, and left the main part of this task to be executed by some more inquisitive successor".

This waspish conclusion led to the despatch, in February 1644, of another expedition of three ships, the *Limmen* and *Zeemeeuw*, both jachts, and the *Bracq*, a galiot, this time with Visscher as captain and Tasman as commander-in-chief.

Their orders were to discover whether there was a strait between New Guinea and the Southland and—having resolved this—to sail south down what was still thought to be the west coast of New Guinea, the Cape York Peninsula, as far as 17.8S, the farthest point reached by Carstenszoon, and then continue along it until a channel was found to the Pacific. If they found it they were to sail as far

south as Van Diemen's Land, where they were to find out whether it was part of the same land discovered by Nuyts in the Australian Bight, or a part of New Guinea. From Nuyts Land they were to sail west-wards, double Cape Leeuwin and explore the still unsurveyed sections of the west coast of the continent.

If there was no way to the Pacific from the Gulf of Carpentaria they were to explore its shores westwards and sail the entire way along the north and northwest coasts; then south as far as Houtman's Abrolhos, where they were to try to salvage a chest of dollars sunk there in the *Batavia* and also attempt to rescue two men marooned by Pelsaert 15 years before.

What they actually accomplished is shown on a map, probably made by Tasman with the co-operation of Visscher. The Torres Strait was again not passed, for some unknown reason, so that the explorers still believed that New Guinea and Australia were one at this point, a belief that was confirmed to them when they sailed the whole way round the shore of the Gulf of Carpentaria without finding any outlet.

West along the coasts of Arnhem Land, they probed into Van Diemen Gulf, east of the present city of Darwin and along the whole north and northwest coasts, the first Europeans to do so; then along the section of coast discovered by de Witt in 1628 to Northwest Cape, finally sailing into Shark Bay, inshore of Dirk Hartog Island, in 25S, where they turned back.

The Australian continent was now beginning to gain some recognizable shape, with its north, west and part of its southern shore known. The company named it Compagnis Niew Nederland—the Company's New Holland. Tasman was again icily received by the Governor-General and the council, who stated that in future voyages of discovery would be carried out by "more vigilant and courageous persons than have hitherto been employed on this service: for the exploration of unknown regions can by no means be entrusted to the first comer".

Tasman sailed no more on voyages of discovery. Not very grandly rewarded for his services by being promoted commander, he was sent in 1648 to attack a Spanish fleet with eight vessels and—unsuccessful in his mission—was discharged. Later he was reinstated, but retired and became a merchant in Batavia, dying in 1659.

Tasman's unsatisfactory record (so far as the company was concerned) and the information he brought back with him about the barren lands on the coasts of New Holland brought to an end any further serious exploration by the Dutch for 50 years.

The Pacific: new men, new motives

HISTORY, IN A BROAD rather than a particular sense, has few if any clearcut dividing lines. The great age of maritime discovery, ushered in by the Portuguese in the 15th century, did not end suddenly as though the seas had parted and a Divine voice said "Enough". It was to continue—and still does—but the 17th century, by the time of the Dutch landings on the west coast of Australia and in New Zealand, marked the end of an epoch.

For 200 years the nations of western Europe had sent their seafarers into a world that was at best sketchily known; a world of fierce and indescribable hazards to men certain only of the prospects of heaven and hell. The technology at their disposal, improved in terms of ships, was less so where navigation—the scientific, as opposed to the practical side of seamanship—was concerned. The 18th century, the "Age of Reason", brought to exploration the new, scientific approach and provided its pioneers with new equipment and facts on which to base their work. The motives, also, underwent a change. A greater part of the world—or at least, the silhouettes of its landmasses—had been unveiled and spheres of influences established. What now followed the earlier searches for wealth and aggrandisement was a scientifically based examination of what had already been found. The Pacific Ocean, greater by far in area than the land surfaces of the world put together, offered an apposite challenge, particularly to the French and the British.

In the last decade of the 17th century French interest in the Pacific Ocean led to the formation of the Compagnie Royale de la Mer Pacifique, and in 1698 Beauchêne Gouin was sent out from La Rochelle on a three-year voyage. It took him to the coasts of Tierra del Fuego, Chile, the Galapagos Islands and, on his homeward voyage, to Cape Horn (for which he produced a new, correct latitude) and to the Falkland Islands, which later became a French place of call under the name of the Iles Malouines. Further voyages followed, most of them from St Malo, and in 1709, when the Compagnie de Chine was formed, French ships began making their homeward-bound voyages across the Pacific.

An important trip, because of the immense influence it had subsequently, was the voyage of the French explorer Jean-Baptiste Bouvet de Lozier, who was sent by the Compagnie des Indes to look for a southern continent. He sighted land in 54.26s in the southern Atlantic on January 1, 1739—either Bouvet Island west of the longitude of the Cape of Good Hope, and about 1,600 miles southwest of it, or an iceberg. He believed it to be the "Southern India" which a nobleman, the

An outstanding navigator and hydrographer who made his first sea voyage at 16, William Dampier was an "academic" buccaneer. In 1679, his life took a picaresque turn when he joined a band of pirates to ravage the South American coast. In his lifetime he survived shipwreck and marooning, was court martialled for cruelty and variously accused of drunkenness, brutality and cowardice; but despite his shortcomings he was a great explorer and added to knowledge of the southern seas

Sieur de Gonneville, had discovered early in the 16th century. De Lozier named the headland he sighted Cape Circumcision, having discovered it on that feast day. Unfortunately he made an enormous error in calculating its longitude and complicated the lives of later explorers of the southern ocean.

In France and England the search for a southern continent was given fresh impetus by the writings of Charles de Brosses, President of the Parliament of Burgundy, John Callander, a Scottish advocate, and Alexander Dalrymple, an experienced hydrographer, also a Scot.

In 1740, Admiral Lord Anson began a voyage round the world, one of the last in the old tradition. He took his squadron round Cape Horn in terribly cold and stormy weather, looted Spanish possessions on the coast of Peru, crossed the Pacific to Manila, where he took a Spanish galleon, and returned home with its treasure and an immense quantity of other booty, some of it stolen from churches. His debit account included the loss of nearly two-thirds of the crews of his three ships from disease and other maritime hazards.

More important in intention—if not in result—was the voyage of Commodore John Byron in 1764, to discover "lands and islands of great extent, hitherto unvisited by any European power ... in the Atlantic Ocean between the Cape of Good Hope and the Magellanic Streight, within the latitudes convenient for navigation, and in climates

adapted to the produce of commodities useful in commerce".

Byron sailed in July 1764 with the *Dolphin*, a sixth-rate man-of-war, and the *Tamar*, a frigate commanded by Captain Mouat. Byron charted and took possession of the Falkland Islands (although the French were already on one of the coasts), and had a long and difficult voyage through the Strait of Magellan, where he and his crews saw giant Patagonians and came to appreciate the anti-scorbutic value of the fresh fish, scurvy grass, wild celery, berries and other vegetables which abounded.

Having reached Más Afuera, one of the Juan Fernandez Islands, he sailed west-northwest, but failed to find the mysterious land supposed to have been discovered by the buccaneer Edward Davis in 1687. He passed along the north side of the Tuamotu Islands (French Polynesia), naming them the Disappointment Islands—because he was unable to land—in June 1765.

Two hundred miles farther west, with his crews suffering from scurvy, he reached Takaroa, in what he named the King George Islands, where he forced a landing against opposition to get coconuts and scurvy grass. He saw there tools and part of one of Jacob Roggeveen's boats, left by the Dutch explorer on his round-the-world voyage in 1722. On July 30, after sighting various other islands and seeing birds which led him to believe that there must be a large land mass to the south, he reached Tinian in the Marianas, north of New Guinea. He returned home by way of Batavia and the Cape, reaching England after a voyage of only 22 months, in May 1766.

This was followed almost immediately by the voyages of Captain Samuel Wallis, also with the *Dolphin*, and Phillip Carteret in a sloop, the *Swallow*. They sailed together at first but parted company beyond the Magellan Strait because of the poor sailing qualities of Carteret's ship. The passage of the strait took four months and in the course of it Wallis had some of the Patagonian giants measured. He was unable to discover one who was more than five feet seven inches tall.

After calling at the Tuamotu islands for scurvy grass, coconuts and water he reached Otaheite (Tahiti), where he and his men experienced all the joys of Pacific island life and where the sick recovered from the scurvy which had broken out in spite of Wallis's precautions. The rations included wort—an infusion of malt, sauerkraut and vinegar—and "three thousand weight of portable soup".

On July 26 they sailed westwards from Tahiti to the distress of the inhabitants, who, after giving them an initially hostile reception, wanted them to stay for ever. On September 19 they reached Tinian, having seen only a few small islands on the way, and arrived in

England by way of the Cape of Good Hope in May 1768, after an absence of 626 days.

Meanwhile Carteret in the wretched *Swallow*, which should never have been allowed to go on the voyage at all and was less well equipped with anti-scorbutics, had reached Más Afuera after a stormy voyage, where he took on water with difficulty because of the weather. He then sailed west in about latitude 28s, to the south of the course steered by Wallis, reaching the reported position of "Davis Land" but failing to find it.

Then, on July 2, 1767, in 25s, 130w, a member of the *Dolphin*'s company, the "son to Major Pitcairn of the Marines" sighted the tiny island which now bears his name and which was to become famous as the refuge of the mutinous crew of Captain Bligh's *Bounty* when they sailed there 22 years later.

Bad weather and sickness now forced Carteret to stand farther north when he was in about 170w, and in August he noticed a southerly set in the current which led him to think, correctly, that there must be open water between New Zealand and New Holland (Australia). He sailed on to rediscover the Santa Cruz group, forgotten since Mendaña discovered them two centuries earlier, and later he sighted Buka at the north end of the Solomons without realizing that he was in the group (Mendaña's estimate of the distance he had sailed to them from his last landfall in the Ellice Islands was exaggerated and misleading).

From here Carteret sailed west, discovering St George's Channel between New Ireland and New Britain, and reached the Celebes in December 1767. Here he remained until May the following year while the sick convalesced and the *Swallow* was repaired by Dutch shipwrights. Her timbers were so rotten and shrunken that a man's hand could be inserted between the butt end of the planks at the stern.

By this time 24 of the crew had died and another seven died on the way to the Cape of Good Hope on the homeward trip. It was fortunate that Carteret had been able to recruit more British seamen in the Celebes. He reached England in May 1769, a year after Wallis, he and his crew having made one of the most courageous voyages of the 18th century, in one of the most unseaworthy vessels ever despatched on a voyage around the world.

The first French navigator to sail round the world on a voyage of discovery was Louis Antoine, Comte de Bougainville, a disciple of de Brosses. Two other Frenchmen had preceded him, Pierre Olivier Malherbe and Legentil Labartinais. Malherbe encircled the world in the 16th and 17th centuries, but he travelled overland part of the way and took 25 years to do it. Labartinais did actually sail round it, but in the course of business—he was a smuggler.

Bougainville, a humane, humorous and highly intelligent product of the age (his *Voyage Autour du Monde* is an entertaining book), was 37 when he sailed from Nantes in November 1766. His parents intended him to be a lawyer but instead he became, successively, soldier, mathematician (he wrote a treatise on integral calculus), secretary at the French Embassy in London and aide-de-camp to the Marquis de Montcalm, who was killed in the fighting with General Wolfe on the Heights of Abraham. When the Seven Years' War ended he colonized the Iles Malouines (the Falklands) at his own expense and it was his settlers who were there when Byron took possession of them.

Bougainville's ship was a frigate, *La Boudeuse*, with a complement of 214. This was one of the first voyages in which scientists took part and Bougainville had with him Philibert de Commerçon, a naturalist, and M Verron, who was to make observations for determining longitude.

Transfer to Spain

As France had decided to hand over the Iles Malouines to Spain, Bougainville was given the job of carrying out a transfer which must have been distasteful to him. Then, having been joined by the transport *L'Etoile*, Bougainville sailed through the Magellan Strait, experiencing very bad weather, passing Cape Pilar at the Pacific end 52 days after entering the narrows.

Sailing first northwest through large tracts of ocean, between the routes followed by Wallis and Carteret, in search of "Davis Land", Bougainville abandoned the search and turned his ships more to the west and on March 22 he sighted Vahitahi atoll at the eastern end of the Tuamotu Archipelago. It was impossible to land on other low islets seen in the course of the next few days because of the surf and the absence of any anchorage.

One of these islands, Akiaki, he named Ile des Lanciers. "The sea broke much to the north and south and a great swell beating all along the eastern side, prevented our access to this isle in that part," he wrote. "However the verdure charmed our eyes, and the cocoa-trees everywhere exposed their fruits to our sight, and overshadowed a grass plot adorned with flowers; thousands of birds were hovering about the shore, and seemed to announce a coast abounding in fish, and we all longed for a descent . . . some of our people cried out that they saw three men running to the sea-shore . . . and my first conjectures were, that some Europeans must certainly have been ship-wrecked on it. I presently gave orders to

lay-to; as I was determined to do all I could to save them . . . soon after they came out again, fifteen or twenty in number, and advanced very fast; they were naked, and bore very long pikes, which they brandished against the ships, with signs of threatening. . . . These men seemed very tall, and of a bronze colour—Who can give an account of the manner in which they were conveyed hither, what communications they have with other beings, and what becomes of them when they multiply on an isle, which is no more than a league in diameter? . . . I made the signal to the Etoile to sound; she did so with a line of two hundred fathoms, without finding any bottom."

With some reason Bougainville named this group L'Archipel Dangéreux.

In April, eight months after Wallis, he reached Tahiti, naming it Nouvelle Cythère, where the ships were surrounded by outrigger canoes whose occupants offered them fruit.

Two days later they anchored and more canoes came out, the occupants crying "'tayo' which means friend. . . . They pressed us to choose a woman and to come on shore with her. . . . It was very difficult to keep at their work four hundred young French sailors, who had seen no woman for six months. In spite of all our precautions, a young girl came on board, and placed herself upon the quarter-deck, near one of the hatch-ways, which was open, in order to give air to those who were heaving at the capstern below it. The girl carelessly dropt a cloth, which covered her, and appeared to the eyes of all beholders, such as Venus shewed herself to the Phrygian shepherd, having, indeed, the celestial form of that goddess. Both sailors and soldiers endeavoured to come to the hatch-way; and the capstern was never hove with more alacrity than on this occasion."

They sailed on April 16, having planted wheat and barley, giving presents of turkeys and ducks to the chief, Ereti, and taking with them his brother, Ahutoru, who wished to see the world. Later, in Paris, although he never learned French, Ahutoru developed a passion for opera.

Then they sailed west, just to the north of Wallis's track, seeing the more savage and less trustworthy inhabitants of Manua and Tutuila in Samoa, whom Ahutoru was unable to understand, people whose triangular-sailed canoes were so fast that they made rings round Bougainville's ships even when they were sailing at eight knots "with the same ease as if we had been at anchor". He named these islands L'Archipel des Navigateurs. Scurvy now made its appearance for the second time (in spite of Bougainville having taken the precaution of giving his crews lemon juice and distilled water, it had broken out on the

The Pacific: new men, new motives

voyage from South America to Tahiti) and now there was nothing to eat except pulse (the seeds of leguminous plants) made into a pottage and salt meat. Also there was venereal disease, contracted at Tahiti.

"Have the English brought it thither?" Bougainville speculated, "or ought the physician to win, who laid a wager, that if four healthy stout men were shut up with one healthy woman, the venereal complaint would be the consequence of their commerce?"

On May 22 they reached the New Hebrides, which he named the Grand Cyclades, about 500 miles west of Fiji, and there, after an opposed landing, they managed to get some fruit, wood and water from the inhabitants. "These islanders are of two colours, black

and mulattoes. Their lips are thick, their hair woolly, and sometimes of a yellowish colour. They are short, ugly, ill proportioned, and most of them infected with leprosy."

At this point Bougainville was convinced that he had rediscovered Quiros's Austrialia del Espiritu Santo. "Has this Spanish navigator seen things in a wrong light? Or, has he been willing to disguise his discoveries? Was it by guess that the geographers made this Tierra del Espiritu Santo the same continent with New Guinea? To resolve this problem, it was necessary to keep in the same latitude for the space of three hundred and fifty leagues further.
I resolved to do it, though the

Until Cook's time, a successful oceanic navigator needed instinct and some luck to be sure of a successful passage. Such equipment as he possessed was simple and imprecise; at the height of a long passage at sea a captain would know no more than approximately where he was—and an expected landfall could be much more sudden and disastrous than he would hope. Thanks to new equipment—sextants and octants which were technically superior versions of the old Davis quadrant and, most important of all, the chronometer, which enabled a longitudinal position to be established accurately—Cook was the first commander of a ship to know almost exactly where he was at any point in his journey

The invention of the chronometer (above) marked the greatest step forward in marine navigation since the compass. An accurate timekeeper is critical in establishing longitudinal position at sea, but until Harrison's invention, no timepiece could retain its accuracy aboard ship. Harrison's chronometer, developed between 1729 and 1760, kept near perfect time despite buffeting and climatic changes. The model shown (above) was made by Larcum Kendall and was taken by James Cook on his third and last voyage

The dipping needle used by Cook on his second voyage. When it was aligned north–south with the aid of a conventional compass, its needle dipped to measure the vertical component of the Earth's magnetic field—its depth beneath the horizon

A Ramsden sextant, used by Cook and his officers. Like the backstaff of John Davis, it measured the angular distance of objects by means of reflection to establish latitude and longitude, but far more precisely

A sextant (above) and an azimuth compass (above right) fitted with vertical sights to bear on the altitude of a star

condition and quantity of our provisions seemed to give us reason to make the best of our way to some European settlement."

He had in fact sailed through the strait between Espiritu Santo and Malekula and was now in the Coral Sea, about 1,200 miles east of the coast of Queensland. From this day forward, with the intention of raising the east coast of New Holland, Bougainville sailed steadily west in latitude 15S, learning on the way that M de Commerçon's valet, Baré, who had become an expert botanist, was in fact a woman in disguise, Commerçon himself having been completely deceived. "It must be owned", said Bougainville, "that if the two ships had been wrecked on any desert isle in the ocean, Baré's fate would have been a very singular one." On June 4, having seen a small flat island covered with birds, which he named La Bâture de Diane, the Shoal of Diana (now the Diane Bank in 15.4S, 149.37E), he was only about 260 miles from the Australian coast.

In spite of the fresh southeast wind there was now a sinister smoothness about the sea and the weed, driftwood and strange fruits floating on it, all indications pointing to the nearness of land.

Breakers ahead

On the afternoon of January 6 they saw a sand bank and breakers and "at half past five o'clock, the men at the mastheads saw fresh breakers to the N.W. and N.W. by W. about a league and a half from us. We approached nearer to see them better. . . . The sea broke, with great violence on these shoals, and some summits of rocks appeared above water from space to space. This last discovery was the voice of God, and we were obedient to it." What his men saw from the mastheads was the Great Barrier Reef, and he had just

missed running on to what is now called the Bougainville Reef about 125 miles east of Cooktown on the coast of Queensland. It was too dangerous to set a fresh course in such waters with night coming on, but after making short tacks all night Bougainville clawed off and sailed northeast by north the following morning.

Four days later they sighted the southeast coast of New Guinea from the approaches to the Torres Strait. "Long before the break of day, a delicious smell announced us the vicinity of this land, which forms a great gulph open to the S.E. I have seen but few lands, which bore a finer aspect than this; a low ground, divided into plains and groves, lay along the sea-shore and from thence it rose like an amphitheatre up to the mountains, whose summits were lost in the clouds. There were three ranges of mountains; and the highest chain was above twenty-five leagues in the interior parts of the country. The wretched condition to which we were reduced, did not allow us, either to spend some time in visiting this beautiful country . . . nor to stand to westward in search of a passage on the south side of New Guinea, which might open a new and short navigation to the Molucas, by the gulph of Carpentaria. Nothing, indeed, was more probable, than the existence of such a passage." What hardship it would have saved them; but the risk was great. By now they only had bread for two months and pulse for 40 days although "the salt-meat was in greater quantities; but we preferred the rats to it, which we could catch".

Now the wind died away and they were nearly carried on to the coast off which there were no soundings at two leagues. This calm was succeeded by strong winds from the southeast, accompanied by fog; and now they were on the southern edge of the dangerous labyrinth of the Louisiade Archipelago in wild seas that hurled shells, sand and weed

from the bottom on to the decks of the ships.

With rations still further reduced Bougainville had to forbid the eating of the leather chafing gear from the yards. The goat they had brought from the Iles Malouines was slaughtered—the butcher shedding tears— and so was a dog bought from the natives in the Magellan Strait.

On June 20 they finally succeeded in doubling Cape Deliverance on Rossel Island at the eastern extremity of the Louisiades and a week later reached the Solomon Islands.

On the shores of what Bougainville named Ile Choiseul they were attacked, the natives deploying their canoes in a masterly way to surround the ships. Even the discharge of firearms failed to stop them and it took a second volley to put them to flight. "Our people took two of their periagues [canoes] . . . on the head of one of these . . . they had carved the head of a man; the eyes were of tortoise-shell, and the whole figure resembled a mask with a long beard. The lips were dyed of a bright red. In their periagues our people found bows, arrows in great quantity, lances, shields, cocoa-nuts, and several fruits, of what species we could not tell . . . some nets with very fine meshes, very well knit, and the jaw of a man, half broiled. These islanders are black, and have curled hair, which they dye white, yellow or red. . . . We called the river and creek from whence these brave islanders came, the Warriors River. . . ."

New Britain

Sailing from these perilous shores and not realizing that he had been in the Solomon Islands—they were to be the subject of long searches in the future—Bougainville reached the coast of New Britain, where there was wood and water; no food but an abundance of giant ants. Here, in what he named Port Praslin, a lead plaque was found, left there by Carteret in his camp, four months earlier.

At the beginning of September they reached Buru Island, west of Ceram in the Moluccas. "The provisions which we had now left were so rotten, and had so cadaverous a smell, that the hardest moments of the sad days we passed, were those when the bell gave us notice to take in this disgusting and unwholesome food."

On Buru they were well treated by the Dutch and feasted on fresh meat and venison. They arrived at Batavia 12 days after Carteret had left, and from there sailed to Mauritius, overhauling and making contact with Carteret in the Atlantic.

Bougainville arrived back at St Malo on March 16, 1769, having lost only seven men in two years and four months. At first it was not believed that he had sailed round the world, as he had not touched on China!

Cook's great voyages

THE PUBLIC INSTRUCTIONS to Lieutenant James Cook, RN, by the Lords of the Admiralty in 1768 were brief and uncomplicated. He was to sail with a team of scientists to the island of Tahiti, in the Pacific, there to observe the transit of Venus—the passage of the planet between the Earth and the Sun—in June the following year. There were other instructions.

They were contained in a sealed envelope, not to be opened until the transit had occurred, almost as if the Lords of the Admiralty had arranged the celestial phenomenon as a cover for the real purpose of the journey. What they ordered Cook to do in great detail shows the radical changes in the whole concept of exploration by the late 18th century.

". . . Whereas there is reason to imagine that a Continent or Land of great extent, may be found to the Southward of the Tract lately made by Captn Wallis in His Majesty's Ship the Dolphin (of which you will herewith receive a Copy) or of the Tract of any former Navigators in Pursuits of the like kind; You are therefore in Pursuance of His Majesty's Pleasure hereby requir'd and directed to put to Sea with the Bark you Command so soon as the Observation of the Transit of the Planet Venus shall be finished and observe the following instructions.

"You are to proceed to the southward in order to make discovery of the Continent above-mentioned (Southward of the Tract lately made by Captain Wallis in His Majesty's Ship the Dolphin or of the Tract of any former Navigators in Pursuits of the like kind) until you arrive in the Latitude of 40 degrees, unless you sooner fall in with it. But not having discover'd it or any Evident signs of it in that Run, you are to proceed in search of it to the Westward between the Latitude before mentioned and the Latitude of 35 degrees until you discover it, or fall in with the Eastern side of the Land discover'd by Tasman and now called New Zeland."

In the true spirit of the scientific age, Cook was also instructed to produce a detailed survey of the coastline of the southern continent and to observe its flora, fauna and inhabitants. With the latter he was to "cultivate a Friendship and Alliance" and try to establish "Traffick". He was also to obtain their consent before taking possession "of Convenient Situations in the Country . . . or if you find the Country uninhabited take Possession for His Majesty by setting up Proper Marks and Inscriptions, as first discoverers.

"But if you should fail of discovering the Continent before-mentioned, you will upon falling in with New Zeland carefully observe the Latitude and Longitude in which the Land is situated, and explore as much of the Coast as the Condition of the Bark, the health of her Crew, and the State of your Provisions will admit of, having always great Attention to reserve as much of the latter as will enable you to reach some known Port where you may procure a Sufficiency to carry you to England, either round the Cape of Good Hope, or Cape Horn, as from Circumstances you may judge the Most Eligible way of returning home. . . ."

It was unheard of for a man of Cook's humble origins to be selected for such a command and it would not have happened a few years later, but at the time he was the only man in the Royal Navy with the necessary qualifications and it is to the credit of the Admiralty that they realized it.

Cook was a genius. Forty years old, more than six feet tall, broad shouldered, blue-eyed, with his brown hair tied behind his head in the manner of the time, he was a typical professional officer of the Royal Navy, capable, reserved, determined. The only erratic thing about him was his spelling, a fault, however, that has its own charm.

Humble origins

His background, however, was very different to that of the conventional officer. Born in 1728 in a clay cottage at Marton-in-Cleveland, Yorkshire, the son of an agricultural labourer, he received a minimal education at the village school, in spite of which he was reported to show "a remarkable facility in the science of numbers". At 12, he was apprenticed first to a shopkeeper at Staithes, a place on the Yorkshire coast now under the North Sea, then to a firm of shipowners at Whitby, sailing in their coal ships to Scandinavia and the Baltic.

With the outbreak of the Seven Years' War between Britain and France and Spain, Cook joined the navy as seaman in the *Eagle*, a 60-gun ship commanded by Captain Hugh Palliser, an officer who was to be of great assistance to Cook in his future career. In just over a month the young Yorkshireman became master's mate and subsequently saw action in the Channel and the northern Atlantic.

Four years later, as master of the *Mercury*, he sailed to the St Lawrence, where he laid the foundations of his reputation as a master navigator and surveyor.

When Cook finally left Canada in 1767, he was still a non-commissioned officer and it was not until May 1768—only three months before he sailed on his first great voyage—that he was made Lieutenant in command of the *Endeavour*, an ordinary Whitby collier of 368 tons which the Admiralty had chosen for the venture. It was the sort of ship that Cook knew better than any.

The *Endeavour* carried a complement of 97, including a one-handed cook whom Cook had received after protesting at the appointment of a man with only one leg—one of his few unsuccessful skirmishes with naval bureaucrats.

The scientists, among whom Cook himself was included (while in Newfoundland in 1766 he had observed a solar eclipse and recorded the details for the Royal Society), were Charles Green, Assistant to the Astronomer Royal; Joseph Banks, a wealthy young naturalist and member of the Society, who put up £10,000 to help the expedition and supplied some of the telescopes and other scientific equipment; and Dr Carl Solander, a Swedish botanist and pupil of Linnaeus, and his assistant. There were also two artists, Alexander Buchan, a landscape painter, and Sydney Parkinson, who specialized in natural history.

Cook sailed from Plymouth in August 1768, much to the chagrin of Alexander Dalrymple, the Royal Society's nominee, who had hoped to be in command. The fact that he was a conceited, didactic, narrow-minded and vindictive character might not have debarred him in an age of patronage; but fortunately for the ship's company and posterity he was not a sailor and the First Lord of the Admiralty, Sir Edward Hawke, vetoed his appointment with the words that he would rather lose his right hand than give a King's ship to a man not of the service.

Cook's chief preoccupation was with scurvy. The dreadful example of the three ships of Admiral Anson on their circumnavigation of the world in which, out of a total complement of 961 men, 626 were dead by the time they reached the Juan Fernandez Islands, was constantly before him. He also had first-hand experience of its effects. While serving in the *Eagle* under Palliser, a humane commander who thought one of its causes might be inadequate clothing, 22 men had died out of a crew of 400 and another 130 had been put ashore—and this in a well-run ship operating off the coasts of Europe.

To combat it Cook made radical changes in the ship's diet, taking the advice of Pelham,

The death ship

Secretary to the Commissioners of Victualling to the Navy.

Butter and cheese were banned and so was suet, and the ration of beef and pork preserved in brine was reduced and issued without the fat (in the 20th century there were still outbreaks of scurvy in sailing ships on long passages due to over-consumption of pickled meat without sufficient fresh foods to counterbalance it). Cook also took with him more than 7,000 pounds of sauerkraut, "portable soup", mustard, vinegar, wheat, "saloop" (salep, a sort of meal which could be made into a hot drink), raisins, malt, with which the infusion called wort was made, and citrus juices. Citrus fruits had been used effectively as long before as 1593 by Sir Richard Hawkins on a privateering voyage to the west coast of South America and by Schouten and le Maire in their voyage to the East Indies by way of Cape Horn in 1615. Some of these special stores had been taken by Wallis on his voyage; but it was the combination of them with other new ingredients, and the reduction in intake of salt meat, that was decisive.

Principal causes of mortality among Royal Navy warship crews during the late 18th century

Enemy action 8.3pc

Fire, sinking, wreck 10.2

Accident 31.5

Disease 50

Eye-patch, hook-hand and peg-leg, equipment of the pantomime pirate, are theatrical details with origins of historical accuracy. Throughout its history, the sailing ship was a death trap to the men who sailed in it and mutilation often the lot of those who survived a lifetime at sea.

During the late 18th century, when British sea power was approaching its peak, press-gangs roamed the seaports, clubbing senseless unwary passers-by and carrying them off to lives of hardship and likely death—not in action, but from accident or disease.

A breakdown of the principal causes of death in the Royal Navy of that time is shown. Within those overwhelming proportions of disease and accident there was an awful variety of individual items. A ship, on leaving port, might have gleamed from stem to stern, but after months at sea, the air below decks was rank and foetid and bilges fouled. Respiratory diseases—tuberculosis, pneumonia—were rife; stomach disorders, caused by bad food and bad water, were things with which every sailor had to live.

Headroom below decks was so limited that cracked heads were common (lunacy among sailors and former sailors was seven times higher than the national average); ruptures caused by lifting weights meant that Nelson's flagship included hundreds of trusses in its inventory. If a man found his way to the surgeon, he was in the hands of a man who supplied his own drugs and instruments and knew as little about his job as the men he treated.

To these everyday hazards, a passage in the tropics added many more. Yellow Jack, or the black vomits, and malaria reduced crews to a point where, unless more hands could be pressed, a ship sailed undermanned and was more prone to foundering or running aground. Finally there was scurvy, a horrifying deficiency disease leading to disfiguration and death. Although it could be countered by a balanced diet, it remained common until steam came along to shorten time on passage and reduce the crew's reliance on stored foods

1 Falls were an everyday hazard to men racing aloft to take in sail at the onset of a squall. They meant either broken bodies on deck or "man lost overboard"

2 A fall into a billowing sail would catapult a sailor far into the sea

3 An added storm hazard was electrocution, if lightning struck a mast

5 Snapping cables whiplashed, severing the limbs of bystanders if not killing them

4 Rupture, caused by hauling on ropes or reefing heavy sails, was common among crew members

6 On deck, a gun breaking loose from its mount would crush anyone in its path and had to be tripped on its side to stop it

7 Cramped quarters below decks, bad air and foul bilges generated the respiratory and other diseases to which sailing ship crews fell victim

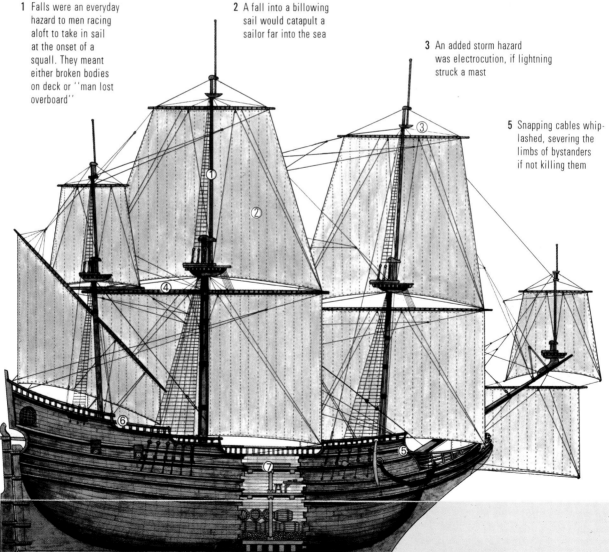

Cook's great voyages

He also took every opportunity of stocking up with fresh foods—in Madeira he bought meat, vegetables and also wine—and although he was a humane man for the times in which he lived, he had two members of the crew flogged for refusing to eat their rations of fresh meat.

He was also careful about cleanliness. His men had to take at least one cold bath a day and twice a week they were made to bring their clothes and bedding on deck for an airing. Once a week the ship was fumigated—"smoked clean with a mixture of vinegar and gunpowder"—and a strict eye was kept on the quality of the drinking water and the cleanliness of the cooking utensils.

As a result of his care, which at first made Cook unpopular with some of his men, there was very little illness and only four or five men suffered from scurvy during the entire voyage.

In the middle of January 1769, before passing through the Le Maire Strait between Tierra del Fuego and Staten Island, where Cook began charting, they saw the Fuegians, whose condition had not changed for the better since the time of Drake.

Finding a convenient bay in which to take on wood and water, Banks and a party went into the interior to look for plants. Apart from the specimens they brought back the expedition was a disaster—the weather was bitterly cold, Alexander Buchan suffered an epileptic fit (he died at Tahiti) and two of Banks's Negro servants died of exposure, after passing out as the result of a drinking bout.

On February 13, 1769, six months after leaving home, Cook was able to write in his *Journal*: "... we are now advanced about 12 degrees to the westward of the Strait of Magellan and 3½ degrees to the north of it [about 53S, 79W], having been 33 days in doubbling Cape Horn or the Land of Terra del Fuego. ..."

Now that he was in the Pacific, Cook shaped a course northwest for Tahiti far to the west of any sailed previously, and on March 1 *Endeavour* was in longitude 110.33W, 560 leagues (1,680 nautical miles) west of the coast of Chile, "which exactly agrees with the Longitude given by the Log from Cape Horn." Cook, as ever, knew where he was. "This agreement of the two longitudes after a run of 660 leagues [1,980 nautical miles] is surpriseing and much more than could have been expected. ..."

On April 4 the first coral atoll was sighted, Vahitahi in the Tuamotu Archipelago. A week later they arrived at Matavi Bay.

In spite of Cook's rather optimistic *Rules to be observe'd by every person in or belonging to His Majestys Bark the Endevour, for the better establishing a regular and uniform Trade for Provisions &c* *with the Inhabitants of Georges*

The oceanic 'continent'

Trivial incident with a fatal outcome; James Cook was killed in a skirmish with natives in Hawaii—a sorry end for a man who always displayed concern for the islanders

After the loss of their leader, Cook's men carried on with one of his tasks—the search for a northwest passage. The drawing of Kamchatka is by one of his artists

"In ten years, he explored more of the earth's surface than any other man in history." This tribute was to James Cook, who by sheer competence as a navigator, sailor and leader of men rose in his lifetime from obscure origins to a permanent place in history. In his youth and early twenties he served in collier brigs working out of Whitby, a busy port in his native Yorkshire, before joining the Royal Navy in 1755 as a seaman. In two years he was master—warrant officer in charge of handling a warship—aboard the 64-gun "Pembroke" and by his navigational skills was instrumental in the successful assault on Quebec by General Wolfe in 1759. The talents that had gained him promotion made him a giant among explorers

If the Pacific were a land mass, fringed by sea, it would be a super-continent. In area, it is greater by far than all the land surfaces of the globe. Much of the land along its margins—the west coasts of the Americas, New Zealand, Indonesia, Japan and the Aleutians—is volcanic, giving to these margins the name of the "Ring of Fire". The oceanic islands, too, are volcanic upthrusts from the seabed, making the journeys of Cook and his contemporaries voyages from mountain-top to mountain-top. Coral reefs, surrounding many islands with a rampart marked only by broken water (how the reefs "grow" is shown below), brought disaster to many ships; even Cook was caught out, on the Great Barrier Reef. He won his battle, but others were not so lucky. The French navigator La Pérouse was lost in this way

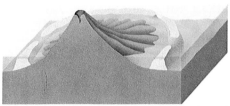
An island is formed by vulcanism; around its margin, coral grows in the warm shallows—water temperature at least 21°C—to enclose an area of calm lagoon

Coral is formed by a substance secreted by millions of polyps, small marine animals. As the volcano is weathered away, coral continues to grow, like a living graveyard

Continued erosion of the volcano results in the disappearance of the original island, but the upward growth of the coral forms a typical atoll, or group of coral islands

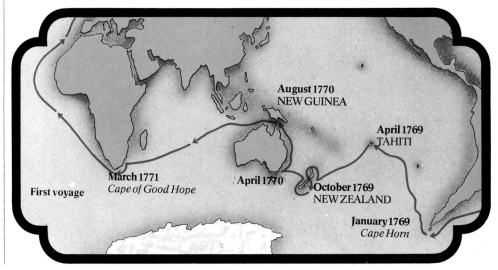
August 1770
NEW GUINEA

April 1769
TAHITI

March 1771
Cape of Good Hope

April 1770

October 1769
NEW ZEALAND

First voyage

January 1769
Cape Horn

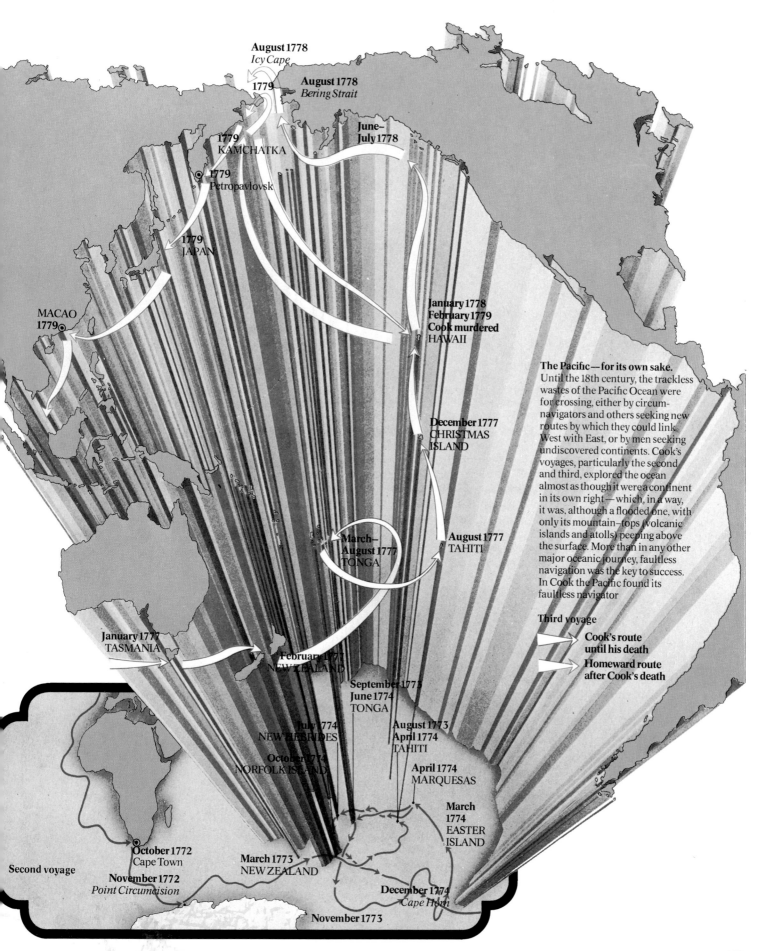

August 1778
Icy Cape

1779

August 1778
Bering Strait

1779
KAMCHATKA

June–
July 1778

1779
Petropavlovsk

1779
JAPAN

MACAO
1779

January 1778
February 1779
Cook murdered
HAWAII

December 1777
CHRISTMAS
ISLAND

August 1777
TAHITI

March–
August 1777
TONGA

The Pacific — for its own sake.
Until the 18th century, the trackless
wastes of the Pacific Ocean were
for crossing, either by circumnavigators and others seeking new
routes by which they could link
West with East, or by men seeking
undiscovered continents. Cook's
voyages, particularly the second
and third, explored the ocean
almost as though it were a continent
in its own right — which, in a way,
it was, although a flooded one, with
only its mountain–tops (volcanic
islands and atolls) peeping above
the surface. More than in any other
major oceanic journey, faultless
navigation was the key to success.
In Cook the Pacific found its
faultless navigator

Third voyage

➡ **Cook's route
until his death**

➡ **Homeward route
after Cook's death**

January 1777
TASMANIA

February 1777
NEW ZEALAND

September 1773
June 1774
TONGA

July 1774
NEW HEBRIDES

August 1773
April 1774
TAHITI

October 1774
NORFOLK ISLAND

April 1774
MARQUESAS

March
1774
EASTER
ISLAND

October 1772
Cape Town

November 1772
Point Circumcision

Second voyage

March 1773
NEW ZEALAND

December 1774
Cape Horn

November 1773

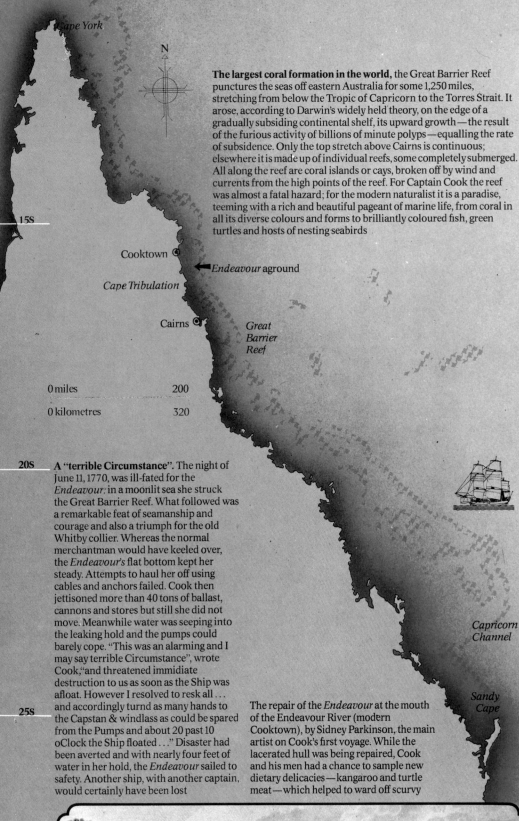

The largest coral formation in the world, the Great Barrier Reef punctures the seas off eastern Australia for some 1,250 miles, stretching from below the Tropic of Capricorn to the Torres Strait. It arose, according to Darwin's widely held theory, on the edge of a gradually subsiding continental shelf, its upward growth—the result of the furious activity of billions of minute polyps—equalling the rate of subsidence. Only the top stretch above Cairns is continuous; elsewhere it is made up of individual reefs, some completely submerged. All along the reef are coral islands or cays, broken off by wind and currents from the high points of the reef. For Captain Cook the reef was almost a fatal hazard; for the modern naturalist it is a paradise, teeming with a rich and beautiful pageant of marine life, from coral in all its diverse colours and forms to brilliantly coloured fish, green turtles and hosts of nesting seabirds

Cape York

N

15S

Cooktown

← Endeavour aground

Cape Tribulation

Cairns

Great
Barrier
Reef

0 miles   200
0 kilometres   320

20S A "terrible Circumstance". The night of June 11, 1770, was ill-fated for the *Endeavour*: in a moonlit sea she struck the Great Barrier Reef. What followed was a remarkable feat of seamanship and courage and also a triumph for the old Whitby collier. Whereas the normal merchantman would have keeled over, the *Endeavour*'s flat bottom kept her steady. Attempts to haul her off using cables and anchors failed. Cook then jettisoned more than 40 tons of ballast, cannons and stores but still she did not move. Meanwhile water was seeping into the leaking hold and the pumps could barely cope. "This was an alarming and I may say terrible Circumstance", wrote Cook,"and threatened immidiate destruction to us as soon as the Ship was afloat. However I resolved to resk all . . .

25S and accordingly turnd as many hands to the Capstan & windlass as could be spared from the Pumps and about 20 past 10 oClock the Ship floated . . ." Disaster had been averted and with nearly four feet of water in her hold, the *Endeavour* sailed to safety. Another ship, with another captain, would certainly have been lost

Capricorn
Channel

Sandy
Cape

The repair of the *Endeavour* at the mouth of the Endeavour River (modern Cooktown), by Sidney Parkinson, the main artist on Cook's first voyage. While the lacerated hull was being repaired, Cook and his men had a chance to sample new dietary delicacies—kangaroo and turtle meat—which helped to ward off scurvy

Cook's great voyages

Island, the inhabitants were so "prodigious expert" as Cook put it, at pilfering—"they clime like Munkeys"—that they not only stole every iron object they set eyes on but also Dr Solander's spy glass, Banks's snuff-box and Cook's stockings, which, for some extraordinary reason, he had behind his pillow. They also put the whole of Operation Venus in danger by stealing the heavy metal quadrant which was essential to the observation of the planet's transit. Banks recovered it only with the greatest difficulty.

On June 3 the long-awaited Transit of Venus took place, one of the results being that Cook was able to deduce the longitude of Venus Point, the most northerly of the island, where his observations were made to within 3 minutes 45 seconds of what it is accepted to be today.

By the beginning of July Cook was anxious to put to sea, having finished his exploration of the island in the company of Banks, seeing the great temple and burial place and gathering the material for an account of the way of life of the inhabitants, and their religion. "The misteries of most religions are very dark and not easily understud," he wrote.

With much lamentation on the part of islanders and crew Cook sailed on July 13 with two supernumeraries, a chief named Tupaia, who volunteered, and his servant. Tupaia was a priest and showed his capacity by sometimes calling up a favourable wind. He was also an excellent pilot.

In the next three weeks, with his help, Cook was able to visit a number of islands west of Tahiti, most of them high volcanic mountains surrounded by coral reefs. He surveyed Huahine and hoisted the flag on Raiatea, Tupaia's birthplace, where he took possession of the entire group, naming them the Society Islands, "as they lay contiguous to one another".

From Raiatea, obeying his secret orders, he sailed southwest on August 9 for almost 1,500 miles in search of the supposed continent, although what Tupaia told him reinforced his own opinion—that there were only islands to be found.

The question whether New Zealand formed the west coast of a great continent was soon to be resolved. At 2 p.m. on October 7, two months after sailing from the Society Islands, Nicholas Young, one of the ship's boys who was at the mast-head, sighted the east coast of the North Island of New Zealand, for which he received the usual reward of a gallon of rum and the honour of having the white-cliffed promontory named after him—Young Nick's Head, the southwestern point of an open bay with low-lying wooded land behind, backed by mountains. Here, Cook's landing parties had an unfriendly reception from the

Maoris, and although Tupaia was able to talk to them, fighting broke out.

On October 11 Cook weighed anchor and sailed out of the bay, naming it Poverty Bay, "because it afforded us no one thing we wanted".

After rounding the Mahia Peninsula, 40 miles to the south, and entering what he named Hawke Bay, after the First Lord of the Admiralty, he found bad anchorages and poor land on shore. Cook turned the *Endeavour*'s head to the north again and in Tolaga Bay, north of his first landfall, found Maoris who were prepared to trade and an abundance of flora and fauna on which no scientist had ever laid eyes.

Here, Sydney Parkinson, the surviving artist, was able to produce some remarkable portraits of the fantastically tattooed inhabitants, who were dressed in skins.

Then, doubling Cape Runaway, where the ship was pursued by giant canoes containing anything up to a hundred ferocious Maoris, Cook put into a bay on the northwest side of the rich and cultivated Bay of Plenty where, together with Green, he observed the Transit of Mercury and saw a *Pa*, a well-fortified Maori village.

"All hands drunk," Banks wrote disapprovingly on Christmas Day 1769; that day Cook sighted Tasman's Three Kings Islands, northwest of Cape Maria Van Diemen.

Sailing down the west coast Cook named Mount Egmont, 8,260 feet high and known to the Maoris as Taranaki, and three days later, in a leaking ship (the *Endeavour* had struck a rock, but without serious damage) entered the western end of the strait between the North and South Islands that was to bear his name.

In what he named Ship Cove, on the north coast of the South Island, he had the ship careened and her hull scraped and caulked and here he climbed a hill and saw for himself what the Maoris had told him and Tasman had failed to discover—that the great inlet was in fact a strait.

On February 7 *Endeavour* began the dangerous passage eastwards through Cook Strait in the course of which ". . . the tide Ebb makeing out we were carried by the rapiddity of the stream in a very short time close by one of the Islands where we narrowly escaped being dashed against the rocks by bringing the Ship to an Anchor in 75 fathom water with 150 fathoms of Cable out. . . ."

After clearing the strait, Cook was obliged to sail up the east coast as far as Cape Turnagain on Hawke Bay in order to satisfy some of his officers that the North Island really was surrounded by water, thus completing its circumnavigation in four months.

At Cape Turnagain he put the ship's head to the south and on February 9 began the clockwise circumnavigation of the South Island, passing round Stewart Island, which he thought was part of the mainland at the southern end. He then followed Tasman's route up the west coast, reaching Queen Charlotte Sound on March 24, 1770. Although less rewarding to the scientist—fewer landings were made and not a single native seen—the voyage round the South Island was of the greatest importance. By making it, Cook proved that New Zealand formed no part of any continental land mass and Banks, up to then a supporter of Dalrymple's theory, was forced to admit "the total demolition of our aerial fabrick calld continent". In less than six months Cook had charted 2,400 miles of coast on both islands and he had discovered that the country, the North Island particularly, was rich and able to support colonists, if only the inhabitants, highly intelligent and skilful cultivators of the soil, could be persuaded not to consume them.

On March 31 Cook made a momentous decision, in consultation with his officers, the *Endeavour* and her crew being ready for sea. In order to prove the existence or otherwise of a southern continent it would be necessary to sail to Cape Horn in high latitudes—beyond 40s—which, with winter coming on, would be very hazardous. Even more unthinkable in such a ship as the *Endeavour* was the prospect of beating against the westerlies on a direct course to the Cape of Good Hope, again without any possibility of taking on provisions, and with little possibility of making fresh discoveries.

A new route
It was therefore decided to return by way of the East Indies; not however by the route used by Tasman, by way of Fiji and the north coast of New Guinea, but, as Cook himself wrote: "Upon leaving this coast to steer to the westward untill we fall in with the East Coast of New Holland and than to follow the deriction of that Coast to the northward or what other direction it may take until we arrive at its northern extremity, and if this should be found impractical than to endeavour to fall in with the lands or Islands discover'd by Quiros."

Cook sailed westwards at daylight on March 31. On April 16 birds of a kind that indicated the nearness of land were seen in 39.40N, to the east of the Bass Strait, of which neither Tasman nor Cook (who had a copy of Tasman's *Journal*) knew the existence, both believing that Van Diemen's Land (Tasmania) was part of the Australian continent.

That night Cook kept leadsmen at work, hoping that he would be on soundings; but the next day *Endeavour* was forced to bear away before a southwesterly gale and as a result the Bass Strait was not discovered. On April 9, while *Endeavour* was down to close-reefed topsails in cloudy, squally weather and "a large Southerly Sea", Hicks, the First Lieutenant, sighted a coast of sandy hummocks, partly covered with trees and scrub, trending northeast to west. Cook named its headland Point Hicks, and the coast New South Wales.

On April 29, having sailed first east to Cape Howe and then north in search of a safe anchorage, and seeing on the way the smoke of fires, Cook saw a bay "which appeared to be tollerably well shelterd into which I resolved to go with the ship". It was Botany Bay, later named by Cook for the wealth of plants found there.

The following morning he took the *Endeavour* in, seeing his first aborigines—naked dark-brown men, women and children on the southern point.

Cook spent eight days in Botany Bay, making no real contact with the aborigines. The crew feasted on giant stingray (Cook's first name for the harbour was Stingray Bay) and explored the bay's surroundings—mangrove swamp and sandy soil on which coarse grass, shrubs and palm trees grew; and woods of gum trees and a tall straight tree like a pine. Cook's description of the bay, "Capacious, safe and commodious," with "a variety of very boutifull birds such as Cocatoo's, Lorryquets, Parrots &cᵃ and Crows exactly like those we have in England", was one of his few inaccurate reports. The harbour was in fact exposed to easterly winds and when the first British colonists arrived in 1783 Governor Phillip soon moved from it to Sydney.

On his departure Cook sailed north, passing the Sydney Heads at the mouth of a harbour which he named (without entering it) Port Jackson, after a Secretary of the Admiralty. He thought it might be a good anchorage but did not realize that inside it was the largest and safest harbour on the east coast of Australia.

The next five weeks were spent sailing northwards and charting the coast, although Cook missed two good sites for settlement, the mouth of the Hunter River, where Newcastle now stands, and the Brisbane River.

On May 20 he passed and named Sandy Cape on the coast of Queensland in 24.39s and five days later Cape Capricorn, on the Tropic.

The *Endeavour* was now entering some of the most dangerous, shoal-infested waters in the world, those inshore of the Great Barrier Reef. No new hazard to maritime explorers, time and time again the world's great reef

Cook's great voyages

formations were to claim their victims, including such gallant and able commanders as la Pérouse. Cook was one of the more fortunate ones. At 11 o'clock on the night of June 11 the *Endeavour* struck the reef, north of what Cook named Cape Tribulation, "because here began all our troubles". Cook's troubles were to be fairly short-lived, however, for, by a supreme combination of luck, seamanship and courage, the leaking ship was floated again the following night and sailed to safety.

The following morning Cook stood in towards the land, 20 miles off to the northwest. "At Noon we were about 3 Leagues from the land . . . in this situation had 12 fathoms water and sever[1] Sand Banks without us", Cook wrote in his *Journal*, "The leak now decreaseth but for fear it should break out again we got the Sail ready fill'd for fothering." Cook then describes the difficult operation of "fothering", or stopping an underwater leak while at sea: "The manner this is done is thus, we mix ockam [oakum—loose fibre obtained by untwisting and picking old rope] & wool together . . . and chop it up small and than stick it loosly by handfulls all over the sail and throw over it sheeps dung or other filth. Horse dung for this purpose is best. [There must have been little chance of finding either in the *Endeavour* and one can only speculate on what was actually used.] The sail thus prepared is hauld under the Ships bottom by ropes and if the place of the leak is uncertain it must be hauld from one part of her bottom to a nother untill the place is found where it takes effect; while the sail is under the Ship the Ockam &c[a] is washed off and part of it carried along with the water into the leak and in parts stops up the hole."

In what is now called Cook Harbour, at the mouth of the Endeavour River, they examined and repaired the damage. The fothering had been successful, partly blocking holes four planks wide, "the whole was cut away as if it had been done by the hands of Man with a blunt edge tool". One of these holes was jammed with a large piece of coral, which had probably saved the ship.

Here, they warded off scurvy by eating the meat of turtles, which they captured 15 miles out at sea on the rare occasions when the weather allowed, the herb called purslane and "beans which growes on a creeping kind of a Vine . . . but the best greens we found here was the Tarra or Cocco tops call'd in the West Indias India Kale . . . these eat as well or better than spinnage."

The aborigines never approached them except to ask for turtle meat and tried to drive them away by firing the grass around their camp.

Cook was impressed by their indifference to any material objects that were given them: "From what I have said of the Natives of New Holland," he wrote, "they may appear to some to be the most wretched people upon Earth, but in reality they are far more happier than we Europeans; being wholly unacquainted not only with the superfluous but the necessary Conveniences so much sought after in Europe, they are happy in not knowing the use of them. . . ."

On August 4, in a ship that was taking water "at not quite an inch an hour", with pumps in bad order and rotten sails, Cook sailed north through a labyrinth of shoals for eight days until, finding a narrow gap in the Great Barrier Reef, now called Cook's Passage, he took the *Endeavour* into the open sea.

Cape York
On August 17 he took his ship inshore of the reef and on August 21 doubled the northernmost point of northeastern Australia, which he named Cape York, having formally taken possession of the whole east coast of Australia from latitude 38s. A week later, sailing westwards through the Endeavour Channel between the Banks Islands and the mainland, Cook raised the coast of New Guinea, where the naturalists went ashore. The most important part of Cook's first voyage of discovery was over. He had already come to the conclusion that New Holland had no connection with Quiros's Austrialia del Espiritu Santo, more than a thousand miles to the east beyond the Coral Sea. By sailing through the Torres Strait he had reaffirmed what Torres had shown 150 years before—and Dalrymple himself, to give him credit, had always believed—that Australia was separated from New Guinea.

Sailing west from New Guinea Cook passed south of Timor, getting fresh provisions from the Dutch, who treated his crew kindly, on Savu Island. The Dutch also gave them every help when they reached Batavia (now Jakarta) on October 10, 1770. By this time almost everyone was sick and seven of

The "Endeavour" leaves Whitby. The ships of this port were perfect for exploration, for the "Endeavour" was followed by "Resolution", "Discovery" and "Adventure"

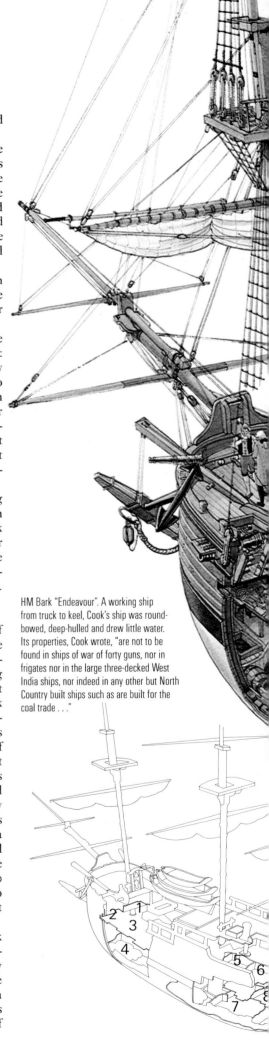

HM Bark "Endeavour". A working ship from truck to keel, Cook's ship was round-bowed, deep-hulled and drew little water. Its properties, Cook wrote, "are not to be found in ships of war of forty guns, nor in frigates nor in the large three-decked West India ships, nor indeed in any other but North Country built ships such as are built for the coal trade . . ."

"Endeavour" data: ship-rigged cat of 368 tons; 98 feet long on the lower deck; keel 81 feet; maximum beam 29 feet 3 inches; hold depth 11 feet 4 inches. Cost to the Admiralty, £2,840 10 shillings and 11 pence

As the collier "Earl of Pembroke", the bark "Endeavour" had a cabin aft for two officers, with fo'c'sle space for crew; converted for Cook, ten new cabins were built into the ship to give accommodation for nearly 100

1 Galley	6 Captain's cabin
2 Boatswain's quarters	7 Steward's stores
3 Sail locker	8 Surgeon's quarters
4 Ship's stores	9 Officers' quarters
5 Draughtsman's cabin	10 Great cabin

Cook's great voyages

the crew died from dysentery and malaria.

The *Endeavour*, by now "an hospital ship", sailed for England on Christmas Day, arriving in the Channel and anchoring in the Downs on July 13, 1771.

The principal reason for Cook's second world voyage was to discover once and for all if any continental land mass really existed in the Southern Ocean. His purpose was to encircle it in the course of two southern summers in latitudes higher than 40S, sailing eastwards from the Cape of Good Hope to Queen Charlotte Sound, New Zealand, to Cape Horn before winter set in, then eastwards again until the longitude in which the circumnavigation had begun was reached.

If, however, no land was discovered in the southern Indian and southern Pacific oceans he would haul to the north in the Pacific for the winter, visit Tahiti, where he could be sure of getting stores, and then sail westwards to rediscover Quiros's Austrialia del Espiritu Santo. Another, political, reason for the voyage was to attempt to forestall French discoveries in all these regions.

Cook, now a Commander, sailed from Plymouth in July 1772, in command of two ex-Whitby colliers—the *Resolution*, 460 tons, of which he himself was in command, and the *Adventure* of 330 tons, commanded by Captain Tobias Furneaux, who had sailed with Wallis in the *Dolphin*.

This time Banks did not go. The scientists included two astronomers, an able but cantankerous German naturalist, Dr Johann Reinhold Forster and his son Georg (a natural history draughtsman), Anders Sparrman, a Swedish botanist and pupil of Linnaeus who was to be picked up at the Cape of Good Hope, and William Hodges, a landscape artist.

At the Cape Cook heard of two other expeditions, both French, one commanded by Yves Kerguelen-Tremarec, who had earlier that year discovered the Kerguelen group of about 300 small islands between 40 and 50S

and 68 and 70E, in the southern Indian Ocean.

The other French commander was Marion-Dufresne who, with Lieutenant Crozet, had sailed from Mauritius and discovered the Marion and Crozet islands in the Indian Ocean before being killed in New Zealand.

On November 22 Cook began the first part of his quest, sailing in search of the so-called Point Circumcision, discovered by Pierre Bouvet in 1739, who believed it to be a point of the Southern Continent.

Cook's two ships first encountered ice in 52S on December 12, "Six Islands this 24 hours, some of which were near two miles in circuit and about 200 feet high, on the Weather side of them the Sea broke very high, some Gentlemen on Deck saw some Penguins". In 54.55S, "at half past six we were stopped by an immence field of Ice, to which we could see no end. . . . We now bore away SSE, SE, SE and SEBS as the Ice trended, keeping close by the edge of it, where we saw many Penguins and Whales and many of the Ice Birds, small grey Birds and Pintadoes."

Ice field cleared

It was bitterly cold with snow, fog and sleet, but on December 18 they were able to clear the ice field when a freshening gale veered to northeast.

On December 25, in 57.50S, 29.32E, Cook sent a jolly boat to try to extract some drinking water from a 100-foot-high iceberg, but there was not sufficient thaw, and "At Noon seeing that the People were inclinable to celebrate Christmas Day in their own way, I brought the Sloops under a very snug sail least I should be surprised with a gale wind with a drunken crew," he wrote.

By now his search for "Point Circumcision" had taken him about 1,000 miles to the east of Bouvet Island; but he did not reach a point within two degrees of Bouvet's supposed meridian for it until January 3, 1773, when exceptionally clear weather allowed him to

see from the masthead that it did not exist within 11 degrees to the north. Cook concluded that Bouvet must have seen an iceberg.

He therefore decided to abandon any search to the west and concentrate on looking for the continent to the south. On January 17 they crossed the Antarctic Circle, "undoubtedly the first and only Ship[s] that ever cross'd that line", and at noon that day were in 66.36S, 39.35E with the mainland of Antarctica, Enderby Land, unknown and invisible to them, 300 miles to the east. From the masthead, Cook could see nothing to the south but ice, "an immense Feild . . . composed of different kinds of Ice such as high Hills or Islands, smaller pieces packed close together and what Greenland men properly call field Ice, a piece of this kind of such extend that I could see no end to it, lay to the SE of us, it was 16 or 18 feet high at least and appeared of a pretty equal height".

Cook now set a course to the east; but on February 9 the *Resolution* and the *Adventure* lost contact in thick fog.

The arrangement was that if this happened both ships would cruise in the area for three days before sailing on to New Zealand; when two days had elapsed without any sign of the *Adventure*, Cook continued his voyage, heading southeast to 60S in a fresh gale with a high sea, still in search of land. His course, had he continued on it, would have brought him to the coast of Wilkes Land in Antarctica, which was not discovered until 1840.

On March 27 *Resolution* anchored in Dusky Bay (now Dusky Sound) on the southeast coast of New Zealand, having been 117 days at sea and sailed 3,660 leagues (10,980 nautical miles) without sight of land.

The *Adventure* was found in Queen Charlotte Sound. Furneaux had reached Van Diemen's Land (Tasmania) on March 11 and had sailed northwards along its east coast, seeing the islands named after him at the eastern end of the Bass Strait without entering it. Tasmania retained the secret of its

insularity until Flinders and Bass circumnavigated it in 1798. Furneaux had not been diligent in his anti-scorbutic measures in the *Adventure* and the health of his crew was much worse than Cook's, but as soon as Cook arrived both crews were put on a regime which included wild celery and scurvy grass.

They sailed out through Cook Strait on June 7, running the easting down in the southern winter, mostly in the low forties. Then, having found no land (they were in longitude 133W), Cook turned north to sweep the waters south of those he had sailed through on his voyage from Tahiti to New Zealand, narrowly missing Pitcairn Island and reaching Tahiti on August 16, 1773.

After visiting various islands of the Society group Cook finally sailed west, naming the Friendly Islands (Tonga), which had been first discovered by Tasman in 1643. Cook lost contact with Furneaux in stormy weather on the way to Cook Strait and when he failed to appear at the rendezvous in Queen Charlotte Sound, sailed without him for the Antarctic on November 25. They never made contact again. Furneaux, arriving in the sound a few days after Cook's departure, had one of his men killed and partly eaten by the Maoris. He then sailed to the Cape of Good Hope by way of Cape Horn, always in high latitudes, which indicated what Cook was to prove by an even more thorough investigation —that whatever Cape Circumcision was, it was not part of a southern continent. Furneaux reached England a year before Cook, in July 1774, the first explorer to sail round the world from west to east.

On December 21, having already been among loose field ice and huge flat-topped bergs, "so numerous that we had to luff for one and bear up for a nother" Cook wrote: "At 7 o'Clock we came the second time under the Polar Circle and stood to the SE till 6 o'clock in the am when being in La^t 67° 5′ South Longitude 143° 49′ West, the fogg being exceeding thick we came close aboard a large Island of ice . . . very high and rugged terminating in many peaks. . . ."

It was bitterly cold and foggy on December 24 and blowing a strong gale. The *Resolution* was under double-reefed topsails. "Our ropes were like wires. Sails like boards or plates of Metal and the Shivers [sheaves] froze fast in the blocks so that it required our utmost effort to get a Topsail down . . . under all these unfavourable circumstances it was natural for me to think of returning more to the North. . . ." Taking *Resolution* north to 47S, 122W "at Noon being little more than two hundred Leagues [600 miles] from my track to Otaheite [Tahiti] in 1769 in which space it was not probable anything was to be found", Cook and his equally courageous crew again plunged south, and on January 30, 1774, became the first men to cross Latitude 70S, reaching 71.10S, in 106.54W, where they were stopped by an immense ice field in the Amundsen Sea in which "we counted Ninety Seven Ice Hills or Mountains, many of them vastly large". Nearest of all to the South Pole was one of Cook's midshipmen, George Vancouver, himself to be a famous explorer who, at the moment before his captain put *Resolution* about in order to return north, is said to have gone out to the end of the bowsprit where he waved his hat, shouting "Ne plus ultra".

Cook's next landfall was Easter Island with its enormous, enigmatic statues. He then sailed for Tahiti, where an immense armada of canoes containing nearly 8,000 men was seen, assembled to attack the nearby island of Moorea. On June 5 Cook sailed through the New Hebrides—Quiros's Austriala del Espiritu Santo.

Standing for home

The *Resolution* made its way back to Queen Charlotte Sound by way of Norfolk Island, before Cook stood for Cape Horn and the last leg of his journey home. Once past the great cape he took possession of the "Isle of

Until the 18th century, all visual knowledge of the South Pacific, its people and wildlife was limited to the recollections of the captains and crews who had sailed there—a situation quite alien to the age of scientific curiosity. From then on skilled natural history draughtsmen and landscape artists were to accompany the voyages, to record in minute and lasting detail the flora and fauna of the lands visited, the native peoples and the landscape itself. One of the most talented of this new breed of men who accompanied Cook on his three voyages was Sydney Parkinson. His output was, not surprisingly, prolific—over 1,500 drawings—for in one bay alone so many specimens were collected that it was named Botany Bay—later the notorious penal settlement. The final voyage was probably the most richly illustrated of all and offered its artists, John Webber and William Ellis, widely contrasting landscapes as well as a diversity of wildlife and people, from the barren Kerguelen Island in the south to the wastes of Alaska in the north. Above is a selection of illustrations from the three voyages. From left to right: freshwater mangrove; New Zealand honeysuckle; varied thrush and American robin; New Zealand native; "kaka beak" (Clianthus puniceus); crested auklet; bearded penguin; ant house (tropical Australian plant); walrus massacre

Georgia" (South Georgia), which, although it was the southern summer, was encased in snow and ice, and discovered the South Sandwich Islands.

"Saturday 29th July we made the land about Plymouth." Cook was home again after a three-year, 70,000-mile voyage in which he lost only four men, none from scurvy.

On July 12, 1776, less than a year after his return, Cook sailed from Plymouth on his third and last voyage. He had been promoted to Post-Captain, been given an appointment at Greenwich Hospital (which he must have found a bit tedious), spent one of his rare leaves with his wife (in 1762 he married a London girl, a Miss Batts, and by her had six children), had an audience of George III, was elected to the Royal Society and as a Fellow read a paper on fighting scurvy.

The aim of the third expedition was to search for a passage from the Pacific to the Atlantic round North America, exploring

Cook's great voyages

along the west coast any river or inlet that might lead either to Hudson or Baffin Bay.

Cook himself sailed in the *Resolution*, which had been refitted, with William Bligh, later of the *Bounty*, as master. The other ship, a new *Discovery*, yet another Whitby collier, of 298 tons, was commanded by Charles Clerke, who had already been round the world twice with Cook and before that with Byron. With Clerke was William Bayly, the astronomer, who had been on the previous voyage. William Anderson, Cook's surgeon, doubled as natural historian and Lieutenant King carried out the astronomical observations in Cook's ship. Large quantities of livestock were carried.

Sailing past the Cape of Good Hope and Kerguelen Island, "which from its stirility I shall call Island of Desolation", Cook went by way of Tasmania and New Zealand to the Friendly Islands, where he arrived at the end of April 1777, his crews enjoying an unusual period of repose until the middle of July—he, too, may have needed a rest—before heading north, later in the year, for unknown waters. On December 4 he discovered the uninhabited Christmas Island, the largest atoll in the Pacific, where a solar eclipse enabled him to determine his position accurately, and six weeks later sighted the high, volcanic mountains of the Hawaiian Islands, which he named the Sandwich Islands.

The next day he stood in to Kauai Island, from which the inhabitants (who were of the same race as the Society Islanders and many other South Sea peoples, but darker) brought off "roasting pigs and some very fine Potatoes, which they exchanged . . . for whatever was offered for them; several small pigs were got for a sixpenny nail or two apiece, so that we

again found our selves in the land of plenty".

"How shall we account for this Nation spreading it self so far over this Vast ocean?" Cook wrote. "We find them from New Zealand to the South, to these islands to the North and from Easter Island to the Hebrides; an extent of 60° of latitude or twelve hundred leagues [3,600 nautical miles] north and south and 83° of longitude or sixteen hundred and sixty leagues east and west, how much farther is not known, but we may safly conclude that they extend to the west beyond the Hebrides."

He sailed on February 2, 1778, for "New Albion", the west coast of North America and just over a month later raised the coast of Oregon in 44.33N. On March 29 he was off the coast of Vancouver Island, having missed the entrance to the Juan de Fuca Strait at the southern end, as Drake had done. Here, in Nootka Sound, they traded with the Indians, swarthy people with straight black hair, flat broad faces and high cheek bones "with the Strictest Honisty on boath sides, taking from them the skins of many sorts of animals, and in particular the Sea Beaver [Sea Otter]."

Sailing north and then west along the coast of Alaska, naming many islands on the way, he reached Cook Inlet on the east side of the Kenai Peninsula, having careened the *Resolution*, which was leaking badly, in Prince William Sound. After entering the inlet in the vain hope of finding a passage and taking possession of the region, he sailed southwest along the Alaska Peninsula, north by a channel through the Aleutians and passed "the Western extremity of all America hitherto known", which he named Cape Prince of Wales, east of the Bering Strait.

On the Asian side of the strait Cook saw the Chukchi inhabitants, who were of excellent physique, friendly though timid, and lived in solid houses. He thought them the most civilized race he had met with in the Pacific. On August 18, having passed through the Bering Strait and crossed the Arctic Circle into the Chukchi Sea, he reached his northernmost latitude, 70.44N, off Icy Cape on the northwest coast of Alaska, having encountered pack ice three days before, on which "lay a prodigious number of Sea Horses [Walrus]" which they hunted.

He attempted to sail westwards along the north coast of Siberia, but met impassable ice, so he turned his ships south, reaching Unalaska Island on October 3, 1778. Here he repaired the ships and strengthened his men against scurvy by giving them wild berries, spruce beer and plenty of fresh fish, including salmon. Here, too, he was able to correct his charts with the help of a Russian fur trader.

Cook now decided to winter in the Sandwich Islands before making another attempt beyond the Bering Strait. Sailing from Unalaska on October 24 he reached Maui Island a month later, from there moving to Kealakekua Bay on Hawaii where the two ships were met by between 800 and 900 canoes with many thousands of people on board, most of whom, unlike the inhabitants of Maui, were accomplished thieves.

Here, in an extraordinary ceremony, Cook was deified, being identified by the inhabitants with Lono, a divine chieftain, who had left the island long before saying that he would return in a great ship, bringing gifts.

Cook remained at Hawaii for nearly three months. His crews had almost certainly by this time overstayed their welcome. When, six days later, they returned—the *Resolution* having sprung her foremast in a gale—it was to a cooler reception. On the night of February 13 the *Discovery*'s cutter was stolen. In the fight which broke out on the shore Cook was first stabbed, then bludgeoned to death in the water.

Despite the tragedy of Cook's death, his captains continued to carry out the instructions with which they had sailed from England. Cook's remains were handed over to Clerke, who had taken command, and the ships sailed for Petropavlovsk in Kamchatka, which was reached towards the end of April. Conditions were even worse beyond the Bering Strait than they had been the previous year and Clerke, who was in the advanced stages of tuberculosis, was only able to bring the ships to a point 15 miles short of their previous highest latitude before he died at sea on August 22.

With Lieutenant Gore commanding the *Resolution* and King the *Discovery*, the home-

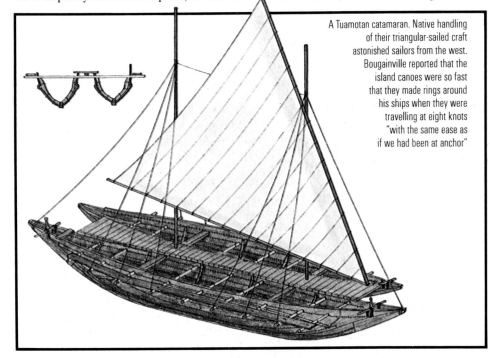

A Tuamotan catamaran. Native handling of their triangular-sailed craft astonished sailors from the west. Bougainville reported that the island canoes were so fast that they made rings around his ships when they were travelling at eight knots "with the same ease as if we had been at anchor"

ward voyage was made by way of Petropavlovsk, where Clerke was buried, the Kurile Islands, Japan, Macao, the Strait of Sunda and the Cape of Good Hope. They made their first anchorage in the British Isles at Stromness in the Orkneys whence they had been blown by gales. On October 4, 1780, they anchored at the Nore in the Thames Estuary, after an absence of four years and almost three months. A great though unsuccessful voyage was over and one of the greatest explorers of the sea was dead.

In spite of Cook's enormously long voyages, and those of his predecessors, there were still areas of the Pacific which needed further exploration, and it was the French who took up the search. In the late summer of 1785, François Galaup de la Pérouse, a gallant man and expert navigator who had commanded a daring raid on the English trading posts in Hudson Bay in 1781, left Brest with two corvettes, *L'Astrolabe* and *La Boussole*. The impulse for the voyage was provided by the Academy of Science and of Medicine, which selected the scientists who accompanied the expedition. La Pérouse himself was briefed by Louis XVI.

The principal aims of the expedition were to find Cape Circumcision; to explore the other islands of the Hawaiian group not visited by Cook, of whom la Pérouse was an ardent admirer; and to explore further the Pacific west of Tahiti and re-discover the Solomon Islands (which had already been reached by Mendaña and Quiros and also by Bougainville, but had not been recognized by him for what they were). La Pérouse was also to explore the Gulf of Carpentaria on the north coast of Australia; to visit the coasts of China and Kamchatka; and to search for the passage from the North Pacific eastwards to the Atlantic. Not all these aims were realized and necessarily the expedition covered a lot of ground that had already been explored.

After rounding Cape Horn la Pérouse landed on Maui in the Hawaiian Islands, before exploring the west coast of America southwards from the Gulf of Alaska as far as the Bay of Monterey to the south of San Francisco.

He then sailed across the Pacific to Macao without making any significant discoveries, touching at the Hawaiian Islands. From Macao he sailed to the Philippines, which he reached in April 1787. There he refitted and took on board French seamen from a frigate commanded by Antoine Bruni d'Entrecasteux as replacements for some of the 21 men lost in a boating accident on the coast of Alaska.

From the Philippines he sailed through the strait between Japan and Korea and then, after following the mainland coast of Asia, turned east through the La Pérouse Strait which separates Hokkaido, the northernmost island of Japan, from the Russian Island of Sakhalin. He then sailed north along the edge of the Kurile Islands to Avacha Bay, on the east coast of Kamchatka.

Too late

The ships sailed from Kamchatka on September 30, visiting Bougainville's Navigator's Islands and the Friendly Islands in Samoa on the way south but failing to find the Solomon Islands.

In January 1788 they reached Port Jackson, where the newly arrived British colonists, including convicts, gave them help. Too late to claim Australia for France, la Pérouse sailed north with the intention of exploring the Solomon Islands and the Gulf of Carpentaria. He and his men were never seen again and their fate remained a mystery until 1827, when an English merchant captain learned that both ships had been wrecked on Vanikoro in the Santa Cruz Islands.

The following year Jules Dumont d'Urville, who was on a secret expedition in Polynesia and also searching for la Pérouse, reached Vanikoro in the *Astrolabe*. "Lying at the bottom of the sea, three or four fathoms below the surface, our men saw anchors, cannons, shot, and a huge quantity of lead plates." According to the inhabitants about 30 men had succeeded in getting ashore but had been massacred. Others, who were better armed, had managed to keep alive for seven months, after which they left for the Moluccas in a makeshift boat.

In the course of its voyage round the world d'Urville's expedition amassed the largest collection of scientific material that had so far been brought to Europe.

The disappearance of la Pérouse led to the despatch of a scientific expedition under d'Entrecasteaux. Sailing from Brest on September 28, 1791, with two ships, *La Recherche* and *L'Espérance*, the latter commanded by Huon de Kermadec, he reached Recherche Bay on the south coast of Tasmania on April 23, 1792. There surveys and astronomical observations were made and the D'Entrecasteaux Channel between the mainland and Bruny Island was discovered. From here he sailed up the east side of the Tasman Peninsula, his hydrographer, Charles Beautemps-Beaupré, producing charts that were models of their kind.

From Tasmania he sailed to New Caledonia, where de Kermadec died; then to Bougainville Island in the Solomons, and from there through the St George Strait between New Ireland and New Britain to the Admiralty Islands, where he had hopes of finding la Pérouse, a hopeless task. After refitting at Amboina Island in the Moluccas, he set off for the southwest coast of Australia, reaching King George Sound on December 6. Unable to enter it because of heavy gales, he sailed to Esperance Bay, 250 miles to the east.

Finding no water there, d'Entrecasteaux sailed along the shores of the Great Australian Bight to the head of it and from there to Adventure Bay on the south coast of Tasmania, which was reached on January 21, 1793, the day Louis XVI was guillotined in Paris. Accurate surveys were made from a base line on the isthmus connecting the north and south parts of Bruny Island.

From Adventure Bay, having sailed some way up the coast, he made for Tongatabu in the Friendly Islands and from there to New Caledonia, which he reached in May 1793.

On May 19, by an extraordinary coincidence, both ships narrowly missed going ashore on the reefs of Vanikoro Island where, unknown to d'Entrecasteaux, la Pérouse's ships were lying on the bottom.

Perilous waters

He now sailed south of the Solomons into the perilous waters off the eastern end of New Guinea and among the islands of Bougainville's dreaded Louisiade Archipelago, on the way finding the Trobriand Islands and other islands which he named after his officers. He also discovered the much larger D'Entrecasteaux Islands. By this time he, like many of his crew, was seriously ill with both dysentery and scurvy. On July 29 he died and was buried at sea.

The command of the expedition now devolved on d'Auribeau, who had taken command of *L'Espérance* after the death of de Kermadec, de Rossel taking over *La Recherche*.

Reaching Surabaya in eastern Java, they learned from the Dutch that war had broken out between France and almost everyone else in Europe including Holland, and some of the more important members of the expedition were imprisoned for several months. D'Auribeau appeared in a rather unfavourable light when he managed to arrange special terms for his own repatriation. De Rossel had even worse luck. While on his way back to France he was taken prisoner by the British and was kept in captivity in London for months. All the precious documents and charts made on the voyage were taken from him and they were not returned until the end of the war in 1797, when de Rossel began work on one of the three narratives of the voyage that were eventually published.

The 18th century was nearing its end and so was the great pioneering work of Pacific exploration. Science, as well as the extraordinary courage and perseverance of the navigators, had served discovery well.

Asia: the Cossack pioneers

UCH OF ASIA that was known to the West in the 16th century was based on the reports of either commercially minded men such as the Polos, or monkish men seeking to spread the word of Christianity. Their knowledge tended to be of routes from one community to another, and of the communities with whom they came into contact. Beyond the caravan routes, which in the main followed steppe, desert and mountain pass in southern-central Asia, there lay a huge expanse of territory waiting to be crossed.

Between 1400 and 1600, the iron grip in which the Tartars held European Russia was loosened. A new sovereign state, Muscovy, came into being and began to push its frontiers eastwards across the Ural Mountains as—centuries later—hardy pioneers moved westwards across North America.

Russia had its frontiersmen, too, men of a wild and free nature who were to appear on the stage of Russian history whenever it was at its most turbulent—the Cossacks. They were a mixture of people whose name, stemming from Kazakh, was an indication of a way of life rather than that of a family.

Cossacks were to be found at the head of almost all the first expeditions to feel their way across the northern wastes of the continent.

The first of these was Yermak Timofeiev, who, in 1579, set off with a force of 1,600 men across the Urals to open up by force of arms what was soon to be known as Siberia. He was backed by the Stroganoff family, to whom Ivan IV had given immense tracts of land in the Urals to colonize, and whose capital was at Perm. Yermak captured Sibir, the residence of the Tartar Kuchum Khan, and in 1587 Tobolsk was founded.

In 1610, Russian fur traders reached the Yenisei, beyond the Ob, and by 1638 the Russians were on the shores of the Sea of Okhotsk, facing the northern Pacific—the whole breadth of the continent, nearly 3,000 miles from the Urals, had been crossed.

Another Cossack, Semeon Ivanovich Dezhnev, began an immense journey in 1648 through the country of the Chukchis in northeastern Siberia, one of numberless similar journeys that are unrecorded.

He sailed down the Kolyma River, reaching the East Siberian Sea at Kolyma Bay, from which he may very well have sailed through the Bering Strait to reach the Gulf of Anadyr. After his ship was wrecked, he and his men travelled overland to the Anadyr River, eventually reaching the River Lena, some 1,200 miles to the west.

Many of the records, if they kept any, of what the tough fur traders and Cossack representatives of the Tsar accomplished in exploring the immensity that is Siberia,

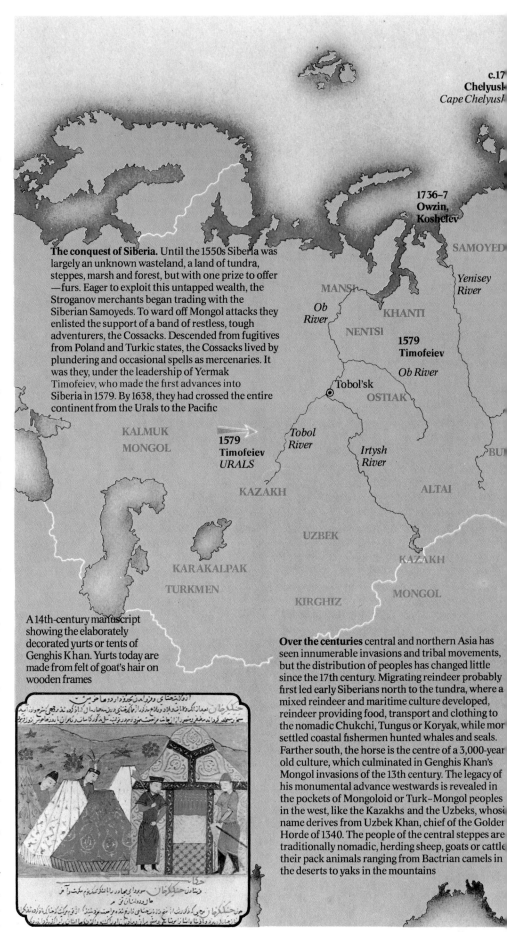

The conquest of Siberia. Until the 1550s Siberia was largely an unknown wasteland, a land of tundra, steppes, marsh and forest, but with one prize to offer —furs. Eager to exploit this untapped wealth, the Stroganov merchants began trading with the Siberian Samoyeds. To ward off Mongol attacks they enlisted the support of a band of restless, tough adventurers, the Cossacks. Descended from fugitives from Poland and Turkic states, the Cossacks lived by plundering and occasional spells as mercenaries. It was they, under the leadership of Yermak Timofeiev, who made the first advances into Siberia in 1579. By 1638, they had crossed the entire continent from the Urals to the Pacific

A 14th-century manuscript showing the elaborately decorated yurts or tents of Genghis Khan. Yurts today are made from felt of goat's hair on wooden frames

Over the centuries central and northern Asia has seen innumerable invasions and tribal movements, but the distribution of peoples has changed little since the 17th century. Migrating reindeer probably first led early Siberians north to the tundra, where a mixed reindeer and maritime culture developed, reindeer providing food, transport and clothing to the nomadic Chukchi, Tungus or Koryak, while more settled coastal fishermen hunted whales and seals. Farther south, the horse is the centre of a 3,000-year old culture, which culminated in Genghis Khan's Mongol invasions of the 13th century. The legacy of his monumental advance westwards is revealed in the pockets of Mongoloid or Turk-Mongol peoples in the west, like the Kazakhs and the Uzbeks, whose name derives from Uzbek Khan, chief of the Golden Horde of 1340. The people of the central steppes are traditionally nomadic, herding sheep, goats or cattle, their pack animals ranging from Bactrian camels in the deserts to yaks in the mountains

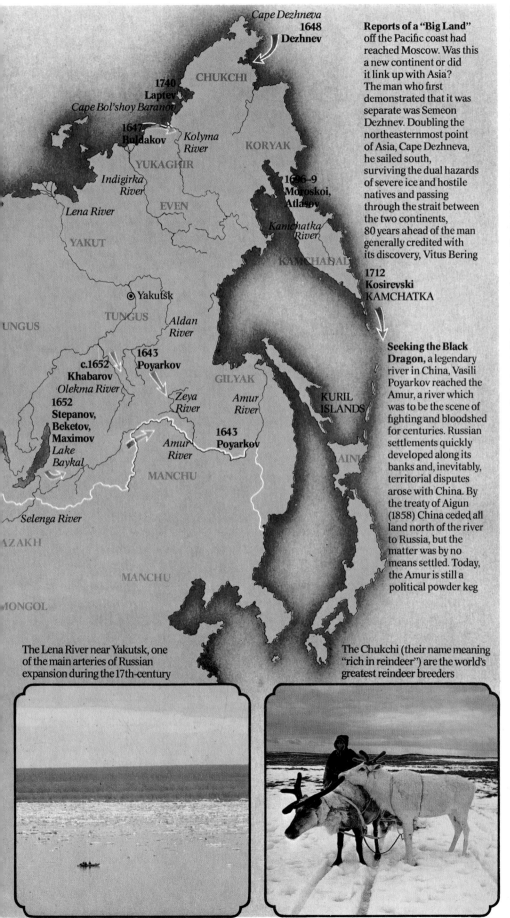

Cape Dezhneva
1648
Dezhnev

CHUKCHI

1740
Laptev
Cape Bol'shoy Baranov

1647
Buldakov
Kolyma River

KORYAK

YUKAGHIR

Indigirka River

Lena River

EVEN

YAKUT

1696–9
Moroskoi, Atlasov

Kamchatka River

KAMCHADAL

Yakutsk

TUNGUS

Aldan River

UNGUS

c.1652
Khabarov
Olekma River

1643
Poyarkov

GILYAK

1652
Stepanov, Beketov, Maximov
Lake Baykal

Zeya River

Amur River

KURIL ISLANDS

1712
Kosirevski
KAMCHATKA

1643
Poyarkov

Amur River

MANCHU

Selenga River

AZAKH

MANCHU

AINU

MONGOL

Reports of a "Big Land" off the Pacific coast had reached Moscow. Was this a new continent or did it link up with Asia? The man who first demonstrated that it was separate was Semeon Dezhnev. Doubling the northeasternmost point of Asia, Cape Dezhneva, he sailed south, surviving the dual hazards of severe ice and hostile natives and passing through the strait between the two continents, 80 years ahead of the man generally credited with its discovery, Vitus Bering

Seeking the Black Dragon, a legendary river in China, Vasili Poyarkov reached the Amur, a river which was to be the scene of fighting and bloodshed for centuries. Russian settlements quickly developed along its banks and, inevitably, territorial disputes arose with China. By the treaty of Aigun (1858) China ceded all land north of the river to Russia, but the matter was by no means settled. Today, the Amur is still a political powder keg

The Lena River near Yakutsk, one of the main arteries of Russian expansion during the 17th-century

The Chukchi (their name meaning "rich in reindeer") are the world's greatest reindeer breeders

disappeared as completely as those of the Portuguese and Spanish discoverers; but enough remain to prove that, in many ways, they had much the same approach to the primitive peoples they encountered as did the Spanish Conquistadors.

Five years before Deznev set out, Vasili Poyarkov set off from Yakutsk on the River Lena and ascended one of its tributaries, the Aldan, and its feeders to the sources in the Stanovy Khrebet. Here he wintered, and after descending various tributaries (and having incited the Daurians, the primitive people of the region, to kill off half his men) reached the Amur River. The Amur runs on the borders of Russia and Inner Mongolia and flows for 1,800 miles to its mouth in the strait opposite Sakhalin Island, near the Sea of Okhotsk, which Poyarkov reached after a three-month voyage downstream.

From here, with his depleted force he sailed north to the mouth of the Ulya River, crossed from its upper waters to the Aldan and reached Yakutsk in June 1646, having navigated half of the last great, unknown Siberian rivers.

Other expeditions of a similar military character took place in these regions between 1648 and 1652 led by Khabarov, an adventurer who discovered an easier route to the Amur, by way of the Olekma River.

Onufrei Stepanov and the Cossacks Beketov and Maximov, who crossed Lake Baykal in 1652, the following spring ascended the Selenga from its mouth on the lake, crossed the divide south of the Yablonovy range (itself part of the watershed between the rivers flowing to the Arctic and the Pacific) and descended the Shilka and Ingoda rivers to the Amur.

These explorations along the Amur, which forms the Chinese border for much of its course, brought a growing Russia into contact with the great and ancient nation in the east. It resulted in bloodshed. In 1653, the Russians sent an envoy to the Manchu emperor, Kang-hi, but the unfortunate emissary was murdered by his guides *en route* to Peking.

Twenty-three years later, another Russian envoy was sent, one Nicolas Spafarik, a Greek. He reached Peking having crossed the Tien Shan (Ta-Hsing-an-ling) from the west. Finally, in 1689, a treaty was negotiated between the two nations at Nerchinsk on the Shilka River, by which the Russians abandoned all their new-found territory on the lower reaches of the Amur, which completely halted their movement down it to the Pacific. The treaty endured until 1855, and anyone attempting to approach the river was severely punished by the Russians.

The year in which Russia and China signed

Asia: voyages of Bering

the treaty marked the ascent to the throne in Moscow of Peter the Great. His 26-year reign, one of the most important in the history of his country, saw the consolidation into an empire of much of what had been explored over the past century.

By this time the pioneers had almost done their work and the main geographical outlines of an enormous area of northern Asia were known. The last area of unknown territory, that between the Anadyr River in the extreme northeast of Siberia, where the Russians already had a post, and the Kamchatka River on the Kamchatka Peninsula, was explored by Moroskoi, another Cossack, and Vladimir Atlassov, sometime between 1696 and 1699.

What the new Tsar now required was a scientifically organized survey of the north and east coasts of Asia and information as to whether they were joined at any point to the mainland of America.

An expedition sent out by Peter in 1719 to discover how close Asia was to the New World, northeast of Kamchatka—that of the surveyors Evreinov and Lushin—was not successful; it was not until 1725, the year of his death, that another one was organized to undertake the same mission, under the command of Vitus Bering, a Danish captain in the Russian Navy.

He and his lieutenants, Martin Spanberg and Alexei Chirikov, had the herculean task of transporting their equipment across the whole of Russia and Siberia to the shore of the Sea of Okhotsk, and when they finally reached it in 1727 they set off in a ship specially built for the purpose and landed on the west coast of Kamchatka. After crossing mountain ranges with sledges in the depths of the Siberian winter to the Kamchatka River, they built yet another vessel, the *Gabriel*, in which they set out in July 1728, ". . . along the shore which bears northerly and which (since its limits are unknown) seems to be part of America".

After charting the coast on the way, they sighted St Lawrence Island in the Bering Sea in 63.40N, 170W and reached a point on the Siberian mainland where the coast trended to the northwest. They were beyond East Cape, the extreme eastern point of Asia, in the Bering Strait.

From here, because of the danger of being ice-bound and because "it seemed to me that the instructions of his Imperial Majesty had been carried out", Bering turned his ship for Kamchatka, where he spent the winter before setting out again in June 1729.

On this voyage he was thwarted in his attempts to sail northwards by contrary winds. Instead, he sailed round the extreme southerly point of the Kamchatka Peninsula to Okhotsk, by doing so proving conclusively

Sea covered by pack ice in spring

1728 Bering Okhotsk

Sea of Okhotsk

1728 Bering Kamchatka River

KURIL ISLANDS

HOKKAIDO

Gulf of Avacha

1739 Spanberg, Sheltinga HONSHŪ

1738 Spanberg

1728 Bering

1730 Gvosdov

1728 Bering ST LAWRENCE ISLAND

1741 Bering † BERING ISLAND

ALEUTIAN ISLANDS

1741 Bering

Secure in her newly won empire, 18th-century Russia set out to explore her maritime horizons. Exploration spelt extinction for

Steller's sea cow (right), observed in the seas off Bering Island by Bering's naturalist, Steller. The sea cow was a species of dugong

that it was not connected with Yezo (the Japanese island of Hokkaido).

Bering did not sail again until 1741, on what was to be his last and most memorable journey. During the intervening decade a series of explorations took place around the coastline of northeastern Siberia. Each added to the sum of knowledge of one of the most inhospitable regions of the world, and the hardy men whose work it was added their names permanently to the world atlas.

Northernmost cape doubled

In 1735, Prontchishchev and Chelyuskin sailed down the Lena from Yakutsk, and after wintering at the mouth of the Olenek River, westwards of the Lena delta, finally succeeded in reaching latitude 77.25N on the eastern side of the barren, desolate Taymyr Peninsula near the cape (which now bears Chelyuskin's name), where they were stopped by ice. Both Prontchishchev and his wife, who was with him, succumbed as a result of the privations the party endured. Chelyuskin finally doubled the cape, probably the northernmost point of the Old World, in about 1743.

On June 4, 1741, Bering in the *St Peter* and Chirikov in the *St Paul* sailed from Avacha Bay on the east coast of the Kamchatka Peninsula (their ships are now commemorated in the name of the town of Petropavlovsk-Kamchatskiy. With them were the scientists

Steller and de la Croyère. The ships were soon separated in a storm and did not meet again. On July 29 the *St Peter* was in the Gulf of Alaska and Bering sighted the great, looming mass of Mount Elias, the 18,000-foot-high mountain in southeastern Alaska which has the largest ice field outside the polar regions. In foggy weather, he altered course and sailed along the seaward side of Kodiak Island off the Alaskan Peninsula and southwestwards along the Aleutians, the chain of islands which extends from the end of it towards Kamchatka. Here he encountered gale force winds which lasted for 40 days.

During this time Bering and his crew were attacked by scurvy and so many of them were struck down that it became impossible to work or navigate the ship properly. The *St Peter* came under the command of Lieutenant Waxel, with Steller giving him what help he could.

On November 15 the *St Peter* drifted into an inlet on Bering Island (Ostrova Beringa), one of the Komandorskiye Group (also named after Bering), about 100 miles west of the Kamchatka Peninsula. Here they spent a winter of extraordinary privation. Their only habitations were holes which they excavated in the sandhills and covered with sails, eating the flesh of sea otters and seals. Bering died of scurvy, along with many of his crew. Steller was one of the 45 men who survived out of a complement of 77 and in the

Exercises in imperialism

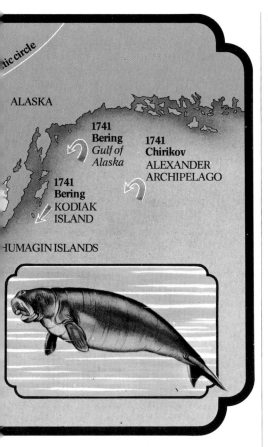

THE REIGN OF the absolute despot, Tsar Nicholas I (1825–55), marked the beginning of the Russian conquest of Central Asia, and the foundation of the Russian Eastern Empire. His explorers, who formed the vanguard were, like their British counterparts across the Himalayas, mostly soldiers skilled in surveying, their work an exercise in Imperialism as much as in discovery.

In 1819, Count N. Muraviev, who had done surveying work in the area of the Caspian Sea, reached the Khiva oasis across the Kara Kum Desert, although it was not taken until 1873. Later Muraviev became Governor of Eastern Siberia and took a force down to the mouth of the Amur River in 1854. The Aral Sea was discovered in 1844 and the mouth of the Syr-Dar'ya, on its northeastern shore—the Jaxartes of the Ancient World—three years later.

Central Asia

The 1850s saw the exploration of the Orenburg region of the southern Urals, the crossing of the great 90,000-square-mile Ust Urt, a desert plateau between the Caspian and Aral seas, and the beginning of the 30-year charting of the Syr-Dar'ya and the Amu-Dar'ya, upstream from its mouth at the southern end of the Aral Sea.

In 1857, the Russian exploration of Central Asia really began with the exploration of the great Tien Shan (the Celestial Mountains), a mountain system bigger than all the European mountain ranges put together, by Professor P. Semenov, an astronomer. He reached Khan Tengri, a peak in the main range. The following year Valikhanov pioneered the route southwards over the range to Kashgar.

That year, 1858, Russian influence began to make itself felt in Persia, when a scientific expedition under Nicholas de Khanuikov travelled through the eastern parts of the country and succeeded in penetrating the Lut, the central desert.

Persian exploration was by tradition the preserve of British military and political adventurers. It was, after all, on the road to the imperial jewel of India. Among the first were the surveyors Henry Pottinger and Captain C. Christie, who were sent to Persia when a rather dotty plan of Bonaparte's—to invade India with the help of the Russian and Persian armies—was unmasked. Pottinger and Christie set off from the coast of Baluchistan disguised as horse traders, and travelled to Nushki on its frontier with Afghanistan. There they separated, Christie travelling to Isfahan by way of Herat and Yezd, Pottinger moving westwards across Baluchistan to join Christie again at Isfahan.

Other great travellers of this early period were J. B. Fraser, who, in 1821, explored the region south of the Caspian, and Captain Arthur Conolly of the Bengal Light Cavalry. Conolly rode from Tabriz to Herat in 1830, tried to reach Khiva, failed and, disguised as an Indian merchant, eventually succeeded in reaching India by way of the Bolan Pass. Ten years later he finally reached Khiva, and in November 1841 Bukhara. Here another unfortunate explorer, Colonel Charles Stoddart, had been placed by the crazy Emir Nasrullah, in the *Siah Cha*—the Black Well, a hideous pit full of human filth, bones and vermin specially bred to torment the occupants. Both Conolly and Stoddart were murdered on his orders. At the end of the 1820s a remarkable American traveller, Charles Masson, set off from Tiflis, reached the Caspian by way of Teheran, entered Afghanistan at Herat and crossed into Sina. He then went back into Afghanistan from Peshawar and explored part of Kafiristan, eventually, after a journey too involved to follow here, reaching Bushire on the Persian Gulf. Later Masson spent seven more years in Afghanistan and became its greatest explorer.

Russian influence in Central Asia continued to increase throughout the 1830s, and in 1839 the East India Company had become so alarmed at reports that Dost Mohammed Khan, the ruler of Afghanistan, was about to ally himself with Russia that they sent a force to Kabul, deposed him and substituted a puppet ruler, Shah Shuja.

In 1841, the Afghans rose against the invaders and that winter a British–Indian Army, under the inept General Mountstewart Elphinstone, began a retreat through the snow-filled Afghan defiles which culminated in its almost complete destruction. Dost Mohammed recovered his throne and when the Indian Mutiny broke out in 1857 the British paid him £10,000 a month to purchase his neutrality.

The next 20 years or so saw "The Great Game" being played flat out by both the British and the Russians, with great intrigues being conducted at both the Afghan and Persian courts. The chief British aim was to keep the Russians out of Herat, which they regarded as the key to India. The Russians were of the same opinion about its importance. They offered the Shah of Persia the entire province of Erivan for it.

Three of the great explorers of the 1850s were not Russians but the sons of a Munich oculist—the brothers Hermann, Adolf and Robert von Schlagintweit. On the recommendation of Humboldt the East India Company commissioned them to carry out scientific exploration, especially in the field of terrestrial magnetism. After working in the Deccan, Kashmir and the Himalayas they

---

course of that dreadful winter kept a detailed record of the wildlife of the island and its topography. Here, he saw the great sea mammal Steller's Sea Cow (*Hydromalis stelleri*), which was extinct, wiped out by sealers, by the end of the century.

During the winter the ship became a total wreck and the following spring the construction of a boat to take them to the Asian mainland was begun under the supervision of a Cossack who had had some experience of ship-building at Okhotsk. On August 21, 1742, they sailed for Kamchatka, reaching Petropavlovsk a fortnight later.

Chirikov with the *St Peter* was more fortunate. He raised the American coast in about 56N, in the Alexander Archipelago, where two of his boat crews went ashore and were never heard of again. Boatless, Chirikov could no longer land, and after passing through the Shumagin Islands, where Bering had also been, with his men suffering from scurvy and desperately short of water, he finally made Avacha Bay with the few survivors on October 11, 1741. The astronomer de la Croyère died soon after landfall was made. At a great cost in life, including that of Bering, the division between the continents of Asia and America had been defined, but the Russians were able to establish a foothold in North America, and to explore its coasts, beyond the 49th parallel, until the United States bought Alaska from them in 1867.

Exercises in imperialism

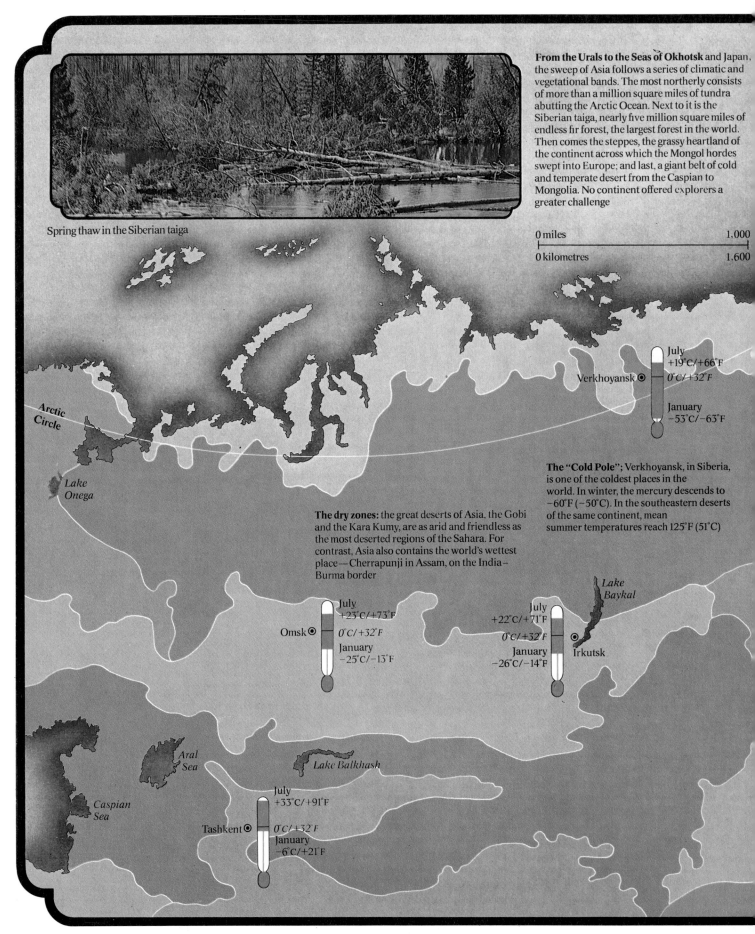

Spring thaw in the Siberian taiga

From the Urals to the Seas of Okhotsk and Japan, the sweep of Asia follows a series of climatic and vegetational bands. The most northerly consists of more than a million square miles of tundra abutting the Arctic Ocean. Next to it is the Siberian taiga, nearly five million square miles of endless fir forest, the largest forest in the world. Then comes the steppes, the grassy heartland of the continent across which the Mongol hordes swept into Europe; and last, a giant belt of cold and temperate desert from the Caspian to Mongolia. No continent offered explorers a greater challenge

0 miles	1,000
0 kilometres	1,600

Verkhoyansk ◉
July
+19°C/+66°F
0°C/+32°F
January
−53°C/−63°F

Arctic
Circle

Lake
Onega

The dry zones: the great deserts of Asia, the Gobi and the Kara Kumy, are as arid and friendless as the most deserted regions of the Sahara. For contrast, Asia also contains the world's wettest place—Cherrapunji in Assam, on the India–Burma border

The "Cold Pole"; Verkhoyansk, in Siberia, is one of the coldest places in the world. In winter, the mercury descends to −60°F (−50°C). In the southeastern deserts of the same continent, mean summer temperatures reach 125°F (51°C)

Omsk ◉
July
+23°C/+73°F
0°C/+32°F
January
−25°C/−13°F

Lake
Baykal

July
+22°C/+71°F
0°C/+32°F
January
−26°C/−14°F
◉
Irkutsk

Aral
Sea

Lake Balkhash

Caspian
Sea

Tashkent ◉
July
+33°C/+91°F
0°C/+32°F
January
−6°C/+21°F

Sea of Okhotsk

July
22°C/+71°F
0°C/+32°F
January
−18°C/0°F
Vladivostok

Sea of Japan

July
+31°C/+87°F
0°C/+32°F
January
−2°C/+28°F

...ing

decided to extend their explorations beyond the Company's dominions, and in 1856—taking with them bales of wool and cotton in an endeavour to pass as merchants—they crossed the Karakorams, losing seven of their 19 horses on the way. They were the first Europeans to cross the great Kun Lun (Kuenlun) range between the high plateau of western Tibet and the deserts of Sinkiang. In the course of their journeys the Schlagintweits produced 84 volumes of notes, hundreds of beautiful drawings and watercolours and collected large numbers of specimens.

In 1857, Hermann and Robert returned to Europe. Adolf, who stayed to carry on their work, was murdered at Kashgar the same year.

The most unusual traveller of this period was undoubtedly Arminius Vambéry, born in Hungary in 1832. At the age of 20 he migrated to Constantinople, where he worked as a tutor and published a Turkish–German dictionary. During his six-year stay in Turkey he became a Turk in everything except nationality, and acquired a knowledge of something like 20 eastern languages and dialects. He was particularly interested in the Turco–Tartar dialects and resolved to travel to Turkestan. Setting off for Teheran, he stayed at the Turkish Embassy for eight months until he was able to join a party of pilgrims returning to Eastern Turkestan from Mecca, having impressed them by his piety and knowledge of Islam. They believed him to be a Muslim.

Great suffering

Wearing the great turban of a dervish (a Muslim friar), and with the assumed name of Reshid Effendi, he left Teheran with this motley band, some of whom had endured great suffering on their enormous pilgrimage, and after a difficult journey reached Karatepe on the Caspian. He crossed the inland sea in a dugout boat, in which the passengers were packed like salted herrings, to Gomush-tepe, a Turcoman settlement that was nothing more than a collection of bee-hive tents—a perilous voyage because the sea was infested with Turcoman pirates who were always on the look-out for suitable persons to capture and sell as slaves.

From here they travelled to Etrek through the grasslands and marshes which border the Caspian and joined a camel caravan under a caravan-bashi who was deeply suspicious of Vambéry's origins.

Eastwards of Etrek the caravan, which numbered 80 persons and 40 camels, entered the Kara Kum, the Black Sands, and began the 400-mile journey across it to Khiva.

By day they took their course from the Sun, by night from what was known as *Temir Kazik* (the Iron Peg), the Pole Star. They suffered from shortage of water and terrible heat, and the camels lost themselves in the morasses of the salt pans, while Vambéry himself narrowly escaped being executed as a spy. At last they reached the foothills of the Little Balkan range and from its eastern spurs turned northeast into an even more terrible expanse of desert in which the only water available at the wells gave them diarrhoea. Of this wilderness Vambéry wrote: ". . . the interminable hills of sand, the dreadful stillness of death, the yellowish-red hue of the sun rising and setting, yes, everything tells us that we are here in a great, perhaps the greatest, desert on the surface of the globe." At last, when all hope seemed to be gone, they reached a fresh-water lake and the rest of the journey to Khiva was without incident.

At Khiva, after once again nearly suffering death as an infidel, Vambéry had two audiences with the Khan, who offered him money, which Vambéry, in his guise as a dervish, declined to accept.

The next part of the journey took the party across the Oxus, passing through country infested with marauders, and sandy wastes in which they suffered agonies of thirst, Vambéry's tongue turning black. They were saved from almost certain death by a party of shepherds, who gave them what food and drink they could, and after another night's journey came to the green outskirts of Bukhara, where Vambéry maintained his reputation for extreme holiness—the only way in which he could survive the three weeks he remained in this perilous place.

At Samarkand, Vambéry left the pilgrims to continue their journey and travelled to Herat by way of Kerki on the Oxus and the Paropamisus Mountains.

Herat had just fallen to an Afghan army and was in ruins. At an audience with the new ruler, the 16-year-old son of the King of Afghanistan, he came dangerously close to being identified for what he wasn't. "By God," said the prince, rising from his chair and pointing a denunciatory finger at him, "I swear that you are an Englishman."

"Have done, Sire," said Vambéry. "You know the saying: 'He who takes, even in sport, a believer for an unbeliever, is himself an unbeliever.' Give me rather something in return for my blessing, so that I may continue on my way." And this the prince did.

In November 1863 Vambéry left Herat for Meshed, having joined a caravan of 2,000 pilgrims and merchants, where he was assisted by an English Colonel in the Shah's service. In January 1864 he reached the Turkish Embassy at Teheran, ten months after setting out from it. From there he

Central Asia: Przewalski's journeys

travelled to London by way of Constantinople and Budapest.

In London all doors were opened to him and he met the Prince of Wales, Swinburne, Dickens and many other famous people, all of which failed to spoil him. "My wanderings", he wrote, "have left powerful impressions upon my mind. Is it surprising if I stand sometimes bewildered, like a child, in Regent Street or in the saloons of British nobles, thinking of the deserts of Central Asia, and of the tents of the Kirghiz and the Turcomans?"

An explorer who, in his time, ranked with Stanley (both received the Royal Geographical Society's Founder's Medal for outstanding work in 1873), but is now almost forgotten, was the Englishman Ney Elias, who led or took part in eight major expeditions to Central Asia, all of them hazardous.

Elias was born in 1844, the son of Jewish parents. Perhaps his most famous journey was begun in September 1872, when with a Chinese servant, a camel driver, an interpreter, six camels and two ponies he set out to cross the Gobi Desert from Kuei Hua Cheng, 150 miles west of Kalgan on the Great Wall.

The crossing proceeded at a rate of about 18 miles a day, Elias taking aneroid and boiling-point readings on the route (the thermometer he carried was incapable of readings at the low temperatures he encountered in the desert).

After 55 days on the road he reached the Chinese garrison post of Ulias-sutai (Uliastay), having lost a camel and a great part of the food when his interpreter deserted. The town was awaiting an attack by Tungan rebels so he set off again with a guide who proved such a nuisance that Elias got rid of him.

Travelling westwards by way of the Jabkhan River (Dzavhan Gol) he crossed the frozen Hara Lake (Har Us Nuur) to reach the town of Kobdo (Hovd), which was full of corpses and burned tents, having been sacked by the rebels a few days previously.

A month later he crossed the Altai range to Suak, on the Chinese–Siberian border, 79 camel stages from his starting point.

From there he reached Biysk on the upper waters of the Ob, and then travelled the remaining 2,300 miles to Nijni-Novgorod by horse-drawn sleigh, in the depths of the Siberian winter and camping out the entire way (the horrors of such a journey were recorded two years later by Colonel Frederick Burnaby—himself a rather idiosyncratic traveller—on his journey from St Petersburg to Khiva). At Nijni-Novgorod Elias caught a train going towards England, after a journey in which he had travelled 4,800 miles.

Elias was a modest man. At a dinner given in his honour another guest made much of having once crossed a certain Central Asian pass. Elias said nothing, but when asked how many he had crossed was forced to reply, "eighteen".

The great explorer in China at this time was Baron Ferdinand von Richthofen, grandfather of the German fighter ace of the First World War.

Von Richthofen went to China with a commercial mission in 1860 and made seven expeditions to the interior between 1868 and 1872, the last one in 1872 being into the wilds of Szechwan. The results of his work—he was the first to make a systematic survey of the mineral wealth of the country—are contained in a monumental book, *China*, with an *Atlas*.

IN CENTRAL ASIA the greatest Russian explorer was Nikolai Przewalski, descendant of a landed Cossack family. He made his first explorations on the Usuri River, a tributary of the Amur, while serving as a young Staff Officer.

On his first great Central Asian journey in November 1870 he set off for Peking from Kyakhta, south of Lake Baykal, with two companions, a young man named Michail Pyltseff and a Cossack. They travelled by conventional means in a Chinese cart of a sort which was used to carry important official papers. "In such a cart", Przewalski wrote, "the traveller must preserve a recumbent position head foremost, in order that his legs may not be on a higher level than his head. The shaking in this kind of cart baffles description. The smallest stone or lump of earth over which one of the wheels may chance to roll produces a violent jolting of the whole vehicle and consequently of its unfortunate occupant. It may easily be imagined how his suffering may be aggravated when travelling with post horses at a trot."

A week later they reached Urga (now Ulan Bator), a Mongol–Chinese town, which was second in sanctity, according to the Buddhists, only to Lhasa. Here they saw a statue of the Maidari, the Buddha-next-to-come, a beaming brass figure which weighed 125 tons. The Mongol part of the town was rendered hideous by the numbers and the filth of male and female beggars who lay on the streets, surrounded by packs of savage curs waiting for them to die. "In the cold winter nights the stronger beggars drag the feeble old women out into the snow, where they are frozen to death, crawling themselves into their holes to avoid their fate."

No foreign travellers liked Urga. A later one, a quite rightly horrified English lady, visited the prison, in which the inmates were nailed up in coffins from which they never emerged, being fed through a hole in the lid.

From Urga, where they exchanged their cart for camels, they entered the Gobi Desert, which was mostly covered with reddish gravel, small pebbles and occasional agates. In some places where there was moisture a sort of grass grew in clumps five feet high, as tough as wire. Here and there too Przewalski noted, "some solitary little flower finds an asylum, or if the soil is saline the budarkhana [*Kalidium gracile*] the favourite food of camels may be seen.

"Everywhere else the wild onion, scrub wormwood, and a few other kinds of Compositiae and Graminea, are the prevailing vegetation of the desert. Of trees and bushes there are absolutely none."

Following the central caravan route to the southeast, and marching from noon to midnight through these vast, depressing solitudes at between 27 and 30 miles a day and meeting tea caravans along the way, they eventually entered the more fertile country of the Chakhar Mongols and reached the Great Wall at Kalgan (Chang-chia-k'ou) northwest of Peking, where it climbs in a spectacular fashion over the range separating the freezing plateaux of Mongolia (the temperature fell below −34°F on Przewalski's crossing) and the warmer plains of China. From there they travelled on horseback to Peking.

At Peking they were hampered by lack of funds—the Russian Imperial Government seems to have been extremely parsimonious in its dealing with Przewalski—but somehow they managed to assemble seven pack-camels and two riding horses and, having added a second Cossack to the party, set off northwards for the Tari-Nor (lake), passing through an interminable region of sandhills covered with willow bushes. "There are no landmarks to steer by," Przewalski wrote, "one hill is exactly like another, and as soon as you have ascended one, dozens more, all as though in the same mould, rise up in front of you."

On cold stormy days the lake, the largest in southeastern Mongolia, was crammed with ducks and geese on passage across the deserts; but when the weather improved it emptied until it changed again when fresh flights took their place.

Here, they saw a great fire on the steppes which the Mongols had lit to burn the withered grass of the previous year. "The heavens were cloaked with clouds refulgent with a purple glow, which threw a lurid glare far and wide over the steppe; columns of smoke rose in fantastic shapes till they were lost to the eye in a confused, indistinct mass. In the foreground lay the vast plain lighted up by the burning belt; behind, the darkness of the night, which seemed blacker and more impenetrable than ever; the lake resounded

Peter the Great of Russia, whose reign saw his country's expansion to the Pacific. Intent also on maritime growth, he studied shipbuilding in London's Deptford yard (right). (Below) St Petersburg, his capital, and capital of Russia until the 1917 revolution

The weather was now cooler and after passing through a boundless yellow plain of sand they reached Ting-yuan-ying, a town below the range of the Ho-lan Shan, which rose in a great rampart to the east. It was surrounded by a mud wall and presided over by the Amban, ruler of the Ala-Shan Mongols, who were among the poorest of all the Mongols because of the wretchedness of their country. "The Prince himself is a man of forty, with a good-looking face, but rather pale, owing to his being addicted to smoking opium. A few years ago his wife died and he now lives with concubines. In character he is corrupt and despotic to the last degree. The gratification of a whim, a sudden outburst of passion, or the desire for revenge, override the dictates of calm judgement and discretion; in fact his own sweet will replaces every law and is implicitly obeyed without the slightest opposition from anybody. But the same system prevails throughout the whole of Mongolia and China. Nothing but the ignorance of masses could allow such a state of society to continue, which under other circumstances would inevitably lead to the dismemberment of the empire."

From the town they climbed into the Ho-lan Shan, where they saw the remarkable long-eared pheasant (*Crossoptilon auritum*) which had bunches of feathers on the back of the head like the ears of an owl; and there they hunted the kuku-yaman, a mountain sheep with a tawny-grey or tawny-crimson coat, which had the strange facility of being able to whistle like a man when giving the alarm at the approach of danger.

Here, 400 miles (a month's journey) from the Koko Nor, they were forced to turn back through lack of money—they sold two of their guns to get some—and by the unreliability of their two Cossacks.

They had a difficult return journey to Kalgan, 800 miles to the east. Almost at once Pyltseff was struck down by typhoid, which detained them for nine days at a well. Then, when they had crossed the Hara Nara Ulin range, and were travelling north of the Yangtze, a storm struck them which Przewalski compared to a December blizzard in Siberia. Early in December they left the valley of the Hwang-Ho for the Mongolian plateau, where they again experienced severe cold. "The Thermometer at sunrise descended to −32.7C (−26°F); and the frost was often accompanied by strong winds and sleet. All this happened in the very place where in summer we had 37C (98F) of heat. . . . My companion, still weak and shaken in health, was obliged to sit on horseback day after day, wrapt in a sheepskin coat. We, who usually went on foot, did not feel the cold so much whilst on the march; but in camp the severity of the winter

with the loud cries of startled birds, while all was still and quiet on the plain."

On May 7 they reached Kalgan. Spring had come, and eight days later they set off westwards through the mountains to reach the Hwang-Ho, seeing on the way the remarkable mountain sheep (*Ovis argali*) which were able to jump from a height of 20 or 30 feet and still land on their feet.

At one Chinese settlement one of the inhabitants, in a spirit of curiosity, loosed a savage mastiff on them. It attacked Faust, the expedition's dog. "I drew one of my revolvers from the holster and shot it on the spot," Przewalski wrote, stoutly. "One must act promptly in these countries, for if you let them kill your dog one day, they may try to kill you the next, and then it becomes more serious."

They then crossed the Yin Shan range southwards to Pao-t'ou, where a general gave them a passport to continue their journey through the dangerous Ordos region. Here, almost the entire garrison were sunk in a torpor, induced by perpetual opium smoking, from which they only roused themselves to terrorize the inhabitants. "The general, un-able to cure his men of this vile practice . . . entreated us to tell him if there was not some antidote for opium, and offered a handsome reward if such could be found."

Having been ferried across the Hwang-Ho with their camels—which objected to going in a boat—they travelled westwards for nearly 300 miles along the river bank in a region of great yellow dunes. "A dull heaviness oppresses the senses in this inanimate sea of sand," he wrote. "No sounds are heard, not even the chirping of the grasshopper; the silence of the tomb surrounds you."

"Deathlike solitude"

Then, having again crossed the Hwang-Ho, the travellers entered the wild and barren desert of the Ala-Shan, a southern extension of the Gobi, the worst parts of which were nothing but bare sand drift. "Some of these sands are so extensive," Przewalski wrote, "as to be called by the Mongols, Tingeri, i.e. 'sky'. Not a drop of water is to be found in them; no birds, no animals are visible; and their deathlike solitude fills with involuntary dread the soul of the man who has wandered there."

Tibet: the lost horizon

was felt by us all with a vengeance . . . one of the Cossacks usually rode forward to the nearest Mongol yurts to buy argols if we had not already laid in a supply. . . . Once, at our wit's end for fuel, we were obliged to cut up a saddle in order to boil a little tea, and had to content ourselves with this frugal supper after a march of 23 miles in severe cold and storm. My companion slept with Faust, and was very glad of such a bedfellow. . . ."

This was not the end of their troubles. Their camels were stolen and when they applied for help to the lamas at a monastery they were told: "We are not the guardians of your camels; seek them as best you can."

They finally reached Kalgan on the evening of the Russian New Year (January 12) 1872. "The first act of the expedition was ended. . . . We could say with clear consciences that so far we had fulfilled our task; and this amount of success only whetted our passionate desire to plunge once again into the heart of Asia, and strive to reach the distant shores of Lake Kok-nor."

And they did. Hastily putting together more stores, arms and merchandise to sell on the way, with two fresh Cossacks, a youngster named Pamphile Chebayeff and Dondok Irinchoff, they set off again from Kalgan, this time taking with them an extremely savage Mongol dog called Karza as well as the amiable Faust.

After suffering the horrors of the Ordos Desert in high summer, they entered the Nan Shan ranges in Kansu and reached the sacred Demchuk Lake at 13,100 feet, where the superior of the Chertinton Monastery, who had lived for seven years in a cave, befriended them. "He told us that he once saw a large cow rise from the lake, swim on its surface for some time and again disappear in its depths. Ever since it has been held in high repute."

On October 25, 1872, they reached the north shore of the Koko Nor. "The dream of my life was accomplished," Przewalski wrote, "and object of the expedition gained! It is true that this success had been purchased at the cost of many hardships and sufferings; but all past trials were forgotten, as we stood in triumph on the shore of the great lake, and gazed with admiration on its beautiful dark blue waves."

They were not the first Europeans to reach it; but none had surveyed the whole route as they had done, or made such a scientific collection of specimens. From here, with winter coming on, they pressed on over the ranges to the Yangtze-Kiang, which they reached on January 22, 1873. Here, 500 miles and 27 days' journey from Lhasa, three of their 11 camels having died, they were again forced to turn back, for they were practically penniless and had few stores left.

In 1876, he made another attempt to get to the Tibetan capital, Lhasa. Reaching the Lop Nor—being the first European to see it since Marco Polo—he surveyed it, noting that it really consisted of a number of small lakes which shifted their position when the river found new courses. To its south he discovered the Astin Tagh range and proved that it formed a continuous whole with the Nan Shan to the east and the Kun Lun to the west, thus forming the great northern battlement of Tibet. He was unable to cross it because it was midwinter.

His next attempt to reach Lhasa was in 1879, reaching a point only 170 miles from it when his camp was attacked by Tibetan guards, the Chinese there having spread a rumour that he was intent on capturing the Dalai Lama. His return route took him into the country south of the Koko Nor and then across the Gobi to Kiatka—an immense journey.

Przewalski tried once again to attempt to reach Lhasa from the north in 1888. He never did reach it. He died at Karakol near the Issyk Kul Lake in the Tien Shan on October 20 that year. In his honour the Russians erected a monument there and changed the name of the place to Przhevalsk.

Przewalski was a great explorer, a better naturalist than surveyor (he failed to locate accurately the Koko Nor). Nothing would divert him from his task except the possibility of hunting. He discovered the wild camel, an ancestor of the domesticated species, and the wild horse (*Equus przewalskii*), of which the surviving examples in Russia are in a game reserve in the Crimea.

Towards the end of the 16th century a native traveller who had returned to India from western Tibet told Jesuit missionaries at the court of the Emperor Akbar that he had seen a religious ceremony in which wine was used. It led the fathers to believe what they had long hoped—that Christianity was being practised beyond the Himalayan range. Two years later the Jesuit mission to the Mogul court was withdrawn and no use was made of the information.

When, in 1598, the mission was once more established, Father Jerome Xavier, grandnephew of St Francis Xavier, suggested that an effort should be made to contact the Christian community in Cathay, which, if it still existed, had been cut off from contact with the Church of St Peter for centuries.

The man chosen for this extremely hazardous journey was Benedict de Goes, a 42-year-old Spaniard, who set off from Agra in January 1603, having assumed the name Abdullah, "which signifies Servant of the Lord, with the addition of Isai, or the Chris-

tian. . . . So he was to pass for an Armenian, for in that character he would be allowed to travel freely, whilst if known as a Spaniard he was certain to be stopped. He also carried with him a variety of wares, both that he might maintain himself by selling them, and to keep up his character as a merchant."

At Lahore he joined the annual caravan that was setting off for Kashgar, beyond the Pamirs, and which consisted of about 500 persons and a large number of mules, camels and carts.

It took the caravan six months to reach Kabul, where the priest, after waiting eight months, joined another caravan bound for Yarkand, and with it crossed the Hindu Kush from Parwan, the last outpost of the Mogul Empire, where Akbar's authority ended.

From Talikhan the caravan went into Badakshan, constantly harassed by robbers, and then followed the Polos' route up the Oxus valley. De Goes was the first European to march in the footsteps of the great Venetians. The caravan then crossed the "Pamech Desert" (what is now laughingly known as the Pamir "Plateau", which, although it may be "The Roof of the World", is certainly not flat).

Of de Goes's horses "five had perished through the intense cold and the entire lack of fuel together with the uncongenial state of the atmosphere, which makes it almost impossible for the animals to breathe. Hence both men and beasts felt oppressed beyond

endurance and gasped for breath. Against this evil, men armed themselves by eating garlic, onions and dried apples, whilst the gums of the animals are rubbed with garlic. The journey through this desert takes forty days, if there is snow on the ground; otherwise it is shorter. The country, moreover, is notorious for its marauding bands, who lie in wait for the caravans to rob or murder them."

The high passes

Then, from Sarikol the caravan climbed to the 14,200-foot "Ciecalith" (Chichiklik) Pass and reached Tanghetar, a place belonging to the Kingdom of Cascar. Here de Goes and his companion, an Armenian trader, secured the necessary passports to continue their journey, and in November 1604 they joined a caravan, which, like all other caravans bound for China, had to pretend to be an embassy in order to satisfy the officials on the frontier. It took months as there were innumerable halts along the road. Having skirted the western end of the Takla Makan Desert they met some Muslim merchants outward bound from Peking, and this proved to them, more or less conclusively, that China and Cathay were identical.

At a town at the foot of the Tien Shan mountains, "a grand dance happening to be performed before them, the young prince [he was only 12 years old] asked Benedict how the people of his country used to dance; and so Benedict, not to be churlish with a prince about so small a matter, got up and danced himself to show the way of it. He also visited the prince's mother. . . . To her he presented some little things that women like, a looking glass, Indian muslin, and so forth. . . ."

From Ha-mi, to the east of T'u-lu fan (Turfan, in the Depression), it took nine days to cross the 300-mile-wide neck of the Gobi Desert to Chia-yu kuan in northwest Kansu. This was the "Jade Gate" in the Great Wall, otherwise known as "The Last Gate of the World", where the old Silk Road went out towards Central Asia. There they waited 25 days for permission to pass through it.

It was the end of 1605. De Goes had reached China and Cathay at last, the first European since the Polos to set foot on Chinese soil from the west; but he never reached the capital. After waiting more than a year to continue his journey through the Great Wall and beyond, de Goes contracted a mysterious and fatal illness. No European was to make a similar journey for another 250 years.

De Goes was the first of a number of Jesuit missionaries who were to explore the high passes of the Himalayas in their efforts to spread Christianity into the fastnesses of Buddhist Tibet.

Not unnaturally their work was strongly objected to by the Buddhist Lamas (one has to imagine the effect that would have been created in 17th-century Portugal if a band of Buddhists had arrived and converted the king without consulting the Catholic hierarchy); and when the king was baptised by the Jesuit de Andrade in 1630 (the ceremony having been delayed because of his reluctance to give up the pleasures of fornication) they rebelled under the leadership of his brother, the Chief Lama. The king became a prisoner and many of the 400 converts were enslaved.

In 1656, John Grueber, a Jesuit missionary and mathematician born at Linz in 1623, set out from Rome with Father Bernard Diestel on the long journey to Peking, arriving there towards the end of 1658, having reached the Portuguese colony of Macao on the China coast in an English ship.

At this time it had become almost impossible for Portuguese ships to sail out of Macao because of the presence of Dutch sea-raiders from Batavia in the South China Sea, and it was therefore decided that Grueber should attempt to pioneer an overland route less hazardous than that followed by de Goes, through Tibet to India.

His companion was to be Father Albert d'Orville, a member of an aristocratic Belgian family, who had been given special training in geography and surveying at Peking.

They set off in April 1661 and two months later, after crossing the Yellow River, reached Hsi-ning, the western gate of the empire, "a great and populous city built at the vast wall of China", almost 1,000 miles to the west of Peking.

The city was on a now non-existent southerly, probably earthen, loop of the Great Wall, "so broad that six horsemen may run abreast on it", and it was possible to travel along the top of it and the main wall as far as the Jade Gate near Chiu ch'uan, where de Goes had died, a journey of 18 days to the northwest.

The salt lake

Leaving Hsi-ning in July 1661 Grueber and d'Orville travelled westwards across the "Tartar Desert" to the Koko Nor (now Ch'ing Hai), the great dark-blue salt lake in northeastern Tsing-hai province, and then southwest through the plains on the edge of the Tsaidam, the "Salt Swamp", one of the most desolate regions in Central Asia, where, according to the explorer W. W. Rockhill, who attempted to reach Lhasa in disguise by this route in 1892, "there is but swamp and sand, willow, brush and briars; where mosquitoes and spiders thrive; where the wind always blows, the heat of the day is intense, and the cold of night piercing".

Then they travelled southwest across the 15,000-foot Burkan, Buddha and Shuga ranges, over a high plateau infested with

Giant panda

Przewalski's horse

The secretive giant panda and Przewalski's horse are two animals of which the West has knowledge as a result of the travels of Europeans. The giant panda, a native of the forests of Szechwan, was first reported by the French missionary Père Jean-Pierre David, a great naturalist, and Przewalski's horse, the only surviving species of wild horse, by the Russian explorer of Asia

Tibet: the lost horizon

bandits, to the Baian-Kara range and on to the present borders of Tibet in the Tanghla range, the great climatic divide between the dry and arid country they had passed through and a plateau deluged with rain, hail and snow for six months of the year. They reached Lhasa, the first Europeans to set eyes on it, in October 1661.

Lhasa had been the capital of Tibet only since the final overthrow of the Red Hat sect by the Yellow Hats under the Fifth Dalai Lama, the great Ngawang Lobzang Gyatso, in 1641.

At Lhasa, Grueber noticed numbers of remarkable things: prayer wheels which, up to now, were not known in Europe; the luxurious clothes worn by the courtiers; the loathsome habits of the ordinary citizens, who slept on the ground, ate raw meat and never washed; and the horrible custom whereby once a year a young man, armed with a sword and bow and arrows, was given the power by the high priests to kill anyone he met. ("Whomever he slays obtains eternal happiness.") He also discovered that a medicinal pill much in demand was compounded from the Dalai Lama's urine and excrement.

Grueber and d'Orville left Lhasa towards the end of November and probably travelled by way of Shigatse to cross the Himalayas and reach Nepal. The descent of the Bhote Kosi, which rises in the glaciers of the massif, must have been hair-raising if it was anything like the journey down it made by a native surveyor, working for the Indian Government, in 1871. "The explorer had to cross the . . . river fourteen times, by means of three iron suspension and eleven wood bridges. . . . At one place the river ran in a gigantic chasm, the sides of which were so close to one another that a bridge of twenty-four paces was sufficient to span it. . . . Near the bridge the precipices were so impracticable that the path had of necessity to be supported by iron pegs let into the face of the rock, the path being formed by bars of iron and slabs of stone stretching from peg to peg and covered with earth. This extraordinary path is in no place more than eighteen inches in width and is carried for more than one-third of a mile (775 paces) along the face of the cliff, at some 1500 feet above the river, which could be seen roaring below in its narrow bed. The explorer, who has seen much difficult ground in the Himalayas, says he never in his life met with anything to equal this bit of the path."

It took Grueber and his companion 11 days to reach Kathmandu from Nilam on the Tibetan side of the mountain, and when they did, Grueber was no more impressed by the habits of the Nepalese than he had been by those of the Tibetans.

Eleven months after leaving Peking they reached India and travelled by way of Patna to Benares and from there to Agra. There, worn out by privation, d'Orville died—"Midway on his journey between China and Europe he departed for his heavenly home"—on April 8, 1682.

After resting for some weeks, Grueber went on by way of Delhi to Lahore with a Father Henry Roth. They then descended the Indus, crossed the dreadful Makran Desert region into southern Persia and eventually reached Rome, by way of Hormuz and Smyrna, in February 1664.

Whatever has come down to us about Grueber's journey is contained in Athanasius Kircher's *China Monumentis Qua Sacris Qua Profanis Nec Non Variis Naturae et Artis Spectaculis, Aliarumque Rerum Memorabilium Argumentis Illustrata*, Amsterdam 1667. It is a pity that Grueber did not write his own account of his travels. After serving for two years as a chaplain with the Austrian Army in Transylvania he lived quietly in Hungary until his death in 1680, at Tyrnau.

The Jesuits appeared again in Tibet when Father Ippolito Desideri, a 30-year-old Italian, and Father Manuel Freyre, a Portuguese and somewhat younger, set off from Lahore in October 1714 with the intention of opening up once more the Jesuit mission in Tibet, which had been assigned to the Capuchins as a mission-field in 1702.

Indian Venice

They crossed into Kashmir and reached "Calixmir" (Srinagar) on November 13, where Desideri partly recovered from dysentery (which had been made worse by having to wade through ice-cold streams on the way) and a haemmorhage of the lungs. Nevertheless he loved "the Venice of India", as much as Freyre seems to have loathed it.

Leaving Srinagar in May 1715 with passports and letters of recommendation to the King of Ladakh, they travelled eastwards to the capital, Leh, over the 11,758-foot-high pass of Zoji La, which they began to climb, to Desideri's amusement, on Ascension Day, the porters cutting steps for them in the snow with hatchets. On this and other passes on the way from "Little Tibet" they suffered from snow-blindness. To combat it they wore masks made from cloth impregnated with charcoal, which gave them some relief.

On June 20 they reached Leh, in "Second Tibet", where Desideri had hoped to open a mission station; but by this time Freyre, who was not the equal of his companion, insisted on returning to India.

Fortunately for Desideri he refused to return by the route by which they had come, and it was Desideri who now planned a route that would take them southeastwards along the upper waters of the Indus into "Third Tibet".

On August 17, 1715, they set off and travelled by way of the Pangong Lake along the edge of the vile Chang Tang desert plateau, on which pools of stagnant water produced sulphurous gases which caused swellings of the gums and lips.

At Tashigong, where they were helped by the Lama at the monastery, they saw the monks in their red mitre-like hats and Freyre got thoroughly mixed up about the Buddhist belief in transmigration of souls and reincarnation, which he attributed to demoniacal possession. From Tashigong they travelled with a military convoy bound for Lhasa, in company with a beautiful Tartar princess, the widow of the governor, who was as kind and prudent as she was beautiful. "If I help you on the journey and give of my provisions," she said, "it will not be because of money but because of God. In the meantime listen to my counsel. Horses are not dependable for they die of hunger; in the desert there is no fodder but grass withered by the cold or covered with snow; so besides horses, be sure to take some oxen which, moreover, are better for your loads."

They set off on October 9, from Gartok, near Tashigong, following a route that no European travellers were to traverse until 1904 (C. G. Rawling and Captain C. H. D. Ryder after Younghusband's expedition to Lhasa that year). The weather was fearfully cold and the Princess Casals comforted them with cha (tea). "Through the mouth of her interpreter she would tell us to have courage," Freyre wrote, "for no dangers from the mountains nor avalanches had power to harm us if we kept to her side."

The following month, on "the highest region we have traversed, during the whole of our peregrinations . . . a complete desert, called Ng-nari Giongar", they saw the 22,000-foot Mount Kailas north of the Mansarowar and Rakas Tal lakes, near to which rise the Indus, the Sutlej and the Tsangpo (the Brahmaputra). Hindus believe that this is Kailash, the abode and paradise of Siva, who caught Ganga as she fell from Heaven for the good of all mankind. It is equally sacred to the Buddhists and the 32-mile circuit of the mountain was made when Desideri was there and until recently by Hindu and Buddhist pilgrims alike many times and sometimes by measuring their length on the ground.

Having passed by the shores of the Mansarowar Lake, which Desideri thought, very reasonably, must be the source of the Ganges, they continued their journey, Freyre nearly losing his life when his horse collapsed in the snow (he was saved by a search party that went back to find him), and on March 18, 1716, they reached Lhasa, five of their seven horses having died on the way from Leh, from where Freyre left almost immediately for India, by way of Nepal.

Desideri remained at Lhasa until April 1721. He met the King of Tibet, a Mongol named Latsang Khan, who had seized power in 1705, some years after the death of the Fifth Dalai Lama. Latsang had murdered his successor, who was a licentious but popular young man, and shut up the next reincarnation in a monastery. The two men got on well together and the king encouraged Desideri to study Buddhism and the Tibetan language, which he did, retiring to a monastery for the purpose, where he wrote a book in Tibetan refuting Buddhism.

In April 1721, Desideri was ordered to return to India, the Capuchins having been awarded Tibet as their parish. Bitterly disappointed, he obeyed. After spending nearly five more years in India he returned to Europe by sea and reached Rome in 1728, where he died in April 1733 at the age of 49.

The last members of the Capuchin mission were withdrawn from Tibet in 1745 and no European visited it again until a Scotsman, George Bogle, on a diplomatic mission from Warren Hastings, Govenor of Bengal, reached Shigatse, where he stayed at the great lamasery, from India. In 1783, Hastings despatched Lieutenant Samuel Turner, a kinsman, to Shigatse on the occasion of the announcement of the incarnation of the Fourth Panchen Lama, a child of 18 months.

Turner reported that the infant wore the garb of the Yellow Hat (Gelugpa) hierarchy, and when he addressed him he felt impelled to speak of the matters which he had come to discuss, as if to an adult ruler: "The little creature looked steadfastly towards me", he wrote, "with the appearance of much attention while I spoke, and nodded with repeated but slow movements of the head, as though he understood every word, but could not utter a reply."

A forbidden land
Both these missions were unsuccessful in their aim, which was to bring about an increase in British influence in Tibet, and when in 1788 the new governor-general—Charles Cornwallis, the invader of Virginia in 1781—neglected to send assistance to the Panchen Lama when the Regent asked him for help against the Nepalese who had invaded the country, Tibet turned to China for assistance and from that time it became a forbidden land to the British.

The exception was Thomas Manning, a brilliant and eccentric member of the East India Company, who, having been refused permission to go to Lhasa as its representative, went just the same, accompanied by a Chinese servant, who was a bore. After a journey of three months he reached Lhasa in December 1811, the first Englishman to do so, having disguised himself in a pseudo-oriental costume which fooled nobody, and which he was forced to exchange for a warmer outfit on the way through Bhutan.

Manning was impressed by the Potala, although his description of it can scarcely be called vivid; but he wrote of Lhasa: "If the palace exceeded my expectations the town as far fell short of them. The habitations are begrimed with smut and dirt. The avenues are full of dogs, some growling and gnawing bits of hide which lie about in profusion, and emit a charnel-house smell; others limping and looking livid; others ulcerated; others starved and dying, and pecked at by ravens, some dead and preyed upon. In short, everything seems mean and gloomy, and excites the idea of something unreal. Even the mirth and laughter of the inhabitants I thought dreamy and ghostly. . . ."

He was, however, impressed by the Ninth Dalai Lama, to whom he kow-towed and handed over his gifts. Then, having had his newly shaven head blessed by the Dalai Lama, and having drunk a cup of buttered tea, he was able to observe the seven-year-old ruler, whose throne was situated some way above his extraordinary guest. "Sometimes, particularly when he looked at me, his smile almost approached to a gentle laugh. No doubt my grim beard and spectacles somewhat excited his risibility, though I have afterwards, at the New Year's festival, seen him smile and unbend freely while sitting myself unobserved in a corner, and watching his reception of various persons, and the notice he took of the strange variety of surrounding objects."

Later he confided to his diary, in rather Pickwickian terms: "This day I saluted the Grand Lama! Beautiful youth. Face poetically affecting. Very happy to have seen him and his blessed smile. Hope often to see him again."

In April 1812, Manning returned to India, having been more or less forced to leave by the Chinese officials who swarmed in the city and who made no secret of the fact that to them his presence was unwelcome. He was the last Englishman to visit Lhasa until the Younghusband expedition reached it in August 1904.

That same year, 1812, disguised as Hindu fakirs, William Moorcroft, a veterinary surgeon to the Bengal Government, and Hyder Jung Hearsey, an army officer whose mother was a native of the country, travelled up the Ramganga, a tributary of the Ganges, to its source, crossed the mountains into western Tibet by the 16,628-foot Niti Pass, east of Mount Kamet, and reached Mansarowar Lake, the first Europeans to visit it since Desideri in 1715. On their way back they were imprisoned and brutally treated in Nepal. The information they gathered on this expedition was of immense value to the Great Trigonometrical Survey of India, which had been begun by William Lambton in 1802.

AFTER GRUEBER AND D'ORVILLE'S journey no further attempts were made by Europeans to reach Lhasa from China until 1844. In the autumn of that year two French Lazarist missionaries, Father Evariste Regis Huc and Father Gabet, both of whom spoke Chinese and Mongolian, shaved off their pigtails to the distress of their Chinese converts, disguised themselves as lamas and set off westwards through Inner Mongolia from what were known as the "Contiguous Defiles", to the north of the Great Wall.

Huc's account of the journey, *Travels in Tartary, Thibet and China*, which was translated into English by William Hazlitt, gives us all the splendours and miseries of the journey and the humour, too.

On the way west they saw the great Imperial forest, which teemed with tigers, panthers, bears, wild boars, wolves and stags. Hunting had been abandoned since the previous Manchu Emperor (Kia-King) had been struck by lightning while hunting in it; but poachers still braved the divine wrath, killing large numbers of stags to obtain half-coagulated blood from their antlers, a highly prized ingredient in Chinese medicine.

Passing the city of "Tolon-Noor", where bells were made for Buddhist lamaseries, "a vast agglomeration of hideous houses, which seem to have been thrown together with a pitchfork . . . the carriage portion of the streets . . . a marsh of mud and putrid filth, deep enough to stifle and bury the smaller beasts of burden that not infrequently fall within it", Huc and Gabet entered, on October 1, a blistering desert and eventually emerged from it into the vast, fertile prairies of the "Tchakar" (Borderland), where they saw great herds and flocks—the Imperial horses running in herds of 1,200 (there were 360 herds).

From now on, as they continued through this beautiful country, they visited the Mongols in their conical tents, taking snuff with them from bottles that they carried on their girdles and asking the obligatory questions: "Is the pasturage with you rich and abundant? Are your herds in fine condition? Does tranquillity prevail?", and so on.

In their tents, too, they inhaled the ghastly odour "occasioned by the mutton grease and

Tibet: the lost horizon

butter with which everything on or about a Tartar is impregnated", and on the occasion of the Festival of the Loaves of the Moon the two of them were given the fat tail of a sheep to eat, which weighed between six and eight pounds. They drank distilled mare's milk and learned of the horrible practice which attended the burial of the Tartar kings, whereby children of both sexes were killed by a dose of mercury, which was also said to preserve their bodies and the pristine freshness of their complexions. The dead children were then stood upright around the corpse of the ruler in order to keep him company, the door of the tomb being guarded against intruders by an infernal machine which discharged flights of arrows at whoever attempted to enter.

They now entered the inundated country on the banks of the flooded Hwang-Ho, in which their camels just managed to keep their heads and humps showing above the water, and after crossing it in a rowing boat passed through the Ordos Desert region before reaching the Koko Nor, having been again forced to cross the Yellow River. Here, they waited until October 1855 to join the great ambassadorial caravan to Lhasa, spending the intervening months in monasteries. In one, Kumbum, southeast of the lake, they saw the Miraculous Tree of Ten Thousand Images, said to have sprung from the shorn locks of a 14th-century sage. The leaves of this ancient tree, which resembled a plane, and the bark, too, were covered, apparently quite naturally, with the words *Om Mani Padme Hum* (Hail O Jewel of the lotus blossom), a miracle which the Lazarists were unable to account for or refute.

The caravan of 2,000 men and 4,000 animals followed a route roughly parallel to that of Grueber and d'Orville and over the same ranges.

The wild ass
Then having crossed the frozen "River of Gold Dust" (the Yangtze) they saw wild cattle and mules of Tartary, "which our naturalists call cheval hemione, a horse half ass which were so fast that no horseman in the caravan could overtake them". And here a terrible north wind blew, so cold that, crossing the Yangtze, they saw a herd of wild yaks frozen in the ice. Men and animals were killed off and those who could go no farther were left behind.

When they reached the Tanghla range the weather improved, just in time to save Father Gabet from what had seemed to Huc certain death, and on January 29, 1846, they reached Lhasa, and took lodgings in one of the lime-washed houses that Huc compared to whitened sepulchres, being clean outside, in-

describably filthy within. "In the town itself", he wrote, "all is excitement, and noise, and pushing, and competition, every single soul in the place being ardently occupied in the grand business of buying and selling. Commerce and devotion incessantly attracting to Lha-Ssa an infinite number of strangers, render the place a rendezvous of all the Asiatic peoples; so that the streets, always crowded with pilgrims and traders, present a marvellous variety of physiognomies, costumes and languages."

Their stay was short. In spite of getting on well with the Regent, who gave them a house, where they opened a chapel, to live in, the Chinese ambassador demanded their expulsion and they left Lhasa on their way eastwards to Canton in March 1846. Travelling with a Tibetan escort provided by the Regent they had a hazardous journey across the upper waters of the Salween and the Mekong. On the way they had an exciting descent of a glacier on the Lha-Ri, the Mountain of Spirits, wearing snow goggles made of horsehair against the glare. "A magnificent long-haired ox opened the march; then after stretching out his neck, smelling for a moment at the ice, and blowing through his large nostrils some thick clouds of vapour, he

manfully put his two front feet on the glacier, and whizzed off as if he had been discharged from a cannon. He went down the glacier with his legs extended, but as stiff and motionless as if they had been made of marble. Arriving at the bottom, he turned over, and then ran on, bounding and bellowing over the snow.... We seated ourselves carefully on the edge of the glacier, we stuck our heels close together on the ice, as firmly as possible, then using the handles of our whips by way of helm, we sailed over these frozen waters with the velocity of a locomotive."

Finally they reached the Yangtze, which they had already crossed far to the north on their outward journey. They had put the frozen lands behind them. "A delicious warmth gradually penetrated our limbs . . . it was nearly two years since we had perspired, and it seemed very odd to be warm without being before a good fire."

From the Chinese frontier they continued their journey in palanquins—"our legs had bestrid so many horses of every age, size, quality, and colour that they refused to have anything further to do with horses at all."

After a journey of more than two years, the Lazarists reached the Portuguese colony of Macao in October 1846.

Mapping the Himalayas

THE FOUNDER OF the Great Trigonometrical Survey of India, Colonel W. Lambton, may well be commemorated in the more specialized textbooks on the history of the subcontinent. Few men, however, have been commemorated to a more singular degree than his successor as the head of the survey, George Everest, whose name was given to the world's highest mountain and is now a synonym for the height of achievement. Everest an indefatigable military engineer who had come out to India as an East India Company cadet in 1806, established the "gridiron" system of triangulation, which was the basis of the survey of the entire subcontinent.

Of his work Kenneth Mason, one of his successors, wrote: "By means of accurate observations he, with very few assistants, measured the great meridional arc passing from Cape Comorin (the southernmost point of India) through the centre of India to the Himalayas. This arc forms the foundation on which was calculated the mathematical spheroid—Everest's spheroid—which most closely fits the figure of the Earth, or geoid,

The Annapurna group of mountains in Nepal (the highest is 26,504 feet above sea level), part of the breathtaking barrier of the Himalayas which separates India from Tibet

in India. The positions and officially accepted heights of Himalayan mountains, and in fact all places in India, are calculated on this spheroid. On the completion of his arc and the network of primary series of triangulation associated with it, it became possible to add by observation a framework of triangulation covering the Himalayas, and to fix with considerable accuracy the positions and heights of the highest summits without visiting them. No man before or since has done so much for the geography of Asia. . . ."

When he retired in 1843 he was succeeded by Andrew Waugh and the work was carried on of mapping the northeastern and northwestern Himalayas between 1846 and 1855, 79 of the highest peaks in the world being fixed by measurements with the great theodolites from the stations in the northeastern section. The greatest of mountains was not named Everest until 1865, and then only because it had been impossible to find a local one. Chomo Lungma, the Tibetan name, is incorrect as it refers to the district. "Tibetan scholars have found in sacred writings descriptive expressions for it, such as *Mi-thik Dgu-thik Bya-phur Long-nga* ('You cannot see the summit from near it, but you can see the summit from nine directions, and a bird which flies as high as the summit goes blind'). No Tibetan would recognise these names (an alternative with the same meaning is *Mi-ti Gu-ti Cha-pu Long-nga*)," wrote Mason. "Surely after a hundred years the world should be content with 'Everest'."

The detailed work of the Great Trigonometrical Survey, beyond the frontiers of India, would have been impossible without what were known as the Pundits, the Hindi for what in this sense of the word is "Learned Experts". The first of these very gallant native surveyors were recruited in 1863 by Captain Thomas George Montgomerie, who himself had been in charge of the survey of some 70,000 square miles of the Himalayas in Kashmir and Ladakh, in the course of which many trigonometrical stations were set up at heights of between 15,000 and 20,000 feet and 19 peaks in the Karakoram over 25,000 feet were measured, including K2, at 28,250 feet second only to Everest. By 1862, the survey of the high peaks of the Himalayan range had been completed.

The Pundits were equipped with all the apparatus for secret surveying. Some of them travelled as merchants, others in the guise of Buddhist pilgrims, and their prayer wheels concealed paper for taking notes and prismatic compasses instead of the customary rolls inscribed with the words *Om Mane Padme Hum*. Some carried hollow books decorated with cabalistic signs, which contained plane tables for mapping and they had

specially made pocket sextants. Their prayer rosaries, which would normally consist of 108 beads, numbered 100, and each tenth bead was larger, enabling them to count their paces in thousands—the Pundits literally counted every carefully regulated step they took.

Their names never appeared in the reports of their work, only initials. One of them, "KP", whose name was Kintup, was unlike most of the others, a completely untrained and illiterate native of Sikkim. On a four-year mission in Tibet, in the course of which he was sold into slavery, he was provided with metal tubes and a drill so that he could insert messages in marked logs, which he was to float down the Tsangpo in the hope that they would be picked up in the Brahmaputra, thus proving that they were the same river. While he was enslaved he lost the drill and had to lash the tubes to the logs with bamboo strips. When he finally reached India, in 1884, he found that all the logs had floated unnoticed into the Bay of Bengal.

Disguised as merchants

The first two students to emerge successfully from the two-year training course at Dehra Dun, near Simla, were two Bhotian cousins, Nain Singh and Mani Singh, who had accompanied the Schlagintweit brothers on their journeys.

In 1864, they set out for Tibet by way of Kumaun, but were turned back at the Tibetan border. On their second attempt, disguised as a Ladakh merchant and wearing false pigtails, Nain Singh reached the Tashilhunpo Monastery, near Shigatse, where he had an audience with the 11-year-old Panchen Lama. Nain Singh had been forced to turn back through Nepal.

Still with his disguise unpenetrated Nain Singh, with a servant, Chumbel, reached Lhasa on January 10, 1866, where, in the course of his three-month stay, his secret was discovered by two Kashmiri merchants, who kept quiet about it. He established the position of the city with the aid of solar and stellar observations and established its approximate altitude by boiling a thermometer. He returned to India by way of the Mansarowar Lake and Kumaun, having paced a route of 1,200 miles, mapped 600 miles of the Tsangpo and surveyed the great southern trade route into Tibet.

He became "No. 1", the Chief Pundit. His brother Kalian Singh became "GK", his cousin Mani Singh, "GM", and his brother Kisn, or Krishna Singh, "AK".

In May 1867, Nain Singh with two companions entered western Tibet by the 18,400-foot Mana Pass, where their luggage was given a terrific going over by Chinese frontier guards. Soon afterwards their disguise was

Mapping the Himalayas

penetrated, but they escaped by bribery and reached Thok-Jalung, 16,000 feet up on a plateau, in a terrible blizzard. Here gold was extracted from shallow trenches washed by streams (the Tibetans believing that digging deep into the Earth was a crime against it). There the workers, who used antelope horns as scrapers, lived in black tents made of yak hair, the site being guarded by a giant black mastiff. One of the gold nuggets he saw weighed about two pounds.

In 1871, Hari Ram ("MH") made a great journey from Darjeeling, in the course of which he encircled Everest. He found that the watershed was "far behind or north of the lofty peaks that are visible from Hindustan". By this journey alone he opened out nearly 30,000 square miles of what had been mostly *terra incognita*. On his return journey he descended the Bhote Kosi, of which he left a frightening account. Two years later he made a great traverse of northern Nepal, from west to east.

Krishna Singh's ("AK") greatest journey took him from Darjeeling, which he left in April 1878, to Lhasa, into Chinese Turkestan and on into China and Szechwan before returning to India four years after he had set out.

One of his remarkable feats was to count, for 230 miles, the paces of a horse on which he had been forced to mount when passing through bandit-infested territory, and make the necessary calculations to reduce them to human steps.

Most of the Pundits were Tibetan-speaking people from the Indian side of the frontier. An exception was Sarat Chandra Das, known as "the babu", an educated Bengali who had been headmaster of a school in Darjeeling and who was the original of Kipling's Hari Chunder Mukerjee in *Kim*. Together with Ugyen-Gyatso, a Tibetan Lama from Sikkim, he travelled to Lhasa, after being nursed through a serious illness by physicians at the Samding Monastery. The monastery was under the rule of a handsome 26-year-old Abbess, known as the "Thunderbolt Sow", and here he saw many strange and sometimes horrible religious images.

They reached Lhasa in May 1882, Das still very ill, to find that smallpox was raging, as it had been along the route. Here, Das had an audience with the Thirteenth Dalai Lama, a child of eight, who received him with the same aplomb as his predecessors had received earlier travellers. Das and his companion managed to return to India without their identities being discovered; but later those Tibetans who had helped them during their stay were punished when the secret was revealed.

Some great Muslim explorers also worked for the Survey: Ata Muhammad, "the Mullah", was the first to pass through the upper gorges of the Indus to Bunji in Kashmir by "the route of the hanging chains", which had been traversed by Hsuan-Tsang, the Chinese Buddhist traveller, in the 7th century. The Mullah made the first map of Swat (now in Pakistan) in the course of his journey. In 1868, Mirza Shuja, "the Mirza", reached the Oxus (one of the sources of which, the Sarikol Lake, was reached by Captain John Wood in 1838), and from it travelled to Kashgar. That same year Lieutenant G. S. Hayward, a member of the Survey, travelled from Peshawar to Leh, crossed the Karakorum Pass to Yarkand, explored the Yarkand and Kara Tash rivers and went on to Kashgar. He was murdered on a subsequent journey in the Pamirs.

In 1864, Fazl Huq, once a Muslim priest and now a Christian convert, who was not working for the Survey but for the Church Missionary Society, managed to enter Kafiristan by way of Swat, and floated down the Kunar River on a raft of inflated skins.

"Kill the Mussulmans"

In 1883, W. W. Macnair, an officer of the Survey, accompanied by a native surveyor "known in the Profession as the Saiad", penetrated the eastern marches of Kafiristan to the Bashgul valley. Macnair hid his plane table in an enormous book and stained his skin with a disagreeable mixture of weak caustic soda and walnut juice. He noticed that the Kafirs drank wine and that the punishment for adultery was a mild beating for the women, a fine of cattle for men and that one of their prayers ran: "Ward off fever from us. Increase our stores. Kill the Mussulmans. After death admit us to Paradise."

On his return to India, Macnair, who had gone to Kafiristan without permission, was given a tremendous ticking-off by Lord Ripon, the Viceroy, and then taken round the back and congratulated in private. "Jolly good show, Macnair!"

The two colossi of the modern period of Central Asian exploration were Sven Hedin and Aurel Stein. Even an outline map of the routes they followed looks as if it was the work of a centipede whose feet had been dipped in ink.

Hedin was born in Sweden in 1869. By the time he was 22 he had already crossed the Elburz Mountains, travelled through Persia on horseback, crossed the Kara Kum, visited Bokhara and Samarkand, and crossed the Tien Shan from Andizhan, in Ferghana, to Kashgar. "When I reached home, in the spring of 1891, I felt like the conqueror of an immense territory," he wrote. "... I therefore felt confident that I could strike a fresh blow and conquer all Asia, from west to east. . . . Step by step I had worked my way deeper and deeper towards the heart of the largest continent in the world. Now I was content with nothing less than to tread paths where no European had ever set foot."

On his second expedition he reached Tashkent in a "tarantass", a sort of cart, from Orenburg, a frightful journey in the Siberian winter. He had in 19 days "traversed eleven and a half degrees of latitude, passed thirty thousand telegraph-poles, employed one hundred and eleven drivers, used three hundred and seventeen horses and twenty-one camels, and passed from a Siberian winter to a temperature that, in the daytime rose to 54 degrees".

He left Tashkent on February 23, 1894, and succeeded in making his way across the Pamirs in mid-winter, suffering temperatures down to $-37°F$, on the way seeing if it was possible to climb the 25,500-foot Mustagh-ata. He managed to reach a point above 20,000 feet with Kirghiz tribesmen, his equipment being carried on yaks. "I felt as if I were standing on the edge of the immeasurable space where worlds revolve for ever and ever. Only a step separated me from the stars. I could touch the moon with my hand; and under my feet I felt the globe of the earth, a slave to the unyielding laws of gravitation, continuing to revolve in its orbit through the night of universal space."

On April 23, with four men and eight camels, having reached the edge of the Takla Makan Desert about 90 miles east of Kashgar, he began what was to be the most difficult and agonizing journey he ever made in Asia.

The way was through a sand-sea in which the ridges rose to a height of 150 feet, where there was no sound except the funereal tolling of the bronze bells worn by the camels. To Hedin it was like a vast graveyard in which only the headstones were wanting.

On the night of April 26 they dug for water, deeper and deeper, using up their own meagre supplies to give themselves strength. At ten feet, having previously been moist, the sand became dry again. Abandoning all unnecessary possessions, and with only enough water to give them two cups each for three days and one for the sheep they had with them, they struggled on through higher dunes. Two of their camels, the "Old Man" and "Blackie", died.

All through April 28 a sandstorm blew, at a velocity of 55 mph. That night only two small iron jars of water remained to them. The next day one of the party was found drinking from one of the iron pots; now only one single cup of water remained and Hedin told them that he would moisten their lips with it at midday.

On May 1 the camels were given the last drops of rancid oil out of a goatskin and Hedin drank the methylated spirits for the primus stove, which none of the others—being Muslims—would touch. He nearly died.

The next morning, mad with thirst, two of the men drank camel's urine mixed with vinegar and sugar, holding their noses while doing so. They cut the sheep's throats and tried to drink the coagulating blood. Here, two of the party were left to die.

By the next night, all but one of Hedin's companions, Kasim—the man who had first stolen water—were left behind. The two survivors crawled on under the terrible sun, sometimes burying one another in the sand on the cool north sides of the hills to get relief. At sunrise on May 3 they saw a tamarisk, three hours later an olive branch, at ten o'clock another tamarisk; but could go no farther. They lay there for nine hours until night fell, then staggered on and found poplars growing.

On the morning of May 4 Kasim collapsed. "I lit my last cigarette," Hedin wrote. "Kasim had always received the butts; but now I smoked this one to the end. I wondered whether I was still on earth, or whether this was the valley of the shadow."

But Kasim did not die: overtaking Hedin he was able to bring him the terrible proof, by showing him their footprints, that they had been walking in a circle.

On May 5 they saw the woods of the Khotan Daria (river), but when they reached them Kasim could go no farther. That night Hedin crept on all fours through the trees to a dry plain, devoid of vegetation, that was the river bed. "Suddenly I started and stopped short. A water-bird, a wild duck or goose, rose on whirring wings, and I heard a splash. The next moment, I stood on the edge of a pool, seventy feet long and fifteen feet wide. The water looked as black as ink in the moonlight. . . . Then I drank and drank again. I drank without restraint. . . . My dried-up body absorbed the moisture like a sponge. All my joints softened, all my movements became easier. . . . My skin, hard as parchment before, now became softened. My forehead grew moist. The pulse increased in strength; and after a few minutes it was fifty-six (it had been forty-nine). I drank again and sat caressing the water in this blessed pool. Later on, I christened this pool Khoda-verdi-Kol, or 'The Pool of God's Gift'."

Ruined cities

This was not the end of Hedin's journey. Having acquired more scientific equipment (he revisited the Pamirs while waiting for it to arrive) he set out from Kashgar in December 1895. In the course of the next 15 months he crossed the Takla Makan, discovering the remains of ruined cities in the sands there and near the Lop Nor, crossed the Kun Lun range to the Koko Nor, crossed the Ordos Desert and then the Gobi northwards from Kalgan. "It proved to be a journey which lasted three years, six months, and twenty-five days, and covered a distance greater than that from Pole to Pole. About 10,500 kilometres—equivalent to one-fourth the circumference of the earth—was mapped out. The charts, in five hundred and fifty-two sheets, measured three hundred and sixty-four feet. Of this mapped portion, nearly one-third, or 3,250 kilometres, represented land hitherto absolutely unknown. The expense of the trip was less than £2,000."

Stein's discovery—the Caves of the Thousand Buddhas, the greatest archaeological find ever made in Asia

Between 1899 and 1908 Hedin was three times in Tibet and his routes criss-crossed the Tibetan Plateau. His last expedition, undertaken to survey roads for the Chinese Government, took him far and wide through their dominions. He died in 1952.

Sir Aurel Stein (1862-1943) was a great archaeological surveyor and scholar as well as an explorer. Unlike Hedin he was a shy man. He was a Hungarian, born in Budapest, who emigrated to England, where he took up oriental studies.

Inspired by Hedin's discovery of the ruined cities in the Takla Makan Desert and supported by the Indian Government, in 1900 he visited the desert, having previously made an adventurous journey through Gilgit to the Hindu Kush and the Pamirs. He returned to England with a large number of objects, which he excavated on the sites of Yotkan and Dandan Uilik and the great ancient city of Takla Makan, which had been abandoned when the waters that flowed down from the Kun Lun range had dried up.

His second expedition in 1906-8 was even more rewarding. This time he managed to cross the Hindu Kush to the wakhan—the narrow appendage of Afghan territory between India and Russia—finding on the way great numbers of Buddhist remains, and from there went through the Pamirs to Khotan, where he carried out excavations, and the Lop Nor. He then crossed the southern Gobi.

His greatest discovery, however, was made near Tun-huang, where he found the amazing frescoes in the Ch'ien Fo-Tung, The Caves of the Thousand Buddhas, and a vast collection of priceless manuscripts, dating from the 5th to the 10th centuries and which had been walled up in the 11th century. It was probably the greatest archaeological discovery ever made in Asia.

The manuscripts and the tombs were in the hands of a self-appointed custodian named Wang Tao-shi and it was only after protracted and diplomatic discussion and a present of silver for the upkeep of the temple that Stein eventually succeeded in removing some 9,000 manuscripts and paintings which filled 29 cases, half of which were destined for the British Museum, the rest for India. Whatever the morality of this transaction, which in some ways resembles Lord Elgin's removal of the friezes of the Parthenon, it was perhaps fortunate that Stein acted as he did. In 1920, White Russian fugitives from the Communists did great damage in the caves and they were again damaged during the Sino–Japanese war in the 1930s. In 1943, the Chinese Government declared the place a national monument and it is now protected.

This was not the end of Stein's journey. In the summer of 1907 his expedition explored 20,000 square miles of the Nan Shan range, which had been visited by Przewalski, and that winter he crossed the Takla Makan at its widest point. It only ended when he became badly frostbitten while exploring the great Kun Lun Mountains in the summer of 1908, and had to have all the toes of one foot amputated at Leh.

Between 1913 and 1915 he made further great discoveries. At Kan-chou he found a hoard of manuscripts in the Tangut and Tibetan languages, and while he was in the region his Indian assistant surveyed the headwaters of the Kan-chou River. In 1915, he found the first Sassanian wall paintings in Sistan, having travelled to Persia from Kashgar by way of the Pamirs, Bokhara and the Amu Darya. From Sistan the expedition reached the Indus by way of Afghanistan.

The results of the expeditions of both Hedin and Stein are to be found in their enormous, multi-volumed works, which are probably among the last of such scope to be written and published by travellers.

North America: the colonial cockpit

BY THE MIDDLE of the 18th century, North America had become the focus of international rivalry between four major powers, Britain, France, Spain and Russia. The rivalry was to become intense, finally expressing itself in open economic and political warfare among the colonizing powers.

The 13 English colonies were stretched along the eastern edge of the continent, the Atlantic seaboard. By 1750 the density of population in this area was approaching ten people per square mile, and the need for expansion was pressing. Hemmed in by the French to the north and the Spanish to the south, the only possible direction for expansion from the 1750s was westwards. As waves of immigrants from other European countries supplemented the land-hungry English settlers of the eastern seaboard, the British Government found it difficult to control the expansion of their colonies into the Indian lands of the trans-Appalachian west.

In the northeast, economic factors had, since the end of the 17th century, caused a gradual but determined expansion of the French Empire. The French were a trading nation. Settlement of French citizens in North America was strictly controlled from Paris, and since the Indians of the area had been more or less subdued and no longer tried to impede their ambitions, the French could now afford to expand the fur trade to meet the ever-increasing demand from Europe. The Indians in turn were becoming slowly more dependent upon the fur trade for the goods which the Europeans could supply, and the western tribes were eager to participate. As the fur supplies of the St Lawrence and Great Lakes area became exhausted, French traders began to move west.

In the northwest the Russians had moved into Alaska. Furs once again provided the magnet for this, another trading nation. Russian penetration of the continent went unnoticed by the western powers for some time, but the discovery, after 1750, that Russian ships were sailing the northern Pacific seaboard, and that *promyshleniki*— Cossack fur traders—were exploiting the fur trade of the northwestern extremes of the continent, and expanding into the east, caused much consternation among the colonial nations.

The China and far eastern trade, which had been the impetus in the first place for European exploration in the New World, played a major part in the rivalries between the European powers during this period. Chinese goods such as silks and spices, porcelain and tea, were much in demand in the West, where they could fetch a high price. In contrast, few European goods were required by the Chinese. As a result, bullion

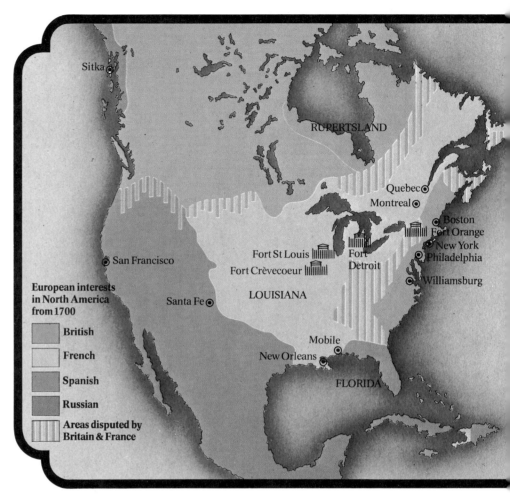

European interests in North America from 1700

- British
- French
- Spanish
- Russian
- Areas disputed by Britain & France

was being exported to the East in increasingly large quantities; a development which was regarded with extreme disfavour in this era of mercantilism. During the 18th century, however, it was discovered that furs, in particular the sea otter, black fox and sable, were highly prized by the Chinese at Canton, and as the Chinese market expanded the rivalry for the trapping areas of the North American continent reached crisis level.

Spanish on their guard

Most jealous of the infiltration of rival western powers on the continent were the Spanish, the oldest colonial power in the Americas. Ensconced in the south, in modern New Mexico and Florida, Spain sought to prevent encroachment into her territories by consolidating and expanding her control over the southwest regions, California and Arizona.

The first half of the 18th century had been a period of retrenchment in the distant colonies of the Spanish Empire. In Mexico, Arizona and Texas, the Spanish had confined their activities to missionary and welfare work among the Indians, setting up a network of missions and attempting—by using Indian labour—to establish more efficient ways of cultivating and irrigating the land.

The topography of California, a barely explored part of the continent, was little known and as late as 1700 the Spanish still believed that it was an island. In 1687, a Jesuit priest, Father Kino, was sent to the northern territories. He founded missions in present-day Sonora, and on the northwest Mexican mainland, the land of the Pima Indians, he created Pimería Alta, a new Spanish province. His work inspired the occupation of Baja (Lower) California and his vision foresaw the conquest and eventual conversion to Christianity of the Indians in Alta (Upper) California.

Kino was an explorer and map-maker. In his diary he noted on one occasion that: "In these twenty-one years up to the present time, I have made . . . more than forty expeditions to the north, west, north-west and south-west of fifty, eighty, one hundred, two hundred and more leagues, sometimes accompanied by other fathers. . . ." His map, drawn up on the basis of actual explorations, is the earliest extant showing the Gila and Colorado rivers and southern Arizona. It was Kino who finally established that Lower California was not an island but a peninsula.

By 1711, Kino and his brother Jesuits had advanced the frontier of Spain through

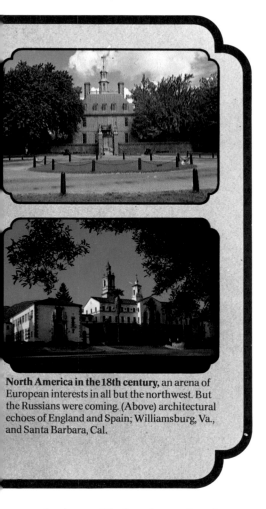

North America in the 18th century, an arena of European interests in all but the northwest. But the Russians were coming. (Above) architectural echoes of England and Spain; Williamsburg, Va., and Santa Barbara, Cal.

northwestern Mexico into what is now southern Arizona.

As a colonial power Spain was not interested in trade and settlement as much as occupation and exploitation. The scant population of the mother country hardly provided the basis of settlement and consolidation of the New World territories and, unlike the British Empire at this time, the Spanish Empire did not allow people of other nationalities to settle in her colonies. Jesuit and, after 1767, Franciscan and Dominican priests were entrusted with the task of extending Christendom to the west, and military and colonial officers set up *presidios*, military forts, to effect an official presence in the outposts of the empire.

In 1719, a French trader, Bénarde de la Harpe, exploring into the southwest, reached Santa Fe via the Red River. This expedition, though not official, was tangible proof to the Spanish of the French commercial threat to their territories through domination of the Indian trade. In 1733, the English settled Georgia, which the Spanish considered part of Florida, their own possession.

The Spanish reacted by sending out from Mexico a military expedition to settle the Seno Mexicano, a stretch of deserted land from Támpico, Mexico, to Matagordo Bay, Texas. The expedition, which set out in 1743, consisted of 750 soldiers and 2,500 civilians under José de Escandón, and succeeded in founding 23 towns and 15 missions. At the same time, a new *presidio* was established around the San Gabriel River, in Apache country. The establishment of new missions from 1743 onwards led the advance into Apache country as far as the San Sabá River.

Seven years' war

In 1752, a garrison and a new *presidio* were established at San Ignacio de Tubac on the Santa Cruz River after an uprising of the Pima Indians in western Pimería Alta. The garrison, it was hoped, would "facilitate Spanish advance to the Gila and Colorado Rivers"; in 1756, another *presidio* and mission were set up on the gulf coast to forestall French encroachment on the Trinity River.

The seven years' war, or the French and Indian War as it was called on the North American continent, was preceded in 1739 by the quarrel between Spain and England which began with the War of Jenkins's Ear. Complicated by events in Europe, the war of 1756–63 became a struggle for North America.

The war went badly for England until 1758, when William Pitt became Secretary of State. In 1759, the tide turned with the surrender of Quebec to the British and the elimination of French power on the North American continent, despite the support of some of the northern Indians for her cause.

By the Treaty of Paris of 1763, all of French Canada, and the Spanish Floridas, were ceded to Great Britain, and France ceded Louisiana and all French claims west of the Mississippi to Spain. The British Empire in North America was more than doubled, a great victory, but one that was short-lived, for the new acquisitions carried problems of administration and control which Britain proved unable to solve. In 1776, the face of the continent changed once again with the American War of Independence, which left England in control of newly created Canada and an independent American nation along the eastern seaboard of the continent. Spain meanwhile retained the lion's share of the continent—all territories west of the Mississippi as well as to the south of latitude 31N. As a reaction to these events, Spain adopted a policy of defensive expansion, designed also to thwart the ambitions of the Russians, who were, through their fur traders, beginning to move southwards. In 1768, the visitor-general of New Spain decided to colonize Vizcaíno's harbour of Monterey.

Captain Fernando de Rivera y Moncada, with 25 soldiers and 40 mission Indians, was sent to blaze a trail northwards to San Diego.

Meanwhile, the Spanish Commander-in-Chief, Portolá, and a Franciscan missionary, Father Junípero Serra, who was working among the Pame tribe in the Sierra Gorda mountains, were sent with 12 soldiers and 44 mission Indians to search for Monterey. The expedition under Portolá trekked more than 600 miles, working northwards to Monterey by land, and explored up the coast as far as San Francisco Bay in search of Vizcaíno's "fine harbour", becoming the first Europeans to walk the shoreline of California. The two parties eventually united at San Diego. In June 1768 a new *presidio* was set up and from 1773 emphasis was laid on finding a land route to the new province.

Father Francisco Garcés, another Franciscan priest, stationed at San Xavier del Bac, thought that California could be reached from Arizona. An expedition under Captain Juan Bautista de Anza was despatched from Arizona and, with Father Garcés, travelled southwestwards to the junction of the Gila and Colorado rivers to the San Gabriel Mission, in California, near what is today Los Angeles. A mission was established among the Yuma Indians on the far side of the Colorado River in 1775, and a new settlement was founded on San Francisco Bay.

In the year of American Independence, Father Garcés had the idea of linking Santa Fe and California by an overland route. Travelling up the Colorado River for 15 days to the site of Needles in California, he headed west, accompanied only by Mojave Indian guides, and reached the San Gabriel Mission. In the same year, another expedition, consisting of two Franciscan priests, Fathers Dominguéz and Escalate, left Santa Fe and explored as far as Utah's Wasatch Mountains and the Great Salt Lake.

But the provinces of California, linked to New Spain only by a tenuous water route, were left, by and large, to develop by themselves. Spain was unable to prevent American encroachments into Texas and Mexico.

Finally, in 1801, the Louisiana area was retroceded to France. Louisiana had been the province of Spain since the Treaty of Paris, but unsettled, with few trading posts or even garrisons; the area was in the hands of its Indian inhabitants and slowly being infiltrated by European settlers from the east. The retrocession was kept secret for over a year, but news of it was leaked to the American President, Jefferson, who, fearing a strong power at the mouth of the Mississippi, opened negotiations for the purchase of a sufficient area to guarantee freedom of navigation and commerce.

In 1803, Napoleon sold Louisiana to the United States for 80 million francs, doubling the size of the young nation almost overnight.

A new world, an old people

DURING THE LAST ICE AGE, more than 20,000 years ago, the ancestors of the American Indians first began to migrate from Asia over a land bridge which in those times stretched across the strait from Siberia to Alaska. Those Asian races carried with them into the New World the lore and culture of the Old. They spread throughout the Americas, and over a period of thousands of years settled the land from the northern tundra to the southern straits.

More than 400 different tribal groups evolved from among the early Indians, whose 1,000 or more languages arose from 160 major stocks. Each group was Mongoloid in appearance, but their cultures varied greatly, the result of adaptation to different ways of life. The Indians of the Great Plains were nomadic hunters whose homes were portable skin tepees; the Pueblo Indians of New Mexico and Arizona were sedentary farmers who developed irrigation and terracing techniques for cultivating plants such as maize, beans and squash. They lived in fortress towns of adobe, with tenement buildings and community courts. The Indians of the forested northwestern coast, the Bella Coola and the Shalish Indians, lived in elaborately carved plank houses and subsisted mainly on fish; some were very poor, but those of British Columbia and Alaska were famous for their totem poles, dugout canoes and masks.

Subjugation

At the time of the discovery of America the indigenous population of the area north of Mexico is thought to have been a little more than one million, and that of Mexico, 20 million or more. Spain, the first colonial power in North America, subjugated the Indians of Mexico and the southwest in the name of God and the king, imposing military organization wherever they ruled and commandeering native labour to work the land and the mines. After the arrival of the Spanish, the Indian populations of Arizona, Mexico and New Mexico declined as a result of dangerous working conditions and of European diseases to which the Indians were susceptible, particularly smallpox, measles, mumps and venereal diseases. A fever epidemic which spread through California in 1830 was officially estimated to have killed 70,000 Indians.

A papal bull of 1537 declared the American Indians to possess immortal souls. Spanish, and later, French and Russian priests and missionaries, founded missions from which they proselytized in the surrounding area, sometimes imposing Christianity upon the natives. By the time the influence of these various nations had declined many Indians had, for good or ill, adopted their customs.

English and French fishermen of the Newfoundland and New England coasts first began to make contact, through trade, with the Indians of the northeastern coasts as early as the 16th century. On the Atlantic coastline dwelt the Penobscot, Pequot, Powhatan, Massachusetts and Delaware tribes, who shared the Algonquian tongue with the Fox, Winnebago, Sauk and Illinois nations of the Great Lakes region. These Indians made their own tools and utensils from wood, bone, skin and stone. The coming of the Europeans with their iron or brass axes, knives, nails and cooking pots produced an insatiable desire for these things among the Indians—a desire that spread throughout the continent. In the early days, such goods were exchanged for fresh foods and some services from the Indians, but by 1600 this casual barter had become a full-scale trade in iron goods and later firearms and alcohol, exchanged for furs which were highly valued in Europe. Within a single century the Indians had begun to lose their traditional proud independence and become reliant upon the manufactured goods of the white man. As the fur trade grew in scale and spread westwards, many Indian tribes abandoned their traditional pursuits to hunt the beaver, otter and other animals whose skins were in demand in Europe. When, in the 1840s, the demand for furs declined, the Indians were deprived of their means of existence.

The Spanish Conquistadors introduced the horse to historic America (it is now known to have lived there in prehistoric times) for

The Indians of the densely forested northwestern regions of North America were—and are—adept carvers of timber. The totem pole (right) is the emblem of a mystical kinship between tribal groups. At the foot of the page, an old photograph of a Blackfoot Indian tepee encampment

their own use. Horses then began to be sold to or were pilfered by the natives with an unforeseeable result—a massive transition of many tribes from their sedentary agricultural pursuits to a nomadic hunting life on the Great Plains. The tribes that took to the horse most readily arrived from the north—the Blackfoot, Gros Ventre, Sarsi, Assiniboine, Comanche and Kiowa—and by the time the settlers arrived there were more than 30 tribes on the plains.

Early settlers on the Atlantic seaboard

An Indian craftsman embellishes a totem pole. Totemism manifested itself on a world-wide basis among tribes whose lives were close to nature

enjoyed, by and large, uneasy peace with the natives. Indians were not expected by the Puritan immigrants to work as manual labourers, as the Spanish had required under their *encomienda* system, and the men did not take Indian wives, but the Indians, as a general rule, mistrusted the settlers who took over and cultivated the lands. Trouble occurred in 1622 when the first Indian uprising broke out in Virginia as a result of the intolerant policies of Anglican missionaries.

The Indians of the southeastern United States—the Apalachee, Chickasaw, Choctaw, Creek, Natchez and Seminole—who were regarded as the élite among Indians by the east coast settlers, taught the Europeans how to raise maize, beans, pumpkin and tobacco. In turn these Indians learned from the Europeans how to plant orchards and to keep cattle.

Farther north, in the French territories, the situation was without conflict for some time. The French Canadians were interested more in trading with the Indians than in settling their lands, and the Proclamation of 1763 laid down that no Indian could be un-lawfully dispossessed of his land since the destruction of the bison had reduced many tribes to starvation. The peace was broken by inter-tribal wars, especially by those between the Iroquois and the Hurons, and by conflicts with the missionaries. Towards the end of the century, when competition between the French and the English for the fur trade in the interior was at its height, many Indians were bribed and corrupted with alcohol.

Some North American Indians remained largely unaffected by the coming of the Europeans. The Eskimoes of central and eastern Canada, encountered by the seekers of the Northwest Passage, are notable for their adaptability to changing conditions. They subsist upon sea mammals, fishing and hunting the caribou, whose seasonal migrations they accompany. Because of their isolation along the Arctic shores, their culture has changed little during the last 200 years.

In the southwest of the continent, the Hopi and Zuñi, Navajo and Apache, Mohave and Yuma of Arizona, and the Yaqui and Tarahumara of New Mexico were less affected by western settlement than the more northerly tribes. The Navajo in particular survived to become the largest tribe in the United States, with a present-day population of about 100,000. Similarly in northeast Mexico, the Chichimecs, a desert tribe who caused the Spanish much trouble in colonial days with their expert use of the bow and arrow, have retained much of their cultural identity, and still live in traditional small farming communities.

The explorers and trappers in North America were quick to adopt Indian ways and methods of survival when faced with the prospect of living in the trackless wilderness. The Indians of the sub-Arctic interiors of Alaska and Canada, the Cree and the Chipewyan of the Mackenzie River, had invented the toboggan and the snow-shoe. The extensive forests provided birch bark for their unique canoes and wood for their dugouts; light canoes were the only feasible method of travel in forested areas ribboned with waterways. The plains Indians passed on to the Europeans the idea of surviving long journeys on pemmican, a concentrated food of dried buffalo meat mixed with berries.

Dispossession

When the settlers flowed west, they inevit-ably came into contact with the Indians in their path. Tribes were dispossessed of their land by the easiest means available in a land where frontier life required every man to be a law unto himself. In 1788, the first treaty was made with the Delaware Indians and by 1871, when treaties with the Indians were stopped by Congress, 389 had been drawn up and remade. Forty-two successive treaties were agreed with the Potawatomi and Chipewyan alone. Large tracts of land were bought cheaply—for an average of ten cents per acre —from the Indian nations, who were resettled into reservations, usually confined to arid and unwanted lands where the inhabitants often succumbed to idleness, disease and alcohol.

The Russian foothold

SURVIVING CREW MEMBERS of Bering's disastrous 1741 expedition to the coasts of North America returned to Kamchatka with news of islands to the east richly populated with the world's most valuable fur-bearing animals. The location of these islands was established only approximately, for neither Bering nor Chirikov had surveyed or charted the seas they explored, but the attraction of wealth to be gained was such that the Cossack fur traders, the *promyshleniki*, were prepared to risk crossing dangerous and unknown waters to achieve their object.

Within two years of the expedition's return, the first Cossack fur trader had found his way to Bering Island and returned with a rich cargo of furs. After him followed a stream of *promyshleniki*, who reached the Komandorskiye Islands and worked their way eastwards across the Aleutian island chain to the Alaskan mainland, and to the Pribilof Islands in the north. The trade was a hazardous undertaking. The Siberian fur traders were unfamiliar with ocean sailing and navigation, and many were lost at sea through shipwreck or starvation, for food was in short supply and on their long voyages they were forced to rely upon fish they could catch from the seas. Moreover, since iron for their ships had to be imported to Kamchatka, they generally travelled in fragile vessels constructed from wooden planks secured with strips of leather instead of nails.

Near extinction

Despite these hazards, Russian fur traders continued to obtain pelts from the natives of the offshore islands and the mainland of Alaska for the next 60 years. In the Aleutian Islands they found the blue and the Arctic foxes, the Alaska seal and the sea otter, whose pelt was the most valuable. The populations of these creatures were reduced almost to extinction during the 18th century. In the Pribilof Islands, the breeding grounds of the fur seal, the population was reduced by 90 per cent in 20 years as a result of the demand for its fur and for its sex glands, greatly esteemed by the Chinese, who believed they possessed rejuvenating powers.

The inhabitants of the 1,000-mile-long chain of the volcanic Aleutian Islands were the friendly and peaceable Aleuts, who also occupied the western part of the Alaskan peninsula. Originally of Asian stock, the Aleuts were distinct from the American Indians and related to the Eskimoes. They lived mainly on sea mammals. Whales, sea lions, seals and walruses were hunted from the kayak or the umiak, the Eskimo open skin boat, and the sea otter was caught with a bone harpoon cast from a throwing board. The Aleuts of the peninsula hunted caribou

and bear, and trapped the annual runs of salmon, which were dried in the sun and stored in the stomachs of seals or sea lions.

The Russians employed the hunting skills of the Aleut. Many natives were transported to the Pribilof or the Commander islands and to California to hunt the seal and the otter—the latter a dangerous task, for the otter lived in the rocky clefts along the turbulent shorelines of the islands and out on the coastal kelp beds. Notorious for their total disregard for human life in their treatment of the natives of Siberia, the Cossack fur hunters treated the Aleuts with similar contempt, seizing the furs they required as tribute rather than by trading, and using their firearms as a means of coercion to enslave the native population. The result of their excesses was the near extermination of the Aleuts; by 1885 it is estimated that only 3,000 of the original 25,000 were left alive, the rest having died from accidents at sea, torture and the depletion of their food supplies.

Until 1775 only Russian ships had sailed the Alaskan coast, and the northern Pacific coast had been explored only superficially. Official Russian expeditions in the 1760s had reached the Seward and Alaskan peninsulas, but no attempt was made to consolidate the discoveries. News of the Russian exploits in the Aleutian Islands and the Alaskan peninsula reached the ears of the European governments after 1750, causing much alarm, especially among the Spanish, who feared encroachment upon their unsettled western territories.

Several expeditions set out from Mexico to explore northwards; in 1774, Juan Pérez discovered the Queen Charlotte Islands and, in 1775, Lieutenant Juan Francisco Bodega y Cuadra reached the site of modern Sitka in southern Alaska and claimed it for Spain. In 1778, the English staked a claim through Cook, who charted the southern Alaskan coasts with such accuracy that the Russians themselves used his charts.

As the fur-bearing populations of the Aleutian Islands began to decline due to over-trapping, the *promyshleniki* began to explore towards the northeast as far as Kodiak Island, searching for new, ever more profitable, trapping areas. In 1781, a Siberian merchant, Gregor Ivanovich Shelikov, formed a trading company with the purpose of investigating and exploiting the fur trade on the North American continent. Russian influence was at last established in 1783 when an expedition under Shelikov founded the first settlement at Three Saints Bay on Kodiak Island. In accordance with Catherine the Great's policy of converting the Aleuts to Christianity, an Orthodox Mission was set up. Its onion dome can still be seen today on

the small Pacific island which is also the home of the largest and most dangerous bear in the world. The Russian colony at Kodiak became the centre of the fur trade in the east for the next 21 years. From it, traders sent out expeditions to the mainland—as early as the year in which it was founded an expedition under Potan Zaikof reached Prince William Island, and the Copper River was discovered and probed.

The Kodiak post flourished as its sphere of influence widened, and in 1792 Alexander Andreivich Baranov was put in charge of the company's North American interests. Baranov eliminated the competition of smaller companies and under his leadership a shipyard was established on Prince William Sound. In 1799, the company was granted a charter as the Russian–American Company under an Imperial ukase, with the rights of exclusive trade and occupation of that part of America north of latitude 55N. Alaska was placed in the hands of this company for the next 60 years.

In 1804, the company moved its headquarters to Baranov Island in the Alexander Archipelago, naming the site Fort Archangel Gabriel. Here Tlingit Indians massacred the entire garrison, but were subdued the following year by 1,000 men and cannon. The trading post grew into a glittering metropolis, "the St Petersburg of the Pacific", dominated

Seward Peninsula

The Sitka spruce, from southeastern Alaska, is now one of Europe's most important forestry trees

ALEUTIAN ISLANDS

UNALASKA ISLAND

by Baranov's castle, the cosmopolitan centre of a network of fur posts stretching from Bristol Bay in the north to California in the south. By 1860, the town was launching 60 vessels a year from its shipyards, and produced engine parts, church bells and nautical charts complete with observations made by its magnetic observatory. The company sent traders south as far as modern San Francisco, and in 1811 Fort Ross was established near Bodega Bay to counter foreign influence.

The Yukon

Much important exploration was carried out under the auspices of the company. An expedition under Kramchenko, Etolin and Vasilief spent two years investigating the coastlines of Bristol Bay and Norton Sound. The northern and southern coasts of the Alaskan peninsula were mapped by Captain Lütke and Vasilief respectively. Andrei Glasunof later crossed from the Russian post at St Michael, Norton Bay, to the Yukon and on to the Kuskokwim River, which opened up possibilities for the fur trade on the Yukon. In 1842–3, Lieutenant Zagoskin of the imperial navy ascended the Yukon to the Tanana, and explored the lower stretches of the Koyukuk and the Innoko, a tributary of the lower Yukon.

Eventually Fort Archangel Gabriel declined, partly as a result of the restrictive Russian policies towards its inhabitants, who were barred from remaining there longer than ten years, and partly because of competition from the Hudson's Bay Company. Since 1750 the company had been pushing westwards, slowly encroaching upon the Russian–American Company territory, reaching out as far as the Yukon River in 1850. American trade with the northwest had also had the effect of weakening the Russian monopoly; the sale of liquor and firearms to the natives brought strong protests from the Russian Government.

Russia eventually answered the challenge with a renewed charter to the Russian–American Company, proclaimed in September 1821, which attempted to exclude American and English ships from trading in the coastal waters of the North Pacific. The ukase declared that the company was granted "the privilege of carrying on to the exclusion of other Russians and of the subjects of foreign states, all industries connected with the capture of wild animals and all fishing industries on the shores of northwestern America which have from time immemorial belonged to Russia, commencing from the northern point of the Island of Vancouver, under 51° north latitude to Bering Straits and beyond them, and on the islands which belong to that coast, as well as on the other situated between it and the eastern shore of Siberia, and also on the Kurile Islands where the Company has carried on industries, as far as the outer tip of the Island of Urup. . . ."

In the ensuing negotiations, Russia's position was challenged both by Great Britain and by the United States, who demanded to be treated on an equal basis. Negotiations lasted from 1822 until 1825. The Monroe Doctrine of 1823 regarding non-colonization of unoccupied parts of the American continent was implicit in the United States' attitude towards the discussions. Russia and the United States eventually agreed that the parallel of 54.40N would be the southern limit of Russian occupation or settlement, and that all parts of the northern Pacific Ocean were to be open to subjects of both powers, provided that they did not encroach on each other's territory without permission.

Purchased by United States

The Crimean War finally brought home to the Russian Government the fact that in wartime Alaska could become an expensive liability from the point of view of strategy and of defence. Steps were taken to ensure Alaska's neutrality in case of war and eventually the Russians agreed to lease the southeast mainland to the Hudson's Bay Company in exchange for an annual supply of 20,000 land otter skins. Russia finally sold the entire colony to the United States in 1867 for a price of $7,200,000.

Food and fur of the north; a Kodiak bear hooks a salmon for its supper

Yukon River

Tanana River

ALASKA

Fort Wrangel

54°40N

51°N

Prince William Sound

New Archangel (Sitka)

KODIAK ISLAND

Mount Edgecumbe

The sea otter (top) and the fur seal (above) were slaughtered for their pelts by Russian hunters in the seas off Alaska

The Russians in America. By the mid-18th century, one of the mainstays of the Russian economy, Siberian sables, was almost exhausted. The "Big Land" across the Bering Strait promised a new source of wealth. The main architect of Russian empire-building in Alaska was Alexander Baranov, the head of the all-powerful Russian-American Fur Company. Under Baranov, New Archangel (Sitka) became the centre of interests stretching from the Bering Sea to Fort Ross in California. The Russians finally sold their "Big Land" of Alaska to the US in 1867 for 7,200,000 dollars

Fort Ross

Towards the 'Western Sea'

AS LATE AS THE 18th century Europeans and Americans alike continued to be fired by the conviction that it would be possible to reach the Orient by travelling westwards. Until the Russians began to penetrate the northwestern reaches of the Americas, little was known about the Pacific coasts and it appeared to the geographers and explorers of the times that China—and the riches to be won by exploiting the China trade—might lie close to the western edges of the New World, and that the two continents might even be joined by a land bridge.

There was no conception of how wide America could be. At the beginning of the century the geography of North America was known in any detail only as far as a line drawn between Hudson Bay and the Gulf of Mexico; the nature of the lands to the west of this line remained an enigma well protected by the certainty of Indian hostilities, and by the uncertainties and costs in store for those who attempted to cross it. The only clue had been supplied two centuries before by the Italian navigator Verrazano, who thought he glimpsed a great sea in the interior of the continent. Travellers' tales and the obliging affirmations of native Indians embroidered the myth until by 1700 it was firmly believed that to the west could be found a great river leading across the interior to a "Western Sea", whose outlet surely pointed the way to the Orient.

In 18th-century America only fur traders with the eternal incentive of larger profits would venture into the unknown west. As the Russian *promyshleniki* were exploring the northwest, French voyageurs, threatened on the one hand by fluctuating fur prices and on the other by the encroachments of the English in the east, were probing the area around the Great Lakes and the headwaters of the Mississippi, fostering good relations with the Indians. They planned to intercept the supply of furs to the Hudson's Bay Company by constructing a chain of trading posts deep into the heart of Cree Indian country to the west, and also northwards, on the Assiniboine River, which rises in eastern Saskatchewan and after flowing through Manitoba joins the Red River at Winnipeg.

Pierre Gaultier de Varennes, Sieur de la Vérendrye, was a *coureur de bois*, a fur trader, controller of trading posts on Lake Nipigon in southern Ontario, and on the Kaministik-wia River. In the course of his work, he learnt from Indians of a river flowing west from the Lake of the Woods to a "great water that ebbed and flowed". This news of the "Western Sea" inspired him to journey to Montreal in order to ask the governor for help. He was granted a trading monopoly in any new territory he might discover, and with

this was able to raise money for the expedition from merchants.

In the summer of 1731 La Vérendrye set off with a party of 50, including three of his sons and a nephew, La Jemeraye, up the Pigeon River, as far as Rainy Lake. At the point where the Rain River flows out of the lake, they built Fort St Pierre. A simple structure, it followed the usual plan of French forts of the period with two main rooms and two gates, each protected by a bastion.

The following year, La Vérendrye and family reached the Lake of the Woods at the tri-junction of Minnesota, Manitoba and Ontario. A beautiful lake, 1,485 square miles in extent, its surface scattered with thousands of islands, the Lake of the Woods drains into Lake Winnipeg through the Winnipeg River. On its southwestern shore they built Fort St Charles, which was to be their head-quarters from 1732 to 1738. Using the fort as a base, La Vérendrye's eldest son, Jean Baptiste, and his nephew reached Lake Winnipeg in 1733—the first known white men to do so.

From the Indians they learned that the outlet river of Lake Winnipeg flows into Hudson Bay, and also heard of a group of Indians on "the River of the West", 750 miles from the Lake of the Woods, which discharges into the "Western Sea". These would have been the Arikaras, Hidatsas or Mandans who lived on the southward bend of the Missouri River.

More money

By now their means were exhausted and La Vérendrye returned to Montreal to extract, with difficulty, more money from the merchants, not returning until 1736. In the meantime, Jean Baptiste and Pierre built Fort Maurepas, at the mouth of the Winnipeg, since the Crees and the Assiniboines had promised not to trade with the English if the French would build a fort for them. Two other sons had explored Lake Winnipeg northwards and the Assiniboine. On the site of modern Portage la Prairie they established Fort la Reine. Good beaver country lay just to the north.

La Vérendrye's nephew died in the spring of 1736 at Fort Maurepas, and another disaster occurred later that year. In order to win the confidence of the Crees, La Vérendrye had had to sell firearms to their war parties, who traditionally fought against the Sioux of the Mississippi. Jean Baptiste and a party that had set out to help bring up the supplies were massacred by a band of Sioux. Jean's head was cut off and wrapped in beaver skins *pour encourager les autres*.

These misfortunes inhibited further explorations until October 1738, when La

Vérendrye set out for the country of the Mandan Indians on the upper Missouri, near the borders of North and South Dakota. He was accompanied by his two sons, some compatriots, and Assiniboine Indians as guides. Following an Indian trail across the prairie roughly west-southwest, they crossed the 100th meridian west of Greenwich, the first known Europeans to do so, and on December 2 arrived in the country of the Mandans. Here the guides defected and the party was forced to turn back in freezing weather and, with its leader seriously ill, arrived in February 1739 at Fort la Reine. In 1742, François and Louis-Joseph, Le Chevalier, set out for the Mandan villages to find the western "Horse Indians" and travel to the sea. From the Mandan villages they took guides and headed southwest, crossing the Little Missouri and entering the country of the Crow Indians.

By this time they may either have been nearing the main chain of the Rocky Mountains near the source of the Missouri or the Bighorn Mountains, outriders of the main range to the south. They joined a war party of Bow Indians which was setting out on a raid against the Shoshoni (Snake) Indians, eventually reaching a deserted encampment at the foot of high, snow-covered mountains.

Finding that there was no loot or any possibility of slaughter, the Bows refused to go any farther and the Les Vérendrye were forced to return with them, reaching Fort St Pierre in July 1743 after a journey of at least 1,500 miles, mostly on foot. This great feat was their last, apart from one more journey, in the course of which one of the sons may have reached the Saskatchewan River, at least 600 miles west-northwest of their base at the Lake of the Woods.

La Vérendrye died in 1749, his great accomplishments grudgingly recognized, but too late, by the bestowal of a Captaincy and a decoration. After his death his sons were refused permission to engage in any more exploration and all their equipment and the posts they had set up were taken from them.

In his lifetime of exploration, La Vérendrye clarified the topography of the rivers and lakes of the "crossroads of the continent", around Lake Winnipeg, establishing the routes by which the first transcontinental crossings were later to be made. He also discovered and mapped the upper Missouri and revealed that the Saskatchewan "is to-day the most convenient route by which to pursue the discovery of the Western Sea", since it "came from very far, from a height of land where there were exceedingly high mountains, and that they had knowledge of a great lake on the other side of the mountains, whose water was undrinkable".

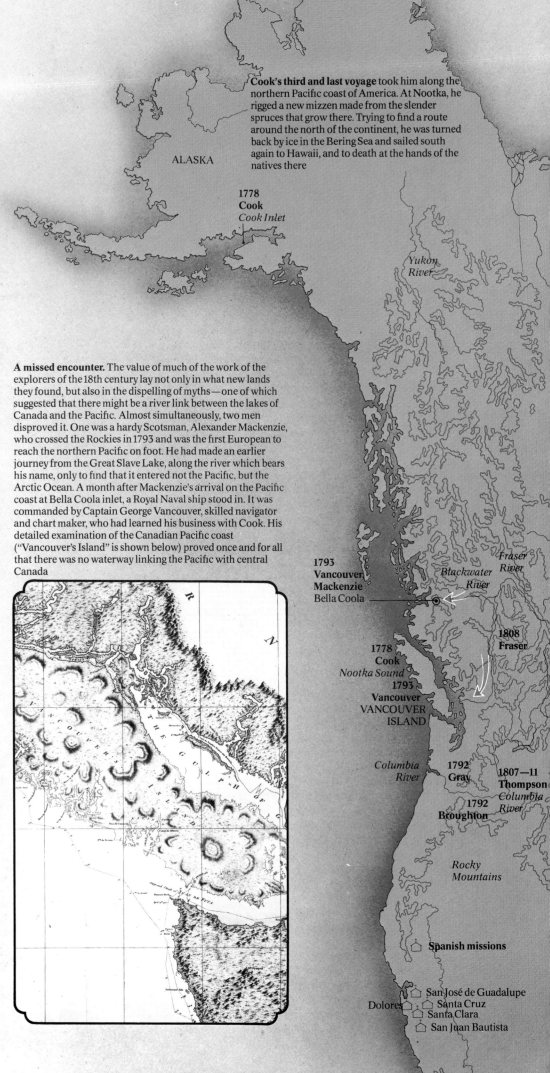

SEA OTTER PELTS picked up for an old cooking pot on the northern Pacific coast around Sitka could, in the 1780s, fetch as much as $60 each in China; profits of $50,000 on a single trading expedition have been cited as not unusual.

By the 1780s the news of the success of Captain Cook's company in selling sea otter furs in Canton had spread. John Ledyard, one of Cook's midshipmen, reported: "We purchased while here about fifteen hundred beaver, besides other skins, but took none but the best, having no thoughts at that time of using them to any other advantage, than converting them to the purposes of clothing; but it afterwards happened that skins, which did not cost the purchaser sixpence sterling, sold in China for one hundred dollars." After 1788, English ships dominated the trade with Nootka.

The Americans followed as the demand for oriental teas, spices and silks grew in the eastern states. An expedition financed by merchants from Boston, Salem and New York set out in 1787 for Nootka in two ships, the *Columbia* under John Kendrick, and the *Lady Washington* under Robert Gray. Gray reached Nootka in 1788, Kendrick shortly after him, but both arrived too late in the year to be able to trade and sail on to China.

In September 1789 four English ships under John Meares, an entrepreneur, arrived in Nootka to trade, but were appropriated by a Spanish expedition sent out under the command of Estévan José Martínez. In 1790, Spain signed the Nootka Convention, abandoning to the British and Americans her territorial pretensions on the northwest coast.

Robert Gray returned to Nootka two years later, in 1792. In the *Columbia* he traded northwards as far as the southern tip of Alaska, and southwards as far as Oregon. At latitude 46.10N he discovered signs of a river mouth, but was prevented by bad weather from investigating further. In 1774, Bruno Heceta and Juan Pérez, sailing along the coast of northern Oregon, had felt and described currents that led them to believe "that the place is the mouth of some great river, or of some passage to another sea", but did not follow up the discovery because the crew was racked with scurvy.

Gray went on to discover Gray's Harbor, and returned to the same latitude on May 11, 1792, to investigate, crossing the bar into the Columbia River, which he named. Until May 18 he continued to explore a few miles upstream, then returned to Nootka, where he met George Vancouver, in command of a Royal Navy ship, who had set out in 1792 to explore the Pacific coast and had circumnavigated Vancouver Island. In 1793 and 1794, Vancouver made accurate surveys of

Cook's third and last voyage took him along the northern Pacific coast of America. At Nootka, he rigged a new mizzen made from the slender spruces that grow there. Trying to find a route around the north of the continent, he was turned back by ice in the Bering Sea and sailed south again to Hawaii, and to death at the hands of the natives there

A missed encounter. The value of much of the work of the explorers of the 18th century lay not only in what new lands they found, but also in the dispelling of myths — one of which suggested that there might be a river link between the lakes of Canada and the Pacific. Almost simultaneously, two men disproved it. One was a hardy Scotsman, Alexander Mackenzie, who crossed the Rockies in 1793 and was the first European to reach the northern Pacific on foot. He had made an earlier journey from the Great Slave Lake, along the river which bears his name, only to find that it entered not the Pacific, but the Arctic Ocean. A month after Mackenzie's arrival on the Pacific coast at Bella Coola inlet, a Royal Naval ship stood in. It was commanded by Captain George Vancouver, skilled navigator and chart maker, who had learned his business with Cook. His detailed examination of the Canadian Pacific coast ("Vancouver's Island" is shown below) proved once and for all that there was no waterway linking the Pacific with central Canada

ALASKA

1778 Cook *Cook Inlet*

Yukon River

1793 Vancouver Mackenzie Bella Coola

Blackwater River

Fraser River

1778 Cook *Nootka Sound*

1793 Vancouver VANCOUVER ISLAND

1808 Fraser

Columbia River

1792 Gray

1807—11 Thompson *Columbia River*

1792 Broughton

Rocky Mountains

Spanish missions

Dolores

San José de Guadalupe
Santa Cruz
Santa Clara
San Juan Bautista

Towards the 'Western Sea'

thousands of miles of the southeast Alaska coastline. Hearing of Gray's discovery of the Columbia, Lieutenant Broughton, one of Vancouver's men, crossed the bar into the Columbia River where he reported that he found an English sailor, James Baker, exploring the river in a small vessel, the *Jenny*.

The accidental discovery of the Columbia solved the problem of the "Great River of the West"; but because the discovery was made within such a short space of time by both English and American explorers, the ensuing English–American dispute over the possession of Oregon continued for many years.

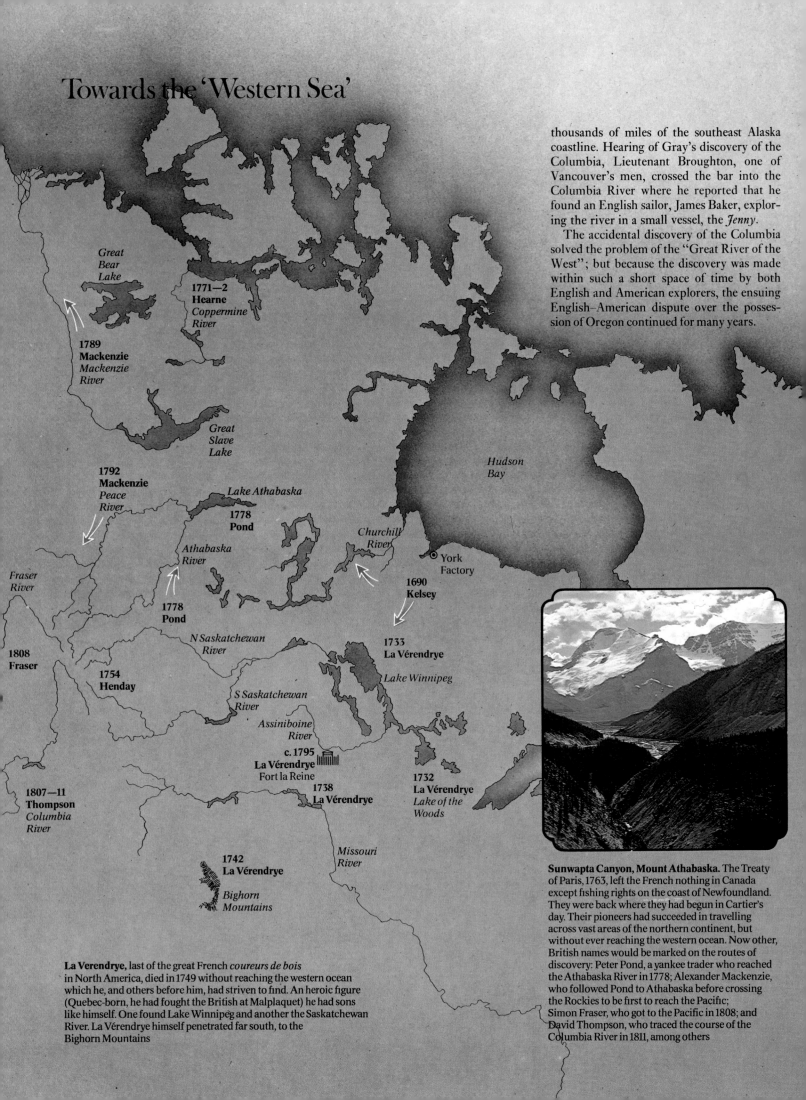

Great Bear Lake

1771—2 Hearne *Coppermine River*

1789 Mackenzie *Mackenzie River*

Great Slave Lake

1792 Mackenzie *Peace River*

Lake Athabaska

1778 Pond

Athabaska River

1778 Pond

Fraser River

1808 Fraser

1754 Henday

1807—11 Thompson *Columbia River*

N Saskatchewan River

S Saskatchewan River

Assiniboine River

c. 1795 La Vérendrye Fort la Reine

1738 La Vérendrye

1742 La Vérendrye

Bighorn Mountains

Missouri River

Churchill River

York Factory

1690 Kelsey

1733 La Vérendrye

Lake Winnipeg

1732 La Vérendrye *Lake of the Woods*

Hudson Bay

Sunwapta Canyon, Mount Athabaska. The Treaty of Paris, 1763, left the French nothing in Canada except fishing rights on the coast of Newfoundland. They were back where they had begun in Cartier's day. Their pioneers had succeeded in travelling across vast areas of the northern continent, but without ever reaching the western ocean. Now other, British names would be marked on the routes of discovery: Peter Pond, a yankee trader who reached the Athabaska River in 1778; Alexander Mackenzie, who followed Pond to Athabaska before crossing the Rockies to be first to reach the Pacific; Simon Fraser, who got to the Pacific in 1808; and David Thompson, who traced the course of the Columbia River in 1811, among others

La Verendrye, last of the great French *coureurs de bois* in North America, died in 1749 without reaching the western ocean which he, and others before him, had striven to find. An heroic figure (Quebec-born, he had fought the British at Malplaquet) he had sons like himself. One found Lake Winnipeg and another the Saskatchewan River. La Vérendrye himself penetrated far south, to the Bighorn Mountains

SEVEN WEEKS AFTER Vancouver's ship nosed its way into the Bella Coola inlet on the northern Pacific coast in 1793, Alexander Mackenzie, a Stornaway Scot in the employ of the North West Company of Montreal, reached the same point by an overland route. At the age of 29 he was the first man to cross the northern part of the continent and reach the Pacific.

Mackenzie's great journey had been preceded by a number of expeditions by fur traders into the northwest, notably by agents of the Hudson's Bay Company.

The first white man to see the broad plains of Canada, which lay south and west of Lake Winnipeg, was "The Boy Henry Kellsey", described by the committee of the Hudson's Bay Company as "A very active Lad, Delighting much in Indians Company, being never better pleased than when he is Travelling amongst them", Kelsey made the first company explorations of significance.

During the 1680s the company was attempting to establish good relations with the Indians of the interior in order to prevent their trade falling into French hands. With this object in mind and with an Indian boy as his only companion, Kelsey was sent to survey the lands north of the Churchill River in 1689. Though he failed to meet the Indians of these barren lands, Kelsey was able to put his pioneering abilities to a rigorous test which served him well when, in 1690, he was again sent on an expedition that led him up the Hayes River, across to the northern edge of Lake Winnipeg and up the Saskatchewan River into Cedar Lake.

In 1754, Anthony Henday, an outlawed smuggler from the Isle of Wight, was sent by the company to seek the co-operation of the Blackfoot Indians. Crossing the prairies between the North and South Saskatchewan rivers to the foothills of the Rockies, he tried unsuccessfully to lure the Blackfoot to the bay. The next year Henday tried again, returning to York Factory with 60 richly laden canoes.

Exploration of North America began in earnest in 1763 with the end of the French and Indian War, especially as news of Russian exploits in Alaska reached the east. In the late 1760s the rumours of mineral wealth to be found in the north were revived by Indians who brought copper from the Arctic coast to the company. Samuel Hearne (1745–92), a Londoner, described by a contemporary as a man of enlightened and benevolent character, and a scientific observer of the regions in which he travelled, volunteered to survey the Coppermine River, thought to be the source of the samples.

After two unsuccessful beginnings, Hearne was able to begin his explorations in December 1770. His way was paved by Matonabbee, a Chipewyan chief who claimed knowledge about the Mountain of Copper. Matonabbee led the party along the timbered belt south of the Great Slave Lake, where there was an adequate supply of game for winter food. In May they turned north to the Coppermine River, which they reached on July 14, 1771.

At their destination, they found no "Mountain of Copper", but only what Hearne frustratedly described as "a jumble of rocks of gravel", containing only a few traces of copper, though large blocks of the metal have since been unearthed at the site. Disappointed, Hearne returned to Fort Churchill, considering his journey a failure, although he had succeeded in travelling overland to the Arctic and had established a firm foothold for the company among the Chipewyan Indians, who had told him that "the continent of America is much wider than many people imagine".

From 1776, the Montreal fur trade expanded rapidly in the hands of the French and a group known as "Pedlars", backed by American, English and Scottish money, to challenge the Hudson's Bay Company.

The most famous of all the Pedlars was Peter Pond, a Yankee emigrant, who led an expedition to Lake Athabaska in 1778. He organized his trading expeditions well, so that on his 1778 journey he purchased more furs than his canoe could easily carry. More important, perhaps, than his discoveries on that expedition (he was the first white man to cross from the Saskatchewan–Churchill country to the Mackenzie basin), was the information he had gleaned from Athabaskan Indians of a river "called Peace River, which descended from the Stony or Rocky Mountains, and from which mountains the distance to the salt lake, meaning the Pacific Ocean, was not great". On the basis of this and other information from the Athabaskans, he calculated the distance between Athabaska and the sea to be about 350 miles.

Into the Arctic

His useful, if inaccurate, information interested his young protégé, Alexander Mackenzie, whose previous exploring and trading experience qualified him in the eyes of the company to explore the then unknown regions of the northwest.

In three canoes, Mackenzie and his party set out up the Peace River in June 1789. Crossing the ice-covered 300-mile-long Great Slave Lake, they eventually entered the Mackenzie River after a six-day search, at what is now Fort Providence on the western arm of the lake. For 40 days the expedition travelled down-river through an increasingly stark landscape, broken only by the wild splendour of the Mackenzie Mountains and a tantalizing glimpse of the Rockies. They passed the Arctic Circle and eventually, on July 12, reached the Arctic delta.

Realizing that the river did not drain into the "Hyperborean", or northernmost, Sea, Mackenzie was forced to make his way upstream against the massive flow of the Mackenzie before winter set in, to Fort Chipewyan, which he reached on September 12. His journey was one of the most remarkable exploits in the history of inland discovery, whether regarded in the light of the achievement or the fact that he travelled 2,990 miles in 102 days.

On October 12, 1792, Mackenzie and a second party of nine embarked on the Peace River, intending to "reach the Pacific across the mountains from the Source of that River". The party wintered at Forks Fort, where they built a 25-foot-long birchbark canoe capable of loading 3,000 pounds, yet portable by three men. In May of the following year they travelled up through beautiful, unexplored country rich with game, making a difficult ascent of the Peace River canyon, during which his men threatened to abandon the journey. Persuaded to continue, however, they eventually reached the Finlay–Parsnip River junction.

On June 12 the expedition reached the Parsnip headwaters in insect-ridden heat and four days later crossed to the Fraser, named after its subsequent explorer, Simon Fraser. Mackenzie's leadership qualities were severely tested when a group of Indians informed the party that the river canyon soon became impassable and that the sea was farther away than they thought. With his stores and ammunition almost exhausted, and his men reluctant to undertake the passage, Mackenzie wrote "the more I heard of the river the more I was convinced it could not empty itself into the Ocean to the North West of what is called the River of the West". Instead he set off across the mountains.

Mackenzie and his men struggled on for ten days across the jumbled, rugged mountains of the coast ranges, tormented by sandflies, blackflies and mosquitoes, forcing their way through thickets, forests and deep snow in a spectacular landscape of snowy peaks, jewel-like lakes and numerous streams. Finally they reached present-day Bella Coola. There, among the totems and high walls of the inlet, Mackenzie saw the ocean on the evening of July 19, 1793. He "mixed up some vermilion in melted grease and inscribed in large characters on the south-east face of the rock on which we had slept, this brief memorial: 'Alexander Mackenzie, from Canada by land, the 22nd of July 1793'".

Breakout from the East

TO THE 1,500,000 RESIDENTS of the British colonies lying along the narrow eastern seaboard of North America the defeat of the French in 1763 meant one thing; they could now realize their long-suppressed ambitions to expand west to the Mississippi.

Up to the turn of the century, it had been possible for new immigrants to the colonies to obtain free land grants in the urban or agricultural settlements. Profits were made from the rents of prosperous farmers. The new wave of immigration from continental Europe after 1713 gave the settlers the opportunity to turn a fast dollar by buying unsettled land, and selling it at a high price to the new pioneers. A class of English and colonial speculators arose who sought settlers to buy and occupy the new land.

By the 1740s, land hunger had become land fever among the eastern settlers. Between 1746 and 1749, several major land companies were formed to further expansion and to push the frontier line a little farther west.

The Loyal Land Company was formed in 1749 by a group of prominent Virginians to secure 800,000 acres of land in southwestern Virginia. The land grant was eventually made without any provision to settle families on it, but the Loyal Land Company immediately took steps to survey and claim it. It was decided to send Dr Thomas Walker, a graduate of William and Mary College with considerable experience in surveying frontier lands, southwest to the area of the company's holdings, and across the mountains to locate an area suitable for settlement.

On March 6, 1749, Dr Walker set out to travel down the Virginia ridges of the Appalachians, crossing the mountains at Cave Gap, which he later called the Cumberland Gap after the Duke of Cumberland. He then travelled down the Cumberland River and turned northeast across the mountains of present-day Kentucky and West Virginia, returning to Albemarle County on July 13.

On his journey, Dr Walker kept a journal describing the abundance of game on the frontier and listing the number of animals killed by his party, but failed to locate any land suitable for settlement, much to the company's displeasure.

At the conclusion of the French and Indian War in 1763, the British Government altered its policy towards its American colonies. On October 7, 1763, the Crown issued a *Royal Proclamation Concerning America*, in which it fully recognized and accepted the rights of the Indians to their lands west of the Allegheny Mountains. The Proclamation set out strict rules for the conduct of the flourishing fur trade in those regions and prohibited the purchase of Indian lands.

The Proclamation inevitably caused much

Indian fighter and folk hero Daniel Boone (1734–1820) led settlers out of the seaboard colonies into virgin territory beyond the Blue Ridge Mountains

ill feeling within the colonies, but the independent and eternally restless pioneers of the American frontier had always taken great pride in outwitting their own government and wasted no time in finding ways around this impediment to their desire to expand.

Ignoring the Proclamation was the easiest way to fight it. Between 1664 and 1774 immigrants and settlers simply crossed the mountains from West Virginia and began to farm the lands around the tributaries of the Ohio, extending the frontier of settlement ever westwards.

The activities of the anonymous fur traders and trappers, "loners" by nature, were also difficult, if not impossible, to control. Dwelling in log cabins on the very edges of the settlements, the backwoodsmen of the trans-Appalachian frontier eked out a poor living from farming and grazing cattle in the surrounding woods and from hunting and trapping whatever their skills would bring them. They traded in pelts, dried buffalo hides and tongues, and tallow. Deerskin was the most profitable commodity. Doe would sell for 50 cents and the skin of a buck would bring in a dollar or more—hence the origin of the term "buck" meaning dollar. These backwoodsmen were the "long hunters" of 1760–70, so called because of the length of time they spent out in the wilderness on their hunting trips and also, perhaps, because of the long rifles they used. They lived around the central area of the frontier, towards West Virginia, where it reaches towards the Cumberland Gap. The Yadkin Valley in North Carolina bred the most famous among them, Daniel Boone.

The long hunters explored sometimes in parties sometimes alone. They hunted in the upper Tennessee and Cumberland river regions, across the mountains, around the Ohio and the Mississippi, as far as Natchez

and the area where Nashville now stands. The country was wild and treacherous, but they came to know its hazards well as they traversed the falls and boulder-strewn narrows, the "sucks" and whorls of its tortuous streams, and evaded the hostile Indians to whom it rightfully belonged.

Hunting parties would set out simply equipped with blankets, cooking equipment, traps and powder and lead, with just enough food supplies to take them into hunting territory. Occasionally a trading post was set up in the more familiar territory, like the one at French Lick (now called Nashville) by a hunter called Timothe Demunbreun. Buffalo, deer and elk gathered around the licks, fissures that exuded a saline deposit.

From Tennessee country, the long hunters began, towards the last half of the decade, to cross the mountains and explore into Kentucky. Daniel Boone on one of his trips had passed through the Cumberland Gap and spent some time in the valleys which led towards the Pine Mountain range. While out on their expeditions, the hunters would keep an eye open for suitable land for settlement, often by previous arrangement with a member of one of the land companies. Boone had a "grubsteak" arrangement with a Judge Henderson from North Carolina, an oratorical back-country speculator with an ambition to found a new colony.

Prisoner of Indians

On his return from Kentucky, Boone met an old acquaintance, an Indian trader called John Finlay who knew the Kentucky country in some detail from previous canoe expeditions; he had once been captured by the Shawnee Indians. During the winter of 1769 the two organized a hunting party of seven trappers to spend the summer exploring the region behind the mountains.

On May 1, 1769, the party set off from the Yadkin Valley towards the Cumberland Gap, following the south fork of the Kentucky River to Station Camp Creek; on down the Kentucky and then the Red rivers to the Eskippikithiki, the Indian Old Fields on the land between the mountains and the Bluegrass plain. Here they camped. Out hunting one day, Boone and his brother-in-law, another member of the party who had once followed the Cumberland River to its junction with the Ohio, were captured by Indians, but managed to escape, collect their horses and return safely to their camp.

They spent most of the summer at the camp, located beside a small creek at the edge of the bluegrass plain, which they used as a base for hunting and exploring trips, whiling away uneventful hours by reading *Gulliver's Travels*. The site has since been named

"Lullbegrud", a name inspired by Boone's brother, Squire, one of the party, who remarked after a series of Indian attacks that they had "driven the Lullbegruds away".

Boone did not return to North Carolina after the summer, but remained behind with his brother and two other companions, Stuart and Neeley. When they went away, Boone himself remained there, often alone, for two years; Stuart was killed by Indians. Boone explored the Kentucky and Green river valleys, walked over most of central Kentucky and also the Cumberland country of north central Tennessee.

By the time his sojourn in the wilds had come to an end, Boone had collected a wealth of furs. With these packed on the horses, he set off back to North Carolina with his brother, but on the way they were attacked by Cherokee Indians, who appropriated their catch. Thus he returned to his cabin with no more wealth than when he set out, but with a host of stories and descriptions of the new lands he had discovered—of game and buffalo, salt licks and wild grapes and strawberries, nuts and acorns in rich forests—all of absorbing interest in the atmosphere of mounting land fever, which had its hold on all the frontier communities at that time.

Boone returned to troubled times. While he had been away in the wilds, farmers protesting at the refusal of the North Carolina Government to allow them to settle the Tennessee country had organized themselves into armed groups called the Regulators which, in 1771, had been defeated by the Colonial Militia at the Battle of the Alamance. Farmers flocked to the mountainous border between North Carolina and northeastern Tennessee, Cherokee country, which they were able to lease from the Indians. The Watauga Association was formed to govern the settlement and was occupied with petitions to the North Carolina Government for annexation of the Cherokee lands.

Boone decided to move his family into the new territory, setting off in September 1773, risking the disgruntled Cherokees and the Colonial laws. Accompanied by six families as well as his own, together with all their possessions and livestock, they set off along the trail which led through the Cumberland Gap, later named the "Wilderness Road", for Kentucky. Along the trail the party was joined by another. In the Cumberland Gap, however, the Cherokees attacked, and among those killed was Boone's eldest son. The party, hysterical, retreated against Boone's advice to the Clinch valley, where they remained for two more years.

New company

Trouble with the Shawnee Indians prevented further thought of land-hunting for some time, but by 1775 settlers found it safe enough to continue their explorations into Kentucky. In 1774–5 another land company, the Transylvania Company, was formed by Judge Henderson and other wealthy speculators with the object of settling Ohio and Kentucky. The first settlement was made in Powell's Valley during the first year of the company's existence. Abundant guns and ammunition played an important part in seducing the Indians to surrender lands in both Kentucky and Tennessee, and a trail was opened across the territory of the Cherokee to the Cumberland Gap.

Before the treaties with the Indians were concluded, Daniel Boone was sent out by Henderson to blaze a trail to Kentucky. Following the route of the Wilderness Road, Boone and his party, which included an ardent young journalist, Felix Walker, crossed from the Columbia to the Kentucky River. Walker described an experience on entering the wild Kentucky countryside: "On entering the plain we were permitted to view a very interesting and romantic sight. A number of buffaloes of all sizes, supposed to be between two and three hundred, made off from the lick in every direction; some running, some skipping and bounding through the plain."

The following day they were attacked by Indians. Two of Boone's party were killed and Walker was seriously injured, but the attack did not deter the settlers. A party that had set off after Boone, arrived at the Kentucky River shortly afterwards and began the construction of a fort, the first building to mark the beginning of the new settlement of Boonesborough. On April 19, 1775, Henderson led the first party of settlers down the brand new Wilderness Trail to the new settlement.

By May 1775 three settlements were under construction in Kentucky, in defiance of the Proclamation. Despite continuing trouble from the Indians the settlement persevered and prospered, and by 1784 the white population of Kentucky was 30,000. In 1792 Kentucky was admitted into the Union as a state.

A legend even in his own day, Daniel Boone became a symbol of the pioneering American frontiersman. In later years the image of the long hunter dressed in buckskin leggings, leather hunting shirt and coonskin cap, hatchet and hunting knife at the ready in his thick leather belt, and rifle at his side, expressed the rugged restlessness and the resourcefulness of the frontier. The spirit of conquest communicated itself to later generations of settlers along the Wilderness Trail, one of whom wrote: "Perhaps no Adventurer Since the days of donquicksotte ever felt So Cheerful & Ilated in prospect, every heart abounded with Joy & excitement."

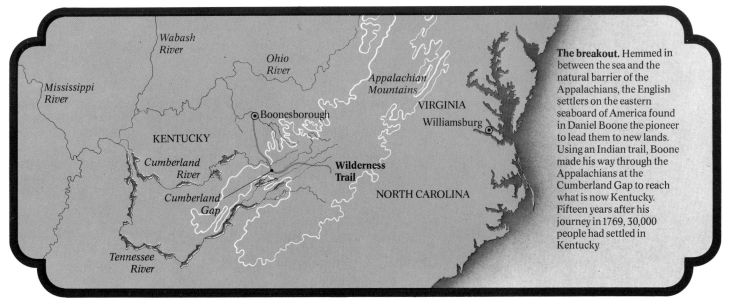

The breakout. Hemmed in between the sea and the natural barrier of the Appalachians, the English settlers on the eastern seaboard of America found in Daniel Boone the pioneer to lead them to new lands. Using an Indian trail, Boone made his way through the Appalachians at the Cumberland Gap to reach what is now Kentucky. Fifteen years after his journey in 1769, 30,000 people had settled in Kentucky

'For the purposes of commerce'

BEFORE 1803, THE YEAR of the Louisiana Purchase Treaty, the Americans had not played any significant part in the exploration of their own country, which was the work in the main of French, Spanish, British and French Canadians. The North West Company of Montreal played an important part in moving the frontier westwards. After Mackenzie had succeeded in crossing the northern part of the continent, the company decided to send David Thompson, a surveyor, from the headwaters of the Saskatchewan, across the mountains of the present Banff and Jasper parks to the Columbia River.

David Thompson had been employed as surveyor to the Hudson Bay Company at Fort Churchill in 1785. He gained an unrivalled knowledge of the country from the lakes towards the Pacific, building on and extending the work of Mackenzie. His abilities went unrewarded by the Hudson Bay Company and in 1797 he joined the North West Company.

Between 1797 and 1806 he explored the region around the headwaters of the Mississippi, and travelled through Manitoba, Saskatchewan and Alberta. In 1807, he founded Fort Kootenay, the first post on the Columbia River, and uncovered the whole Columbia water system, leading to the establishment of a chain of posts by the St Lawrence traders and an early Canadian hold on the Columbia River. Thompson spent the last years of his life surveying central Canada, and died in 1857, having travelled 50,000 miles in the most extensive and rugged journeys of the New World.

Alexander Mackenzie's book *Voyages from Montreal through the Continent of North America* first inspired Thomas Jefferson to organize a search for an overland route to the Pacific. In January 1803, Jefferson proposed to Congress that "an intelligent officer, with ten or twelve chosen men, fit for the enterprise . . . might explore the whole line [of the Missouri] even to the Western Ocean. . . ."

Instructions

Having obtained Congressional approval, Jefferson selected his private secretary, Captain Meriwether Lewis, to lead the expedition, and Lieutenant William Clark to be second-in-command. "The object of your mission," Jefferson instructed him, "is to explore the Missouri River, and such principal streams of it, as by its course and communication with the water of the Pacific Ocean, whether the Columbia, Oregan [sic], Colorado, or any other river, may offer the most direct and practicable water-communication across the continent, for the purposes of commerce."

Thus Captain Lewis, joined by Captain Clark at Louisville, Kentucky, arrived at St

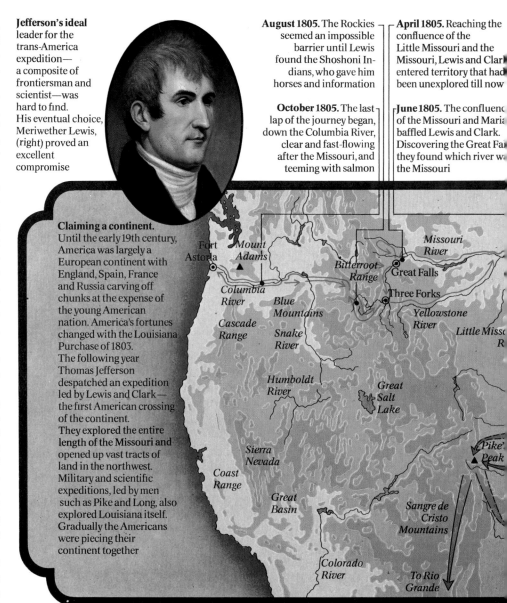

Jefferson's ideal leader for the trans-America expedition— a composite of frontiersman and scientist—was hard to find. His eventual choice, Meriwether Lewis, (right) proved an excellent compromise

August 1805. The Rockies seemed an impossible barrier until Lewis found the Shoshoni Indians, who gave him horses and information

October 1805. The last lap of the journey began, down the Columbia River, clear and fast-flowing after the Missouri, and teeming with salmon

April 1805. Reaching the confluence of the Little Missouri and the Missouri, Lewis and Clark entered territory that had been unexplored till now

June 1805. The confluenc of the Missouri and Maria baffled Lewis and Clark. Discovering the Great Fal they found which river wa the Missouri

Claiming a continent. Until the early 19th century, America was largely a European continent with England, Spain, France and Russia carving off chunks at the expense of the young American nation. America's fortunes changed with the Louisiana Purchase of 1803. The following year Thomas Jefferson despatched an expedition led by Lewis and Clark— the first American crossing of the continent. They explored the entire length of the Missouri and opened up vast tracts of land in the northwest. Military and scientific expeditions, led by men such as Pike and Long, also explored Louisiana itself. Gradually the Americans were piecing their continent together

Louis, where they passed the winter of 1803–4 in disciplining the men of their party and making preparations for leaving in the spring. "The party consisted of the two officers, nine young men from Ky, fourteen volunteer soldiers of the US Army, two French watermen, an interpreter and hunter (of French-Shawnee extraction), named Drewyer, and a black servant (York) belonging to Captain Clark."

The expedition set out along the Missouri on Monday, May 14, 1804. They travelled 1,600 miles through an endless ocean of undulating prairie of present-day Missouri, along the borders of modern Kansas, Nebraska and Iowa, and into Dakota. At Council Bluffs near Omaha they smoked their first peace pipe with an Indian nation—the much-feared Sioux, who allowed them to cross their hunting grounds. They reached the Mandan villages in time to winter.

The way so far was well plied by fur

traders. For the next leg six dugout canoes were built to cope with the narrowing river. The party, now 32 people, included Toussaint Charbonneau, a Montrealer, with his wife Sacajawea and their baby. Sacajawea, "bird-woman", a Shoshoni Indian, was responsible for the success of the expedition as only she knew the way to the Lemhi Pass in the Rockies between the Missouri and the Columbia. By April 25, 1805, the party had reached the confluence with the Yellowstone River in the foothills of the "little Rocky Mountains", where the air was "so pure that objects appear much nearer than they really are".

Escape from death

At the confluence of the Marias and Missouri rivers, they cached some of their baggage in a hole lined with brushwood and topped with sod. Captain Lewis then set out to find the correct branch of the Missouri, and

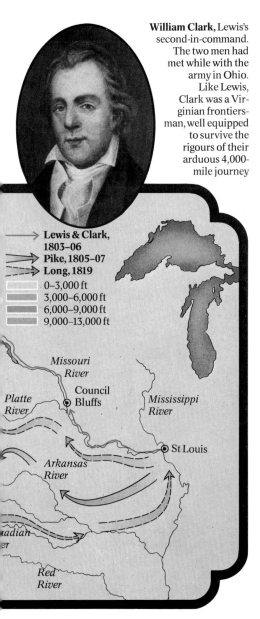

William Clark, Lewis's second-in-command. The two men had met while with the army in Ohio. Like Lewis, Clark was a Virginian frontiersman, well equipped to survive the rigours of their arduous 4,000-mile journey

Lewis & Clark, 1803–06
Pike, 1805–07
Long, 1819
0–3,000 ft
3,000–6,000 ft
6,000–9,000 ft
9,000–13,000 ft

Missouri River
Council Bluffs
Platte River
Mississippi River
St Louis
Arkansas River
...adian ...er
Red River

on June 13 he unexpectedly came upon the Great Falls of the Missouri.

The next day Lewis narrowly escaped death when confronted by a large brown bear, which ran open-mouthed at him and "as if the beasts of the field had conspired against him, three buffalo bulls . . . ran . . . full speed towards him".

The falls obliged the party to make an 18-mile portage with a wagon built on the spot, and by July 25 they had reached the three forks of the Missouri, which they named after the statesmen Jefferson, Madison and Gallatin, and went up the Jefferson to the two forks, beyond which the river was unnavigable. Lewis took the southern fork and then followed an Indian path leading to the fountain head of the Jefferson. From there they crossed the Great Divide, the watershed from the Atlantic to the Pacific river system, as far as is known the first white men to do so in this part of North America.

Lewis then followed the Lemhi River on the Pacific side and found a troop of nearly 60 mounted warriors approaching at full speed. These proved to be Shoshoni, with whom the party smoked a peace pipe. This was the homeland of Sacajawea. They halted among the Shoshonis and purchased horses for the next leg of the journey.

Clark had attempted to travel the Indian route along the Lewis (now Salmon) River, but was forced to turn back after 70 miles. The weather was growing colder. On September 4 the expedition crossed the Bitterroot Mountains at the Nez Percé Pass to the Clark River, and again at the Lolo Pass, which they crossed with the help of friendly Shoshoni Indians and Sacajawea's interpretation.

The expedition travelled by water down the Clearwater River valley to its junction with the Snake River, having left their horses with the Choppunish Indians in the plains at the foot of the Bitterroot Mountains. By October 16 they had reached the confluence of the Columbia River by way of the Kooskooske and Lewis rivers in their newly constructed canoes, negotiating many rapids in the process. On October 23 the Columbia Falls were circumvented by a portage; on November 1 they reached the Cascade Falls, passing through the Coast Range on November 4. On November 19, the party reached "Cape Disappointment at the Entrance of the Columbia River into the Great South Sea or Pacific Ocean". They found a suitable site for settlement a little way back from the coast which they called Fort Clatsop, after the local Indians, and where they built a fort for the winter. Here they kept a meteorological register, made a compilation of Indian tribes and of the flora and fauna of the region, which they also mapped.

On March 23, 1806, they left Fort Clatsop, travelling back up the Columbia to the cascades beyond present-day Portland, Oregon. On June 11 they reached their route of the previous year across the Bitterroot Mountains via Lolo Pass and at the beginning of July the expedition halted at Travellers Rest Creek to plan further operations. It was decided that Lewis's party would travel overland by what is now known as the Great Blackfoot Valley, by a short cut to the falls of the Missouri. This it did, rejoining Clark on August 12 after a skirmish with the Minnetarees, in which two of his men were killed. Clark's party, having explored the Willamette, returned to the Jefferson River and the three forks, from where Clark, ten men and about 50 horses followed the present-day railway route via Gallatin City, Bozeman and Livingstone to the Yellowstone, descending the Big Horn in the process, and returned to St Louis on the Missouri.

Lewis and Clark had travelled 7,689 miles in two years, four months and ten days, across a totally unexplored country. Annotated topographical sketches brought back resulted in the first map of the Pacific route, and 200 botanical species were added to those already known. They had also noted 122 species and sub-species of fauna, some of which they had preserved and skinned, and had encountered 50 tribes of Indians, some of the chiefs of which later visited Washington. Lewis and Clark uncovered the whole interior drainage system of the Columbia and the mountain systems of the west.

As the Lewis and Clark expedition was making its way back to St Louis, Zebulon Montgomery Pike, a 26-year-old lieutenant and army acquaintance of Meriwether Lewis, was sent out by Jefferson to explore the headwaters of the Mississippi, leading a small party of 20 soldiers.

With exemplary efficiency, Pike had had built a 70-foot-long keelboat for the expedition. At the junction of the Mississippi and Minnesota rivers he negotiated the purchase of a 100,000-acre military reservation for the government, and from there journeyed to the headwaters of the Mississippi, which he explored, but missed its true source.

The southwest

In 1806, Pike was despatched by General James Wilkinson to "ascertain the direction, extent and navigation of the Arkansas and Red Rivers".

The southwest territories were unknown to the Americans at the time of the Louisiana Purchase. Pike left St Louis to first escort a group of Indians to Osage and Pawnee villages. From the villages Pike turned away to the northern bend of the Arkansas River, which he followed to the Rocky Mountains, to the front range of the Royal Gorge. He sighted and named Pike's Peak, which he declared to be unclimbable. In 1807, he was discovered by the Spanish and turned back. Under escort Pike was taken to Santa Fé, on to Albuquerque and to Chihuahua, and then returned to the United States via San Antonio and Nacogdoches to Natchitoches in Louisiana. On the way he was able to gain a wealth of information about the geography of the Spanish southwest.

The explorations of such explorers as Zebulon Pike were in a sense filling in the gaps in a picture that had only been outlined. Major Stephen H. Long spent the year of 1817 locating suitable sites for military posts around the headwaters of the Minnesota and St Croix rivers. From the knowledge brought home by these explorers, the map of North America was filled in in greater detail and the way paved for the opening up of the West.

Following their own star

F UR TRADERS PLAYED an important part in extending the geographical knowledge of the country; but after 1803 they were replaced by the mountain men, a wild breed of white American trappers who became the symbol of the fur trade, and explored the territories of the trans-Mississippi west as they trapped the beaver to supply the markets of Europe.

The first organized American fur trapping expedition was arranged by a Spanish fur trader, Manuel Lisa, who, even before the Louisiana Purchase, had moved north to St Louis and the Missouri River. He quickly realized the possibilities of the new beaver traps then being introduced—traps baited with castoreum, a secretion of the beaver's perineal gland which exerts a powerful attraction upon other members of the species —and devised a plan for setting up a trading post among the Mandan Indians and another on the Yellowstone River to exploit the area for furs.

In 1807, he set off against the Missouri current with 40 hired hands, two of whom, George Drouillard and John Potts, had accompanied Lewis and Clark.

Up river, the hostile Arikara Indians attacked them, convinced that white men had murdered their envoy to Washington; Lisa overawed the Indians with his two swivel cannon. Later the party was attacked once again by the Mandans. Lisa won the trust of the natives, however, and on reaching the Big Horn built Fort Raymond, "Manuel's Fort", the first trading post in the region.

John Colter, a legendary figure of the fur-trapping era who had joined Lisa's party, also set out to search for Indian trade and to explore the locality for beaver. During the winter of 1807-8, Colter trekked over 500 miles alone.

He walked up Pryor's Fork to Pryor Mountains and across them to Clark's Fork and the upper Big Horn basin. In the canyon of the Shoshone River's north fork he discovered the travertine deposits, spectacular hot springs and geysers and sulphurous gas vents, later known as "Colter's Hell" to the trappers. He crossed the Owl Creek Mountains to the headwaters of the Wind River, and the continental divide. It is believed that he explored the present-day Grand Teton National Park and on his way home crossed the Teton Pass to the hot springs and geysers region of the present-day Yellowstone National Park.

Trapping in the Three Forks area, by October Colter's autumn party had made 20 packs of beaver, nearly a ton of prime fur. At Jefferson Fork Colter and Potts were attacked by Blackfoot, in spite of the precaution of working at night. Potts was shot and the furs stolen. Colter was stripped, ordered to run and given a 30 seconds start—across a rugged plateau of prickly pear and sharp stones. Robust and strong, Colter outran all but one Indian, whom he managed to kill with his own spear. Making for the Madison River, he dived under a log jam, and hid in an air pocket. Staying until night in the icy water, he waded six miles downstream and climbed up a sheer cliff. Stark naked he walked through the brush to Fort Raymond, where he arrived over a week later, sunburnt and covered with insect bites.

Indian attack

In the spring of 1809 he was off on another journey up the Yellowstone River to Three Forks, where he and his party were again attacked by Indians. Colter again escaped, hewed a small dugout from a cottonwood tree and travelled 2,000 miles home to leave the fur trade and devote his time to farming.

The success of his first trapping expedition led Lisa to form the Missouri Fur Company with his associates William Clarke, Pierre Chouteau and Andrew Henry. The company undertook to make explorations into the west in return for monopolistic privileges. The first expeditions failed after more trouble with Indians, but later John Thomas Evans, a Welshman and member of the Caradogian Society, was sent out to the Mandan villages with instructions to advance towards the Pacific via the Missouri or one of its western tributaries. Evans mapped territory west of the Missouri, realizing that the distance between the river and the mountains was greater than generally realized. Jefferson was kept up to date on the results of all these expeditions. Meanwhile, Andrew Henry had ascended the Madison River with a detachment of men, crossed the continental divide and established Fort Lisa. Though he did not trap much beaver and was forced to subsist on roots for some time, he discovered Henry's River, a northern branch of the Snake, and explored several headwater streams, discovering new passes through the mountains.

In 1808, when Lisa founded the Missouri Fur Company, John Jacob Astor, a German immigrant and fur trader from Montreal, founded the American Fur Company. Astor was one of the first men to realize the economic significance of the Lewis and Clark expedition, which brought back reports of the rich fur country west of the Rockies. Astor planned to set up a line of trading posts across the continent along their route. He selected the mouth of the Columbia River as his base, Fort Astoria. Ships loaded with supplies were to sail from New York round the Horn to Astoria, and from there, loaded with furs, they would travel to trade in China.

Recruiting Canadian mountain men from the rival North West Company, Astor sent a ship from New York in September 1810 as an advance party, but the crew was massacred by Indians at Nootka. Meanwhile, an overland party led by Wilson Price Hunt had set out across the scorching prairies with 45 hired hands, 11 trapper hunters and 82 horses, to cross the virtually unexplored country between the Missouri and the Big Horn.

The party was guided by Crow Indians across the Big Horn Mountains to the river. They marched northwest through Wyoming over the Wind River Range and crossed the Union Pass at the junction of the Wind River, Absaroke and Gros Ventre ranges.

Following his own star. The greatest of North American explorers was a lonely, anonymous and probably unlettered hunter and trapper. Such a man, with only his horse and perhaps a pack mule for company, was one to whom the lonely and dangerous life appealed—a man who, like the Indians with whom he came into contact, was always retreating before the advance of a civilization for which he cared little. Such men were the first to trace the tracks over which large, sponsored expeditions travelled during the 19th century

On September 24 they crossed the swift Hoback River, named after a guide, which they followed to its junction with the Snake. Building dugouts they cached their saddles, entrusted their horses to the Shoshoni, and set out on the green waters of the 1,800-foot-wide Snake. After an accident in the rapids they continued on foot. Dogged by hunger, in the Snake River canyon the 19 remaining men were forced to share one dog, one beaver, a handful of cherries and the baked soles of their moccasins. Travelling up the Burnt River valley, they finally reached Astoria on February 14, 1812. The Astorians had completed the exploration of the Snake River, begun by Henry, discovered the Green River and the Union Pass and claimed to have discovered a short cut around the south end of the Wind River Mountains, the famed South Pass.

Between 1815 and 1830, St Louis was the gateway to the northwest. From St Louis the Americans set off for the beaver hunting grounds. The town expanded as fast as her trade, which rose to nearly four million dollars in its heyday. In St Louis, William Henry Ashley, a Virginian businessman who had suffered a financial loss in the Panic of 1819, entered the fur trade, and thought to make a profit from trapping parties to the upper Missouri. His company of 1822 was the largest party of trappers to set out from St Louis, but on the second of his Missouri expeditions Ashley encountered such violence from the treacherous Missouri Indians that he decided to change his tactics. With a party which included such future heroes of the fur trade as William and Milton Sublette, David E. Jackson, Hugh Glass, Jedediah Smith and Jim Bridger, these St Louis traders trapped along the Missouri, the Big Horn, the Platte, the Green, Wind and Sweetwater rivers, and found the South Pass. Later, they hunted around the headwaters of the Missouri, crossed the Great Divide, trapped at the Columbia River headwaters and traced the Snake to its junction. Ashley opened a new route to the Rocky Mountains along the North Platte.

Though a pious man who carried a Bible wherever he went, Smith was a typical mountain man. In 1826–7 he led a party of trappers southwest to California. They reached what is now the Zion National Park and the Mohave Indian settlements on the Colorado River, and crossed the San Bernardino Mountains to San Gabriel, near Los Angeles, where they clashed with the Mexican authorities. Released with the help of some American sea captains, Smith and his party set off northwards through the San Joaquin valley. Trapped by snow in the foothills of the Sierra Nevada, Smith and two companions crossed the sierra at Ebbetts Pass in May 1827, and traversed the saline Utah Desert to Bear Lake in time for the next rendezvous. After returning to California the party was twice attacked by Indians, but succeeded in travelling as far as Fort Vancouver in Oregon via the Sacremento valley.

Smith became the most experienced—and one of the longest lived—of the mountain men. Jim Bridger was perhaps one of the most famous. In the winter of 1824, one of Ashley's parties were trapping along the Bear River. Bridger followed the Bear to its outlet on a vast sheet of water, which he tasted. Finding it salt, he declared that he was standing on an arm of the Pacific. He had discovered the Great Salt Lake.

Bridger himself once said: "They said I was the damnedest liar that ever lived . . ." when he described the Fire Hole River which ran cold at the top but hot at the bottom; the Yellowstone Falls "three times as high as Niagara", and the Mammoth Hot Springs in what is now the Yellowstone National Park.

Walker's Pass
Joseph Reddeford Walker was one of the historical trail blazers of the far west. In 1833, he reached San Francisco and Monterey, having travelled from the Salt Lake, down the Humboldt River and across the Sierra Nevada. He explored Owens valley and first described the Yosemite valley and the Tuolumne Redwood Grove, and discovered Walker's Pass through the sierras.

The discoveries of the mountain men attracted the attention of the Hudson's Bay Company, who from 1825 sent Peter Skene Ogden on a series of explorations into the west. In May 1825 he led an expedition to the Great Salt Lake, and in 1826 to the Deschutes and John Day rivers in unexplored territory. He explored the Klamath River as far as Mount Shasta in 1827. Ogden was the first person to discover the Unknown River, which Frémont was later to name the Humboldt. Setting out from Fort Vancouver every year from 1824, Ogden explored California as far as the gulf. In 1829–30 he crossed from the mouth of the Snake River

The great migration

to the Humboldt sink, to the Sevier, Virgin and Colorado rivers, following the latter to its mouth, and returning through Yuma country to San Joaquin. Information provided by both Smith and Ogden was used for maps of the west produced during the 1830s.

Seemingly as rapidly as they had come, by the 1830s the days of the lone hunter were gone. In the overtrapped valleys of the west, bitter competition set in.

In 1845, Captain John Charles Frémont was sent westwards by the American President on a journey of exploration. With the famous mountain man and fighter Kit Carson as a guide, he reached the Great Salt Lake, followed the Humboldt River, crossed the sierra and headed for Sutter's Fort in California; ordered out of Monterey province by the Mexican Civil Government, he made his way north to Klamath. This was the last of a series of such expeditions. In 1841, he had won a commission to explore the Des Moines River and in 1842 the Wind River chain of the Rocky Mountains. The following year he took an expedition to Colorado and Oregon, returning via Nevada and California.

Frémont, on his return, publicized his discoveries and was hailed in his time as the "Great Pathfinder". From "Pathfinder" to "Pathfollower" he was demoted as it was realized that he had simply followed the trails of the old mountain men, naming Ogden's Unknown River the Humboldt, and using the mountain men themselves as guides.

THE FIRST WAGON TRAIL to be opened was the road to Santa Fe, the capital of New Mexico, and Spanish territory until 1821. In September of that year, William Becknell, a Missouri merchant, set off on a trading trip into the southwest, following the left fork of the Arkansas River, and finding a way over the Rockies through the boulder-strewn Raton Pass. He heard of Mexico's newly won independence only after encountering a contingent of Mexican soldiers farther down the trail. Spanish trading restrictions were now removed and Americans could trade at Santa Fe. Becknell, losing no time, traded his goods in Santa Fe at profit estimated to have been in the region of 15 times his investment. On the way home he pioneered a short cut to avoid the Raton Pass along the Cimarron River.

After 1821, the Santa Fe trade prospered. One or two caravans from Missouri, the number of wagons increasing each year, arrived laden at Santa Fe every summer. After 1826, Mexican caravans added to the commerce of the prairies. By 1831, a caravan of 100 wagons carried goods worth $200,000. The Santa Fe Trail opened the southwest of the continent to emigrants, but the trail remained largely a trading trail. No mass migrations set out to Mexico, but the movement of settlers was instrumental in the creation of the Texan Republic in 1836. The Santa Fe Trail was not a difficult trail, even for the blundering Conestoga wagons built to carry the trade goods to Mexico. The Old

Spanish Trail, pioneered by two Spanish Fathers during the 18th century, was far more gruelling and could only be used by traders with pack mules.

In 1829, the Old Spanish Trail was pioneered as a trade route by a New Mexican merchant, Antonio Armijo, attempting to discover a route to Upper California. Travelling northwest to the "Four Corners" region near the Mesa Verde, his party passed through the Goose Neck Gorge of the San Juan River to the "Crossing of the Fathers", stone steps leading to the point where the trail crossed the great Colorado River, impossible to negotiate by wagon. Despite its difficulty, the Old Spanish Trail became an important trade route for the next 20 years, but as late as 1846 there was still no practicable wagon route from Santa Fe to California.

Missionaries, traders and merchants followed closely on the heels of the mountain men to become the first settlers in the far west. They sent home urgent requests for more settlers to join them and by the 1840s the movement to the far west had begun.

Many were the adventures and disappointments of the wagon trail pioneers, but as prosperity returned to the east after the depressions of the 1830s, land hunger found an outlet and the fever to go west increased.

The mass migrations to Oregon began in 1843. The first comprising nearly 1,000 emigrants and more than 1,800 cattle and oxen, blazed a new section of the Oregon

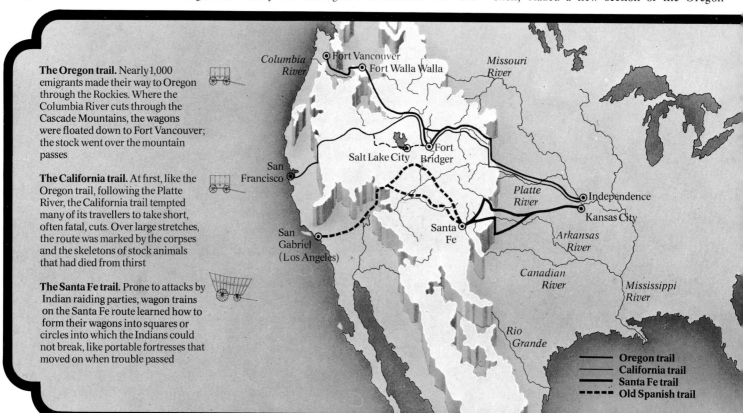

The Oregon trail. Nearly 1,000 emigrants made their way to Oregon through the Rockies. Where the Columbia River cuts through the Cascade Mountains, the wagons were floated down to Fort Vancouver; the stock went over the mountain passes

The California trail. At first, like the Oregon trail, following the Platte River, the California trail tempted many of its travellers to take short, often fatal, cuts. Over large stretches, the route was marked by the corpses and the skeletons of stock animals that had died from thirst

The Santa Fe trail. Prone to attacks by Indian raiding parties, wagon trains on the Santa Fe route learned how to form their wagons into squares or circles into which the Indians could not break, like portable fortresses that moved on when trouble passed

——— Oregon trail
——— California trail
——— Santa Fe trail
----- Old Spanish trail

Trail by turning to the southwest after fording the Green River instead of taking the northern route followed two years earlier by the Western Emigration Society. After reaching Fort Hall, they travelled along the south bank of the Snake River and turned northwest to the valley of the Grande Ronde, and across the Blue Mountains to Oregon. On reaching the Columbia River the wagons were rebuilt as boats and floated to Fort Vancouver.

The second mass migration to California, in 1844, became the first train to take wagons across the sierras, and their route became the usual emigrant route to California.

There were many disasters along the trail. In 1844, the Donner Party, taking a misguided short cut across the terrible Salt Lake Desert, met an early winter storm while crossing the sierras. Snowbound, and eating the dead of their party to survive, some of their members scaled the summit to find a relief party. Out of 89 emigrants, only 45 survived. The Donner route was improved and used later by the Mormons, who in 1847 trekked from Nauvoo to settle in Salt Lake Valley.

Liberty and expansion were the key concepts behind the American movement west. In December 1845, John L. O'Sullivan, editor of the New York *Morning News* wrote: "It is our manifest destiny to overspread and to possess the whole of the continent which Providence has given use for the development of the great experiment of liberty and federated self-government entrusted to us."

"Some had waggons drawn by oxen; others, waggons drawn by horses; a few had hacks . . . many were to make the journey on horseback; and a few brought nothing but themselves." The migration of a people to make a new home for themselves is a story as old as that of mankind. The families that set out in wagon trains to populate western North America were in many cases continuing a journey that had begun in the Old World of Europe, or who were at most first or second generation Americans themselves. The wagons in which they travelled were simple, durable farm carts fitted with bows of bent hickory over which canvas covers were stretched. They did not provide a comfortable ride; few wagons had springs, and for braking a log was towed behind the wagon. Apart from food and water, bedding and tools, each wagon had a tar bucket. Its contents were used for lubrication and for caulking whenever the wagon had to be floated across a river.

It was in trains of wagons such as these that a generation of migrants made their rough and ready, mobile homes, and explored the land they were to settle. Not all of them were to reach their destination in the West and for the unlucky ones, the remains of a wagon marked a family's resting place

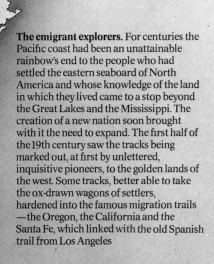

The emigrant explorers. For centuries the Pacific coast had been an unattainable rainbow's end to the people who had settled the eastern seaboard of North America and whose knowledge of the land in which they lived came to a stop beyond the Great Lakes and the Mississippi. The creation of a new nation soon brought with it the need to expand. The first half of the 19th century saw the tracks being marked out, at first by unlettered, inquisitive pioneers, to the golden lands of the west. Some tracks, better able to take the ox-drawn wagons of settlers, hardened into the famous migration trails —the Oregon, the California and the Santa Fe, which linked with the old Spanish trail from Los Angeles

South America: a land for scientists

FROM THE DAY Christopher Columbus first set foot on the continent in 1492, South America was to exert a strong fascination on European explorers—men who would risk hardship, disease and death to navigate its dark water-courses, map its coastline, penetrate its jungles and trudge across its deserts and plains. Besides the discoverers and the Conquistadors, there came, too, adventurers and gold-seekers, slave-hunters, merchants, missionaries and others keen to exploit the wealth and diversity of a vast new continent. But, two centuries after Columbus made his historic landfall, a fresh breed of explorers came to South America. These were the scientists—physicists, astronomers, mathematicians, geologists and botanists—who peopled a whole new era of exploration during which expert knowledge and discovery were fed back from the New World to the Old.

The background to this age of scientific discovery was a dispute in the French Académie des Sciences, where, in the first half of the 18th century, there was controversy as to the shape of the Earth: was it slightly flattened at the poles as Isaac Newton suggested, or was the Astronomer Royal of France right in thinking of it as a "prolate spheroid"—elongated at the poles and constricted in the middle? The Académie chose to resolve the dilemma by measuring the meridian of an arc of a degree of latitude in the Arctic and at the Equator, and comparing the results with measurements taken in France. In 1734, two expeditions were mounted; one to Lapland, the other to the Peruvian province of Quito, the only place along the Equator where work of this nature could be carried out.

The brilliant mathematician Charles-Marie de la Condamine—an academician since the age of 29—was chosen to lead the equatorial expedition, heading a distinguished scientific team. Also, since Quito lay under Spanish rule, the French agreed to take along two young Spanish mathematicians, Juan and Ulloa, who were to provide some of the most detailed and conscientious observations of all.

La Condamine and the French contingent set sail in May 1735, travelling by way of Martinique, Cartagena, Panama and Guayaquil. It was on the way to the high Andes, during a sidetrip along the Rio Esmeraldas, that La Condamine first discovered rubber, which he used to make a protective casing for his quadrant. He was the first man to bring rubber to Europe.

Quito, ancient northern capital of the Incas, proved a tolerable city, although the scientists soon noticed a high incidence of disease—spotted fever, pleurisy, *mal de valle* (probably gangrene of the rectum), venereal disease and *peste*, an inflammation unknown in Europe, in which the symptoms were delirium and blood vomiting.

The Earth-measurers based themselves on the plain of Yarqui, northeast of Quito. At an altitude of 8,000 feet, this windswept expanse of semi-desert was to tax them to the limits with its terrible day and night temperature extremes. The work, they now realized, would take years rather than months and would be costly, too, in human terms. Already one young Frenchman had died of fever. Later two more men would die and Jussieu, the distinguished botanist would suffer a mental breakdown. Ironically for the French the final observations (completed in 1743) confirmed Newton's theory: like the Lapland contingent, La Condamine and his companions in Peru had proved that the Earth was round. After eight years the Andean party split up and turned for home.

With his main task completed, La Condamine now became the first scientist to descend the River Amazon, travelling by raft as far as Manaus and penetrating some way up the River Negro before striking east for Belém on the Atlantic coast.

Adventurous wife

Jean Godin des Odonais, who had lingered in Quito after the expedition broke up, was to make a similar descent of the Amazon six years later. More spectacular still, however, were the adventures of his wife, Doña Isabel: in 1769 she set off to rejoin her husband, travelling with a small party by raft and dugout canoe along the Pastaza, Maranon and Amazon rivers. The sole survivor of this terrible journey, she was found wandering alone in the jungle and was finally reunited with her husband after 20 years. The Godins arrived in Paris in 1773.

When La Condamine and his party had set out 38 years earlier no one could have foreseen just what epic proportions the exercise would assume. What began as a geophysical expedition soon widened into an extensive study of much of the continent as the members followed up their individual interests. Besides yielding results in various fields, the Earth-measuring episode proved the spur for intensified scientific interest in South America which was to continue throughout the following century.

Meanwhile, besides the wider issue of the shape of the Earth, there had for many years been speculation as to the exact position of South America itself and it was this that inspired the first truly scientific expedition of the century, that of Pere Louis Feuillée. Between 1707 and 1711, Feuillée, an accomplished astronomer and physicist, not only surveyed the coasts of Peru and Chile and observed the southern skies in his attempt to put South America firmly on the map, but also collected a considerable number of plants and animals.

After Feuillée, maritime exploration was interrupted to some extent by the unsettled situation in Europe. It was not until after the Treaty of Paris (1763) that European sailors were able to turn their attention once again to the business of mapping the southern continent. The most comprehensive scientific survey of this kind was launched in 1789 under the leadership of Alessandro Malaspina, a Lombard nobleman who had entered the service of Spain.

Malaspina planned to explore the coastlines of the Spanish territories in South America. He had two objectives; to make hydrographic charts "for the most remote regions of America" and sea charts to guide the navigator, and to make a political and economic assessment of the Spanish Empire. Planning his voyage in microscopic detail, he turned for advice to Ulloa, now Lieutenant-General of the Spanish fleet and a valuable ally both on account of his vast knowledge of South America and of his "true love of solid progress in the sciences".

In five years the Malaspina expedition surveyed a massive territory, including the Rio de la Plata, the coastlines of Argentina, Brazil, the Valdes Peninsula, Patagonia, the Malvinas Islands, Tierra del Fuego, Chile and Peru (also, after leaving the expedition, the Bohemian botanist Haenke went on to make a detailed botanical survey of Bolivia). Even so, Malaspina himself, who favoured emancipation of the colonies, came home to Spain to face arrest and imprisonment. Much of this great explorer's work was lost and his maps gathered dust for 30 years. Yet because of the sheer scope and brilliance of his work, the expedition was still of lasting significance.

Scientific interest was not, however, limited to Earth-measuring and the minutiae of navigational charts. The lush plant-life of South America had attracted attention, too. But it was not until the 18th century that the continent's botanical riches came to be studied in their own right. This was an interest fostered by the Spanish authorities, who were constantly soliciting rare specimens, especially medicinal plants, from all over the empire. Carlos III of Spain commissioned three expeditions to the New World in order to enlarge his collection.

Particularly outstanding was the contribution of Father Mutis, physician and naturalist, who set out from Spain in September 1760. As physician to the viceroy of Nueva Granada, Mutis did most of his work in the environs of Bogotá, identifying and classifying little-known plants, and corresponding with the great Swedish botanist

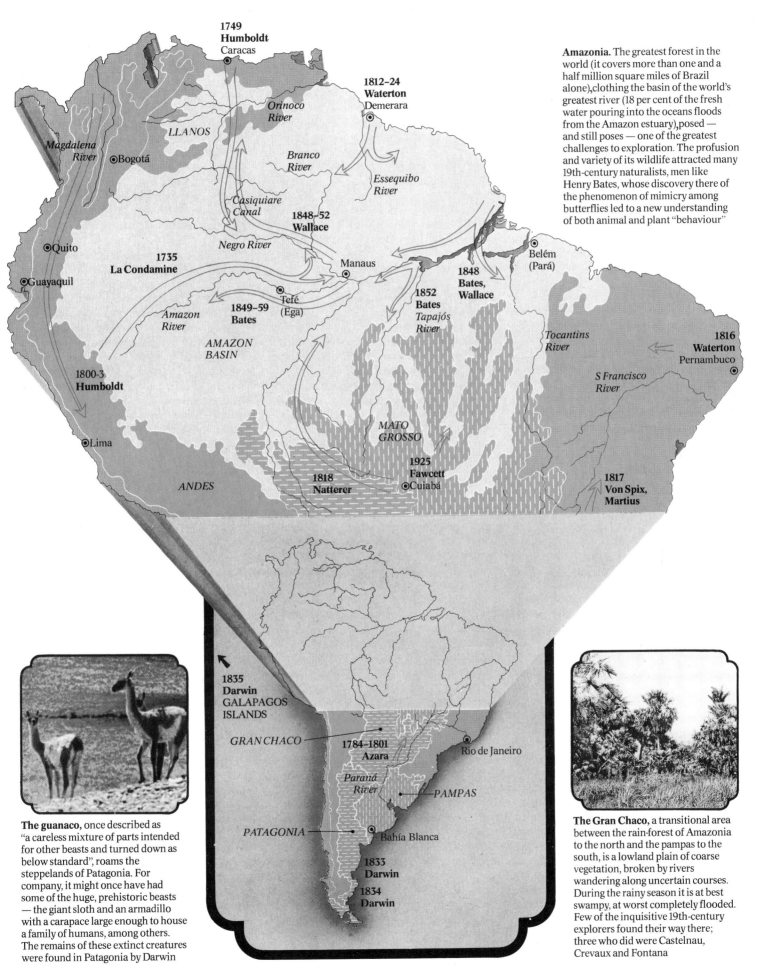

1749
Humboldt
Caracas

1812–24
Waterton
Demerara

Orinoco River

LLANOS

Branco River

Essequibo River

Magdalena River

⊙Bogotá

Casiquiare Canal

1848–52
Wallace

Negro River

⊙Quito

1735
La Condamine

⊙Guayaquil

Amazon River

1849–59
Bates

Manaus ⊙

⊙Tefé
(Ega)

1848
**Bates,
Wallace**

Belém
(Pará) ⊙

1852
Bates
Tapajós River

Tocantins River

1816
Waterton
Pernambuco ⊙

AMAZON BASIN

1800-3
Humboldt

S Francisco River

⊙Lima

ANDES

MATO GROSSO

1818
Natterer

1925
Fawcett
⊙Cuiabá

1817
**Von Spix,
Martius**

Amazonia. The greatest forest in the world (it covers more than one and a half million square miles of Brazil alone),clothing the basin of the world's greatest river (18 per cent of the fresh water pouring into the oceans floods from the Amazon estuary),posed — and still poses — one of the greatest challenges to exploration. The profusion and variety of its wildlife attracted many 19th-century naturalists, men like Henry Bates, whose discovery there of the phenomenon of mimicry among butterflies led to a new understanding of both animal and plant "behaviour"

1835
Darwin
GALAPAGOS
ISLANDS

GRAN CHACO

1784–1801
Azara

Rio de Janeiro ⊙

Paraná River

PAMPAS

PATAGONIA

Bahía Blanca ⊙

1833
Darwin

1834
Darwin

The guanaco, once described as "a careless mixture of parts intended for other beasts and turned down as below standard", roams the steppelands of Patagonia. For company, it might once have had some of the huge, prehistoric beasts — the giant sloth and an armadillo with a carapace large enough to house a family of humans, among others. The remains of these extinct creatures were found in Patagonia by Darwin

The Gran Chaco, a transitional area between the rain-forest of Amazonia to the north and the pampas to the south, is a lowland plain of coarse vegetation, broken by rivers wandering along uncertain courses. During the rainy season it is at best swampy, at worst completely flooded. Few of the inquisitive 19th-century explorers found their way there; three who did were Castelnau, Crevaux and Fontana

The great traveller

Linnaeus for 18 years until the latter's death in 1778. Mutis, who was to be described by Humboldt and Bonpland as the "patriarch of botany in the New World", had the satisfaction of obtaining the *Aristoloquia* (highly prized as a remedy for snakebite) and of seeing the *chinchona*, the quinine tree.

In 1774, a request by France for permission to send a botanist out to Peru was granted with the proviso that Dombey, the French nominee, should take with him two young Spanish botanists, Ruiz and Pavon. Ruiz was appointed leader of the expedition which, according to Carlos III's directive, was to undertake "the methodical examination and identification of the products of nature of my American dominions . . . not only in order to promote the progress of the physical sciences, but also to banish doubts and adulterations that are found in medicine, painting, and the other important arts. . . ."

Arriving in Peru in 1778, Dombey and his companions passed through a variety of climatic zones, collecting specimens from each. Some of this material, they were told, had medicinal properties: the maw of *huacha* birds would dissolve a goitre; shoots of *quiscar* boiled in water were supposed to cure colds (or, mixed with urine, to ease toothache); and there were other plants to take care of anything from haemorrhoids to infertility. The botanists were intrigued, too, by the *zerbatana*, the blowpipe used by the Indians for hunting: the poisoned darts caused the quarry's blood to clot immediately, and yet the flesh remained edible.

While Haenke, Mutis, Dombey, Pavón and Ruiz were hard at work elsewhere on the continent, a Spanish naval officer called Azara was busy with explorations of the Parana–Paraguay basin that were to occupy 20 years. Though not a scientist—he was posted to South America in 1780 for military reasons—Azara was able to make seven important mapping expeditions from his base at Asuncion. During these long years of isolation he developed a keen interest in zoology and natural history, and became an authority on the quadrupeds of the region.

Azara was the first person to give a scientific basis to the geography of the Rio de la Plata, and to define the region watered by this and the rivers Uruguay, Parana and Paraguay. Moreover, his biographer credits him with propounding the germ of evolutionary theory. Azara comes over as a careful observer of nature and as a man preoccupied with genetic concepts way ahead of his time. He provides, therefore, a significant link between the early students of the South American scene and the great naturalists of the 19th century—men of the stature of Humboldt and Darwin—who were shortly to occupy the stage.

HUMBOLDT WAS NOT the first man of science to feel the lure of South America —nor, at that stage, was he by any means the most distinguished. Certainly the passport introduction was modest enough: "Friedrich Heinrich Alexander, Baron von Humboldt, born at Berlin, age 28, five feet eight, light brown hair, grey eyes, large nose, rather large mouth, well-formed chin, forehead open, marked with scars of smallpox. . . . Travelling for the acquisition of knowledge." But in a few brief years this gentle young man was to establish himself as a colossus of exploration, earning from no less a figure than Charles Darwin the accolade of being "the greatest scientific traveller who ever lived".

Born in 1769, Humboldt developed an interest in science in his teens. At the age of 20 he took part in a scientific expedition up the Rhine and it was this experience that sparked a passion for exploration. In preparation for the momentous years ahead, he studied languages, biology, astronomy and geology.

At first there were frustrations, when various planned expeditions—including one which would have taken him round the world —fell through. But from the beginning the omens for the South American odyssey were set fair. While in Spain with his friend and collaborator Aimé Bonpland, a young French physician and botanist, Humboldt learned that the authorities might agree to the two men visiting the Spanish Americas at their own expense.

Royal support

His way smoothed by friends in high places, Humboldt had an audience with the Spanish king in March 1799. Carlos IV was quickly persuaded to provide them not only with passports, but with a royal authorization assuring them of the assistance of all governors and other officials they might encounter and of access to any place they might wish to visit. It was, Humboldt later conceded, an extraordinary privilege. There had been no Spanish expeditions to South America since that led by the ill-fated Malaspina (from 1789 to 1794). Now he, a Prussian, was being given the freedom of the continent—*carte blanche* to go where he pleased—without being saddled, as the Earth-measuring La Condamine and the botanist Dombey had been, with Spanish extras.

Quickly Humboldt and Bonpland did the rounds of the museums and instrument-makers. Also, they visited such eminent botanists as Ruiz and Pavón (Dombey's companions in Peru) and Née (who had gone out with Malaspina), all of whom opened their collections to them. By June 5, 1799, the preparations were complete and the two young scientists set sail from Coruña.

After they had crossed the Tropic of Cancer, on June 27, typhoid fever broke out, and so on July 16 Humboldt and Bonpland disembarked at Cumaná on the coast of New Andalusia (now northeastern Venezuela). The next few weeks were spent calibrating the instruments and examining traces of the earthquake which had rocked the city two years previously.

From Cumaná there were frequent trips into the surrounding countryside. On these excursions, Humboldt, a Protestant, met the first of the many missionary friars who were to offer so much guidance and hospitality to the two young explorers throughout their stay in South America. At Caripe the Capuchin friars took them to see the great Cavern of the Guacharo, where they shot several *guacharo* birds, hitherto unknown to naturalists.

On November 16 Humboldt and Bonpland took ship for La Guaira, from where they planned to go on to Caracas. The idea at this stage was to remain at Caracas until the end of the rainy season, then cross the *llanos*, the vast, dust-filled river plains of central Venezuela, to the Orinoco mission settlements and follow this river to the River Negro and the Brazilian frontier, returning to Cumaná via Angostura (now Ciudad Bolivar).

Meanwhile, La Guaira proved to be one of the hottest places on Earth. In contrast, the climate of Caracas—"agreeably placed" at an altitude of 3,200 feet—was "a perpetual spring". The two men stayed in the capital until February 7, 1800, when they set out for the *llanos*. Passing through the *cordillera*, they were struck by a mass of detail—great veins of garnet where the track was cut through rock, a profusion of coffee trees and giant fig trees. Particularly fascinating was the *palo de vaca*, or cow-tree, yielding a thick vegetable milk.

In March they entered the *llanos*, where they encountered ground temperatures up to a merciless 50°C (122°F) and mirages beckoning in the shimmering heat. Halfway across the *llanos*, having had an unnerving meeting with an alligator while attempting to bathe in a water-hole, they reached a place called Calabozo, where they observed another of the continent's deadly creatures, the red-eyed electric eel or *Gymnotus*. Anything from three to nine feet long, *Gymnotus* gives off shocks up to 650 volts in output, enough to stun or even kill a large beast. Consequently, Humboldt and Bonpland watched in amazement as the Indians chased terror-stricken horses and mules—some of which drowned—into the mud-pools to provoke the eels into coming to the surface. Eventually the eels tired, temporarily losing "charge", and some specimens were harpooned for the naturalists. Both men suffered

Forever seeking gold, the 16th-century Spanish travellers through Amazonia had eyes—according to their records—only for its prospect. The magnet for the 19th-century explorer-scientist was its real nature; its terrain, its vegetation and its animal life. Rain-forest is the most secretive of habitats and Humboldt and the men who were to follow him would have heard the sounds of more wildlife than they would have seen—but what they did see were many species without parallel in other continents. The Amazonian forest is the largest in the world, the river running through it—with 17 of its tributaries more than 1,000 miles long—by far the greatest. Forest and water are therefore largely indivisible and the wildlife, if it doesn't fly, must be able to take to the trees, or water, or both, if it is to survive. In neither context does it offer the observer much more than a fleeting glimpse

Bane of the Amazon explorer, the ''zancudo'' fly (right) penetrates the thickest material, its bites remaining swollen and painful for weeks afterwards

The largest rodent in the world, the capybara (left) grows to three feet or more in length. It swims with ease and when ashore trots like a horse

The spectacled cayman, once numerous on the Amazon's banks, has been reduced by hunters to near-extinction

Short shrift to any living creature which falls into the water is given by the piranha (below). In a school it strips a capybara of all its flesh in under a minute

The electric eel of the Amazon (below) can deliver shocks of up to 650 volts—enough to stun or kill a man or a large animal

nausea and pain in the joints from shocks received while handling the eels before they started to dissect them.

By March 29 they had reached the Capuchin mission on the River Apuré and the trek across the arid, treeless expanse of the *llanos* was over. For the next three months they would endure a steamy, sweating, insect-ridden ordeal, making their way painfully along the rivers and past the dark rain-forests. Now all the equipment was transferred to a *lancha*, or dugout canoe, where the only shelter was a crude palm-thatched cabin rigged up on the stern.

Nevertheless, the days on the Apuré were filled with fascination. For company there were vast flocks of flamingos, spoonbills and herons, small jet-black monkeys, sting-rays, *caribito* fish (relatives of the bloodthirsty piranha), manatees, turtles and fresh-water dolphins. On the banks they saw 20-foot-long alligators, large swimming rodents called capybara, snakes, jaguars, peccaries and tapirs. The nights were filled with the racket of howler monkeys and parrots.

On April 5 they reached the junction with the Orinoco and a dramatic change of terrain. Here the river seemed limitless; wide as a lake and lined with vast beaches against the encroaching forest. Next morning they arrived at one of the three islands in the Orinoco where the turtles laid their eggs in the sand. They were in time to see the turtle egg harvest, attended each year at low water by several hundred Indians, who collected the eggs to make turtle oil. Humboldt estimated that there were about a million turtles laying eggs along the Orinoco.

Priest–guide

Soon the river narrowed and the water became discoloured, evil-smelling and unfit to drink—changes brought about by the putrefied remains of caymans lying along the banks. At Carichana they found a mission station, and one of the priests, Father Zea, though weak with malaria, agreed to guide them to the River Negro and back. They bought a smaller canoe to negotiate the 40-mile-long Great Cataracts, at Atures and Maipurés, strewn with granite rocks and one of the longest and most perilous series of rapids in South America.

While the Indians manhandled the dugout through the rapids, Humboldt and Bonpland stayed with Father Zea. They were quick to make use of the tree-house he had built to escape the worst of the mosquitoes and other insects. These pests were now a major problem, especially the villainous little *zancudo* flies, which penetrated the thickest material, leaving a series of savage bites that would be swollen and painful for weeks.

The great traveller

Beyond the rapids lay an unknown land, territory which no trained observer had yet penetrated. As the days passed they drew nearer to the watershed between the Orinoco and the Amazon basins. On the night of April 24 they turned right into a tributary, the Atabapo—a "black-water" river, fit to drink—and by dawn it seemed as if they had been whisked into paradise; gone were the insects, and in the cool, clear water fish were visible at depths of up to 30 feet.

They continued along this river, sometimes accompanied by 14-foot-long anacondas swimming alongside, as far as a smaller tributary, the Temi. The forest was flooded at this time so they sailed the canoe between the trees, hacking a way clear with machetes. Once, in the depths of the forest, they were surrounded by freshwater dolphins—a remarkable sight 1,200 miles from the sea.

At the end of April they turned off into an even smaller tributary, the Tuamini, heading southwest. Soon they reached the mission of Javita, run by Father Ceresco.

It took 23 Indians four days to drag the canoe on tree-trunk rollers across the seven-mile isthmus of land separating the Orinoco and Amazon basins. Impatient with this portage, Humboldt sat down and wrote to Carlos IV suggesting that a canal should be built to replace this cumbersome link between the Orinoco and Amazon waterways. Then, frustrated at the botanical limitations—most of the leaves and flowers were in the tree canopy, over 100 feet high—he and Bonpland trudged through the jungle in the wake of their canoe. Within hours of re-embarking they entered the Negro, one of the greatest and most beautiful of Amazon tributaries.

On May 10 the expedition arrived at the point Humboldt had come so far to see, the bifurcation of the Orinoco. Here the main stream flows to the west, and an offshoot, the Casiquiare Canal "as broad as the Rhine" flows 180 miles southwest to the Negro. The main objective of the Orinoco trip had been achieved; they had proved the existence, hitherto disputed, of the Casiquiare, the only natural waterway in the world connecting two gigantic river systems.

Triumphant but exhausted, the naturalists unpacked their theodolites and sextants to determine the point of connection astronomically. But Humboldt never became so engrossed in the stars as to forget the tropical richness around him. "Every object," he wrote, "declares the grandeur of the power, the tenderness of Nature, from the boa constrictor, which can swallow a horse, down to the humming-bird, balancing itself on a chalice of a flower."

Plagued once again by insects, they now began the return journey through a region of dense jungle inhabited by cannibal tribes. Rejoining the Orinoco, they made a stop at Esmeralda, where they learned the secrets of curare, the poison used by the Indians to kill their prey. They then carried on downstream to the Great Cataracts.

Now Humboldt and Bonpland lost no time in returning to civilization. The last 300 miles were covered in less than a week, and by June 13 they had reached Angostura. "It would be difficult for me to express the satisfaction we felt on landing," Humboldt wrote. "Long privations give a value to the smallest enjoyments; and I cannot express the pleasure we felt when we saw for the first time wheaten bread on the Governor's table."

A heart-breaking postscript to this 1,500-mile marathon was the discovery that one-third of their collection of 12,000 botanical specimens had been ruined by the humidity. Also, weakened by the privations of the past months, both men fell ill with typhoid fever, which delayed their return to Cumaná. Finally, however, they were fit enough to trudge back across the *llanos*, and in November they took ship to winter in Cuba.

After his exploration of the great rivers of Venezuela, Humboldt had planned to visit North America, but a sudden change of plan launched him on a two-year expedition that was to establish him once and for all as an international figure. Returning in the spring of 1801 for this second phase of the South American epic, Humboldt turned his attention to the exploration of one of the world's highest volcanic regions, the Andes of Colombia, Ecuador and Peru.

Torment

From Cartagena, access to the eastern cordillera was by way of the River Magdalena, a 500-mile journey through uninhabited forests. Once again Humboldt and Bonpland, the faithful companion who was still at his side, found themselves cramped in an Indian canoe, tormented by insects. The journey, with the river in full spate, was miserably slow, and it was six weeks before the two men could begin the 9,000-foot ascent to Bogotá.

Here their main purpose was to visit Father Mutis, physician and botanist, who had been in South America since 1760. Mutis, now 70 years old and a leading authority on the flora of the region, showed them part of his vast collection of 20,000 plants and made Humboldt a present of 100 botanical drawings.

On September 8 the expedition left Bogotá for Quito by way of the arduous, snow-covered Quindiu Pass. Gratefully they reached the comforts of Quito early in January 1802.

The province of Quito contains some of the highest peaks in the Andes, among them the 20,577-foot-high volcano Chimborazo, which had never been climbed. Humboldt and Bonpland now made their minds up to conquer this peak. But first there were several months' preparation, which included climbing the smallest of the neighbouring volcanoes, Pichincha, a relative midget at 15,672 feet. Apart from preparing them physically, this ascent furnished more scientific data. Humboldt already knew that, advancing towards the poles, mean temperature drops one degree Fahrenheit for each degree of latitude. Climbing Pichincha, he found a temperature drop of one degree for every 300 feet of altitude.

At dawn on June 23, accompanied by Bonpland and Carlos Montúfar, son of the provincial governor, Humboldt began the ascent of Chimborazo. On the snow-line all the Indian guides but one deserted. By 17,000 feet the mist had thickened, obscuring the summit, and all three men were suffering with *soroche*—mountain sickness. They began to experience nausea and giddiness, their eyes became bloodshot and blood seeped from their lips and gums. Still they pressed on, until the mist lifted briefly to reveal ahead of them a ravine 400 feet deep and 60 feet wide. There was no way forward.

Humboldt and his companions had reached 19,286 feet—an altitude record which remained unbroken for more than 30 years—but they had no choice but to turn back. On the descent they were hampered first by a hailstorm and then by a blizzard.

The ascent of Chimborazo brought Humboldt world recognition, and to the end of his days he regarded it as the greatest of his achievements. But in the summer of 1802 there was other work to be done. Returning to Quito, Humboldt and Bonpland prepared to move on from Ecuador into Peru, where, in Lima, they planned to observe the transit of Mercury across the Sun.

The road south led through forests of *chinchona*, the quinine-producing tree. After a year at high altitude Humboldt reported, "it is delightful to descend gradually through the more genial climate of the Cinchona or Quina Woods of Loxa, into the plains of the Upper Amazon. There an unknown world unfolds itself, rich in magnificent vegetation." Leaving the upper Amazon, they followed the Inca highway, which eventually took them across a series of *páramos*, cold, wind-swept regions. Here Humboldt located the magnetic equator.

Now, from a vantage point on the western slopes of the Andes, they caught their first glimpse of the Pacific. The mule road wound down the last mountain ridge to Trujillo, founded by Pizarro, now a mere ruin in the vast barrenness of the Peruvian coastal desert. At last, as they moved south along the coast, Humboldt understood a remark made to him in Quito: "When you see no more trees, it is Peru."

Clearly it had not rained here for centuries. But why? The atmosphere was humid, rain clouds hung over the cordillera. How was it that the coast of Peru was a desert, while farther north the coast of Ecuador was clad in thick jungle with a rainfall of over 100 inches a year? Humboldt took a series of readings and found that the sea temperature was much lower than that over the land: there was a cold current running north, lapping the entire Peruvian coastline. Also, they noticed the terrible, eye-watering stench of *guano*, the nitrogen-rich fertilizer which the Incas had used on their terraces. Humboldt, who was to introduce *guano* to Europe, was now convinced that it had not rained here for hundreds of years. This vast deposit had built up from the droppings of sea-birds living on fish swarming in the cold current. The current came to be named after Humboldt.

At length, on October 22, 1802, the expedition arrived in Lima. Two weeks later Humboldt observed the transit of Mercury, completing his observations. Their work at an end, he and Bonpland set off for the coast. And, though his loyal companion was to come back to settle in South America, Humboldt sailed for Mexico in February 1803, never to return.

On his arrival in Europe, Humboldt was positively lionized. Learned societies honoured him, geographical features were named after him, and the king of Prussia gave him a handsome pension. Although he had prepared himself for a lifetime of travel, he made only one more expedition. This was a rapid trip, made at the age of 60, across Russia and Siberia to the Altai Mountains. The latter years of his life were spent in research, in completion of the *Cosmos*—his vision of the nature of the universe—and on various diplomatic missions. He died in Berlin in May 1859.

Humboldt's contribution to Europe's hitherto scanty knowledge of South America was immeasurable. His *Personal Narrative of Travels to the Equinoctial Regions of America* ranks among the greatest of explorers' records. It was the first written account describing in detail, and with considerable accuracy, the continent's flora and fauna. It was, moreover, particularly valuable since this was a man as intrigued by the height of a mountain as he was by the eating habits of a tribe of savages or the voice-box of a howler monkey or the killer mechanism of an electric eel. Here was one of the world's last great polymaths whose width of thought and vision has seldom been equalled.

"The greatest scientific traveller who ever lived" was Darwin's tribute to Alexander von Humboldt (right). As a young man, Humboldt had made his first scientific journey along the Rhine in his native Germany and worked for several years as a mining inspector in Freiberg. Like Darwin, his fame rests on one great journey to South America—although, unlike Darwin, he was to make another journey of exploration, into Asia, at the behest of the Tsar of Russia. Like Darwin's, his was a five-year journey in which he amassed geographical information more comprehensive than anything before or since his time. Despite the approbation he received on his return to Europe, and the vision of the nature of the world that his travels had given him, he regarded his ascent of Chimborazo as his greatest achievement. It was then thought to be the world's highest mountain

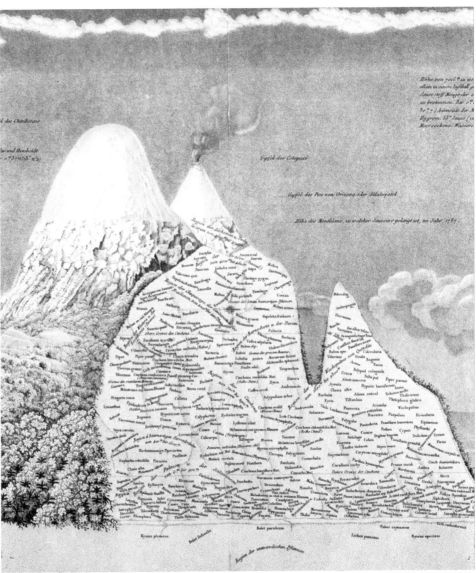

Humboldt's profile of Mount Chimborazo, simplified in outline yet packed with information on the mountain's plant geography, from the tropical vegetation at low altitudes to the close-growing cushion plants and lichens in the Alpine meadows close to the snow-line. Humboldt and his companions failed to reach the summit, 20,577 feet high, being forced back by mountain sickness little more than 1,000 feet from the top. Thirty years passed before anyone climbed higher than Humboldt had done and it was not until 1880 that Chimborazo was conquered by the English mountaineer Edward Whymper

Darwin and the *Beagle*

DARWIN'S OPINION OF his own qualities was modest enough. Of them he wrote: "The most important have been the love of science, unbounded patience in reflecting over any subject, industry in observing and collecting facts, and a fair share of invention as well as of common sense." Taken singly or together, these were the qualities of a diligent man whom history might have passed by. In Darwin's case, they must have been supplemented by some other virtue, perhaps intangible, that marks a man out for greatness.

Charles Darwin was the son of a doctor in Shrewsbury; his mother was the daughter of Josiah Wedgwood, the potter. His grandfather was the eminent botanist, Erasmus Darwin. His career at school, at Edinburgh University, where he had studied medicine, and at Cambridge, where he had taken a degree with the intention of going into the church, had not been brilliant; but at Edinburgh he had begun to study zoology and at Cambridge Professor John Henslow, the botanist, had persuaded him to take up geology. It was Henslow who secured his place for him in the *Beagle*, as unpaid naturalist to the expedition.

The *Beagle* was commanded by Captain Robert Fitzroy, who (with Commander P. P. King, the hydrographer who had charted the coasts of Australia) had already surveyed the coasts of South America from the Rio de la Plata to Chiloé Island on the coast of Chile. The *Beagle* expedition was to continue the charting of the coast and "to carry a chain of chronometrical measurements round the World", which would enable a number of meridians of longitude to be established.

Fitzroy was an aristocrat. His paternal grandfather was a duke, his mother was the daughter of a marquess. He was a first-class sailor and hydrographer, but he was also rather moody and intolerant. It was not long before differences of opinion arose between him and Darwin, particularly when Darwin's scientific investigations began to lead him to question the Biblical account of the creation of the world and the inhabitants' survival of the Flood by going on board the Ark.

With a crew of 74, there was not much room in the *Beagle* for a laboratory and Darwin's was nothing more than a small space at the end of the chart-room, where he also slept.

They sailed by way of the Cape Verde Islands, where Darwin collected and sent home specimens of dust brought by the wind from Africa which were found to contain 67 organic forms. They were all ". . . with the exception of two marine species . . . inhabitants of fresh water. . . ."

It was here, on St Jago, that he saw a white stratum with shells embedded in it, resting on ancient volcanic rocks and overlaid by a stream of basalt. The sight of it began a train of thought to which he was to return when he reached South America and determined him to write a book on geology.

In the spring of 1832 they reached Bahia, on the coast of Brazil, where Darwin saw his first tropical forest. "The noise from the insects is so loud, that it may be heard even in a vessel anchored several hundred yards from the shore; yet within the recesses of the forest a universal silence appears to reign. To a person fond of natural history, such a day as this brings with it a deeper pleasure, than he can ever hope to experience again. . . ."

Bones of the giants

Reaching Rio de Janeiro, Darwin travelled 100 miles inland to a coffee plantation, collecting specimens of the teeming insect life. In September Fitzroy began to survey the coast of Patagonia and it was on the shore at Punta Alta, near Bahia Blanca, that Darwin made an important discovery—the bones of "numerous gigantic extinct Quadrupeds". They were "parts of three heads and other bones of the *Megatherium* (a giant sloth), the huge dimensions of which are expressed by its name. Secondly, the *Megalonyx*, a great allied animal. Thirdly, the *Scelidotherium*, also an allied animal, of which I obtained a nearly perfect skeleton. It must have been as large as a rhinoceros. . . . Fourthly, the *Mylodon Darwinii*, a closely related genus of little inferior size. Fifthly, another gigantic edental quadruped. Sixthly, a large animal, with an osseous coat in compartments, very like that of an armadillo. Seventhly, an extinct kind of horse. . . . Eighthly, a tooth of a Pachydermatous animal . . . a huge beast with a long neck like a camel. . . . Lastly the

Charles Darwin, whose one great journey in the "Beagle" uncovered the secrets of man's own origins

Toxodon, perhaps one of the strangest animals ever discovered: in size it equalled an elephant or megatherium, but the structure of its teeth . . . proves indisputably that it was intimately related to the Gnawers, the order which, at the present day includes most of the smallest quadrupeds: in many details it is allied to the *Pachydermata*: judging from the position of its eyes, ears, and nostrils, it was probably aquatic, like the Dugong and Manatee to which it is also allied. How wonderfully are the different orders, at the present time so well separated, blended together in different points of the structure of the *Toxodon*!"

All these remains, which were found embedded in a bank of shingle or else scattered about the beach, were encrusted with seashells, some of them of extinct species and the fact that these creatures had been alive "whilst the sea was peopled with most of its present inhabitants" was a matter of great importance and seemed to cast some doubt on the then widespread belief that no change had taken place in any species since the Creation, which, itself, had taken place in the course of only six days.

In January 1833, having visited the Falkland Islands, Fitzroy sailed into the Beagle Channel between Navarin Island and the mainland of Tierra del Fuego with the intention of returning to their home country three Fuegians whom he had educated at his own expense—York Minster, Jemmy Button and Fuegia Basket. York Minster was a powerful, surly man but, according to Darwin, "his affections were very strong towards a few friends on board; his intellect good". Jemmy Button, "whose name expresses his purchase-money", was everyone's favourite. He used to console Darwin during his attacks of seasickness by saying "Poor, poor fellow!" Jemmy was short and fat but a great dandy. Fuegia Basket was "a nice, modest, reserved young girl, with a rather pleasing but sometimes sullen expression, and very quick at learning anything, especially languages. . . . York Minster was very jealous of any attention paid to her; for it was clear he determined to marry her as soon as they were settled on shore." To complete the party there was a missionary, a Mr Matthews, whose unenviable job it was to go ashore with them to convert the rest of the heathens in this, one of the most inhospitable regions of the world where cannibalism was indulged in—only females being eaten, however.

The meeting with their own people was not a success. Jemmy had forgotten how to speak the language and refused to stay with them; but the encounter was enlivened by the male Fuegians, who were obsessive about facial hair and shaved with sea-shells.

PAMPAS

Montevideo

Remains of *Macrauchenia* (now extinct) found by Darwin

Bahia Blanca
Punta Alta

PATAGONIA

On the bleak coast of Patagonia, at Punta Alta and farther south, Darwin made discoveries — of the fossils of giant prehistoric creatures resembling smaller extant animals — which equalled the importance of his later work in the Galápagos

Giant sloth. Darwin found its bones in Patagonia

S Julian

Eventually, the trio, together with the unfortunate Mr Matthews, were put ashore at Ponsonby Sound, where Jemmy's tribe, the Tekeenika, lived and there, before the *Beagle* left, the sailors dug gardens for them and erected wigwams.

A week later Fitzroy returned. Mr Matthews was taken off, otherwise he would have lost his life or his reason. "From the time of our leaving, a regular system of plunder commenced; fresh parties of natives kept arriving.... York and Jemmy lost many things, and Matthews almost every thing which had not been concealed underground. ... Matthews described the watch he was obliged always to keep as most harassing; night and day he was surrounded by the natives who tried to tire him out by making an incessant noise close to his head.... Another party showed signs that they wished to strip him naked and pluck all the hairs out of his face and body. . . ."

After doubling the Horn in terrible weather Darwin had further opportunities of meeting other tribes whose way of life was exactly as it had been when Drake had sailed on this coast, 250 years before. "Whilst beholding these savages, one asks," he wrote, "whence have they come? What could have tempted, or what change compelled a tribe of men, to leave the fine regions of the north, to travel down the Cordillera or backbone of America, to invent and build canoes which are not used by the tribes of Chile, Peru, and Brazil, and then to enter on one of the most inhospitable countries within the limits of the globe ... yet ... there is no reason to believe that the Fuegians decrease in number; therefore we must suppose that they enjoy a sufficient share of happiness, of whatever kind it may

be, to render life worth having. Nature by making habit omnipotent, and its effects hereditary, has fitted the Fuegians to the climate and the productions of his miserable country."

From August 1833 to the end of September Darwin, accompanied by an Englishman named Harris on the first part of the journey —and by gauchos who hunted with *bolas* and the *lazo* (a kind of weighted lasso)—travelled north across the Argentinian pampas, seeing flocks of rhea, a form of ostrich of which he managed to acquire a living specimen, and the pichiego armadillo, which could bury itself in the earth in the time that it took a man to dismount from his horse.

The gaucho life

In the course of this journey, which took him all the way to Buenos Aires by way of Bahia Blanca, a distance of at least 600 miles, Darwin became even fitter than the gauchos: "There is high enjoyment in the independence of the Gaucho life," he wrote "to be able at any moment to pull up your horse, and say, 'Here we will pass the night'. The death-like stillness of the plain, the dogs keeping watch, the gipsy-group of Gauchos making their beds round the fire, have left in my mind a strongly-marked picture of this first night, which will never be forgotten."

Fitzroy's work on the coast of Patagonia was almost finished by the end of December. In the meantime Darwin had travelled from Buenos Aires to Santa Fé and up the Panama, contracting fever on the way, as well as making a journey from Mercedes to Montevideo. In March 1834, having again visited the Falkland Islands, the *Beagle* was back in Ponsonby Sound. "Soon a canoe with a little flag flying,

was seen approaching, with one of the men in it washing the paint off his face. This man was poor Jemmy,—now a thin haggard savage, with long disordered hair, and naked, except a bit of blanket round his waist. . . . As soon however as he was clothed, and the first flurry was over, things wore a good appearance. He dined with Captain Fitz Roy and ate his dinner as tidily as formerly. He told us that he had 'too much' (meaning enough) to eat, that he was not cold, that his relations were very good people, and that he did not wish to go back to England: in the evening we found out the cause of this great change in Jemmy's feelings, in the arrival of his young and nice-looking wife. With his usual good feeling, he brought two beautiful otter-skins for two of his best friends, and some spear-heads and arrows made with his own hands for the Captain. . . . Jemmy had lost all his property. He told us that York Minster had built a large canoe, and with his wife Fuegia, had several months since gone to his own country, and had taken farewell by an act of consumate villany; he had persuaded Jemmy and his mother to come with him, and then on the way deserted them by night, stealing every article of their property. Every soul on board was heartily sorry to shake hands with him for the last time. I do not doubt that he will be as happy as, perhaps happier than, if he had never left his own country. . . ."

In April that year Fitzroy, having again sailed up the coast of Patagonia, put into the mouth of the Santa Cruz River to carry out some repairs.

On April 18, Fitzroy and Darwin with 23 men and three whaleboats set off up the river. In the course of a long, hard journey they saw the smoke of Indian fires, the hoof-

Darwin and the *Beagle*

prints of their horses, herds of guanaco up to 500 strong and the pumas that stalked them; condors, that lived among the basaltic cliffs along the river (Darwin shot one with an eight-foot wing span), and carrion hawks.

On April 29 they had their first sight of the snow-covered peaks of the cordillera and were among great angular rocks that had come down from the mountains, more than 60 miles away. Five days later—to Darwin's great disappointment—when they were 140 miles from the Atlantic and about 60 from the Pacific, they were forced to turn back because of shortage of time and food.

By the time they reached the ship, Darwin was more cheerful. "Every one, excepting myself, had caused to be dissatisfied; but to me the ascent afforded a most interesting section of the great tertiary formation of Patagonia."

At the end of May they entered the Strait of Magellan, where they met "the famous so-called gigantic Patagonians, who gave us a cordial reception. Their height appears greater than it really is, from their large guanaco mantles, their long flowing hair, and general figure: on the average their height is about six feet, with some men taller and only a few shorter; and the women are also tall; altogether they are certainly the tallest race which we anywhere saw."

Once again Darwin saw the great woods on the shores of the strait of which he had written in his *Journal* during the previous February: "In the deep ravines, the death-like scene of desolation exceeded all description; outside it was blowing a gale, but in these hollows, not even a breath of wind stirred the leaves of the tallest trees. So gloomy, cold and wet was every part, that not even the fungi, mosses or ferns could flourish. In the valleys it was scarcely possible to crawl along, they were so completely barricaded by great mouldering trunks, which had fallen down in every direction. . . ."

What fascinated Darwin most of all was the kelp *Macrocystis pyrifera*, which grew everywhere in the waters of the strait, and was so strongly anchored to the rocks that it formed natural breakwaters against the heaviest gales. In one place Fitzroy found it growing from the bottom in 45 fathoms.

"The number of living creatures of all Orders whose existence intimately depends on the kelp, is wonderful. . . . We find exquisitely delicate structures, some inhabited by simple hydra-like polypi, others by more organised kinds. . . . On shaking the great entangled roots, a pile of small fish, shells cuttle-fish, crabs of all orders, sea-eggs, starfish, beautiful Holuthuriae, Planariae, and crawling nereidous animals of a multitude of forms, all fall out together . . . if in any

country a forest was destroyed, I do not believe nearly so many species of animals would perish as would here, from the destruction of the kelp. Amidst the leaves of this plant numerous species of fish live, which nowhere else could find food or shelter; with their destruction the many cormorants and other fishing birds, the otters, seals and porpoises, would soon perish also; and lastly the Fuegian savage, the miserable lord of this miserable land, would redouble his cannibal feast, decrease in numbers, and perhaps cease to exist."

They sighted Mount Sarmiento, a 6,800-foot-high mountain on the mainland of Tierra del Fuego. "Owing to the abundance of light reflected from the white and glittering surface," Darwin wrote, "no shadows were

The Galápagos Islands, situated 600 miles west of Ecuador, have been called the strangest islands in the world. Their lunar landscape of volcanic rock is the home of species of flora and fauna peculiar to the archipelago—land and marine iguanas, tortoises (*galapagos* means giant tortoise in Spanish), birds and plants which, central to Darwin's theory of evolution, were shown by him to have developed in isolation to the mainland and therefore to be unique

cast on any part; and those lines which intersected the sky could alone be distinguished: hence the mass stood out in the boldest relief. Several glaciers descended in a winding course from the upper great expanse of snow to the sea-coast: they may be likened to great frozen Niagaras; and perhaps these cataracts of blue ice are full as beautiful as the moving ones of water. . . ."

Fitzroy now decided to sail out of the strait into the Southern Ocean by way of the Magdalen Channel between Clarence and Santa Ines islands, where he would be on one of the most dangerous coasts in the world. "June 10 . . . we made the best of our way into the open Pacific. . . . We passed out between the East and West Furies; and a little farther northward there are so many breakers that the sea is called the Milky Way. One sight of such a coast is enough to make a landsman dream for a week about shipwrecks, peril, and death; and with this sight we bade farewell to Tierra del Fuego." It had taken them a month to pass through only half the strait.

From Valparaiso, which they reached on July 23, Darwin, still in search of further evidence that the land had risen from the sea,

made a journey into the surrounding country, where he found that "the proofs of the elevation of this whole line of coast are unequivocal: at the height of a few hundred feet old-looking shells are numerous, and I found some at 1300 feet".

Then "for the purpose of geologising the basal parts of the Andes, which alone are not shut up by the winter snow" he set off on a long journey into the mountains with two guasos, the Chilean equivalent of the gaucho of the pampas. He found them more subservient, and for this reason less agreeable. On the way he saw gold mines in which men brought up 200 pounds of stone on their backs from a depth of 450 feet, climbing on notched tree trunks.

In November Fitzroy took the *Beagle* south to Chiloé Island, where those Indians who were not converted to Christianity practised polygamy on an heroic scale, ". . . a cacique will sometimes have more than ten: on entering his house, the number may be told by that of the separate fires. Each wife lives a week in turn with the cacique; but all are employed in weaving ponchos, &c. for his profit. To be the wife of a cacique is an honour much sought after by the Indian women."

Here, Darwin secured a specimen of the very rare Chilotan fox by walking up behind it and hitting it on the head with his geological hammer. Here, too, he saw an extraordinary flight of petrels, *Adamastor cinereus*. "I do not think I have ever saw so many birds of any other sort together. . . . Hundreds of thousands flew in an irregular line for several hours in one direction. When part of the flock settled on the water the surface was blackened. . . ."

On February 20, at Valdivia on the coast of Chile, they experienced earth tremors that completely destroyed the city of Concepción and its port to the north. "A bad earthquake at once destroys our oldest associations," Darwin wrote, "the earth, the very emblem of solidity, has moved beneath our feet like a thin crust over fluid;—one second of time has created in the mind a strange idea of insecurity, which hours of recollection would not have produced."

When they did reach Concepción Darwin found that the land around the bay had been raised permanently by two or three feet and on an offshore island by ten feet.

In March 1835 Darwin's preoccupation with geology took him across the Andean cordillera by the dangerous Portillo Pass. The high point of his observations was the discovery of fossilized shells on the uppermost ridge, at over 13,000 feet above sea level.

In September they reached Chatham Island in the Galápagos Archipelago, where the sands were so hot that it was difficult to walk on them, even when wearing thick boots.

They remained among these volcanic islands for almost a month, Darwin identifying 26 kinds of land-birds, all of which, except one finch, were to be found nowhere else.

He also spent a lot of time studying the giant tortoises, *Testudo nigra*. Some were so heavy that it took eight men to lift them off the ground; yet in spite of their size they were able to travel about eight miles in two or three days. When Darwin overtook one, "the instant I passed, it would draw in its head and legs, and uttering a deep hiss fall to the ground with a heavy sound, as if struck dead".

Less agreeable to look at but equally interesting were the Galápagos lizards, both land and marine varieties.

The land lizards were only to be found on the central island of the group: "Like their brothers the sea-kind, they are ugly animals, of a yellowish orange beneath, and of a brownish red colour above: from their low facial angle they have a singularly stupid appearance. They are, perhaps, of a rather less size then the marine species. In their movements they are lazy and torpid. . . ."

Darwin was particularly struck by the variety of wildlife on these islands and noted that the majority of species of plants, shells, reptiles, birds, fish and insects were to be found nowhere else in the world. He deduced that their isolated habitat had allowed them to develop in peace and harmony in directions which a normal habitat, with its predators, would preclude. An entry in Darwin's *Journal* of 1837 shows how the pieces of the puzzle of life were beginning to fall into place in his mind: "In July opened first notebook on Transmutation of Species. Had been greatly struck from about the month of previous March on character of South American fossils, and species on Galapagos Archipelago. These facts (especially the latter) origin of all my views."

Disappointing Maoris

From the Galápagos they sailed to Matavai Bay, Tahiti, where Darwin did comparatively little in the way of original research.

Towards the end of December 1835 they reached the Bay of Islands, off the coast of the North Island of New Zealand. After having

known the Tahitians, Darwin found the Maoris, who were dressed in dirty blankets, disappointingly drab. They, too, were suffering from an overdose of white men. He was, however, very interested in the complex patterns which they had tattooed on their faces, "heraldic ornaments, distinctions far more intelligible to the natives than our own armorial bearings are to many of us".

He also approved the friendly ceremony of ongi, the nose-rubbing with which they greeted one another. Here, too, he learned of the giant Moa, *Dinornis robustus*, a flightless bird between ten and 12 feet tall which had only comparatively recently become extinct.

After visiting Sydney, they sailed via Tasmania and King George Sound in southwestern Australia to the Cocos Islands in the Indian Ocean, 1,700 miles northwest of Perth. A group of beautiful coral atolls, they were populated by people from the East Indies, who had been brought there as slaves.

Darwin found that plants and trees from Java and Sumatra, 600 miles away, had established themselves in the islands, their seeds having been carried by the Northwest Monsoon to the coast of Australia and from there to the islands by the northeast trade wind. Canoes from Java had also been driven up on the windward shores.

While studying the formation of coral atolls with Fitzroy, Darwin discovered that coral can only build a reef at a maximum depth of between 20 and 30 fathoms and that therefore their foundations must be mountains and

Close, as Pacific islands go, to the continental mainland of South America, the Galápagos Islands remained undisturbed by man—or indeed by any outside influence—until discovered by the Spanish in the 16th century. Understandably, the Spanish called the islands Las Encantadas, the Bewitched, after seeing the life-forms that had evolved in an isolation where predation was unknown. Monstrous tortoises (left), older perhaps than any living creature, stalked the volcanic surface. Nightmarish but completely vegetarian marine iguanas (below) stared fearlessly at the new arrivals and birds without the power of flight hopped aside. To Charles Darwin it was a laboratory of life itself, and from his observations of the small Galápagos finches (inset below left)—least dramatic of all the animals in the group—he drew much of the inspiration for his "Origin of Species"

The naturalist adventurers

islands which had slowly sunk beneath the water to that depth. In a process lasting, in Darwin's estimation, a million years, first a barrier reef was formed and then an atoll.

Here, too, he saw some remarkable creatures, a bluish-green fish of the genus *Scarus*, which fed on the coral, as did "the slimy disgusting Holuthuriae [allied to our starfish] which Chinese gourmands are so fond of"; an enormous crab which could open coconuts and extract the flesh; and the gigantic chama, a shellfish "into which, if a man were to put his hand, he would not, as long as the animal lived, be able to withdraw it".

One of Fitzroy's last ports of call was Pernambuco, on the coast of Brazil. "On the 19th of August we finally left the shores of Brazil," Darwin wrote. "I thank God, I shall never again visit a slave-country. To this day, if I hear a distant scream, it recalls with painful vividness my feelings, when passing a house near Pernambuco, I heard the most pitiable moans, and could not but suspect that some poor slave was being tortured, yet I knew that I was as powerless as a child even to remonstrate. Near Rio de Janeiro I lived opposite to an old lady who kept screws to crush the fingers of her female slaves. . . . I have seen a little boy, six or seven years old, struck thrice with a horse-whip (before I could interfere) on his naked head, for having handed me a glass of water not quite clean; I saw his father tremble at a mere glance from his master's eye."

The *Beagle* reached Falmouth on October 2, 1836, and there Darwin left her, "having lived on board the good little vessel for nearly five years".

All Darwin's field research was concentrated in this one great journey, for he never went abroad again. Suffering increasing illhealth (it is thought that he may have contracted Chaga's disease after allowing himself, presumably in the interests of science, to be bitten by the Bechuga Bug), he devoted the rest of his life to research and writing. His greatest work, *The Origin of Species* (to give it its full title, *On the Origin of Species by Means of Natural Selection or the Preservation of Favoured Races in the Struggle for Life*), appeared in 1859 and set the worlds of religion and natural sciences in a turmoil. The fossils at Bahia Blanca, with their similarity to living animals and the mutations of living creatures, even within the Galápagos Archipelago, spelt evolution to Darwin. His basic arguments were not altogether new— there were suggestions of his hypothesis in the writings of Malthus, and Wallace, who was working towards the same conclusion independently—but what Darwin had to say was, for the first time, backed by concrete evidence. He died, aged 73, in 1882.

IN THE EARLY YEARS of the 19th century Charles Waterton, squire of Walton Hall, Yorkshire, and the splendidly eccentric descendant of an ancient Catholic family, went to live in what had just become British Guiana and set off in 1812 on the first of four journeys into the interior. This first journey—in search of *curare*, the poison used by the Indians on their arrows and which he believed might be a cure for rabies—took him to the savannas near the Brazilian border, by way of the Demerara and Essequibo rivers. In 1816 and 1817 he made a second journey, spending six months collecting birds and observing wildlife in the neighbourhood of Pernambuco, Cayenne and Demerara.

Having visited Rome (where he climbed the lightning conductor on top of St Peter's and did a handstand on the head of an angel in the Castel Sant' Angelo) in the winter of 1817, he returned once more to South America and ascended the Essequibo, collecting in the course of a voyage of 11 months a menagerie which included some 200 birds, five armadillos, serpents, an ant bear and a sloth. His most exciting capture was a live cayman, which seven Indians drew out of the water on a barbed wooden hook. When it emerged Waterton jumped on its back and held its forelegs until its jaws could be bound. "It was", he wrote, "the first time I was ever on a cayman's back." In 1824, he was again on the Essequibo, studying exotic birds, vampire bats and sloths.

In 1825, he published his *Wanderings in South America*, which is illustrated with some highly original drawings of how the capture of the cayman was carried out.

Waterton was one of the first of the 19th-century explorers of South America—certainly the most eccentric of them—whose interest in natural history drew them to the continent. Among them was the Frenchman Auguste de Saint-Hilaire, who, in the course of five journeys into the interior collected 2,000 birds, 6,000 insects, 125 quadrupeds, 35 reptiles, 58 fishes and shells and 7,000 plants.

The shining example set by Humboldt attracted many Germans, including a distinguished soldier, Prince Maximilian of Wied-Neuwied, the Bavarians Johann Baptist von Spix and Carl Friedrich Phillipp von Martius and the Austrians Johann Pohl and Johann Natterer.

Most of these men explored in the eastern half of South America. The last four named had travelled out from Trieste on the ship carrying the Archduchess Leopoldina of Austria to join her future husband the Crown Prince of Brazil. Spix, a zoologist, and Martius, a botanist, who were both travelling on behalf of the King of Bavaria, set off from São Paulo along the line of the São Francisco River. In it, and on its banks, they saw vast quantities of pink spoonbills, storks, Jaburu and Tujuju birds, ducks, waterhens and plovers.

Crossing northeastern Brazil to the Amazon they ascended the river to its junction with the Japura. There they separated in order to cover more territory; Spix continuing up the main stream for several hundred miles to its junction with the Javari, Martius following the Japura to the Andes.

On their way through the primeval forest they saw enormous trees, one of which the nine Indians who accompanied them were unable to encircle with outstretched arms because it was 82 feet in circumference. This was the first scientific expedition to the Amazon since that of La Condamine. It eventually returned to Munich with 3,300 animals and 6,500 plant specimens.

The Mato Grosso

The Austrian expedition of Pohl, Natterer and Schott, together with an artist, Thomas Ender, who made hundreds of drawings and watercolours, explored the interior of Minas Gerais and Goiás. Natterer himself succeeded in crossing the Mato Grosso to the Guyapore River and descended it to the Amazon, while Pohl went down the Tocantins, which rises on the central plateau and enters the Pará near Belém, as far as Carolina.

Between 1826 and 1833 Alcide Dessalines d'Orbigny, a zoologist and ethnologist, on a mission for the Musée d'Histoire Naturelle at Paris, explored in southern Brazil, Uruguay, Argentina, Patagonia and west of the Andes in Chile, Bolivia and Peru. His *Voyage dans l'Amérique Méridionale* included a study of the Indian tribes, which he tried hard to save from destruction.

Another German, Robert Hermann Schomburgk, born at Freiberg in Silesia, began a series of explorations in 1835 from British Guiana. He was the first to reach the source of the Essequibo River in the Guiana highlands and discovered the lily, *Victoria Regia*. He crossed the country between the Essequibo and Esmeralda on the Orinoco, in the country visited by Humboldt, and laid out a line of astronomically determined points across the watershed.

In 1839, he set out from Esmeralda and almost succeeded in reaching the source of the Orinoco, returning by the Casiquiare Canal and the Negro, a journey of more than 3,000 miles.

Between 1843 and 1847, Comte François de Castelnau carried out extensive explorations, some of them in the regions visited by Natterer. He went down the Araguaia and ascended the Tocantins. He also discovered the source of the Paraguay in the central Mato Grosso, near Diamantino, beyond the great swamps through which it runs south, explored part of El Gran Chaco, a huge, still largely uninhabited region, and went on through Bolivia to Lake Titicaca, the largest lake in South America (3,500 square miles) and the highest in the world (12,500 feet).

Later he travelled from the Urubamba, which rises in the Andes northwest of Cuzco, down to the Ucayali, which rises in the dividing range between Peru and Brazil and then into the Amazon above Iquitos reaching Pará. On this journey all the astronomical and meteorological records were lost when his companion, the Vicomte d'Osery, was murdered by his two guides.

Between 1827 and 1832 the German Eduard Poeppig crossed the cordillera from Lima, went down the Huallaga, one of the headstreams of the Amazon, a 550-mile-long river which rises in the central Peruvian Andes, reached the Amazon and crossed the continent.

By the 1850s, three great areas remained to be explored and mapped—much of the Amazon basin, El Gran Chaco and parts of Patagonia.

In 1848, Henry Walter Bates, who had been a clerk in a brewery at Burton-on-Trent, and Alfred Russel Wallace, a schoolmaster at Leicester, inspired by reading the works of Humboldt and Darwin, and William Edwards's *A Voyage up the River Amazon*, decided to make an expedition of their own. From Pará (Belém) the two friends went up the Tocantins, the 1,680-mile-long river which rises on the central plateau of Brazil and enters the Pará near Belém. The following year, they made their way separately up the Amazon, meeting up in Manaus in January 1850. Here they split up again, "finding it more convenient to explore separate districts and collect independently".

Wallace set off up the Negro to the Casiquiare and the Uaupés. Bates continued upstream to Ega (now Tefé) and also made several expeditions up the Tapajós River. At Ega alone he discovered 500 new species of butterfly and during his 11 years in these unhealthy regions he collected more than 14,000 specimens of creatures, 8,000 of them unknown.

His book, *The Naturalist on the River Amazon*, is filled with marvellous observations on birds, beasts, plants, insects and man and the fantastic trees "fifty to sixty feet in girth at the point where they became cylindrical, 100 feet to the lowest branch". Of an insect (*Hetaira esmeralda*)—a description taken from the book at random—he wrote: "It has one spot only of opaque colouring on its wings, which is of a violet and rose hue;

but this is the only part visible when the insect is flying low over dead leaves in the gloomy shades where alone it is found, and then it looks like a wandering petal of a flower."

Bates, the brewery clerk from Burton, was to carve for himself a permanent niche in the pantheon of great naturalists by his observation of mimicry among butterflies, a behavioural phenomenon that is a biological study in itself.

Between 1860 and 1880, the pace of exploration gathered momentum in these wild and dangerous regions. Acevedo and Pinto, Chandless, Orton, Tucker, Church, Brown, Selfridge, Reyes, Crevaux, Labre and Coudreau probed deep into the Amazon

Percy Fawcett, whose death after he set out to find a lost city—with buildings and statues of quartz—in the depths of the Mato Grosso remains one of the great unsolved mysteries of 20th-century exploration

basin. Crevaux met an untimely end at the hands of native Indians as he explored the Gran Chaco, the marshy zone between the forests of Amazonia and the pampas.

South beyond the pampas, the bleak and arid uplands of Patagonia drew the attention of Argentine explorers, the greatest of whom was Carlos Moyano, during the late 1870s and early 1880s; but some years before, the region had been crossed from south to north by one of those splendid individuals who appear from time to time in the annals of exploration. He was George Chaworth Musters, a commander in the Royal Navy, who made an astonishing journey through Patagonia from Punta Arenas on the Strait of Magellan to the mouth of the River Negro, travelling with a band of aborigines of the Tehuelche tribe who regarded him as their king, and from Santa Cruz following the

River Chico to the foothills of the Andes.

The first of the 20th century's explorers of South America, and one of its most important, was an American surgeon, Hamilton Rice, who in 1907 began the systematic exploration of every tributary in the vast northwestern basin of the Amazon. He tried to reach the source of the Orinoco, but in its upper reaches the tribes were so ferocious that Rice had to turn back. The source was not located until 1951, by a Franco–Venezuelan expedition.

In 1925, he explored in Brazilian Guiana and was one of the earlier surveyors to make use of wireless and seaplanes in South America. The hero of exploration in the southern Amazon basin was a Brazilian military engineer, Colonel Cândido Rondón, who on three occasions penetrated the Mato Grosso in conditions of extreme hazard, for the Indians of the region were among the most unwelcoming. Rondón's personal bravery eventually won them over—a factor which was to prove important in 1913, when the Brazilian teamed up with a former president of the United States, Theodore Roosevelt, in what was to prove one of the most famous modern journeys in South America.

The Rondón–Roosevelt expedition set out early in 1914 along the waterway they called the River of Doubt. The former president describes the journey.

"On February 27, 1914, shortly after midday, we started down the River of Doubt into the unknown . . . no civilized man, no white man, had ever gone down or up this river or seen the country through which we were passing. The lofty and matted forest rose like a green wall on either hand. The trees were stately and beautiful. The looped and twisted vines hung from them like great ropes. Masses of epiphytes grew both on the dead trees and the living; some had huge leaves like elephants' ears. . . ."

It was no easy trip. On the way they encountered torrential rain, endless rapids and whirlpools in which one of the party was swept away and drowned; another was murdered; the doctor's undershirt and various other items of equipment were devoured in a single night by carregadores ants; they were bitten by horseflies as big as bumblebees, and a concealed Indian killed one of the expedition's dogs with a poisoned arrow.

Finally, after six weeks, they entered the Madeira River, having "put on the map a river about 1500 kilometres in length running from just south of the 13th degree to north of the 5th degree and the biggest affluent of the Madeira".

In 1906, an English surveyor, Percy Fawcett, began the first of the long series of explorations when he undertook the work of demarcating the new frontier between Bolivia

Africa: a new challenge

and Brazil. It took him up the unknown waters of the Alto Acre and then down the Abuna River, tributaries of the Madeira.

He then performed the same work on the eastern frontier of Bolivia with Brazil, where he explored the River Verde, which forms part of the boundary. It was impossible to drag the boats up the rapids so they were abandoned, together with the provisions. "For nearly three weeks we lived upon occasional palm tops," Fawcett wrote. "We were eaten up by insects; were drenched by a succession of violent storms with a southerly wind, bitterly cold for wet and blanketless people." Nevertheless, they reached open country near the source of the river in the Serra de Huanchaca. On this journey five members of the party died.

After learning of the outbreak of the First World War, Fawcett returned to England and was a colonel when the conflict came to an end. The powerful magnet that was South America continued to exert its power over him and, more, he was now firmly convinced that there were still to be found traces of lost civilizations deep in the Amazonian hinterland.

He had first heard the rumours when conducting his boundary work before the war, and they had now become something of an obsession with him. The conviction grew and grew that there remained in South America the evidence which would show that there once existed a vast continent across the southern Atlantic Ocean, and that there was a lost city with buildings and statues of quartz.

Fawcett managed to obtain support for his quest from an American newspaper group, and in 1925 set out with his son Jack and Jack's friend, Raleigh Rimell, from Cuiabá, on the edge of the Mato Grosso.

From Cuiabá he intended to go north with mules across the watershed of the Mato Grosso and descend a river called the Paranatinga by canoe until he reached approximately 10S. He would then turn eastwards to the Xinqu, a 1,200-mile-long river which flows to the Amazon delta, and from there reach the Tocantins by way of its principal tributary, the Araguaia. His final destination was Barra do Rio Grande on the São Francisco River.

Nothing more was heard of Fawcett or his companions. In 1928, Commander G. M. Dyott succeeded in tracing their route and actually found some objects belonging to them, including an airtight case. They were almost certainly killed by a hostile tribe, but a strange belief that he might have survived persisted for many years, although Dyott's evidence of Fawcett's end seemed to have been confirmed by another expedition along Dyott's route in 1933. It was a mysterious end to the search for an ancient mystery.

"THAT AS NO SPECIES of information is more ardently desired, or more generally useful, than that which improves the science of Geography; and as the vast continent of Africa, notwithstanding the efforts of the Ancients, and the wishes of the Moderns, is still in great measure unexplored, the members of this Club do form themselves into an Association for Promoting the Discovery of the Inland Parts of that Quarter of the World."

With this sonorous resolution, passed on June 9, 1788, at the St Albans Tavern, London, the Saturday Club, a gentlemen's dining club, became the Association for Promoting the Discovery of the Interior Parts of Africa. The aims of the Association and the explorers it sent into the field were to discover the whereabouts of the River Niger and of the by now equally fabulous city of Timbuktu, both of which had been reached by the Arab traveller Ibn Battuta in 1335, but most of whose records had disappeared.

The Association lost no time in despatching its first explorers. Soon after its foundation Simon Lucas, an Arabic-speaking oriental interpreter at the Court of St James's, set off for Tripoli, to cross the desert. He reached Marzuq, 500 miles to the south, before being forced to turn back.

At the same time John Ledyard, a highly eccentric American traveller, who, starting from Ostend, had got as far as central Russia on a walk round the world, and had been on Cook's last expedition, began preparations for an attempt to find the Niger by travelling westwards from Cairo. He died there after drinking an unseemly mixture of vitriol and tartar emetic in an attempt to quell a stomach upset. Ledyard had recommended himself to the Association's secretary by replying, "Tomorrow morning", when asked when he would be ready to leave London.

More successful—and indeed he might have reached the Niger if he had been more generously treated by the Association—was Daniel Houghton, a gallant but impetuous major with a wife and family to support. He was given £260, part of which was to be invested in trade goods, and £10 for his wife, and set off from Pisania, a trading post on the Gambia run by a Dr John Laidley, who was to act as his postbox to the outside world.

From this point, travelling with five mules and a horse, Houghton (who spoke Mandingo, the local language) reached Medina, the capital of the Kingdom of Woolli. While he was there a fire destroyed part of the town and most of his equipment, including his gun. Wounded by a replacement gun, which burst in his hands, racked with fever, and with only a couple of animals (his interpreter had made off with the remainder), he struggled on into

the Kingdom of Bondou, where the monarch relieved him of still more of his possessions. His last letter, dated September 1, 1791, from Simbing gave the news that he had been robbed of all his trade goods. Nevertheless, he had learned two vital facts: that the Niger flowed eastwards and that quite large vessels navigated it, and in one of these he proposed to travel when he reached the river.

He never reached it. Five years later Mungo Park learned that he had joined some Moors going north from Bambouk to Tisheet, and that near Jarra they had left him to die.

The next agent to be sent out from the Association's headquarters in Soho Square was Mungo Park, a tall, handsome young doctor of 24, the seventh son of a Scottish farmer near Selkirk. He had sailed to Sumatra in an East Indiaman and returned with a botanical collection, which he had presented to Sir Joseph Banks. This recommended him to Banks and the Association briefed him "to ascertain the course and, if possible, the rise and termination of the River Niger, and that he shall use his utmost exertion to visit the principal towns or cities in its neighbourhood, particularly Tombuctoo [sic] and Hausa."

Park shipped to the Gambia and spent the latter half of 1795 at Dr Laidley's house at Pisania learning Mandingo before setting off on his great journey accompanied by some slave merchants, Johnson, a Negro servant, a slave boy named Demba, who turned back when he reached the Muslim country of Mali, one horse and two asses. Park had with him some beads, amber and tobacco as currency, a pocket sextant, compass and thermometer as scientific instruments, a minimum of food, two sporting guns, four pistols, some changes of linen and an umbrella.

His route took him first northeast on Houghton's route towards the Senegal, into the Kingdom of Woolli, where he was well received by the ruler, then across the Falemé into Bondou, where the king relieved him of his umbrella and his coat.

On his way through the various Negro kingdoms he was progressively robbed of his possessions, and at Benown he was imprisoned by the "Moorish" king, Ali, for four months. All Muslims were Moors to Park. "Never", he wrote, "did any period of my life pass away so heavily; from sunrise to sunset was I obliged to suffer with an unruffled countenance, the insults of the rudest savages on earth."

At the end of June 1796 he succeeded in escaping alone with his wretched horse (Johnson having refused to continue beyond Benown) and a year after landing in Africa reached Ségou, some 700 miles from the Atlantic, where he saw "with infinite pleasure the great object of my mission; the long-

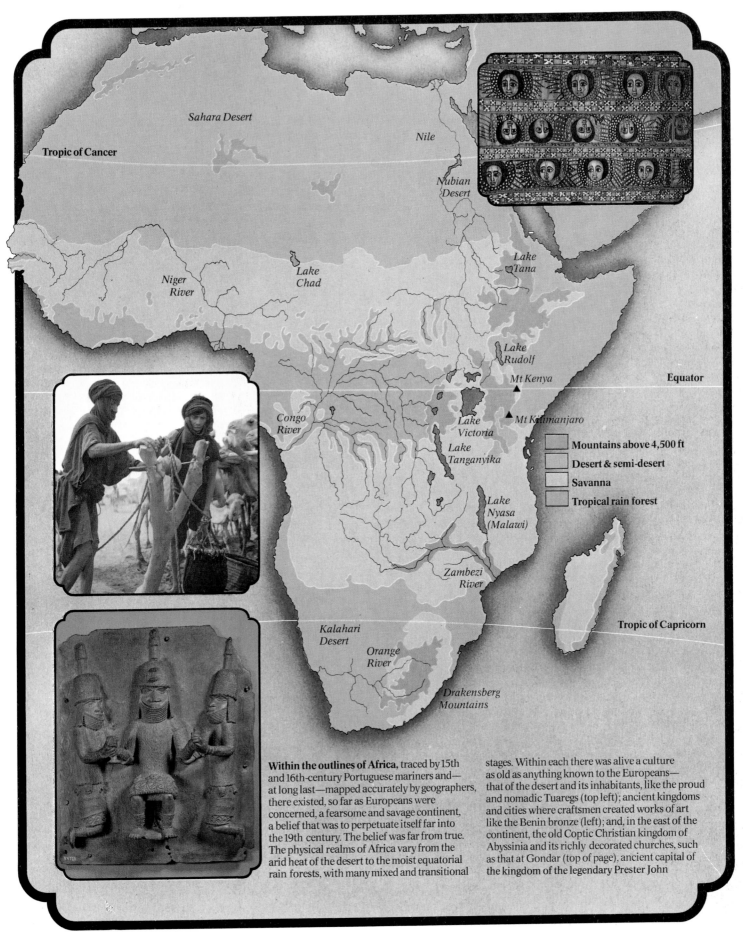

Sahara Desert

Nile

Tropic of Cancer

Nubian Desert

Lake Tana

Niger River

Lake Chad

Lake Rudolf

Mt Kenya

Equator

Congo River

Mt Kilimanjaro

Lake Victoria

Lake Tanganyika

Mountains above 4,500 ft

Desert & semi-desert

Savanna

Tropical rain forest

Lake Nyasa (Malawi)

Zambezi River

Tropic of Capricorn

Kalahari Desert

Orange River

Drakensberg Mountains

Within the outlines of Africa, traced by 15th and 16th-century Portuguese mariners and—at long last—mapped accurately by geographers, there existed, so far as Europeans were concerned, a fearsome and savage continent, a belief that was to perpetuate itself far into the 19th century. The belief was far from true. The physical realms of Africa vary from the arid heat of the desert to the moist equatorial rain forests, with many mixed and transitional stages. Within each there was alive a culture as old as anything known to the Europeans—that of the desert and its inhabitants, like the proud and nomadic Tuaregs (top left); ancient kingdoms and cities where craftsmen created works of art like the Benin bronze (left); and, in the east of the continent, the old Coptic Christian kingdom of Abyssinia and its richly decorated churches, such as that at Gondar (top of page), ancient capital of the kingdom of the legendary Prester John

A new challenge

sought-for, majestic Niger, glittering to the morning sun, as broad as the Thames at Westminster, and flowing to the eastward...."

From here he pressed on a little farther to Silla. Here, with the rainy season coming on, he turned back to the Gambia by a more direct and southerly route.

While Park was engaged on his first expedition to the Niger the Association sent out Friedrich Hornemann, a young German Arabic-speaking theological student, to follow the route originally intended for Ledyard. Of all the Association's agents, apart from John Lewis Burckhardt, who set out for the Niger in 1812, he was the best prepared linguistically and scientifically. Hornemann travelled from Cairo to Marzuq in the Fezzan by way of the Siwa Oasis, he and his companion Frendenburgh, a convert to Islam who posed as his servant. They were the first known European travellers in North Africa to disguise themselves successfully as Muslims, Hornemann giving as a reason for his pigmentation and imperfect knowledge of Arabic the fact that he was a Mameluke.

Frendenburgh died of fever at Marzuq and Hornemann's last letter to the Association was sent from Tripoli in April 1800, when he was on the point of joining a caravan for Bornu by Lake Chad (still unknown to Europeans), from where he hoped to reach the Gulf of Guinea by way of Katsina. It was later established that he passed beyond Katsina and died just short of the Niger at Bokani, the first known European to cross the Sahara since Roman times and the first to set eyes on Lake Chad.

Park, who worked as a country doctor in Scotland after his return from Africa in 1799 (his book, *Travels in the Interior Districts of Africa*, became a best-seller), went back to Africa in 1805. In April that year he left Pisania with a large, unwieldy expedition of about 40 Europeans, including 30 soldiers from the garrison at Goree. It was the beginning of the rainy season, a bad moment to set off with untried men (the soldiers were wearing thick red coats), and by the time Park reached the Niger at Bamako, where it

A group of slaves awaiting shipment from West Africa to the American colonies. The trade in humanity was already old when the Portuguese first visited the coast

was in flood, "rolling its immense stream along the plain", only 11 Europeans were still alive. The rest were dead from malaria and dysentery. More men died at Sansanding, a town of about 11,000 inhabitants a little to the east, where two months were spent preparing for the journey down the Niger to the sea—for by now Park was convinced that the river flowed to the Atlantic. Here two decayed canoes were converted into a vessel 40 feet long and six feet wide.

On November 19 Park set out on the last stage of the journey with the only survivors—a Lieutenant Martyn and three soldiers (one of them insane), three slaves and one Amadi Fatouma as guide and interpreter. A thousand miles downriver, past Timbuktu and Gao at the rapids of Bussa, Park and his European colleagues were either drowned or killed in an encounter with the forces of the king of Haoussa, 500 miles short of the Niger delta.

Park had failed. He had been rash and impatient in his dealings with some of the petty

For centuries, Arab traders had rounded up slaves in tropical Africa to take them to the markets of the Near East (above right). Livingstone estimated that ten Negroes were killed for every six captured, and out of the six, five died

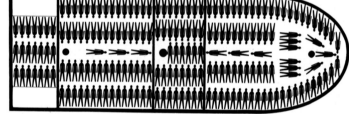
Shipment to the Americas was equally horrifying. Slaves were packaged with a grisly skill into ships' holds (below) and rarely more than half survived. Stories of slavery horrified Europe and renewed its interest in Africa

rulers he encountered along the river, but he had also behaved heroically. The news that the Niger turned to the south eventually reached England.

Park's wife never gave up hope that her husband was alive and one of her three sons, Thomas, a midshipman in the Royal Navy, was given leave in 1827 to search for his father. He died of fever on his way to Bussa.

In 1822, the British Colonial Office sponsored another expedition, the Bornou Mission, to the interior from Tripoli. It consisted of Walter Oudney, a Scottish naval surgeon and botanist, Lieutenant Hugh Clapperton, another naval officer, and a soldier, Major Dixon Denham, an unpleasant man who spent much time sending the British Consul at Tripoli scurrilous reports about Clapperton, suggesting that he had homosexual relations with his native servants.

By the time their caravan reached Marzuq they were in poor health from fever; but finally, on February 4, 1823, "the great lake Tchad, glowing with the golden rays of the sun in its strength, appeared to be within a mile of the spot on which we stood. . . . My

heart bounded within me at the prospect, for I believed this lake to be the key to the great object of our search. . ." Denham wrote in his *Narrative of Travels and Discoveries in Northern and Central Africa*, in which he characteristically took most of the credit for the success of the expedition.

From here Denham went southeast to reach the Chari River, which feeds the lake, while Clapperton and Oudney moved westwards to Kano. Clapperton reached it alone, for Oudney died on the way.

From Kano, Clapperton reached Sokoto, where he was about 150 miles from the Niger, but was unable to find a guide to take him to it and was forced to return to Kukawa. From there, after rejoining Denham, he returned to Tripoli. They had not been able to find the answer to the problem of the Niger, but they had crossed the Sahara, discovered Lake Chad and learned a great deal about the caravan route and the country between the lake and the Niger.

In 1824, Major Alexander Laing was ordered by the Colonial Secretary, Lord Bathurst, to attempt to reach the source of the Niger by way of Timbuktu. His route took him first south into the Sahara and then north to Ghadames, a town that had not been visited by any known European; and from here he followed a caravan route along the edge of the shifting sand dunes of the Grand Erg Oriental to Ain Salah and joined a large caravan of merchants for the dangerous passage through the country of the Ulad Delim, an Arab tribe who were sworn enemies of the Ahaggar Tuareg ("the people of the veil") and who disputed with them the road to the south. Sixteen days out they were attacked by Tuareg while encamped in Wadi Ahennet and Laing was dreadfully injured. Nevertheless, on August 18, 1826, he reached Timbuktu, never to return. Nearly six weeks after his arrival he was killed by Tuareg at his camp outside the city.

Among Laing's preoccupations had been the fear that Clapperton might precede him. In November 1825, with a party which included a young Cornishman, Richard Lander, Clapperton had travelled from Bagadrion, the Bight of Benin, to Bussa on the Niger. From Bussa, Clapperton and Lander succeeded in reaching Sokoto, where Clapperton became ill with fever. He died on April 18, 1827, one of the great African explorers, to whom real fame has been denied.

It was left to Lander, with one slave boy, to make the return journey to the coast; he did not reach England until July 1828. It was the French explorer Réné Caillié, a young and penniless man from a humble family, who finally succeed in reaching Timbuktu and returning from it in one piece. As a boy he had been inspired to become an explorer while reading Robinson Crusoe. From 1824 to 1827 he lived in Senegal, preparing to reach Timbuktu, which, like most Europeans, he imagined to be infinitely more rich and grand than it was, learning Arabic and living in every way as a local inhabitant.

He set off in April 1827 from the Rio Nuñez north of Sierra Leone. "Our caravan consisted of five free Mandingoes, three slaves, my Foulah porter, my guide, and his wife. All except the last two and myself carried enormous burdens." In June they reached the upper waters of the Niger at Kouroussa, having suffered severely from scurvy and having walked the best part of 1,000 miles. The following March Caillié reached the island of Djenne in the Bani River and the marshes above its confluence with the Niger.

From Djenne he travelled down the Niger to Kabara, the port of Timbuktu, and on April 20 he reached the city. "I looked around," he wrote, "and found that the sight before me, did not answer my expectations of Timbuctoo. The city presented, at first view, nothing but a mass of ill-looking houses, built of earth. Nothing was to be seen in all directions but immense plains of quicksand of a yellowish white colour. The sky was a pale red as far as the horizon; all nature wore a dreary aspect, and the most profound silence prevailed; not even the warbling of a bird was to be heard. Still though I cannot account for the impression, there was something imposing in the aspect of a great city, raised in the midst of sands, and the difficulties surmounted by its founders cannot fail to excite admiration."

This was the desert city that, since the 12th century, had been the hub of the North African world, where salt and food and Guinea gold had changed hands and, later, merchandise from Europe; a city where, according to Leo Africanus, there were plates and sceptres of solid gold, "some whereof weigh 1300 pounds". Now the gold-fields were largely exhausted and the city was a rather banal place of mud houses, dependent for its food supplies on what came down the Niger from Djenne and other places. Only two mosques testified to whatever grandeur it may have formerly possessed. Here, Caillié remained for a fortnight, well treated by the Muslims as he had been all along the way, until he left to cross the Sahara northwards with a caravan of more than a thousand camels, slaves and merchandise. After a terrifying and dangerous journey through the eastern Sahara he reached Tangier in July 1828, where the French authorities refused to believe that he had made the journey at all. He was subsequently awarded 10,000 francs by the Geographical Society of Paris, founded seven years earlier.

The mouth of the Niger was finally discovered by Richard Lander and his brother John on an expedition sent out by Lord Bathurst. They set off in February 1830 from Badagri, at a time when its king was setting up arrangements for a mass sacrifice of 300 human beings. They reached Bussa on June 17 and then travelled 100 miles upriver to a place called Bin Yauri, where they found a book of logarithms which had belonged to Park. From there they travelled downstream in canoes, were robbed, came close to being massacred and were imprisoned by the king of Ibo, who succeeded in obtaining a ransom for their release of goods to the value of 35 slaves. They eventually reached the sea at a settlement called Brass Town on the Nun branch of the river in November.

As a result of this feat Richard Lander received the Royal Premium from the newly founded Royal Geographical Society. The Niger had now yielded up most of its secrets.

Desert tribesmen; they live a life which has remained unchanged since time out of mind

Across the Sahara

THE YEARS FOLLOWING Caillié's journey to Timbuktu were not propitious ones for the Europeans who attempted to emulate him. Many perished, either at the hands of the Tuareg or from disease. These were the years when France extended its influence into Algeria and Morocco and distinguished German scientific explorers—Berbrugger, von Puekler-Muscau, Wagner and von Müller—carried out their explorations in these regions.

In the 1850s the greatest and most scientific explorer was Heinrich Barth, an Arabic-speaking archaeologist, historian, geographer and law student from the University of Berlin. At 28 he joined an expedition sent out by the British Government, which was intended not only to explore the regions about Lake Chad and westwards to the Niger, but also to negotiate trade treaties with the rulers in West Sudan before carrying on across the continent in an attempt to reach Zanzibar.

This well-equipped expedition was commanded by James Richardson, who had already made a successful journey to Ghat, a once-important caravan centre; the third member was another German, a geologist named Adolf Overweg.

They left Tripoli in April 1850 and crossed the Sahara to Marzuq and Ghat. From here they reached Agadès by way of the Aïr Mountains and now the expedition split up, Richardson taking a direct route to Lake Chad while Barth and Overweg travelled farther to the west. A further subdivision took place when Barth went off alone to Katsina and Kano, passing himself off as a Muslim scholar. Of Kano, a town of about 30,000 people, he wrote: "The great advantage of Kano is that commerce and manufacturers go hand in hand, and that almost every family has its share in them. There is really something grand in this kind of industry, which spreads as far as Murzuk, Ghat, and even Tripoli; to the west, not only to Timbuktu, but in some degree even as far as the shores of the Atlantic, the very inhabitants of Arguin dressing in the cloth woven and dyed in Kano . . . in fact, if

Timbuktu, "a mass of ill-looking houses" to Réné Caillié, the first European to reach there and return alive

we consider that this industry is not carried on here as in Europe, in immense establishments, degrading man to the meanest conditions of life, but that it gives employment and support to entire families without compelling them to sacrifice their domestic habits, we must presume that Kano ought to be one of the happiest countries of the world. . . ."

By the time Overweg and Barth reached Kukawa, in Bornu, by Lake Chad, Richardson had died of fever and Barth took command. The Sultan was interested in trade but not in the abolition of slavery and from there, after visiting Lake Chad—which Barth found to be unsurveyable because it was impossible to penetrate the swamps—he travelled with Overweg into the Adamawa country and reached Yolu on the Benue River, a great tributary of the Niger, which flowed from east to west, finding that it was navigable by steamers. Altogether they spent about 15 months in the region of Lake Chad, Barth making a great, lone journey southeastwards to Bougomène on the Chari River early in 1852, where he was imprisoned by the Sultan. Soon afterwards Overweg died at Bornu of malaria, aged 29. In November Barth set off for Timbuktu.

Accumulated rubbish

"Having then traversed the rubbish which has accumulated round the ruined clay wall of the town," he wrote on September 7, 1853, when he finally reached it, "and left on one side a row of dirty reed huts which encompass the whole of the place, we entered the narrow streets and lanes, or, as the people of Timbuktu say, the tijeraten, which scarcely allowed two horses to proceed abreast. But I was not a little surprised at the populus and wealthy character which this quarter of the town, the Sane-Gungu, exhibited, many of the houses rising to the height of two storeys. . . ."

Here he remained until May the following year, then sailed down the river to Say and reached Kukawa in December, where he was joined by another German explorer, E. Vogel, who had been sent out to carry on exploration south of Lake Chad, from which he hoped to reach the Nile. Vogel was murdered at Ouadai, 500 miles to the west of the lake.

Barth finally left Kukawa in May 1855, and reached Tripoli at the end of August that year. He had made a most remarkable series of journeys and—what was even more important—he had recorded them. No travellers up to this time in these regions had shown such genius for getting on with the African people. He was the only one, too, who learned about them and their history, describing them in their own right, not comparing their societies and methods of government to any European model; he had explored a tract

Exploration inland from the west coast of Africa attracted the British, whose traders were settled on the Gambia at Pisania. Beyond there, travellers were at the mercy of the whims of local potentates. The first to make a journey into the heartlands was Mungo Park (above), who, in 1796, reached the Niger at Ségou to confirm that it flowed eastwards. On his second journey, in the rainy season, he followed the Niger as far as the Bussa rapids and died there in 1806, probably drowned while under attack from natives

> **Mungo Park, 1795-7**
>
> **Hugh Clapperton, Dixon Denham, Walter Oudney, 1822-5**
>
> **Alexander Laing, 1825-6**
>
> **Réné Caillié, 1827-8**
>
> **Richard & John Lander, 1830-2**
>
> **Heinrich Barth, 1850-5**

St Lo...

Mungo
Pis...

Penniless and uneducated, Réné Caillié was inspired by Park's travels, which he determined to emulate for the honour of France—and for a 10,000-franc prize offered by the French Geographical Society. He learned Arabic, passed himself off as a Muslim and set out from Sierra Leone for Timbuktu, which he had to visit to obtain the prize. He reached it in 1828, but was disappointed in the "mass of ill-looking houses". After a 2,000-mile journey across the Sahara, he arrived home—and received his prize

The white man's grave. "Beware and take care of the Bight of Benin; for one that comes out, there are forty goes in..." The seafarer's shanty sums up the endemic dangers of West Africa. Tropical medicine has now brought under control the three deadly diseases—malaria, bilharzia and sleeping sickness—which earned for the region the title of the "white man's grave". The vectors, or carriers, of all three diseases are small forms of life: the anopheles mosquito (malaria); water snail (bilharzia) and the tsetse fly (sleeping sickness)

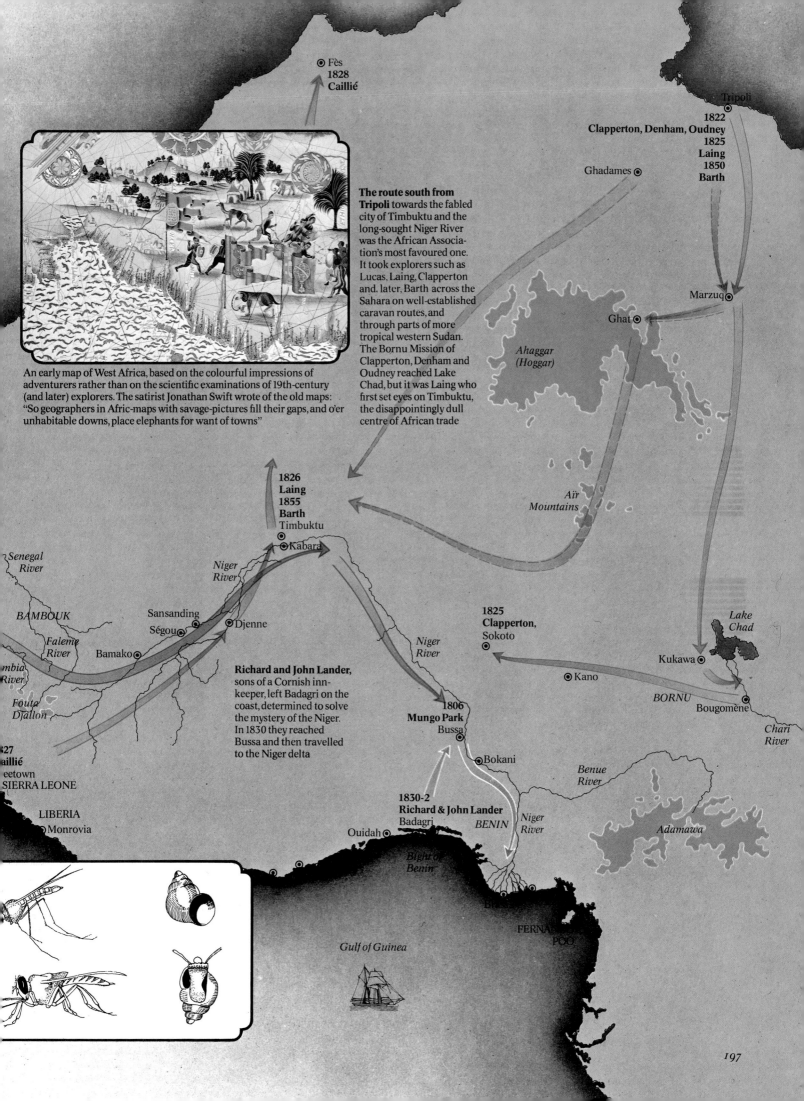

Fès
1828
Caillié

Tripoli
1822
Clapperton, Denham, Oudney
1825
Laing
1850
Barth

Ghadames ⊙

Marzuq ⊙

Ghat ⊙

Ahaggar (Hoggar)

The route south from Tripoli towards the fabled city of Timbuktu and the long-sought Niger River was the African Association's most favoured one. It took explorers such as Lucas, Laing, Clapperton and, later, Barth across the Sahara on well-established caravan routes, and through parts of more tropical western Sudan. The Bornu Mission of Clapperton, Denham and Oudney reached Lake Chad, but it was Laing who first set eyes on Timbuktu, the disappointingly dull centre of African trade

Air Mountains

An early map of West Africa, based on the colourful impressions of adventurers rather than on the scientific examinations of 19th-century (and later) explorers. The satirist Jonathan Swift wrote of the old maps: "So geographers in Afric-maps with savage-pictures fill their gaps, and o'er unhabitable downs, place elephants for want of towns"

1826
Laing
1855
Barth
Timbuktu
⊙ Kabara

Senegal River

Niger River

BAMBOUK

Faleme River

Sansanding
Ségou ⊙   ⊙ Djenne
Bamako ⊙

mbia River

Fouta Djallon

Niger River

1825
Clapperton,
Sokoto
⊙

Lake Chad

Kukawa ⊙

⊙ Kano

BORNU

Bougomène ⊙

Chari River

Richard and John Lander, sons of a Cornish inn-keeper, left Badagri on the coast, determined to solve the mystery of the Niger. In 1830 they reached Bussa and then travelled to the Niger delta

1806
Mungo Park
Bussa

⊙ Bokani

Niger River

Benue River

327
aillié
eetown
SIERRA LEONE

LIBERIA
⊙ Monrovia

1830-2
Richard & John Lander
Badagri

BENIN

Niger River

Ouidah ⊙

⊙

Bight of Benin

B

FERNA
POO

Adamawa

Gulf of Guinea

197

of Africa which extended over 24 degrees of latitude and 20 degrees from east to west.

A less scientifically inclined traveller, but equally indefatigable, was Gerhard Rohlfs, a German who enjoyed exploration for its own sake and was fascinated by the Muslim character and way of life. He served as a soldier in the French Foreign Legion and later as a surgeon with the forces of the Grand Sherif in Morocco. In 1862, passing himself off as a Muslim, he reached Tafilelt with a caravan from Fez, the first European since Caillié to do so. The following year he tried to reach Timbuktu but failed and then, after being the first European to reach Tuat, in 1864 he was persuaded by Barth to try and discover the relationship between the rivers flowing into Lake Chad and the Niger–Benue system. In 1865, he crossed from Tripoli to Bornu, reached the Benue and sailed down it and the Niger to the Gulf of Guinea.

In 1869, another German, Gustav Nachtigal, physician to the Bey of Tunis (in which position he had acquired a great knowledge of Arab life), was sent by the King of Prussia to take gifts to the Sultan of Bornu at Kukawa. At the court he found that the Sultan's soldiers dressed in extraordinary costumes which ranged from the vestigial to suits of armour and others wearing yellow, green and red costumes, like harlequins. Nachtigal also visited Timbuktu and finally reached Cairo by way of Ouadai and Darfur.

Great explorations were also made by the French, who began a systematic campaign of military conquest in the Sahara in the 1890s, and by the Italians Matteucci and Massari, who, in 1882, set off from Suakin on the Red Sea and travelled to the Niger by way of Kordofan, Ouadai, Bornu and Kano.

Of the innumerable modern explorers of the Sahara the most recent to use the ancient method of camel transport was the English writer Geoffrey Moorhouse, who, in October 1972, set off from Chinguetti in Mauritania to make the 3,000-mile crossing of the continent to the Nile, by way of Timbuktu, a journey never before attempted by a European. In March the following year with one companion, Ibrahim, he reached Tamanrasset, where he was forced to give up, the camels having died one by one, the explorers themselves being *in extremis*; but having crossed 2,000 miles of the Sahara, the last 300 on foot, "I knew I could not go on," he wrote in his book *The Fearful Void*. "I did not wish to go back. But I must do this, I must return to my own people. Only with them could I replenish what had been poured out of me in the ride across Mauritania, in the collapse before Timbuktu, in the sandstorms near the well of Asler, and in the long march with Ibrahim by the edge of the Tanzerouft."

F OR NON-MUSLIMS ARABIA was a dangerous region. The holy places, Mecca and Medina, were completely denied to them. Discovery within the sacred precincts of Mecca meant, under the old law, as the explorer Burton wrote, "a choice thrice offered between circumcision and death".

Arabia is, evidently, a land of extremes, both physical and spiritual: of heat and cold, abundance and nothingness. Of the splendours and miseries of this land, no European knew more than the Victorian explorer Charles Doughty. "The desert day dawns not little and little, but it is noontide in an hour. The sun, entering as a tyrant upon the waste landscape, darts upon us as a torment of fiery beams, not to be remitted till the far off evening."

The first non-Muslim and European to travel in Arabia after Covilhão's presumed journey to Mecca in 1492 was Ludovico di Varthema. Having reached Damascus in April 1503 by way of "Baruti", Tripoli, Aleppo and Ma'an, Varthema managed to enrol himself in the Mameluke escort to the great Haj (pilgrim) caravan, which was on the point of setting off on the annual pilgrimage to Mecca. (To do this he must have become ostensibly a Muslim.)

The caravan reached Mecca some time after the middle of May and the accuracy of the account that Varthema wrote of it was on the whole confirmed by later travellers. In the midst of the city was Al Haram, the Great Mosque. There, probably the first European to do so, he saw the Kaaba, "The Cube". This is the Holy House of Islam, which Muslims believe was constructed in heaven 2,000 years before the creation of the world, where it was adored by the angels before its re-erection on Earth by Adam below the point it had occupied in heaven.

After remaining at Mecca for 20 days, Varthema deserted from the Mameluke guard and was hidden in the house of an Arab merchant, who believed the lies Varthema told him: that he was the most skilful cannon founder in the world, and that he hated Christians (these together made a powerful recommendation).

Three days later, after the Haj caravan had left for Syria without him, Varthema joined a caravan bound for Jiddah and sailed from there to Aden.

At Aden, he was accused of being a Christian spy, loaded with chains and cast into prison, from where he was sent into the interior to be interrogated by the Sultan of Aden.

After a 160-mile camel journey to Rada' that took eight days, Varthema failed to impress the Sultan. He ordered Varthema to say the words "La ilah illa Allah; Mohammed

The challenge of Arabia. Richard Burton (below) is associated for ever with exploration in Arabia because of his translations of oriental erotica and the "Arabian Nights", and for his vivid account of a pilgrimage to Mecca which he made, impenetrably disguised as a faithful Muslim. In fact, his Arabian travels covered little new ground, for the German Burckhardt had already visited the holy cities of Islam. Burton had intended to cross Arabia and the Rub'al Khali (Empty Quarter),but penetration of this desolate region by Europeans had to wait until the journeys of Thomas and Philby by motor vehicle in the 1930s and those of Wilfred Thesiger, by camel and on foot, in the 1940s

Rasul Allah" ("There is no god but the God; Mohammed is the Prophet of God"). Unfortunately, "whether such was the will of God, or through the fear which had seized me", he was unable to reply and the Sultan threw him into prison before going to war.

In the prison Varthema feigned madness and kindled the interest of a lascivious wife of the Sultan. She was neither impressed by his madness nor believed in it. "The following day she had prepared for me a bath according to their custom, with many perfumes, and continued these caresses for twelve days. Afterwards, she began to come down to visit me every night at three or four o'clock. . . ."

When the Sultan returned from his campaign his wife persuaded him to release Varthema. While waiting for a ship to travel to India, he made further expeditions into the hinterland of the Yemen, known to the Romans as Arabia Felix (the Fortunate), reaching the walled city of San'a, 7,500 feet up in the mountains.

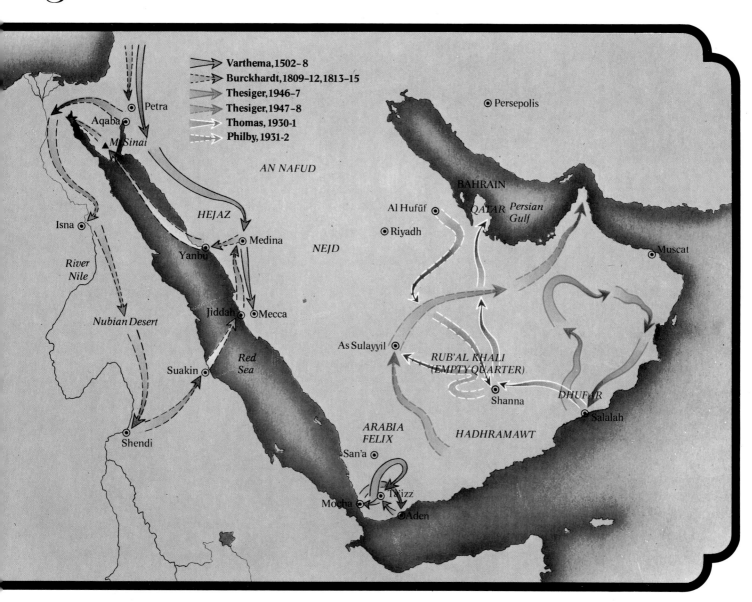

Varthema, 1502–8
Burckhardt, 1809–12, 1813–15
Thesiger, 1946–7
Thesiger, 1947–8
Thomas, 1930–1
Philby, 1931–2

Petra
Aqaba
M Sinai
AN NAFUD
Persepolis
BAHRAIN
Al Hufūf
QATAR
Persian Gulf
Isna
HEJAZ
Riyadh
Muscat
River Nile
Medina
NEJD
Yanbu
Nubian Desert
Jiddah
Mecca
As Sulayyil
RUB'AL KHALI (EMPTY QUARTER)
Red Sea
Suakin
DHUFAR
Shanna
Salalah
ARABIA FELIX
HADHRAMAWT
Shendi
San'a
Taizz
Mocha
Aden

The next recorded visit by a European to Mecca (where he met an unnamed Irishman who had become a Muslim) was that of Joseph Pitts of Exeter in Devonshire. He was a ship's apprentice who had been captured by Barbary pirates in 1678 and sold into slavery. Forced by torture to become a Muslim, in 1685 he made the pilgrimage to Mecca by way of Cairo and Jiddah with his master and also visited Medina. He finally succeeded in escaping from his bondage in Smyrna (Izmir) and reached England in 1694.

Danish expedition

The first scientific expedition to Arabia, and the first of its kind ever to leave Denmark, was sent out by King Frederick V in 1761. Its five members (foolishly no leader was appointed) were Friedrich von Haven, a Danish linguist, Peter Forrskål, a Swedish botanist, Engineer-Lieutenant Carsten Niebuhr, a German described as "Mathematicus and Astronomus", Christian Kramer, a Danish physician and zoologist, and George Baurenfeind, a German artist. There was also a Swedish ex-soldier named Berggren. They were singularly ill-assorted and on the outward voyage various members of the party threatened to murder one another.

The expedition spent a year in Egypt and then, in October 1762, "disguised" in Muslim dress, they boarded a pilgrim ship bound for Jiddah. There Forrskål collected natural history specimens, which he was able to send back to Europe.

The next part of the voyage to Arabia Felix was made in a "tarrád", an open boat that resembled half a barrel sliced longitudinally but with pointed ends. Each night the vessel hove to and Niebuhr went ashore to make astronomical observations for his maps, while Forrskål observed the bird-life and collected shells. On December 29, 1762, they landed at Al Luhayyah in the northern Yemen.

The following February they set off through the sandy coastal plains of Tehama on don-keys, bound for Beit al Faqih. On the way Niebuhr continued his survey, and by taking solar and stellar observations was able to initiate a map of the Yemen that was still being used by explorers a century later.

At Beit al Faqih, but without recognizing the symptoms, both Niebuhr and von Haven contracted malaria; continuing their travels through the plain in temperatures of up to 100°F, the expedition next reached Mocha, a ruinous and unhealthy port on the coast, where its members were subjected to many indignities by the authorities.

Forrskål suffered the worst treatment. His specimens, which were preserved in alcohol, were poured from their jars by customs officials who believed that he was preparing poisons—which made his collection of snakes in alcohol particularly suspect.

Here, too, von Haven died. He was not much mourned, having been both incompetent and lazy. On June 28, 1763, the five survivors set off on a gruelling journey for

Abundance and nothingness

San'a. By now Forrskål had also contracted malaria and he died at Yarim on July 11.

On July 12 the remainder of the party pressed on towards San'a. All of them were now to some degree sick—and for the first time Niebuhr's will-power deserted him. From this point onwards blank spaces appear on his map of the route.

At San'a they waited impatiently for an audience with the Imam, knowing that they were due to sail from Mocha for India in mid-August; but the Imam was paying his troops and would not interrupt this necessary work to receive them. When he did, however, they were dazzled by his wealth and graciousness.

Finally, on July 26, having received a generous present of money from the Imam, they set off on a desperate, forced march with camels in an attempt to reach Mocha before the ship sailed. If they missed it they would have to wait until the following year.

Nine days later, on August 5, they reached the port in a state of collapse. On the voyage to Bombay, Baurenfeind and Berrgren died. Kramer succumbed later, in February 1764.

Niebuhr was the only survivor. He remained in India until the autumn of 1764, writing up his notes and recovering to some extent. Then, in December, he sailed for the Persian Gulf in a small English warship.

Niebuhr returned to Copenhagen in November 1767. He was one of the greatest scientific travellers who ever lived, and one of the few Westerners to see that the world of Islam was approaching a state of crisis and that great changes were about to take place.

The upheaval, when it came, was inspired by Abd-al Wahhab, born about 1703 at 'Ayeina in southern Nejd. Abd-al Wahhab had made the pilgrimage to Mecca and had returned from it convinced that the religion would have to be reformed and reduced to its original simplicity. Abd-al Wahhab believed, Niebuhr wrote, "that God is the only proper object of worship . . . and forbade the invocation of saints and the very mentioning of Mahomet or any other Prophet in prayer as practices savouring of idolatry".

By about 1740 Abd-al Wahhab had succeeded in converting Muhammad ibn Sa'ud of Dar'iyah, and ibn Sa'ud became the head of the Wahhabi community and its Caliph when the sect was founded in 1745. A holy war was launched and after a series of campaigns Wahhabi rule spread as far as lower Iraq. In 1791, Abd-al Wahhab died and 'Abdul 'Aziz, the son of ibn Sa'ud, marched to the shore of the Persian Gulf.

In 1803, the Wahhabis reached the Red Sea at Hali, 250 miles south of Jiddah. That year they took Mecca and sacked it, stripping the Kaaba and forcing the Sharif Ghalib of Mecca to flee. 'Abdul 'Aziz was murdered in November 1803 and the Wahhabis were eventually driven out of Mecca. However, the cause was furthered by 'Abdul's able son, Sa'ud, and by 1806 Yenbo (Yanbu), the port of Medina on the Red Sea, Medina and Jiddah were in his hands.

Almost all Arabia was now forced to conform to the Wahhabis and in 1810 they advanced beyond Jordan and almost to the gates of Damascus. In this year, the tide began to turn against them and they later suffered defeats at the hands of Mehemet Ali, the Viceroy of Egypt, but violent uprisings continued until after 1840. Their effect was to make travel in the peninsula more hazardous than ever.

The next European to visit Mecca was Ali Bey al-'Abbasi, otherwise Domingo Badia y Leblich, a wealthy Spaniard who seems genuinely to have been converted to Islam. He arrived in Jiddah in 1807 with a retinue of servants and a number of scientific instruments. His book, *Travels*, published in London in 1816, is the best description of Mecca and the Hejaz under Wahhabi domination.

Dervish disguise

Two years later, in 1809, Ulrich Jaspar Seetzen reached Mecca and Medina. A distinguished German botanist and Arabist, he had spent 20 years preparing himself for his eastern travels.

After performing the pilgrimage in the guise of a dervish, he went on to San'a and Aden and from there attempted to cross Arabia with an eastbound caravan, having assumed the name of Hajji Musa. He was murdered at Ta'izz, and all his diaries were lost, which deprived him of his due fame.

The next great Arabian traveller is also famed for his journeys in Africa. John Lewis Burckhardt was born of well-to-do parents at Lausanne in 1784. At Göttingen he made the acquaintance of the famous naturalist Professor Blumenbach, who gave him an introduction to Sir Joseph Banks, founder of the Association for Promoting the Discovery of the Interior Parts of Africa.

One of the principal objects of the Association was the exploration of the Niger, and after Mungo Park's death at the Bussa Rapids in 1806 it was decided to make a further attempt by infiltrating an explorer from the Nile westwards to Timbuktu with a caravan returning from Mecca. Burckhardt volunteered and was accepted.

He reached Aleppo in July 1809, where he lodged with the British consul, John Barker. In the course of the next two and a half years he became fluent in Arabic and an authority on Islamic law and doctrine.

In the spring of 1810 he went into the surrounding country and lived with the nomadic Ryhanlu Turkmans. Later that year he reached Tadmur (Palmyra) and saw the golden colonnades of the great ruined Arab city of the desert.

From the autumn of 1810 onwards he began to travel more extensively, and by June 1812 he felt himself ready to start for Egypt and the journey to the Niger. The route he took to Egypt was southwards along the side of the Jordan Valley, then west across Sinai. Travelling under the name of Ibrahim ibn Abdullah—a name he maintained throughout all his subsequent travels—he arrived on August 22 before one of the wonders of the world, the astonishing classical façade of the temple-tomb known by the Arabs as Khaznet Firaun, Pharaoh's Treasure, more than 60 feet high and carved from the living red rock.

From there he went down into Petra, the city of the Nabateans, but was prevented by a suspicious local guide from exploring the fantastic agglomeration of tombs, temples and chapels carved in the sheer sandstone cliffs, "but I knew well the character of the people around me; I was without protection in the midst of a desert where no traveller had ever been before me".

Arriving in Cairo on September 3 he decided, before setting off for the Fezzan, to do what no other European had done—to travel into Nubia and Dongola by following the great bend of the Nile southwards. Early in 1813, he left Esne in Upper Egypt and travelled south as far as Tinareh, a place north of the Third Cataract on the east bank. On his way back, on March 22, he made the second great discovery of his life, the great rock temple of Abu Simbel, on the west bank of the river, with its four 60-foot figures of Rameses II carved in the rock.

Back at Esne, where he suffered two bad attacks of ophthalmia, he learned that there was no possibility of a caravan setting off through the African desert that summer. He made a courageous decision—to perfect his knowledge of Islam and provide himself with an unbreakable alibi for his journey to the Niger by making the pilgrimage to Mecca.

The route he chose was through the Nubian Desert and, after exploring in Nubia, he proposed to cross the Red Sea to Arabia from Massawa in Ethiopia.

On April 17, 1814, his caravan reached Shendi, a great entrepôt for slaves and merchandise on the routes between Egypt, Ethiopia, Arabia and Lake Chad. Here Burckhardt bought a Negro slave boy for 11 Spanish dollars (thereby saving him, at least for a while, from the vile treatment that owners customarily meted out).

Forced to abandon his plan to reach Massawa because there was no practicable route to it, Burckhardt next joined a caravan

of about 150 merchants, 300 slaves, 200 camels and 30 horses bound for Suakin.

From Suakin, which he reached towards the end of June, Burckhardt took passage to Jiddah in a small open boat filled with Negro pilgrims. When he arrived there he found that the letter of credit that he had arranged in Cairo was out of date and he was forced to sell his slave, making a profit of 32 dollars.

From Jiddah he went inland to Ta'if, southeast of Mecca, where the Viceroy of Egypt, Mehemet Ali, who knew of Burckhardt by reputation, arranged for him to be pronounced not only a Muslim but an extremely devout and well-informed one. In this fashion Burckhardt became the first and probably the last non-Muslim European to visit Mecca openly and in safety.

Burckhardt left Mecca for Medina with a caravan in January 1815. By this time he was suffering from malnutrition and at Medina he had a bad attack of malaria. He decided to cut short his travels and return to Cairo, which he reached, after a long and hazardous journey, on June 24, 1815, after an absence of two and a half years.

At Cairo he set about writing the account of his journey. The opportunity to join a caravan to the Sahara never presented itself and he died at Cairo in 1817 from dysentery.

The defeat of the Wahhabis by the Egyptians led indirectly to the first crossing of Arabia by a European. In 1819, Captain George Sadlier was sent by the Bombay Government to congratulate Ibrahim Pasha, Mehemet Ali's adopted son, on the capture of Dar'iya and to propose a plan for the complete destruction of Wahhabi power with the help of a British expeditionary force.

When he reached Al Qatif, north of Bahrain on the Persian Gulf, Sadlier found that Ibrahim's forces were already pulling out of Arabia. Nevertheless, he made the courageous decision to attempt to overtake Ibrahim, if for nothing else but to present him with the sword of honour, which was a gift from his government. Eventually his party, in company with some Egyptian troops, caught up with the main Egyptian army southwest of Aneiza, where Sadlier found that Ibrahim had gone on to Medina.

He decided to turn back; but now he was not allowed to and he and his party were forced to travel on to the outskirts of Medina. He was not allowed to enter the city and was lodged outside it. There he met Ibrahim, who told him that he was not allowed to treat with a British envoy from Bombay so Sadlier went on to reach the Red Sea at Yenbo on September 20, having crossed the peninsula in three months from east to west.

The first scientific exploration of the interior of the Hadhramawt, the mountainous

Abundance and nothingness

region on the south coast of Arabia, was carried out by Lieutenant Wellsted of the surveying ship *Palinurus*. This was one of a number of vessels that was being used to search out suitable sites for coaling stations for East India Company ships on the route from Suez to Bombay.

Wellsted had already explored parts of the hinterland of Sinai from Tor and also the island of Socotra. In May 1834, he visited the site of the ancient port of Cana, at Husn al Ghorab on the Hadhramawt coast.

The following year, with Lieutenant Charles Cruttenden, he penetrated 50 miles inland from Bal Haf, west of Husn al Ghorab, to the ruins of Naqab al Hajar in Wadi Meifa'a, a great city of the Himyarite people in the 2nd century BC. Also that year he visited Muscat in Oman, and from the summit of Jebel Akhdar saw the vast plains of the South Arabian Desert, the Rub'al Khali.

Four years after the British seized Aden, in June 1843, Adolph von Wrede, a Bavarian, made a journey into the interior from Mukalla on the coast of the Hadhramawt. Disguised as a pilgrim, he reached the edge of the great desert of Al Akhaf, part of the Rub'al Khali.

In 1893, the German archaeologist Leo Hirsch discovered the great Wadi Hadhramawt in its upper course, near Shibam. That same year the English explorer and archaeologist James Theodore Bent and his wife Mabel, one of the few European women to travel in the interior of Arabia, followed a similar route into the interior.

They reached the coast of Shihr, east of Mukallah, in March 1894, after a very dangerous journey. From there, roughly following the line of the coast, they travelled eastwards for about another 150 miles as far as Raida.

Further exploration in the Hadhramawt was carried out by a Dutch ex-diplomat and Orientalist named van der Meulen, together with a German, von Wissman. Of more modern explorers in the Hadhramawt the best known is the Englishman Harold Ingrams, who became a resident adviser to the Sultans on the coast in 1935 and more or less completed its exploration.

In 1853, another European reached Mecca in disguise, Richard Burton, a 32-year-old officer of the Bengal Army, who was later to travel extensively in Africa, the Middle East and South America. Burton was the son of an Irish colonel in the British Army. Intended for the Church, he was sent to Trinity College, Oxford, where he spent only a year but learned Arabic. In 1842, he went to India, where he joined the Bombay Infantry. One of the great linguists of the 19th century, he eventually spoke 29 languages and 11 dialects.

By his own admission he was driven by the Devil and there was certainly something Satanic about his face. Frank Harris later wrote of him: "Catholic in his admiration and liking of all greatness, it was the abnormalities and not the divinities of men that fascinated him. . . . Deep down in him lay the despairing gloom of utter disbelief."

On July 6, 1854, having been circumcised for the purpose, Burton set sail from Suez in a 50-ton pilgrim ship bound for Yenbo; he was disguised as an Indian-born Afghan hakim, or doctor, and took the name Al Haj (the Pilgrim) Abdullah. His aim was "to cross the unknown Arabian Peninsula, in a direct line from either El Medinah to Muscat, or diagonally from Meccah to Makallah on the Indian Ocean."

Twelve days later he reached Yenbo and set off for Medina with two servants. On January 24, seven days and 110 miles from the Red Sea, he had his first view of the holy city, having climbed a flight of steps cut in the black basalt ridge.

Burton left an account of the city and its shrine to which, apart from the Englishman J. F. Keane, who succeeded in reaching both it and Mecca in 1878, he was the last non-Muslim visitor until 1908.

On August 31, he set off with a caravan for Mecca along the Darb al Shakri, the inland road which traversed the Harrat lava fields.

On September 7 they reached the valley of El Zaribah, where they prepared for their entry into Mecca. Their heads were shaved, their moustaches and toenails trimmed and, after bathing, they donned the two white cotton cloths with red stripes and fringes, the Ihram, the pilgrim garb. From now on they were forbidden to kill any living thing—they were not even allowed to scratch themselves in case they killed their own vermin.

On the day of Id al Khabir, Burton took part in the Ramy, the ceremony in the course of which pilgrims throw seven stones at stone pillars at the place where Iblis, the Devil, was driven away by stones thrown by Abraham, Hagar and Ishmael.

At the end of September, "worn out with fatigue and the fatal fiery heat", he embarked on a steamer for Egypt, intending to return later and make his journey across Arabia. Ill-health prevented it and he returned to India.

A courageous successor to Burton was the distinguished Dutch Arabist J. Snouck Hurgronje. His book *Mekka* (Hague, 1888) was published with two remarkable portfolios of photographs, the first ever taken in the city.

In 1908, A. J. B. Wavell became the first European to reach Medina by the newly constructed Hejaz railway from Damascus, later badly damaged by T. E. Lawrence's raiding Arabs. Wavell travelled in the guise of a Swahili-speaking pilgrim from Zanzibar,

with two companions. The 1st class tickets cost £3 10s each, "not a great deal for a ride of over a thousand miles".

From Medina they travelled with a caravan and then by steamer to Jiddah and Yenbo and by camel to Mecca. He described the scenes at Mount Arafat, a pyramidal hill only about 400 feet high, when half a million people arrived at the foot of it between sunrise and 10 o'clock. "The roar of this great column is like a breaking sea," he wrote, "and the dust spreads for miles over the surrounding country. . . . The hill was literally black with people, and tents were springing up round it, hundreds to the minute, in an ever-widening circle. As we approached, the dull murmur caused by thousands of people shouting the formula, 'Lebēka lebēka, Allohoomka lebēka', which had long been audible, became so loud that it dominated every other sound."

Swedish Arabist

". . . the last of the original pioneers, who, since Niebuhr, had been opening up Arabia, the last to force the barriers of a great unexplored region of the first importance" was the Swedish Arabist, George Augustus Wellin; the region, the Nejd, the 420,000-square-mile area of northern and central Arabia. Disguised as a learned Bedouin Sheikh, in 1842 he travelled across the Nafud desert. Six years later he crossed the volcanic mountains of the northern Hejaz to the oasis of Tabuk. From there he journeyed to Tayma' on the edge of the Nafud, the first European to do so. His last journey, that same year, took him across part of the southern Nafud and an enormous expanse of gravel steppe to Meshed Ali near the Euphrates, and from there to Baghdad.

The next traveller to enter the Nejd was William Palgrave, born in 1826, who was commissioned by Emperor Napoleon III to report on the attitude of the Arabs to France—an important matter as it was now certain that the Suez Canal would be built.

In July 1862, Palgrave and a Syrian teacher named Barakat Jurayjuray set off from Ma'an disguised as Syrian doctors and crossed the Nafud desert to Ha'il. From Ha'il, where they were well treated by the Qatif Emir of Shammar, they succeeded in reaching Riyadh and Al Qatif on the Persian Gulf, Palgrave being the first European to make the crossing of the peninsula from west to east.

Perhaps the greatest of all Arabian explorers, certainly the writer of the greatest prose work about Arabia in the English language, was Charles Montagu Doughty.

In November 1876, he set off with the Haj caravan from Damascus to Mecca. At Meda'in Salih, where he left the caravan, he began the wanderings that in two years took him, at the same speed as the Bedouin in whose *menzils* (encampments) he lived, to Tayma, then east to Boreida and southwest to Jiddah.

Here he writes of the desert south of Ha'il: "I saw in the morning the granite flanks of Ajja strangely blotted, as it were with the shadow of clouds, by the running down of erupted basalts.... Rock-partridges were everywhere calling and flying in this high granite country, smelling in the sun of the resinous sweetness of southern wood."

Very different was the peregrination of the Blunts in 1878–9. Wilfrid Scawen Blunt, poet and British diplomat, and his wife, Lady Anne Blunt, grand-daughter of Lord Byron and an accomplished artist, went down from Damascus to Jawf, ostensibly to buy horses but also to see the Nejd. They made no pretence at disguise although they wore Arab clothes and their journey was more like a medieval royal progress in appearance.

The next traveller in the Nafud was Edward Nolde, a German adventurer who crossed it with a considerable retinue in 1893 on his way to visit the Emir at Ha'il. He went through it by a more easterly route than others had used before him and reached the wells of Haiyanniya after travelling for 180 miles without water.

The Arab revolt against the Turks in the First World War, chronicled by T. E. Lawrence in *The Seven Pillars of Wisdom*, led to the exploration of large areas of the Hejaz, previously unknown, in which even the longitudes of the stations on the railway line were undetermined.

By the 1930s the last great unexplored region of Arabia, and one which amounted to a quarter of its entire area, was the 250,000-square-mile expanse of the Rub'al Khali, "The Abode of Emptiness". Among those who had seen it were Wellsted in 1836, from Jebel Akhdar, and von Wrede in 1843, from north of the Wadi Hadhramawt. In 1929, Lawrence wrote to Marshal of the Royal Air Force Lord Trenchard suggesting that a British airship (the R-100 or the R-101) should fly over it: "Nothing but an airship can do it, and I want it to be one of ours which gets the plum."

The first successful crossing was made in the winter of 1930–1 by Bertram Thomas, a former British political officer in the Middle East. In October 1930, after preliminary reconnaissance the year before, he landed near Salala, on the coast, and in December set off northwards with a party of Rashidi Bedouin under Sheikh Salih bin Yakut, who, after much bargaining, had sworn loyalty to him.

Six marches through steppe country took them to Shishur, where they found, in Thomas's words, "the southern bulwark of the sands of my desire".

Later they entered the region of Uruq adh Dhaiyah. There Thomas saw "dunes of all sizes, unsymmetrical in relation to one another, but with the exquisite roundness of a girl's breasts, rise tier upon tier like a mighty mountain system".

Early in January they reached the waterhole of Shanna, in about latitude 18.59N, 50.45E, 990 feet above the sea and 330 miles south of Doha, their destination on the Persian Gulf. From Shanna Thomas made the last dash northwards with 12 picked men and camels and five pack animals. On January 27 they reached the well of Banaiyan, only about 80 miles from the sea. The crossing of the central sands had taken 18 days. Finally, on

The addax, a perfect desert creature—it survives on an entirely waterless diet—has been driven to near-extinction by jeep-mounted hunters with firearms

the morning of February 5: "The Badawin moved forward at a sharp pace, chanting the water chants. Our thirsty camels pricked up their ears with eager knowingness. . . . Half an hour later we entered the walls of the fort. The Rub'al Khali had been crossed."

The second explorer to cross the Rub'al Khali was Harry St John Philby, another former British political officer in Iraq and a convert to Islam. He began his crossing from the wells of Dulaiqiya, near Hufuf, due west of Qatar, on January 7, 1932. Part of his mission was to find Wabar, a legendary city which, the Arabs believed, had been destroyed like Sodom and Gomorrah because of its wickedness, the fire of God's wrath having turned it into an iron block the size of a camel.

At Al Hadida, in the very heart of the sands, in about 50E, 21N he found the "ruins" of Wabar, two meteoritic craters about 300 feet wide and 30 feet deep. He also came upon a fragment of rusted meteoritic iron, weighing about 25 pounds, that probably was the lump to which the Bedouin considered the city had been reduced.

Now following the route parallel to Thomas's, and very close to it, Philby reached Shanna, and on February 22 he set off from it to make the crossing of the desert to the Suleivil Oasis at the mouth of Wadi Dawasir, arriving there on March 11.

No further attempts on the Rub'al Khali were made until after the Second World War, when Wilfred Thesiger, one of the last great explorers of modern times, joined the Middle East Anti-Locust Unit, which gave him the opportunity to travel in Saudi Arabia; for the next five years his life was spent in and around the Rub'al Khali.

The reward

Thesiger made his first crossing of the Rub'al Khali in 1946–7. Of it he wrote, "To others my journey would have little importance. It would produce nothing except a rather inaccurate map which no one was ever likely to use. It was a personal experience, and the reward had been a drink of clean, nearly tasteless water. I was content with that."

Thesiger's second crossing was made from the Manwakh well, north of Hadhramawt, in the winter of 1947–8, again with Rashid tribesmen. No other man will ever make such a journey and his book, *Arabian Sands*, is a classic description of a way of life that is now no more.

"I shall always remember", he wrote, "how often I was humbled by those illiterate herdsmen who possessed, in so much greater measure than I, generosity and courage, endurance, patience, and light-hearted gallantry. Among no other people have I felt the same sense of personal inferiority."

The Nile: 'father of waters'

The statues of Abu Simbel were unknown outside Egypt until found by Burckhardt. They have now been re-erected on higher ground to avoid the rising waters behind the Aswan dam

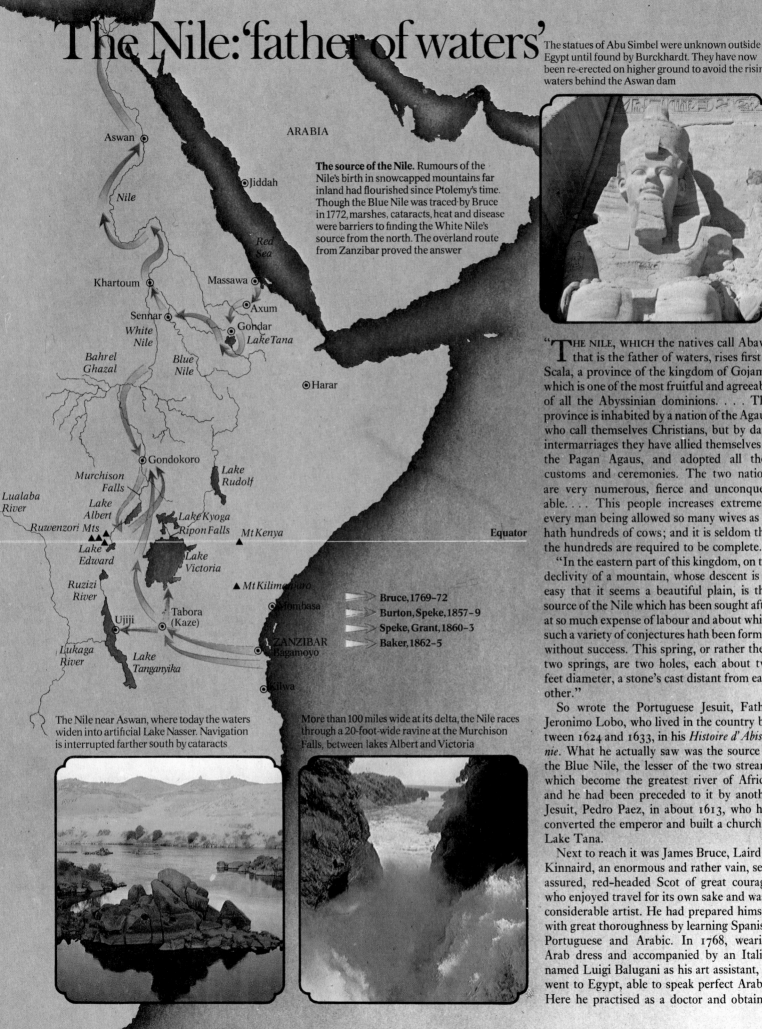

The source of the Nile. Rumours of the Nile's birth in snowcapped mountains far inland had flourished since Ptolemy's time. Though the Blue Nile was traced by Bruce in 1772, marshes, cataracts, heat and disease were barriers to finding the White Nile's source from the north. The overland route from Zanzibar proved the answer

ARABIA

Aswan

Nile

Jiddah

Red Sea

Khartoum

Massawa

Sennar

Axum

White Nile

Gondar

Bahr el Ghazal

Lake Tana

Blue Nile

Harar

Gondokoro

Lake Rudolf

Murchison Falls

Lualaba River

Lake Albert

Ruwenzori Mts

Lake Kyoga

Ripon Falls

Mt Kenya

Equator

Lake Edward

Lake Victoria

Ruzizi River

Mt Kilimanjaro

Ujiji

Tabora (Kaze)

Mombasa

Lukaga River

Lake Tanganyika

ZANZIBAR

Bagamoyo

Kilwa

⟩	Bruce, 1769–72
⟩	Burton, Speke, 1857–9
⟩	Speke, Grant, 1860–3
⟩	Baker, 1862–5

The Nile near Aswan, where today the waters widen into artificial Lake Nasser. Navigation is interrupted farther south by cataracts

More than 100 miles wide at its delta, the Nile races through a 20-foot-wide ravine at the Murchison Falls, between lakes Albert and Victoria

"THE NILE, WHICH the natives call Abawi, that is the father of waters, rises first in Scala, a province of the kingdom of Gojama, which is one of the most fruitful and agreeable of all the Abyssinian dominions. . . . This province is inhabited by a nation of the Agaus, who call themselves Christians, but by daily intermarriages they have allied themselves to the Pagan Agaus, and adopted all their customs and ceremonies. The two nations are very numerous, fierce and unconquerable. . . . This people increases extremely, every man being allowed so many wives as he hath hundreds of cows; and it is seldom that the hundreds are required to be complete.

"In the eastern part of this kingdom, on the declivity of a mountain, whose descent is so easy that it seems a beautiful plain, is that source of the Nile which has been sought after at so much expense of labour and about which such a variety of conjectures hath been formed without success. This spring, or rather these two springs, are two holes, each about two feet diameter, a stone's cast distant from each other."

So wrote the Portuguese Jesuit, Father Jeronimo Lobo, who lived in the country between 1624 and 1633, in his *Histoire d'Abissinie*. What he actually saw was the source of the Blue Nile, the lesser of the two streams which become the greatest river of Africa; and he had been preceded to it by another Jesuit, Pedro Paez, in about 1613, who had converted the emperor and built a church at Lake Tana.

Next to reach it was James Bruce, Laird of Kinnaird, an enormous and rather vain, self-assured, red-headed Scot of great courage, who enjoyed travel for its own sake and was a considerable artist. He had prepared himself with great thoroughness by learning Spanish, Portuguese and Arabic. In 1768, wearing Arab dress and accompanied by an Italian named Luigi Balugani as his art assistant, he went to Egypt, able to speak perfect Arabic. Here he practised as a doctor and obtained letters of recommendation to various potentates, one of them from the Patriarch of Ethiopia to the Christian Greeks there.

At Aswan he was forced to abandon his journey up the Nile because of hostile tribes to the south and instead crossed the desert to the Red Sea, sailed to Jiddah and from there to Massawa, arriving there in September 1769. He eventually reached Gondar, the capital of Abyssinia, where he was received with honour by the young emperor, Tecla Haimanot, and the extremely cruel Ras Michael of Tigre, who had made Tecla his puppet. He was able to do this, having ingratiated himself with the Queen Mother, a remarkable woman, by curing the palace children of smallpox during the emperor's absence on a campaign.

Michael gave him command of a troop of Imperial horses and he reached the source of the Little Abbai, believing it to be the main source of the Nile, having first struck the river at the Tississat Falls, near its exit from Lake Tana 6,000 feet up in the mountains, fixing its position with considerable accuracy.

"I ran down the hill", he wrote in his *Travels to Discover the Source of the Nile*, "towards the little island of green sods, which was about two hundred yards distant; the whole side of the hill was thick grown over with flowers, the large bulbous roots of which appeared above the surface of the ground, and their skins coming off on treading upon them, occasioned me two very severe falls before I reached the brink of the marsh; I after this came to the island of green turf, which was in the form of an altar, apparently the work of art, and I stood raptured over the principal fountain which rises in the middle of it. It is easier to guess than to describe the situation of my mind at that moment—standing in that spot which had baffled the genius, industry and inquiry of both ancients and moderns, for the course of nearly three thousand years."

After returning to Gondar, where he took part in a campaign against the Galla tribes and visited Sennar, also on the river, Bruce followed it to its confluence with the White Nile. There, at what was later to be the site of Khartoum, he noticed that the White Nile was the deeper of the two; but still believed that the Blue Nile was the principal river.

He reached Aswan at the end of November 1772 and arrived in London in 1774, having visited an Italian marchese who had married his wife during his long absence—she had given him up for dead—and learning in Paris from the great cartographer d'Anville that he was not the first to discover this source.

In Britain the only recognition that he received for his journey was an audience with George III, but no one could convince him that what he had seen was not the principal

source of one of the world's great rivers.

His good and on the whole accurate book was not published for 17 years, and then it was not believed (one of his principal critics was Samuel Johnson, who had written *Rasselas*, a book about Abyssinia, without having been there). Bruce died in 1794, having fallen down a flight of stairs while on his way to help a lady into her carriage.

Napoleon's invasion of Egypt in 1789 let loose a horde of savants in the country and under Mehemet Ali's rule the country was conquered as far south as Kordofan. This enabled the German Burckhardt to make his journey through the Nubian Desert and to

John Hanning Speke and Lake Tanganyika. The beauty of the lake captivated Speke and Burton when they reached it

Suakin in 1813 and on to Arabia—he died while planning a journey to the Niger. In 1815, Mehemet Ali sent the French explorer Frédéric Cailliaud—the son of a locksmith, who had taught himself geography, archaeology and history—to Nubia, and on the way to the Red Sea Cailliaud found the emerald mines at Jebel Zobara, which had been worked in ancient times. In 1820, he took part in the Egyptian expedition which founded Khartoum. By 1841, other expeditions, accompanied by French and German explorers, had reached the rapids of Gondokoro, in about 4N, using sailing boats. They were unable to negotiate them, but by 1850 Austrian missionaries had founded a mission station there.

By this time Ludwig Krapf (a German

missionary who had been expelled from northern Abyssinia in 1842) and Johann Rebmann had followed up some remarkable rumours about mountains covered with some white substance which they had heard at their mission at Mombasa, from Arabs who had reached Lake Tanganyika and who knew of the existence of Lake Nyanza to the northeast.

In May 1848, Rebmann himself saw the peak of Kilimanjaro. "He conversed with the natives in reference to the white matter visible upon the dome-like summit of the mountain, and he was told that the silver-like stuff, when brought down in bottles, proved to be nothing but water."

In December the following year Krapf himself saw Mount Kenya, as well as Kilimanjaro. "That both mountains are covered with perennial snow is proved by the multitude of rivers rising amidst them," Krapf wrote in his *Travel Researches, and Missionary Labours During the Eighteen Years' Residence in Eastern Africa*. "I was not then aware that Ptolemy had alluded to a mountainous country, and that these mountains were covered with perennial snow, and considered by him as the real sources of the Nile."

This news of the existence of snow on mountains—one of which, Kilimanjaro, was just over three degrees from the Equator, the other, Mount Kenya, practically on it—was greeted in Europe with some scepticism.

"One lake"

Then, in 1855, Rebmann and Erhardt produced a map based on Arab and Negro reports of a huge lake in Central Africa, as big as the Caspian, in which the lakes that were eventually to be named Nyasa, Tanganyika and Victoria Nyanza were shown as one.

Richard Burton was swift to propose an expedition, "primarily for the purpose of ascertaining the limits of the Sea of Ujiji, and secondly to determine the exportable produce of the interior and the ethnography of its tribes". In 1856, the Royal Geographical Society decided to send him to East Africa. "The great object of the expedition", the Society wrote in their instructions to Burton, "is to penetrate inland from Kilwa or some other place on the east coast of Africa and make the best of your way to the reputed Lake Nyasa.... Having obtained all the information you require in this quarter you are to proceed northwards towards the range of mountains marked on our maps as containing the probable source of the Nile, which it will be your next great object to discover ... you will be at liberty to return to England by descending the Nile ... or otherwise, always having regard to the time at your disposal."

Burton's companion was to be John Hanning Speke, like Burton an officer in the

The Nile–'father of waters'

Indian Army but otherwise of a very different temperament. They had already made a disastrous expedition to Somaliland in 1854–5 from Aden (which the British had annexed in 1839), in the course of which Burton and Speke were wounded, the latter severely, by raiding tribesmen.

In August 1857, they left Bagamoyo on the mainland opposite Zanzibar for the interior. With them they had a guide, Sidi Bombay (who was to become a legendary figure in the story of the search for the sources of the Nile), 130 porters, 30 donkeys and sufficient trade goods for two years.

Following the Arab caravan route, and suffering terrible hardships on the way, they reached Kazé (Tabora) in Unyamwezi, the Land of the Moon, a centre of the slave trade, where they were given a good reception by the Zanzibar Arab slavers. One of these told them that the great sea was, in fact, three separate lakes.

By this time Burton was suffering from fever, and he and Speke had great difficulty in recruiting fresh porters to replace those who had either fallen sick or defected; but on February 13, 1858, 900 miles out from Bagamoyo, they looked out on the blue waters of Lake Tanganyika 2,500 feet up in the Great Rift Valley, hemmed in by mountains which rise to 8,000 feet, the second largest lake in Africa and the second deepest in the world after Lake Baykal.

"Nothing", Burton wrote in his book, *The Lake Regions of Central Africa*, "could be more picturesque than this first view of the Tanganyika Lake, as it lay in the lap of the mountains, basking in the gorgeous tropical sunshine. The shores of this vast crevasse appeared doubly beautiful to me after the silent and spectral mangrove-creeks of the East African seaboard, and the melancholy, monotonous experience of desert and jungle scenery, tawny rock and sun-parched plain or rank herbage and flats of black mire. . . . Forgetting toils, dangers and the doubtfulness of return, I felt ready to endure double what I had endured; and all the party seemed to join with me in joy."

By this time Burton was partly paralysed and was suffering from an abscess of the jaw, while Speke was partly blind. Subsequently Speke wrote: "From the summit the Eastern horn of the lovely Tanganyika Lake could be seen in all its glory by everybody but myself."

Here, at Ujiji, a miserable slave and ivory post, they established that the height of the lake was only about ten feet higher than the Nile at Gondokoro, 600 miles to the north, which would seem to make it impossible for the lake to be a source of the Nile. Nevertheless they hired boats and visited another post towards the northern end of the lake, failing however to discover the important fact that instead of a river flowing out of it, which might have connected with the Nile a river, the Ruzizi, flowed into it from Lake Kivu to the north; nor did they know that the Lukaga, part of the Congo river system, flowed out of it to the west.

Too ill to continue their journey they returned to Tabora, by which time the two men were on bad terms; and from Tabora, Burton being unable to travel, Speke set off through scrub at first, then through wide plains with vast granite boulders like grotesque fungi sprouting from them and discovered 200 miles to the north the lake he named Victoria Nyanza—Victoria after the monarch, Nyanza (the Great Water) being the name by which the dwellers on its shores knew it.

Displeased

On August 3, 1858, gazing across the lake, he was convinced that he had found the source of the Nile. "It was early morning," he wrote. "The distant sea of the north horizon was defined in the calm atmosphere between north and west . . . I no longer felt any doubt that the lake at my feet gave birth to that interesting river, the source of which had been the subject of so much speculation, and the object of so many explorers."

Burton was more than displeased when Speke told him this on his return six weeks later and the two men returned to Zanzibar on even worse terms than they had previously been, if this were possible. They were so ill, anyway, that they had to be carried.

Speke immediately departed for London, which he reached in May 1859, leaving Burton to wind up the affairs of the expedition at Aden. There, with indecent haste, and without waiting for the arrival of Burton, Speke described the expedition to Sir Roderick Murchison, the President of the Royal Geographical Society, and even before Burton arrived home 12 days later, he had spoken at a meeting of the Society, another expedition had been organized and a sum of £2,500 voted for it. Burton's feelings can be imagined. Both men longed for the limelight.

Speke's companion on his next expedition was James Grant, a Scotsman who was far more to his taste: self-effacing and, like Speke, a sportsman as well as being a zoologist, botanist and painter in watercolours, whose pictures of flowers have a rare quality. The pair left Zanzibar in October 1860 with a number of Hottentot policemen and Indian soldiers, 75 freed slaves, Bombay, a cook and two black servants from a man-of-war, a guide, 100 Negro porters and an Arab caravan leader—plus 12 mules, three donkeys and 22 goats to provide milk. Speke also took with him 50 carbines, ammunition and a number of gold watches as gifts for their native hosts.

"My first occupation", he wrote, "was to map the country." By the time the caravan had reached Tabora half Speke's property had been stolen, Grant had fever, many of the party were also ill and 98 of the porters had deserted. Things looked black, but Speke pressed on, travelling by way of Karagwe, west of Lake Victoria, which they reached in November 1861. Here Rumanika, the Galla chieftain, gave them great hospitality and they were able to hunt white rhinoceros. Speke discovered the Sitatunga (*Tragelaphus spekei*), an antelope with splayed, elongated toes that enable it to traverse marshy ground, and which feeds on the tops of papyrus rushes. At Karagwe the explorers recorded a strange tribal practice.

In order to inflate their women to an acceptable size they fattened them on milk, one of Rumanika's sisters-in-law being so enormous that she was unable to rise except on all fours. "It was desirous to obtain a good view of her, and actually to measure her," Speke wrote, in one of those strange aberrations that the Victorians were prone to, "and I induced her to give me facilities for doing so, by offering in return to show her a bit of my naked legs and arms. The bait took as I wished it, and after getting her to sidle and wriggle into the middle of the hut, I did as I promised, and then took her dimensions as noted. . . . Round arm, 1 ft 11 in; chest 4 ft 4 in; thigh, 2 ft 7 in; calf 1 ft 8 in; height, 5 ft 8 in. . . . Meanwhile, the daughter, a lass of sixteen, sat stark naked before us, sucking at a milk-pot, on which the father kept her at work by holding a rod in his hand, for as fattening is the first duty of fashionable life, it must be duly enforced if necessary. I got up a bit of flirtation with missy, and induced her to rise and shake hands with me. Her features were lovely, but her body was as round as a ball."

Speke and Grant became the first Europeans to enter Uganda, which they reached in January 1862. There, they stayed at the court of the young king Mutesa of Buganda, who extinguished human life with the same indifference as another might swat a fly. There they remained until July among the royal palaces. These were constructed from palm trunks, and some were 50 feet high.

On July 21 Speke reached the Nile at Urondogani and six days later what he named the Ripon Falls, known to the Waganda people as "The Stones", where the Nile flowed out of Victoria Nyanza. "Though beautiful," he wrote, "the scene was not exactly what I expected; for the broad surface of the lake was shut out from view by a spur of hill, and the falls, about 12 feet deep, and 400 to 500 feet broad, were broken by rocks.

Still it was a sight that attracted one to it for hours—the roar of the waters, the thousands of passenger fish, leaping at the falls with all their might, the Wasoga and Waganda fishermen coming out in boats and taking post on all the rocks with rod and hook, hippopotami and crocodiles lying sleepily on the water, the ferry at work above the falls, and cattle driven down to drink at the margin of the lake,—made, in all, with the pretty nature of the country—small hills, grassy-topped, with trees in the folds, and gardens on the lower slopes—as interesting a picture as one could wish to see."

Then after "marching down the north slope of Africa" to reach the Nile farther downstream, they paddled down it in canoes, until just south of Lake Kyoga they encountered a hostile chief, and were forced to leave the river without seeing it. Travelling overland they also failed to discover Lake Albert, into which the Victoria Nile flows.

On February 15, 1863, they reached Gondokoro, on the way down the river having found a tree with the letters MI scratched on it by an Italian, Miani, who had come in search of them. At Gondokoro they met the remarkable explorer Samuel Baker and his even more remarkable and beautiful wife, Florence, a Hungarian girl, who had travelled up the Nile through the Sudd with 100 men.

"My men", Baker wrote in his journal, "rushed madly to my boat, with the report that two white men were with them who had come from the *sea*! Could they be Speke and Grant? Off I ran, and soon met them in reality. Hurrah for Old England! . . . All my men were perfectly mad with excitement. Firing salutes, as usual with ball-cartridges, they shot one of my donkeys—a melancholy sacrifice as an offering at the completion of this geographical discovery.

"Speke," Baker said, "appeared the more worn of the two: he was excessively lean, but in reality was in tough condition; he had walked the whole way from Zanzibar, never having once ridden during that wearying march. Grant was in honourable rags; his bare knees projecting through the remnants of trousers that were an exhibition of rough industry in tailor's work. He was looking tired and feverish, but both men had a fire in their eye, that showed the spirit that had led them through."

From here, provisioned by Baker and in Baker's vessels, Speke and Grant travelled down the Nile to Khartoum and on to Europe, reaching London in June 1863.

Baker and his wife went on upriver with only 13 porters, and were detained by Kamrasi, the extortionate king of Unyoro, who had been such a headache to Speke. Kamrasi told Baker that he wished to have Florence for himself, and that she must stay behind. "If this were to be the end of the expedition I resolved that it should also be the end of Kamrasi, and, drawing my revolver quietly, I held it within two feet of his chest, and looking at him with undisguised contempt, I told him that if I touched the trigger not all his men could save him: and that if he dared to repeat the insult I would shoot him on the spot. . . . My wife, naturally indignant, had risen from her seat, and maddened with the excitement of the moment, she made him a little speech in Arabic (not a word of which he understood), with a countenance almost as amiable as the head of the Medusa. . . . With an air of complete astonishment, he said, 'Don't be angry! I had no intention of offending you by asking for your wife; I will give you a wife, if you want one, and I thought you might have no objections to give me yours; it is my custom to give visitors pretty wives, and I thought you might exchange. Don't make a fuss about it; if you don't like it, there's an end of it; I will never mention it again.'"

Their efforts were rewarded when they discovered Lake Albert Nyanza, the other source of the White Nile—actually the real source is far to the south, beyond Lake Edward, in the Ruwenzori Highlands and flows through Lake Albert. ". . . I hurried to the summit. The glory of our prize burst suddenly upon me! There, like a sea of quicksilver, lay far beneath the grand expanse of water—a boundless sea its horizon on the south and southwest glittering in the noon-day sun; and on the west, at fifty or sixty miles' distance, blue mountains rose from the bosom of the lake to a height of about 7000 feet above its level."

Swarms of crocodiles

"It is impossible to describe the triumph of that moment—here was the reward for all our labour—for all the years of tenacity with which we had toiled through Africa. England had won the sources of the Nile! . . . I felt too serious to vent my feelings in vain cheers for victory, and I sincerely thanked God for having guided and supported us through all dangers to the good end."

They then went on to discover the Murchison Falls, "where the river drops in one leap 120 feet into a deep basin, the edge of which literally swarms with crocodiles". They reached Khartoum, after a journey of two and a half years, in May, 1865 to learn that Speke had died the previous September in a shooting accident, thus bringing to an end his long feud with Burton.

The shape of Victoria Nyanza was now roughly known and the Victoria Nile, with some gaps, mapped from the Ripon Falls, more or less to the north end of Lake Albert, which Baker had reached but Speke had mapped more accurately from hearsay.

Among the Germans whose names were increasingly to be found in the story of African exploration and travel, one of the most outstanding was the botanist and ethnographer Georg Schweinfurth. He had already explored the Red Sea coast of Africa when he set off from Khartoum in December 1868 to examine the plant life of the western tributaries of the White Nile.

Schweinfurth was not only a botanist with a wonderful talent for drawing, which enabled him to make pictures as accurate as photographs, he was also an excellent zoologist; and in his work he was a man of the stature of Barth, as his great book, *The Heart of Africa*, shows.

On his way to the watershed of the Nile and Congo by way of the Bahr el-Gazal, a western tributary of the White Nile, he passed through jungles of papyrus grass 15 feet high, and once across the divide found himself in forest that was West African. "In the innermost recesses of these woods one would come upon an avenue like the colonnade of an Egyptian temple, veiled in the leafy shade of a triple roof above. Seen from without, they had all the appearance of impenetrable forests, but, traversed within, they opened into aisles and corridors which were musical with many a murmuring fount. Hardly anywhere was the height of these less than seventy feet, and on an average it was much nearer one hundred . . . and then there was the marvellous world of ferns, destitute indeed of stems, but running in their foliage to some twelve feet high . . . high above these there rose the large, slim-stemmed Rubiaceae, which by regularity of growth and symmetry of leaf appeared to imitate, and in a measure to supply the absence of, the Arboraceous ferns. Of all the other ferns the most singular which I observed was that which I call the elephant's ear. This I found up in trees at a height of more than fifty feet, in association with the Angroecum orchis and the long gray beard of the hanging Usnea."

On March 19, 1870, Schweinfurth discovered the upper waters of the Welle River, which flows to the Congo, and saw for the first time the pygmies of the Congo, in the dense forest on the north side of the watershed. He saw also the semi-civilized Mangbettu people on the divide, the cannibalistic Niam-Niam (so called by the Arabs because of the gusto with which they ate human flesh), the Mittoo and the Loobahs, whose women forced cones of polished quartz through their lips and circular plates made of quartz, ivory or horn, enlarging them to an enormous size. His journey lasted three years.

Missionaries to the unknown

BY THE END of the 18th century European Christians had become seriously concerned about the state of the heathen.

In Africa the reformed churches were first in the field, the Moravian Brethren establishing themselves at the Cape in 1792. Soon missions proliferated: the Anglican Church Missionary Society in Sierra Leone in 1804; the Basel Mission on the Gold Coast in 1828, followed by the Bremen Mission; the Rhenish Mission opened in South West Africa; the Berlin Society and the High Anglican Universities Mission in central, southern and eastern Africa and the Mission of Scottish Presbyterian Churches in the southwest and the east. Among Roman Catholic Missions, the Congregation of the Holy Ghost worked in vast fields in western and central Africa, while Cardinal Lavigerie's Society of our Lady of Africa, known as the White Fathers, ramified through central Africa eastwards. Benedictines, Jesuits and Franciscans were also in the field, as well as female orders.

Generally speaking the influence of the missionaries only began to be felt after the great explorers had opened the way; but it was dangerous unhealthy work—on the west coast alone, in 1825 more than 50 missionaries perished from various sorts of fever.

Strangely, except in the north of Africa, not all Muslims were hostile to missionaries. David Livingstone, the greatest of all missionary explorers, was often helped by Arab slavers. Even Seyyid Said, the Sultan of Oman and Zanzibar, whose riches were largely based on the profits from slavery,

assisted one missionary. "This letter", he wrote, "is written on behalf of Dr Krapf, the German, a good man who wishes to convert the world to God. Behave well to him and be everywhere serviceable to him." This, from a ruler whose subjects were engaged in slave-catching on a vast scale. From the great hunting grounds around the lakes, slaves were taken down to the coast at Bagamoyo, opposite Zanzibar, or to Kilwa, 200 miles to the south, in journeys that could last three months or more, in the course of which Livingstone estimated that five out of six slaves perished, and that for every six captured ten Negroes were killed.

Factory worker

Livingstone was born at Blantyre, Lanarkshire, in 1813, second son of a tea tradesman. At ten he started work in a cotton factory and educated himself by constant reading.

At 19 he went to Glasgow University, where he studied Greek and Divinity; then to London, where he graduated in medicine. While working in the London hospitals he joined the London Missionary Society and was ordained in 1840.

In May 1841, he landed at Algoa Bay in South Africa, and after travelling for ten weeks with horses and ox wagons reached Kuruman, the Society's most remote South African station. Quickly adapting to the practical difficulties of African life, he soon set off northwards in search of a suitable place for a mission station deeper in the bush.

The following year he made a four-month

journey into Bechuanaland, where he studied the customs of the tribes and their dialects, and in 1843 he founded a mission station at Mabotsa, 250 miles north of Kuruman, in country infested with lions that constantly attacked the herds, he himself only escaping death by a miracle when one attacked him.

In 1844, he married Mary Moffatt, daughter of the minister at Kuruman, and they went to live at Mabotsa. During this time he had great trouble with the Boer farmers, who either shot down or enslaved the Bechuana tribesmen, their supremely arrogant attitude being, according to Livingstone: "We make the people work for us, in consideration of allowing them to live in our country." One of Livingstone's missions was eventually destroyed by the Boers.

In June 1849, Livingstone set off north across the Kalahari Desert, where the wheels of his wagons sank deep into the white sand, and water could be found only by digging down through the sand to the sandstone shield which held the water below. He was accompanied by William Oswell, one of the several wealthy English sportsmen who often played some part in exploration in southern Africa. Eight years earlier, Oswell, with another hunter, Mungo Murray, and several Hottentots and Bechuanas of the Bakwena tribe, had tried to reach the arid country of the Makololo, a tribe ruled by a powerful, apparently enlightened chief called Sebituane.

Having passed through a region of salt pans, they followed the beautiful River Zouga (now the Botletle), and on August 1 they

discovered the shallow Lake Ngami (now a marsh).

The king of the lake tribe refused to provide them with a guide to take them to Sebituane and they had to turn back. Two years later, travelling with his pregnant wife and their three children, who were only four, three and one year old, he made another unsuccessful attempt to reach the Makolo.

On his third attempt in April 1851, the whole family set off by a different route across the Kalahari, crossing waterless wastes, their only guide an inefficient bushman named Shobo, who finally deserted them; but on the fifth day of their agony, with the possibility that the children would die before their eyes from thirst, they found water.

They then entered an area infested with tsetse flies and as a result 43 of their oxen died; but at last they reached the River Chobe (now Linyote), a tributary of the Zambezi, where they found Sebituane, who had travelled 400 miles to meet them, waiting on an island in the river.

"Sebituane was about forty-five years of age; of a tall and wiry form, an olive or coffee-and-milk colour, and slightly bald; in manner cool and collected, and more frank in his answers than any other chief I have ever met," Livingstone wrote.

The strange encounter with the great chief, in the course of which they learned the story of his life and of his aspirations, was recorded by Oswell, who had accompanied Livingstone and his family. "In the dead of night he paid us a visit alone, and sat down very quietly and mournfully at our fire. Livingstone and I woke up and greeted him, and then he dreamily recounted the history of his life, his wars, escapes, successes and conquests, and the far-distant wanderings in his raids. . . .''

From here Livingstone and Oswell reached the Zambezi, which flowed to the east. "This was a most important point," Livingstone wrote, "for that river was not known to exist there at all."

It was now that Livingstone confessed to Oswell his plan to cross to the Atlantic coast, 1,800 miles to the west. Then, realizing that it would be wrong to subject his family to such dangers, he took them on a six-month journey to the Cape (his wife giving birth to a son on the way), from where he sent them to England before setting out on the first of the great journeys that were to make him the most famous explorer of Africa, and of the Victorian Age.

It was at this period that his mission at Kolobeng was sacked by the Boers, who

disapproved of his efforts to put down slavery.

On November 11, 1853, with 27 porters and canoes lent to him by Sebituane's son Sekeletu, Livingstone set off from Linyanti, the Makololo capital, to cross the continent to the Atlantic. He had with him a tent, a change of clothes, five guns, scientific instruments and some ivory tusks given him by Sekeletu to sell when he finally crossed the divide.

They travelled along the Upper Zambezi, at first through rich, park-like country before entering the great rain-forest, where they were permanently drenched, suffering from fever and dysentery. After skirting Lake Dilolo, he crossed a terrible, swampy plain and in February 1854 descended from the watershed into the basin of the Congo, where he found the Kasai River, which flows northwards to join the Congo, the Zaire or "Great River" of its people.

By this time Livingstone was almost a skeleton and rode an unfriendly ox named Sinbad while his followers marched on foot. Now they entered the country of the hostile Kioko and Chiboque peoples, who wanted "a man, tusk, gun, or even an ox" in exchange for food. Livingstone indignantly refused to sell his Makololos as slaves and the party were soon on the verge of starvation.

They now crossed the River Cuango and entered Portuguese territory, meeting a Portuguese sergeant at an advance post. He gave them food and set them on their way to a trading outpost of the Angola colony, where as always they were well treated by the Portuguese, and Livingstone was impressed by the lack of colour discrimination. "Nowhere in Africa is there so much goodwill between Europeans and natives," he wrote.

On May 31, 1854, they reached the sea at Luanda. "My companions looked upon the boundless ocean with awe," Livingstone wrote. "On describing their feelings afterwards, they remarked that 'we marched along with our father, believing that what the ancients had always told us was true, that the world has no end; but all at once the world said to us, "I am finished; there is no more of me."' They had always imagined that the world was one extended plain without limit." They had covered 1,500 miles through unmapped country.

Accurate map

Dissatisfied with the route he had pioneered, Livingstone decided to re-cross the continent. His party set off in September up the Cuanza River, and a year later, on September 11, 1855, reached Linyanti, having lost both his horse and Sinbad. Livingstone himself nearly died from rheumatic fever on the journey, during which he plotted a route that was a wonder of accuracy.

Only seven weeks later he set off for the east coast and on his way had his first sight of the Victoria Falls, "the most wonderful sight I had witnessed in Africa".

His next expedition was a much grander affair, sponsored by the British Government. Livingstone's secret intention was to lay the foundations of a British colony "in the healthy high lands of Central Africa". The expedition arrived at the mouth of the Zambezi in May 1858, sailing from there up the river to Tete in a paddle-launch called the Ma-Robert—the name given to Mrs Livingstone by the tribesmen, after her first-born son. There, in September, he and his party were given a great welcome by the Makololo. On this journey they were not able to take the boat, which they named "The Asthmatic", farther upstream than the Quebrabasa rapids.

Livingstone then attempted to go up the Shire, a tributary of the Zambezi, but was forced to turn back. In September 1859, together with John Kirk, a doctor and naturalist, he succeeded in travelling overland with 36 Makololo porters through the Shire Highlands and discovered Lake Nyasa (now Lake Malawi), the third largest lake in Africa.

Almost a year later, after a difficult ten-week journey, Livingstone reached Sekeletu's kraal, to find that his faithful friend was suffering from leprosy, which he was able to do something to alleviate. There, among other stores left by his expedition seven years before, he found the magic lantern and the slides that he had used to make Christianity more vivid to the tribespeople.

His next expedition took him up the Ruvuma (Rovuma) River, which rises east of Lake Nyasa and enters the Indian Ocean north of Cape Delgado. The party, which had among it members of the Universities Mission and the Bishop of Central Africa, Charles Mackenzie, reached the Shire Highlands in their search for a suitable place to establish a mission station and met with terrible, heart-rending sights—long lines of manacled men, women and children, escorted by black drivers, "blowing exultant notes on their tin horns", who fled when the Europeans approached, leaving the slaves to be released. One of the slaves released in the Shire country was Shuma, who became Livingstone's personal attendant until the end.

What Livingstone discovered on his great trans-continental journeys was that far from being the sandy desert which many had thought it to be, in which the rivers led nowhere, the interior of Africa was "a well-watered country, with large tracts of fine fertile soil covered with forest, and beautiful grassy valleys, occupied by a considerable population. . . ."

David Livingstone's involvement with the

Missionaries to the unknown

Nile quest began in 1866, when he set off from the east coast along the Ruvuma River, to explore the watersheds of the Nile, the Congo and the Zambezi. He had with him his attendant, Susi, who had been with him to the Zambezi, two boys whom he had saved from slavery who remained with him until he died and a number of unreliable porters. He also had with him camels, buffaloes, donkeys and mules.

In spite of the letters of recommendation that he carried from the Sultan of Zanzibar, many of the Arab traders were hostile. His journey took him round the south side of Lake Nyasa to the southern end of Lake Tanganyika, which he reached in April 1867, plotting its position accurately. Sick with fever, having lost his medicine chest with the vital quinine—"I felt as if I had received my death sentence"—seeing many dead and dying slaves along the route, he crossed the Muchinga Mountains in present-day Zambia, which rise to 5,000 feet, living on maize. "I took my belt up three holes," he wrote.

That November, very ill, he rediscovered Lake Mweru, originally found by Dr de Lacerda, the Portuguese explorer, in 1798. Eight months later, in July 1868, now with only five companions, he found Lake Bangweulu, a shallow lake on a plateau fed by another Congo headstream, the Chambezi, and drained by the Lualaba.

He then went north to Ujiji on Lake Tanganyika, where he found that his stores had been stolen, then northwest to Nyangwe on the Lualaba, where he witnessed a dreadful massacre of Negro men and women, who were mown down in their dozens by Arab slavers as they attempted to escape down the river.

On November 10, 1871, having crossed Lake Tanganyika eastwards to Ujiji, he met Henry Morton Stanley, the intrepid American newspaper correspondent, born Rowlands and brought up in a Welsh workhouse. Stanley had been sent out by James Gordon Bennett, the proprietor of the *New York Herald*, to find Livingstone. "As I advanced slowly towards him I noticed he was pale, looked wearied, had grey whiskers and moustache, wore a bluish cap with a faded gold band around it, had on a red-sleeved waistcoat, and a pair of grey tweed trousers," Stanley wrote. "I would have run to him, only I was a coward in the presence of such a mob—would have embraced him, but that I did not know how he would receive me. So I did what moral cowardice and false pride suggested was the best thing—walked deliberately up to him, took off my hat and said, 'Dr Livingstone, I presume?' 'Yes,' he said, with a kind smile, lifting his cap slightly." Stanley, aged 30, had scooped the world.

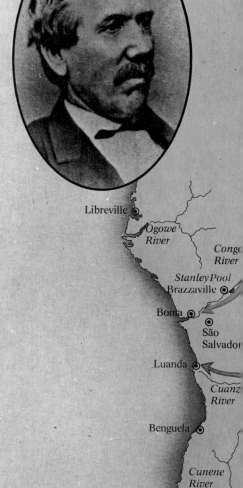

"The greatest man of his generation" was how Florence Nightingale described David Livingstone, who became a legend in his own lifetime, the only explorer to be given a full state funeral in Westminster Abbey. He was happiest when tramping through unexplored parts of Africa, where he covered more than 30,000 miles, mostly on foot, as he mapped the river systems, intent on eradicating the Arab slave trade. Much of his Christian teaching was to upset native tribal traditions, but of all African explorers he was the truest friend of the African people

After almost ten years Livingstone tired of his first missionary spell in South Africa — his religious spirit was challenged by a drive to explore. In 1850 he set out across the Kalahari Desert, which he eventually crossed three times, on foot — twice with his wife and children

In 1858 Livingstone was sent to head an expedition up the Zambezi to prove the river navigable, and demonstrate the potential for British settlement and cotton cultivation. The result was a failure; sandbanks and rapids prevented navigation by steamers above Tete. When Livingstone returned to Africa for the last time in 1866, he was officially dubbed "Her Majesty's Consul, Inner Africa"

Life as an explorer was not simple for Livingstone. He suffered constantly from tropical diseases, and a few days before his death wrote: "It is not all pleasure, this exploration"

Libreville

Ogowe River

Congo River

Stanley Pool
Brazzaville

Boma

São Salvador

Luanda

Cuanza River

Benguela

Cunene River

The *Ma-Robert* (the local name for Mrs Livingstone, the mother of Robert), built specially for work on the Zambezi

When David Livingstone first saw the Zambezi in 1851, he was so much reminded of his native Clyde that he envisaged steamers plying up and down, carrying missionaries and traders into the heart of the continent. He believed that by using rivers as communications routes he could introduce legitimate trade, help wipe out slaving and spread Christianity. Steamers built in Scotland to sail the Niger had been responsible for opening up the interior to English commerce. Livingstone saw them in use in the same way on the southern rivers, linking inland mission stations and trading centres. (Right) Stanley's *Lady Alice*, dismantled for cross-country portage beside the Congo

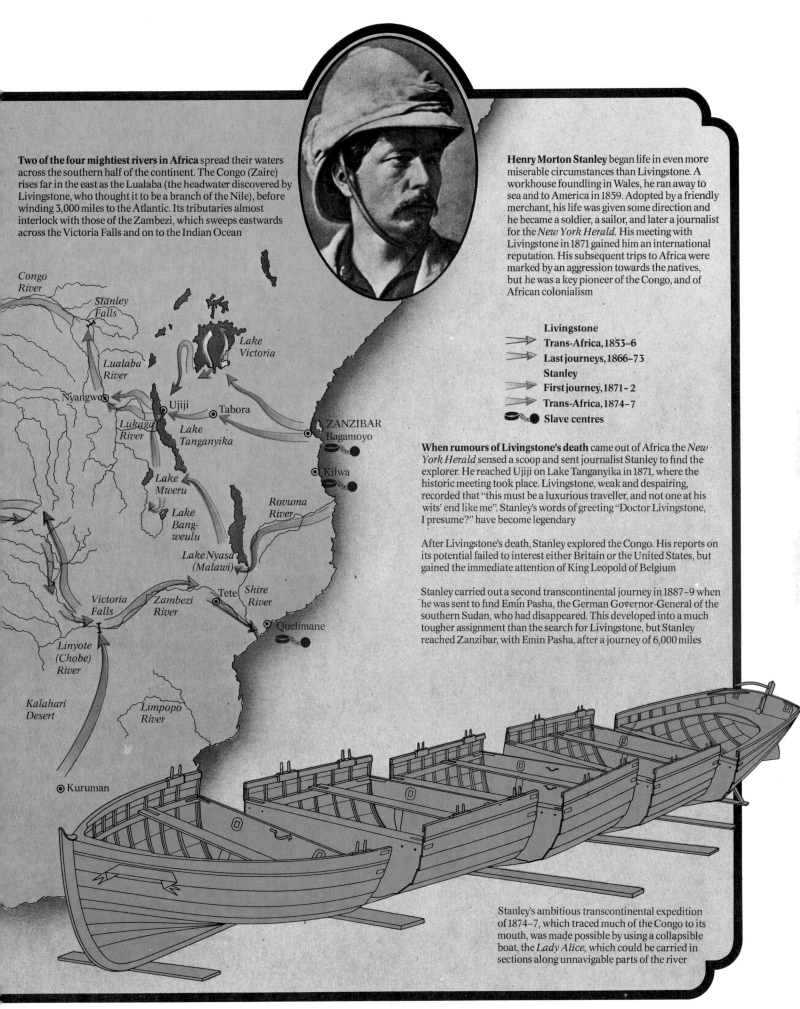

Two of the four mightiest rivers in Africa spread their waters across the southern half of the continent. The Congo (Zaire) rises far in the east as the Lualaba (the headwater discovered by Livingstone, who thought it to be a branch of the Nile), before winding 3,000 miles to the Atlantic. Its tributaries almost interlock with those of the Zambezi, which sweeps eastwards across the Victoria Falls and on to the Indian Ocean

Congo River

Stanley Falls

Lualaba River

Nyangwe

Ujiji

Tabora

Lukuga River

Lake Victoria

Lake Tanganyika

ZANZIBAR
Bagamoyo

Kilwa

Lake Mweru

Lake Bang-weulu

Rovuma River

Lake Nyasa (Malawi)

Tete

Shire River

Victoria Falls

Zambezi River

Quelimane

Linyote (Chobe) River

Kalahari Desert

Limpopo River

Kuruman

Henry Morton Stanley began life in even more miserable circumstances than Livingstone. A workhouse foundling in Wales, he ran away to sea and to America in 1859. Adopted by a friendly merchant, his life was given some direction and he became a soldier, a sailor, and later a journalist for the *New York Herald*. His meeting with Livingstone in 1871 gained him an international reputation. His subsequent trips to Africa were marked by an aggression towards the natives, but he was a key pioneer of the Congo, and of African colonialism

	Livingstone
→	**Trans-Africa, 1853–6**
→	**Last journeys, 1866–73**
	Stanley
→	**First journey, 1871–2**
→	**Trans-Africa, 1874–7**
●—	**Slave centres**

When rumours of Livingstone's death came out of Africa the *New York Herald* sensed a scoop and sent journalist Stanley to find the explorer. He reached Ujiji on Lake Tanganyika in 1871, where the historic meeting took place. Livingstone, weak and despairing, recorded that "this must be a luxurious traveller, and not one at his wits' end like me". Stanley's words of greeting "Doctor Livingstone, I presume?" have become legendary

After Livingstone's death, Stanley explored the Congo. His reports on its potential failed to interest either Britain or the United States, but gained the immediate attention of King Leopold of Belgium

Stanley carried out a second transcontinental journey in 1887–9 when he was sent to find Emin Pasha, the German Governor-General of the southern Sudan, who had disappeared. This developed into a much tougher assignment than the search for Livingstone, but Stanley reached Zanzibar, with Emin Pasha, after a journey of 6,000 miles

Stanley's ambitious transcontinental expedition of 1874–7, which traced much of the Congo to its mouth, was made possible by using a collapsible boat, the *Lady Alice*, which could be carried in sections along unnavigable parts of the river

Missionaries to the unknown

In August 1872, Livingstone left Tabora on what was to be his last journey, sure that the river flowing into Lake Bangweulu was the source of the Nile. By the end of April 1873 he was struggling through terrible swamps infested with mosquitoes, poisonous spiders and stinging ants, to the south of the lake.

On April 9 he made his last entry in his notebook. Carried in a litter to the village of a chief named Chitambo on April 30, he asked how far it was to the Lualaba and, when told that it was three days' journey, said: "Oh Dear! dear!" At four o'clock on the morning of May 1 his devoted servants, Susi and Chuma, found him dead kneeling by his bed in an attitude of prayer.

They buried his heart, embalmed his body, wrapped it in bark and carried it 1,000 miles to the coast in a sailcloth hammock slung from a pole—a journey of 11 months and a tribute to the loyalty that he inspired in his men. Then, still accompanied by Susi and Chuma, his remains were taken to England and buried in Westminster Abbey.

His epitaph reads: "For thirty years his life was spent in an unwearied effort to evangelize the native races, to explore the undiscovered secrets, to abolish the desolating slave trade of Central Africa, where with his last words he wrote 'All I can add in my solitude is may Heaven's rich blessing come down on everyone, American, English or Turk, who will help to heal this open sore of the world'."

The horrors of the massacres he had witnessed were not in vain. Soon afterwards the Sultan of Zanzibar bowed to opinion and closed the slave market on the island for ever.

AFTER THE DEATH of Livingstone, Stanley set off, in November 1874, from Bagamoyo with the most lavishly equipped expedition ever to penetrate into the interior of Africa. It was sponsored by the London *Daily Telegraph*. Stanley took with him two young English boatmen, Edward and Frank Pocock, and a young clerk named Frederick Barker. They had with them a 40-foot-long steel boat, the *Lady Alice*, which was built in sections so that it could be more easily transported, eight tons of equipment subdivided into 60-pound packs, 356 porters and followers, and numerous dogs and donkeys.

By the time the expedition reached Lake Victoria in March 1875, 26 men had been killed or wounded in an attack on the column by 2,000 tribesmen and only half the original force of porters remained. Disease and desertion had accounted for the remainder. Barker was dead—soon to be followed by Edward Pocock.

On the shore of the lake the boat was assembled and Stanley and Frank Pocock made a circumnavigation of the lake, menaced by storms and ill-disposed hippopotamuses who tried to upset their craft. Stanley proved conclusively that it was a single lake, fed by the Kagera and drained by the Victoria Nile. Thus Speke's belief, which was nothing but an inspired guess about the Nile source, was completely vindicated. The country between Lake Victoria and Lake Edward was also explored this time and another voyage, round Lake Tanganyika, proved that both Speke and Livingstone were right in their belief that no river of sufficient importance to be identified as a possible source of the Nile flowed into it.

In October 1876, the expedition—now numbering about 130 persons, of whom 30 bore arms—reached, with the expenditure of immense effort, the confluence of the Luana and the Lualaba rivers on what was to be the epic first crossing of the continent, most of it within a few degrees of the Equator. At this time Stanley had no means of knowing whether he would emerge from it at the Atlantic or the Mediterranean.

At Nyangwe, in the dark heart of the continent—Livingstone's farthest point in 1871 and the farthest point known to Europeans, and to only a few Arabs—Stanley struck a bargain with Tippoo Tib, a half-Arab, half-Negro slaver of fearful reputation, to provide an escort of 700 men, together with women and children, down the Lualaba for 60 marches, in exchange for 5,000 Spanish dollars. The expedition set off on November 5, 1876, following the course of the Lualaba River on foot, passing through dense mouldering tropical rain-forest that was so dark that Stanley was unable to read his notes in daylight.

The *Lady Alice* and a number of canoes were launched on November 19, and from then on the expedition was partly waterborne, partly on foot.

Two hundred miles north of Nyangwe, Tippoo gave up. His men were dying at the rate of two or three a day from smallpox, ulcers and dysentery. After the slave master's party had left, Stanley continued with the *Lady Alice*, and with 149 men, women and children and some donkeys loaded into canoes. The map of what lay before him was a vast blank.

Cannibals dogged their way constantly as they sailed down the Lualaba to the point where it becomes the Congo. On this great river further hazards awaited them—seven cataracts. Here the boats had to be carried up cliffs and a way cut through the bush. It was here, too, above the present town of Stanleyville (Kisangani), that Stanley discovered the depressing fact that the altitude of the river was 14 feet below that of the Nile at Gondokoro, which meant that wherever he was bound, it was not for Cairo. Neither did he know a fact that would have cheered him—that before him, now that he had passed the cataracts, were some 1,000 miles of unobstructed sailing.

In March they were six degrees east of the Congo delta and about 450 miles from its nearest mouth in a direct line. Now they encountered further rapids so swift that the boats had to be "walked" down them, held in check with ropes. They passed high white cliffs, which they named Stanley Pool, the first Europeans to reach this area since some Capuchin missionaries in the 17th century. From here they entered the chasms of the Crystal Mountains, where they had to persuade a tribe, fortunately friendly, to help them to haul the *Lady Alice* and the 17 remaining canoes over the intervening, precipitous terrain.

In the succeeding cataracts eight canoes were lost and on June 3, 1877, Frank Pocock, crippled by ulcers on his feet, but for all that "joyous and light-hearted as a linnet," was drowned in the Massassa Rapids.

When they were only five days from Boma, the port on the north bank of the Congo, they left the river and abandoned the *Lady Alice* on a cliff top; on August 1, the 115 survivors, who included three mothers with new-born babies, set off again on foot. Nine hundred and ninety-nine days after setting out from Zanzibar they reached Boma.

Stanley kept his promise to take the survivors back to Zanzibar, instead of accepting the tempting offer of a quick voyage to Lisbon, and reached it in November 1877.

This was the end of the great heroic phase of African exploration. In the course of it the Niger, the Zambezi, the Nile and the Congo had all been explored. The great outline had been delineated—the details still remained to be filled in. Some of them would take many years to be completed.

This was not the end of Stanley's endeavours. From 1879 onwards he spent five years in the Congo, working for the Belgian Government, and in 1885 he set out with a British expedition by way of the Congo to rescue Emin Pasha, otherwise Eduard Schnitzer, a German naturalist who had been appointed as governor in Wadelai by General Gordon and who, now that Khartoum had fallen to the Mahdi and Gordon was dead, was reputed to be in great danger. After suffering appalling difficulties in reaching Emin—and reaching the Ruwenzori Mountains (the "Mountains of the Moon") in the Congo—Stanley discovered that Emin didn't want to be rescued. Together, he and Stanley drank five half-bottles of champagne on the shore of Lake Albert Nyanza.

BETWEEN 1831 AND 1833 the British and French treaties for the suppression of the slave trade came into operation and it soon became obvious to the French that Senegal, their nearest base to the chief centres of the slave trade around the Congo and Dahomey rivers, was too far off from them to be able to intercept the slave ships—and worse, they were losing bounties by failing to do so.

In 1838, the French took possession of the mouth of the Gabon River, where Libreville now stands, and established settlements there. In the 1840s they set up other forts along the coast, where they soon found that "the exuberance of the vegetation was not a proof of the fertility of the soil". Then the missionaries arrived, among them members of the Roman Catholic Congregation of the Holy Ghost, which set up stations on the Gabon and in the lower Congo.

One of the first laymen to reach the Congo basin was Ladislaus Magyar, who in 1849 began a journey from Benguela, a slave port on the Angola coast, and marched eastwards to the valley of the upper Zambezi before crossing into the basin of the Congo.

In 1853, Silva Porto crossed Africa, starting from Benguela, travelled along the Congo–Zambezi watershed and continued eastwards south of Lake Nyasa and the Ruvuma River.

These were the years when Paul Du Chaillu, the son of a French trader in Gabon and an American citizen, made three journeys into the unexplored interior of Gabon.

Du Chaillu found little to fear from the inhabitants. "The very fact that a white man could travel alone, single-handed, and without powerful backers, through this rude country, without being molested or robbed is sufficient evidence that the negro race is not unkindly natured," he wrote in his *Explorations and Adventures in Equatorial Africa*. His great discovery was the gorilla, which he was the first white man to see, while he was exploring the N'tem highlands. "The underbush swayed rapidly ahead," he wrote in his book, which became a best-seller, "and presently before us stood an immense male gorilla. He had gone through the jungle on his all fours; but when he saw our party he erected himself and looked us boldly in the face. . . . Nearly six feet high with immense body, huge glaring large deep gray eyes . . . thus stood before us the king of the African forest."

Du Chaillu's book about the gorillas was derided as a pack of lies by many knowing reviewers—two young specimens which he had tried to take out of the forest failed to survive, and the existence of the gorilla was unconfirmed until further sightings were made three-quarters of a century later.

While Stanley was fighting his way across the continent from east to west, King Leopold II of the Belgians convened an International Conference at Brussels, which discussed African exploration, the civilizing of the country and the suppression of the slave trade. It was attended by large numbers of savants and explorers—Germany was represented by the great traveller and geologist Baron von Richthofen and by Nachtigal, Schweinfurth and Rohlfs. Against them was matched a British contingent, which included Grant and Verney Lovett Cameron, who had searched for Livingstone in 1873, had gone on to Lake Tanganyika, which he discovered was connected with the Congo, and had then gone on to cross the continent to the west coast near Benguela. He was the first European to cross Equatorial Africa from east to west, a journey that took him 31 months.

The conference decided to set up a chain of what it called *stations civilisatrices* along Livingstone's cross-continent route. At these stations Africans would be educated in various skills by scientists and artisans, scientific research would be carried out, maps would be drawn, specimens collected. The stations would also serve as bases for further exploration. One was to be in the southern Congo. In the event the scheme failed and only one station was built; and when Stanley emerged, triumphantly, at the mouth of the Congo, only to be rebuffed by the British Government when he proposed that the entire river should be claimed by them, it was Leopold who employed him in a vast scheme to open up the entire river basin.

The French viewed these developments with alarm. In 1878, they decided to send out Pierre Savorgnan de Brazza, a French naval officer of aristocratic Italian extraction, to go up the river and take possession of the territory in the region of Stanley Pool, so far unappropriated by any European nation.

De Brazza was an experienced explorer. Setting out in 1875, he had already, in a two-year journey, reached the source of the Ogowe, a river which rises in the Baleke plateau of the Congo and flows through the thick forests of Gabon to reach the Atlantic in a delta by Cape Lopex and Port Gentil. He had also found two tributaries of the Congo.

Now, to beat Stanley, he set off with a tiny force of 11 Senegalese marines, reached the Ogowe, where he set up a *station civilisatrice* and then, with incredible speed, crossed the watershed to the Congo, on the way inducing local chiefs to acknowledge French sovereignty with the aid of small gifts and his own pleasing personality—he was an extremely humane man and the Africans liked him. His greatest "convert" was the important chief Makolo, this alliance giving France part of the right bank of the Congo and the adjacent territory. And now, having established a post (the future Brazzaville) under his Senegalese sergeant, Malamine, de Brazza went down the river to meet Stanley, whom he had out-manoeuvred—a famous, but somewhat cool confrontation.

De Brazza then continued to the coast at Libreville, where he expected to find men and supplies to consolidate his gains. Instead, he received orders to return to France. Leopold had prevailed on the French to leave the Congo to Belgium.

Eventually, de Brazza had the satisfaction of persuading the French Government to uphold its claim and the French Congo became a reality.

A colonizer of the old sort, he never forgot that he was dealing with human beings. "Do not lose touch with the Negroes," he wrote. "Do not forget that you are the intruder who was not invited!"

Contrasting splendours of Africa: termitarium, swamp birds and a mountain rising in solitary splendour from the savanna

Land of the Masai

ONE OF THE great explorers of East Africa was Joseph Thomson, a young Scottish geologist. In his early twenties, he led an East African expedition, sponsored by the Royal Geographical Society, and in 1883, the Society put him in command of an expedition, the aim of which was "to ascertain if a practical direct route for European travellers exists through the Masai country from any one of the East African ports to Lake Victoria Nyanza", a journey that would open up one of the last unknown regions of East Africa.

The great, open country of the Masai people was difficult and dangerous. The Masai, cattle-owning and cattle-lifting nomads, were formidable warriors and intensely xenophobic. A people of Hamitic origin, with Mongol eyes and a chocolate complexion, they were a fearsome sight when fully dressed for battle, wearing great ostrich-feather headdresses, their legs adorned with the hair of the colobus monkey, which simulated wings, and armed with broad-headed spears, swords and clubs and with a six-foot length of cotton streaming from their hair.

The only explorers who had done any work in this direction up to now were two missionaries, New and Wakefield, and Klaus von der Decken, who died on the Juba River in Somaliland after five years in East Africa exploring the area around Kilimanjaro.

In March 1883, Thomson left the coast opposite Zanzibar, taking with him a Maltese sailor named James Martin. The expedition travelled in the footsteps of the German explorer Gustav Adolf Fischer, who had reached Kilimanjaro the previous year and who later explored the Great Rift Valley.

Now began the first of Thomson's hair-raising encounters with the Masai, in the course of which they took a sadistic pleasure in humiliating him by making him take his boots off and wriggle his toes, pinched him and attempted to take down his trousers. His only defence was the performance of a slight piece of European magic—adding some Enos fruit salts to a glass of water—and this gave him some temporary reputation among them. In July 1883, they joined a north-bound Swahili caravan for security and with it reached the Great Rift Valley, where Thomson climbed the extinct volcano Longonot.

They had a terrible time at Naivasha, surrounded by arrogant, threatening Masai; but fortunately rival tribesmen were massing to attack, which probably saved the explorers.

Thomson then crossed the 13,000-foot Aberdare range, which he named after Lord Aberdare, who became President of the Royal Geographical Society, and saw Mount Kenya, towering in its snow-capped splendour, finally reaching the northeast shore of Lake Victoria in December 1883.

The return journey was one of horror. After discovering the 14,000-foot Mount Elgon, an extinct volcano on the present borders of Uganda and Kenya, and also the remarkable prehistoric caves on its southern slopes, Thomson was badly gored by a buffalo.

After being semi-conscious for six weeks in a grass hut, in April 1884 he was strong enough to resume his journey by litter and the expedition eventually reached Rabai, inland from Mombasa, on May 24 after a journey of 3,000 miles.

In 1885, on behalf of the National African Company, he went up the Niger to the West Sudan, and, three years later, explored at his own expense in the Atlas Mountains, climbing some of the high peaks.

In 1891, Captain J. R. L. MacDonald began his survey for the projected 657-mile-long railway between Mombasa and the shore of Lake Victoria. It took him through the midst of more than 300,000 square miles of what is now Kenya, then unknown country, on which the explorers who had their sights on the Nile sources had had neither time nor will to explore.

Work started on the railway, after much public opposition in the British Press and Parliament, in December 1895, the Chief Engineer being a young Englishman named George Whitehouse.

The rest of the story is one of disasters and ultimate triumph. Looking at a cross-section of the route it suggests the temperature chart of a patient who is suffering from an undulant fever which grows steadily worse. The line was pushed forward by thousands of Indian coolies through the coastal belt—where 500 workers became hospital cases, suffering from malaria, dysentery and jungle sores—through the terrible Taru Desert and a tsetse fly belt, 160 miles wide, in which 1,500 out of 1,800 transport animals died. At Tsavo, two man-eating lions ate 28 of the workers before they were finally shot after a ten-month hunt. At one stage in the construction hordes of caterpillars held up the locomotives.

The summer of 1900 took them across the Great Rift with relatively easy going; but the ascent of the east side to the Mau Escarpment, over 8,000 feet above the sea, reached early in 1901, was a nightmare, with heavy rain, thick mud, sleet and ice.

The downhill section to Port Florence (Kisumu) on Lake Victoria took a year, in which survey parties were raided by the Nandi tribes, dysentery and malaria again caused havoc among the workers and two engineers were killed in a train smash; but on Friday, December 20, the last 10,400 feet of line were laid in record time and the Florence Station was reached, 581 miles from the starting point on the coast at Mombasa.

Empire building—the hard way. All the hazards faced by explorers in tropical lands were compressed into the experience of the men who built the East African railway from Mombasa to Lake Victoria between 1896 and 1901. As a feat of Victorian engineering, it was impressive; from sea level the lines eventually climbed to 9,000 feet across the Rift Mountains before descending to the lake. The engineering problems were far from being the only ones. For almost a year, the construction of one bridge was held up by man-eating lions. who killed and ate 28 workers before they were shot. Rhinos sent construction gangs running, ants undermined embankments—even seas of caterpillars brought locomotives to a halt. Outbreaks of malaria and dysentery added to difficulties, almost as though the whole of nature had decided to stop the railway

An African lion. The king of beasts gave ground reluctantly to the railway builders of East Africa and elsewhere picked off an occasional explorer. Livingstone was badly hurt by one

Among the fiercest of Africa's tribes, the nomadic Masai—like the lion—gave an uncomfortable welcome to the first white men to make their way into the tribe's lands

Giant groundsels form a frame for Mount Kenya, one of the two great mountains (the other is Kilimanjaro) which rise in solitary splendour from the plains of East Africa

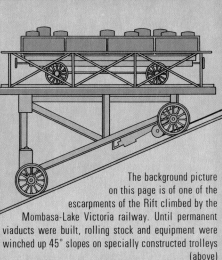

The background picture on this page is of one of the escarpments of the Rift climbed by the Mombasa-Lake Victoria railway. Until permanent viaducts were built, rolling stock and equipment were winched up 45° slopes on specially constructed trolleys (above)

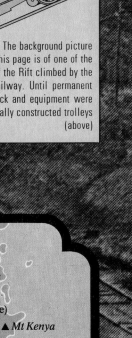

▲ Mt Elgon

Kisumu
(Port Florence)

▲ Mt Kenya

Lake
Victoria   ◎ Nairobi

Mt Kilimanjaro ▲

Mombasa ◉

Railway
Mountains
over 4,500 ft

Advance from the Cape

THE EPIC STORY of African exploration in the 18th and 19th centuries was almost all in that part of the continent properly called the Tropics—the area between the tropics of Cancer and Capricorn, the one to the north, the other to the south of the Equator and each about 23 degrees 28 minutes from it.

North of the Tropic of Cancer, Arab influence had been present for centuries and had largely excluded the European, unless he was disguised as a Muslim. To the south of Capricorn the European planted the seeds of permanent settlement in a region where both climate and terrain were more hospitable to northerners than anywhere else in the continent—the Cape of Good Hope.

The Dutch East India Company had begun to use the Cape of Good Hope as a revictualling station on the sea route from Europe to the East in the 17th century. Soon it had a small population, consisting of members of the Company, who tried their hands at market gardening, in order to have fresh produce to sell to the ships.

They had a hard time of it, and they were on the verge of starvation until 1657 when the Company conferred on nine of them the right to own 13 acres of land, providing that they continued to provide foodstuffs for its vessels.

These "free burghers" as they were called soon learned that the answer to increased food production was to enslave the Hottentots and the Bushmen, who had all been driven out of their ancient pastoral lands and hunting grounds by the Bantu. As a result their tribal organization now rapidly collapsed, assisted by outbreaks of smallpox.

The Boers, as the settlers called themselves, were of Calvinist or Huguenot origin and saw life in terms of the Old Testament —they believed that they had a Divine right of enslaving and taking the land of what they called "the sons of Ham". Livingstone, in the 1840s, recorded one of them as saying: "We make the people work for us, in consideration of allowing them to live in our country." They had become cattle-owning farmers by buying stock from the Bantu, and when their ivory hunters pushed eastwards across the Orange River and found the fertile regions of Natal in the middle of the 18th century, their eyes turned in that direction.

The impulse that was to force the Boers farther north and east came when Britain took over the government of the Cape during the Napoleonic Wars. Slavery was abolished throughout the British Empire in 1833, missionary societies made their appearance, and land—which the Boers had regarded as something which one simply took—was in future to be auctioned by the government to the highest bidder. To make matters worse

for the Boers the government demarcated a frontier beyond which they were forbidden to pass. Along it were planted some thousands of British settlers who had been landed at Port Elizabeth to act as a buffer between the Boers and the tribes whose lands they coveted.

In the autumn of 1836 what became known as the Great Trek began, with the Voortrekkers moving out across the Orange River over the mountains and on to the vast plain of the veld.

The trek was neither exploration nor discovery in the traditional sense, but it took whole communities, rather than intrepid individuals or armed bands of Conquistadors, into lands about which they knew little or nothing at all. More importantly, it took them into the tribal lands of warrior people; a hazard met and overcome, whatever the ultimate result, by Europeans from the time of Alexander onwards.

The first attacks on them were made by the Matabele, beyond the Vaal River, where 53 men, women and children were massacred. The survivors, under Hendrick Potgieter and Sarel Cilliers—who preached about hell and damnation and the wrath of God before his trekkers went into action—formed a great laager at Veg Kop, between the Rhenoste and Wilge rivers, which was attacked by 6,000 Matabele on October 16, 1836. The attack was beaten off, the Matabele losing 400 warriors, the Boers only two men with a dozen wounded. What was worse, they lost 55,000 cattle, sheep and goats, which were driven off by the Matabele when they retreated.

Potgieter retaliated by leading a commando against the Matabele, catching the army unawares and asleep in the Mosega Valley. Heavy losses were inflicted on the tribe, their kraals were put to the torch and as a result they retired beyond the Limpopo, leaving their territory in the hands of the Boers.

While Potgieter's trekkers consolidated their gains, 1,000 wagons, under Piet Retief, went on across the great mountains of the Drakensberg border range. From the escarpment they looked down on to the fertile country of the great Zulu king, Dingaan, who had murdered his predecessor Chaka, the man who had turned the Zulu nation into a formidable war machine. From here, near Van Reenen's Pass, Retief set off down the precipitous slopes with 15 men and four wagons and rode to Umgungundhlovu (the Place of the Elephant), Dingaan's capital. There, Dingaan agreed that if Retief would recapture some cattle, which a chief named Sikonyela had stolen, he and his trekkers could have land in Natal. Unfortunately Retief's men had disregarded his instructions to remain on the pass and had descended with

their 1,000 wagons into the plain, where they were already engaged in occupying Zulu lands.

Dingaan did not forgive what he regarded as an act of treachery; he requited it in full by luring Retief and 70 of his companions into his kraal where, after being induced to lay aside their weapons, they were set upon and their brains beaten out with knobkerries.

The Zulus now attacked the main body of the settlers, taking them by surprise at night and killing 550 Boers and Africans, of whom more than 150 were children. Dingaan then sent his Zulu against Port Natal, which was a British settlement, and razed it to the ground. Fortunately there had been time to evacuate the inhabitants by ship.

Potgieter now sent reinforcements from what had been the Matabele country and the tide turned against Dingaan, this time for ever, when, on December 16, 1838, a strong commando of 500 men under Andreus Pretorius shattered a Zulu army of between ten and 12,000 men.

This was the beginning of the end of the Zulu nation. In December 1839 a commando under Pretorius and a number of Zulu regiments, which had defected from Dingaan, invaded Zululand. The capital was sacked, 65,000 head of cattle were taken and Dingaan

In the manner of the American migrants moving west in wagon trains, and at about the same time in history, the Boers of 19th-century southern Africa trekked north from the Cape to superimpose a European country upon the tribal lands of a native people. Unlike North America, where the new arrivals rapidly came to outnumber the indigenous peoples, the South African settlers remained—and remain—a minority, reflecting itself in their defensive attitudes towards the native inhabitants.
The country through which the Boers passed and where they made their homes was excitingly rich in game. Antelopes of a variety of species provided a moving carpet of life, but their numbers were soon to diminish rapidly as the pastoral arrivals extended their farms, and the ivory and big game hunters, drawn by stories of the sport to be had, found their way to the country. (Left) one of the trekkers' "waens"; (below) wildebeest at a waterhole

himself fled into Swaziland where he was assassinated. The triumph of the Boers was complete. The Great Trek was over. Soon the Orange Free State and the South African Republic, the Transvaal, came into being; but the fear that the Boers had always felt for the coloured people, who so vastly outnumbered them, never died.

Confronted as they were by some of Africa's finest fighting men, who were defending their traditional pastures, the Boers paid little heed to the richness of the wildlife surrounding them; but 100 years before the Great Trek, Europeans had made their way to southern Africa to gather plants and to observe the animals that abounded there.

Earliest in the field, in 1722, was Carl Peter Thunberg, a graduate of Uppsala University, who had studied under Linnaeus. His companion was Anders Sparrman, also of Uppsala, who interrupted his journeys with Thunberg to accompany Cook on his voyage to the Antarctic.

Between them in the course of their travels in what is now Cape Province, between 1722 and 1726, the two Swedes sent back great quantities of seeds and specimens including Ixias and more than 50 varieties of Pelargonium.

They were followed by François Le Vaillant, the son of the French consul at Paramaribo in Dutch Guiana, where he had already travelled extensively in the forests. An eccentric character, he was accompanied by a tame baboon called Kees. He spent four years exploring Great and Little Namaqualand and the Hottentot country, returning to France in 1785 with the first giraffe skin Paris had ever seen and large numbers of stuffed birds.

In 1810, after first learning the colonial Dutch patois, an Englishman, William Burchell, began a journey with a Cape frontier wagon, which took him across the Karroo and over the Orange River to the edge of the Kalahari where, finding no water, he was forced to turn south through Bechuanaland, reaching the sea at Port Elizabeth. From there he returned to Cape Town.

Altogether he travelled 4,500 miles with his Hottentot assistants and collected about 63,000 specimens of plants and animals.

At the same time that Burchell was making his journeys John Campbell, a member of the London Missionary Society, discovered the course of the Orange River and found the source of the Limpopo (the Crocodile River) in the Transvaal.

By about 1815 big game hunters began to appear on the scene, following in the footsteps of the Boer ivory hunters. It was estimated that in one area alone of South Africa, between the Karroo and the Kalahari, there were tens of millions of springbok and vast quantities of rhinoceros, elephant, giraffe, zebra, kudu and hartebeest.

One hunter who raised great hecatombs of game was Roualeyn Gordon Cumming, a former soldier. He travelled in South Africa for five years between 1843 and 1848, with what was practically an arsenal of weapons and wearing a kilt. Cumming reached the Limpopo valley and beyond, killing 105 elephants, 80 lions and 800 antelopes.

In the following decades, big game hunting took on the aspect of a military campaign against the great herds, which were reduced to a fraction of what they had been. One of the last great hunters, Frederick Courtenay Selous, wrote a sad, savage epitaph to the bloody era in 1900: "The traveller by rail will journey at his ease it is true, in a saloon carriage, through seemingly endless wastes of low forest and scrubby bush, and will probably think it terribly uninteresting country; but no man will ever again sit by a camp fire by one of the little rivers that the railways will cross, eating prime pieces of fat elephant's heart roasted on a forked stick, nor watch the great white rhinoceroses coming to drink just before dark."

Australia: motives and first moves

"COOK HAD REAPED the harvest of discovery but the gleanings of the field remained to be gathered." So wrote one of the "gleaners", Matthew Flinders, at the end of the 18th century; the harvested field was the Australian coast. Cook had indeed placed Australia's coastline firmly on the map, but the vast interior still slumbered, undisturbed by European man, sparsely peopled by a primitive man and by strange, divergent life forms.

The impetus to open up this huge land mass —at three million square miles almost as big as the present-day United States—was provided indirectly by that very country. When the American colonies shook off their British yoke in 1776, Britain had to find an alternative overseas gaol for her convicts. The domestic prisons and hulks—old rotting merchantmen or warships—were filled to overflowing. Africa was regarded as too unhealthy for the convicts and, perhaps more importantly, their guards. Monetary rather than salutary considerations ruled out the next candidate, the West Indies; a convict settlement might interfere with the lucrative slave trade. Only one possibility remained, Botany Bay on the east coast of Australia, visited by Cook on his voyage of 1779. Curiously, the idea was warmly recommended by one of Cook's fellow travellers, the naturalist Sir Joseph Banks, who had previously painted an off-putting picture of the area, declaring it to be "so barren that it could not yield much to the support of man". Banks now took a far more optimistic view of the new land's potential, a view shared by Cook, who had firmly believed that "most sorts of grain, fruit, roots, etc., would flourish were they once brought hither".

Another decisive factor in Australia's favour was the abundance of flax and timber noted by Cook on Norfolk Island, about 1,000 miles northeast of Sydney. Both commodities were essential for the maintenance of Britain's seapower and Britain could not risk her great European rivals, the French, pre-empting this new supply source or founding settlements there.

So, on January 18, 1788, what became known as "The First Fleet", under the command of Captain Arthur Phillip, anchored in Botany Bay. On board there were more than 1,000 people, about 820 of whom were convicts, the remainder being merchant seamen, marines who were to act as guards, and their families.

The first settlement

A quick reconnaissance showed that the area was, after all, unsuited for settlement, the bay itself affording poor anchorage and the surrounding country consisting of low-lying land and swamps with an inadequate water supply. The ideal harbour, Port Jackson, was found a few miles to the north, and Phillip moved his ships there, to a cove that he named Sydney Cove, after the British Home Secretary, Lord Sydney.

He was just in time—two French ships appeared in the bay. Sent out by Louis XVI, they were engaged in a survey of the north, west and south coasts of Australia, with a view to annexing for France any parts not claimed by Cook. As it was, the French commander, La Pérouse, made a dignified retreat and sailed off to a mysterious death.

Phillip himself, preoccupied with the numerous teething problems of the new settlement, not least among them ensuring adequate food supplies, was not able to devote as much time to the exploration of the hinterland as he would have wished. By the end of his governorship, in 1792, farms had been established on all suitable land round Port Jackson. To the west the settlers had come up against a seemingly impassable barrier, the Blue Mountains, part of the Great Dividing Range, which extends in the form of an enormous boomerang from the Cape York Peninsula almost as far as Mount Gambier in South Australia. Both convicts and guards found themselves literally in a prison, on a narrow strip of soil between the Pacific and the mountains.

Exploration, so it seemed, would have to begin by sea. With this realization coincided, most opportunely, the arrival of the new governor, John Hunter, aboard the *Reliance*, and with him two members of its crew ideally suited for the task: Matthew Flinders, the Master's mate, who had been a midshipman on one of Bligh's voyages to the South Seas; and George Bass, the ship's surgeon, who was also an enthusiastic amateur explorer.

Together they began, on their own initiative, to explore the dangerous, surf-bound coast. For this purpose they acquired the *Tom Thumb*, a boat only eight feet long, and in 1795, with Bass's servant, a boy named William Martin, they made a hazardous voyage to Botany Bay and rowed up the Georges River. On a second voyage the following year, in a slightly larger *Tom Thumb*, they reached the next opening in the coast to the south, which they found to be a harbour and not the mouth of a river as had been previously supposed. This was named Port Hacking after the pilot who first discovered it.

In December 1797, Bass made an even more remarkable voyage, this time in an open whaleboat, just over 28 feet long. After reaching Cape Howe, the southeastern extremity of Australia, he sailed along the south coast, discovering a fine natural harbour, Western Port. On his return voyage he visited an island off Wilson's Promontory.

Off the promontory, they encountered a strong current running to the west. Bass, already convinced that he was in a strait between the mainland and Tasmania, wrote: "Whenever it shall be decided that the opening between this and Van Diemen's Land is a 'strait', this rapidity of tide, and that long southwest swell that seems to be continually rolling in upon the coast to the westward, will then be accounted for."

Bass's suspicion was confirmed the following October when he sailed with Flinders in the *Norfolk*, a sloop, for Tasmania. Sailing round it anti-clockwise, they finally demon-

"Wreck Reef" by W. Westall, shows Flinders's "Porpoise" aground, its ensign upside down as a distress signal

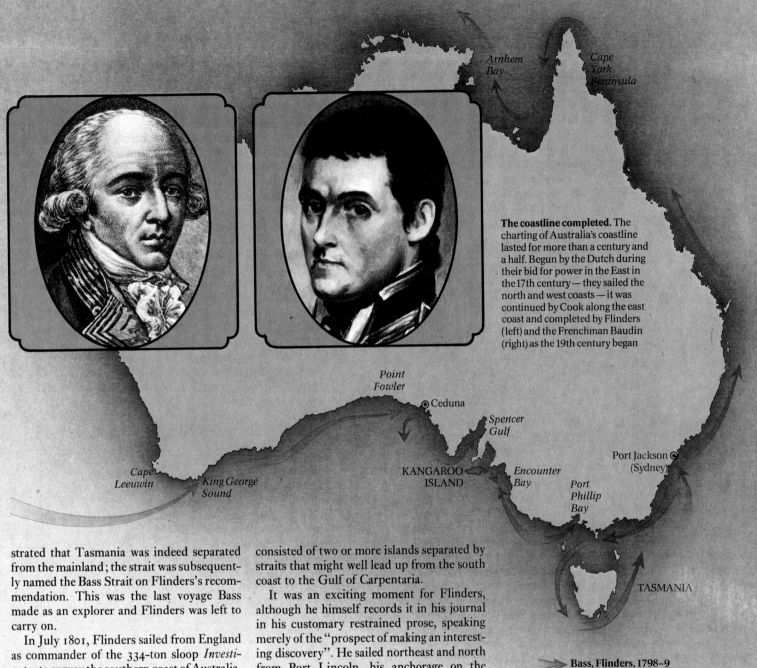

Arnhem
Bay

Cape
York
Peninsula

The coastline completed. The charting of Australia's coastline lasted for more than a century and a half. Begun by the Dutch during their bid for power in the East in the 17th century — they sailed the north and west coasts — it was continued by Cook along the east coast and completed by Flinders (left) and the Frenchman Baudin (right) as the 19th century began

Point
Fowler

◉ Ceduna

Spencer
Gulf

KANGAROO
ISLAND

Encounter
Bay

Port Jackson ◉
(Sydney)

Cape
Leeuwin

King George
Sound

Port
Phillip
Bay

TASMANIA

➤➤ **Bass, Flinders, 1798–9**
➤➤ **Flinders, 1801–2**
➤➤ **Flinders, 1802–3**
➤➤ **Baudin, 1802**

strated that Tasmania was indeed separated from the mainland; the strait was subsequently named the Bass Strait on Flinders's recommendation. This was the last voyage Bass made as an explorer and Flinders was left to carry on.

In July 1801, Flinders sailed from England as commander of the 334-ton sloop *Investigator* to survey the southern coast of Australia. On December 8 he entered King George Sound, which had been discovered by Captain George Vancouver. Here he made a new survey and found that the aborigines spoke a different language from those of New South Wales. Following the coast of the Great Australian Bight, he sailed to Point Fowler, east of the head of the bight, and from there through the islands discovered by Nuyts, naming them the Nuyts Archipelago.

From now on he was on a completely unexplored coast and on February 20, 1802, he found that the coast trended northwards. It was now 14 years since the first settlers had arrived, and the heart of Australia was still a mystery. Some believed it to consist entirely of desert; others imagined a vast inland sea, a second Caspian, or even a second Mediterranean with an outlet on some part of the unexplored south coast, which Flinders was now sailing along. A third party held the theory, based on evidence of tides and currents adduced by Dampier, that Australia

consisted of two or more islands separated by straits that might well lead up from the south coast to the Gulf of Carpentaria.

It was an exciting moment for Flinders, although he himself records it in his journal in his customary restrained prose, speaking merely of the "prospect of making an interesting discovery". He sailed northeast and north from Port Lincoln, his anchorage on the eastern side of the York Peninsula. He was soon disappointed, for what he believed to be a strait turned out to be a rapidly narrowing gulf, the Spencer Gulf, which runs for 200 miles into what is now the great wheat-growing country of South Australia.

Scientific foray

Undaunted, Flinders set out in a ship's boat to explore the upper reaches, taking with him what he called his "scientific gentlemen". William Westall, the expedition's landscape draughtsman, whose delicate drawings captured the mysterious stillness of the coasts of the continent, Ferdinand Bauer, a painter of natural history, and Robert Brown, the naturalist, who made a collection of nearly 4,000 species of plants in the course of the voyage. North of Port Augusta they landed and climbed Mount Brown in the Flinders Range.

From the gulf Flinders sailed to Kangaroo Island, across the Investigator Strait, which,

like much of the coast that he had visited, was uninhabited, but teemed with seals and kangaroos. Of the two creatures, Flinders deemed the seal the more "discerning . . . for its actions bespoke a knowledge of our not being kanguroos, whereas the kangaroo not unfrequently appeared to consider us to be seals". Whatever their intelligence level, the kangaroo proved a welcome addition to the diet for men who had been largely without fresh food for four months. In gratitude for so "seasonable a supply", Flinders christened the island after its inhabitants. He then sailed into Gulf St Vincent, where Adelaide now stands; yet again his hopes of finding a strait to the north were dashed.

On April 8, while in what he named Encounter Bay, southeast of Gulf St Vincent, Flinders sighted a foreign sail—that of a rival

Australia: the rival interests

French expedition commanded by Nicolas Baudin. A naval officer, Baudin had already been in charge of an Austrian expedition to the Indian Ocean that had acquired plants for the collection at Schönbrunn Palace in Vienna. This time he had been sent out by Napoleon to carry out scientific and geographical surveys on the coasts of Australia, and to collect plant life and mineral samples.

Flinders prepared for action, but the encounter was amicable enough, the two men breakfasting together the next morning. The expeditions then continued on their respective courses, Flinders eastwards via Port Phillip Bay to Port Jackson, Baudin to Kangaroo Island and then west to the Spencer Gulf.

At the beginning of May, Flinders reached Port Jackson, his survey of the entire south coast from west to east completed. In the process he had finally proved that Australia was one great continent and that no south–north strait existed.

Two months later he sailed north to complete Cook's chart of the east coast, searching for new harbours as he went. The voyage does not belong to the annals of exploration in the strict sense of the word; much of it was along previously charted coasts. Yet this by no means detracts from Flinders's importance as a hydrographer; he ranks second only to Cook in his work on the Australian coasts.

More fortunate than Cook, Flinders found a passage through the Great Barrier Reef at the northern end and sailed into the Torres Strait to the Gulf of Carpentaria by a new route, the Prince of Wales Channel. Although shorter, it proved too difficult and dangerous for general use. Contrary winds prevented him from returning through the strait and instead he sailed westwards round Australia, reaching Port Jackson on June 9, 1803.

This was the end of Flinders's career as an explorer–hydrographer and the beginning of his misfortunes. As the *Investigator* had been found to be beyond repair, Flinders and 26 officers and men sailed for England in the *Porpoise*, a Spanish prize, with a greenhouse erected on its deck to hold the plant collection, which was destined for the Botanical Garden at Kew.

The voyage home was fraught with difficulties. Seven days' sail from port, the *Porpoise* foundered on a reef. Flinders's next attempt to reach England ended even more tragically, in imprisonment. His ship, the *Cumberland*, a schooner of only 29 tons, began to leak in the Indian Ocean and Flinders was forced to put in to Port Louis, Mauritius, a French possession.

There, the governor refused to recognize the authority of Flinders's letter of protection from Bonaparte on the grounds that it applied only to the *Investigator*. As a result

Cave and rock paintings (this one is at Emily Gap, Northern Territory) were an integral part of aboriginal culture

Flinders and his men were imprisoned, Flinders for six and a half years.

When he eventually reached England in October 1810, a worn and broken man, he was promoted and received the unprincely sum of £500 as compensation. This paltry amount certainly could not compensate for the fact that Flinders's long years of captivity had prevented him from completing his account of his voyages. His book, *A Voyage to Terra Australis,* was finally published in 1814, the year of his death. It is not only a narrative of a voyage but a scientific record of his achievements in the fields of meteorology, hydrography, navigation and magnetism.

One factor marred Flinders's satisfaction in having finished his great work—the French had stolen all his glory by publishing an

account of the Baudin expedition in 1807. Two maps of "Terre Napoléon" appeared in it, liberally sprinkled with French names; the French had even taken the credit for much of Flinders's work.

There had been two ships in the Baudin expedition: the *Géographe,* commanded by Baudin himself, and the *Naturaliste,* commanded by Jacques Félix Emmanuel Hamelin. With him were Louis-Claude de Freycinet, also a naval officer, and François Péron, a naturalist. The expedition included a landscape painter, Lesueur.

On May 27, 1801, Cape Leeuwin was sighted and three days later the two ships anchored in what Baudin named Géographe Bay, north of the cape.

On the night of June 9 they were separated in a storm. A rendezvous had been arranged at Rottnest Island, off the present port of Perth; but instead Baudin waited at Bernier

Island in Shark Bay, north of the island on which the Dutch explorer Vlamingh had left a pewter plaque in 1697. The two ships and their commanders were not reunited until the *Naturaliste* arrived at Kupang on Timor Island at the end of September.

Dysentery wrought havoc with the crews on Timor and numbers of men died. On November 13 the two ships sailed for Sydney westabout, scurvy breaking out on the voyage. Two months later they reached the south coast of Tasmania. Sailing up the east coast, they discovered that what had been thought to be an island was the Tasman Peninsula. In the course of this voyage a landing party from the *Géographe* was lost in a storm and, to add to Baudin's misfortunes, he now lost contact with the *Naturaliste* which, by a miracle, picked up the missing boat and its crew.

Hamelin then sailed for Sydney, where he waited for three weeks for Baudin, who by this time was exploring the Australian mainland. It was during this stage of the expedition, in April 1802, that Baudin's encounter with Flinders took place.

The two French commanders were finally reunited on June 20, when the *Géographe* arrived at Sydney, having been driven off the coast of Tasmania by bad weather conditions.

In November 1802 they sailed with a third vessel, the 39-ton *Casuarina*: Hamelin in the *Naturaliste* for France, which was reached in June 1803; Baudin in the *Géographe* and Freycinet in the *Casuarina* for Kangaroo Island (which Baudin had named Decrès on his first visit) and then to Cape Denial, from where they surveyed about 100 miles of the coastline westwards as far as Cape Adieu (by Cape Nuyts), entering Murat Bay on which the present town of Ceduna stands.

They then sailed to Timor, intending to go on from there to explore the Gulf of Carpentaria and the Torres Strait; but by this time (June 1803) the crew was so debilitated by sickness that, on July 7, Baudin altered course for Mauritius, where he later died.

It was left to Freycinet to take home the combined crews of the *Casuarina* and the *Géographe* in Baudin's ship. He arrived at Lorient on March 25, 1804.

The result of this enormous operation—100,000 zoological and 2,500 botanical specimens were brought back for evaluation—was Péron's vast work, *Voyage de découvertes aux Terres Australes*, finally completed by Freycinet in 1816, six years after Péron's death.

One of the unusual aspects of the expedition was the charting method used by Baudin. In the course of his brief meeting with Flinders, Baudin told him that all the bearings, observations and sketches of the coast from seaward that would normally have been incorporated in charts made on board a surveying vessel

were sent to Paris, where they were kept until all the necessary information could be collated. "This mode", Flinders wrote, "appeared to me extraordinary and not worthy of imitation. . . ."

In 1817, Louis XVIII put Freycinet in command of the corvette *l'Uranie*, and on September 17 he sailed from Toulon to extend the work of Baudin. Among his staff were Gaudichard, a botanist and pharmacist, and Jacques Arago, the expedition's artist, who was also a playwright, theatre director and novelist.

The most bizarre member of the crew was Madame Rose de Freycinet, the young and beautiful wife of the leader of the expedition who, with her husband's consent, slipped aboard the ship disguised as a sailor before it left Toulon. The disguise was soon abandoned, but fortunately Madame de Freycinet proved to be as brave and resourceful as she was good to look at and her presence on board helped to keep up Gallic morale.

Musical encounter

The expedition lasted three years. Sailing to the west coast of Australia by way of the Cape of Good Hope and Mauritius, Freycinet made a landfall near Shark Bay and anchored in Denham Sound on September 13, 1818. Here an observatory was erected.

Here, too, the aborigines came down to the shore and exchanged weapons for coloured handkerchiefs and bead necklaces. As more and more aborigines arrived a dangerous situation began to develop, the day being saved by Arago, who began to play the castanets, which soon had one of the aborigines dancing. *L'Uranie* had two stills for producing fresh water from salt water, and as there was a desperate shortage of water, one of them was set up on the shore.

This time Freycinet removed the Vlamingh plaque and eventually it was taken back to Paris and placed in the Académie des Inscriptions. It was missing from 1821 until 1940, when it was discovered behind a collection of papers. It is now in the museum at Perth in Western Australia.

None of the members of the expedition, including Madame de Freycinet, thought much of Shark Bay and its surroundings, and on September 26 Freycinet sailed for Timor. There, everyone was impressed by the sane and simple life of the inhabitants, who were practically vegetarians, lived in houses made of bamboo and palm leaves and played a complex sort of backgammon. In Dīli, the capital of the Portuguese sector, Madame de Freycinet helped to show the flag by appearing in the latest Paris fashion: mauve muslin with a plunging neckline and a straw hat decorated with an ostrich feather—much

to the amazement of the local Portuguese ladies, who were still dressed in the fashions of the 18th century.

From Timor Freycinet visited the Moluccas and from there sailed through the Pacific, the crew suffering from dysentery and fever, to Sydney.

Freycinet was even less of a "discoverer" than Flinders; he belonged to the growing tradition of scientific explorers, men anxious to increase their scanty store of knowledge of the world. Freycinet certainly succeeded in achieving this end; his mammoth work, *Voyage autour du Monde*, published posthumously, comprised no fewer than 13 volumes and four atlases.

By 1817, the year Freycinet set out on his last voyage, most of the Australian coastline had been charted; the only section which still invited speculation, a section which had escaped even Flinders's seemingly exhaustive survey, was the stretch between Arnhem Bay and the North West Cape. It was to this relatively unknown area that the Admiralty Commissioners despatched Captain Phillip Parker King. His instructions emphasized the importance of examining all gulfs and other openings "as the chief motive for your survey is to discover whether there be any river on that part of the coast likely to lead to an interior navigation into this great continent". The theory, put forward by Sir Joseph Banks, of a great river system leading into the interior still persisted, and fertile imaginations eagerly resurrected Dampier's theory that a passage to the Pacific was to be found behind the group of islands now known as the Dampier Archipelago.

Between 1817 and 1822 King made four voyages along the Australian coastline, the first three in the *Mermaid*, a cutter of only 84 tons, ill-equipped for survey work, and the fourth and last in the brig *Bathurst*. He also surveyed the coast of Tasmania.

The opening into the interior proved elusive. King suggested two possibilities: the stretch of coast between Depuch Island and Cape Villaret, including Eighty Mile Beach, and the gulf behind the Buccaneer Archipelago, which he had been prevented from exploring by strong winds and high tides. Both suggestions were way off the mark, the first, ironically, being one of the driest stretches of the west coast.

The Admiralty was far from satisfied with King's results and in 1837 sent out HMS *Beagle*, commanded first by Captain Wickham and later by John Lort Stokes, to complete the investigation of the northwest coast. They discovered various rivers that King had missed, including the Victoria, but none was the hoped-for waterway into the interior. The myth was never to be realized.

By 1843, THE YEAR of the last voyage of the *Beagle*, and some 230 years since the Dutch first sighted Australia, the outline of this massive continent had been finally pieced together. By this time, too, land exploration was well under way. Already, by the beginning of the 19th century, the early settlers had begun to break out of their natural prison.

As the colony expanded, the need for good grazing and arable land grew desperate. The land immediately to the north and south of Port Jackson had been explored; the sea hemmed the settlers in on the east; the only possibility left was the unknown territory to the west, across the Blue Mountains. Forty miles west of Sydney, their sandstone escarpments rise up in a series of walls and ridges more than 3,000 feet high, concealing within them a labyrinth of ravines and chasms, some of them almost as deep as the mountains are high—gulleys which lead nowhere, except into deadends choked with scrub, where waterfalls pour down into them over vertical cliffs. Beyond the eastern walls are more ridges, like a succession of huge waves, with others breaking across them in confusion; far on the horizon the dividing range looms like a pooping sea.

Across the Blue Mountains

The earliest explorers of the Blue Mountains were mostly marines. Escaping convicts also attempted to cross them. Many, particularly the Irish, believed in an Arcadian, well-watered land beyond the mountains to the west, populated by a white race. Other attractions of this blessed land were an "abundance of every sort of provision without the necessity of so much labour". Some even believed that if they succeeded in crossing the mountains they would find an overland route to China.

In January 1798, Governor Hunter attempted to put an end to these rumours by sending out, under guard, a party of four convicts and two bushmen in search of the mysterious land. Their guide was John Wilson, a time-expired convict who had been transported for the major transgression of stealing nine yards of cotton cloth. He now lived with the aborigines, had been ritually scarred by them and wore garments made from kangaroo skins.

The party set off from Parramatta, now a suburb of Sydney. By the time they had reached the mountains both convicts and soldiers were tired of the venture; but Wilson and the bushmen pushed on, returning on February 9 with the news that they had reached the banks of "a large sluggish river as big as the Hawkesbury". The river was possibly the Lachlan. They also reported having seen level country on the far side.

Another attempt was made by Ensign Barrallier of the New South Wales Corps at the end of 1802. Because Paterson, his commanding officer, would not release him for the expedition, King, the governor, made him his aide-de-camp and sent him on an embassy to the "King of the Mountains".

Barrallier had previously surveyed the country round the Hunter River for King and shown himself to be both industrious and competent. There is little reason to doubt the accuracy of his map of his 1802 expedition, which shows that he succeeded in crossing the mountains. Barrallier certainly believed that he had done, for he noted in his diary on November 25, 1802, that "everyone . . . congratulated themselves with having succeeded in accomplishing the passage of the Blue Mountains without accident" and also records "a view of a plain as vast as the eye could reach". Yet, sadly, Barrallier's exploits were largely overlooked and credit for crossing the mountains was given to a later expedition led by Gregory Blaxland.

The year 1813 was one of appalling drought. Crops were destroyed; water sources dried up; cattle and sheep started to die off in hundreds. Blaxland was one of the many farmers who faced the prospect of economic ruin. Determined to force a crossing through the mountains rather than stand by and see all his livestock die, he set off from his farm at the foot of the mountains in May 1813. With him went two other land-owners, Lieutenant Lawson and William Charles Wentworth, and James Burnes, an experienced bushman, together with three convict servants, four packhorses and some hunting dogs. The party tackled the mountains in a new way. Instead of descending into the canyons which separated them, they kept to the ridges, and finally succeeded in crossing the greater part of the range from the Nepean River at Emu Ford.

Following a dividing spur to the west, on May 28 they reached Mount York and looked down on to wooded pastures, sufficient, Blaxland maintained, to support the entire stock of the colony for the next 30 years. There, on the shores of the Lett River, a tributary of the Nepean, a few miles south of the present town of Lithgow, they feasted, the animals on lush grass, the explorers on kangaroo and fish.

Unwittingly Blaxland's party had diverged from the central ridge, and had not crossed the main range. What they had done, however, was to bequeath a new, highly successful technique for approaching the mountains, a technique taken up by George Evans, a surveyor, sent out by Governor Macquarie later that year to follow up Blaxland's findings.

The challenge of the Australian interior. By the end of the 18th century the coastline of Australia had been charted in all but subtle detail. The first permanent settlement had been established in the southeastern corner of the continent—if only, at first, as a penal colony. Beyond the limits of settlement and far within the known coastline there slept a land quite unlike any other in its undisturbed antiquity. Its explorers were to find conditions that were to put fierce demands upon their resolution—at first a seemingly impenetrable barrier of mountains and, beyond it, a series of baking plains of stone, clay and sand capable of supporting small, specially adapted communities of plant and animal life. Slender, too, were the numbers of native aboriginals; about 300,000 (one to 10 to 15 square miles) at the time of the first settlements. The pictures (right) show some of the contrasting terrains of the continent; the Macdonnell Ranges (top left); the hills and pastures of the Great Dividing Range in Queensland (top right); ephemeral blooms in the Simpson Desert (below left); and the Blue Mountains

Mountains
Desert
Semi-desert & seasonal grassland
Temperate grassland
Temperate rain-forest & woodland
Evergreen forest
Tropical & sub-tropical grassland
Tropical rain-forest

Great Sandy Desert
Macdonnell Ranges
Gibson Desert
Simpson Desert
Great Victoria Desert
Nullarbor Plain
Great Dividing Range

Accompanied by two freed men and three convicts, Evans followed Blaxland's route to his westernmost point and from there succeeded in crossing the Great Dividing Range. On November 30 he saw with his own eyes what had up to now been nothing but a dream —fertile land on the banks of a west-flowing river, to which he gave the name "Fish" after its abundance of Murray cod.

Following its course downstream they reached its junction with the Campbell, and named the combined rivers the Macquarie, after the governor who had inspired the expedition. They were now in the grass plains close to what was to be, two years later, the site of Bathurst, the first settlement west of the Dividing Range. Later it was to become one of the great sheep-farming and wheat-growing regions of Australia and the scene of the gold rush of 1851. They followed the river downstream until December 17 and then turned back. After surveying the whole of Blaxland's route in detail, a task rendered difficult by bushfires, they arrived back on the Nepean River near Penrith on January 8, 1814. The only people they had seen in the course of their journey were four aboriginal women and two children.

As soon as Governor Macquarie heard the news of the fertile land to the west he ordered the construction of a road. Although it was more than 100 miles long the road was completed in six months, built by convicts who were then given their freedom. Soon flocks and herds were being driven over it. The great break-out had begun.

In his report of his travels, Evans had expressed the belief that his west-flowing river led to the west coast, a theory enthusiastically snatched up by Macquarie. Evans was duly despatched on a second expedition southwards from Bathurst and on May 26, 1815, he sighted and named the Lachlan River, following it downstream for four days before turning back. Its general direction was less northerly than the Macquarie, a little north of west, and he had little doubt that it joined forces with the Macquarie or some other river farther west to form one big waterway, an Australian Mississippi.

Macquarie pressed on with the investigation of the enigmatic rivers, sending out a further expedition led by his surveyor-general, John Oxley, who had been a lieutenant in the navy. Evans was second-in-command and Allan Cunningham, himself to be an explorer of note, and Charles Fraser were the botanists. Altogether the party numbered 13—the largest organized expedition so far. The general intention was to follow the Lachlan to its end.

They left Bathurst on April 28, 1817, with 14 pack horses, two boats and rations for

Australia: breakout beyond the mountains

five months. A week later they reached Byrne's Creek on the Lachlan, where Evans had turned back.

Up to then the country, in which tall grass alternated with scrub, had been melancholy and waterless, apart from the river, which abounded with fish; but now they entered a region of morass, the boats making slow progress on the river, which was full of sunken acacia trees.

Now, mysteriously, under a rainless sky, the river rose and, at a place they named Field's Plains, overflowed into the surrounding marshland, its course being lost to view in a vast expanse that extended from west to northwest for as much as 30 miles. On May 18 they abandoned the boats, and a week later reached a prominent hill, not far from the present town of Griffith.

Oxley now decided to make for Cape Northumberland, on the coast of South Australia, thinking that this would be the most likely course on which he could intersect a river arising from the Lachlan. The expedition moved southwestwards into an equally dreary but almost waterless region of light red sand, in which acacia scrub and cypress grew. This was succeeded by an even more desiccated country, choked with scrub, creepers and prickly acacia.

The scrub became thicker and thicker; the only water to be found was rain water in holes and rock crevices. Oxley decided to abandon his course and march northwest towards the Lachlan. It was an unfortunate decision, as he was only about 25 miles from the Murrumbidgee River.

On June 21 he wrote, in one of his uniformly gloomy pronouncements, of what was later to be one of the more fertile and productive regions of the continent: "The farther we proceed north-westerly the more convinced I am that for all the practical purposes of civilised man the interior of this country, westward of a certain meridian, is uninhabitable, deprived as it is of wood, water and grass."

Two days later they reached the Lachlan and once more encountered vast swamps, through which the river moved sluggishly, as if on the point of expiring. Convinced that this was so, Oxley decided to return upstream until he could find a suitable crossing place and from there make for the Macquarie. Before they set out a wine bottle was buried under a eucalyptus tree at this most westerly camp site, in 144.30E, and the words DIG UNDER carved on it. It was never found.

On August 4 they crossed the Lachlan, but with great difficulty because the current in this unpredictable river was at this point extremely swift. After travelling through varied country, ranging from good to unspeak-

able, they reached Bathurst on August 29.

Macquarie's lofty ambitions for the Lachlan were dashed. The river would not, after all, serve as an artery for commerce, either internal or international. His hopes were now pinned on the Macquarie.

Oxley's next expedition down this great river, in April 1818, was much more successful. Together with Evans, Fraser, a surgeon named John Harris, 12 other men and 19 horses he left Wellington Valley and had an easy passage down the first reaches on foot and by boat.

Soon, however, heavy rain began to fall; the river rose and by June 30 overflowed its banks. The expedition was forced to retreat upstream to higher ground.

Oxley and four volunteers continued downstream in one of the boats, through a region in which the land was almost completely under water; but on the second day their way was blocked by an enormous barrier of reeds, growing six or seven feet above the water, in what are now called the Macquarie Marshes. Again Oxley believed himself to be on the edge of the inland sea, probably a "shoal", one that was gradually being silted up by "depositions from the higher lands".

Meanwhile Evans had travelled westwards, discovering the Castlereagh River, and Oxley now decided to cross it and make for what he had named the Arbuthnot Range, which lay beyond. With great difficulty they crossed the river, by this time swollen to a seething torrent by the heavy rains.

The journey to the Arbuthnot Range was equally difficult, through quagmires and water waist deep, but, after crossing its northern slopes, they were rewarded by the sight of mile upon mile of fertile grassland, the Liverpool Plains.

Grazing problem solved

They then battled their way over the Great Dividing Range, losing a horse which "literally burst with the violent exertion". By September 16 the worst was over and a week later they sighted the Pacific. "Bilboa's ecstacy at the first sight of the South Sea could not have been greater than ours . . ." Oxley wrote.

Macquarie's hitherto unbounded optimism had been dealt a severe blow. Neither the Lachlan nor the Macquarie had fulfilled his expectations. His one consolation was the discovery of the Liverpool Plains, the long-awaited solution to the colony's acute grazing shortage. The only drawback was that Oxley's tortuous route across rivers, swamps and waterlogged plains was impracticable for sheep and cattle. A new route had to be found.

The man who succeeded was Allan Cunningham, the botanist on Oxley's first expedi-

tion. In June 1823, in the course of a very difficult journey of over 500 miles, which took him 11 weeks, Cunningham discovered a way through the Liverpool Range from Bathurst, Pandora's Pass. From now on, an ever-increasing flood of squatters and their livestock poured across the mountains.

The most important of Cunningham's various expeditions began in May 1827, when Governor Darling sent him to explore the country between Bathurst and the Queensland border in order to find out whether it was suitable for settlement. He set off from Segenhoe on the upper Hunter River with a party of six men and 11 horses, and, with the help of a guide named Macintyre, crossed the Liverpool Range to the Plains and discovered the Namoi River. He then went north and discovered the Gwydir, Dumaresq and Macintyre rivers. On June 8, from a hill above the Macintyre, he made his greatest discovery: before him lay an enormous tract of open country filled with waving grass and backed by distant mountains. With true colonial loyalty he named it Darling Downs.

Not only did he discover the best pastoral country in Queensland but, equally important, a way into it from the coast across the Dividing Range, Cunningham's Gap.

Meanwhile, further important discoveries had been made in the south. In June 1823, Captain John Currie, a naval officer, and Major Ovens, the Governor's private secretary, set off from Lake George, the westernmost settlement, near what is now Canberra, and discovered the Murrumbidgee, seeing to the south the snow-capped mountains of the Australian Alps.

The following year an expedition set out to explore the country between Sydney and Port Phillip Bay. The two leaders were Hamilton Hume, an experienced bushman, and William Hovell, a ship's captain turned settler. Together with six convicts, they left Lake George and crossed the Murrumbidgee on October 22, using their wagon covered with a tarpaulin as a raft. They went on to discover and cross the upper reaches of the Murray, which they named the Hume, in honour of Hamilton's father. This time their improvised boat was a sort of coracle made from wicker and tarpaulin.

Continuing their journey southwest they crossed the Ovens and the Goulburn rivers with the aid of a fallen tree. Of the surrounding land, which Oxley had wrongly dismissed as "useless for all the purposes of civilized men", Hovell wrote: "I have seen no country better adapted for feeding sheep, the hills adjoining the Goulburn River being nearly clear of timber, grass to the top, and in the hollows below an abundance of herbage of a very excellent quality."

In contrast, the next stage of their journey took them through nightmarish country—through thick scrub infested with leeches, through acres of razor-edged grass. Finally, having narrowly escaped death in a bush fire, they crossed the Great Dividing Range and reached the coast near Geelong on Port Phillip Bay on December 18.

The combination of leaders had proved unfortunate. Throughout the journey Hovell had refused to bow to Hume's superiority as a bushman and pathfinder, and the two men had quarrelled bitterly. Most of the credit for the success of the expedition lies with Hume. Hovell's main contribution was a negative one: mistaking Port Phillip Bay for Western Bay, on his return to Lake George in January 1825 he gave such an enthusiastic account of the fertility of the soil that the government sent settlers to the real Western Bay, where the land was found to be so poor that it was soon abandoned, a mistake that delayed the settlement of Victoria.

Although this expedition had been very successful, the mystery of where the rivers ended was still unsolved. "My opinion", wrote Hovell, "is that they empty themselves, first into one immense lake, and the waters from the lake are carried off into the ocean in the N.E. or S.W. coast, as part of the coast in these directions is low."

The consensus of opinion, although some thought in terms of an immense river system of Amazonian complexity, was that the centre of Australia was saucer-shaped, containing within it an inland sea, possibly below sea level, fed by water from the coastal ranges, a theory echoing Flinders's belief in the existence of a vast, landlocked lagoon beyond the mountains at the head of Spencer Gulf. The reports of water-birds flighting inland from the coast of New South Wales and the existence of the marshes discovered by Oxley suggested that there was a lot of water somewhere to the west. The theorists were wrong, although there were rivers of a sort and lakes too, ghostly, ghastly, dazzling white saline expanses, capable of supporting nothing in the way of human or animal life.

One of the believers in the existence of an inland sea was Captain Charles Sturt (1795–1869), a soldier who had fought in the Peninsular War and had come out to Australia with his regiment to guard convicts. He subsequently became Military Secretary to Governor Darling.

Between November 1828 and January 1829, together with Hamilton Hume and a small party of soldiers and convicts, he crossed the Blue Mountains and explored the Macquarie Marshes. It was midsummer, one of the hottest, driest summers experienced by the early colonists, and the Macquarie was a mere trickle compared with the furious torrent encountered by Oxley; the boggy marshland a series of isolated, stagnant ponds. From here he pressed on, dogged by cannibals, to the banks of a broad river, covered with wildfowl. He and his men had reached the Darling, near the present town of Burke.

Salt-water shock

Their joy was short-lived: "Its banks were too precipitous to allow of our watering the cattle," Sturt wrote, "but the men eagerly descended to quench their thirst, which a powerful sun had contributed to increase; nor shall I ever forget the cry of amazement that followed their doing so, or the look of terror and disappointment with which they called out to inform me that the water was so salt as to be unfit to drink. . . . Whence this arose, whether from local causes or from a communication with some inland sea, I know not, but the discovery was certainly one for which I was not prepared. . . . We placed sticks to ascertain if there was a rise or fall of tide, but could arrive at no satisfactory conclusion, although there was undoubtedly a current in it. Yet as I stood upon its bank at sunset, when not a breath of air existed to break the stillness of the waters below me, and saw their surface kept in constant agitation by the leaping of fish, I doubted whether the river could supply itself plentifully, and rather imagined that it owed much of its abundance, which the pelicans seemed to indicate was constant, to some mediterranean sea or other."

They were saved by the discovery of a pool of fresh water. Leaving the rest of the party by it, Sturt and Hume explored the river for a further 60 miles downstream, where its appearance was much the same.

Although no inland sea had materialized, Sturt had begun to solve the mystery of the great river system, ascertaining on his return journey that the Castlereagh, Bogan and Macquarie rivers all flowed into one major river, the Darling.

In November 1829 Darling sent Sturt out again; this time to follow the Murrumbidgee to its end or, if this was impossible, to try to reach the Darling, which was presumed to flow to the northwest of it.

Accompanied by his servant, by George Macleay, the son of a former Colonial Secretary, and a number of soldiers and convicts, four of whom had been on his previous expeditions, Sturt reached the upper waters of the Murrumbidgee, just above its junction with the Lachlan. Here two boats were built, a 27-foot whaleboat, put together with materials taken to the site on a horse-drawn dray, and a skiff, which was built with timber cut and carpentered on the spot.

On January 7, 1830, Sturt and Macleay, with a small party which included the four convict explorers, began the hazardous descent of the turbulent river, which was full of underwater obstructions.

On the second day the skiff carrying the provisions hit a trunk and went to the bottom in 12 feet of water. On January 14 they found that the river began to turn from southwest to south. "At 3 pm Hopkinson called out that we were approaching a junction, and in less than a minute afterwards, we were hurried into a broad and noble river."

They had reached the Murray, 300 miles downstream of the point where Hume and Hovell had reached and crossed it in 1824. Here it was 350 yards wide, between 12 and 30 feet deep, and had beautiful reaches up to three-quarters of a mile long. Not realizing that it was the so-called "Hume" River, Sturt christened it, "in compliment to the distinguished officer, Sir George Murray [Secretary of State for the Colonies]".

They floated down the great river, always in a more or less northwesterly direction, which led Sturt to think that they must be bound for the centre of the continent.

On January 21 they came to a sandbank, where a great concourse of ferocious-looking aborigines armed with spears was gathered. Sturt estimated that there were about 600. " . . . A dead silence prevailed among the front ranks, but those in the background, as well as the women, who carried supplies of darts, and who appeared to have had a bucket of whitewash capsized over their heads, were extremely clamorous." Sturt's party was saved at the last moment from an undoubtedly grisly fate by the arrival of four men with whom they had become friendly farther up the river, one of whom, a giant, "struggled across the channel to the sandbank, and in an incredibly short space of time stood in front of the savage, against whom my aim had been directed. Seizing him by the throat, he pushed him backwards, and forcing all who were in the water upon the bank, he trod its margin with a vehemence and an agitation that were exceedingly striking. . . . All wrangling ceased, and they came swimming over to us like a parcel of seals. . . ."

To Sturt and his men their timely salvation was little short of a miracle. Anthropologists later offered a more down-to-earth explanation: the aborigines had rescued the explorers because they believed that one of them was a reincarnation of a legendary hero who had supposedly led the tribe down the Darling to the mouth of the Murray.

It was shortly after this dramatic moment that, drifting downstream, they came to a river flowing into the Murray from north by east. It was the Darling again, here 100 yards

Australia: breakout beyond the mountains

wide, its grassy banks covered with splendid trees. Another section of the river system had been pieced together: the Darling and its tributaries all flowed into the Murray, as did the Murrumbidgee and the Lachlan.

The combined stream flowed southwards and they continued down it. Finding the skiff an encumbrance they burned it, keeping the nails and iron-work. Five days later, on January 29, they were among cliffs with fossil shells in the strata, and here they met an old man who described to them the roaring of the sea which he had visited. On February 4, 33 days after leaving their depot on the Murrumbidgee, and 1,000 miles from it, they reached the mouth of the Murray, a large, shallow, tidal lake, which Sturt named Alexandrina. The only outlet from the lake was blocked by sandbanks.

Vainly they hoped that the ship that was supposed to rendezvous with them in Gulf St Vincent beyond the Mount Lofty Range might have come in search of them; but even if it had, it would have been impossible to launch a boat through the surf.

By now they were not strong enough to cross the Mount Lofty Range to the gulf and it was decided to go back by the same route; in itself a strenuous journey for men in their weak condition.

When they reached the depot they found it abandoned. For 17 more days, in the course of which one man became insane, they continued to row upstream in a river that was now in flood. Finally, they reached a point near Hamilton Plains where Sturt set up camp, sending the two fittest men over the mountains to the nearest station. On April 18

they returned with horses, cattle and drays loaded with provisions. They were just in time: the flour supply was finally exhausted.

The party reached Sydney at the end of May, where they were given a well-deserved heroes' welcome. From here Sturt, whose sight was failing, went on sick leave to England. On the way home he became totally blind, but recovered.

His contribution to the knowledge of the interior was one of the most outstanding in the history of Australian exploration. Not only had he pieced together the continent's only great river system, but he had opened up vast new areas for the land-hungry colonists.

Filling the gaps

The missing details of the river system were filled in by Major Thomas Mitchell, who became Surveyor-General on Oxley's death in 1828. A fine surveyor and an excellent artist, Mitchell was jealous of Sturt. He considered that being a professional surveyor, which Sturt was not, he should have been given command of Sturt's last expedition.

Mitchell's first expeditionary foray in 1831 was inspired by the desire to outdo Sturt and to track down the north-flowing, navigable river which an escaped convict, George Clarke "The Barber", was said to have reached north of the Liverpool Range. The river, so Mitchell hoped, would flow into one of the openings on the northwest coast suggested by Captain King. He travelled from the Namoi River to the Darling near the Nundawar Range, following it downstream to its junction with the Gwydir. Here, he was

forced to give up when two of his men were killed by aborigines and all his stores were stolen. He had, however, proved to his own satisfaction that all the rivers south of latitude 29S flowed into the Darling and that if there was a river flowing to the northwest it must be north of that parallel.

The scepticism of the British Colonial Office provided Mitchell with a pretext for a second expedition. Not entirely convinced by Sturt's report that the Darling flowed into the Murray, they demanded conclusive proof. By this time, Sturt, the obvious candidate, was taking much-needed leave in Britain and the choice of expedition leader fell on Mitchell. Among the party was Allan Cunningham's brother, Richard, also a botanist. They set out from Parramatta in 1835 for the upper waters of the Bogan River. Soon after reaching it Cunningham went missing. On April 25 his horse was found dead and on April 30 a piece of his coat was found near a native camp fire, but it was not until the following November that a search party discovered the place where he had been killed, and the reason for his death. After wandering for five days he met some aborigines who fed him and treated him well. He then became delirious and the aborigines, fearing that he was possessed, killed him.

Mitchell reached the Darling via the Bogan River on May 25. Contrary to his expectations the water was fresh, although he was only a few miles upstream from the point reached by Sturt and Hume where it had been undrinkable.

Here, he established a depot, which he named Fort Bourke. Finding the river to be unnavigable downstream, he and his party set off along the bank, two days later discovering a gum tree with Hume's initials on it, which marked the farthest limits of his journey with Sturt.

They trekked 300 miles through uninhabitable country without seeing a single tributary to the main river, and eventually, on July 9, reached a point, near the present town of Menindee, where the Darling changes course from southwest to south.

For the first 100 miles or so the aborigines had been friendly. They then became increasingly hostile and now began singing war-songs, looting and threatening the explorers. This resulted in some indiscriminate shooting by one of the convicts, two aborigines being killed and a mother and child wounded: "I was liable to pay dear for geographical discovery, when my honour and character were delivered over to convicts, on whom, although I might confide as to courage, I could not always rely for humanity," Mitchell wrote, somewhat hypocritically, for he himself tended to rely more on fire-arms than bargaining power.

Here, 150 miles from the Darling's confluence with the Murray, Mitchell turned back, confident in his own mind that this was the river that Sturt had seen when going down the Murray.

Mitchell had not fulfilled his instructions; he had not traced the course of the Darling to the sea, if indeed it led there, and it was with the intention of completing his mission that he set out again in March 1836. With him he took 24 men wearing a sort of para-military uniform (red shirts and white braces), an aboriginal interpreter, who got married on the way, seven carts, two boats, oxen and a herd of sheep. Following in Oxley and Sturt's tracks, he went down the Lachlan and the Murrumbidgee to the Murray. Here a skirmish took place with the natives; this time Mitchell did not hesitate to shoot the "lynx-eyed" enemy.

When he reached the confluence of the Murray and the Darling, Mitchell followed the latter upstream for a short way until, quite suddenly, it dried up completely. Deeming further exploration along "this impossible river" a waste of time and dwindling resources, Mitchell took his men up the west bank of the Murray to the base camp.

The next stage of his journey was to be his great triumph. Passing Swan Hill (about 200 miles north-northwest of Melbourne) he

In the early years of the colony, the main impetus for exploration was not curiosity but a far more practical cause — the need for good grazing land, a need that grew more and more desperate as the colony expanded and an increasing number of sheep and cattle were imported. It was in these early days, too, that the foundations of Australia's booming wool industry were laid. In 1796, a farmer named John Macarthur imported a few merino sheep from the Cape of Good Hope. Samples of the wool so impressed English manufacturers that they guaranteed Macarthur large orders — at the expense of Spain, which then had a monopoly of fine wool—if he could produce sufficient quantities. Macarthur returned from England with nine merino rams and sheep from the private collection of King George III. Macarthur's sheep thrived and so did those subsequently imported by other farmers. The main problem was the shortage of grazing, exacerbated by serious drought, and it was the search for new pasturage that drove out men such as Blaxland and Evans, and resulted in the discovery of some of the lushest grazing areas in the world. The merino, a native of Spain, was well adapted to the semi-arid climate which characterizes much of the Australian interior. It now predominates over cattle and other species of sheep in areas with an average annual rainfall of under 20 inches. Although semi-arid, such areas are rich in natural fodder, including the nutritious saltbush. After the rains the diet is supplemented by ephemeral plants. Through scientific breeding over the years Australia developed a merino strain with high-quality wool and a high average fleece weight and is now the leading wool exporter in the world, supplying roughly one-half of all merino wool

turned southwest and there before him lay endless tracts of verdant country. Mitchell was, understandably, delighted at this magnificent prospect and his ego was truly flattered by the moment of the occasion: "... I felt conscious of being the harbinger of mighty changes; and that our steps would soon be followed by the men and animals for which it seemed to have been prepared." He pressed on, discovering various ranges and rivers, including the Grampian Mountains and the Glenelg River, by which he reached the sea at Discovery Bay.

Australia Felix
Disappointed to find no suitable harbour, he travelled eastwards to Portland Bay and from there across the Great Dividing Range. He finally reached Sydney in November 1836, having covered some 2,400 miles. Not only had he discovered a new river and mountain system but what he named Australia Felix, the marvellously fertile country between the Murray and the sea, today the rich wool and wheat area of western Victoria.

From the outset, interest in the west coast had been negligible. The early colonists were too intent on securing their parcels of land in the east to concern themselves with exploring the opposite side of their vast continent. Only the threat of a possible French or Dutch settlement stirred them out of their apathy and prompted the occasional, half-hearted attempts at exploration and colonization. One colony founded in such circumstances, in 1829, was Perth.

Interest revived slightly in 1836 with the arrival of two army officers from England, Captain George Grey and Lieutenant Lushington. Their bravery keener than their topographical knowledge of Australia, the two men were determined to travel overland from the mouth of the Prince Regent River on the northwest coast to Perth, a journey of 1,200 miles. After four months of great privation and terrible heat they had accomplished little beyond the exploration of the river and the Glenelg of Mitchell. On the slopes of the King Leopold Ranges to the east of the Glenelg, Grey made the most momentous discovery of the entire expedition: a series of amazing cave paintings of human figures, one of them a man more than ten feet tall, dressed in a scarlet robe. Originally thought to be of Malay origin or the work of some unknown people from overseas, the paintings, referred to as the Wondjina figures, are now believed to be the work of aborigines. According to legend, the Wondjinas lived in the area of the Kimberley Range. When they died, the impression of their bodies remained on their cave walls, whilst their spirits sought eternal refuge in nearby rock pools.

Two prize merino rams.
These fine-wool sheep are
the basis of Australia's wool industry

Australia: the middle years

THE EXPLORERS OF WHAT might be called the middle period of Australian exploration, from 1836 onwards, were, with a few exceptions, almost unbelievably intrepid and courageous men, some to the point of folly. Most of them walked in the fear of the Lord and were not ashamed to call upon him when they were *in extremis*.

For these men there was no possibility of opening up the interior as the first explorers in North America had done, by working their way through the Great Lakes and then going down into the heart of the country by way of the Mississippi. Here the rivers in the interior led nowhere, dwindling away, exasperatingly and sometimes fatally for the explorers, into a series of water-holes, then nothingness. Typical of the rivers of "The Centre" is the Finke, which the aborigines call the Larapinta (the Snake). It goes nowhere, finally expiring after 1,000 miles of pointless meandering in a vast, uncharted area of flood flats on the southern edge of the Simpson Desert, in South Australia.

Yet in spite of Australia's size, exploration progressed rapidly. It took only 75 years from the crossing of the Blue Mountains in 1813 for most of the interior to be known in outline, if not in detail, whereas it took more than four times as long to gain a similar amount of knowledge about North America.

The Australian explorers enjoyed one advantage over their American counterparts: unlike the North American Indians, in Australia the aboriginal tribes offered no serious organized resistance to the settlers, and it was a long time before the Europeans began to drive them from their tribal grounds.

By 1840, with something like a third of the mainland known to some extent, the great grasslands discovered by Sturt and Mitchell were filling up with settlers and their animals. Yet again, the colony's voracious appetite for land had to be satisfied.

Among the first to attempt to find new pasturage and a practicable route for cattle overland to the west coast was Edward John Eyre, the 25-year-old son of an English vicar. Eyre's search for new land took him into the Flinders Range, from which he had seen the "broad glittering stripe" of Lake Torrens to the north. That same year, 1839, he explored the Eyre Peninsula on the west side of Spencer Gulf and reached Streaky Bay on the Great Australian Bight.

Eyre's next, far more ambitious, plan was to reach the centre of the continent and if possible to cross to Port Essington on the north coast.

In June 1840, he started out with seven other men, 13 horses, two drays and 40 sheep for Lake Torrens, which Eyre and an aboriginal boy reached on July 8: "... the dry bed

Charles Sturt

Ludwig Leichhardt

John McDouall Stuart

Robert O'Hara Burke

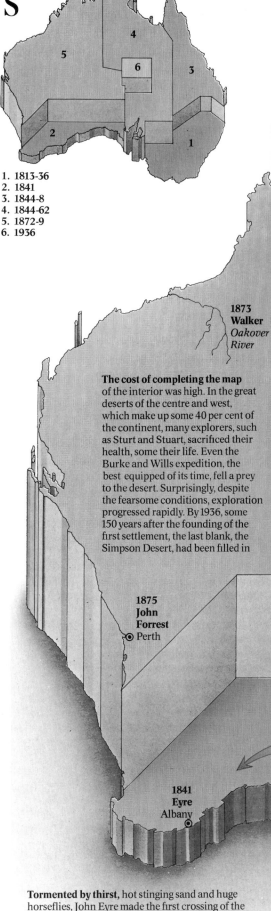

1. 1813-36
2. 1841
3. 1844-8
4. 1844-62
5. 1872-9
6. 1936

1873
Walker
Oakover River

The cost of completing the map of the interior was high. In the great deserts of the centre and west, which make up some 40 per cent of the continent, many explorers, such as Sturt and Stuart, sacrificed their health, some their life. Even the Burke and Wills expedition, the best equipped of its time, fell a prey to the desert. Surprisingly, despite the fearsome conditions, exploration progressed rapidly. By 1936, some 150 years after the founding of the first settlement, the last blank, the Simpson Desert, had been filled in

1875
John Forrest
⊙ Perth

1841
Eyre
Albany ⊙

Tormented by thirst, hot stinging sand and huge horseflies, John Eyre made the first crossing of the continent, from east to west. His route proved impracticable for livestock, but, as a feat of courage and endurance, the journey is one of the most outstanding in Australian exploration

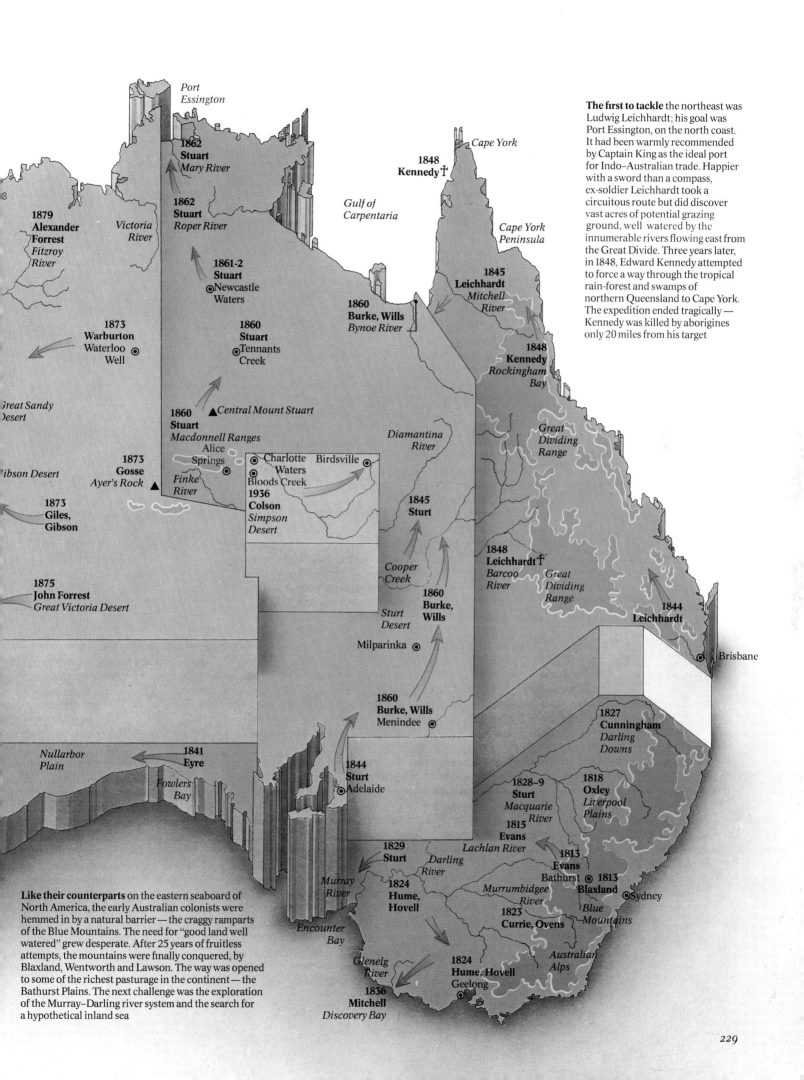

Port
Essington

1862
Stuart
Mary River

1879
Alexander
Forrest
Fitzroy
River

Victoria
River

1862
Stuart
Roper River

Gulf of
Carpentaria

Cape York

1848
Kennedy †

Cape York
Peninsula

The first to tackle the northeast was
Ludwig Leichhardt; his goal was
Port Essington, on the north coast.
It had been warmly recommended
by Captain King as the ideal port
for Indo–Australian trade. Happier
with a sword than a compass,
ex-soldier Leichhardt took a
circuitous route but did discover
vast acres of potential grazing
ground, well watered by the
innumerable rivers flowing east from
the Great Divide. Three years later,
in 1848, Edward Kennedy attempted
to force a way through the tropical
rain-forest and swamps of
northern Queensland to Cape York.
The expedition ended tragically —
Kennedy was killed by aborigines
only 20 miles from his target

1861-2
Stuart
⊙Newcastle
Waters

1860
Stuart
⊙Tennants
Creek

1860
Burke, Wills
Bynoe River

1845
Leichhardt
Mitchell
River

1848
Kennedy
Rockingham
Bay

Great Sandy
Desert

1873
Warburton
Waterloo ⊙
Well

▲ *Central Mount Stuart*

1860
Stuart
Macdonnell Ranges
Alice
Springs ⊙

Diamantina
River

Great
Dividing
Range

ibson Desert

1873
Gosse
Ayer's Rock ▲

1873
Giles,
Gibson

Finke
River

⊙ Charlotte
Waters
⊙
Bloods Creek

Birdsville ⊙

1936
Colson
Simpson
Desert

1845
Sturt

1848
Leichhardt †
Barcoo
River

Great
Dividing
Range

1875
John Forrest
Great Victoria Desert

Cooper
Creek

1860
Burke,
Wills

1844
Leichhardt

Sturt
Desert

Milparinka ⊙

⊙ Brisbane

1827
Cunningham
Darling
Downs

1860
Burke, Wills
Menindee ⊙

Nullarbor
Plain

1841
Eyre

1844
Sturt
⊙ Adelaide

Fowler's
Bay

1828-9
Sturt
Macquarie
River

1818
Oxley
Liverpool
Plains

1815
Evans
Lachlan River

1813
Evans
Bathurst ⊙

1813
Blaxland
⊙Sydney

Blue
Mountains

1829
Sturt

Darling
River

Murrumbidgee
River

1824
Hume,
Hovell

Murray
River

Encounter
Bay

1823
Currie, Ovens

Australian
Alps

Glenelg
River

1824
Hume, Hovell
Geelong
⊙

Like their counterparts on the eastern seaboard of
North America, the early Australian colonists were
hemmed in by a natural barrier — the craggy ramparts
of the Blue Mountains. The need for "good land well
watered" grew desperate. After 25 years of fruitless
attempts, the mountains were finally conquered, by
Blaxland, Wentworth and Lawson. The way was opened
to some of the richest pasturage in the continent — the
Bathurst Plains. The next challenge was the exploration
of the Murray–Darling river system and the search for
a hypothetical inland sea

1836
Mitchell
Discovery Bay

Australia: the middle years

of the lake coated over with a crust of salt, formed one unbroken sheet of pure white, and glittering brilliantly in the sun. On stepping upon this I found that it yielded to the foot, and that below the surface the bed of the lake consisted of soft mud. . . ."

Without prospect of water they moved into the Flinders Range to the east, where they found a water-hole in Scott Creek. On August 15, he saw what he thought was a continuation of Lake Torrens, shimmering to the northeast. Actually it was Lake Eyre South, to the north of it. Mirages had prevented him from seeing the land bridge between the two lakes. From his most northerly point, Mount Hopeless, northwest of the range, he saw, to the north and east, more expanses of salt lake (lakes Blanche and Callabona), a seemingly impassable barrier.

Abandoning his attempt on the centre from this direction, he decided to strike westwards in the hope of finding a route leading off into the interior. From Streaky Bay he managed, in temperatures in excess of 110°F, to penetrate to the head of the bight, but could get no farther with so many men and animals.

He now made what to everyone, including the Governor of South Australia, who forbade him to go on, seemed a foolhardy decision—to make a series of forced marches along the shores of the treeless, almost waterless Nullarbor Plain to Albany on King George Sound, 1,000 miles to the west. Just how arid it is can be appreciated by anyone who has ever travelled across the southern part of the plateau on the Trans-Continental Railway. In 1,000 miles the line does not cross a single permanent watercourse.

On February 25, 1841, he set off from Fowlers Bay with his servant, John Baxter, three aboriginal boys, nine pack horses, a pony and foal, six sheep and what he hoped would be enough food to see them through.

Their route took them through endless sandhills and at every step they were tormented by sand that "floated on the surface of the water, penetrating into our clothes, hair, eyes, and ears, our provisions were smothered with it, and our blankets half buried when we lay down at nights".

On March 2 they reached the westernmost water-hole and then entered a completely waterless region, where any grass that existed was withered. For 130 miles, following the edge of steep limestone cliffs, they tramped along under a tantalizingly cloudy sky from which not a drop of rain fell.

Lack of water was a constant nightmare throughout the journey. Had it not been for his aboriginal guides, Eyre might well have died. It was they who led him to their wells dug in the sand and to rock water-holes; it was they who showed him how to extract water

Survival in the desert calls for ingenious adaptation on the part of plant, beast and man. Desert plants withstand drought by mechanisms ranging from drought-resisting seeds which lie dormant until rain triggers off germination, to water-storing underground roots, and tough leathery leaves, coated with wax or encrusted salts

Birds of prey, such as the grey goshawk (above), are a common sight in the desert sky. Their victims—other birds, reptiles and small marsupials—provide both food and water

As well as basic foods, the aborigine diet has its delicacies, notably the witchetty grub—the larva of the longicorn beetle—found in the roots of certain acacias

Drought avoidance is the key to survival for flowering annuals such as Sturt's desert pea. The seeds lie dormant until enough rain falls to dissolve its growth-inhibiting coating. The life cycle lasts no more than eight weeks

Most vertebrates are adapted to obtain water from food and digestion of fat; many are nocturnal and thus escape the relentless heat. Nomadism is the key to survival for many birds, the kangaroo and also the aborigine—perhaps the most resourceful members of the desert community.

It was the aborigine who showed the explorers where to find water—often from such unlikely sources as tree trunks—and who introduced them to the wide range of food that the desert has to offer, however unpalatable some of it was to European taste-buds. Without the help of the aborigine, without his intimate knowledge of desert conditions, many explorers might never have survived the rigours of the Australian heartland

The second largest bird, the flightless emu has to rely on its powerful legs to escape the aborigine hunter; on level ground it can reach 35 mph

A basic aboriginal food, Gould's goanna, like many desert species, is paler and redder than species of wetter areas; its lighter colour reflects heat and acts as camouflage

The water-holding frog survives droughts of over a year by storing water in its body and burrowing deep in mud. It surfaces only when rain comes, laying its eggs immediately. The hibernating frogs provide water for aborigines

from the long lateral roots of the gum scrub, one tree yielding about two-thirds of a pint. In one place, not far from the shores of the bight, Eyre even collected water by brushing the leaves of a salt bush with a sponge.

Near the present telegraph station at Eyre, 160 miles from the previous water-hole, they found a supply by digging six feet in the sand. Here they remained for three weeks, during which the gallant Baxter went back 47 miles in order to try to find some provisions they had cached. He was unsuccessful.

To add to their hardships, winter was coming on now and the nights were bitterly cold, with frost. Food rations were running out too, and they had to supplement their meagre supplies by killing a sick horse and, two weeks later on April 22, the last of the sheep. By this time the aborigines were sulky and disobedient and on the night of April 28 two of them murdered Baxter and made off with most of the remaining food and all but one of the guns.

Eyre was now left with only one companion, the aborigine boy, Wylie. "For an instant", Eyre wrote, "I was almost tempted to wish that it had been my own fate instead of his. The horror of my situation glared upon me in such startling reality, as for an instant almost to paralyse the mind. At the dead hour of night, in the wildest and most inhospitable wastes of Australia, with the fierce wind raging in unison with the scene of violence before me, I was left with a single native, whose fidelity I could not rely upon, and who for aught I knew might be in league with the other two, who perhaps even now might be lurking about with the view of taking away my life as they had done that of the overseer." Fortunately, Wylie proved to be loyal; but the two of them had 600 miles to go before there could be any hope of reaching safety.

At last, on May 8, rain fell and they were able to scoop up supplies from depressions in the rocks. Three days later they found grass, some of it green, and here they killed one of the surviving horses, Wylie eating 6½ pounds of meat between supper and breakfast.

They were now in granite country, where water was more plentiful and they could supplement their diet with such delicacies as kangaroos and crabs.

Their luck held out even longer; on June 2 they reached a bay near Esperance, where they found the *Mississippi*, a French whaling ship, at anchor. After a brief rest on board ship, Eyre set out to complete his overland journey.

On June 23 they passed the 120th meridian and two days later heavy rain began to fall. Finally, on July 7, with the rain still pouring down, they entered the deserted streets of Albany on King George Sound. Although Eyre had failed to reach the centre of Australia

and to find a practicable overland route for livestock, in terms of sheer physical endurance and courage his was one of the greatest journeys of Australian exploration.

Attention now shifted briefly to Port Essington on the north coast. Captain King's enthusiastic recommendation of the harbour had inspired many grandiose schemes in Sydney business circles: here was the perfect gateway to Asia, the ideal cornerstone for Indo–Australian trade. Before such schemes could be realized, an overland route had to be found from Sydney. The man who attempted to find it was Dr Ludwig Leichhardt, a 32-year-old deserter from the Prussian Army.

An eccentric figure sporting a Malay coolie hat and a sword (he was terrified of fire-arms), Leichhardt was hopelessly unsuited for the leadership of such an expedition. Most of his two years in Australia had been spent in Sydney; his sense of direction and bushmanship were negligible; he was also extremely short-sighted. Had it not been for his aborigine guides, Charley Fisher and Harry Brown, he might well not have reached his goal. One quality he did not lack, however, was courage.

Staying near water

He set out in October 1844 from Moreton Bay near Brisbane. His route was dictated by the presence of water rather than the compass. As Leichhardt's maps show, he never strayed more than 10 miles from running water—an essential condition of the expedition as the men carried only a two-gallon pot in addition to their individual quart pots.

In June 1845, he reached the Mitchell River on the east side of the Gulf of Carpentaria, where John Gilbert, the expedition's naturalist, was killed by aborigines.

From this point Leichhardt turned south to skirt the gulf, crossing the innumerable rivers that empty into it. In December 1845, the ragged members of the expedition reached Port Essington and returned by sea to Sydney. They were given a heroes' welcome, and the King of Prussia granted Leichhardt a free pardon for having deserted from his army.

Leichhardt may not have blazed a direct route to Port Essington, but he did discover, as he wrote in his journals, "an excellent country, available, almost in its whole extent, for pastoral purposes".

In April 1848, Leichhardt set off from McPherson Station on the Darling Downs with the intention of following Mitchell's route to the Upper Barcoo (the Victoria River, which Mitchell had reached on an expedition in 1845). He then intended going north to the Gulf of Carpentaria and from there to the west coast and south to the Swan River. He and his companions were never

heard of again, although two of his camps were found on the Barcoo.

The same year Edmund Kennedy, a surveyor who had been with Mitchell on his expedition to the Barcoo in 1845, embarked on what was to be one of the most ill-fated of all Australian expeditions up to that time. He landed at Rockingham Bay on the coast of Queensland with the intention of reaching Cape York on the Torres Strait, where his expedition would be replenished from the sea. It was also hoped that a port for trade with Southeast Asia could be established there. The expedition forced its way through tropical rain-forest and swamps, crossed the Atherton Tableland and reached 13S on the Cape York Peninsula. From here Kennedy, with four men, including an aborigine named Jackey Jackey, pressed on towards Cape York. Two days later one of the party wounded himself with a gun and Kennedy left two men to look after him, pushing on alone with Jackey Jackey.

Some time in December, when only 20 miles from their objective, Port Albany, south of the cape, they were attacked by aborigines and Kennedy was mortally wounded. "I asked him," Jackey said, "'Mr Kennedy, are you going to leave me?' and he said, 'Yes, my boy, I am going to leave you. . . . I am very bad, Jackey; you take the books, Jackey, to the Captain, but not the big ones, the Governor will give anything for them.'"

Having buried him, Jackey reached the shore at Port Albany on December 23, 1848, and was taken off by the waiting ship. There were only two other survivors; the rest died of starvation.

Meanwhile, the centre of the continent still aroused general curiosity. In 1844, Sturt, who as assistant commissioner of lands in South Australia had been engaged in surveying the new territories and allocating them to settlers, set out at the head of a large expedition to reach the centre. He was convinced, from his observation of migratory birds, that good, fertile, well-watered land must exist there. He also believed that an inland sea or lake existed somewhere near the centre.

He left Adelaide in August with 15 men, 11 horses, 200 sheep, 30 bullocks, a boat and several carts and drays.

From the Murray he went up the Darling as far as Menindee Lake, then headed northwest, east of the salt pans sighted by Eyre, to cross the Main Barrier Range near Broken Hill. Here he found water, but not in sufficient quantities to support his animals, which were consuming 1,000 gallons a day.

On January 27, 1845, desperately short of water, he set up a camp at Depot Glen, near Milparinka, the largest water-hole they had so far discovered. It proved to be their salvation.

Australia: the middle years

The heat was scarcely bearable; in the shade the temperature rose to 132°F, in the sun to 157°F: "... every screw in our boxes has been drawn ... our hair, as well as that of our sheep ceased to grow ... and we found it difficult to write or draw, so rapidly did the fluid dry in our pens and brushes," he wrote. They even resorted to digging an underground room as a refuge from the relentless heat.

At last, on July 17, the rains broke: "... the ripple of waters in a little gully close to our tents was a sweeter and more soothing sound than the softest melody I ever heard ... the moment of our liberation had arrived."

With the cooler weather they went on to establish another camp, this time in fertile country on the west side of the Grey Range. On August 8 Sturt, with three companions, set off for the centre.

On August 18 they crossed the Strzelecki Creek, which they named after the Polish explorer, Paul Edmund de Strzelecki who had discovered gold in the Bathurst district and, in 1840, vast new areas of grazing land in Gippsland. They then entered a region that Sturt described as being "a gloomy stone-clad plain, of an extent such as I could not form any just idea. Ignorant of the existence of a similar geographical feature in any other part of the world, I was at a loss to divine its nature." He named it Sturt's Stony Desert.

The following month, having crossed the Diamantina River, near the present town of Birdsville, Sturt reached Eyre Creek and from a sandhill looked westwards towards the ridges of a terrible desert (the Simpson Desert, which was not crossed until 1936). Two days later, more than 400 miles out from Fort Grey with the water-holes drying up rapidly behind him, he admitted defeat. "I turned from it with a feeling of bitter disappointment," he wrote. "I was at the moment only a degree from the Tropic, and within 150 miles of the centre of the continent. If I had gained that spot my task would have been gratified."

A new incentive to explore the continent had arisen: Australia needed to establish a transcontinental telegraph line that would link up with India and the rest of the world. To encourage the opening up of a route, the South Australian Government offered £2,000 to the first expedition that succeeded in crossing the coast from north to south.

The first to attempt the crossing, and the first to finally reach the centre, or as near the geographical centre as anyone but a pedant would allow, was John McDouall Stuart, a surveyor who had been with Sturt on his 1844 expedition.

Having discovered and passed through the Macdonnell Ranges west of Alice Springs, on April 22, 1860, the three members of the expedition, who were suffering from scurvy, reached a hill about 125 miles north of Alice Springs. Stuart named it Central Mount Sturt (now changed to Stuart), "after the Father of Australian Exploration, for whom we gave three hearty cheers and one more for Mrs Sturt and family".

From here Stuart pushed on to Tennant Creek, 175 miles to the north. He was only about 300 miles from the Gulf of Carpentaria, but an attack by aborigines and the debilitating scurvy forced the party to turn back. By this time Stuart was nearly blind.

On September 1 they reached Chambers Creek, south of Lake Eyre, and safety. Back in Adelaide they were given a great welcome and the government voted Stuart funds for a further attempt on the centre.

Through to the north

On January 11, 1861, Stuart set out with 13 men and 49 horses from Mount Margaret Station, a farm west of Lake Eyre, on a second attempt to cross the continent.

They reached the most northerly point of Stuart's previous expedition on April 25 and from north of it made a number of attempts to break through to the Gulf of Carpentaria to the northeast or the Victoria River to the west, but the difficult terrain and the absence of any water beyond Newcastle Waters caused them to give up on July 12.

In the hope of forestalling Stuart's attempt to forge a route for the overland telegraph on behalf of the South Australian Government, the Government of Victoria fitted out the best-equipped and most expensive expedition of its kind. Camels—better adapted to desert conditions than the horses used hitherto—were specially imported from India; ample stores and equipment were provided. The main flaw in the expedition was the choice of leaders, Robert O'Hara Burke and William John Wills.

Neither man was an experienced explorer. Burke was a 40-year-old Irishman from Co. Galway, who had been a soldier in the Belgian and Austro–Hungarian armies and was now a police inspector in Victoria. Wills, who was 27, had been a medical student, a surveyor and was working in the meteorological office in Melbourne. He acted as surveyor.

The 15-man expedition set out from Melbourne in a blaze of glory on August 20, 1860. By the time it reached Menindee, in mid-October, the expedition had split into two factions, the fault of Burke, who had no skill in handling an expedition or its members; and it was here, while waiting for the remainder of the party to arrive, that Burke decided to press on to Cooper Creek, taking with him Wills, John King, who was in charge of the camels, Charles Gray, one of the assistants, and William Brahe, the foreman.

They left on October 19 and 23 days later reached Cooper Creek, near Innamincka, where the temperatures soared to 140°F in the sun. From here, having established a depot and put Brahe in charge of it, Burke left on December 16 to make a dash for the Gulf of Carpentaria, taking with him Wills, the only one who kept a journal, and Gray.

From now on only fragmentary information exists about their movements, but some time in the middle of February 1861 they reached the swamps on the shore of the gulf by the Bynoe River at its southwestern end. The swamps prevented them from reaching the sea, but they came close enough to ascertain that it was there.

The return journey, begun on February 13, was one of the most nightmarish in the annals of Australian exploration. For the first few weeks it rained incessantly, and the party had to plough its way through treacherous mud. Rations became dangerously low.

On March 25 Gray was discovered eating stolen rations—at the time he was extremely ill with dysentery. According to Wills's diary he was given a "good thrashing" by Burke. Five days later they had to resort to killing a camel, which they "jerked" (dried in the sun), and then Burke's horse, which they ate fresh. On April 17, giving the lie to the belief held by the other two that he was shamming, Gray died.

Four days later, with only two camels left, they reached Cooper Creek to find it deserted. Brahe, having given them up for lost, had left only eight hours previously. He had, in fact, exceeded his instructions in waiting so long. Naturally, they spoke of him bitterly, but they did find a tree with "Dig 3ft N.W. Apr. 21 1861", carved on it and there they found food and a letter from Brahe, telling them that he had left that very morning. The rear party had never reached the creek at all. Wills and King wanted to overtake Brahe, who by that evening was camped only 14 miles away; but Burke decided that they would never catch him up. Instead he decided to follow the Strzelecki Creek in an attempt to reach Stuart's Mount Hopeless, 150 miles to the south.

By May 17 they had killed both their camels; and from now on they were kept alive only by the kindness of the aborigines, who fed them with a sort of cake made with "nardoo seeds", fish and "fat" rats, which they enjoyed. On May 28, having wandered aimlessly, they were back where they had been a month previously, close to the camp at Cooper Creek.

By this time Brahe, whose conscience was troubling him, had already returned to the

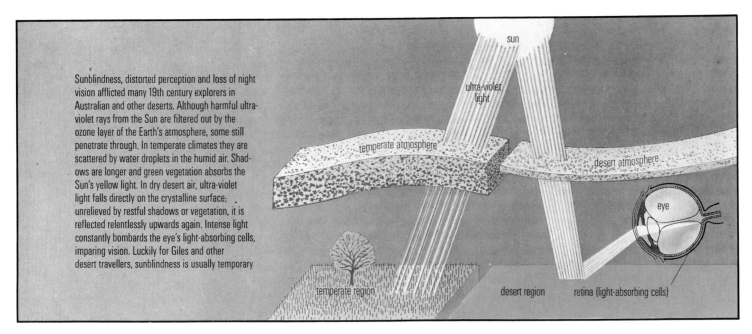

Sunblindness, distorted perception and loss of night vision afflicted many 19th century explorers in Australian and other deserts. Although harmful ultra-violet rays from the Sun are filtered out by the ozone layer of the Earth's atmosphere, some still penetrate through. In temperate climates they are scattered by water droplets in the humid air. Shadows are longer and green vegetation absorbs the Sun's yellow light. In dry desert air, ultra-violet light falls directly on the crystalline surface; unrelieved by restful shadows or vegetation, it is reflected relentlessly upwards again. Intense light constantly bombards the eye's light-absorbing cells, imparing vision. Luckily for Giles and other desert travellers, sunblindness is usually temporary

Creek. He and his party arrived on May 8 but, seeing no sign of the other party—incredibly, without bothering to find out whether the buried provisions had been touched—turned back, only a few miles from the dying men.

Burke and Wills died on or about June 30. King was the only survivor. The aborigines kept him alive with food until a relief expedition under Alfred Howitt of Melbourne, one of four that were sent out between 1861 and 1862 to search for the missing men, found him on September 18 "... wasted to a shadow, and hardly to be distinguished as a civilized human being but by the remnants of the clothes upon him."

THIS WAS NOT the end of exploration and discovery in the ghastly, heartless centre of the continent. Throughout the 1860s and the 1870s the Victorian explorers continued their attempts to force their way across the continent in various directions, across the great deserts, the spinifex plains and sandhills, the gibber stone plains, the endless ranges of quartzite, granite, gneiss, schists and red sandstone, which turn to the most improbable colours, according to the time of day and the season of the year, ranges that are like tidal waves rising from the land. They battled through dense stands of desert oak in the midst of which a traveller can see nothing but a few feet in front of him. They suffered from scurvy. Their camels died, poisoned by strange vegetation.

In the far north they came across swamps on the banks of rivers filled with estuarine alligators and became infested with leeches. There was little to choose, in terms of unpleasantness, between swamp, rain-forest and the great emptiness.

There were many who ventured into the unknown; so many that it is not even possible to mention more than a small number. Some were the discoverers of the great gold and coal fields. All the time they were forced to tack miles off course by one consuming need, to find water, so that a map of their combined explorations looks as if it had been drawn by centipedes whose feet had been dipped in ink.

One of the most determined of all Australian explorers, Stuart made a final attempt to reach the north coast in 1862. This time his efforts were rewarded. On July 24 he and his men finally reached the Indian Ocean at the mouth of the Mary River on Van Diemen Gulf. "Thring, who rode in advance of me, called out 'The Sea!' which took them all by surprise, and they were so astonished, that he had to repeat the call before they fully understood what was meant. They immediately gave three long and hearty cheers ... I dipped my feet, and washed my face and hands in the sea, as I promised the late Governor Sir Richard Macdonnell I would do if I reached it."

Debilitated

Stuart had reached his goal, but at the expense of his health. "For three months I had to be carried between two horses on a stretcher. I completely lost the use of my limbs and had to be carried about like an infant." He also lost his power of speech periodically and suffered from night blindness. Four years later, in 1866, he died, worn out and blind.

Within nine years of Stuart's return, an overland telegraph cable had been set up along his route, stretching from Adelaide to Darwin, from where an undersea cable linked Australia with the rest of the world.

Despite the herculean exploits of men such as Sturt and Stuart, in 1868 roughly one-fifth of the continent was still unexplored, an area to the west of Stuart's route encompassing some half a million square miles—one of the largest blanks on the face of the globe, with the exception of the polar regions. The general feeling was that this *terra incognita* would largely consist of "an inhospitable and dreary desert".

The first to test the validity of this belief was Ernest Giles, a man who loved exploration for its own sake: " ... The romance was in the chivalry of the tasks," he wrote in his book *Australia Twice Traversed, The Romance of Exploration*.

In 1872, Giles, with a party of five, attempted to cross the continent from Charlotte Waters on the Overland Telegraph line to the Murchison River, more than 1,000 miles to the west. He failed, but discovered the extraordinary collection of monoliths known as Mount Olga. "The appearance of Mount Olga from this camp is truly wonderful," he wrote, "it displayed to our astonished eyes rounded minarets, giant cupolas, and monstrous domes." He also discovered *Livistona Mariae*, a palm that is a relict of the prehistoric period (some are nearly 2,000 years old), and the mysterious River Finke.

On his next attempt, in 1873, with Alfred Gibson—a strange choice of companion for Gibson was illiterate and had little sense of bushmanship or direction—he penetrated the great Gibson Desert, west of the Petermann Range. Gibson was lost in the sands while returning to the depot to seek help. Giles walked out of the desert alone, often semi-delirious, carrying a 45-pound keg of water on his shoulders for 60 miles. At the end of his great trek, he came across a small, dying wallaby weighing not more than two pounds,

Australia: a continent completed

and, in his own terrible words "the instant I saw it I pounced upon it and ate it, living, raw, dying—fur, skin, bones, skull and all".

By this time rival expeditions were afield, seeking a crossing from the Overland Telegraph to the west coast. In July 1873, William Gosse, a young surveyor, set out at the head of an expedition sponsored by the South Australian Government. Travelling through the country beyond the Macdonnell Ranges he reached Ayers Rock. An immense sandstone monolith with walls 1,100 feet high, it looms over the surrounding plain like a tidal wave that never breaks.

In the Townsend Range, about 100 miles inside Western Australia, Gosse had to turn back, his horses " . . . very distressed by the sand and the spinifex. We are obliged to punish them severely to make them face the spinifex when their legs are raw and fly-blown. I have pushed on as far as is safe."

Giles's second rival was Colonel Peter Egerton Warburton, a 60-year-old Indian Army officer. In April 1873, Warburton set off from Alice Springs in drought conditions with his son, a surveyor, John W. Lewis, two Afghan camel drivers, Dennis White as cook, an aboriginal boy and 17 camels. His aim was to cross to the Indian Ocean.

After passing Central Mount Wedge, north of the main Macdonnell Range, they entered a terrible plain covered with spinifex. On June 18 they reached some water-holes, full of dead rats, which they named, as it was the anniversary of the battle, Waterloo Wells.

They then went on, first northwest and then west, into the Great Sandy Desert, their camels dying from eating poisonous herbs, some running away, others simply collapsing. Those that collapsed were either cut up and "jerked" or eaten on the spot. "No shred was passed over. Head, feet, hide, tail all went into the boiling pot. . . . The tough, thick hide was cut up and parboiled. The coarse hair was then scraped off with a knife and the leather-like substance replaced in the pot and stewed until it became like the inside of a carpenter's glue pot, both to the taste and the smell. . . . "

Finally, on December 11, when they were nearing the end of their strength, they reached the Oakover River on the edge of the desert, and from there Lewis rode, with the two surviving camels, in search of an outstation where he could find food. He succeeded, returning in time to save his dying leader. The debilitated party eventually reached the coast, having covered more than 2,000 miles, the first men to cross from the Overland Telegraph to the west coast.

The first to cross the continent in the other direction, from west to east, was John Forrest. His skill as a bushman had already been tested—in 1869 he led a search party for Leichhardt and the following year he was sent out by the government to find a practicable route for livestock along the Great Australian Bight to Adelaide. Forrest had no more success than Eyre in finding such a route through these waterless wastes, but he did map much of the country through which the Overland Telegraph from Perth to the eastern colonies was soon to pass.

Forrest then proposed to explore the country between the west coast and the telegraph line set up along Stuart's route, and in April 1874 left Geraldton, 250 miles north of Perth, with his brother Alexander and four others. Five and a half months later he reached the Peake telegraph station.

Giles had been beaten. Nevertheless, on May 6, 1875, with Henry Tietkins as second-in-command, a party of five, which included Saleh, an Afghan camel driver, Tommy, an aborigine, and 22 camels he left Port Augusta, on Spencer Gulf, and crossed the southern part of the Victoria Desert. They reached Perth in mid-November, their longest march without water being 330 miles.

On January 13, 1876, he left Perth with the same team, except that Alec Ross replaced Tietkins as second-in-command. Their route eastwards took them across the "ceaseless undulations of sand" of the Gibson Desert.

Dual triumph

The heat was intense; they were continually tormented by flies and stinging ants. At one stage Giles went completely blind. They reached the Peake telegraph station on August 23, 1876, the first to cross the continent in both directions.

In February 1879, Alexander Forrest left Nickol Bay near Roebourne on the northwest coast to explore the country beyond the Fitzroy River. There, they failed to break through the King Leopold Ranges and were forced back to the Fitzroy. After some survey work Forrest then decided to attempt to reach the Overland Telegraph.

They left the river towards the middle of July, at first passing through good pastoral country, Forrest over-optimistically estimating its extent as 25 million acres. They then entered waterless country and the agonies of thirst were added to those of hunger. The last part of the journey assumed a nightmarish quality. Forrest and one companion rode ahead for 100 miles to the telegraph line to get help for the rest.

On August 30, Forrest recorded " . . . we were so thirsty that we could hardly speak. We shot a hawk and cut his throat in order to drink the blood, but it did not seem to do us any good." The next day they reached their goal, where, to their immense relief, they found an adequate supply of water.

Surveyors, gold-prospectors and farmers quickly filled in the details between the "centipede" trails of the explorers. Only one area consistently defied all attempts at exploration until the 1930s—the Simpson Desert, sprawling over 30,000 square miles on the borders of the Northern Territory, South Australia and Queensland. Its forbidding sandstone ridges, running "like waves of the sea, varying from 70 to 200 feet in height", turned back many explorers, including Charles Sturt on his 1845 attempt to reach the heart of the continent. The core of the desert remained inviolate (unless, as some people believe, Leichhardt and his men perished there) until 1936, when Edmund Colson, a 55-year-old farmer and an aborigine named Peter crossed it from Bloods Creek to Birdsville in 16 days. The northern end was crossed by Dr C. T. Madigan between 1935 and 1937.

The final detail had been filled in, some 160 years after the arrival of the first settlers in Botany Bay. Although roughly one-third of the continent had proved to be inhospitable desert, the colonists had found compensations —millions of acres of lush grazing ground and, from the 1850s on, gold and other minerals.

The debt to the men who opened up these areas was immense. It had been a story of fortitude and almost superhuman endurance in the face of some of the most appalling physical conditions to be found in any continent in the world. Snatched from death, often by what seems nothing less than a miracle—reading of their escapes even an atheist might be persuaded of the possibility of divine intervention—the explorers would return again and again to the quest until they succeeded, or else perished. The names on the maps that they bestowed on their discoveries are rarely their own. They are usually the names of other explorers (sometimes their own companions who perished on the way) or of royalty, cartographers, colonial governors, politicians, their own patrons, members of learned societies and so on—some of them now very obscure people. Generally speaking, if the explorers got a mention on their own explorations they were already dead, so that a knowledge of the circumstances in which some of these Australian rocks, ranges, peaks, deserts and swamps received their rather out-of-place names, endows them with a sinister quality.

To Ernest Giles, who survived the rigours of Western Australia exploration, only the polar regions presented explorers with a greater challenge. In his telling words ". . . exploration of a thousand miles in Australia is equal to ten thousand miles in any other part of the earth's surface. . . ."

Return to the northern passages

AFTER THE DEFEAT of Napoleon at Waterloo in 1815 large parts of the Old and New Worlds were able to enjoy a period of relative peace. Britain pledged herself to maintain the freedom of the seas, and the new Hydrographic Department of the Royal Navy, which had been established in 1811, began to carry out intensive scientific surveys to make navigation safer for merchant shipping.

It was now that the Navy returned to the quest, more or less abandoned since Baffin's last attempt to discover it in 1616, for the Northwest Passage. By this time, strange as it now seems, Baffin's discoveries had been discredited.

The Navy was not interested in pioneering a commercial route to Cathay and the Indies. It was interested in the passage for scientific reasons, but there was also alarm at the rapid extension of Russian influence on the shores of the Arctic Ocean, the Bering Sea and the Pacific seaboard. It seemed possible that the British and Americans might have to contend with a third power on the American continent and it was only a matter of time before the Russians began to search for the passage between the Pacific and the Atlantic. National honour, that costly abstraction, was at stake.

It was also decided that an attempt would be made to cross the Arctic by ship by way of the Pole, providing that no land mass lay across the route. By this time more than 40 years had passed since the Navy had mounted a well-organized but unsuccessful expedition to reach the Pole—that of Captain Constantine Phipps, who, in 1773, had reached the edge of the icepack in latitude 80.50N, north of Spitsbergen, some miles beyond the farthest point north reached by Hudson in 1608. It was in the course of Phipps's voyage that a 15-year-old midshipman named Horatio Nelson distinguished himself by rescuing a boat's crew from a pack of angry walruses. It was not until 1806 that Phipps's latitude was passed when the Scottish whaling captain, William Scoresby, sailing from Whitby, reached 81.31N, east of Spitsbergen.

The prime mover and principal planner of this fresh assault on the Arctic was Sir John Barrow, Secretary to the Admiralty. In 1817 his opportunity came. That year William Scoresby the younger, who also became a distinguished explorer on the coast of Greenland, returned from a whaling voyage and reported to Sir Joseph Banks of the Royal Society that he had encountered exceptionally mild conditions inside the Arctic Circle. "I observed about 2,000 square leagues [18,000 square miles] of the Greenland Seas included between the parallels 74 and 80 perfectly void of ice," he wrote, "whereby I was enabled to penetrate within sight of the eastern coast of Greenland, to a meridian usually considered

inaccessible", and he proposed "the examination of the coasts of Spitzbergen and Greenland, explorations affecting the whale-fishery, and researches toward deciding whether or not a navigation into the Pacific by a northeast or northwest passage existed."

Banks communicated this information to Barrow, who lost no time. The First Lord of the Admiralty, Lord Melville, gave his sanction, the Royal Society gave its support and four whaling ships were bought and reinforced against the ice. Great care was taken of the crews' comfort—beds were installed instead of hammocks, the ships were very adequately heated and fur-lined clothing supplied. Two of the ships, the *Dorothea* (370 tons) under the command of Captain David Buchan and the *Trent* (250 tons) with a Lieutenant John Franklin, were to head north and cross the Arctic to the Bering Sea, passing as close to the Pole as possible; while the other two ships the *Isabella* (385 tons) and the *Alexander* (252 tons), under Captain John Ross and Lieutenant Edward Parry were to head west and attempt the Northwest Passage by way of the Davis Strait, which was thought to have an island named James Island lying in it. When he reached the Bering Sea, Buchan was to remain in the area to give assistance to Ross and Parry.

Buchan's expedition was a failure. From the time he sailed from the Thames in April 1818 the *Trent* leaked badly and required continuous pumping, and the whereabouts of the leak was not discovered until the two ships had been beset in the icepack off the northwest point of Spitsbergen for 13 days. It was hopeless. The *Trent* was forced four feet out of the water by the pressure of the pack and the *Dorothea* sprung some of her timbers, and when they escaped from the ice Buchan was forced to retire in the face of its inexorable southerly drift.

Ross's first journey

Before Ross sailed north in April, Barrow summed up the knowledge that existed about the Northwest Passage at that time and also the aims of the expedition: "With regard to the North-West Passage . . . it has been ascertained that there is no passage on the coast of America, below the Arctic Circle [Hearne and Mackenzie had proved this by reaching the mouths of two rivers on the Canadian mainland to the north of it in the 1770s]; but it has not been ascertained whether this coast joins Greenland or trends away to join the north coast of America. . . . Indeed, the best geographers are now of opinion that Greenland is either an island or an archipelago of islands . . . although a communication . . . in all probability does exist between the two oceans it by no means follows that

there must be found a navigable passage for large vessels; though it is not unfair to infer that, where large mountains of ice can float and find their way, a ship may do the same. This, however, is the point to be ascertained by the expedition under Captain Ross."

In short nothing was known of the vast area from east of Baffin Land to Icy Cape on the north coast of Alaska, reached by Cook in 1778, apart from the two points reached by Hearne and Mackenzie.

On June 17 Ross and his ships reached Hare Island off the west coast of Greenland in 70.30N, where he met a fleet of 45 whaling ships. Here, having been advised by one of their captains to "stick by the land floe", he sailed north with them.

Ross reached 76.54N before his ships were temporarily beset and he was forced to turn away westwards towards Ellesmere Land, where he failed to penetrate Jones Sound. Instead, he sailed into Lancaster Sound (both sounds had been discovered by Baffin in 1616), but after about 50 miles he turned back, convinced that it was a bay.

It is one of the enigmas in the history of discovery. The strait is 40 miles wide and 120 miles long, the southernmost passage leading to the Polar Sea and the Bering Strait, the true approach route for the Northwest Passage. Sailing into it as he did it was impossible for Ross to have seen what he claimed—"land round the bottom of the bay forming a chain of mountains connected with those which extended along the north and south side", which he named the Croker Mountains.

If it was a mirage it was visible to no one else. The kindliest explanation is that he was suffering from an hallucination, and for the rest of his life he was known by his detractors as "Croker Mountains". Parry was aghast at his decision to turn back. What Ross had succeeded in doing was confirming the truth of Baffin's discoveries and proving that there was no such place as James Island. The Admiralty was as dismayed as his officers had been when Ross returned, and within a month they decided to mount two new expeditions. One was to be commanded by John Franklin and was to travel overland from Hudson Bay to the Coppermine River; the other was to return to Lancaster Sound and find out the truth about the "Croker Mountains". It was commanded by Parry, a superb navigator and an excellent scientist, the author of a work on astronomy and already, at 29, a Fellow of the Royal Society.

In May 1819 Parry sailed from Yarmouth in command of the bomb (a bombardment warship) *Hecla* (375 tons) with Lieutenant Liddon in the gun-brig *Griper* (180 tons), an extremely unhandy vessel. Both officers and

Return to the northern passages

their crews were exceptionally young.

By August 1 Parry's ships were at the mouth of Lancaster Sound, having narrowly escaped destruction in a storm among the bergs off Greenland, and now they sailed into it, past cliffs "like an immense wall in ruins, rising almost perpendicular from the sea" under a crowd of sail, the mastheads filled with officers and men anxious to know whether Ross's Croker Mountains were as mythical as Parry believed them to be.

"Our Course", Parry wrote, two days later, "was nearly due wést, and the wind, still continuing to freshen, took us in a few hours nearly out of sight of the Griper. The only ice which we met with consisted of a few large bergs very much washed by the sea. And, the weather being remarkably clear, so as to enable us to run with perfect safety, we were by midnight in a great measure relieved from our anxiety respecting the supposed continuity of land at the bottom of this magnificent inlet, having reached the longitude of 83 degrees 12 minutes, where the two shores are above 13 leagues apart, without the slightest appearance of any land to the westward of us for four or five points of the compass." The Croker Mountains had melted away.

Increasingly, the ships' compasses became sluggish and Sabine and Parry realized that they were somewhere in the vicinity of the Magnetic Pole, which at that time was located on Boothia Peninsula; when they turned south through Prince Regent Inlet, which leads into the Gulf of Boothia, the compasses became useless. Here, they were only about 250 miles from the Magnetic Pole.

A hundred miles inside Prince Regent Inlet Parry turned back, having come to the correct conclusion, that it connected with Hudson Bay and warned by ice-blink that there were great obstacles ahead. Returning to Lancaster Sound he endeavoured to force his ships westwards along the southern shores, but encountered thick drift ice, and it was only when he crossed to the coast of Devon Island, on the north side of the sound, that he was able to find a passage.

On the evening of August 22 they emerged from the sound and saw a magnificent strait, stretching away to the north at right angles to their course, which Parry named Wellington Channel, "after His Grace the Master General of the Ordnance". Ahead was another strait, 30 miles broad, which he named after Barrow. It led to the great inverted triangle of Melville Sound, 160 miles to the west, and beyond that into the permanent polar ice of the Beaufort Sea.

From now on their progress was painfully slow, bedevilled by contrary winds, calms, fog, snow and ice; but on September 4, off the southern shore of Melville Island in Melville Sound, they at last crossed the 110th meridian west of Greenwich amid much rejoicing. By doing so the ships' crews became entitled to the £5,000 reward offered by Parliament to the first men to cross this meridian within the Arctic Circle.

After this they made little progress. The icepack in the sound was being pressed northwards by the wind on to the shores of the island and the ships with it. East of Cape Hearne they encountered the impenetrable ice that was pressing down through the Banks Strait (now McClure Strait) to the west from the Beaufort Sea. Already the new autumn ice was seven inches thick in the sound and it was imperative to find sheltered anchorage in which the ships could winter. On September 24, having reached a farthest

Edward Parry, Royal Navy officer and brilliant scientist, who failed in an early attempt to reach the North Pole

point of 112.29w, Parry ordered the cutting, with saws, of a channel more than two miles long to the head of what he named Hecla and Griper Bay (later Winter Harbour). Once the ships were at anchorage, Parry had the topgallant and topmasts sent down and the decks roofed in so that they could be used as a running track.

Inside the ship heat was evenly distributed from the stoves by air ducts. Great precautions were taken against scurvy. Beer was brewed, fresh bread baked and each day they drank lemon juice. They were made to eat broth and vegetables preserved in vinegar and watercress was grown. Another remedy was Burkitt's essence of malt, hops and spruce.

The Arctic night closed in on November 4 and lasted for three months. At times the temperature fell to 50 degrees below zero and the water in the harbour froze to a depth of seven feet six inches; while bears prowled about the ship and famished wolves howled.

It was a remarkable achievement on Parry's part that during the entire winter only one man died (of some disease unconnected with being in the Arctic); another had to have his fingers amputated because of frostbite.

With the arrival of summer he set off with a small party of officers and men and a cart loaded with supplies on a 14-day journey across Melville Island. This was the first overland expedition made by the Navy in the Arctic. Meanwhile, parties were out shooting musk oxen, deer, hares, brent geese, ducks and ptarmigan, and produced nearly 400 pounds of fresh meat.

On August 1, with the return of warm weather, Parry set sail to the west in the teeth of contrary winds, but only succeeded in reaching 113.48w near Cape Dundas. From a hill on the island they could see the loom of what they named Banks Land across the strait of the same name to the southwest; while to the west the polar floe stretched away towards the Beaufort Sea, rising in great hummocks up to 25 feet above the water.

On August 16, with new ice already forming on the sea, he turned back. He and his men had penetrated more than 500 miles into the Arctic, beyond the Magnetic Pole and more than half-way from Greenland to the Bering Strait. The Arctic winter had been vanquished, and information of great value to the whaling industry about Lancaster Sound had been collected. But the Northwest Passage, Parry now knew, would have to be forced in a lower latitude than that of Melville Sound.

Parry was promoted to the rank of commander and in May 1821 he sailed again. This time with the *Hecla* and the *Fury*, a duplicate of the *Hecla* with interchangeable fittings and gear; an ingenious idea which he himself had devised in case disaster overtook one of the vessels. Wintering in the Arctic, he spent three summers attempting to find a passage westwards from the northeast corner of Hudson Bay, in waters explored by Baffin and Middleton, exploring Frozen Strait and Repulse Bay at the base of the Melville Peninsula. When these proved to be dead-ends, he attempted to force his ships through the Fury and Hecla Strait at the northeast point of the American mainland. The strait, 100 miles long and only two miles broad in places, leads into the Gulf of Boothia, but it was choked with ice.

The expedition was given great help by an Eskimo tribe, who drew accurate maps for them, insisted on eating the soap that was given to them and offered their naked children and even the loan of their wives to the explorers in exchange for the mirrors and other Western wonders that they were given. Parry studied the Eskimo way of life—

their hunting methods, the way they built igloos and their dog teams and sledges—but failed to draw the conclusion which Peary, the eventual conqueror of the Pole came to, that their clothing and means of transport were also the most efficient for Europeans living in the Arctic.

In 1824, he again sailed through Lancaster Sound and into Prince Regent Inlet; but after surviving an exceptionally severe winter on its eastern shore, his ships were driven ashore by gales on the opposite coast of Somerset Island. There, the *Fury* remained for ever and the crews returned home in the *Hecla*.

Attempt on the Pole
It was Parry's last attempt to find the Northwest Passage. The Admiralty, discouraged by the setbacks, turned its attention away from the elusive seaway and towards the problem of reaching the North Pole, and Parry was the man chosen to make the attempt. It proved to be one of the most arduous and disheartening journeys in the

long history of northern polar exploration.

With two flat-bottomed boats equipped with runners to act as sledges on the ice, Parry, three other officers and 24 seamen and marines set off from Spitsbergen in June 1827 and the party was soon on the pack-ice in 81.12N. Hauling the boats, a weight of more than 260 pounds per man, the party struggled north, while the ice beneath them drifted imperceptibly southwards, nullifying most of their efforts.

A month after setting out, they turned back. They had travelled 580 miles from their ship, the *Hecla*, but they were only 172 miles to the north of it because of the ice drift. The latitude they had reached—82.45N—was not to be surpassed for 48 years.

John Ross, the unfortunate officer of "Croker Mountains" fame, submitted a new plan to the Admiralty in 1828. It was for a new search for the Northwest Passage in Prince Regent Inlet, south of the point reached by Parry with the *Hecla* and the *Fury* in 1824; but he had not been forgiven for his

mythical mountains and the Government had withdrawn the prize money it had offered for Arctic discovery. It was left to Felix Booth, a distiller of gin, to put up the £18,000 necessary to equip the expedition.

In May that year Ross sailed in what seemed an extraordinarily unsuitable vessel for the purpose, the 87-ton paddle steamer *Victory*, which had been employed on the ferry service between Dover and Calais. Luckily it was also rigged as a sailing ship.

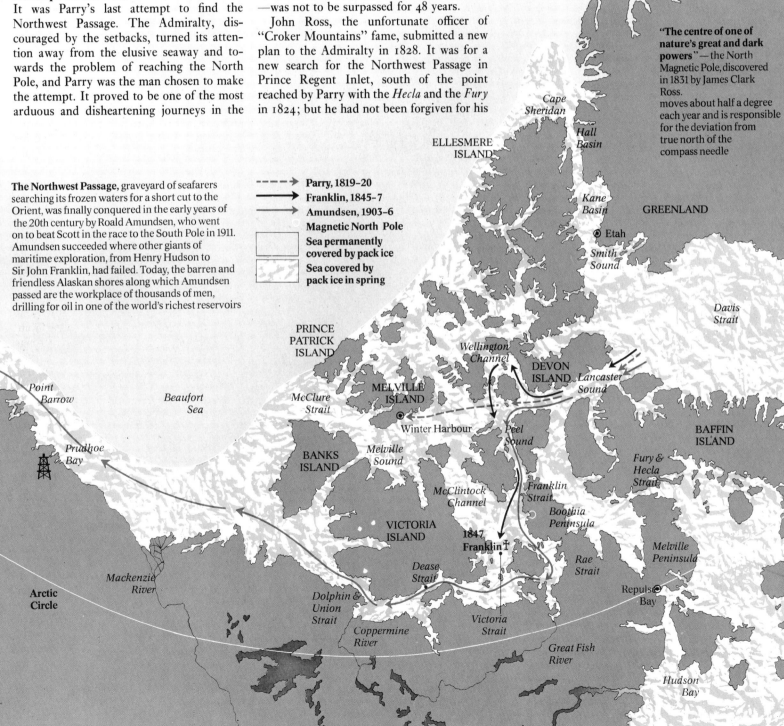

The Northwest Passage, graveyard of seafarers searching its frozen waters for a short cut to the Orient, was finally conquered in the early years of the 20th century by Roald Amundsen, who went on to beat Scott in the race to the South Pole in 1911. Amundsen succeeded where other giants of maritime exploration, from Henry Hudson to Sir John Franklin, had failed. Today, the barren and friendless Alaskan shores along which Amundsen passed are the workplace of thousands of men, drilling for oil in one of the world's richest reservoirs

"The centre of one of nature's great and dark powers"—the North Magnetic Pole, discovered in 1831 by James Clark Ross.
moves about half a degree each year and is responsible for the deviation from true north of the compass needle

- - - → **Parry, 1819–20**
——→ **Franklin, 1845–7**
——→ **Amundsen, 1903–6**
Magnetic North Pole
Sea permanently covered by pack ice
Sea covered by pack ice in spring

Return to the northern passages

His most fortunate acquisition was his nephew Commander James Clark Ross as second-in-command. James Ross, who was 29, was a specialist in terrestrial magnetism, knew a great deal about natural history and had already been six times within the Arctic Circle (by 1836 he had served 14 navigable seasons in the Arctic and eight winters).

Under the power of its monstrous engine the *Victory* could only make three knots. The boiler leaked and had to be plastered with a nasty mixture of dung and potatoes. Ross soon gave up using it and set sail instead.

After reaching the mouth of Prince Regent Inlet on August 10, they followed the shore of North Somerset Island south to where Parry's ship the *Fury* had been driven ashore. The *Fury* had disappeared, but they found some of its canned stores in excellent condition.

Pressing south, Ross reached the peninsula, which he named Boothia Felix, after his patron. There he and his men wintered, at Felix Harbour—the first men to make a landfall on the American continent from the north. And there they cast the useless engine away on the shore.

The winter was enlivened by school work for the men, lectures on "Total Abstinence" by Ross and by visits from Eskimoes, who were extremely well informed about the topography of Boothia Gulf and who drew maps for Ross, as they had done for Parry on the other side of the Melville Peninsula, to the east. They also taught the explorers how to make sledges, and in the spring of the following year James Ross made the first of his long journeys overland, taking with him two Eskimo guides, five seamen and two sledges, one of them drawn by a team of dogs. On this first great journey he crossed the Boothia Peninsula, followed its western shore northwards and crossed the James Ross Strait to discover Cape Felix, the north point of King William Island. He believed the cape

to be part of the North American mainland and showed it as such on his chart—with tragic results, years later, for Franklin, who failed to recognize the existence of the straits on the east side of the island and took the fatal passage into the ice of the Victoria Strait to the west.

North Magnetic Pole

The high point of James Ross's journey was the discovery, in May 1831, of the North Magnetic Pole in 70.5N, 96.46W, where he suspended several magnetic needles, which remained inactive. "Nature had erected no monument to denote the spot which she had chosen as the centre of one of her great and dark powers," he wrote. He erected a cairn to remedy the deficiency, and hoisted the flag.

At the end of May 1832 John Ross abandoned the *Victory* to the ice and with his men made a terrible boat journey of 300 miles to Fury Bay. Here the remainder of Parry's provisions saved them from death by starvation, and after an abortive attempt to reach Lancaster Sound they spent the winter in a house that they had built. On August 26, 1833, at four in the morning, having reached Lancaster Sound, they met a whaler, and when Ross hailed it he found that it was his old ship, the *Isabella*.

John Ross was knighted and made a rear-admiral and, together with his crew, received a prize of £5,000 from Parliament. He

and his men had earned it. Four consecutive winters had been passed in the Arctic with the loss of only one life due to the conditions (two men died from other causes); important information had been gained about the geography of the North American mainland and the meteorology of the Arctic, and the North Magnetic Pole had been discovered. Ross had finally justified himself.

After Ross's return in 1833, the following decade was devoted to filling in details of the North American mainland. Still haunted by the fear that the Royal Navy might be forestalled by the Russians—even by the Americans, whose fleet was growing—the Admiralty decided on another attempt to reach the Bering Strait from the east in 1845.

The man chosen to lead it, Sir John Franklin, was 59—old for an Arctic explorer. He sailed in May that year with two ships, the *Erebus* and the *Terror*, both of which had seen service in Antarctica. They had special screw propellers that could be raised to avoid damage by ice, but drove the ships at only four miles an hour. This was in the transitional period between paddle ships and screw-driven warships.

The ships had provisions for three years. They had a form of central heating and carried every kind of equipment from cut-glass and silver for the officers' wardroom to slates and school books for the men. What was lacking, surprisingly when one considers how knowledgeable the experts should have been by now about Arctic conditions, was proper clothing. Thick blue, official-issue uniforms, warm underclothing and wolfskin blankets were deemed adequate. The boats and sledges provided were cumbersome.

Erebus and *Terror* sailed from Britain in May 1845. Franklin sent his last letter to the Admiralty from the Whalefish Islands in Disco Bay, Greenland, on July 12 and a fortnight later a whaler captain found the ships

A two-way journey through the Northwest Passage was made in 1969 by the oil tanker "Manhattan" to prove that the once-impenetrable waterway could be a commercially viable route

moored to an iceberg at 74N, 66W in Baffin Bay, while on their way to Lancaster Sound. He dined on board with Sir John and his officers. This was the last that was ever seen of the *Erebus* or the *Terror* by civilized man and, alive, of their crews.

What happened to them is partly conjecture, partly the result of discoveries made over a period of many years by Eskimoes and explorers. In the summer of 1846, Franklin took his ships through the Peel Sound and Franklin Strait. This was the moment when, having cleared them, he made the fatal error, forced on him by the charts based on the findings of James Ross, which showed King William Island as part of the mainland, linked to the Boothia Peninsula by an isthmus. Instead of taking the navigable passage through the straits to the east and south of the island, the keys to a northwest passage, he turned his ships southwest into what was to be for them a valley of death; the Victoria Strait between the island and Victoria Land, which receives the full force of the polar ice-stream as it flows down from the Beaufort Sea.

On September 12, 1846, they were beset and so they remained all through 1847. The following June Franklin died and was succeeded by Crozier, his second-in-command, with James Fitzjames taking over the *Erebus*. That winter the ships were carried infinitely slowly farther into the strait with scurvy rampaging among the crews, and the inferior rations, supplied by a rascally victualler, nearing their end. On April 22, 1848, Crozier gave the order to abandon the ships, and the record of what had happened was committed to a single sheet of paper and left in a sealed canister in a cairn on King William Island, 15 miles from the place where the ships had been abandoned. By this time 24 men had died and 105 were still alive.

According to what was written, they began what was to be their death march on April 26 in the hope of eventually being able to reach the Hudson's Bay Company's post at Fort Resolution. Although they met Eskimoes on the way who might have helped them, it seems that the natives were frightened by their ghastly appearance; they were in the last stages of starvation and scurvy.

A year before Crozier abandoned his ships, alarm began to be felt among men who knew the Arctic about the safety of Franklin and his men, but the first relief expeditions were not sent out until 1848. Captain Henry Kellett was ordered to search north and west of the Bering Strait. Sir John Richardson and Dr John Rae, of the Hudson's Bay Company, were to follow the north coast eastwards from the Mackenzie River to the Coppermine River and the shores of Wollaston Land in the southern part of Victoria Land. Sir James Ross was to search in the area of Melville Sound, Banks Island, which was not known to be an island, and the Wellington Channel. Among Ross's officers were Leopold McClintock and Robert McClure, soon to become famous in their own right.

All failed, although Ross's expedition, which wintered only 70 miles from the site of Franklin's first winter camp, made every effort to contact the missing men. Foxes were caught and released wearing engraved collars, guns and rockets were fired at frequent intervals, cairns were set up and kegs set afloat with messages in them.

In 1850, 15 vessels were deployed for the search, including two US Navy brigs under Lieutenant E. J. De Haven, which had been fitted out by a New York shipping magnate, Henry Grinnell.

De Haven's ships, the *Advance* and the *Rescue*, were later beset in the Wellington Channel and drifted far to the north, where he discovered Grinnell Land, the northerly extremity of Devon Island.

Four years of continuous search and exploration followed on the expeditions of 1850. In the course of them great blanks were filled in on the charts of the Canadian Arctic archipelago, many ships were lost and great sufferings were endured by those who took part.

Among the searchers was Richard Collinson, who worked eastwards in the *Enterprise* from the Bering Strait with his second-in-command, McClure, in the *Investigator*. On this voyage in the Arctic Collinson covered 128 degrees of longitude (64 each way), a record not broken until Nordenskiöld's Northeast Passage in the steamer *Vega* in 1878 and 1879.

McClure, after separating from Collinson and becoming beset in the ice, joined up with a naval sledging party from the west and thus, with his men, became the first man to have made the Northwest Passage, although partly on foot, and almost to circumnavigate the North and South American continents (they had sailed from Britain to the Bering Strait by way of South America). McClure and his men were awarded £10,000 as the first to discover the passage.

If in life he had failed, Franklin's death brought a sort of triumph. The years of searching for him added new names to the roll of Arctic pioneers, and their experiences greatly expanded mankind's stock of knowledge of one of the world's most desolate regions and of the means of survival there.

The long-sought passage was finally navigated between 1903 and 1906 by the Norwegian Roald Amundsen in the cutter-rigged *Gjøa*. Even as late as this, Amundsen found the skeletons of two of Franklin's men.

Voyage of the Vega

THE 1860s AND 1870s were the years of the great northern explorations by Baron Nils Adolf Erik Nordenskiöld, the son of a distinguished Swedish mineralogist and traveller, born in 1832 at Helsinki in Finland, then under Russian domination.

He was in his thirties when he led the first of two Swedish North Polar Expeditions and reached 81.42N, 17.30E, up to that time the highest northern latitude reached by man. On the second expedition, having wintered in Spitsbergen, he tried to reach the Pole, using reindeer to haul his sledges, but the sea-ice in the Arctic Ocean was so rough that he was forced to give up. He did, however, succeed in crossing the ice of Nordaustlandet, the most northerly island of Spitsbergen.

For the next five years Nordenskiöld devoted himself entirely to the problem of forcing the Northeast Passage, which he believed had commercial possibilities.

In 1875 and 1876 he made two preliminary voyages through the Kara Sea to the mouth of the Yenisei, the first in a walrus-hunting sloop, the *Proeven*, the second in a steamer, the *Ymer*. He was convinced "that the open navigable water, which two years in succession had carried me across the Kara Sea, formerly of so bad repute, to the mouth of the Yenisei, extended in all probability as far as Bering Strait, and that a circumnavigation of the Old World was thus within the bounds of possibility."

Steam whaler
The King of Sweden and Norway approved Nordenskiöld's plan and the expedition was financed by Baron Oscar Dickson and a Russian merchant.

The vessel chosen for the voyage was an Arctic whaling ship, the barque-rigged steamer *Vega* (300 tons). It was built of oak with an ice-skin of greenheart, and had an effective speed of about six or seven knots under steam. Its captain was Lieutenant Palander of the Swedish Navy. A tender, the *Lena*, a smaller, steel-built steamer specially built for the expedition, was under the command of one of the walrus-hunting captains, Christian Johannesen. In addition, two other ships, the *Fraser* and the *Express*, were to carry coal to the mouth of the Yenisei.

The expedition included a number of scientists, one of whom, O. Nordquist, was not only a zoologist but a lieutenant in the Imperial Russian Regiment of Guards. The crew were mostly naval men or walrus-hunters.

In July 1878, the expedition sailed from Tromsö, on the north coast of Norway, and reached Port Dikson on August 6. Four days later the *Vega* and the *Lena* left on their historic voyage.

Voyage of the Vega

On the evening of August 19, after steaming along the coast, mostly in fog which, when it lifted, revealed great, rough unbroken ice-fields fast to the land, they anchored in a bay on Cape Chelyuskin, the northernmost promontory of the Taymyr Peninsula (Polustrov Taymyr) and of Asia, where they were welcomed by a large polar bear. "We had now reached a great goal," Nordenskiöld wrote, "which for centuries had been the object of unsuccessful struggles. For the first time a vessel lay at anchor off the northernmost cape of the old world. . . ."

The cape was nothing more than a low promontory, divided by a bay and with hills about 1,000 feet high running inland from it. "No glacier rolled its bluish-white ice masses down the mountain sides, and no inland lakes, no perpendicular cliffs, no high mountain summits, gave any natural beauty to the landscape, which was the most monotonous and the most desolate I have seen in the High North."

Here, they dredged the sea bottom, determined their position astronomically, saw signs of reindeer and lemming, but no sign of man, and studied the vegetation, which included various sorts of mosses, lichens and grasses and "twenty-three species of inconsiderable flowering-plants, among them eight species belonging to the Saxifrage family, a sulphur-yellow poppy, commonly cultivated in our gardens, and the exceedingly beautiful, forget-me-not-like *Eritrichium*". They also saw a great flock of barnacle geese, "evidently migrating to more southerly regions, perhaps from some Polar land lying to the north . . .", a loon, kittiwakes and the remains of snowy owls.

They sailed again on August 20, encountering drift-ice, large flows and fog, seeing loons and kittiwakes. The presence of loons, birds scarcely ever seen in the Kara Sea, seemed to indicate that here the sea did not freeze completely in winter, as they would be unlikely to fly across the frozen Kara Sea in search of food and breeding grounds.

By this time they were in a labyrinth of ice and Nordenskiöld stood in close to the land on the east side of the peninsula on the morning of August 23, having escaped from the impenetrable ice by steaming the *Vega* out through the only escape route—a sack-shaped opening to the north through which they had passed the previous day.

For four days they sailed south along the peninsula, for the first two through sea which was marked on the most recent maps as land and on the night of August 27, off the Lena delta, Nordenskiöld sent the *Lena* back to Port Dikson. By now Nordenskiöld had come to the conclusion that if the ships had kept close in to the land on the voyage from the Yenisei to the Lena they would have

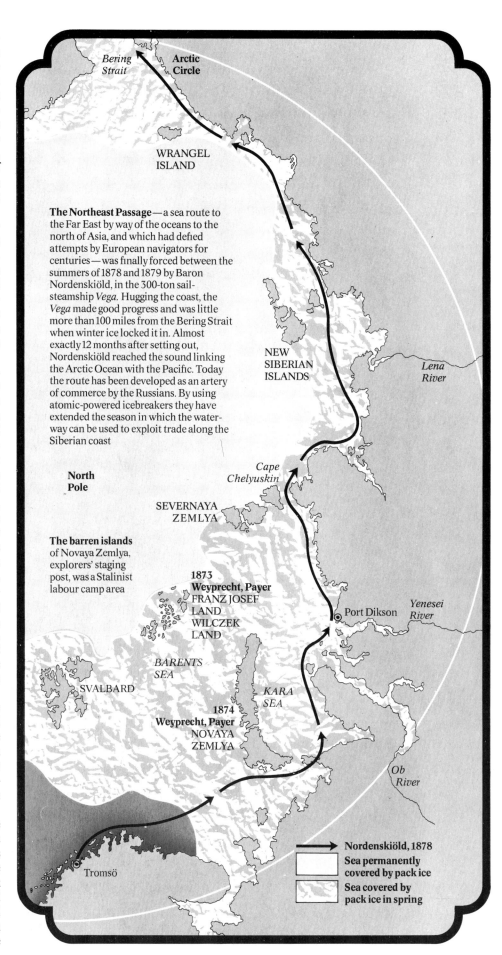

The Northeast Passage—a sea route to the Far East by way of the oceans to the north of Asia, and which had defied attempts by European navigators for centuries—was finally forced between the summers of 1878 and 1879 by Baron Nordenskiöld, in the 300-ton sail-steamship *Vega*. Hugging the coast, the *Vega* made good progress and was little more than 100 miles from the Bering Strait when winter ice locked it in. Almost exactly 12 months after setting out, Nordenskiöld reached the sound linking the Arctic Ocean with the Pacific. Today the route has been developed as an artery of commerce by the Russians. By using atomic-powered icebreakers they have extended the season in which the waterway can be used to exploit trade along the Siberian coast

The barren islands of Novaya Zemlya, explorers' staging post, was a Stalinist labour camp area

1873
Weyprecht, Payer
FRANZ JOSEF
LAND
WILCZEK
LAND

1874
Weyprecht, Payer
NOVAYA
ZEMLYA

Bering Strait

Arctic Circle

WRANGEL ISLAND

NEW SIBERIAN ISLANDS

Lena River

North Pole

Cape Chelyuskin

SEVERNAYA ZEMLYA

Port Dikson

Yenesei River

BARENTS SEA

KARA SEA

SVALBARD

Ob River

Tromsö

→ Nordenskiöld, 1878
☐ Sea permanently covered by pack ice
☐ Sea covered by pack ice in spring

encountered no serious obstruction from ice, "and I am convinced", he wrote, "that this will happen year after year during the close of August. For I believe that the place where ice obstacles will perhaps be met with most frequency will not be the north point of Asia, but the region east of the entrance to the Kara Sea. . . . "

The *Vega* now continued on a north-easterly course and on August 30 was off the west side of Ljakoff Island (Lyakhovskiye Ostrova), the southernmost of the New Siberian Islands (Novosibirskiye Ostrova) and first visited by the Russian traveller of that name in 1770. "These have, from the time of their discovery, been renowned among the Russian ivory collectors for their extraordinary richness in tusks and portions of skeletons of the extinct northern species of elephant known by the name of mammoth," Nordenskiöld wrote. In these waters the *Vega*'s dredge brought up half-decayed pieces of such tusks.

This western side of the island was dangerous, with shallow water offshore and with a lot of rotten (melting) ice piled up on it. Fearing a sudden frost that might seal the *Vega* in for the winter, or a sudden storm that might make it a lee shore, Nordenskiöld decided, reluctantly, not to land.

For the next two days the weather was fine, the sea ice-free, and even when they did meet masses of sea-ice off the mouth of the Kolyma River, east of the Bear Islands, they were still able to find a clear channel close in to the coast.

By now the short summer was nearing its end and already at midnight the sun was about 13 degrees below the horizon. There was also much more ice and the fog had returned. "The navigation along the north coast of Asia began to get somewhat monotonous," Nordenskiöld wrote. "Even the most zealous polar traveller may tire at last of mere ice, shallow water; and mere fog, shallow water and ice."

But now they were diverted by the appearance off the cape of two skin boats loaded with cheerful local inhabitants, the first human beings they had seen since leaving the Proliv Yugorskiy Shar, the strait connecting the Barents and Kara seas.

These people were Chukchis and soon they swarmed on board. They were dressed in suits of reindeer skin and the men wore their thick, bluish-black hair in a sort of rough fringe over their foreheads. The women were tattoed on their brows, noses, and some on their chins and cheeks; some of the young girls "were not even absolutely ugly . . . and had a beautiful, almost reddish-white complexion". One or two of the men were so fair that Nordenskiöld believed they must

have been descendants of Russian fugitives, or prisoners of war. They were extremely hospitable, their children were happy and hardy, and their visitors had little they wanted.

By September 12, having spent two days negotiating fields of ice in often dense fog, they were off Cape Irkaipij (Mys Shmidta), near the 180th meridian, 150 miles south of Wrangel Island (Ostrov Vrangelya), sighted and named—rather misleadingly—Cape North, by Cook in 1778. (In the 1930s the Soviet authorities renamed it after Otto J. Schmidt, who was in charge of the development of the Northern Sea Route.)

Here, just beyond the Gulf of Kolyuchin, only 120 miles west of Cape Dezhnev (Mys Dezhneva) at the mouth of the Bering Strait, they were finally hemmed in by a belt of ice only six miles broad, and here they stayed for nearly ten months. "It was an unexpected disappointment," Nordenskiöld wrote, "which it was more difficult to bear with equanimity as it was evident that we would have avoided it if we had come some hours earlier to the eastern side of Kilyuchin Bay."

Rampart of ice

On September 29, 1878, the *Vega* was moored to a piece of ground ice "about 40 metres long and 25 metres broad; its highest point . . . 6 metres above the surface of the water. It was thus not very large, but gave the vessel good shelter." By the beginning of October the inshore ice was firm enough to support the weight of a man and Chukchis came out to the ship. In December great storms threw up on the underlying ground ice what Nordenskiöld described as a "toross", an enormous rampart of ice blocks near the ship. All through the winter, beyond the ice on the horizon from northwest to east, they could see the blue-water sky, which denoted the existence of open water in the sea below it.

The sudden, alarming appearance of the toross led Nordenskiöld to establish a depot on the shore with enough provisions for 100 men for 30 days. He also set up a magnetic observatory. To reach this on dark nights was a hazardous business as the ice-field was covered with powdered snow and the slightest wind completely obliterated any footprints.

In the course of the winter various excursions were made to the nomad Chukchis of the interior, who owned reindeer herds. They were also shrewd businessmen, who made immense journeys across the Bering Strait to the islands off Alaska, bringing back furs for the Russian dealers in Siberia. "Many a beaverskin that comes to the market at Irbit belongs to an animal that has been caught in America, whose skin has passed from hand to hand among the wild men of America and

Siberia, until it finally reaches the Russian Market."

In March 1879 they saw astonishing elliptic auroras, which spanned the polar night sky to the north. Sledges drawn by reindeer and laden with reindeer skins and goods from Russian posts began to pass on their way to the Bering Strait. In April great flocks of migratory birds began to arrive. On July 17 the "ice" began to break up on the landward side of the ship and that evening "Palander rushed on deck, saw that the ice was in motion, ordered the boiler fires to be lighted—the engine having long ago been put in order in expectation of this moment". The following day the *Vega* was under steam and sail again.

Once clear of the ice they were free of it forever and "by 11 am [on July 20] we were in the middle of the sound which unites the North Polar Sea with the Pacific, and from this point the *Vega* greeted the old and new worlds by a display of flags and firing of a Swedish salute".

The Northeast Passage had been achieved 326 years after Sir Hugh Willoughby's first attempt in 1553.

It was the Russians who were logically to develop the route. In 1932, the Russian professor Otto Schmidt made the passage in an ice-breaker from Murmansk to Vladivostok in a single season by way of the Severnaya Zemlya Islands. In August 1933, the specially built 4,000-ton ice-breaker *Cheliuskin*—with a complement which included a number of women—sailed from Murmansk, the scientists on board studying solar radiation, currents and the drift of icebergs. The intention was to make the double passage, but at the Bering Strait the ship became locked in the ice and was driven by currents along the coast of Alaska and then to the north, where it sank in February 1934. In intense cold the crew set up a camp on the ice, constructed a landing ground and were rescued by aeroplanes. In 1935, the passage was made by two merchant ships, escorted by ice-breakers.

The first vessel to make the east–west passage was the Canadian-built ice-breaker *Litke* in 1934, which sailed from Vladivostok in June, reaching Murmansk in September. The following year two merchant ships, *Anadir* and *Stalingrad*, made the passage. In July the ships were in the thick ice near Ayon Island. Here, "for forty and fifty hours at a stretch Captain Melefsorov [of the *Anadir*] sat high in his crow's nest with nothing beside him but a samovar of tea, while the steamer, built to sail through a depth of twenty-one feet of ice, was forced to break through ice twenty-two and sometimes twenty-three feet deep." It took the *Anadir* ten weeks and two days to make the voyage.

The ship that died-and the ship that live

The death of the "Jeannette". Years later, relics of its crew's possessions were washed up in Greenland, nearly 3,000 miles from where it sank

By the latter part of the 19th century centuries of ship-building and design had evolved vessels to meet the challenge of almost everything the sea had to offer. Steam was supplementing and about to supplant sail and steel reinforced traditional wood. A well-built ship, capably manned, could make its passage in all but the most extraordinary conditions. De Long's "Jeannette" was such a ship. Sailing through the Bering Strait and into the ice of the Arctic Ocean in 1879, the American steam yacht was crushed and sank, for it had met, and had been defeated by, a natural force to which it had no answer—the power of the ice. What the "Jeannette" failed to do was successfully accomplished, years later, by Fridtjof Nansen's "Fram", which drifted, resisting all the pressure the ice could bear on it, for 35 months. Nansen, the greatest of all Arctic explorers, had planned a ship that, skilfully reinforced, would ride up under the pressure of ice and rest on its surface until a thaw released it to float again—"to slip like an eel out of the embraces of the ice". A cross-section of the hull of the "Fram" is shown (below)

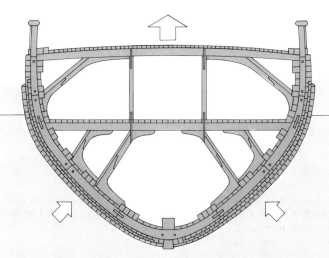

THE HEROIC FAILURE of American Lieutenant George Washington De Long to reach the Pole by sea between 1879 and 1881 was one of the Arctic's great tragedies, but the lessons learned from it helped to prove the existence of one of the natural phenomena of the Arctic—the ice drift.

The De Long expedition sailed from San Francisco in July 1879 with a crew of 32 aboard the steam yacht *Jeannette*. Believing that Wrangel Island, 80 miles off the Siberian mainland in the East Siberian Sea, was part of a northern land mass, De Long decided to use the island as a beachhead for a sledge journey to the Pole, after wintering there.

He never reached it. The *Jeannette* was beset and drifted west in the pack, passing north of Wrangel Island and in sight of it, thus destroying his belief that it was part of a land mass.

The *Jeannette* was then carried northwestwards for 17 months, passing what were named the De Long Islands (Ostrova de-Longa), until June 1881, when she was crushed, and sank 150 miles off the New Siberian Islands.

With boats and sledges De Long and his gallant crew succeeded in reaching the northernmost of the group, but only 12 men survived the cold and hunger of the Siberian tundra. De Long was not among them.

Three years later a list of provisions signed by De Long, a list of the *Jeannette*'s boats, a pair of oilskin breeches marked Louis Noros (the name of a member of the crew) and a hat belonging to one of the survivors were found by Eskimoes in drift-ice near Julianêhab on the southwest coast of Greenland. It was estimated that to reach this point these objects had travelled 2,900 miles in the ice in 1,100 days: 700 days to drift from the longi-

tude of the New Siberian Islands to 80N on the east coast of Greenland and 400 days from it to Julianêhab, rounding Cape Farewell.

This evidence of the existence of a slow, steady current across the polar basin convinced Dr Fridtjof Nansen, the distinguished young Norwegian naturalist and Arctic explorer, that it was possible to drift across it in a vessel, travelling with the ice instead of fighting against it and possibly, at the same time, reach the Pole, providing that the right sort of vessel could be constructed.

Driftwood

There was nothing fantastic about Nansen's conclusions. Driftwood of Siberian origin—larch, fir, alder and aspen—regularly appeared on the coast of Greenland, and was the only wood available to the Greenland Eskimoes for the construction of sledges and other equipment. A throwing stick ornamented with Chinese beads, of a sort used by Eskimo hunters on the Alaskan coast near the Bering Strait, had also been found at Godthåb, more than 300 miles north of Julianêhab: Nansen himself had discovered mud on ice in the Denmark Strait, between Iceland and Greenland, of Siberian or North American origin.

Nansen's plan was greeted with scepticism, if not derision, by most Arctic experts, but in his own country, Norway, however, it was kindly received. He was given financial support by the government and by a number of

private subscribers, headed by King Oscar. The Russians also gave some help, by providing forward bases, and the British Royal Geographical Society made a contribution.

Nansen was an ideal man for such a perilous operation. In 1888, at the age of 27, he had made the first crossing of Greenland with three Norwegians and three Laplanders, using sledges and skis. These Nansen sledges, which he invented, weighed only 31 pounds and were built of ash with very narrow convex runners, which had blades made of an amalgam known as German silver. They were ten feet long and only 27 inches wide. The skis, known in Norway as skates, were very narrow and much more efficient than the snow shoes used by previous expeditions.

No Arctic explorer devoted more attention to preparation and personal fitness than Nansen and, as a result, his party was able to survive during the terrible years in the Polar Sea.

The ship, known as the *Fram*, the "Forward", was designed by Colin Archer, son of a Scottish shipbuilder who had settled in Norway. In Nansen's words, it had been so constructed "that the whole craft should be able to slip like an eel out of the embraces of the ice". In June 1893 the *Fram* sailed from Christiania (Oslo) provisioned for five years and with a crew of 13.

After taking on board 34 Siberian dogs at Khabarova, on the mainland south of Os

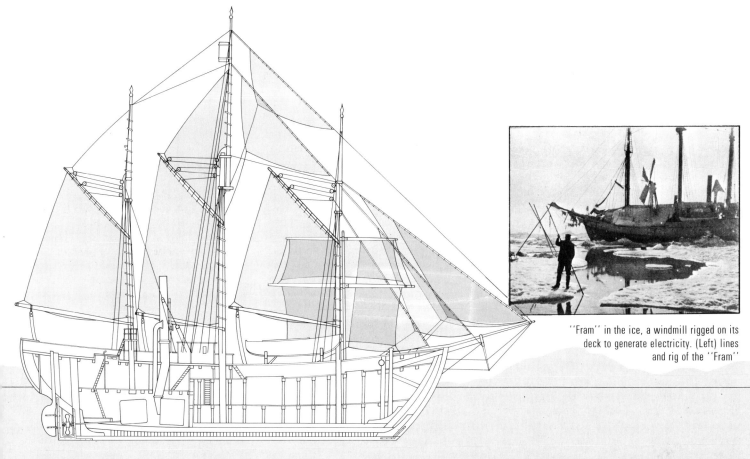

"Fram" in the ice, a windmill rigged on its
deck to generate electricity. (Left) lines
and rig of the "Fram"

Vaygach (Island) on the Kara Sea, Nansen sailed the *Fram* through the sea and along the coast of Siberia, encountering the ice-barrier on September 20. On September 22 they moored the ship to an enormous block of ice.

Five days later, with her rudder removed, her engine dismantled and a windmill set up to work the dynamo, the *Fram* froze in and began her 35-month drift through the ice, while the crew carried on their various scientific tasks. They took meteorological observations every four hours in endless winter night and summer day and astronomical observations every second day when the weather was clear—these were keenly awaited as they told the men their position and the direction of drift. They made observations to determine the magnetic constant in a tent on the ice and later in a snow hut; observations to determine the temperature of the water and its salinity, the formation, growth and thickness of the ice, its temperature at various levels, the currents beneath it, the amount of electricity in the air and of the Aurora Borealis. They collected wildlife, such as it was, and underwater specimens by trawling and dredging. Once a month the men were weighed and their blood was tested.

In the second autumn they were about 300 miles north-northeast of Cape Chelyuskin and about 400 miles south of the Pole. In March of the following year, southwards of the Pole in 84N, Nansen and Hjalmar Johansen left the *Fram*, taking with them two kayaks, three sledges and 28 dogs. Their principal food was dried and powdered fish and meat, biscuits and 86 pounds of butter, and they took shotguns, a silk tent, a sleeping bag covered in reindeer skin and a

Nansen cooker. In addition to their woollen Arctic clothing they wore Laplanders' hats and moccasins. They left the *Fram* to the cheers of the crew, knowing that they could never find her again in the ice. At first the ice was fairly smooth, but later they entered a region of terrible hummock ice, which overturned their flimsy sledges and tore their kayaks, travelling in temperatures down to $-47°$F. Twenty-three days out, in these inhuman conditions, on April 8 Nansen hoisted the Norwegian flag in 86.13N, 95E, 160 miles farther north than any man had ever penetrated, and about 240 miles from the Pole. They could go no farther.

Now began the long retreat to Franz Josef Land. Towards the end of April, they found fresh-water ice from Siberian rivers, a larch tree and footprints travelling eastwards in 85N! Killing their dogs as they grew too weak to travel and with the ice becoming progressively thinner, the two men struggled on all through May and June using sledges and kayaks in the open lanes of water.

Stalking bears

"Our hearts fail us", Nansen wrote on June 11, "when we see the ice lying before us like an impenetrable maze of ridges, lanes, brash and huge blocks thrown together pell-mell, and one might imagine oneself looking at suddenly congealed breakers. There are moments when it seems impossible that any creature not possessed of wings can get further and one longingly follows the flight of a passing gull."

On July 24 they sighted the north coast of Franz Josef Land and a fortnight later reached the edge of the ice, having had a narrow escape from being killed by bears.

"Before me lay the dark surface of the sea, with floating ice-floes," he wrote, "far away the glacier wall rose abruptly from the water; over the whole lay a sombre, foggy light. Joy welled up in our hearts at this sight, and we could not give it expression in words. Behind us lay all our troubles, before us the waterway home."

At the end of August, Nansen and his companion set up a camp in a stone hut, illuminating and heating it with walrus blubber and living on bear meat throughout the winter of 1895, not knowing that the Jackson–Harmsworth Arctic Expedition was encamped only 94 miles away, at Cape Flora.

On June 17, 1896, when they reached Cape Flora, Nansen heard dogs barking and later met a well-groomed man. "I raised my hat; we extended a hand to one another, with a hearty 'How do you do?' but it was sometime before the English explorer, Frederick Jackson, said: 'Aren't you Nansen? . . . By Jove! I am glad to see you!'"

In August, travelling home by sea, Nansen received a telegram at Hammerfest from Sverdrup telling him that the *Fram* had escaped from the pack north of Spitsbergen and was on her way to Tromsö.

So ended one of the most valuable and courageous expeditions in polar history. "Still," Nansen wrote, "we have done nothing but our duty."

A noble, compassionate man of great imagination and vision, Nansen devoted much of the rest of his life to alleviating human misery, securing the repatriation of prisoners after the First World War and by his work in famine relief for the League of Nations. He was awarded the Nobel Peace Prize in 1922 and died in 1930.

The American challenge

"It is the duty of mankind to explore these strange and uncomprehended portions of our globe; and more than this, it is a duty which seems properly to devolve upon our nation. Europe has contributed more than her just proportion of geographical expeditions . . . we Americans now owe it to the world to prosecute these researches."

I N THESE WORDS, a Harvard academic summed up the mid-19th-century spirit of the United States, where popular imagination and sympathy had been caught up by the search for Franklin. A New York shipping magnate, Henry Grinnell, paid for the first American participation in the hunt for survivors of the ill-fated expedition (he bought and equipped the brigs commanded by Lieutenant De Haven, which left New York in 1850) and later subsidized the voyages to northern Greenland of the colourful Dr Elisha Kent Kane and Isaac Hayes.

Kane and his men were the first from civilization to see the mighty Humboldt Glacier in Greenland. In a journey which called for

Robert E. Peary, the American naval officer who learned the secrets of Arctic survival from the Eskimoes—and claimed for his nation the honour of first reaching the North Pole

immense fortitude, a sledge party reached 80.10N at the south end of the Kennedy Channel between Greenland and Ellesmere Island before returning in 1855 to America and national fame.

The story of Arctic exploration has few characters more attractive than the penniless Cincinatti printer Charles Francis Hall, who could almost be said to have "thumbed a lift" to the north on his first voyage with a New London Whaler. Between 1860 and 1871 Hall made three journeys, on the last of which he died, a national hero, having reached 82.11N.

Although Hall's journey was to be followed shortly after by yet another British expedition, led by Captain George Nares, in 1875—somewhat hamstrung by old-fashioned techniques, Nares managed to send one party, under Albert Markham, to 83.20N, closer to the Pole than had been hitherto achieved—the American experience and recognition of the value of Eskimo knowledge was to serve them well, and to culminate in the triumph of Peary.

Before this happened, however, nations other than those with historical roles in Arctic exploration were to appear on the scene. The name of Emperor Franz Josef of Austria was given to an Arctic archipelago by the Austrian officers Weyprecht and Payer, who first reached the islands, in the drift through the ice of their ship, the *Tegethoff*, in 1872–4. Franz Josef Land was later used as a base by an Italian party led by the Duke of the Abruzzi, one of whose officers, Lieutenant Cagni, in 1900, travelled closer to the Pole than even Nansen had done, reaching 86.34N.

On June 8, 1886, Lieutenant Robert E. Peary, a young engineer in the US Navy dockyard service, made his first journey in the north when he set off from Disco Bay on the west coast of Greenland in an attempt to cross the inland ice to the Greenland Sea, more than 500 miles to the east. His only companion was Lieutenant Maigaard, a Dane. For 24 days they battled against the wind and snow-storms until, 125 miles out, they were forced to turn back.

For the next five years Peary's time was entirely taken up by his navy profession, but in 1891, with his wife and five other companions—among them Matthew Henson his

Negro servant, who was eventually to reach the Pole with him—he was put ashore at McCormick Bay in Inglefield Gulf on the east Greenland coast of Baffin Bay, where they stayed for 13 months in a portable house. It was the first of the nine winters Peary was to spend in the Arctic. He made friends with the Etah Eskimoes, who were to be the principal instruments of his success, learning from them the secrets of survival in the farthest north and adapting their sledges to his own needs. His one, single-minded aim was to be the first man to reach the Pole.

In April 1892, he set off with 16 dogs, four sledges and some Eskimoes and after sending back two of the sledge parties with Eivind Astrup—a Norwegian hunter—reached Independence Bay in 82.40N, on the northeast coast, having travelled 500 miles over the inland ice, more or less proving that Greenland was surrounded by water.

From 1897 onwards Peary increased his efforts to find the way to the Pole, using the steamer *Windward* as a supply ship, but he soon came to the conclusion that the attack could not be made successfully from the north Greenland coast. The movement of the ice round its northwest point into the Robeson Channel was too rapid; and he began to set up supply depots in Grant Land, on the north coast of Ellesmere Island.

In January 1899, the temperature at one of these bases, Fort Conger, fell to −58°F and Peary had to have some of his toes amputated. Nevertheless, the following March he set off again for the north coast of Greenland and reached its northernmost point, Cape Morris Jesup in 83.40N, where the polar pack drove in on the shores of the continent with all its force. He sledged over it for another ten minutes of latitude to the north.

During these years, from 1897 onwards, Peary was haunted by the fear that other explorers might beat him to the Pole. In 1897, Otto Sverdrup, Nansen's splendid captain in the *Fram*, was making plans to take the ship through the Robeson Channel and from there sledge along the north coast of Greenland and down the east coast, in order to find out if it was surrounded by water. Sverdrup had no intention of trying to reach the Pole. Like Nansen, but unlike Peary, he was not interested in races; his interest was scientific. Peary, however, took it as an affront and an attempt to make use of stratagems that he regarded as his own property. In any event Sverdrup, like Peary, failed to get his ship through the northern narrows in 1898 because the ice was too thick.

Another contender in the race for the Pole was Salomon August Andrée, a 40-year-old official in the Swedish Patent Office. Financed by Alfred Nobel, the inventor of dynamite, King Oscar and others, he proposed to fly the 690 miles to the Pole from Spitsbergen in an immense balloon of Chinese silk named the *Ornen* (Eagle), which contained 190,000 cubic feet of gas.

On his second attempt on July 11, 1897 (the first had failed for lack of a south wind), he succeeded in ascending from Virgo Harbour, Danes Island, narrowly escaping a ducking and losing his steering gear in the process, a loss that was to prove fatal. He and his companions, Nils Strindberg, a nephew of the playwright, and Knuth Fraekel, an engineer, were never seen alive again.

Some 30 years later, in August 1930, two sailors who had landed from a Norwegian sealer on White Island, about 50 miles east of Nordaustlandet, Spitsbergen, between it and Franz Josef Land, discovered a small boat which contained the body of Fraekel, the log book of the *Ornen*, Andrée's and Strindberg's journals and Strindberg's camera with some exposed film, which was later successfully developed.

Peary believed that it was essential to force a specially constructed ship through the Robeson Channel to the northeast coast of Ellesmere Island, facing the Polar Sea. This belief, which he communicated to his supporters, a group of wealthy New Yorkers who had formed the Peary Arctic Club, led to the construction of the *Theodore Roosevelt*, a steamer of 1,500 tons, 150 feet long with a 33-foot beam, a 1,000-horsepower engine, a wooden hull two feet thick reinforced with steel and a retractable rudder.

The final assault
The *Roosevelt* was successfully pushed through the Robeson Channel and reached Cape Sheridan on the northeast coast of Ellesmere Island in 1905, but the cold was so dreadful (−60°F), that when Peary reached 87.06N, 186 miles from the Pole, he gave the order to retreat—with the satisfaction, however, of having made the nearest approach. In the course of these operations the *Roosevelt* was badly damaged by the ice.

What was to prove to be his final assault on the Pole began in July 1908, when Peary again sailed in the *Roosevelt*. The party of 22 included the indefatigable Matthew Henson, Professor Ross Marvin, Dr J. W. Goodsell, Robert Bartlett, a Newfoundlander and the brilliant captain of the *Roosevelt*, and George Borup, a member of Peary's first expedition.

At Etah they took on board a number of Eskimo families, with many women, and over 200 dogs, and once again the *Roosevelt* was

pushed north to Cape Sheridan in 82.32N. As usual, Peary had sent out teams of Eskimoes to establish caches of stores along the route, construct igloos and as far as possible clear the way of obstructions. There were to be 19 teams of 17 dogs and each sledge was to carry 50 days' rations; pemmican for dogs and men, condensed milk, tea and hardtack, musk-ox and sealskin bedding, snowshoes and Eskimo kamiks as spare footwear, an ice-axe and a snow knife, and cooking apparatus.

Peary had great faith in pemmican, "... the most satisfying food I know," he wrote in *The Secrets of Polar Travel*. "I recall innumerable marches in bitter temperatures when men and dogs had been worked to the limit and I had reached the place for camp feeling as if I could eat my weight in anything. When the pemmican ration was dealt out, and I saw my little half-pound lump, about as large as the bottom third of an ordinary drinking-glass, I have often felt sullen rage that life should contain such situations. By the time I had finished the last morsel I would not have walked round the completed igloo for anything or everything that the St Regis, the Blackstone, or the Palace Hotel could have put before me."

The final battle began on March 1, at Cape Columbia, 420 miles from the Pole, in 83.7N, 70.25W, with other parties travelling ahead of Peary's party. These led the way until the second day, when Markham's farthest was passed in temperatures down to −50°F, and after a very rough journey with numbers of

The rapid development of aircraft during the First World War introduced a new dimension into polar exploration in the 1920s. There were the halcyon years of the airship, two of which entered the story of the Arctic, the first triumphantly the second disastrously. In 1926, the ''Norge'', with its designer, the Italian Nobile, and Roald Amundsen aboard, made the first crossing from Europe to America via the North Pole. Two years later, the ''Italia'' (right), captained by Nobile, flew over the Pole but force-landed on its return journey. Nobile was rescued by aircraft, leaving other survivors behind and was later accused of deserting his men. Among the many rescue teams which set out was Nobile's erstwhile colleague Amundsen. The French seaplane in which Amundsen flew was never seen again

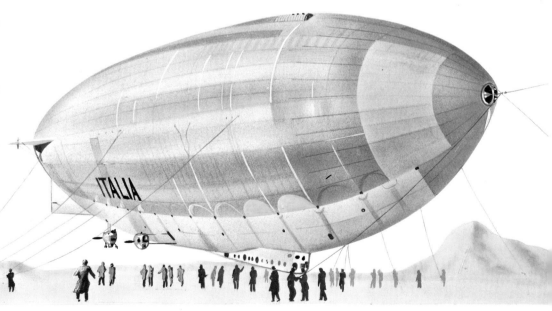

Strange conquest: in 1959, 50 years after Peary prepared to make his successful assault on the North Pole, the United States Navy's nuclear submarine ''Nautilus'' (left) passed successfully beneath the ice cap at the Pole, to be followed a few days later by another, the ''Skate'', which succeeded in breaking through the ice

The American challenge

sledges damaged, a lead (channel) was crossed on rafts of ice (Peary never used kayaks). On March 5 the Sun reappeared and the temperature rose, but 45 miles north of Cape Columbia they encountered an impassable lead of black water in the ice. Peary became desperate at the delay, which lasted six days. They were on soundings of 110 fathoms, which showed that they were still on the continental shelf, which Peary believed had caused the lead to open.

It froze over on March 11 and they went on in temperatures down to −59°F, and on March 14, soundings showed that they were in 825 fathoms and, at last, free of the shelf. At this point Peary's main party numbered 16 men, 12 sledges and 100 dogs. On March 19 Borup's party was sent back at 85.23N, leaving 12 men, 10 sledges and 80 dogs. On March 22 they managed to take the first observations of the Sun, giving their latitudinal position as 85.48N; but now their way was blocked with more leads, over which they ferried the sledges on rafts of ice.

On April 1, 133 miles from the Pole, after the ice had parted, separating the igloos and nearly destroying the entire company, Bartlett's party was sent back. This left Peary and Henson's team of four Eskimoes, five sledges and 40 dogs for the final attack.

From now on, having taken a third hitch in his belt since leaving the mainland, Peary forged ahead with his dog teams trotting, even galloping. "The floes were large and old, hard and level, with patches of sapphire ice. While the pressure ridges surrounding them were stupendous, some of them 50 feet high. ... The brilliant sunshine, the going good save for the pressure ridges, the consciousness that we were now well started on the last lap of our journey, and the joy of being again in the lead affected me like wine."

He was also racing against the waxing Moon, which on April 3 appeared in its full silver beauty, with the golden Sun opposing it on the other side, producing spring tides which began to break the ice asunder. It had a peculiarly sinister air.

April 4 was a good day with the temperature down to −35°F; and on April 5, at 10 am, they reached 89.57N, within three minutes of latitude from the North Pole—since one nautical mile equals one minute of terrestrial latitude.

There the Eskimoes built two igloos, and the dogs that had not been killed as superfluous along the route were given double rations; from this point Peary—his life's ambition realized—pushed on for some miles across the Pole with two Eskimoes to 89.55N, from which point he was looking southwards down the other side of the world. When they took soundings there was no bottom in 1,500

fathoms. " ... In a march of only a few hours, I had passed from the western to the eastern hemisphere and had verified my position at the summit of the world. ... East, west and north had disappeared for us. Only one direction remained, and that was south. Every breeze which could possibly blow upon us, no matter from what point of the horizon, must be a south wind."

The men to make the final part of this truly great journey were Henson, in his own right a great sledge driver and explorer, and four Eskimoes. It is no reflection on Peary to quote the great Arctic explorer Vilhjalmur Stefansson, who spent many years among the Eskimoes of the Canadian Archipelago. Stefansson maintained that without the help of the Etah Eskimoes " ... Peary's name might have been less famous than it is now; for they followed him on all his expeditions, left home and country and kind and put their whole existence at stake, in realizing the fantastic travelling notions of a foreign man".

Another American explorer claimed to have reached the Pole, a year before Peary, on April 21, 1908. This was Dr Frederick A. Cook, who had been with Peary as an ethnologist on his first expedition to Inglefield Gulf in 1891 and had also been a member of Lieutenant A. de Gerlache's Belgian expedition of 1899 to the Antarctic.

Supported by the Explorers' Club—a rival organization to the Peary Arctic Club, which had financed Peary's attempts—Cook and Rudolf Francke set up a base at Anoatok, near Etah, in 1907, where 250 Eskimoes were assembled with their dogs. The preparations Cook made were very similar to Peary's but on a smaller scale. The expedition adopted Eskimo dress, used modified forms of Eskimo sledges and its principal rations were pemmican. It also had with it a collapsible boat.

Non-existent land

In February 1908, Cook claimed that he, Francke, nine Etah Eskimoes, 103 dogs and 11 sledges carrying 4,000 pounds of supplies set off across Ellesmere Island and reached the most northerly point of Axel Heiberg Island, which had been described by Sverdrup as a mountain of flint and lava and by Peary as a bluff about 1,600 feet high with a gravel foreshore. Up to this point the party succeeded in living off the land by hunting.

Here, Cook sent back the majority of his support group and with two Eskimoes, 26 dogs and the collapsible boat set off for the Pole on March 18. Twelve days later he claimed to have sighted land to the west in 84.50°N, which he named Bradley Land (but no such land exists).

On April 21, according to Cook, he reached the Pole. Whether he reached it or not—and

he almost certainly did not—he undoubtedly made a remarkable journey. When he reached Hassel Strait, he was unable to regain his base and the party would probably have perished without the collapsible boat, which enabled it to reach Smith Sound.

Later in his career Cook was involved in criminal proceedings and eventually he was expelled from the Explorers' Club. He subsequently wrote a best-seller, *My Attainment of the Pole*, which sold over 100,000 copies. He died in 1940.

The first aeroplane to be used in Arctic exploration, a 70-horsepower Farman fitted with pontoons, was flown over the Barents Sea by the Russian Lieutenant I. Nagurski while searching for survivors of Georgi Sedov's expedition in the *Foka*, in which he had attempted to reach the Pole. A seaplane was also used by F. G. Binney on the Oxford University Arctic expedition to Nordauslandet in 1924 for photographic surveying.

In 1925, after two abortive attempts to fly over the icepack and land on it, using Junkers and Curtiss machines, Amundsen was financed by Lincoln Ellsworth, son of a millionaire. Two Dornier-Wal (Whale) flying boats were built of duralumin and fitted with twin Rolls-Royce engines in tandem, each of which developed 360 horsepower.

Amundsen and Ellsworth flew from Spitsbergen on May 21, 1925, and with half their fuel gone landed in open leads in 87.43N, 10.30W, having navigated with the help of special solar compasses.

On June 15 the combined crews of Ellsworth's and Amundsen's aircraft succeeded in taking off from the ice in the only one that was still usable. They made a forced landing in heavy seas off Spitsbergen and were rescued by a sealing ship.

The Pole was finally reached by aeroplane on May 9, 1926, when Commander Richard E. Byrd of the US Navy and Floyd Bennet, a warrant officer, flew a Fokker monoplane with three 200-horsepower engines over it from King's Bay, Spitsbergen. On his return, Byrd met Amundsen, who was about to take off for the Pole in an airship, on an expedition again financed by Ellsworth, and Amundsen asked Byrd what his future plans were, to which he answered, "the South Pole".

"You're right," said Amundsen. "The aeroplane alone can triumph in the Antarctic."

Amundsen's airship was the *Norge*, an Italian dirigible designed by a distinguished pilot of dirigibles, Commander Umberto Nobile, of the Italian Military Aeronautic Corps. It was equipped with two 250-horsepower engines, which gave it a speed of 50 mph in windless conditions, and carried seven tons of fuel.

Enormous difficulties had been overcome

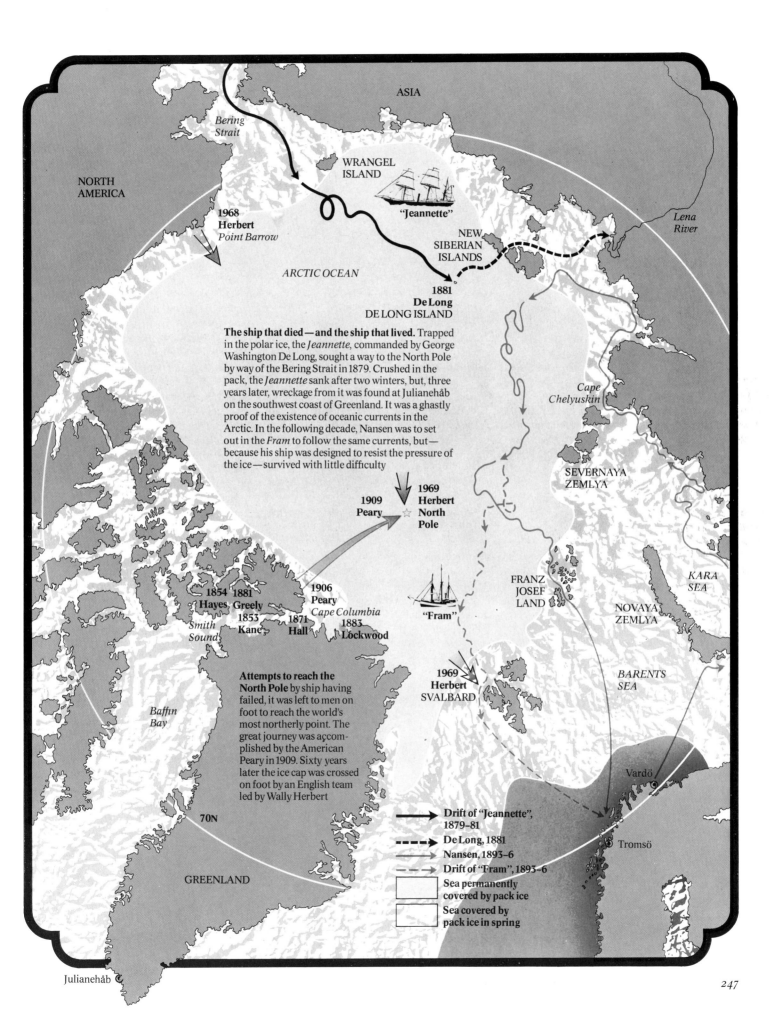

ASIA

Bering Strait

NORTH AMERICA

WRANGEL ISLAND

"Jeannette"

1968 Herbert *Point Barrow*

ARCTIC OCEAN

NEW SIBERIAN ISLANDS

Lena River

1881 De Long DE LONG ISLAND

The ship that died—and the ship that lived. Trapped in the polar ice, the *Jeannette*, commanded by George Washington De Long, sought a way to the North Pole by way of the Bering Strait in 1879. Crushed in the pack, the *Jeannette* sank after two winters, but, three years later, wreckage from it was found at Julianehåb on the southwest coast of Greenland. It was a ghastly proof of the existence of oceanic currents in the Arctic. In the following decade, Nansen was to set out in the *Fram* to follow the same currents, but— because his ship was designed to resist the pressure of the ice—survived with little difficulty

Cape Chelyuskin

SEVERNAYA ZEMLYA

1909 Peary

1969 Herbert North Pole

1854 Hayes **1881 Greely** **1906 Peary** *Cape Columbia*
1853 Kane **1871 Hall** **1883 Lockwood**
Smith Sound

"Fram"

FRANZ JOSEF LAND

KARA SEA

NOVAYA ZEMLYA

Attempts to reach the North Pole by ship having failed, it was left to men on foot to reach the world's most northerly point. The great journey was accomplished by the American Peary in 1909. Sixty years later the ice cap was crossed on foot by an English team led by Wally Herbert

Baffin Bay

1969 Herbert SVALBARD

BARENTS SEA

Vardö

70N

GREENLAND

Tromsö

→ Drift of "Jeannette", 1879–81
⇢ De Long, 1881
→ Nansen, 1893–6
⇢ Drift of "Fram", 1893–6
☐ Sea permanently covered by pack ice
☐ Sea covered by pack ice in spring

Julianehåb

247

The American challenge

in providing the materials to build a hangar for it on Spitsbergen, and the 2,000 tons of building materials had been delivered to the site the previous October by steamer.

On May 11, two days after Byrd's flight, the *Norge* left the ground at 8.55 am in a temperature of −49°F in almost windless conditions. The crew consisted of Nobile, Amundsen, Ellsworth, Riiser-Larsen (navigator), Hogen and Wisting (pilots), two wireless operators, a meteorologist, six mechanics and Frederick Ramm, a journalist. At 1.15 pm they were over the Pole, where Italian, Norwegian and American flags were thrown down.

After a perilous passage, in which ice thrown against the side of the ship by the propellers punctured the canvas, fog was encountered and the radio ceased to function when the aerial frosted up, the *Norge* made landfall at Cape Barrow on May 14, having flown 3,400 miles direct from Europe to America. The Eskimoes, when they saw it, thought that it was a great flying whale.

Amundsen was thus the first to reach both Poles. The acclaim heaped upon him provoked a bitter reaction from Nobile, who thought that his undoubtedly significant contribution to the success of the *Norge* flight had not received due recognition.

He decided to build another dirigible, the *Italia*, make a crossing under the Italian flag, land at the Pole and also carry out a survey among the Siberian Islands and in the Canadian archipelago on the way. Funds were raised by public subscription. Mussolini provided an escort ship, the *Città di Milano*, and at 4 am on May 23, 1928, the *Italia* set off from King's Bay for the Pole, having carried out survey work in the Siberian Islands.

On board were a number of Alpinists who were expert skiers, and three distinguished scientists—Aldo Pontremoli, the physicist, Finn Malmgren, the Swedish meteorologist, who had already flown in the *Norge*, and Franz Behounek, the Czech radium specialist.

The Pole was reached at midnight. The Italian flag and a Papal cross were thrown out, and Mussolini was informed by telegram that "the standard of Fascist Italy is floating in the breeze over the ice of the Pole", while a gramophone played the National Anthem. At 2.20 am on May 24, after circling the Pole, the return flight began, but radio communication ceased at 1.30 am the following day, after the *Italia* had run into fog.

The year before, the Australian Hubert Wilkins and his co-pilot, the Norwegian Carl Eielson, had crashed 500 miles from Point Barrow, outward bound for Spitsbergen, on an attempted crossing.

A few weeks before the *Italia* set off, Wilkins and Eielson took off again in a Lockheed Vega, but it was forced down on Likholmen Island off the west coast of Spitsbergen, after flying non-stop for 20 hours 20 minutes. After a week they were airborne again and reached Gronfjorden, on Spitsbergen.

It was at the banquet given in honour of the pair at Oslo, which was presided over by Amundsen, now 56, that the official news of the disappearance of the *Italia* was given to him, in the form of a telegram. "I am ready to go at once," he said.

The *Italia* had been forced down on the icepack 180 miles northwest of Spitsbergen. On its impact with the ice the gondola, in which Nobile and nine members of the expedition were standing, broke away, and relieved of this load the *Italia* had again risen into the air with the remainder of the crew on board. Neither they nor the *Italia* were ever seen again.

On June 6, a Russian amateur radio operator picked up a radio signal from the radio operator Biaggi, and two days later Amundsen left Tromsö to join the search, in which 16 ships and 21 aircraft were taking part. He flew off in a French seaplane with Lieutenant Commander Guilbaud and a crew of three, and vanished without trace.

On June 24, a plane piloted by Einar Lundborg, a Swede, sighted a red tent on the icepack. He succeeded in landing on it, but took off Nobile alone, leaving the rest behind. Nobile's life was heavily insured and Lloyd's had offered an enormous reward to those who rescued him.

"Desertion and cannibalism"

Three of the survivors, Mariano, Zappi and Malmgren, had already set off on foot. The remainder were picked up by the Russian ice-breaker *Krassin*, which also found Mariano and Zappi. Mariano was *in extremis*, dressed in only one layer of clothing, whereas Zappi was wearing three suits—he said that Malmgren had died a month previously. This conflicted with the evidence of the pilot of the *Krassin*'s reconnaissance plane, who had distinctly seen three men on the ice. As a result Nobile was put under arrest, on the orders of Mussolini, for deserting his men, and Zappi was later accused of cannibalism.

In 1930, an expedition under Gino Watkins, a Cambridge undergraduate aged 23, set off with the British Arctic Air Route expedition from Angmagssalik on the almost unknown coast of eastern Greenland, to survey it to the north and explore the interior. This was to gain information that would help in the opening up of a proposed air route from London to Canada, by way of Iceland, Greenland, Baffin Bay and Hudson Bay. To do so it was essential to know more about the weather and the mountain systems. This expedition made boat journeys along the entire coast between 68N (Kangerlugsuak) and 60N (Prins Christian Sund). One party crossed to the west coast at Holsteinberg and another made an even longer journey from the Angmagssalik base over the icecap to Ivigtut. A remarkable feat was Augustine Courtauld's winter spent alone at the inland ice meteorological station (8,200 feet). After five months Watkins returned to find the ventilator standing alone 12 inches above the surface in a wilderness of snow. Courtauld's home had been buried and he had been unable to dig his way out for over five weeks. Watkins was drowned on a subsequent expedition, when his kayak floated away.

Another expedition, more important scientifically, was the German Greenland Expedition of 1930, under Dr Alfred Wegener, who had been with the disastrous Mylius–Erichsen expedition to Greenland in 1906–8, when its leader and two of its members perished on the inland ice. He also crossed the north Greenland ice from east to west in 1912, with J. P. Koch. His expedition used motor sledges and seismic sounding gear, and established a weather station at latitude 71N, 250 miles from the west coast. On an attempt to reach the coast from it in November 1930, Wegener and his companion, Willemsen, both died.

In June 1931, Sir Hubert Wilkins attempted what then seemed a feat of impossible daring, which was to take the *Nautilus*, a converted submarine which had belonged to the American Navy, under the Pole from Spitsbergen to Alaska—a voyage which, it was calculated, would take 42 days.

The *Nautilus* was equipped with extremely advanced scientific instruments; but due to the mysterious loss of part of the diving apparatus, Wilkins was forced to turn back after having reached 82.15N, where he found it impossible to break through to the surface.

It was not until nearly 30 years later that a second *Nautilus*, this one nuclear powered, succeeded at 11.15 pm on August 3, 1958, in passing under the Pole, 96 hours out from Point Barrow. Nine days later, another atomic submarine, the *Skate*, succeeded in surfacing at it, meeting the occupants of the scientific Alfa Station, who were then drifting at "the Pole of relative inaccessibility".

The last great heroic journey began on February 21, 1968, when the Englishman Wally Herbert, with dog sledges and three companions, set off on what proved to be a 3,700-mile journey to cross the Arctic Ocean on foot by way of the Pole. They reached it, supported by air drops, on April 6, 1969, and the last part of the journey "downhill" to Spitsbergen, which they reached on June 11, 476 days out, was a series of desperate forced marches over disintegrating sea ice.

Antarctica: the coastwise explorers

AFTER COOK'S VOYAGES, in the course of which he three times crossed the Antarctic Circle, no further organized exploration took place in Antarctica for almost half a century, apart from the expedition of the American captain Edmund Fanning in 1805, of which little record remains.

American and to a lesser extent British sealing captains, however, were active in the waters around South Georgia and the South Sandwich group, and some may have reached the South Shetland Islands, off the north-eastern end of the Antarctic Peninsula.

The first recorded discovery of these islands was made in 1819 by an English pilot, Captain William Smith, when wild weather drove his brig 480 miles southeast of Cape Horn across the Drake Passage.

After two further voyages, in December 1819 Smith—now under the command of a naval officer, Edward Bransfield—took his brig south again. Clarence and Elephant islands were charted and then, on January 30, 1820, they saw mainland.

What they had in fact discovered was Trinity Peninsula, the northeast extremity of the Antarctic continent, in 64.30s.

While anchored at Deception Island in the South Shetlands in November 1820, an American sealer, Nathaniel Palmer, saw Trinity Island to the south and a suggestion of mountainous land beyond. He was unable to reach it because of the ice.

While returning to the South Shetlands Palmer's vessel was enveloped in thick fog. On the night of February 4, 1821, at anchor and hemmed in by icebergs, he heard ships' bells echoing his own. When the fog lifted the following morning he found his tiny vessel lying between two Russian ships of Captain Baron Fabian Gottlieb von Bellingshausen's Antarctic expedition. They had sailed from Kronstadt in the Gulf of Finland in July 1819 on an expedition ordered by the Emperor Alexander I.

Bellingshausen, a great admirer of Cook, hoped to add to Cook's discoveries south of the Antarctic Circle. He was a fine sailor and took great care in provisioning his ships and in providing proper clothing for his men.

On January 27, 1820, sailing east-south-east, his ships crossed the Antarctic Circle, the first to do so since Cook's. Soon they were not much more than 20 miles off the Princess Martha Coast on the Antarctic mainland, but heavy weather forced them northwards into the longitude of Cape Town. Bellingshausen now sailed east for Australia, where the ships were to refit. He again penetrated the Antarctic Circle in 41E (where Cook had crossed it 47 years previously) before being driven back by bergs and snow squalls. He arrived in Sydney in March 1820.

The southern winter months were spent charting and exploring the South Pacific. Then, in November, the Russians headed south again and crossed the Antarctic Circle. On January 21, 1821, Bellingshausen reached his farthest point south, 69.52s, 92.10w, in what is now the Bellingshausen Sea, off Ellsworth Land, a coast so heavily protected by ice that no vessel has succeeded in reaching it to this day. The following day an island was sighted—Peter I Øy.

Bellingshausen also sighted the great, mountainous mass of what he named Alexander I Land—actually an island in the great bend of the Antarctic Peninsula. It was the first land to be discovered within the Antarctic Circle.

Surprisingly, Russia, having taken this remarkable initiative, undertook no further Antarctic exploration, except in the course of routine whaling and sealing enterprises, until 1957.

No ice

One of the most remarkable voyages of this pioneering period was that of James Weddell, a 34-year-old English sealing captain. On February 4, 1822, while off Sandwich Land, Weddell sailed to look for fresh sealing coasts to the south.

By February 18 they had reached 73.17s and the weather was summery. "In the evening", Weddell wrote, ". . . NOT A PARTICLE OF ICE OF ANY DESCRIPTION WAS TO BE SEEN. . . ." Contrary winds and the lateness of the season decided him to return.

Weddell named this sea King George IV Sea. It was renamed the Weddell Sea in 1900. No further southward penetration was made in it until Shackleton's voyage of 1914–16.

The greatest unofficial supporters of Antarctic exploration in the following years were the Enderby brothers, whose whaling ships had been active in the south since the late 18th century. Charles Enderby, one of a family of whaling-ship owners, who had been active in southern waters since the end of the 18th century, became a fellow of the Royal Geographical Society in 1830, the year of its foundation, and from this time onwards Enderby skippers combined exploration with whale and seal hunting. That same year they sent out John Biscoe to search for land in the Indian Ocean sector of the Antarctic.

On January 28 Biscoe reached his highest latitude, 69s in 10.43E, off the present Prinsesse Astrid Kyst of Dronning Maud Land.

On the night of February 24 he saw what he took to be land. "The appearance of it was, I think, nearly similar to the North Foreland [a headland on the Kent coast of the English Channel] and I should think the cliffs of it . . .

as high, or nearly so, as the North Foreland." They were the ice cliffs of what he named Enderby Land on the Antarctic continent and although convinced, correctly, that they were solid ice, Biscoe also believed that the ice was formed from the sea and that most of Antarctica was ice with the tops of a number of islands rising above it.

Among other great Enderby skippers was John Balleny, who discovered the Balleny Islands, a group of five mountainous, volcanic ice-covered islands, early in 1839. He later sighted the Sabrina Coast of Wilkes Land.

In a sense it was the end of an era in the Antarctic. The next expeditions were sponsored by great powers, and their ships, which were specially equipped, carried quantities of scientific equipment and men who knew how to use it; but whatever they accomplished with their large crews they could scarcely surpass the courage and endurance of the sealers in their tiny vessels.

One of the few great powers to show any interest in Antarctic exploration at this time was France. In 1836, Jules Sebastien César Dumont d'Urville put forward proposals for another expedition to the Pacific, which were accepted by the French Admiralty. However, when they were submitted to King Louis-Phillipe, he suggested that d'Urville should make a voyage into the Weddell Sea and attempt to better 74.15s, Weddell's farthest.

So it was that d'Urville, partly crippled with gout, sailed from Toulon in September 1837 with two corvettes, the *Astrolabe* and *Zelée*, both ill-suited for polar exploration.

At the end of February d'Urville discovered Joinville Island off the eastern extremity of Graham Land, and then sailed along the coast. No landings were actually made on the Antarctic Peninsula, but numbers of channels and islands were charted and named.

D'Urville's heart had never been in the venture to the Weddell Sea, and it was with genuine enthusiasm that, in January 1840, hearing of Ross's Antarctic expedition, he sailed southeast from Hobart, Tasmania, to search for the South Magnetic Pole.

On January 20 the ships were close to the Antarctic Circle and the following day they found themselves in a flat calm gazing at a coastline of vertical ice-cliffs, about 120 feet high, behind which, rising to between three and four thousand feet, lay a featureless, completely snow- and ice-covered land. D'Urville named it Terre Adélie after his wife, and the first cape seen Cap de la Découverte.

On January 28, while in fog in about 65s, 135E, a brig which hoisted the American colours was sighted running down towards them. This was the *Porpoise*, one of the ships of Lieutenant Wilkes's Antarctic expedition.

On January 30, 1840, the icepack was

Antarctica: the coastwise explorers

encountered and the ice-barrier was lost to sight. The following day d'Urville took his ships northwards once more into the Pacific. There were no further French Antarctic expeditions during the 19th century.

Meanwhile American plans for an Antarctic expedition had been maturing with almost unbelievable slowness. The most consistent supporter of Antarctic exploration was John Reynolds of Ohio, but years passed before he was able to raise any interest. At last, on May 18, 1836, the United States Exploring Expedition, part of which would be concerned with Antarctic exploration, was authorized by Act of Congress.

There followed two years of acrimonious feuding between the Navy, who were to be in charge of the expedition, and the civilians, the principal among them being Reynolds. Eventually the command was offered to Lieutenant Charles Wilkes, a 40-year-old descendant of the English politician John Wilkes, champion of the American colonists.

Unsuitable ships

Wilkes's six ships were incredibly ill-chosen considering the amount of time it had taken the expedition to form. They were the flagship *Vincennes*, a sloop of 780 tons; the sloop *Peacock*, 650 tons; the *Porpoise*, a 230-ton gun-brig; the *Sea Gull* and the *Flying Fish*, two decrepit pilot boats, and the *Relief*, a store ship, which was so slow that it was sent home.

The expedition sailed from Hampton Roads on August 18, 1838, and reached Nassau Bay in the south of Tierra del Fuego in February 1839.

From Nassau Bay Wilkes, with the *Porpoise* and the *Sea Gull*, sailed to the South Shetlands, from where he failed to force his way into the Weddell Sea. The *Relief* carried out a survey in the Magellan Strait. The main honours went to the *Peacock*, which reached the high latitude of 68s in 95.44W, and the tiny *Flying Fish*, which reached Cook's farthest south, 105W in the Amundsen Sea. The fleet then sailed for Valparaiso, on the way north losing the *Sea Gull* with all hands.

The squadron's four ships reached Sydney in November 1839. There, Wilkes did his best to make his ships as weather-proof as possible before sailing south again on December 26. On January 15, land was sighted, possibly one of the Balleny Islands.

What seemed to be land was seen on January 16 and three days later, in about 66.20s, 154.30E, land was sighted to the south-southeast and southwest. They were at the mouth of a bay about 20 miles deep—probably the coast of Oates Land.

On January 22, in sight of land, the *Peacock* found bottom in 320 fathoms with slate-coloured mud, but two days later, the ship drove astern into the icepack. It was so badly damaged that Hudson, her captain, retired to Sydney while Wilkes carried on to the west.

On January 30, in a smooth sea and brilliant weather, he managed to sail the *Vincennes* through a labyrinth of bergs into a bay in the mainland and approached to within half a mile of the rock- and ice-bound shore. Wilkes named this land the Antarctic Continent and the bay Piner's Bay, after the signal-quarter-master of the *Vincennes*. It was at this time that the *Porpoise*, separated from the *Vincennes*, met d'Urville's *Astrolabe* and *Zelée*. D'Urville claimed that he had sighted the Antarctic Continent first, on January 18, Wilkes that he had first seen it on January 19. However, d'Urville had failed to allow for the crossing of the International Date Line and it transpired that both explorers had discovered it on the same day.

Now the *Vincennes* was pounded by another furious gale, and Wilkes was told that the health of the crew was in such peril that the ship would be endangered if the voyage was continued in these latitudes. Nevertheless, with his crew dangerously near to mutiny, he decided to carry on, discovering the Knox Coast in 65.57s beyond 100E.

On February 16, he encountered a barrier stretching northwards across his path, the Shackleton Ice Shelf. Here, in 97.37E, off Queen Mary Coast, he turned to the north, his hopes dashed of reaching Enderby Land.

When Wilkes reached the United States in June 1842, however, it was not to receive a hero's welcome but to face a court martial. He was aquitted on all counts except that of illegal punishment of subordinates.

The reasons which impelled the British Government to organize a naval expedition to the Antarctic were almost entirely connected with the study of terrestrial magnetism, and the man appointed as commander was Captain James Clark Ross, discoverer of the North Magnetic Pole. It was one of those comparatively rare cases in the history of exploration in which the right man was selected not by chance but by design.

No more powerfully built or more suitable ships ever went to the Antarctic than the *Erebus* and the *Terror*, two timber-built, three masted, barque-rigged naval bombs. They were only 370 tons and 340 tons, but they had the advantage of great carrying capacity, small draft, and needed only a small crew. Great care was taken with the provisioning.

Ross's instructions were to set up fixed magnetic observatories at St Helena, the Cape of Good Hope, Kerguelen Island and in Tasmania. Then in the southern summer of 1840–1, to "proceed directly to the south-

Whaling ships reap their harvest of life from the cold, rich oceans of the south

The last continent. Hedged about by ice-strewn stormy seas and fogs, Antarctica in the 19th century posed a challenge, at once inviting and uninviting, to the great maritime nations of the north. It was no accident, therefore, that the first explorers to scout Antarctica's coasts in detail were often naval officers, commanding naval ships; men like the American Wilkes, the Frenchman d'Urville, the Russian von Bellingshausen and the Briton Ross. The oceans of Antarctica, however, knew other vessels than warships—the sealers which reaped a gruesome harvest after Smith's discovery of the South Shetlands in 1819. Busily engaged in their work, these captains paid little attention to the continent itself although one, John Biscoe, first sighted Enderby Land, named after his employers, the Enderby brothers, in 1831. In the 20th century, whaling replaced sealing, with the same devastating effect on stocks

New names, new nations found their way into the story of Antarctica as the 19th century closed and the 20th dawned; the Swede Nordenskjöld (nephew of the man who first navigated the Northeast Passage), the Germans Drygalski and Filchner, the Norwegians Bull and Borchgrevink (the first men to set foot on the continent proper, at Cape Adare, in 1895), and the Belgian de Gerlache

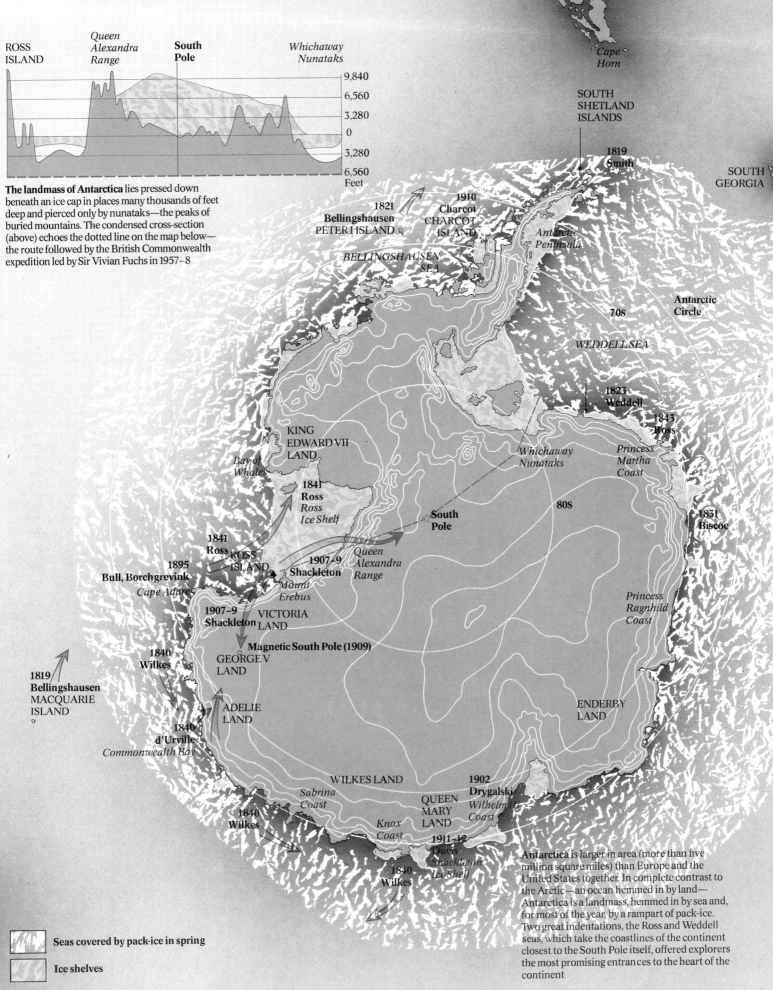

ROSS
ISLAND

*Queen
Alexandra
Range*

**South
Pole**

*Whichaway
Nunataks*

9,840

6,560

3,280

0

3,280

6,560
Feet

The landmass of Antarctica lies pressed down
beneath an ice cap in places many thousands of feet
deep and pierced only by nunataks—the peaks of
buried mountains. The condensed cross-section
(above) echoes the dotted line on the map below—
the route followed by the British Commonwealth
expedition led by Sir Vivian Fuchs in 1957–8

*Cape
Horn*

SOUTH
SHETLAND
ISLANDS

SOUTH
GEORGIA

1819
Smith

1910
Charcot
CHARCOT
ISLAND

1821
Bellingshausen
PETER I ISLAND

*Antarctic
Peninsula*

*BELLINGSHAUSEN
SEA*

Antarctic
Circle

70S

WEDDELL SEA

1823
Weddell

1843
Ross

KING
EDWARD VII
LAND

*Bay of
Whales*

*Whichaway
Nunataks*

*Princess
Martha
Coast*

1841
Ross
*Ross
Ross
Ice Shelf*

**South
Pole**

80S

1831
Biscoe

1841
Ross
ROSS
ISLAND

1895
Bull, Borchgrevink
Cape Adare

1907–9
Shackleton

*Queen
Alexandra
Range*

*Mount
Erebus*

*Princess
Ragnhild
Coast*

1907–9
Shackleton
VICTORIA
LAND

Magnetic South Pole (1909)

1840
Wilkes

GEORGE V
LAND

1819
Bellingshausen
MACQUARIE
ISLAND

ADELIE
LAND

ENDERBY
LAND

1840
d'Urville
Commonwealth Bay

WILKES LAND

1902
Drygalski
*Wilhelm II
Coast*

QUEEN
MARY
LAND

*Sabrina
Coast*

1840
Wilkes

*Knox
Coast*

1911–12
Davis
*Shackleton
Ice Shelf*

1840
Wilkes

Antarctica is larger in area (more than five
million square miles) than Europe and the
United States together. In complete contrast to
the Arctic—an ocean hemmed in by land—
Antarctica is a landmass, hemmed in by sea and,
for most of the year, by a rampart of pack-ice.
Two great indentations, the Ross and Weddell
seas, which take the coastlines of the continent
closest to the South Pole itself, offered explorers
the most promising entrances to the heart of the
continent

Seas covered by pack-ice in spring

Ice shelves

Antarctica: the coastwise explorers

ward in order to determine the position of the magnetic pole, and even to attain it if possible. . . ."

In the following southern summer, 1841–2, he was to sail eastwards in the highest latitude he could reach from the point he had attained the previous year, and search for new positions in which to set up observatories.

Ross in the *Terror*, with Captain Francis Moira Crozier commanding the *Erebus*, sailed from Margate Roads on September 30, 1839. Crozier had sailed with Ross in the Arctic and had been with Parry on his attempt to reach the North Pole in 1827.

Having set up the observatories *en route*, the expedition reached Hobart, Tasmania, in August 1840. There, Ross received information that d'Urville and Wilkes had been operating in the region where he was to search for the South Magnetic Pole. He was annoyed, but as a result he took what proved to be an extremely important decision—to try to reach it farther to the east.

On January 1, 1841, *Terror* and *Erebus* crossed the Antarctic Circle and on the morning of January 5 Ross's ships headed into the pack, the first ever to do so.

After some days the pack became closer, but a darkened sky to the southeast showed that open water lay ahead, and on the morning of January 9 they reached the great expanse of the Ross Sea. It was an historic moment.

At noon they were in 69.15S, 176.15E and after experiencing an easterly gale, which left no ice to be seen, Ross set course on the Magnetic Pole, which the dip of the compass needles proved was not far off. On January 10, a mountainous land was sighted at a distance of about 100 miles with one great peak, nearly 12,000 feet high, rising above the others. Ross named it Mount Sabine.

By the evening of January 11 they were only a few miles off the coast, a lee-shore on which heavy surf broke over the pack-ice that hemmed it in, making a landing impossible. Behind it rose a perpendicular cliff 1,000 feet high, the northern termination of a dark promontory, the northeastern extremity of what Ross named Victoria Land.

They took possession of the new land in the name of the Queen, and on January 14 they again set sail for the south. Eight days later the *Terror* and the *Erebus* reached 74.20S, beyond Weddell's farthest point.

On January 27, about 80 miles from the mainland, a landing was made with great difficulty and danger on what was named Franklin Island, and the following day they had a closer view of an astonishing island, which had been in sight since the previous day and which Ross named High Island (later Ross Island). "It proved to be a mountain twelve thousand four hundred feet of eleva-

tion above the level of the sea, emitting flame and smoke in great profusion. . . . I named it 'Mount Erebus'. . . ."

Ross now intended to sail south of the island, but was soon confronted by a disturbing phenomenon. He had reached the ice-front of what was later named, in his honour, the Ross Ice Shelf, the great breach in the defences of Antarctica from which the attacks on the South Pole would be mounted 60 years later. It covers some 310,000 square miles, an area far greater than France, varying in thickness from about 600 feet on its seaward side to 2,000 feet at its meeting with the inland ice-sheet. It was here, while in 76.12S, 164E, only 160 miles from the South Magnetic Pole, that Ross decided to return to Tasmania.

On November 23, Ross sailed south once again. On this journey, which lasted 137 days, little was accomplished in the way of discovery, but much was learned about the hazards of polar waters.

The following year Ross received permission from the Admiralty to spend a third winter in the Antarctic, this time in an attempt to survey the east coast of Graham Land (the Antarctic Peninsula) and to set up a new record for a farthest south in the Weddell Sea.

Impassable ice

The weather became exceptionally bad and by February 14, 1843, Ross had only succeeded in reaching the impassable pack-ice in the Weddell Sea, 550 miles north of Weddell's farthest. However, he made considerable discoveries on the (until now) unvisited eastern coast of Graham Land, among them the James Ross Island group.

This expedition, apart from that of the *Challenger*, when she crossed the Circle in February 1874, was the last of the great voyaging expeditions in the Antarctic.

The 1890s saw the invasion of the Antarctic by whalers, the Arctic hunting grounds being by this time seriously depleted. The first expeditions were made by some Scottish ships from Dundee, one of which, the *Balaena*, carried William Spiers Bruce, a young Scottish naturalist who later commanded his own expedition to the Weddell Sea. Another was made by the Norwegian Captain Carl Larsen, who met the Scottish expedition's ships at Joinville Island; Larsen himself went on to discover Oscar II Coast on the east side of Graham Land in 1893.

As a result of this voyage, Commander Svend Foyn, a Norwegian whaling ship owner of similar calibre to the Enderbys, sent the whaler *Antarctic* into the Ross Sea under the command of Captain Leonard Kristensen. On board were two young Nor-

wegians, H. J. Bull and Carstens Borchgrevink, and it was these three who finally made the first landing on the Antarctic continent near Cape Adare, Victoria Land, on January 24, 1895.

This voyage was followed, in 1897, by those of the Belgian Lieutenant Adrien de Gerlache and of Borchgrevink.

De Gerlache, who sailed in the *Belgica*, a 250-ton Norwegian sealer, had with him Roald Amundsen as first mate and Dr Frederick Cook, who was later to claim that he had reached the North Pole before Peary. Landings were made on the Palmer Archipelago in January and Alexander Island was reached. Then, in 71.30S, the ship was beset and drifted for a year to the south of Peter I Øy, the first ship to winter in the Antarctic.

The sun disappeared for a period of 70 days on May 15, and the crew suffered from anaemia due to the unsuitable rations and from depression brought on by the appalling monotony and the hideous groaning and crashing of the ice in the interminable night.

Borchgrevink's expedition, financed by Sir George Newnes, the English newspaper and magazine publisher, sailed from the Thames in the *Southern Cross*, a powerful converted Norwegian whaler, in August 1898. His crew included some distinguished scientists and was the first to carry sledges and dog teams.

He finally succeeded in passing through the pack on February 11, 1899, in 70S, 174E. Eight days later, the *Southern Cross* set a new record, becoming the first ship ever to anchor in Antarctica, in Robertson Bay in 71.15S.

Here, in wild weather, they built a hut, the first winter camp on the Antarctic mainland. The *Southern Cross* then sailed away, leaving a party of ten men to endure a terrible winter of 75 days of darkness and blizzards of such fury that it was often impossible to even crawl on all fours to the thermometers outside.

With the return of the sun, Lieutenant William Colbeck of the Royal Navy began making charts and maps in the neighbourhood, while Borchgrevink explored two great glaciers, which he named the Newnes and Murray glaciers. On January 28 the *Southern Cross* returned and they were able to go farther south and explore the area around mounts Erebus and Terror. In February they reached the ice-barrier, which Colbeck's maps showed had receded 30 miles since Ross's time. There they landed the dog teams, and Borchgrevink, Colbeck and a Lapp who was in charge of the dogs reached 78.50S over the ice, the farthest point south so far reached by man. It was a fitting end to the 19th century. Borchgrevink had proved that it was possible to winter on the continent. The attack on the South Pole was about to begin.

Inland to the Pole

As the 19th century drew to its close the Royal Society and the Royal Geographical Society mooted a fresh expedition to the Antarctic. Its objects were to determine the nature and extent of the Antarctic Continent; to penetrate into the interior; to ascertain the nature of the ice-cap; to observe the character of the underlying rocks and their fossils; to obtain as complete a series as possible of magnetic and meteorological observations; to observe the depths and temperatures of the ocean; to take pendulum observations; and to sound, trawl and dredge. Today the exploration of the continent remains incomplete in all these fields.

The command of what was named the National Antarctic Expedition was given to Robert Falcon Scott, a 32-year-old torpedo lieutenant in the Royal Navy, with no experience of the polar regions, but exceptionally able, ambitious and determined.

The ship, specially designed by the Admiralty, was the 735-ton auxiliary barque *Discovery*, powered by an engine which drove a special two-bladed lifting screw. In order that observations could be more accurate an area of 30 feet from the magnetic observatory was made completely free of iron and steel fittings. Among the officers was Ernest Henry Shackleton, who, next to Amundsen, was to become Scott's greatest rival in the attack on the South Pole.

It was decided that the expedition should follow Sir James Ross's route into the Ross Sea, attempt to discover whether the mountains Ross thought he had seen at the eastern end of the ice barrier actually existed, if possible make a landing on the ice-shelf and then winter on the coast of Victoria Land.

On January 21, 1902, the *Discovery* entered McMurdo Sound and then coasted east along the north shore of Ross Island as far as Cape Crozier at the foot of Mount Terror.

Scott now took the *Discovery* along the edge of the ice barrier until, on January 29, in 165E—eastwards of Ross's farthest point—land was sighted stretching northeastwards. Scott named it King Edward VII Land.

Pack-ice prevented him from continuing, and he now took his ship back to a bay in the ice-front in 77.50S and moored alongside it. Here, on February 4, Lieutenant Armitage and the physicist and expert in magnetism, Louis Bernacchi, landed with a sledge and went up the slopes to the ice-shelf. Here Scott made a captive balloon ascent.

The winter was spent in huts erected at Hut Point, a promontory at the southern tip of Ross Island. Before the Antarctic night descended, reconnaissance journeys were made to familiarize the sailors with skis and sledge work. Great difficulty was experienced in dealing with the dogs and their harness and it proved easier to man-haul the sledges. This inability or reluctance to persevere in acquiring these vital skills was one of the contributory factors to the tragic end of Scott's final expedition.

Nightmare return

On November 2, 1902, Scott, Wilson and Shackleton, with 19 dogs and three sledges, set off in an attempt to cross the ice-shelf.

After sledging for 59 days they turned back. Scurvy had broken out—Shackleton suffering particularly—and the return journey to the *Discovery* was a nightmare. They had reached 82.17S, sighted the great Trans-Antarctic Range and travelled 900 miles.

When Scott's party reached the ice-bound *Discovery* they found that a relief ship, the *Morning*, had already arrived and was lying off six miles away in ice-free waters. When the *Morning* sailed for England on March 2 Scott sent a number of invalids home, one of whom was Shackleton. For a man of Shackleton's stamp nothing could have been more calculated to reinforce his determination to return to the Antarctic.

In the following year a rescue operation was mounted by the Admiralty, who had acquired the *Morning* and the whaler *Terra Nova*. Both arrived in McMurdo Sound on January 5, 1904. Meanwhile, Scott, Evans and Lashly had made a major journey to 8,900 feet on the icecap in 77.59S 146.33E. The expedition finally reached Spithead on September 10.

At the same time that Scott was in the field, German, Swedish, French and Scottish expeditions were also working in the Antarctic.

The main achievement of the German expedition, led by Professor Erich von Drygalski, a distinguished physicist, was the discovery of Kaiser Wilhelm II Land. One of the most striking features of this land was an extinct black volcanic cone, about 50 miles from the ship. It was named the Gaussberg.

The leader of the Swedish expedition, which left Gothenburg in October 1901, was Dr Otto Nordenskjöld, geologist, Arctic veteran and nephew of the great explorer of the Northeast Passage. Nordenskjöld had carried out geological work in Tierra del Fuego and wanted to find out if any geological link existed between the southern tip of South America and northeastern Antarctica.

Despite innumerable hardships the Nordenskjöld expedition accomplished a great deal. It accurately surveyed the extremely complicated southwestern regions of the South Shetlands and corrected a number of errors made by Ross and d'Urville, besides discovering new land. Geologically it was able to suggest that the Antarctic Peninsula was connected with the South American continent. Rich hauls of fossils of fresh-water Jurassic flora were discovered at Hope Bay on the peninsula. On Snow Hill and Seymour Island a number of fossil formations of the Cretaceous period were found, which enabled conclusions to be drawn about the whole area as far south as the Antarctic Circle.

While Nordenskjöld's expedition was already working—and nearly perishing—near the Antarctic Circle a French doctor of medicine and science, Jean-Baptiste Charcot, was preparing a 250-ton polar vessel, the *Français*, at St Malo.

Charcot's intention had been to go to the help of Nordenskjöld's expedition, but when he learned that they had been rescued, he decided to continue the exploration of the west coast of the Peninsula and of Alexander Land. Prominent among his discoveries was what is now known as the Loubet Coast of Graham Land, a mountainous coast with long spurs descending from a snow-capped plateau.

The fourth of these almost simultaneous expeditions was that of the Scottish Antarctic expedition led by William Spiers Bruce and financed by the Scottish industrialist Andrew Coats of Paisley.

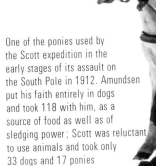

One of the ponies used by the Scott expedition in the early stages of its assault on the South Pole in 1912. Amundsen put his faith entirely in dogs and took 118 with him, as a source of food as well as of sledging power; Scott was reluctant to use animals and took only 33 dogs and 17 ponies

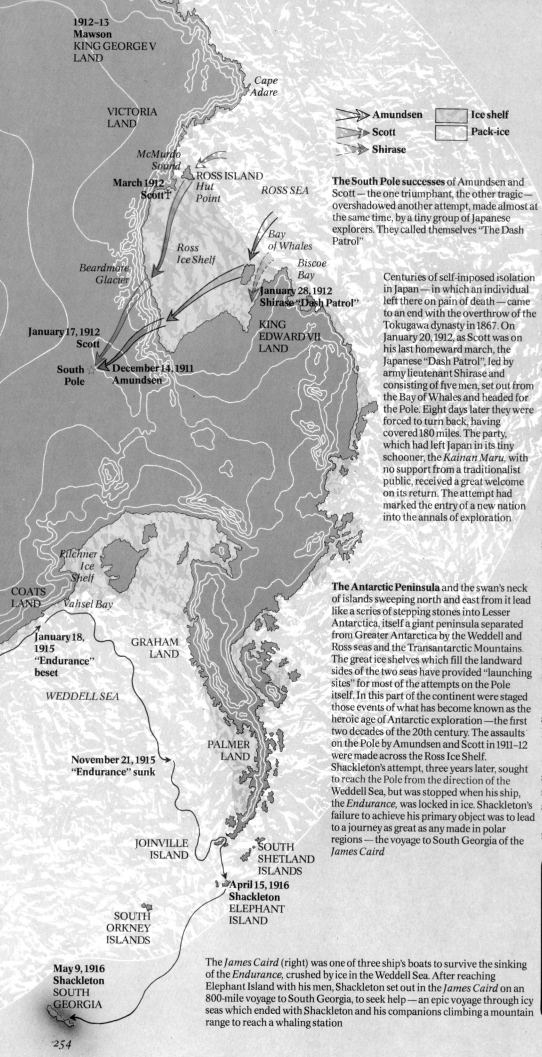

1912–13
Mawson
KING GEORGE V
LAND

Cape Adare

VICTORIA
LAND

McMurdo Sound

**March 1912
Scott †**

ROSS ISLAND
Hut Point

ROSS SEA

Ross Ice Shelf

Beardmore Glacier

Bay of Whales

Biscoe Bay

**January 28, 1912
Shirase "Dash Patrol"**

KING EDWARD VII LAND

**January 17, 1912
Scott**

**December 14, 1911
Amundsen**

South Pole

→ Amundsen   ☐ Ice shelf
→ Scott   ☐ Pack-ice
⇢ Shirase

Kilchner Ice Shelf

COATS LAND

Vahsel Bay

**January 18, 1915
"Endurance" beset**

GRAHAM LAND

WEDDELL SEA

**November 21, 1915
"Endurance" sunk**

PALMER LAND

JOINVILLE ISLAND

SOUTH SHETLAND ISLANDS

**April 15, 1916
Shackleton
ELEPHANT ISLAND**

SOUTH ORKNEY ISLANDS

**May 9, 1916
Shackleton
SOUTH GEORGIA**

254

The South Pole successes of Amundsen and Scott — the one triumphant, the other tragic — overshadowed another attempt, made almost at the same time, by a tiny group of Japanese explorers. They called themselves "The Dash Patrol"

Centuries of self-imposed isolation in Japan — in which an individual left there on pain of death — came to an end with the overthrow of the Tokugawa dynasty in 1867. On January 20, 1912, as Scott was on his last homeward march, the Japanese "Dash Patrol", led by army lieutenant Shirase and consisting of five men, set out from the Bay of Whales and headed for the Pole. Eight days later they were forced to turn back, having covered 180 miles. The party, which had left Japan in its tiny schooner, the *Kainan Maru*, with no support from a traditionalist public, received a great welcome on its return. The attempt had marked the entry of a new nation into the annals of exploration

The Antarctic Peninsula and the swan's neck of islands sweeping north and east from it lead like a series of stepping stones into Lesser Antarctica, itself a giant peninsula separated from Greater Antarctica by the Weddell and Ross seas and the Transantarctic Mountains. The great ice shelves which fill the landward sides of the two seas have provided "launching sites" for most of the attempts on the Pole itself. In this part of the continent were staged those events of what has become known as the heroic age of Antarctic exploration — the first two decades of the 20th century. The assaults on the Pole by Amundsen and Scott in 1911–12 were made across the Ross Ice Shelf. Shackleton's attempt, three years later, sought to reach the Pole from the direction of the Weddell Sea, but was stopped when his ship, the *Endurance*, was locked in ice. Shackleton's failure to achieve his primary object was to lead to a journey as great as any made in polar regions — the voyage to South Georgia of the *James Caird*

Inland to the Pole

After an unsuccessful expedition in 1903, Bruce sailed again for Antarctica the following year. In the Weddell Sea he sighted a low, ice-clad land, faced with ice-cliffs between 100 and 150 feet high extending northeast and southwest. He named the coast Coats Land, but the ice prevented a landing.

After his return to Britain, invalided home from the Antarctic, Shackleton endeavored to join the Royal Navy with a permanent commission. This was stupidly denied him and in an effort to enrich himself he embarked on a number of unsuccessful ventures.

It was during this time that he met the powerful engineer–industrialist William Beardmore, who eventually loaned Shackleton the bulk of the money for an expedition of his own to the Antarctic.

Shackleton's plan was to use Scott's base at Hut Point and from it send out three separate sledging parties: one eastwards across the ice-shelf, to King Edward VII Land; another westwards to the South Magnetic Pole; and a third, the main party, to attempt to reach the South Pole. This he proposed to lead himself, for to Shackleton the Pole was infinitely the most precious prize.

Shackleton made himself personally responsible for the equipment, which was similar to Scott's, except for two innovations. In addition to only nine Siberian dogs he took 15 Manchurian ponies to haul the sledges, an almost fatal error; Shackleton, like Scott, underestimated the value of dogs.

In April 1907, Shackleton wrote a letter to the *London Times* giving details of his plans. It provoked a letter from Scott telling him that he, too, was planning another expedition and asking Shackleton to leave Hut Point free.

This was a serious blow to Shackleton, but he agreed and decided to try and set up a base at the eastern end of the Ross Ice Shelf or in King Edward VII Land.

The change of plan also meant that he would have to find a much more robust ship, and he eventually bought the *Nimrod*, a small Norwegian schooner-rigged sealer of about 200 tons, with an engine that gave her a best speed of about six knots, and had her re-rigged as a barquentine in order to improve

The *James Caird* (right) was one of three ship's boats to survive the sinking of the *Endurance*, crushed by ice in the Weddell Sea. After reaching Elephant Island with his men, Shackleton set out in the *James Caird* on an 800-mile voyage to South Georgia, to seek help — an epic voyage through icy seas which ended with Shackleton and his companions climbing a mountain range to reach a whaling station

her performance under canvas.

Among the scientists chosen for the expedition were Professor Edgeworth David, a professor of geology at Sydney University; Dr Douglas Mawson, a physicist from Adelaide University and Raymond Priestley, a geologist from Bristol University.

The *Nimrod*, commanded by Lieutenant R. N. England of the Royal Navy Reserve, sailed from Lyttelton, New Zealand, on January 1, 1908, and was towed, to save fuel, 1,500 miles to the edge of the icepack through heavy seas.

King Edward VII Land proved unreachable beyond the pack and Shackleton found himself in an impossible dilemma. He had to retreat to the west; but if he wintered in McMurdo Sound he would be going back on the undertaking he had given to Scott. Eventually he had no choice, as England insisted on a withdrawal, and the base had to be set up at Cape Royds at the western end of Ross Island—two days' journey from Hut Point and two days farther from the Pole.

Spring arrives

Depot laying began when the Antarctic spring sun was just showing above the horizon, but it was not until the end of September that Depot A, the expedition's forward base, was set up, 100 miles to the south of Hut Point.

By now, six of the ten ponies had died and as the remainder were all needed for the attack on the geographical Pole, the projected journey eastwards to King Edward VII Land was abandoned.

On September 25, Mawson, David and the surgeon, Mackay, who had earlier reached the summit of Mount Erebus, set off for the Magnetic Pole, man-hauling 2,200 pounds of equipment. From Terra Nova Bay they travelled over the Larsen Glacier to the plateau, and sledged westwards to the vicinity of the Pole, which was then in 72.25S, 155.16E. After a perilous journey they were picked up by the *Nimrod*, having mapped a large amount of new territory and made important geological discoveries.

The greatest event, however, was Shackleton's attack on the South Pole. Together with Lieutenant Adams, Dr Marshall, a cartographer, and Frank Wild he set out on October 29, east-southeast across the ice-shelf, with four pony-drawn sledges, two tents and provisions for 99 days. Shackleton had calculated the distance to the Pole as 800 geographical miles and estimated that the journey out and home would take 91 days, averaging 20 miles a day.

On November 6, the supporting party turned back and 12 days later Depot A was reached. On November 21 the first pony had

Robert Falcon Scott, beaten to the South Pole by Amundsen

Roald Amundsen—first through the Northwest Passage, first to the South Pole

Ernest Henry Shackleton—'the boss' to his men, and regarded as one of the greatest of polar explorers

to be shot and soon two more followed suit, the meat being left at the depots for the return.

With only one pony left, they marched for Mount Hope, a 3,000-foot peak on the inland edge of the ice-shelf. When they reached it an awe-inspiring sight met their eyes—an immense glacier, one of the largest in the world, a sort of frozen Amazon, 100 miles long and 30 miles wide where it met the shelf, pouring down through the ranges to meet the ice-shelf in a chaos of pressure ridges and crevasses. Shackleton named it the Beardmore Glacier. It was the way to the 10,000-foot-high Antarctic Plateau.

The ascent was a slow nightmare, at the rate of about five miles a day. The last pony, "Socks", fell into a crevasse.

By January 1, 1908, they were all suffering from terrible headaches. That night they were still 172 miles from the Pole.

Now the weather worsened, with a terrible wind that drove the temperature down to $-14°F$. "The end is in sight," Shackleton wrote on January 4, when they were 11,200 feet above the sea. "We can only go for three more days at the most, for we are weakening rapidly . . . we were so done up at noon with cold that the clinical thermometer failed to register the temperature of three of us at 94°." On this day they left their last depot.

The end was really near now, and finally, on January 9, Shackleton admitted: "We have shot our bolt." They were only 97 geographical miles from the Pole; but they were 800 miles from their base.

The return was difficult; but at least it was downhill and the searing wind was at their backs. They reached Depot A on February 20, having hoisted a sail on the sledge and scudded before the southerly blizzard. The next depot was east of Minna Bluff and from it Shackleton and Wild pressed on for 60 miles to Hut Point, leaving Adams with Marshall, who was too ill to go on.

Their agony was not yet over, however. When they reached the Point on February 28 it was to discover that the *Nimrod* had already sailed with the other two parties. By a miracle she was still close enough in for the fires that Shackleton and Wild lit and the flags they hoisted to be seen and all four men were saved. They had travelled for 117 days on 99 days' rations. It had been a remarkable expedition. The Magnetic Pole had been reached, the Trans-Antarctic Range crossed to the Antarctic Plateau, the way to the South Pole opened.

While Shackleton's party was still in Antarctica Charcot had also returned to it with an expedition mainly financed by the French Government.

A devoted scientist and a surveyor of exceptional accuracy, Charcot conducted his

Inland to the Pole

exploration in a highly civilized way, carrying excellent wines on board and also an extensive library of classics.

In August 1908, he sailed from Le Havre in the 800-ton, barque-rigged steamer *Pourquoi-Pas?*, which was specially constructed and equipped with the most modern innovations —a motor launch, searchlight and telephones. It even carried electric cables so that the ship could be used as a power source for land stations.

From Puntas Arenas on the Magellan Strait Charcot took the *Pourquoi-Pas?* to Wiencke Island in the Palmer Archipelago, where she hit a rock, doing serious damage to the keel. Nevertheless, Charcot continued his voyage.

In 1909, he found that the land west of the Antarctic Peninsula, between Palmer Archipelago and Alexander Island and named after Queen Adelaide by Biscoe in 1832, was in fact an island. Then, during the summer of 1909–10, he went on to discover the Fallières Coast, inshore of Marguerite Bay on the Antarctic Peninsula, and in January 1910 Charcot Land, off Alexander Island.

The stage was now being set for the most dramatic event in 20th-century Antarctic exploration, the race for the South Pole.

The protagonists were Scott and Amundsen, both highly capable, dedicated professionals. Their backgrounds, however, were very different, as were their characters.

Scott was, by nature and training, a man in whom the desire for discovery for its own sake was overlaid by the realization of the importance of scientific discovery, which had perhaps to some extent been forced upon him by the nature of the sponsored, semi-official expeditions that he had commanded.

Amundsen was a freelance who had been inspired by his spirit of adventure to make the almost impossible Northwest Passage in a puny vessel. In the Arctic he had learned that survival could best be ensured by copying the way of life of its inhabitants, the Eskimoes, and this he did with conspicuous success. Like Peary he employed dog teams to draw his sledges, sacrificing them in what to dog-lovers seems a ruthless way, and he used Eskimo clothing.

Scott seems to have had no intention of taking dogs or ponies to the Pole. He had also been horrified by the slaughter of seals for dog food, which had taken place on his first expedition. Like Shackleton he was a believer in woollen clothing, worn with proofed gabardine smocks, although these tended to freeze solid.

Scott sailed first, on June 1, 1910, in the *Terra Nova*, a barque-rigged steam whaler of 744 tons, with a predominantly naval crew, who had been given special leave. His

The ski-fitted Ford trimotor in which the US naval commander Richard Byrd made the first flight across the South Pole

second-in-command was Lieutenant Edward Evans. Among the scientists were Dr Edward Wilson, Raymond Priestley, Frank Debenham, a geologist, and Dr George Simpson, a meteorologist. Among other volunteers were Apsley Cherry-Garrard and Captain Lawrence Oates of the Inniskilling Dragoons. No particularly revolutionary equipment was taken, apart from three motor sledges with air-cooled engines.

The ship reached Melbourne on October 12 and there Scott received a cable from Madeira. It read: "Beg leave to inform you proceeding Antarctica. Amundsen."

Having borrowed Nansen's *Fram* with the intention of attempting to drift across the North Pole, Amundsen had heard of Peary's successful attack on it in April 1909 and had immediately headed the *Fram* for Madeira. It was not until he reached the island that he disclosed his intention of trying to reach the South Pole.

Winter base

On January 4, 1911, the *Terra Nova* reached Cape Evans on Ross Island, 14 miles north of Hut Point, and began to land equipment for the winter base.

Seven days later, Amundsen reached the Bay of Whales in the ice-shelf, after an easy passage through the pack, where his stores and dogs were landed and "Framheim"— the expedition's hut—was set up. Amundsen was now nearly 500 miles to the east of Scott's base and 60 miles nearer the Pole. His party consisted of eight men with 118 Greenland dogs to set up the attack, against Scott's party of 33, who had only 33 sledging dogs, mostly Siberian, and 17 ponies.

By February 17 Scott and his men had, with the loss of eight ponies and five dogs, laid depots as far south as One Ton Depot in 79.29s, on the ice-shelf. By March 31, Amundsen's sledge and dog teams had set up depots in 80, 81, and 82s. In addition to having depots farther south than Scott's, Amundsen was 60 miles to the south of Scott at the outset.

The Norwegian party, Amundsen, Olav Bjaaland, Helmer Hanssen, Sverre Hassel

and Oscar Wisting, all on skis and dressed in Eskimo clothes—each suit of which weighed about ten pounds, half that worn by Scott and his men—and with four sledges each drawn by 13 dogs, left the Bay of Whales on October 19, 1911. Each sledge carried 1,800 pounds, enough supplies for four months. They travelled very fast, about four and half miles an hour, and as they went they put up numbered snow cairns giving the distance and direction of the next one. Altogether they built 150 on the way to the Pole. They passed the final depot in 82s on November 6.

On November 12 in 84s, with the great Trans-Antarctic range in sight, they left a depot with provisions for five men and 12 dogs for five days, and on November 17 they began the ascent of the Axel Heiberg Glacier, the foot of which was a chaos of great blocks of ice and full of crevasses.

On December 4 they reached the plateau, and there, in what they named "The Butcher's Shop", 10,000 feet above the sea, 40 dogs were shot to provide food for the others and for the men, and to save weight.

From here they advanced into the teeth of a southeast blizzard and on December 7 they reached Shackleton's farthest south in 88.23s.

They were now suffering from frost sores and on December 9, with the temperature down to $-14°F$, they were in agony. South of 88.25s barometer and hypsometer showed that they were beginning to descend; but then they levelled out and by noon on December 14, with the weather cloudy and a light breeze, they were in 89.55s by dead reckoning.

Then "at three in the afternoon a simultaneous 'Halt!' rang out from the drivers. They had all carefully examined their sledge meters, and they all showed the full distance —our Pole by reckoning. The goal was reached, the journey ended." They knew that they were not on the exact spot "but we were so near it that the few miles which possibly separated us from it could not be of the slightest importance", and here they raised the Norwegian flag over what Amundsen named King Haakon VII's Plateau.

They remained at the Pole for three days, during which they made a circle round it of

$12\frac{1}{2}$ miles radius to ensure that they had not missed it. Before leaving they set up a small tent of gabardine from which they flew a Norwegian flag and a pennant with "FRAM" painted on it.

The return journey was comparatively uneventful and they reached Framheim on January 25, 1912, with, as Amundsen wrote, "two sledges and eleven dogs; men and animals all hale and hearty".

Scott's parties set off on November 1, a fortnight later than Amundsen. There were three, each of four men, each self-contained. Ponies drew all but four of the sledges—two dog sledges and two motor sledges, both of which ceased to function on the ice-shelf by November 5.

At Shambles Camp at the foot of the Beardmore Glacier, the surviving ponies were shot. The dogs had done well, as Scott noted frequently, and with some surprise.

The attack on the glacier began the following day. The snow was thick, the result of the blizzard, and there had been avalanches, which concealed the crevasses.

By the evening of December 14, the day Amundsen reached the Pole, they had only reached 2,000 feet. All Scott's efforts were directed to equalling Shackleton's schedule, and the strain was to have a disastrous effect on the polar party.

On December 21, Camp 43, the Upper Glacier Depot, was established at about 7,100 feet in 85.7s and one of the two support parties was sent back.

On January 1, they established 3 Degree Depot in 86.55s. They had caught up with Shackleton's schedule, but the last support party was by now showing signs of exhaustion. On January 4 it was sent back and the decision was made to add Lieutenant Bowers of the Royal Indian Marine—an immensely strong man—to the party for the final assault. It was a bad decision as he, in common with the others of Evans's party had left his skis at the 3 Degree Depot and would have to walk the whole way. His presence also upset the ration schedules and made the only tent very uncomfortable.

The final attack now began, 178 miles from the Pole, the party consisting of Scott, Wilson, Oates, Petty Officer Edgar Evans and Lieutenant Bowers.

On January 7 they reached 10,560 feet, their highest point, and began to descend very slightly towards the Pole, meeting with blizzards and travelling over difficult sastrugi - windcut ridges.

On the morning of January 18, they reached the Pole and found the little tent with the Norwegian flag flying over it. Their chagrin shows in the photograph taken at the time and found later in their last camp.

"Great God! This is an awful place," Scott wrote, "and terrible enough for us to have laboured to it without the reward of priority."

Now began the 800-mile return march to Cape Evans. Both Oates and Evans were soon suffering from frostbite. On January 31 they reached 3 Degree Depot, by which time Wilson had strained a tendon in his leg and Evans had lost two fingernails. On February 9, in a moraine on the glacier below Mount Buckley, although exhausted and starving, they collected 35 pounds of fossils with plant impressions, a piece of coal with leaves in it and others with impressions of thick stems, more important to science than reaching the Pole, and further proof of their devotion.

On February 17 Evans died just short of Shambles Camp. Temperatures were down to $-16°F$. On March 2 they reached Middle Barrier Depot, east of Mount Markham, where they found that the vital fuel oil had leaked, leaving hardly enough to take them to One Ton Depot, about 70 miles to the north.

Death of Oates

They never reached it. By now the temperature was down to $-40°F$ at night, and it was at this point that Oates was forced to admit that both his feet were terribly frostbitten. Gangrene set in and by March 6 he was unable to pull any longer—the going was terrible with thick snow and that day they made only six and a half miles. The end came for Oates on March 16 or 17. "Lost track of dates but think the last correct," Scott wrote. "In the morning, with the blizzard still at its height and with the words 'I am just going outside and may be some time', he left the tent and was never seen again."

The final camp was made on March 21, only 11 miles south of One Ton Depot. By now Scott was in a similar plight to that of Oates. From here Wilson and Bowers hoped to reach the depot and bring back fuel, but a heavy gale was blowing and it was impossible. Scott's last entry in his *Journal* was written on March 29. "Every day we have been ready to start for our depot only eleven miles away, but outside of the tent it remains a scene of whirling drift. I do not think we can hope for any better things now. We shall stick it out to the end, but we are growing weaker, of course and the end cannot be far."

All three men were found dead in their sleeping bags by a search party on November 12. Near Scott were letters he had written to the wives of Wilson and Bowers, to his own wife and son and others. His main concern had been that his dependants and those of his companions should be looked after. A scrawled postscript to his final entry in his *Journal* read: "For God's sake look after our people."

WHILE SCOTT WAS spending his last winter at the edge of the Ross Ice Shelf, Wilhelm Filchner, a Prussian army officer, raised Coats Land and endeavoured to establish a base on the great ice-shelf that bears his name. At the onset of the southern winter, in March 1912, Filchner's ship, the *Deutschland*, was beset in the ice and survived a drift of 600 miles before breaking out in November.

In January that year, an expedition led by Douglas Mawson, sailing in an old sealer, the *Aurora*, discovered King George V Land, east of d'Urville's Terre Adélie, and set up base at Cape Denison. Here an unceasing wind blew, mostly at above gale force, for most of the year. They named it "The Home of the Blizzard".

In September 1912, four parties set off to explore King George V Land. Meanwhile, John King Davis, the *Aurora's* captain, sailed westwards over 40 degrees of latitude to land a party under Frank Wild to the east of Kaiser Wilhelm Land. Davis discovered that the ice-front had receded a great deal since the voyages of d'Urville, Balleny and Wilkes and he now sailed over what was charted as land. He failed to sight the Knox Coast, but discovered the Shackleton Ice Shelf to the west of it.

Before the Antarctic winter set in, Wild's party reached the edge of the continental plateau in Queen Mary Land and in October they began the exploration of the coasts: first as far as Drygalski's Gaussberg, 200 miles to the west; then to the east in the direction of the Knox Coast. Both these journeys were exceptionally arduous due to the fearful wind and the glacier-riven coastline.

Meanwhile, far to the east in King George V Land, a great drama was being enacted. Mawson, with Lieutenant B. E. S. Ninnis, a British army officer, and Dr Zavier Mertz, a Swiss mountaineer and skiing champion, had set out from "The Home of the Blizzard" at the same time as the other parties, to explore the coast eastwards as far as what was later named Oates Land. With them they had three sledges and 17 dogs.

At the end of November one of the sledges fell into a crevasse. They managed to get it out, but the sledge was so badly damaged that they had to transfer the provisions to Ninnis's sledge. On December 14, Ninnis disappeared with his sledge and his entire team of dogs into a crevasse. The only sign that they had ever existed was one wounded dog on an ice-shelf about 150 feet below with another, dead, beside it.

The retreat was a nightmare. Mertz died on January 7, in his sleep, huddled close to Mawson in their makeshift tent. With 100 miles still to go Mawson cut his sledge in half

The 'boss'

and jettisoned every non-essential item of equipment, but with frostbitten, blistered feet he averaged only about six miles a day.

At the end of January, he found a cairn with a bag of food in it left by a search party, and also a message telling him that further supplies had been left 23 miles ahead, five miles east of Commonwealth Bay. He reached this cairn, but there a blizzard pinned him down and when he gained the shore he saw the *Aurora* steam out of the bay. Fortunately he was not alone. Five men from the other parties, which had all returned safely, had volunteered to remain behind in the hope that Mawson's party would turn up.

Throughout the winter the morale of the men at Commonwealth Bay was kept high by the radio link with Australia (Mawson was the first Antarctic explorer to use it). Finally, in mid-December 1913, they were taken off by Davis in the *Aurora*.

The last Antarctic expedition of what with reason has been called the Heroic Age, was Shackleton's expedition to the Weddell Sea. He planned to land in 78s with six men, 100 dogs and sledges, two of which were fitted with propellers, and cross the continent to the Ross Sea by way of the Pole and the Beardmore Glacier.

Shackleton's ship, the *Endurance*, sailed from England in the company of Mawson's old *Aurora* a few days after the outbreak of the First World War in August 1914, and by the following January had closed with the ice barrier off what Shackleton named the Caird Coast. In a few days, 130 miles northeast of Vahsel Bay, the *Endurance* was beset. Through the southern autumn and winter (the sun set on May 1) the *Endurance* drifted in the embrace of the ice; first southwest then northwest. On September 17 a fatal pressure on her hull began.

"In the engine-room," Shackleton wrote, "the weakest point, loud groans, crashes and hammering sounds were heard. The iron plates on the floor buckled up and overrode with loud clangs." Luckily the *Endurance* succeeded in riding above it with a six-degree list to port.

What Shackleton described as the "beginning of the end" for the *Endurance* came on October 24, when the ship, which had been floating in an open pool since the last attack six days earlier, was subjected to a new onslaught by three pressure ridges. ". . . Huge blocks of ice, weighing many tons, were lifted into the air and tossed aside as other masses rose beneath them. We were helpless intruders in a strange world, our lives dependent upon the play of grim elementary forces that made a mock of our puny efforts."

On the night of October 26, Shackleton gave the order to lower the boats to the floe

The "Polar Star", the radial-engined monoplane in which Ellsworth finally succeeded in crossing Antarctica in 1935

and to get all the gear on to flat ice, and the next day, after 281 days in which the *Endurance* had drifted more than 570 miles to the northwest (its actual drift through observed positions was 1,186 miles and it probably covered more), they abandoned ship. The *Endurance* finally sank on November 21.

The nearest point of land where they might find food and shelter was Paulet Island in the Joinville group. This was where Nordenskjöld's expedition had built a hut in 1902, which had been stocked with food by an Argentinian ship. Shackleton decided to try to reach it with the dog sledges and dragging two of the heavy ship's boats, but the ice was so soft that in seven days they made only seven miles.

Northward drift

Drifting slowly north in the Weddell Sea in what they called "Patience Camp", the 28 men waited for the ice to break up. At first the weather was fine but, as the Antarctic summer passed into 1916, southwesterly gales and blizzards set in.

On March 25, 1916, nearly four months after the *Endurance* sank, land was sighted—Joinville Island—but again the ice was too broken and loose to travel over and not loose enough to allow the boats to be launched.

On April 2 the last of the dog teams was shot for food. Apart from the dog meat, their principal food was seal meat, with one biscuit at midday.

On April 9, with Clarence and Elephant islands in sight ahead and the ice breaking up around them, the floe on which they had camped for months suddenly split in two.

By afternoon the pack opened sufficiently for the three boats—the *James Caird*, the *Dudley Docker* and the *Stancomb Wills*—to be launched successfully. Now began the perilous business of navigating through a labyrinth of floes and bergs, all of them in violent motion, and by night hauling the boats out on unstable ice.

They were nearing the edge of the pack now, but in great peril from killer whales, which rose hissing around them. Off Elephant Island they suffered a gale which took them in close to the shore. They were tormented by thirst, for in their hurry to abandon the floe they had failed to bring with them any ice and

they obtained what was only temporary relief by chewing raw seal meat and swallowing the blood. By April 13 they were clear of the ice. "Dark blue and sapphire green ran the seas. Our sails were soon up, and with a fair wind we moved over the waves like three Viking ships on the Quest for Lost Atlantis."

It was bitterly cold and there were several cases of frostbite. Finally, on the morning of April 15, 1916, after sailing close in under great cliffs and glaciers, they found a narrow channel through a reef which led to a small beach at the foot of high cliffs. They were the first men to land on Elephant Island and it was the first land they had felt underfoot since leaving South Georgia in December 1914.

However, they were still in a serious position; nobody would ever find them on this desolate coast and Shackleton decided to try to reach South Georgia. When they had moved to a better beach about seven miles to the west, Shackleton began to prepare the 20-foot-long *James Caird*, the heaviest of the three boats, for the journey to South Georgia—800 miles to the northeast across seas that in May, with winter advancing, are among the stormiest in the world. There was little that could be done except to deck it in, using sledge runners as a framework and the lids of cases, which were then covered with canvas. The carpenter also fitted the mast of one of the other boats fore-and-aft inside the boat as a hog-back to prevent it buckling. Shackleton took with him Worsley, McNeish, Crean, McCarthy and Vincent. They sailed on April 24.

"The tale of the next sixteen days", Shackleton wrote, "is one of supreme strife amid heaving waters. The sub-Antarctic Ocean lived up to its evil winter reputation." It is also a story of amazing courage and superb seamanship of a kind that has rarely been equalled.

On the sixth day, while hove-to in a severe gale, the *James Caird* came near to being lost when the sea anchor carried away and they fell into the trough. By a miracle they were able to get sail on her before she broached-to. The second escape was at midnight on the 11th day (May 5). In the midst of a hard northwest gale they were overrun by a wave so immense that Shackleton, in all his experience of the sea, had never seen the like. ". . . We baled with the energy of men fighting for life, flinging the water over the sides with every effort, receptacles that came to our hands, and after ten minutes of uncertainty we felt the boat renew her life beneath us."

They were now reduced to drinking water from a cask that had been penetrated by sea water and suffered agonies from thirst; but on May 8, 14 days out, they sighted the black cliffs of South Georgia. On the evening of May 9 they managed to run the *James Caird* into a long, narrow bay with a little cove. There, to their inexpressible joy, they found a stream of fresh water.

The cove was inside the southern headland of King Haakon Bay on the uninhabited southwest coast of South Georgia. The condition of McNeish and Vincent made it unwise to put to sea again and the boat itself was so weakened that it seemed unlikely that it would ever make the Stromness whaling station, 150 miles away by sea, on the northeast coast of the island.

Shackleton now shifted camp to the northeast side of the bay, from which it was easier to start inland—across unexplored country— to the whaling station.

On May 29, Shackleton set out, together with Worsley and Crean, leaving the others in a house made from the upturned boat, which they named "Peggotty Camp". They took with them three days' provisions, a Primus stove filled with sufficient oil to cook six meals, the carpenter's adze to use as an ice axe, an Alpine rope and a box of matches. Shackleton had given away his heavy boots

on the floe and the carpenter produced for him a primitive version of a crampon by putting some screws from the *James Caird* into the soles of his light boots.

They left at one in the morning by moonlight and reached about 3,000 feet before descending to a glacier and then climbed to a ridge at 4,500 feet the following evening. As they had no tent it was essential to descend to a lower altitude and, unroping themselves, they slid 900 feet down an ice slope. Then, after a meal, they continued to march into the eye of a full moon. At midnight they turned northeast. With the moon partly obscured by cloud they descended what they soon discovered to be a glacier (the Fortuna Glacier) and were forced to return up it.

At five in the morning, as they were sinking into sleep, Shackleton realized that they might never wake from it. After five minutes he roused the others, telling them that they had slept for half an hour. Travelling to the east, at dawn they saw Husvik Harbour in Stromness Bay far below. At seven o'clock, by their chronometer, they heard the whistle calling the men to work at the whaling station.

So ended the most remarkable combined

The end of an era in polar exploration. Reliable machinery in partnership with man helps scores of anonymous scientists tread the routes which, a few decades earlier, claimed the lives of pioneers

small boat and Alpine journey ever made— and by men in poor physical condition.

The three men who had been left on the other side of South Georgia were soon rescued, but three separate relief ships, which sailed between May and August 1916, failed to get through to the main party at Elephant Island. Finally, on August 30, the Chilean ship *Yelcho*, with Shackleton on board, as he had been on the ships making previous attempts, succeeded in taking them all off.

Apart from the remarkable record kept by J. M. Wordie of the movement and nature of the ice in the Weddell Sea—which was of great assistance to Dr Vivian Fuchs when he entered it—Shackleton's expedition had few tangible results, but the courage of its members and the qualities of leadership and seamanship displayed by Shackleton (known affectionately to his men as "the boss") himself have rarely, if ever, been surpassed.

Arena of the nations

B Y THE END of the First World War, more than half the coastline of Antarctica was still uncharted, the interior largely a featureless blank. Subsequent decades were, however, to see a huge increase in knowledge of the continent. For much of this the aeroplane—a new means of transport in the history of exploration—was responsible.

The first man to use an aeroplane in the southern polar regions was the Australian Sir Hubert Wilkins (he had flown in the Arctic, and had attempted unsuccessfully to take a submarine beneath the North Pole). The flight was made during the course of an Anglo–American expedition in 1928, when Wilkins flew along the east coast of the Antarctic Peninsula. The first flight across the South Pole itself was made the following year by the American naval officer who three years before had been the first to fly across the North Pole—Commander Richard Evelyn Byrd.

The historic flight was made on November 28, 1929, when Byrd, with the Norwegian Bernt Balchen as pilot and H. June and A. C. McKinley as crew, took off from Little America I, near the Bay of Whales, in their Ford tri-motor aircraft.

During the flight they had to jettison two weeks' food rations before the plane gained a satisfactory altitude. They circled the Pole twice, and landed back at base at 8.30 pm after a journey of 15 hours 51 minutes and 1,500 air miles.

On his second expedition, in 1933, Byrd spent seven months alone at the Bolling Advanced Weather Station, 125 miles south of Little America I on the Ross Ice Shelf in a tiny prefabricated hut, buried in snow. It could only be entered by a hatch that would not close properly and had a stove from which certain essential parts were missing.

Twice he came close to death. The first time, in May 1934, he was unable to open the hatch and was marooned outside the hut in the full fury of an Antarctic blizzard. "It is more than just wind," he wrote, "it is a solid wall of snow moving at gale force, pounding like surf . . . you can't see, you can't hear, you can hardly move. . . ." It was in these conditions that, by a miracle, he found a shovel and was able to open the hatch.

In May he was nearly asphyxiated by exhaust gases from the generating engine and carbon monoxide fumes from the faulty stove. A rescue party was sent out using tractors and reached Byrd on August 11, in time to save him from death.

Between 1934 and 1937 the British Graham Land Expedition, under John Rymill, carried out exploration in that region by sledge and air, using a small, single-engined De Havilland Fox Moth aircraft. It conclusively proved that the Antarctic Peninsula was not an island, which it had been believed to be since Wilkins's flight five years earlier.

In November 1935, Lincoln Ellsworth, who had crossed the Arctic by air with Amundsen, succeeded in flying across Antarctica. With a Canadian, Herbert Hollick-Kenyon, as pilot, the crossing was made in a Northrop monoplane, the *Polar Star*, from Dundee Island, southwest of Joinville Island, to a point about 60 miles from the Ross Sea. They reached Little America II at the Bay of Whales on foot on December 15, having been forced to land through lack of fuel.

Despite intense American activity in Antarctica the United States Congress failed to provide funds to maintain permanent bases. No formal claim has been made by the United States to any part of the continent.

South American interest

In 1908, Britain published Letters Patent claiming that sector of the Antarctic lying between 20W and 80W. From 1922 until the Second World War Discovery Investigations made a comprehensive study of the Southern Ocean. In 1942, Argentina and Chile each laid claim to almost identical sectors, including nearly all the British territory. In 1943 Britain despatched HMS *Carnarvon Castle* to obliterate all foreign marks of sovereignty and two permanent stations were set up, followed later by others. So began the work of the British Antarctic Survey which today is solely concerned with Antarctic science and remains the longest continuing Antarctic expedition ever mounted. Argentina and Chile have also maintained stations but political dispute was quieted by the signing of the Antarctic Treaty in 1961.

In the southern summer of 1946–7 the United States mounted Operation "High Jump", the largest and most ambitious Antarctic expedition so far, with 13 ships, including aircraft carriers for the aircraft, ice-breakers and a submarine commanded by Rear-Admiral Richard H. Cruzen. The whole operation was directed by Byrd, now an admiral. In all, 4,000 men took the field, including, for the first time, journalists and news photographers.

It operated in three groups, two in the Ross Dependency and neighbouring waters; the other westwards from Oates Land as far as Prinsesse Astrid Kyst. The principal aim of "High Jump" was large-scale photographic reconnaissance for political and military purposes—to give the United States a basis for future territorial claims and to familiarize men with polar conditions. In all 350,000 square miles of territory were discovered and 60 per cent of the coastline was photographed.

The year 1949 saw the beginning of the Norwegian–British–Swedish Expedition, the brainchild of Professor H. W. Ahlmann, a Swedish glaciologist. Under the direction of Dr H. U. Sverdrup, head of the Norwegian Polar Institute, and led by Captain John Giaever, also a Norwegian, it carried out a seismic traverse of the inland ice-sheet, the first of its kind.

In 1950, France finally returned to the Antarctic, where she established a permanent research station on Terre Adélie, Port Martin.

Operation "High Jump" was the prelude to an even larger onslaught on the Antarctic of a much more scientific character. It took place as part of the vast global programme, which was carried out during the course of the International Geophysical Year (IGY) between July 1, 1957, and December 31, 1958. This vast operation was first proposed by Dr Lloyd V. Berkner (a radio engineer with Byrd on his first Antarctic expedition) in 1950.

Berkner's original proposal for a Third Polar Year (the preceding ones had been 1882–3 and 1932–3) was broadened to comprehend simultaneous geophysical observations throughout the world and in the atmosphere. Eventually, during the IGY, 67 nations were involved. It was described as "the single most significant peaceful activity of mankind since the Renaissance and the Copernican Revolution".

In the Antarctic alone, 12 nations took the field—the United States, Russia, Argentina, Australia, Belgium, Chile, France, Great Britain, Japan, New Zealand, Norway and South Africa. Between them they undertook to set up about 60 stations either on the mainland or on offshore islands.

The two most massive efforts were made by the United States and Russia. The American operation, "Deep Freeze", was led by Byrd and in 1955–6 "Deep Freeze I" established seven stations between the Ross Sea and the Filchner Ice Shelf—the "Seven Cities" of Antarctica.

The construction of the South Pole Base began on November 19, 1956. Prefabricated buildings were parachuted down in sections to the advance party, who had flown in the same day; on November 26, a seven-ton tractor was dropped successfully. By March 1958 the seven bases were more or less ready—the cost, according to Rear Admiral Dufek, who had taken over command from Byrd, being 245 million dollars.

The Soviet Comprehensive Antarctic Expedition, the first Russian operation since Bellingshausen's voyage, sailed from the Baltic in November 1955 commanded by Mikhail Somov. It comprised the icebreaker *Ob*, the *Lena* and a refrigerator ship. There was also a complete air fleet of specially equipped machines commanded by Ivan Cherevishny.

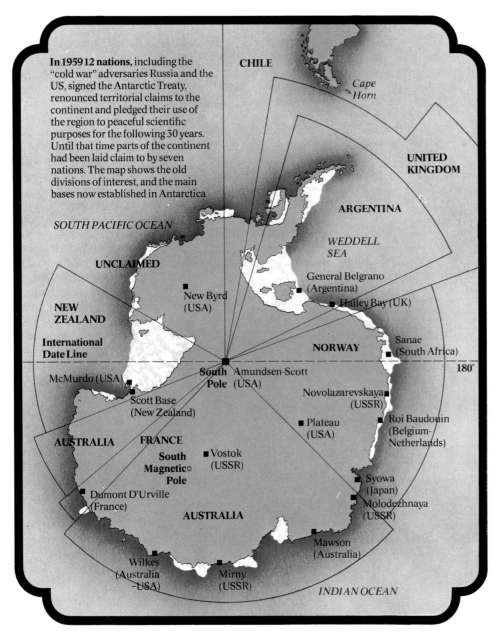

In 1959 12 nations, including the "cold war" adversaries Russia and the US, signed the Antarctic Treaty, renounced territorial claims to the continent and pledged their use of the region to peaceful scientific purposes for the following 30 years. Until that time parts of the continent had been laid claim to by seven nations. The map shows the old divisions of interest, and the main bases now established in Antarctica

CHILE

Cape Horn

UNITED KINGDOM

ARGENTINA

SOUTH PACIFIC OCEAN

WEDDELL SEA

UNCLAIMED

General Belgrano (Argentina)

New Byrd (USA)

Halley Bay (UK)

NEW ZEALAND

International Date Line

NORWAY

Sanae (South Africa)

180°

McMurdo (USA)

South Pole

Amundsen-Scott (USA)

Novolazarevskaya (USSR)

Scott Base (New Zealand)

Plateau (USA)

Roi Baudouin (Belgium-Netherlands)

AUSTRALIA

FRANCE

South Magnetic Pole

Vostok (USSR)

Syowa (Japan)

Dumont D'Urville (France)

AUSTRALIA

Molodezhnaya (USSR)

Mawson (Australia)

Wilkes (Australia -USA)

Mirny (USSR)

INDIAN OCEAN

Altogether the expedition numbered 425 men.

Early in January Somov's fleet reached the Knox Coast, where they erected a prefabricated town, Mirniy (Peace). The following year they built four more stations, from one of which, at Komsomolskaya, the Magnetic Pole was reached. In December 1958 they set up an observatory at the Pole of Relative Inaccessibility, in 82.06s, 54.58E—the place most distant from all the coasts of Antarctica.

Shackleton's plan to cross the continent from the Weddell to the Ross Sea by way of the South Pole was also fulfilled during the IGY, by the British Commonwealth Trans-Antarctic Expedition.

The plan involved two parties. One, under Dr Vivian Fuchs, left Shackleton Base on the Filchner Ice Shelf on November 24, 1957, using the latest tracked vehicles, Sno-cats and Weasels, as well as dog sledges. Soon it

became involved in a dangerous region of crevasses, where the ice-shelf met the continent, and dog teams had to be sent ahead to find a safe route for the tractors, which were clumsy and constantly getting stuck. Furthermore, Fuchs's party had to make a seismic and gravity traverse along the entire route to the Pole, in order to determine the thickness of the ice-sheet and the nature of the underlying land. This was extremely slow work as they moved south along the meridian of 30W, although well worth while, for it revealed depths of as much as 9,000 feet of ice, the peaks of mountains and a great valley under the Pole itself.

The other, New Zealand, party, under Sir Edmund Hillary, was to lay a chain of fuel and food depots from McMurdo Sound to the Polar Plateau. Using modified farm tractors, it made faster progress than Fuchs's, and

pushed on beyond Depot 700, 500 miles from the Pole, where the two parties were supposed to meet. Hillary reached the Pole on January 3, 1958.

Hillary then told Fuchs and the expedition organizers by radio that in his opinion Fuchs should abandon the crossing when he reached the Pole and be evacuated by air. This, not unnaturally, was ill-received by Fuchs, who in spite of the lateness of the season carried on to the South Pole, where he received a great welcome from the Americans at their station and also from Hillary himself.

The expedition finally reached McMurdo Sound on March 2, 1958, after a journey of 2,180 miles in 90 days.

One of the innumerable results of the IGY was the great increase in knowledge of the Antarctic ice-cap. It was found to have an average depth of 8,000 feet and an estimated volume of eight million cubic miles—about as much water as in the Atlantic Ocean.

Traverses carried out by American parties under the seismologist Charles R. Bentley and the glaciologist Vernon H. Anderson before and during the IGY, also revealed the nature of Greater and Lesser Antarctica. The former—roughly west of a line joining the Filchner Ice Shelf with the centre of the Ross Sea ice-front—was found to be composed of very old rocks; denuded of its ice, much of it would be above sea level.

Lesser Antarctica, to the east, which included the whole of Marie Byrd and Ellsworth lands, as well as the entire Antarctic Peninsula would, if iceless, emerge as an archipelago of islands in which a huge channel over 300 miles wide and 8,000 feet deep would link the Ross and the Bellingshausen seas. Another great trough was found to extend for 800 miles from the Ross Sea to the Sentinel Range in Ellsworth Land.

On the Americans' second traverse, between November 19, 1957, and February 28, 1958, they traced out a 1,200-mile quadrilateral from Byrd Station. They also found the track of an Adélie penguin at a height of 4,800 feet above the sea and more than 180 miles from it. The penguin was never found: where it was going and what it was living on is a mystery.

A long-term result of the IGY was the signing of the Antarctic Treaty at Washington in December 1959 by the 12 participatory nations and subsequently by Poland, Czechoslovakia, Denmark and the Netherlands. The treaty, which is to last for 30 years, stipulates that Antarctica should be used for peaceful purposes only. All political claims are frozen for the duration of the treaty. It can only be hoped that this spirit of peaceful co-existence and co-operation will endure beyond the allotted time span.

400 years of mountain conquest

For explorers, mountains are luxuries. Only when the hard work of drawing the maps has been done – when the passes have been found, the rivers charted, the forests penetrated – can men afford to lift their eyes to the peaks they have by-passed and savour the prospect of conquering them.

Most of the traditional motives for exploration – empire, trade, missionary zeal – are left behind by the mountaineer. There is no profit in climbing a mountain: only challenge; the overcoming of fear; the sheer satisfaction of proving oneself in conditions that test muscle, mind and nerve almost beyond endurance; and a hint of glory. Sometimes a mountain is climbed, as George Mallory said before his attempt on Everest, simply because it is there. The panorama below contains 20 of the world's greatest mountains, drawn to a common scale and juxtaposed. Four hundred years passed before they were all climbed; their conquerors ranged from Conquistadors, looking for sulphur on the summit of Popocatepetl, to a woman in an "Eskimo suit" borrowed from a museum. Some, like those on the Alps, provided generations of sportsmen with a playground; others, like those in the Himalayas, were objects of veneration, forbidden to foreigners until relatively recently. But each represents the insatiable desire of man to know his world and to master it. Each is, quite literally, a peak of achievement

Mount Everest 29,028ft, Nepal/Tibet. Chomolungma ("Goddess Mother of the World") was named after Sir George Everest, surveyor-general of India in the 1830s. Access was granted by the Dalai Lama in 1920, but it was not until suitable oxygen apparatus was developed that Everest's conquest became feasible. It fell to Hillary and Tenzing in 1953

K2 (Mount Godwin Austen), 28,251ft, India. The second mountain in the Karakoram range, hence "K2". In 1909 the Duke of Abruzzi surveyed a route to the peak, but K2 was not climbed until 1954, by three Italians: Desio, Lacedelli and Compagnoni

Kangchenjunga 28,208ft, Nepal/Sikkim. One of the most hazardous mountains in the world, its avalanches aggravated by monsoons. The Sikkim government asks climbers to stop before reaching the summit, to appease the gods: two British parties, Brown and Band, Streather and Hardie, got to within 20ft in 1955

Nanga Parbat 26,660ft, Pakistan. Known as "The Naked Mountain", Nanga Parbat was first climbed in 1953 by an Austro-German party led by Herrligkoffer

Annapurna range (Annapurna I 26,504ft), Nepal. Annapurna I was the first 26,000ft peak to be climbed, Annapurna III (24,858ft) the first high peak to be climbed (in 1970) by an all-woman team, from Japan

Communism Peak 24,590ft, USSR. The Pamirs, the range which includes Communism Peak, has some of the world's largest glaciers. The summit was reached by a Russian, Abalakov, in 1933

Lenin Peak 23,405ft, USSR. One of the most frequently climbed mountains in the world, first ascended by a Soviet-German team led by Rickmers in 1928

Aconcagua 22,834ft, Argentina. The highest mountain in the world outside those of the Himalayas. Zurbriggen reached the summit alone in 1897

Huascaran 22,205ft, Peru. In 1908 the northern summit was reached by Annie Peck, the first woman to climb a high peak. She wore the first anorak – an "Eskimo suit" borrowed from the Museum of Natural History

Chimborazo 20,561ft, Ecuador. Humboldt first attempted to climb this extinct volcano in 1802, when it was thought to be the world's highest mountain. It was not until 1880 that Edward Whymper reached the top

Mount McKinley 20,320ft, USA. The highest peak in North America, named after the US president assassinated in 1901. The Indians called it Denali, The Great One. It was climbed in 1910 by Anderson and Taylor

Mount Logan 19,850ft, Canada. The plateau summit was first reached in 1925 by MacCarthy and Lambert in an ascent beset with logistical problems

Mount Kilimanjaro 19,340ft, Tanzania. An extinct volcano, permanently covered with snow, and the highest mountain in Africa. The highest of the three craters, Kibo, was climbed by Meyer in 1889

Popocatepetl 17,887ft, Mexico. The volcano was first climbed in the 16th century by Conquistadors of Cortes who needed sulphur for gunpowder

3. Kangchenjunga

4. Nanga Parbat

5. Annapurna range (Annapurna I)

7. Lenin Peak

8. Aconcagua

10. Chimborazo

11. Mount McKinley

16. Vinson Massif

17. Mont Blanc

20. Mount Cook

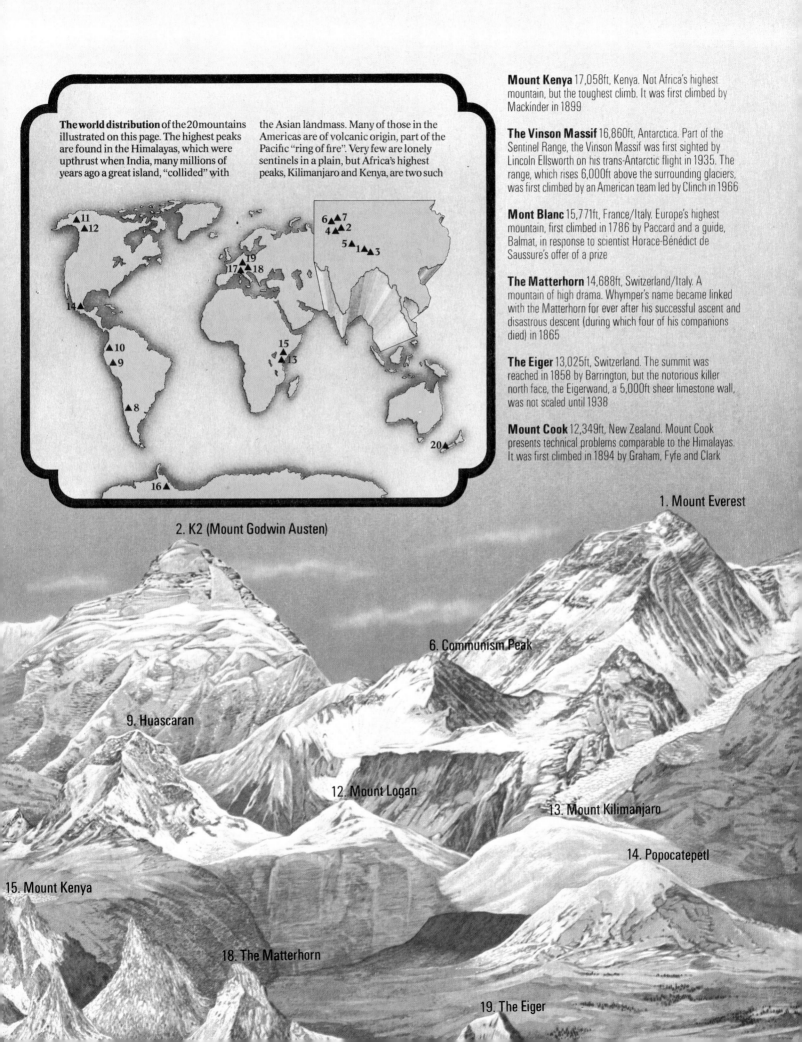

The world distribution of the 20 mountains illustrated on this page. The highest peaks are found in the Himalayas, which were upthrust when India, many millions of years ago a great island, "collided" with the Asian landmass. Many of those in the Americas are of volcanic origin, part of the Pacific "ring of fire". Very few are lonely sentinels in a plain, but Africa's highest peaks, Kilimanjaro and Kenya, are two such

Mount Kenya 17,058ft, Kenya. Not Africa's highest mountain, but the toughest climb. It was first climbed by Mackinder in 1899

The Vinson Massif 16,860ft, Antarctica. Part of the Sentinel Range, the Vinson Massif was first sighted by Lincoln Ellsworth on his trans-Antarctic flight in 1935. The range, which rises 6,000ft above the surrounding glaciers, was first climbed by an American team led by Clinch in 1966

Mont Blanc 15,771ft, France/Italy. Europe's highest mountain, first climbed in 1786 by Paccard and a guide, Balmat, in response to scientist Horace-Bénédict de Saussure's offer of a prize

The Matterhorn 14,688ft, Switzerland/Italy. A mountain of high drama. Whymper's name became linked with the Matterhorn for ever after his successful ascent and disastrous descent (during which four of his companions died) in 1865

The Eiger 13,025ft, Switzerland. The summit was reached in 1858 by Barrington, but the notorious killer north face, the Eigerwand, a 5,000ft sheer limestone wall, was not scaled until 1938

Mount Cook 12,349ft, New Zealand. Mount Cook presents technical problems comparable to the Himalayas. It was first climbed in 1894 by Graham, Fyfe and Clark

1. Mount Everest

2. K2 (Mount Godwin Austen)

6. Communism Peak

9. Huascaran

12. Mount Logan

13. Mount Kilimanjaro

14. Popocatepetl

15. Mount Kenya

18. The Matterhorn

19. The Eiger

The ocean depths

By the beginning of this century the world's great oceans, which cover 70 per cent of the surface of the globe, had barely been probed. Until the 18th century marine exploration was limited to the capacity of a man's lungs. Free divers, unaided by breathing apparatus, risked their lives seeking food and sunken treasure.

Various diving bells and chambers had been in use in Europe from Renaissance times, but the dual problems of lack of air and water pressure restricted their use to the shallows. Eventually, in 1865, a successful prototype of fine steel was built by a Frenchman, Ernest Bazin. The chamber was used—to a depth of 245 feet—to search for treasure at the bottom of Vigo Bay. In 1875, a Venetian engineer, Toselli, added a compressed air cylinder to Bazin's invention, and in the improved version a diver could work for up to 50 hours.

In 1926, Dr William Beebe, an American naturalist and explorer, announced the design of a diving chamber capable of reaching a depth of one mile. Another American, geologist and engineer Dr Otis Barton, concluded that a sphere would be the answer to the problem of water pressure: water presses with equal force all over the surface of a spherical chamber, so, if the construction is sound, no leaks occur.

The two men collaborated and the resulting submersible craft was christened a bathysphere. This vessel was 4 feet 9 inches in diameter and weighed 5,400 pounds. In 1930, Beebe and Barton made the first ever deep-sea descent, off Bermuda. Minor setbacks occurred on subsequent dives, but the breakthrough had been made. In 1934, the two Americans descended to 2,500 feet, to a zone of perpetual darkness.

After 1953 the bathysphere was superseded by the bathyscaphe, the invention of Swiss physicist Auguste Piccard. A keen high-altitude balloonist, Piccard hung his diving chamber from a submersible "balloon" filled with petrol and fitted with water compartments which, when flooded, would cause the device to submerge. On its first test Piccard's invention reached a depth of 10,300 feet.

In 1960, Jacques Piccard, son of the inventor, took the bathyscaphe *Trieste* to the Pacific to explore the Mariana Trench, which is nearly seven miles deep. Laden with 32,000 gallons of petrol, the *Trieste* floated downwards, landing five hours later on the sea-floor, "like a free balloon on a windless day, indifferent to the almost 200,000 tons of water pressing on the cabin from all sides".

Developed almost entirely for military use, submarines have only recently been put to work in the interests of science. Today they are used to observe fish for commercial purposes, and also play an important role in deep-sea rescue and engineering work.

Meanwhile, it was the world's first nuclear submarine, the USS *Nautilus*, that made the most exciting marine expedition of the century—the journey from the Pacific to the Atlantic beneath the North Pole. Designed by Hyman G. Rickover, a Polish-born American admiral, the *Nautilus* was quite unlike conventional submarines: powered by nuclear reactors, she could remain submerged indefinitely.

The vessel's first expedition in 1955—240 miles under the pack-ice between Greenland and Spitzbergen—proved disastrous. First the periscope was smashed. Then, nearing the 86th parallel, the gyro-compass began to swing wildly—a navigation hazard of high latitudes, where a submarine may travel round in circles, unable to find a course without surfacing.

At last, however, *Nautilus* set out for the Aleutian Islands in July 1958, reaching the pack-ice after a journey of more than 3,000 miles. At the Barrow Sea Valley the vessel submerged, and here underwater mountains were sighted, rising thousands of feet from the sea-bed.

Beneath the Pole

Gliding beneath the Pole of Relative Inaccessibility, the Arctic's geographical centre, the submarine finally arrived beneath the North Pole on August 3. Here it was found that the ice descended 25 feet below the surface, that the depth of water was 2,235 fathoms and its temperature 32.4° F.

This achievement was the culmination of a long tradition of marine exploration dating back to the 15th century, to the great voyages of exploration and discovery initiated by the Portuguese. Navigators on these early voyages learned the embryo science of oceanography as they went along, though often their deductions were far from accurate.

One of the early Italian oceanographers, Count Luigi Ferdinando Marsigli, was the first to think of using the naturalist's dredge to collect samples from the sea-bed. He also put forward a theory that currents are produced by variations in density of ocean waters.

In the 1770s, Captain James Cook made regular soundings to a depth of 200 fathoms, and kept records of winds, currents and water temperatures. Also, two of his crew, Johann Forster and his son, made the important discovery that surface and sub-surface temperatures differ. The Forsters were among the first to attempt deep-sea soundings and to collect blue mud from the Pacific, at a depth of 683 fathoms.

In the mid-19th century, an English naturalist, Edward Forbes, turned his attention to marine biology and probed the deep waters off the Isle of Man and in the Aegean Sea. Collecting samples from the sea-bed with a dredge, he found that marine animals become more abundant with depth. Forbes established eight "zones of abundance", but rashly declared that life ceases at 300 fathoms.

Another important contribution was that of Matthew Fontaine Maury, an American naval officer, who condensed a mass of data on winds and currents in his book *The Physical Geography of the Sea*. In 1854, he produced the first map of the North Atlantic to a depth of 4,000 fathoms.

Up to now, however, marine research had been haphazard, and it was not until the first transatlantic telegraph line was laid—it opened in 1866—that it became obvious how much there was still to be done. At this time the English set to work investigating the seas to the north and west of the British Isles. Voyages by the survey vessels *Porcupine* and *Lightning* in 1868 and 1869 proved so fruitful that it was decided to make a systematic exploration across the world. Soon a voyage was planned to investigate "the conditions of the Deep Sea throughout the Great Oceanic Basins".

The British Admiralty provided the *Challenger*, a 226-ft naval steam and sailing vessel, converted to undertake a voyage lasting three and a half years and covering 68,890 nautical miles. With many leading civilian scientists on board, the expedition set sail in December 1872.

Throughout the voyage *Challenger*'s officers were in charge of making observations and soundings of the sea-bed at 360 deep-sea stations. Temperatures were recorded at various depths and currents and atmospheric and meteorological conditions measured and observed. In mid-February 1873 came one of the most exciting finds: a number of blackened, pebble-like objects from a depth of 1,500 fathoms—nodules of manganese.

After long months in the Atlantic, the Indian Ocean and the Pacific, *Challenger* came home in May 1876, bearing "a great freight of facts", as well as 715 new genera and 4,417 species of living organisms. The results of the voyage were published in an official 50-volume report.

The exercise was repeated in 1950, when *Challenger II* set out on a two-year voyage, also covering the Atlantic, Indian and Pacific oceans as well as the Mediterranean. Using new echo-sounding techniques which bounce ultrasonic impulses from the sea-floor they made accurate soundings at far more frequent intervals than had been possible in the 1870s.

The *Challenger II* expedition discovered the mid-Atlantic Ridge, a rift valley scoring the sea-bed for more than 10,000 miles, and the Mariana Trench, one of the deepest spots

A voyage as yet unequalled in its scope or diligence – or in its rewards of scientific knowledge – was that of HMS "Challenger" (above) a converted sail and steam warship of 2,306 tons which, between December 1872 and May 1876, made a voyage of nearly 70,000 miles around the world. The "Challenger" expedition was mounted by the Royal Society with the co-operation of the Admiralty and in its three-and-a-half year journey unveiled for the first time many hidden facts of the ocean depths and floor. Before the ship's departure, its gun decks and many of its cabins were stripped and converted into laboratories (below). The crew, commanded by Captain George Nares, was joined by a team of eminent scientists led by the eminent Scottish naturalist, Charles Wyville Thomson and including the Canadian oceanographer John Murray and the naturalist J. Buchanan. Sailing from Portsmouth, "Challenger's" course took it down through the Atlantic, into the Indian Ocean and on to the Pacific, on the way becoming the first steamship to cross the Antarctic Circle. Hundreds of observations and deep soundings were made during the course of the journey, the deepest in what is now known as the Challenger Trench, off the Marianas Islands in the northern Pacific – 26,850 feet. Throughout the voyage, records were kept of oceanic temperatures, currents and the depths and the contours of the seabeds over which the "Challenger" passed. Samples of life in the ocean depths were dredged, examined and classified and the "Challenger" arrived home "with a great freight of facts", including 715 new genera and 4,417 species. Since that time, more knowledge has been gained but nothing that alters to any degree what Thomson and his men discovered on a voyage that was greater in scope and thoroughness than anything before or since. Charles Thomson was knighted and on his return produced a two-volume preliminary account of the voyage. The full report, which took nearly 20 years to compile in its entirety, made up a total of 50 volumes. It marked the first substantial advance in real knowledge of the oceanic depths and was the foundation of the modern science of oceanography.

in the western Pacific. But this was to be the last great voyage of oceanic exploration. Nowadays information is culled from short cruises with single rather than multiple objectives, from deep-diving vessels or research ships.

Meanwhile, the most tenacious figure of all in the continuing struggle for mastery over the sea is the lone diver. As early as 1838, divers wearing armoured diving suits were employed on coastal salvage and demolition, regularly braving depths of more than 150 feet.

By 1865, the first successful Scuba (self-contained underwater breathing apparatus) was in commercial production and divers could reach even greater depths. But it was not until 1942 that Jacques Yves-Cousteau, a French naval officer, and engineer Emile Gagnan developed the aqualung—a device which ushered in a new era in underwater exploration. Able to descend safely to a depth of 200 feet, unhampered by weighted suits and air cables, aqualung divers could now study and film undersea plant and animal life.

There were commercial applications, too. In the 1950s an American geologist used an aqualung to search for deposits of oil off the California coast. Elsewhere, divers discovered many new mineral deposits—diamonds, tin, magnetic iron ore and phosphorites.

Another important sphere of diving operations is underwater archaeology, a speciality restricted to the shallows until World War II. The arrival of the aqualung, however, provided enormous impetus to the search for

Undersea armour: a modern diving suit which, despite bulk gives its wearer great freedom of movement

long-submerged civilizations. In 1959, aqualung divers recovered priceless treasures from the site of Chichen Itza, an important Mayan city off the coast of Yucatán in Mexico. At about the same time, marine archaeologists were investigating the sunken Greek port of Apollonia, which once served the thriving city of Cyrenia. Many ancient treasures were recovered from the sea in the two-year excavations. Also in 1959, an American archaeologist surveyed the floor of the Mediterranean and discovered 35 ancient wrecks, including a Bronze Age ship.

One of the worst hazards plaguing all divers is decompression sickness—"the bends". Rapid decompression after a deep dive causes gases dissolved in the air supply to diffuse in the blood and tissues. The effect is at best agonizing pain, at worst fatal embolism. This problem has prompted experiments with various combinations of gases, and in 1957 an American naval research officer, George Bond, made the valuable discovery that if a helium-oxygen mixture is used for up to 24 hours, the body becomes saturated with it. Therefore, the decompression period for men spending weeks underwater is no more than for a 24-hour dive.

The previous year Edwin Link, the American who invented flight training simulators and who was also a marine archaeologist, had designed a "submersible decompression chamber". This was an aluminium diving bell from which a diver could make free excursions on to the sea-bed, returning at intervals for decompression. Once the results of Bond's experiments became known, the Belgian diver Robert Sténuit made the first test of the SDC, living for 24 hours in the chamber with frequent sorties outside.

In 1962, Cousteau launched the first of his Conshelf projects with an exercise in which two men lived and worked for a week in a small chamber 33 feet down in the Mediterranean. Conshelf Two, staged a year later in the Red Sea, was more ambitious; here, again at a depth of 33 feet, five men occupied a complex underwater settlement, equipped with full living and working facilities, for a month.

Almost a century after the publication of *Twenty Thousand Leagues Under the Sea*, the novel in which Jules Verne peopled the ocean with human colonists, deep-sea trials have shown that men can indeed live and work in the ocean depths. Pioneers such as Cousteau see the conquest of the deep as a challenge not to be ignored. Describing the third Conshelf project, launched in 1965, Cousteau remarked: "Thus began a test of human ingenuity and adaptability . . . that I am convinced will lead man to greater rewards than the space race."

The last frontier

MORE THAN A CENTURY ago, Jules Verne was one of the most prominent writers to put his imagination to work to project mankind into outer space. In *From the Earth to the Moon*, published in 1865, he made use of the reaction principle—the principle by which a rocket works—to fire his characters into space. Rockets had already been in military use in Europe since the 15th century. Now Verne dreamed up an enormous aluminium cannon to hurl his three-man lunar capsule on its way. From launch to splashdown, Verne's space odyssey was tracked by a reflecting telescope—just as, a century later, the NASA space-shots were tracked by the 200-inch telescope at Palomar.

While Verne's books were selling throughout the world, various scientific discoveries laid the groundwork for real-life space travel. In these early days the most significant contribution was that made by Konstantin Eduardovich Tsiolkovsky, who was born near Moscow in 1857. A devotee of Jules Verne, he dreamed of putting a satellite into orbit round the Earth. Grasping the reaction principle early on, he realized that a rocket would work as well in a vacuum—in space—as inside the Earth's atmosphere.

Twenty years before the first viable aircraft was built, he had produced a mathematical elaboration of the rocket principle—his "basic formula"—which is still applied. He saw the multi-stage rocket as the only solution to the problem of achieving the necessary speeds with existing types of energy. He was also the first to envisage using a series of booster rockets to be jettisoned one by one as their fuel supply ran out and the first to think of using liquid fuel in rockets.

In 1926, an American physicist, Robert Hutchings Goddard, who had worked on rocket weaponry during World War I, launched the world's first liquid-fuel rocket. A bizarre device ten feet long, it had separate tanks for liquid oxygen and petrol and a combustion chamber in which the fuels reacted to produce the hot gas propellant. It rose 184 feet at a speed of 64 mph. The flight lasted for two and a half seconds.

Already another physicist, Hermann Oberth, had put up a scheme for a long-range, liquid-fuel rocket to the German authorities during World War I. But, while this idea was rejected, Oberth sparked off a space fever epidemic during the interwar years with his *The Rocket into Interplanetary Space*. Published in 1923, the treatise explained how a rocket could be sent into space, or a satellite into orbit.

But it was not until October 3, 1942, that the first rocket was fired into space. The launch site was Peenemünde, the small German rocket base on the Baltic, and this

Fictitious forerunner of modern spacecraft, Jules Verne's three-man lunar capsule, launched from an aluminium cannon, in "From the Earth to the Moon".

rocket, the A4, was the forerunner of the notorious V2, the "Vengeance weapon 2" of World War II. Ironically, it was these inventions that paved the way for the exploration of outer space. At the end of World War II the Peenemünde rocket team became dispersed: some, like Werner von Braun, went to the United States, and some went to work in the Soviet Union, and so the space race began almost by chance.

First in space

As the Cold War intensified, both countries developed sophisticated rockets capable of controlled flight. Now, for the first time, the upper atmosphere could be probed. Wind speeds were measured; a hurricane was photographed from above; high-level photographs were taken of the Earth, demonstrating its curvature; and animals mutely preceded man on guinea-pig flights into space. On October 4, 1957, the Russians took the lead with the launching of the world's first satellite, the 20-inch diameter Sputnik 1.

Before the next major breakthrough—putting a man into space—the scientists had to produce even larger rockets. Acceleration had to be closely calculated if men were not to be crushed at take-off. Re-entry was a formidable problem, too, with the risk of space-craft overheating from the friction set up by their speed. Other hazards included damage by meteors and possibly solar radiation.

Even so, less than four years after the launch of Sputnik 1, the Russians achieved yet another space first: on April 12, 1961,

Apollo 11 astronaut investigating "solar wind"—low-energy particles from the Sun—during the first Moon landing in July 1969.

Yuri Gagarin became the first man in space, orbiting the Earth in the cylindrical Vostok 1. It took only weeks for the Americans to catch up: on May 5 Commander Alan Shepard made the first American space solo.

Another four years went by before the first space walk—by Lieutenant-Colonel Alexei Leonov on March 18, 1965. Later that year the Americans made their first space walk, and the first space rendezvous took place—between the American Gemini 6 and 7 space-craft, which orbited the world together.

The first attempt at docking two space-craft came in March 1966, when the Americans put the Agena 8 target satellite into orbit and astronauts Neil Armstrong and David Scott were blasted up shortly afterwards in Gemini 8. Soon after docking, the two space-craft went into an uncontrollable spin when one of the thrusters jammed. Emergency control was used to bring the astronauts back to Earth. In October 1967, the first automatic docking—part of the Russian Cosmos programme—took place.

Meanwhile, lunar reconnaissance was well advanced. From 1958 onwards, 47 probes—some unsuccessful—were sent to the Moon. As early as October 1959, the Russian probe Luna 3 travelled around the Moon and began transmitting photographs of its dark side. Another Russian probe, Luna 9, made the first soft landing in January 1966, and two months later Luna 10, the first Moon satellite, entered into orbit.

Now the Americans concentrated their efforts on putting the first man on the Moon.

Despite the tragic loss by fire of the three-man crew of Apollo 1 in 1967, the Apollo programme forged ahead. Within two years, the Apollo 11 mission was on its way and on July 21, 1969, Neil Armstrong became the first man to set foot on the moon.

Not surprisingly (since the lunar surface had already been minutely probed), Armstrong found no men on the Moon. Now that the Moon has yielded up many of its secrets, the question remains; is there any form of life like ours among the planets?

Radio-telescopes have located many remote objects in the universe—distant galaxies, inter-stellar hydrogen gas, pulsating stars, and traces of the explosions of far-off stars in the distant past. Their sensitive antennae are constantly receiving the signals that find their way here from outer space, and astronomers are on the alert for any regular impulses that may emanate from another civilization.

It was the development of radar during World War II which made it possible for us to send out signals strong enough to be detected by beings on another planet searching for signs of life outside their own solar system. Today, signals are regularly transmitted into the Galaxy. However, the likelihood of making contact with another civilization is remote because distances in space are so vast. The common unit of measurement is the distance light will travel in one year—5,880,000,000 miles. The nearest star, Alpha Centauri, is four light-years away, and our strongest radio waves reach about 100 light-years out into the Galaxy. Signals sent from Earth would take anything from four years to a century in transmission.

Clearly, therefore, signals must be restricted to stars relatively near at hand—those of similar age and intensity to our Sun, which might conceivably have a planetary system comparable to ours. It is thought there could be intelligent life forms on 50 planets.

Undaunted, the Americans sent their own messenger to outer space in March 1972, the Pioneer 10 space probe, which was programmed to travel past Jupiter, and, after relaying back information about that remote planet, to set off beyond the solar system—the first interplanetary space-craft to carry a message from Earth to such alien civilizations as may exist—a process which could last up to 100 million years. Although, despite the technological progress of the past 200 years, man is still largely imprisoned within his own planet, he can send his technology ahead of him, as a scout and as a herald of his existence.

Ready for blast-off, the Saturn rocket of Apollo 13, one of the few missions when near disaster occurred. The service module exploded, but by skilful improvisation the lunar module was used to bring the astronauts safely back to its splashdown in the Pacific.

Men of the world: Asia

On this and the following five pages are listed, continent by continent and with key maps, more than 600 men whose achievements, over a span of 4,000 years, defined the scale and detail of the world in which we live. The key (below) is a list of the abbreviations which have been used in this gazetteer for the nationalities of the explorers and for the physical features—mountains, islands, sounds, etc.—that are mentioned. The letter key following each entry, such as **Fb**, **Fc**, **Ph**, **Lk**, used in conjunction with the continental map, gives a bearing to the penetration of the continent and places visited by the individual explorers

To the ancients of the West, Asia was what is now Asia Minor. The huge continent itself is between 17 and 18 million square miles in extent and is about one-third of the land surface of the Earth. It reaches from Europe to the Pacific Ocean and from above the Arctic Circle to the Equator

Amer	=	American	It	=	Italian	E	=	East
Aus	=	Austrian	Jap	=	Japanese	Est	=	Estuary
Austral	=	Australian	Mex	=	Mexican	G	=	Gulf
Belg	=	Belgian	Norw	=	Norwegian	I	=	Island
Br	=	British	Phoen	=	Phoenician	Is	=	Islands
Can	=	Canadian	Port	=	Portuguese	Isth	=	Isthmus
Chin	=	Chinese	Pruss	=	Prussian	L	=	Lake
Da	=	Danish	Rom	=	Roman	Mt	=	Mountain
Eng	=	English	Russ	=	Russian	Mts	=	Mountains
Flem	=	Flemish	Scot	=	Scottish	N	=	North
Flor	=	Florentine	Sp	=	Spanish	Pen	=	Peninsula
Fr	=	French	Sw	=	Swedish	Pt	=	Point
Gen	=	Genoese	Ven	=	Venetian	R	=	River
Ger	=	German	Vik	=	Viking	S	=	South
Gk	=	Greek	Arch	=	Archipelago	Sd	=	Sound
Hung	=	Hungarian	B	=	Bay	Str	=	Strait
Ice	=	Icelandic	C	=	Cape	W	=	West·
Ind	=	Indian	Ch	=	Channel	Cent	=	Central
Ir	=	Irish					

1 **Scylax** (Gk) Kabul R, Indus R, G of Oman, Red Sea 6th cent. BC Kh, Lh, Me, La-Ma
2 **Alexander the Great** (Gk) Hindu Kush 329 BC; Indus R 327–6 BC Kh, Lh
3 **Hephaestion** (Gk) Khyber Pass 326 BC Kh
4 **Megasthenes** (Ionian) Patna, Indo-Gangetic Plain 302 BC Mk, Mh-k
5 **Chang Chi'en** (Chin) Fergana c.138 BC; Peshawar c.127 BC Ih, Kh
6 **Aelius Gallius** (Rom) Red Sea coast to Arabia Felix 25 BC Ka-la-Ma-Nb
7 **Hippalus** (Gk) Indus R c.AD 14 Lh
8 **Fa-Hsien** (Chin) Ho't'ien c.AD 400; Ceylon c.AD 413 Jj, Qj
9 **Hsuan-tsang** (Chin) Barköl Tagh Mts, Tien Shan Mts, Tashkent, Samarkand, Hindu Kush, Assam, Ceylon, Gujarat AD 629–645 Ik, Ji-j, Ig, Ih, Kh, Ml, Qj, Nh
10 **Soleiman** (Arab) Maldive Is, Ceylon, Malacca, Andaman Is, Canton c.AD 850 Rg, Qi, Rn, Pl, Mq
11 **Rurik** (Vik) Novgorod, Dnieper R AD 862 Fb, Fc
12 **Al Mas'udi** (Arab) Aral Sea 10th cent. If
13 **John de Carpini** (It) Dnieper R,

Don R, Volga R, L Baykal, Karakoram Mts 1245–7 Fc, Gd, Gd, Gm, Ki
14 **William of Rubruck** (Flem) Caspian Sea, Kazakhstan, Karakoram Mts 1253 He-le, Hf-i, Ki
15 **Niccolò** and **Maffeo Polo** (Ven) Bukhara, Samarkand, Hwang Ho R, Peking 1262–9 Ig, Ih, Jp, Ip
16 **Marco Polo** (Ven) Cent Asia, Gobi Desert, China, Burma, E Indies, Ceylon 1271–95 Jj, In, Jn, Nm, Tp, Qj
17 **John of Monte Corvino** (It) Tabriz to Peking 1291 Jd-Ip
18 **Odoric of Pordenone** (It) Constantinople, India, E Indies, Canton, Peking, Lhasa 1318–30 Ha, Pi, Rq, Mq, Ip, Ll
19 **Ibn-Battuta** (Arab) Iraq, Saudi Arabia 1325–30; Hindu Kush, Indus R 1333; Maldive Is, Ceylon 1344; Sumatra, Canton 1345 Kc, Lb-c, Kh, Lh, Rg, Qi, Sn, Mp
20 **Cheng-Ho** (Chin) Indo-China, E Indies, Canton 1407–9 Oo, Sn, Ph, On, Po
21 **Hou-Hsien, Cheng-Ho** (Chin) Maldive Is, E Indies, Ryukyu Is 1417–19 Rg, Tp, Kr
22 **Vasco da Gama** (Port) Calicut, Malabar coast of India 1498 Ph

23 **Lodovico di Varthema** (It) Mecca, Arabia Felix, Persia, India 1502–7 Ma, Nb, Ke, Mi
24 **Lourenço de Almeida** (Port) Ceylon, Maldive Is 1505 Qi, Rq
25 **Ferdinand Magellan** (Port) Malay Arch 1511–12; Moluccas 1521 Qn, Pt
26 **Francisco Serrão** (Port) E Indies 1513 Ss
27 **Andrea Corsali, Giovanni da Empoli** (It) Canton 1514 Mq
28 **Affonso d'Albuquerque** (Port) Malacca, Hormuz 1515 Ru, Le
29 **Francisco Zeimoto, Antonio da Mota, Antonio Peixoto** (Port) Japan 1542 Is-Ht
30 **Richard Chancellor** (Eng) Moscow 1553 Fc
31 **Anthony Jenkinson** (Eng) Moscow, Kazan, Volga R basin, Astrakhan, Bukhara 1557–8; Qazvin 1561–2 Fc, Ff, Gd, Hd, Ig, Jd
32 **Matteo Ricci** (It) Goa, Canton, Nanking, Peking 1578–1601 Oh, Mp, Kq, Ip
33 **Yermak Timofeiev** (Russ) Ural Mts, Tobolsk 1579 Eg, Fg
34 **John Newberry** (Eng) Euphrates R 1581 Kc
35 **Benedict de Goes** (Sp) Lahore, Hindu Kush, Pamirs, Tien Shan Mts, Gobi Desert, Chia-yü, Ku-an 1603–5 Kh, Kh, Ki, Ji-j, In, Ko, Ip
36 **John Jourdain** (Eng) Yemen, Indo-Gangetic Plain 1608; E Indies 1612 Nc, Mh-k, Qs
37 **Antonio de Andrada** (Sp) Srinagar, Tibet 1624–6 Ki, Kk
38 **João Cabral, Estevão Cacella** (Port) Cooch Behar, Shigatse 1626–8 Mk, Lk
39 **João Cabral** (Port) Kathmandu, Ganges R 1631 Lj, Mk
40 **Francisco Azevado** (Port) Ladakh 1631–2 Ki
41 **Vasili Poyarkov** (Russ) Aldan R, Amur R, Stanovoy Khrebet, Sea of Okhotsk 1643 Do, Fo, Eo, Er
42 **Buldakov** (Russ) Kolyma R 1647 Cp
43 **Semyon Ivanovic Dezhnev** (Russ) Chukchi Pen, Siberia, Kolyma R, Lena R, Bering Str 1648 As, Cp, Cp, Cm, At
44 **Khabarov** (Russ) Olekma R, Amur R c.1652 Em, Fo
45 **Onufrei Stepanov** (Russ) L Baykal, Shilka, Amur R 1652 Gm, Gn, Fo
46 **John Grueber** (Aus), **Albert d'Orville** (Belg) L Koko Nor, Tsaidam, Lhasa, Kathmandu, Agra 1661–2 Jn, Jm, Ll, Lj, Nj
47 **Stenka Razin** (Russ) Volga R, Astrakhan 1668 Gd, Hd
48 **Nicolas Spafarik** (Gk) Tien Shan Mts, Peking 1676 Jk, Ip
49 **Vladimir Atlassov** (Russ) Kamchatka Pen 1696–9 Ds
50 **Ippolito Desideri** (It), **Manuel Freyre** (Port) Kashmir, Chang Tang Desert, Mt Kailas 1714–15; Lhasa 1716 Ki, Lj, Lj, Ll
51 **Philip Strahlenberg** (Swiss), **Daniel Messerschmidt** (Pruss) Ob R, Yenesei R 1720–7 Ei, Ej
52 **Samuel van de Putte** (Dutch) Peking 1720 Ip
53 **Vitus Bering** (Da) St Lawrence Is, Bering Str 1728; Bering I 1741 At, As, Dt
54 **Laptev** (Russ) Bol'shoy Baranov 1740 Bp
55 **Semyon Ivanovich Chelyuskin** (Russ) Novaya Zemlya, Taimyr Pen 1742; C Chelyuskin c.1743 Ch, Cj, Bk
56 **Carsten Niebuhr** (Ger) Mt Sinai, Al Luhayyah, San'a, Bombay, Persepolis 1762–7 Ja, Nb, Nb, Mh, Kd
57 **George Bogle** (Scot) Shigatse 1774; Tashilhumpo 1775 Lk, Lk
58 **Samuel Turner** (Eng) Shigatse 1783 Lk
59 **Jean La Pérouse** (Fr) Macao, Philippines, Korean Str, Sea of Japan, G of Tartary, Sakhalin,

Kamchatka 1785 Mp, Nr, Jr, Hs, Fr, Fr, Ds
60 **Harford Jones Brydges** (Eng) Bushire, Isfahan, Qazvin, Tabriz 1807–11 Ld, Jd, Jd, Jd
61 **Ulrich Jaspar Seetzen** (Ger) Mecca, Medina 1809 Ma, La
62 **Henry Pottinger, Charles Christie** (Eng) Baluchistan, Nushki, Isfahan 1810 Lf, Lf, Ld
63 **Thomas Manning** (Eng) Lhasa 1811 Ll
64 **William Moorcroft, Hyder Jung Hearsey** (Eng) Ramganga R, Niti Pass, L Manasarowar 1812 Li, Kj, Lj
65 **Johann Ludwig Burckhardt** (Swiss) Palmyra, Petra, Hejaz 1814–15 Ib, Ja, Ma
66 **George Sadlier** (Br) Arabia 1819 Lb
67 **Alexander von Humboldt** (Ger) Moscow, Molotov (Perm), Tobolsk, Ob R, Altai Mts, Volga R, Don R 1829 Fc, Eh, Fh, Ei, Hk, Gd, Gd
68 **Arthur Connolly** (Eng) Tabriz, Herat 1830; Khiva 1840; Bukhara 1841 Jd, Kg, If, Ig
69 **Evariste Regis Huc, Joseph Gabet** (Fr) Inner Mongolia, Ordos Desert, Hwang Ho R, L Koko Nor, Yangtse R, Lhasa, Mekong 1844–6 Ip, Io, Jp, Jn, Kp, Ll, Oo
70 **Petr Semenov** (Russ) Dzungaria, Tien Shan Mts, Khan Tengri 1846–57 Ik, Ji-j, Ii
71 **Richard Burton** (Eng) Mecca 1853 Ma
72 **Adolf, Hermann** and **Robert von Schlagintweit** (Ger) Karakoram Mts, Kun Lun Mts 1856 Ki, Kj
73 **Nicolas de Khanuikov** (Russ) Lut Desert 1858 Ke
74 **Ferdinand von Richthofen** (Ger) Ceylon, Japan, China 1860–72 Qj, Ht, Ln
75 **William Palgrave** (Eng) Ma'an, An-Nafud Desert, Al Qatif 1862 Jb, Kb, Lc
76 **Arminius Vambery** (Hung) Khiva, Oxus R, Samarkand, Teheran 1863–4 If, Jg, Jg, Jd
77 **Mani Singh** ("GM") (Tibetan) Gartok 1865–7 Kj
78 **Nain Singh** (Tibetan) Tashilhumpo, Lhasa 1865–6; L Manasarowar 1867 Lk, Ll, Lj
79 **Nikolai Przewalski** (Russ) Kyakhta, Ulan Bator, Gobi Desert, Peking, Hwang Ho R, L Koko Nor 1870–2; Astin Tagh Mts 1876–7; Przevalsk 1888 Gm, Hm, In, Ip, Jp, Jn, Jl, Ji
80 **Hari Ram** ("MH") (Ind) Darjeeling, circuit Everest group of mts 1871 Lk, Lk
81 **Ney Elias** (Eng) Hovd, Biysk, Nijni Novgorod (Gorki) 1872–3 Hk, Gi, Ff
82 **Charles Montagu Doughty** (Eng) Saudi Arabia 1876–8 Kb-Lb
83 **Kishen Singh** ("AK") (Ind) Darjeeling, Lhasa 1878; Szechwan 1882 Ml, Ll, Lm
84 **Wilfrid Scawen Blunt** (Eng) Saudi Arabia 1879 Lb-c
85 **Sarat Chandra Das** (Bengali) N Sikkim, Lhasa 1879–82 Lk, Ll
86 **Kinthup** ("KP") (Sikkimese) Tsangpo R, 1879–84 Lk
87 **Francis Edward Young-husband** (Eng) Manchuria 1886; China 1887; Mandalay 1888; Rawalpindi, Yarkand 1889; Kunar Valley, Oxus R 1892–4; Lhasa 1904 Gq, Hn-Ho, Nm, Kh, Ji, Kh, Ml, Ll
88 **Sven Anders Hedin** (Sw) Bukhara, Samarkand, Tien Shan Mts 1891; Tashkent, Kashgar, Pamirs, Khotan, Gobi Desert 1894–7 Ig, Jg, Ji, Ih, Ij, Ki, Jj, Ji
89 **Percy Sykes** (Eng) Cent Persia 1893–4; S Persia 1897–1901; Baghdad, Hindu Kush 1906–10 Ke, Le, Jc, Kh
90 **Leo Hirsch** (Ger) Wadi Hadhramaut 1893 Nb-c

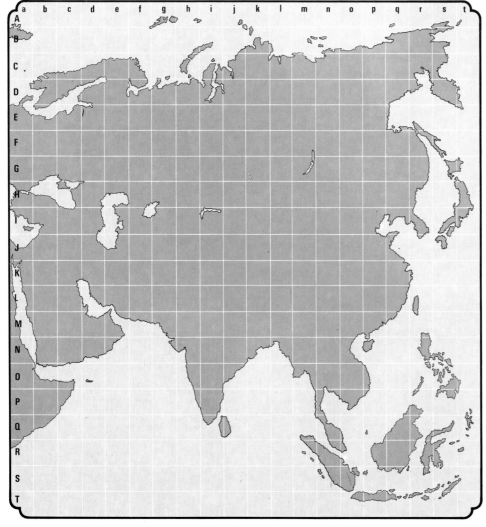

North America

The Trans-Siberian Railway crosses steppe, inhospitable taiga and tundra to link Europe with the Pacific Ocean

The rolling plains of North America's Middle West were once virgin grassland and are now, thanks to farm mechanization, the granary of the world

The Americas and nearby islands cover an area of more than 16 million square miles. North and South America are more or less evenly balanced in area, each covering something between six and seven million square miles. Middle America, including the islands of the Caribbean, accounts for the remainder. The exploration and rapid settlement of the northern part of the Americas owes almost everything to its temperate climate between the Tropic of Cancer and the Arctic

South America

Once separated from, now linked with, the northern continent, South America is two-thirds tropical, with the tropical area largely clad in primeval rain-forest—penetrated by adventurers but still one of the world's great unknown regions. Settlement is mainly coastal except in the pampas

1 Amerigo Vespucci (Flor) Campeche Bay, Amazon est 1497 Ba, Dk
2 Christopher Columbus (Gen) Coast of Venezuela 1498 Ag
3 Amerigo Vespucci (Flor) Coast of Brazil (to 5S) 1499 Eo-Fo
4 Alonzo de Ojeda (Sp) G of Urabá, G of Paria to G of Cumana 1499 Bb, Af-g
5 Amerigo Vespucci (Flor), **Alonzo de Ojeda** (Sp) G of Maracaibo, coasts of Venezuela and Brazil 1499 Ad-Bd, Bh, Dl
6 Pedro Alvares Cabral (Port) Coast of Brazil 1500 Hn
7 Vincente Yáñez Pinzón (Sp) Coast of Brazil 1500 Dl-El
8 Amerigo Vespucci (Flor) Rio de Janeiro, Patagonia 1501–2 Jl, Og
9 Vasco Núñez de Balboa, Martín Fernández de Encisco (Sp) Panama isth 1510 Ba
10 Juan Díaz de Solís (Sp) Rio de la Plata est 1515 Mh
11 Hernando de Soto (Sp) Darien 1519 Ba
12 Ferdinand Magellan (Port) Magellan Str 1520 Ne
13 Sebastian Cabot (Ven) Recife 1526 ; Rio de la Plata, Paraná R, Paraguay R 1527–8 Fo, Mh, Kg, Ig
14 Francisco Pizarro, Diego de Almagro (Sp) Tumbes 1527 ;
Cuzco 1533 ; Lima 1535 Ea-Fa, Hc-d, Hd, Hb
15 Diego Garcia (Port), **Sebastian Cabot** (Ven) Pilcomayo R 1528 Kg-Jf
16 Sebastián de Belalcázar (Sp) Cauca R, Popayán, Cali, Magdalena R valley 1536 Cc, Db, Db, Bc
17 Gonzalo Jiménez de Quesada (Sp) Magdalena R, Guaviare R 1536–7 Bc, Dd
18 Diego de Almagro (Sp) Cuzco, Andes, Concepción 1537 Hc, Hd, Nd
19 Francisco de Orellana, Gonzalo Pizarro (Sp) Napo R, Amazon R to Belém (Para) 1541–2 Ec, Ec-Dk
20 Pedro de Valdivia (Sp) Santiago 1541 Me
21 Alvar Núñez Cabeza de Vaca (Sp) Iguaçú R, Paraná R, Asunción 1542 Ki, Kh, Lh
22 Gonzalo Jiménez de Quesada (Sp) Orinoco R 1569–71 Dd
23 Francis Drake (Eng) Coast of Brazil, Magellan Str, Chile and Peru 1577–8 Lj, Rf-e, Re-Hb
24 Walter Raleigh (Eng) Caroní R 1595 Cg
25 Willem Cornelisz Schouten, Jacob Le Maire (Dutch) Le Maire Str, Desolation I 1616 Sg, Re
26 Pedro Teixeira (Sp) Amazon R, Napo R, Quito 1637–8 Ei, Ec, Eb
27 Matías Abad (Sp) Colombia 1648 Cc

28 Francisco Figueroa, Domingo Fernández (Sp) Marañón R, Ucayali R, Huallaga R 1658 Fc, Gc, Gb
29 Samuel Fritz (Bohemian) Huallaga R, Amazon R to Belém (Pará) 1691–2 Gb, Ec-Dk
30 Amadée François Frézier (Fr) Santa Caterina, Tierra del Fuego 1712 Kj-k, Rf-Sf
31 Charles Marie de la Condamine (Fr) Esmeraldas R, Mt Chimborazo, Marañón R, Amazon R 1735–45 Da, Ea, Fc, Fe, Ef
32 Jorge Juan y Santacilia, Antonio de Ulloa (Sp) G of Guayaquil, Quito 1736 Ea, Eb
33 Jean Godin des Odonais (Fr) Quito 1742–9 ; Amazon R 1749 ; Cayenne 1749–73 Ef, Ci-j
34 João de Sousa de Azevado (Port) Tapajós R, Amazon R, Guaporé R, Arinos R 1749 Fh, Ei, Hg, Gh
35 José Celestino Mutis (Sp) Bogotá and environs 1761–1808 Cc
36 John Byron (Eng) Coast of Brazil, Falkland Is 1764–5 Jl, Rg-h
37 James Cook (Eng) Coast of Brazil, Tierra del Fuego 1769 Jl, Rf-Sf
38 Isabel Godin des Odonais (Sp) Canelos, Pastaza R, Marañón R,
Amazon R 1769–73 Eb, Fb, Fb, Ef
39 James Cook (Eng) C Desolation, C Horn 1772–3 Re, Sf
40 Joseph Dombey (Fr) **Hipólito Ruiz López, José Antonio Pavón y Jiménez** (Sp) Peruvian montana 1779–81 ; Huánuco 1789 Hc, Hc
41 Félix de Azara (Sp) Paraná-Paraguay R basin 1784–1801 Jh
42 Thaddeus Peregrinus Haenke (Bohemian) Rio de la Plata est 1789 ; Chile 1790 ; Peru 1793–4 Mh, Mc, Hb
43 Alessandro Malaspina (Lombard) Coasts of Brazil and Argentina, Falkland Is, Chile, Peru 1787–84 Mh-Qf, Rg-h, Od, Ic
44 Alexander von Humboldt (Ger), **Aimé Bonpland** (Fr) Cumaná, Venezuelan llanos, Orinoco R, Casiquiare Canal, Negro R 1779–80 Af, Be, Cf, Ce, Df
45 Alexander von Humboldt (Ger), **Aimé Bonpland** (Fr) Magdalena R, Ecuador, Peru 1801–3 Bc, Fb, Gb
46 Charles Waterton (Eng) Essequibo R 1812 Ch
47 Johann Baptist von Spix, Karl Friedrich Philipp von Martius (Ger) Rio de Janeiro, São Paulo 1817 ; Minas Gerais, Belém (Pará), Pará R, Amazon R 1818 Jl, Kj, Ik, Dk, Dk, Eh
48 Johann Baptist von Spix (Ger) Solimões R, Tabatinga 1819–20 Ee, Ed
49 Karl Friedrich Philipp von Martius (Ger) Japurá R, Negro R 1819–20 Ee, Df
50 Johann Natterer (Aus) Minas Gerais, Goiás 1823–5 ; Mato Grosso 1826–7 ; Madeira R 1828 ; Solimões R, Casiquiare Canal, Negro R 1832–5 Ik, Ij, Hg, Fg, Ee, Ce, Df
51 Johann Emmanuel Pohl (Aus) Goiás, Tocantins R 1819 ; São Francisco R 1820–1 Ij, Hk, Gl
52 Eduard Peoppig (Ger) Peru, Amazon R 1827–32 Fb, Eh
53 Charles Darwin (Eng) Río de la Plata est, Tierra del Fuego 1832 ; Argentina 1833 ; Falkland Is, Chile 1834 ; Galápagos Is 1835 Mh, Rf, Og, Rg-h, Md
54 Johann Jakob von Tschudi (Swiss) Chiloé I, Chile, Peruvian montana 1839–40 ; S Andes, Minas Gerais Pd, Md, Hc, Le, Ik
55 Robert Hermann Schomburgk (Fr) Essequibo R, 1835–43 Cg
56 François de Castelnau (Fr) Goiás, Tocantins R, Paraguay R, L Titicaca 1843, Cuzco, Amazon R 1843–7 Ij, Hk, Jh, Ie, Hd, Eh
57 William H. Edwards (Amer) Amazon R 1846 Eh
58 Henry Walter Bates, Alfred Russel Wallace (Eng) Tocantins R 1848 ; Amazon R 1849–50 Hk, Eh
59 Alfred Russel Wallace (Eng) Amazon R, Negro R 1849–50 ; Casiquiare Canal, Uaupés R, Branco R 1850–1 Eh, Df, Ce, De, Dg
60 Henry Walter Bates (Eng) Amazon R 1850–1 ; Tapajós R region 1851–5 Eh, Fh
61 James Orton (Amer) Napo R, Amazon R 1868 Ec, Eh
62 George Chaworth Musters (Eng) Falkland Is, Argentina 1869–70 Rh, Pf
63 Carlos María Moyano (Argentine Lake region 1877–8 and coastal region of Argentina 1882–3 Pe-Qe, Qf
64 Jules Crevaux (Fr) Paraguay R, Pilcomayo R, Gran Chaco 1879–82 Ih, Jg, Jg
65 Percy Fawcett (Eng) Acre R, Abuña R, Madeira R 1906–7 ; Corumbá, Verde R 1908–9 ; altiplano Peru-Brazil border 1910–12 ; Mato Grosso 1925 Gd, Ge, Fg, Ih, Hg, Hd, Hg
66 A. Hamilton Rice (Amer) Branco R, Uraricoera R 1924–5 Dg, Cf
67 Candido Rondon (Brazilian) **Theodore Roosevelt** (Amer) Mato Grosso, Roosevelt R, Madeira R, Amazon R 1914 Hg, Gg, Fg, Eh

Africa

Second largest of the continents (treating North and South America as two) Africa is $11\frac{1}{2}$ million square miles in area. Close to Europe, it was one of the last to be explored in detail by Europeans

1 Harfuk (Egyptian) S Sudan c.2275 BC Ej
2 Diogenes (Gk) E Africa (Ruwenzori Mts?) c.630 BC Hm
3 Hanno (Phoen) Sierra Leone c.470 BC Fb
4 Herodotus (Rom) Aswan, Nile R c. 460 BC Ck, Ck
5 Eudoxus (Gk) C Guardafui c.140 BC Eo
6 Petronius (Rom) Napata 25 BC Dk
7 Cornelius Balbus (Rom) Jerma, Fezzan 19 BC Ch
8 Julius Maternus (Rom) Trans-Sahara, possibly to L Chad c.10 BC Eg
9 Suetonius Paulinus (Rom) Trans-Atlas to Ger R AD 42 Bd
10 Nero's centurions (Rom) Nile R to the Sudd c.AD 60 Fk
11 Chinese sailors E coast of Africa, Malindi, Madagascar pre 860 Im, Im, Ln
12 Ibn-Battuta (Arab) Egypt 1325 ; E African coast 1330–2 ; Timbuktu 1351 ; W Sudan, Mali 1352–3 Ck, Hn, Dd, Eh, Ef
13 Gil Eannes (Port) C Bojador 1433 Db
14 Afonso Baldaya (Port) Rio de Oro 1435–6 Cb
15 Nuño Tristão (Port) Senegal R 1444 Db
16 Alvise da Cadamosto (Ven) Gambia R, Cape Verde Is 1455 Ea, Ea
17 Diogo Gomes (Port) Sierra Leone Mts 1457 Fc
18 Fernão do Poo (Port) Fernando Poo 1472 Gf
19 Lopo Gonçalves (Port) São Tome, Principe Is 1474 Hf, Hf
20 Diogo Cão (Port) mouth of Congo R 1482 Ig
21 João Affonso d'Aveiro (Port) Benin 1486 Gf
22 Bartolomeu Dias (Port) C of Good Hope 1488 Ni
23 Pedro de Covilhão (Port) Moçambique, Kilwa, Malindi 1490 Km, Im, Im
24 Vasco da Gama (Port) Great Fish R, Natal 1497 Ni, Nk
25 Diogo Dias (Port) Madagascar 1500 Ln
26 Leo Africanus (Arab) W Sudan, Tuat, Ghadames, Agadèz, Timbuktu 1526 Ej, Ce, Bg, Df, Dd
27 Antonio Fernandes (Port) S Ethiopia, Mashonaland 1505–14 Fm, Kk
28 Francisco Alvarez (Port) Cent Ethiopia 1520–6 Fm
29 Pedro Paez (Port) Blue Nile source 1618 Fm
30 Manoel de Almeida (Port) L Zwai, Ethiopia 1622–33 Fm, Fm
31 Manoel Barradas (Port) Tigre,
Ethiopia 1624–33 Em, Em
32 Jerome Lobo (Port) Blue Nile Falls 1628 Fm
33 André Brüe (Fr) Dramanet, Senegal R 1698 Eb
34 Charles Poncet (Fr) Gondar, Massawa 1699 Em, Fm
35 Carl Thunberg, Anders Sparrman (Sw) SW Africa 1722 Ni
36 James Bruce (Scot) Axum, Gondar, Blue Nile source 1768–73 Em, Fm, Fm
37 Michel Adanson (Fr) Coast of Senegal 1780 Ea
38 Daniel Houghton (Eng) Upper Gambia 1791–2 Ec
39 John Campbell (Scot) Namaqualand 1791–2 ; Limpopo R source 1812 Mi, Mj
40 Francisco Jose de Lacerda (Port) Cunene R 1787 ; L Mweru 1798 Lh, Jk
41 William George Browne (Eng) Darfur 1793–4 Fj
42 Frederick Hornemann (Ger) Marzuq, Katsina 1797–1800 Ch, Ff
43 John Barrow (Eng) Orange R 1801 Ni-j
44 Mungo Park (Scot) Gambia R, Senegal R, Upper Niger 1795–7 ; Niger R to Bussa Rapids 1806 Eb-e, Fe, Fe
45 Johann Ludwig Burckhardt (Swiss) Nile R from Aswan to Dongola, Abu Simbel 1813 ; Nubian Desert, Shendi, Suakin 1814–15 Dl, El, Dl, Dm
46 Frédéric Caillaud (Fr) Nubia 1815 ; Meroe 1821 Dl, Dl
47 Joseph Ritchie, George Lyon (Br) Tripoli to Marzuq 1818 Ag-Ch
48 Hugh Clapperton, Dixon Denham, Walter Oudney (Br) L Chad, Kano, Sokoto 1822–5 Eg, Ff, Ff
49 Alexander Gordon Laing (Scot) Tripoli to Timbuktu 1825 Ag, Dd
50 Hugh Clapperton, Richard Lander (Br) Badagri, Bussa, Kano, Sokoto 1825–7 Ge, Fe, Ff, Ff
51 René Caillié (Fr) Timbuktu 1825–8 Dd
52 Richard and **John Lander** (Eng) Niger R mouth 1830–1 Gf
53 William Cornwallis Harris (Eng) Marico R 1835–7 Mj
54 James Alexander (Scot) Cape Town to Walvis Bay 1836–7 Ni, Mh
55 Antoine and **Arnaud d'Abbadie** (Fr) Lalibela, Ethiopia 1837–48 El, El
56 Johann Rebmann (Ger) Mt Kilimanjaro 1848 Il
57 Johann Ludwig Krapf (Ger) Mt Kenya 1849 Hm
58 Ladislaus Magyar (Hung) Upper Zambezi R, Congo R basin 1849 Ki, Ij
59 David Livingstone (Scot)

Modern works in an ancient land : the giant Kariba Dam on the upper waters of the Zambezi river

Australia

L Ngami 1849 Li
60 Heinrich Barth (Ger) Tripoli to L Chad 1850; Kano, Sokoto, Timbuktu 1852–5 Ag, Eg, Ff, Ff, Dd
61 Paul du Chaillu (Fr/Amer) Ogowe basin, Gabon 1850–9 Hg, Hh
62 David Livingstone (Scot) Zambezi R 1851 ; Luanda to Quelimane 1852–6; Victoria Falls 1856 Kk, Jh-Km, Kj
63 John Petherick (Eng) Niam-Niam territory (Azande) of N Congo 1853 Gj
64 Eduard Vogel (Ger) Ouadai, L Chad 1853–6 Eh, Eg
65 Richard Burton (Eng) Harar, Ethiopia 1854 Fn, Fn
66 Richard Burton, John Hanning Speke (Eng) Somaliland 1854 Fo
67 Robert Moffat (Scot) Orange R 1856 Nj
68 Richard Burton, John Hanning Speke (Eng) L Tanganyika, L Victoria 1858 Ik, Hk
69 David Livingstone (Scot) L Shirwa, L Nyasa, Shire Highlands 1858–63 Kl, Jl, Km
70 John Hanning Speke, James Augustus Grant (Eng) Karagwe, Ripon Falls 1860 Hl, Hl
71 Klaus von der Decken (Ger) Kilimanjaro area 1861–2 Il
72 Alexandrine Tinne (Dutch) Nile R basin 1861 ; Upper Nile R, Azande regions of Congo 1863 Ek-l, Fk, Gj
73 Gerhard Rohlfs (Ger) Atlas Mts 1862 ; Tuat 1863–4; E Sahara 1869; Kufra Oasis 1878 Cd, Ce, Ch, Dj
74 Samuel Baker (Eng) L Albert, Murchison Falls 1863–5 Gk, Gk
75 David Livingstone (Scot) L Mweru, L Bangweulu, Lualaba R 1865–73 Jk, Jk, Hj
76 A. Renders (Ger) Zimbabwe ruins 1868 Lk
77 St Vincent Whished Erskine (Scot) Lower Limpopo 1868–9 Lj
78 Georg Schweinfurth (Ger) Uele R 1868–71 Gj
79 Gustav Nachtigal (Ger) Tibesti, Bornu, Kukawa, Kanem 1869–75 Dj, Ef, Eg, Eg
80 Frederick Courtney Selous (Eng) S Rhodesia 1872–92 Lk
81 Henry Morton Stanley (Br/Amer) L Edward, Congo R 1874–7 Hk, Ih
82 Verney Lovett Cameron (Eng) Lukuga R 1874 Ik
83 Emin Pasha (Edvard Schnitzer) (Ger) Semliki R 1875 Hk
84 Charles Chaillé-Long (Amer) Nile 1874 ; L Kyoga 1875 Gk, Hk
85 Pierre Savorgnan de Brazza (Fr) Ogowe R 1875–8 Hg
86 Romolo Gessi, Carlo Piaggia (It) L Albert 1876 Gk
87 Gaetano Casati (It) S Sudan, Congo R basin 1879–83 Gj, Gk
88 Henry Morton Stanley (Br/Amer) L Leopold II, Congo tributaries 1879–84 Hh, Ij
89 Wilhelm Johann Junker (Ger) Uele R 1879–86 Gj
90 Oscar Lenz (Ger) Morocco to Senegal R 1880 Bd–Eb
91 Hermann von Wissman (Ger) Angola 1880; Nyangwe 1882; Kasai R 1885 Jh, Ij, Ih
92 Gustav Adolf Fischer (Ger) L Naivasha 1883 Hl
93 Joseph Thomson (Eng) L Rukwa, L Baringo, Mt Elgon 1883 Jk, Hl, Gl
94 Robert Flegel (Ger) Benue R source 1883–4 Fh
95 Samuel Teleki von Szek (Hung), **Ludwig von Hohnel** (Aus) L Rudolf, L Stefanie 1887–8 Gl, Gl
96 Louis Gustave Binger (Fr) Niger R and Volta R 1887–9 Gf, Ge
97 Henry Morton Stanley (Br/Amer) Ruwenzori Mts, Semliki R 1888–9 Hj, Hk
98 Jean-Baptiste Marchand (Fr) Niger R source 1890 ; W Sudan 1892; Ivory Coast 1893–5; Congo R to Nile 1896 Fb, Ei, Gd, Ee-I

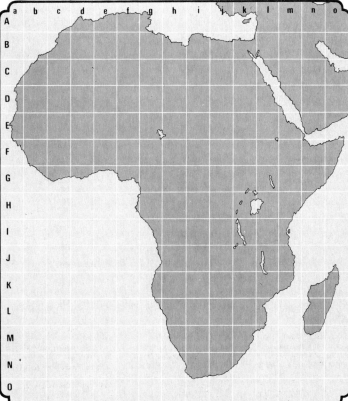

Its outline pieced together by European navigators in the 17th and 18th centuries, Australia, the smallest of the continents, had been criss-crossed by explorers by the end of the 19th century

1 Willem Jantszoon (Dutch) C Keer-weer 1606 Cn
2 Dirck Hartogszoon (Dutch) Dirk Hartogs I, "Eendrachtsland" (28S to 22S) 1616 Jb, Lc-Hb
3 Haevick Claeszoon (Dutch) 21.20S 1618 Hb
4 Lenaert Jacobszoon (Dutch) 22S 1618 Hb
5 Frederik Houtman (Dutch) "Dedelsland" (nr. Perth), Houtman Abrolhos 1619 Ld, Kb
6 The "Leeuwin" (Dutch) C Leeuwin to Point Nuyts 1622 Mc-d
7 Jan Carstenszoon, Willem van Colster (Dutch) Staaten R 1623 Dn
8 Willem van Colster (Dutch) NE Arnhem Land 1623 Bk
9 François Thijszoon, Pieter Nuyts (Dutch) C Leeuwin to Nuyts Arch 1627 Mc-Lk
10 Gerrit de Witt (Dutch) "De Witts Land" (21S) 1628 Hb
11 François Pelsaert (Dutch) 23S, 29.16S 1629 Ib, Lc
12 Pieter Pieterszoon (Dutch) Melville I, Cobourg Pen 1636 Bi, Bj
13 Abel Janszoon Tasman (Dutch) Tasmania, coasts of South and North Is, New Zealand 1642 Pp, Rc-Ng
14 Jacobszoon Visscher, Abel Janszoon Tasman (Dutch) Gilbert R to Port Hedland 1644 Dn-Gc
15 James Cook (Eng) E coast of North and South Is, New Zealand 1769–70; Cook Str 1770; E coast of Australia 1770 Sc-Ng, Qf, Nr-Bo
16 William Dawes (Eng), **George Johnston** (Scot) nr. Linden 1789 Lr
17 Watkins Tench (Eng) Tench R 1789 Lr
18 Antoine Bruni d'Entrecasteaux, D'Entrecasteaux Ch 1792 Pp
19 William Paterson (Scot) Grose R 1793 Lr
20 Matthew Flinders, George Bass (Eng) Georges R 1795; Port Hacking 1796 Lr, Lr
21 John Wilson (Eng) Nr Goulburn 1798 Lr
22 George Bass (Eng) Western Port 1798 Np
23 Matthew Flinders, George Bass (Eng) Bass Strait 1798 Op
24 Matthew Flinders (Eng) Nuyts Arch to Encounter Bay 1802 Lk-Mn
25 Francis Barrallier (Anglo/Fr) Blue Mts 1802 Lr
26 Nicolas Baudin (Fr) C Banks to Nuyts Arch 1802 Nn-Mm
27 Gregory Blaxland (Eng) Lett R 1813 Lr
28 George Evans (Eng) Macquarie R, nr. Bathurst 1813; Lachlan R 1815 Lq, Lg, Kg
29 John Oxley (Eng) Hay District 1817, Liverpool Plains 1818 Lp, Kr
30 George Evans (Eng) Castlereagh R 1818 Kq
31 Phillip Parker King (Austral) Port Darwin 1819; York Sd 1820 Bi, Df
32 Allan Cunningham (Eng) Pandora's Pass 1823 Kr
33 John Currie (Eng), **John Ovens** (Ir) Murrumbidgee R 1823 Mq
34 Hamilton Hume (Austral), **William Hovell** (Eng) Murray R to Geelong 1824 Mp-No
35 Allan Cunningham (Eng) Namoi R, Gwydir R, Dumaresq R, Cunningham's Gap 1827 Kr, Kr, Jr, Ir
36 Dumont d'Urville (Fr) French Pass, New Zealand 1827 Qf
37 Charles Sturt (Eng) Bogan R, Darling R 1829; L Alexandrina 1830 Jp, Ko, Mm
38 Thomas Mitchell (Scot) Darling R 1835; W Victoria 1836 Lo, Nn
39 George Grey, Franklin Lushington (Br) King Leopold Ranges, Glenelg R 1837 Ef-Dg
40 Edward John Eyre (Eng) Flinders Range, L Eyre, Eyre Pen, Streaky Bay 1839; Mt Hopeless 1840 ; Nullarbor Plain 1841 Km, Im, Ll, Lk, Jm, Lk-c
41 Paul Edmund de Strzelecki (Polish) Gippsland, Mt Kosciusko 1840 Np-q, Mq
42 Ludwig Leichhardt (Pruss) Mitchell R, Port Essington 1845 Cn, Bj
43 Charles Sturt (Br) Sturt Desert, Eyre Creek 1845 Im, In
44 Edmund Kennedy (Br) Nr. Port Albany 1848 Bo
45 John McDouall Stuart (Scot) Tennant Creek 1860; Newcastle Waters 1861 ; mouth of Mary R 1862 Ek, Ek, Bi
46 Robert Burke (Ir), **William Wills** (Eng) Bynoe R 1861 En
47 Ernest Giles (Eng) Mt Olga, Finke R 1872; Gibson Desert 1874 ; Great Victoria Desert 1875 Hi, Hk, Hg, Jj-h
48 Peter Egerton Warburton (Eng) Great Sandy Desert, Oakover R 1873 Gf, Ge
49 William Gosse (Anglo/Austral) Ayers Rock, Townsend Range 1873 Ii, Ih
50 Alexander Forrest (Austral) Victoria River Downs 1879 Dj
51 Cecil T. Madigan (Austral) Simpson Desert 1935–9 Gk-I
52 Edmund Colson (Austral) Simpson Desert 1936 Hk-m

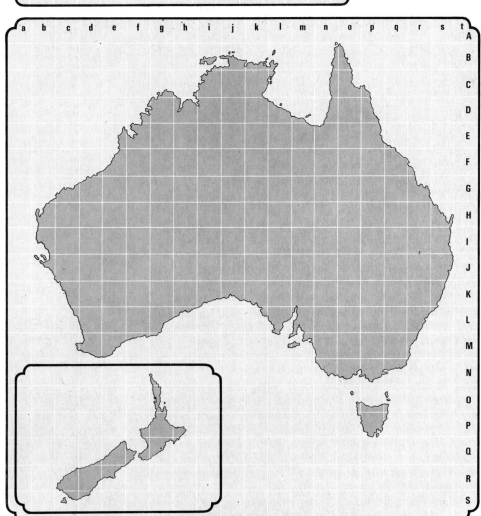

Pacific

Larger by far than all the land masses of the world—with another Africa added—the Pacific Ocean covers 69 million square miles or about a third of the Earth's surface and half its water surface. Its islands, many of them volcanic, are numbered in many thousands—some isolated specks, but more commonly arranged in lines or arcs.

Arctic

The Arctic is predominantly ocean, hidden beneath its frozen cap. The Arctic regions—the land masses fringing the ocean, within the Arctic Circle—are those of North America including Greenland, Europe and Asia

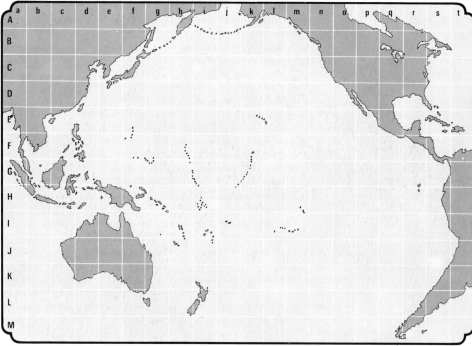

1 **Soleiman** (Arab) Malacca c.850 Ga
2 **Odoric of Pordenone** (It) Sumatra, Java, Borneo 1318–30 Ga, Hb, Gc
3 **Niccolò de Conti** (Ven) E Indies 1400s Gb
4 **Cheng-Ho** (Chin) Java, Sumatra, Philippines 1405–7 Hb, Ga, Fd
5 **Ludovico de Varthema** (It) Malacca, Sumatra, Java, Borneo, Banda Is, Moluccas 1502–8 Ga, Ga, Hb, Gc, Hd, Gd
6 **Diego Lopez de Sequeira** (Port) Malacca 1509 Ga
7 **Ferdinand Magellan** (Port) Magellan Str, Tuamotu Is, Phoenix Is, Ladrones Is, Philippines, Moluccas 1519–21 Mq, Im, Hi, Gi, Fd, Gd
8 **Afonso do Albuquerque** (Port) Malacca 1511 Ga
9 **Antonio de Abreu, Francisco de Serrão** (Port) Moluccas, Banda Is 1512 Gd, Hd
10 **Francisco de Serrão** (Port) Java, Timor, Moluccas 1513 Hb, Hd, Gd
11 **Jorge de Meneses** (Port) N coast of New Guinea 1524 Hf
12 **Alvaro de Saavedra** (Sp) Moluccas, New Guinea, Admiralty Is, Marshall Is 1527 Gd, He, Hf, Ij
13 **Hernando de Grijalva** (Sp) Gilbert Is, New Guinea 1537 Gh, He
14 **San Francisco de Xavier** (Port) Malacca, Moluccas, Japan, Ternate 1540–52 Ga, Gd, Lf, Gd
15 **Iñigo Ortiz de Retes** (Sp) New Guinea, Banda Is, Ternate, Moluccas 1545 He, Hd, Gd, Gd
16 **Alonso de Arellana** (Sp) Philippines, Mariana Is 1564–5 Fd, Ef
17 **Andres de Urdaneta** (Sp) Philippines, Mariana Is, W-E crossing of Pacific 1564–5 Fd, Ef, Fd-Eq
18 **Francis Drake** (Eng) W coast of America, Philippines, Moluccas, Java 1577–80 Do, Fd, Gd, Hb
19 **Thomas Cavendish** (Eng) Philippines, Ladrones Is, Java 1586–8 Fd, Gi, Hb
20 **Alvaro de Mendana** (Sp), **Pedro Fernandez de Quiros** (Port) Solomon Is 1567; Marquesas Is, Ellice Is 1595–6 Hg, Hm, Hi
21 **Cornelius Houtman** (Dutch) Moluccas, Java, Bali 1595–7 Gd, Hb, Hc
22 **Oliver van Noort** (Dutch) Ladrones Is, Philippines, E Indies 1598–1601 Gi, Fd, Gb
23 **John David** (Eng) Moluccas 1601; E Indies 1605 Gd, Gb
24 **Wybrand van Warwijk** (Dutch) Sumatra, Borneo, Malacca, Java 1602 Ga, Gc, Ga, Hb
25 **Stevan van der Hagen** (Dutch) Moluccas, Banda Is 1603 Gd, Hd
26 **Henry Middleton** (Eng) Sumatra, Java, Halmahera 1604–5 Ga, Hb, Gd
27 **Willem Jansz** (Dutch) Java, S coast of New Guinea 1605 Hb, He
28 **Pedro Fernandez de Quiros** (Port) Tuamotu Is, N Cook Is, New Hebrides 1605–6 Im, Il, Ih
29 **Luis Vaez de Torres** (Sp) S coast of New Guinea, Torres Str 1606 He, He
30 **John Saris** (Eng) Java, Sumatra, Buru, Amboina, Halmahera 1611–13 Hb, Ga, Hd, Hd, Gd
31 **Willem Cornelius Schouten, Isaac le Maire** (Dutch) C Horn, Juan Fernández Is, Tuamotu Is, Friendly Is (Tonga), Horno Is, New Ireland, New Hanover, Admiralty Is, N coast of New Guinea, Moluccas 1615–19 Mq, Kq, Im, Ii, Hf, Hf, Hf, Hf, Gf, Gd
32 **Jan Pieterszoon Coen** (Dutch) E Indies 1618 Gb
33 **Abel Tasman** (Dutch) Friendly Is (Tonga), Fiji Is, New Guinea 1642–4 Il, Ii, He
34 **William Dampier** (Eng) New Hebrides 1684–91; New Guinea, New Hanover, New Ireland, New Britain, Dampier Str, Juan Fernández Is 1708–11 Ih, Hf, Hf, Hf, Hf, Hf, Kq

35 **Edward Davis** (Eng) Juan Fernández Is, Tuamotu Is 1687 Kq, Im
36 **Beauchêne Gouin** (Fr) C Horn, Galápagos Is 1698 Mq, Gr
37 **Jacob Roggevven** (Dutch) Juan Fernández Is, Tuamotu Is, Easter I 1722 Kq, Im, Jp
38 **George Anson** (Eng) C Horn, coast of Peru, Pacific crossing to Manila 1740 Mq, Hs, Ec
39 **John Byron** (Eng) Juan Fernández Is, Tuamotu Is, Takaroa, Tinian, King George Is, Gilbert Is 1764–6 Kq, Im, Im, Ff, Im, Gh
40 **Louis Antoine de Bougainville** (Fr) Tuamotu Is, Tahiti, Samoa, New Hebrides, Great Barrier Reef, New Guinea, Louisiade Arch, Solomon Is, New Britain, Buru Is 1766 Im, Il, Ii, Ih, If, He, If, Hg, Hf, Hd
41 **Samuel Wallis** (Eng) Tahiti, Tinian 1767–8 Il, Ff
42 **Philip Carteret** (Eng) Tuamotu Is, Tahiti, Society Is, Más Afuera, Pitcairn I, Santa Cruz Is, Solomon Is 1767–9 Im, Il, Il, Ir-Kr, Jn, Ih, Hg
43 **James Cook** (Eng) Tahiti, Batavia, 1768–71; Society Is, Friendly Is (Tonga), Easter I, New Hebrides 1772–5; Christmas I, Hawaiian Is, Kuril Is 1776–80 Il, Hb, Il, Jp, Ih, Hb, Ek, Bg
44 **François Galaup de la Pérouse** (Fr) Hawaiian Is, Philippines, La Pérouse Str, Navigators Is, Friendly Is (Tonga) 1785–8 Ek, Fd, Bg, Ii, Il
45 **Jules Dumont d'Urville** (Fr) Vanikoro Is, Moluccas 1789 Hg, Gd
46 **Antoine Bruni, Chevalier d'Entrecasteaux** (Fr) Solomon Is, Admiralty Is, Friendly Is, Louisiade Arch, Trobriand I, Récifs d'Entrecasteaux, Java 1791 Hg, Hf, Ii, If, Hf, Jh, Hb
47 **Charles Darwin, Robert Fitzroy** (Eng) Galápagos Is, Tahiti 1831–2 Gr
48 **Charles Wyville Thompson, George Nares** (Eng) Fiji Is, Mariana Is, Hawaiian Is, Tahiti 1872–6 Ii, Fh, Ek, Il ("Challenger" expedition)
49 "Challenger II" (Amer) Mariana Trench (soundings) 1949–50 Ef
50 **Jacques Piccard** (Fr) Mariana Trench (bathyscaphe) 1960 Ef

Lonely atolls provide the setting for man's most violent game—the firing off of nuclear charges

1 **Rurik** (Vik) Novgorod, Dnieper R c.862 Nl, Ol
2 **Scandinavians** Orkney Is, Shetland Is, Faeroe Is 860s Og, Ng, Ng
3 **Irish monks** Iceland 860s Mf
4 **Gardar** (Vik) Iceland 9th cent. Mf
5 **Naddod** (Vik) Iceland 9th cent. Mf
6 **Floki Vilggerdarson** (Vik) Iceland 9th cent. Mf
7 **Gunnbjörn Ulfsson** (Ice) E coast of Greenland c.950 Kg
8 **Snaebjord Galti** (Ice) E coast of Greenland 978 Lf
9 **Erik the Red** (Ice) W coast of Greenland 982 Kc
10 **Icelandic settlers** Greenland c.986 Lc
11 **Erling Sighvatsson, Bjarni Thordarson, Eindridi** (Ice) Greenland 10th cent. Ke
12 **Gregory Istoma** (Russ) N coast of Norway 1469 Lj
13 **Gaspar Corte Real** (Sp) Denmark Str to C Farewell 1500 Lf-Mc
14 **Hugh Willoughby** (Eng) Novaya Zemlya I, Kola Pen 1553 Jk, Lk
15 **Richard Chancellor** (Eng) White Sea 1553–4 Lk
16 **Richard Borough** (Eng) Vaygach I 1556 Jl
17 **Oliver Brunel** (Dutch) Ob R, Kostin Shar 1570s Il, Kk
18 **Martin Frobisher** (Eng) S coast of Greenland, Resolution I 1576; Frobisher Bay 1577; Hudson Str 1578 Le, Kb, Jb, Jb
19 **Arthur Pet, Charles Jackman** (Eng) Pet Str, Yugorskiy Shar 1580 Jl, Jl
20 **John Davis** (Eng) Davis Str, Cumberland Sd, Baffin I 1585–6; Sukkertoppen 1586; C Chidley 1587 Kc, Jc, Jb-c, Kd, Ka
21 **William Barents** (Dutch) Novaya Zemlya I, Orange Is 1594–5; Bear I, NW coast of Spitsbergen 1596–7 Jk, Ik, Ki, Jh
22 **George Waymouth** (Eng) Hudson Str 1602 Jb
23 **Henry Hudson, Robert Bylot** (Eng) Novaya Zemlya I 1608; Salisbury I 1610 Jk, Ib
24 **William Baffin, Robert Bylot** (Eng) Southampton I 1615; Lancaster Sd, Smith Sd, Jones Sd, Baffin Bay 1616 Ib, Id, Ie, Ie, Jd
25 **Ivan Lyakhov** (Russ) Lyakhovskiy I 1770 Fj
26 **Constantine Phipps** (Eng) N Spitsbergen 1773 Ji
27 **James Cook** (Eng) North C, Wrangel I 1778 Dg, Dh
28 **William Scoresby** (Eng) NE Spitsbergen 1806 Ji

29 **M. M. Hedenström** (Russ) Faddeyevskiy I and Mal Lyakhovskiye I, New Siberian Is 1809–10 Fj, Fj, Fj
30 **William Scoresby the Younger** (Eng) E coast of Greenland 1817 Lf
31 **David Buchan, John Franklin** (Eng) NW of Spitsbergen 1818 Jh
32 **James Ross** (Scot), **Edward Parry** (Eng) Lancaster Sd 1818 Hc
33 **William Edward Parry** (Eng) Melville Sd 1819–20; Frozen Str, Fury and Hecla Str 1821; 82.45N from Spitsbergen 1827 He, Ic, Hc, Ih
34 **Ferdinand von Wrangel** (Russ) Coast of Siberia 1820–4 Dh
35 **Frederick William Beechey** (Eng) Pt Barrow, Icy C 1825–6 Dg, Ef
36 **John Ross, James Clark Ross** (Scot) Boothia Pen 1828–33 Hc
37 **James Clark Ross** (Scot) King William I, Magnetic N Pole 70.5N, 96.46W 1829–31 Hc, Hd
38 **George Back** (Eng) Foxe Channel 1836–7 Ib
39 **Capt Fabvre** (Fr) Spitsbergen 1838–9 Ki
40 **Thomas Simpson** (Eng) Simpson Str 1839 Hc
41 **John Franklin, Francis Crozier** (Eng) Wellington Ch, Crozier Ch, Beechey I, Peel Sd, Franklin Str, Victoria Str 1845–7 Hd, Ge, Hd, Hd, Hd, Gd
42 **Graham Gore** (Eng) Victoria I 1847 Gd
43 **John Richardson, John Rae** (Scot) Canadian Arctic Arch 1847–50 Ge
44 **James Ross** (Scot), **Leopold McClintock, Robert McClure** (Ir) Somerset I 1848–9 Hd
45 **Henry Kellet** (Eng) Bering Str, Wrangel I and Herald I 1848–51 Cg, Dh, Dh
46 **E. J. De Haven** (Amer) Grinnel Land 1850–1 He
47 **Richard Collinson** (Eng), Amundsen G, Dease Str 1850–4 Fd, Gl
48 **Robert McClure** (Ir) McClure Str, NW Passage 1850–4 Ge, Fd-Jb
49 **William Kennedy** (Eng), **Joseph René Bellot** (Fr) Bellot Str, Franklin Str 1851–2 Hd, Hd
50 **John Rae** (Scot) Pelly Bay, Boothia Pen 1854 Hc
51 **Bedford Pim** (Eng) Melville Sd, Banks I 1852 Gd, Fe
52 **Edward Inglefield** (Eng) Smith Sd 1852 Ie
53 **Frederick Mecham** (Eng) Eglinton Is, Prince Patrick I 1852–4 Ge, Ge
54 **Leopold McClintock** (Ir) Melville I, Prince Patrick I 1852–4; James Ross Str, Rae Str 1857–9 Ge, Ge, Hc, Hc
55 **Elisha Kent Kane, Isaac Hayes** (Amer) Kane basin, Rensselaer Harbour 1853–5 If
56 **William Norton** (Amer) C Constitution, Greenland 1854 If
57 **Isaac Hayes, William Godfrey** (Amer) Ellesmere I 1854; Greenland 1860; Ellesmere I 1861 If, If, If
58 **Otto Torell** (Norw), **Nils Adolf Erik Nordenskiöld** (Sw) Spitsbergen 1858–61 Ki
59 **Allen Young** (Eng) Prince of Wales I, McClintock Ch 1859; Peel Sd, Franklin Str 1875 Hd, Gd, Hd
60 **W. R. Hobson** (Eng) Prince of Wales I, Erebus Bay, Simpson Str 1859 Hd, Hc
61 **Charles Francis Hall** (Amer) Baffin I 1860–2; Melville Pen 1864–9; Hall basin 1871 Jc, Ic, If

Industry in the Alaskan Arctic: oil drillers at work

272

Antarctica

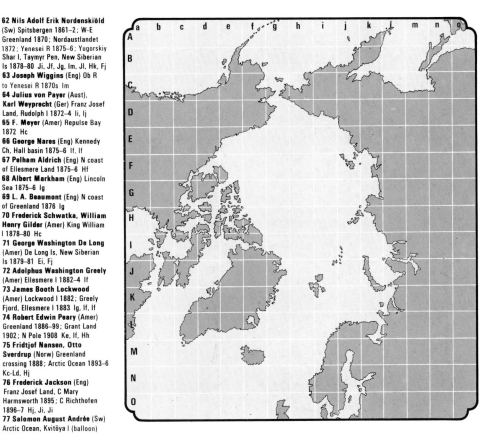

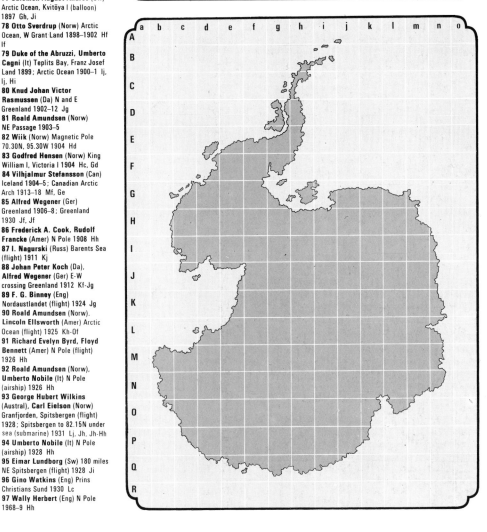

62 Nils Adolf Erik Nordenskiöld (Sw) Spitsbergen 1861–2; W-E Greenland 1870; Nordaustlandet 1872; Yenesei R 1875–6; Yugorskiy Shar I, Taymyr Pen, New Siberian Is 1878–80 Ji, Jf, Jg, Im, Jl, Hk, Fj

63 Joseph Wiggins (Eng) Ob R to Yenesei R 1870s Im

64 Julius von Payer (Aust), **Karl Weyprecht** (Ger) Franz Josef Land, Rudolph I 1872–4 Ii, Ij

65 F. Meyer (Amer) Repulse Bay 1872 Hc

66 George Nares (Eng) Kennedy Ch, Hall basin 1875–6 If, If

67 Pelham Aldrich (Eng) N coast of Ellesmere Land 1875–6 Hf

68 Albert Markham (Eng) Lincoln Sea 1875–6 Ig

69 L. A. Beaumont (Eng) N coast of Greenland 1876 Ig

70 Frederick Schwatka, William Henry Gilder (Amer) King William I 1878–80 Hc

71 George Washington De Long (Amer) De Long Is, New Siberian Is 1879–81 Ei, Fj

72 Adolphus Washington Greely (Amer) Ellesmere I 1882–4 If

73 James Booth Lockwood (Amer) Lockwood I 1882; Greely Fjord, Ellesmere I 1883 Ig, If, If

74 Robert Edwin Peary (Amer) Greenland 1886–99; Grant Land 1902; N Pole 1908 Ke, If, Hh

75 Fridtjof Nansen, Otto Sverdrup (Norw) Greenland crossing 1888; Arctic Ocean 1893–6 Kc-Ld, Hj

76 Frederick Jackson (Eng) Franz Josef Land, C Mary Harmsworth 1895; C Richthofen 1896–7 Hj, Ji, Ji

77 Salomon August Andrée (Sw) Arctic Ocean, Kvitöya I (balloon) 1897 Gh, Ji

78 Otto Sverdrup (Norw) Arctic Ocean, W Grant Land 1898–1902 Hf If

79 Duke of the Abruzzi, Umberto Cagni (It) Teplits Bay, Franz Josef Land 1899; Arctic Ocean 1900–1 Ij, Ij, Hi

80 Knud Johan Victor Rasmussen (Da) N and E Greenland 1902–12 Jg

81 Roald Amundsen (Norw) NE Passage 1903–5

82 Wiik (Norw) Magnetic Pole 70.30N, 95.30W 1904 Hd

83 Godfred Hensen (Norw) King William I, Victoria I 1904 Hc, Gd

84 Vilhjalmur Stefansson (Can) Iceland 1904–5; Canadian Arctic Arch 1913–18 Mf, Ge

85 Alfred Wegener (Ger) Greenland 1906–8; Greenland 1930 Jf, Jf

86 Frederick A. Cook, Rudolf Francke (Amer) N Pole 1908 Hh

87 I. Nagurski (Russ) Barents Sea (flight) 1911 Kj

88 Johan Peter Koch (Da), **Alfred Wegener** (Ger) E-W crossing Greenland 1912 Kf-Jg

89 F. G. Binney (Eng) Nordaustlandet (flight) 1924 Jg

90 Roald Amundsen (Norw). **Lincoln Ellsworth** (Amer) Arctic Ocean (flight) 1925 Kh-Of

91 Richard Evelyn Byrd, Floyd Bennett (Amer) N Pole (flight) 1926 Hh

92 Roald Amundsen (Norw), **Umberto Nobile** (It) N Pole (airship) 1926 Hh

93 George Hubert Wilkins (Austral), **Carl Eielson** (Norw) Granfjorden, Spitsbergen (flight) 1928; Spitsbergen to 82.15N under sea (submarine) 1931 Lj, Jh, Jh-Hh

94 Umberto Nobile (It) N Pole (airship) 1928 Hh

95 Eimar Lundborg (Sw) 180 miles NE Spitsbergen (flight) 1928 Ji

96 Gino Watkins (Eng) Prins Christians Sund 1930 Lc

97 Wally Herbert (Eng) N Pole 1968–9 Hh

1 James Cook (Eng) 1st crossing of Antarctic Circle 1773 Ln

2 William Smith (Eng) King George I 1819 Bi

3 Gottlieb von Bellingshausen (Russ) Kronprinsesse Märtha Kyst 1820; Bellingshausen Sea, Peter 1 Øy, Alexander Land, S Shetland Is 1821 Gm, Ee, De, Dg, Bi

4 Nathaniel Palmer (Amer) Deception I 1820; Palmer Land, S Shetland Is 1821 Bh, Bh, Bi

5 William Smith, Edward Bransfield (Eng) Trinity Pen, Clarence I, Elephant I 1820 Bi, Bi, Ai

6 Nathaniel Palmer (Amer), **George Powell** (Eng) S Orkney Is 1821 Ak

7 James Weddell (Eng) Weddell Sea 1822 Fk

8 John Biscoe (Eng) Prinsesse Astrid Kyst, Enderby Land 1830; Graham Land, Adelaide I 1832 Jn, Mn, Nn, Cg

9 Peter Kemp (Eng) Kemp Coast 1833 Nl

10 John Balleny (Eng) Balleny Is. sighted Sabrina Coast 1839 Na, Qe

11 Jules Sébastien César Dumont d'Urville (Fr) Joinville I 1839; Terre Adélie 1840 Bi, Oc

12 Charles Wilkes (Amer) Sighted Oates Land, Knox Coast, Shackleton Ice Shelf 1840 Ob, Qf, Rg

13 James Clark Ross (Eng) C Adare, Possession I, Victoria Land, Ross I, Mt Erebus, Mt Terror, Ross Ice Shelf 1841; Weddell Sea 1843 Mb, Ma, Mb, Lc, Lc, Lc, Kd, Fi

14 George Nares (Eng) Crossed Antarctic Circle 1874 Pk-l

15 Carl Larsen (Norw) Larsen Ice Shelf 1893 Ch

16 Leonard Kristensen, H. J. Bull, Carstens Borchgrevink (Norw) 1st landing C Adare 1895 Mb

17 Adrien de Gerlache (Belg) S Shetland Is, Palmer Arch, Alexander I Land 1898 Bi, Bh, Cg

18 Carstens Borchgrevink (Norw) Robertson Bay 1899; Lady Newnes Ice Shelf, Newnes Land, Ross Ice Shelf 1900 Mb, Mb-c, Mc, Kd

19 Erich von Drygalski (Ger) Wilhelm II Land, Gaussberg 1902 Qi, Qi

20 Robert Falcon Scott (Eng), **Ernest Shackleton** (Ir) McMurdo Sd, King Edward VII Land, Ross Ice Shelf to 82.17S 1902–3 Lc-d, Jc, Kd

21 Robert Falcon Scott (Eng) Ferrar Glacier 1903 Ld

22 Carl Larsen (Norw), **Otto Nordenskjöld** (Sw) Graham Land 1902–3 Bh-i

23 William Spiers Bruce (Scot) Coats Land 1903 Gk

24 Jean-Baptiste Charcot (Fr) Palmer Arch, Wienckel I, Graham Land 1904 Bh, Ch, Cg

25 Ernest Shackleton (Ir) B of Whales, Ross I, Beardmore Glacier, Polar Plateau (to 88.23S) 1908–9 Jc, Lc, Le, Kg

26 Edgeworth David, Douglas Mawson (Austral) S Magnetic Pole 1909 Nc

27 Jean-Baptiste Charcot (Fr) Graham Land, Marguerite Bay, Fallières Coast, Charcot I 1909–10 Cg, Cg, Ch, Df

28 Roald Amundsen (Norw) S Pole 1911 Jh

29 Robert Falcon Scott (Eng) Ross I, S Pole 1911–12 Ld, Jh

30 Wilhelm Filchner (Ger) Luitpold Coast, Vahsel Bay 1912 Gj, Gi

31 Choku Shirase (Jap) Ross Ice Shelf 1912 Jd

32 John King Davis (Austral) Davis Sea 1912 Qh

33 John King Davis (Austral) Shackleton Ice Shelf 1912 Qg

34 Douglas Mawson (Austral) King George V Land, Terre Adélie 1912–13 Nb, Oc

35 Frank Wild (Austral) Queen Mary Land, Gaussberg, Knox Coast 1912–13 Pi-j, Qh, Qi

36 Ernest Shackleton (Ir) Weddell Sea (drift) 1915 Ci (''Endurance'' sunk)

37 Ernest Shackleton (Ir) Elephant I, S Georgia 1915–16 Ai, Ak

38 Hubert Wilkins (Austral) Graham Land (flight) 1928 Bh-Ch

39 Richard Byrd (Amer) S Pole 1929 Jh

40 Douglas Mawson, John King Davis (Austral) Banzare Coast, Knox Coast 1929–31 Pd, Qf

41 Hjalmar Riiser-Larsen (Norw) Kronprins Olav Kyst, Kronprinsesse Märtha Kyst (flight) 1929–30 Ln, Hm

42 Gunnar Isachsen, Hjalmar Riiser-Larsen (Norw) Prinsesse Ragnhild Kyst 1930–1 Kn

43 Richard Byrd (Amer) Marie Byrd Land (flight) 1933–4 Hc-Ic

44 Lars Christensen (Norw) Ingrid Christensen Coast (flight) 1934 Ok

45 John Rymill (Eng) Coast and Is of Graham Land 1934–7 Bh, Cg

46 Lincoln Ellsworth (Amer), **Herbert Hollick-Kenyon** (Can) 1st trans-polar flight 1935

47 Vivian Fuchs (Eng) S Pole 1957 Jh

Street lights in a frozen ''township''—an American research base set up on the Antarctic peninsula

Bibliography

A list of the literature of exploration in the English language, together with those books which have been translated into English, would be formidably long; the books themselves would require a library of some size. On this and the facing page are some of the works to which a keen student of the subject might be expected to turn, although many, of course, are to be found only in specialist libraries. The titles listed here cover those to which reference has been made in the compilation of this atlas. Our gratitude is due to men of many centuries, from the unknown compilers of ships' logs and chroniclers of old journeys, to contemporary travellers and authors.

GENERAL READING

A History of Geographical Discovery and Exploration J.N.L. Baker (1931); **A History of Geography** J.S. Keltie and O.J.R. Howarth (1913); "The History of Maritime and Inland Discovery", **Lardner's Cabinet Cyclopaedia** (1833); **Geographical Discovery** J. Jacobs (1912); **Maritime Discovery** C.R. Lowe (1881); **DTV Atlas zur Weltgeschichte** vols I & II (1964); **A History of Geographical Discovery in the 17th and 18th Centuries** E.A. Heawood (1912); **Discoveries and Explorations in the 19th Century** C.G.D. Roberts (1906); **Arctic Pilot**, Hydrographic Department of the Admiralty.

ANCIENTS, VIKINGS, MONKS AND TRADERS

The Ancient Explorers M. Cary and E.H. Warmington (1929); **Selections from Strabo** ed. H.F. Tozer (1893); **Anabasis, the Life of Alexander the Great** Arrian, trans. A. de Selincourt (1958); **Alexander the Great** W.W. Tarn (1948); **Alexander the Great** P. Green (1970); **Herodotus, the Histories** ed. A. de Selincourt (1954); **Conquest by Man** P. Hermann (1954); **Ancient Greek Mariners** W.W. Hyde (1947); **Rome Beyond the Imperial Frontiers** M. Wheeler (1954); **The Phoenicians** D. Harden (1971); **Lodestone and Evening Star** I. Cameron (1965). **The Vikings** H. Arbman (1961); **Great Adventures and Explorations** V. Stefansson (1947); **The Norse Discoverers of America** G.M. Gathorne Hardy (1921); **The Norse Atlantic Saga** G. Jones (1964); **Maritime History of Russia** M. Mitchell (1949); **Lodestone and Evening Star** I. Cameron (1965); **The Vinland Sagas, the Norse Discovery of America** trans. M. Magnusson and H. Palsson (1965); **Conquest by Man** P. Hermann (1954); **The West Vikings** F. Mowat (1966); "The Navigation of the Norsemen" G.J. Marcus, **Mariners Mirror** (May 1953); **A History of the Vikings** T.D. Kendrick (1968); **A History of the Vikings** G. Jones (1968). **The Dawn of Modern Geography** C.R. Beazley (1897–1906); **Travel and Travellers in the Middle Ages** A.P. Newton (1926); **The Rise of Christian Europe** H.T. Roper (1965); **The Quest for Cathay** Sir P. Sykes (1936); **Ser Marco Polo** ed., trans. Sir H. Yule (1920); **Cathay and the Way Thither** Sir H. Yule (1866); **The Great Chinese Travellers** J. Mirsky (1965); **Europe and China** G.F. Hudson (1931); **Embassy to the Court of Tamerlane** G. de Clavijo (1928); **The Golden Road to Samarkand** W. Blunt (1973); **Travels of Fah-hian and Sung-yun** trans. S. Beal (1869); **The Life of Huen-Tsang** Hui-Li, trans. S. Beal (1911); **The Silk Road** L. Boulnois, trans. D. Chamberlain (1966); **The Travels of Marco Polo** ed., trans. R. Latham (1958); **A Short History of Geographical Discovery** A. Torayah Sharaf (1963); **The Golden Trade of the Moors** E.W. Bovill (1968); **The Geographical Lore of the Time of the Crusades** J.K. Wright (1925); **Medieval People** E. Power (1963).

PORTUGUESE AND THE AGE OF NAVIGATION

The Quest for India B. Landstrom (1964); **Prince Henry of Portugal** C.R. Beazley (1895); **The Portuguese Pioneers** E. Prestage (1966); **The Portuguese Seaborne Empire** C.R. Boxer (1969); **Vasco da Gama** F. Hummerich (1896); **The History of the Portuguese in India** F.C. Danvers (1894); **The Age of Reconnaissance** J.H. Parry (1963); **Science and Civilisation in China** J. Needham (1954); **The Journal of Christopher Columbus** C. Jane (1968); **Christopher Columbus** C. Markham (1892); **India in the 15th Century** R.H. Major (1858); **The Exploration of the Pacific** J.C. Beaglehole (1934); **Chronological History of the Discoveries in the South Seas, or Pacific Ocean** J. Burney (1803–17); **The Life of Ferdinand Magellan** F.H.H. Guillemard (1890); **The Black Death** P. Ziegler (1969); **Europe and a Wider World 1415–1715** J.H. Parry (1949).

COLLISION OF CULTURES

History of the Conquest of Peru W.H. Prescott (1847); **History of the Conquest of Mexico** W.H. Prescott (1843); **Spanish Explorers in the Southern United States 1528–43** F.W. Hodge and T.H. Lewis (1925); **The Discovery and Conquest of Mexico** B.D. del Castillo, ed. A. Maudslay (1928); **Narrative and Critical History of America** J. Winsor (1886–9); **Five Letters** H. Cortes, ed., trans. J.B. Morris (1928); **Narrative of the Coronado Expedition, 1540–2** G.P. Hammond and A. Rey (1940); **Narratives of the Career of Hernando de Soto** E.G. Bourne (1905); **Expeditions into the Valley of the Amazons** Sir C. Markham (1850); **Pedro de Valdivia, Conqueror of Chile** R.B. Cunningham Graham (1926); **Discovery of the Amazon according to the Account of Fr Gaspar de Carvajal and other documents** ed. H.C. Heaton (1934); **The Aztecs under Spanish Rule** C. Gibson (1964); **Daily Life of the Aztecs** J. Soustelle (1961); **Aztecs of Mexico** G.C. Vaillant (1965); **Highway of the Sun** V.W. von Hagen (1956); **The Ancient Sun Kingdoms of the Americas** V.W. von Hagen (1973); **The Conquistadors** H. Innes (1969); **On the Royal Highways of the Inca** H. Ubbelohde-Doering (1967); **Peru: Incidents of Travel and Exploration in the Land of the Incas** E.G. Squier (1878); **The Conquest of the Incas** J. Hemming (1970).

NORTHWEST AND NORTHEAST PASSAGES

Principal Navigations R. Hakluyt (1589); **The Three Voyages of William Barents to the Arctic Regions 1594, 1595 and 1596** K. Beynen (1876); **Collection of Voyages by the Dutch East India Company** (1703); **Danish Arctic Expeditions** ed. C.A. Gosch (1897); **The Three Voyages of Sir Martin Frobisher 1576–8** ed. Sir R. Collinson (1867); **The Voyages and Works of John Davis the Navigator** ed. Sir A.H. Markham (1880); **Henry Hudson the Navigator** ed. G.M. Asher (1860); **The Voyages of Captain Luke Foxe, of Hull, and Captain Thomas of Bristol** ed. M. Christy (1894); **The Voyages of William Baffin 1612–22** ed. Sir C. Markham (1881); **Northwest by Sea** E.S. Dodge (1961); **John and Sebastian Cabot** C.R. Beazley (1898); **The Voyages of the Cabots and the English Discovery of North America under Henry VII and Henry VIII** J.A. Williamson (1929).

FRENCH AND BRITISH IN NORTH AMERICA

La Salle and the Discovery of the Great West F. Parkman (1912); **Indians of North America** H.E. Driver (1969); **The Explorers of North America 1492–1806** J.B. Brebner (1955); **The European Discovery of America** S.E. Morison (1974); **The Saint Lawrence Basin** S.E. Dawson (1905); **The Precursors of Jacques Cartier** H.P. Biggar (1911); **Cartier Voyages** H.P. Biggar (1930); **Champlain** R. Flenley (1924).

OCEANIC JOURNEYS: THE PACIFIC

The Exploration of the Pacific J.C. Beaglehole (1934); **The Voyages of Pedro Fernandez de Quiros** ed. Sir C. Markham (1904); **The East and West Indian Mirror** ed. J.A.J. de Villiers (1906); **The Discovery and Exploration of Australia** E.H.J. Feeken, G.E.E. Feeken and O.H.K. Spate (1970); **The Dutch Seaborne Empire** C.R. Boxer (1965); **The Discovery of Australia** A. Sharp (1963); **The Journals of Captain James Cook on his voyages of discovery** ed. J.C. Beaglehole (1955); **A Voyage of Discovery to the North Pacific Ocean and Round the World** G. Vancouver (1798); **Vancouver** G. Godwin (1930); **A Voyage to New Holland** W. Dampier, ed. James Williamson (1939); **The Life of Vice-Admiral William Bligh** G. Mackaness (1951); **Voyage to Disaster—The Life of François Pelsaert** H. Drake-Brockman (1963); **Discovery of Van Diemen's Land in 1642** J.B. Walker (1888–99); **The Revolt of the Netherlands, 1555–1609** P. Geyl (1962); **Social History of the Navy 1793–1815** M.A. Lewis (1960); **Treatise on the Scurvy** J. Lind (1757); **Essay on Preserving the Health of Naval Seamen** J. Lind (1762); **Joseph Antoine Raymond Bruni D'Entrecasteaux: an Account of his life, his expedition and his officers** G.H. Hogg.

ASIA

History of Geographical Discovery in the 17th and 18th Centuries E. Heawood (1912); **Early Travels in India, 1583–1619** Sir W. Foster (1921); **The Voyage of John Huyghen van Linschoten to the East Indies** ed. A.C. Burnell and P.A. Tiele (1884); **Akhbar and the Jesuits** C.H. Payne (1926); **The Quest for Cathay** Sir P. Sykes (1936); **Abode of Snow** K. Mason (1955); **Tibet—A Chronicle of Exploration** J. Macgregor (1970); **Papal Envoys to the Great Khans** I. de Rachewiltz (1971); **Tibet Past and Present** Sir C. Bell (1924); **The People of Tibet** Sir C. Bell (1928); **The Religion of Tibet** Sir C. Bell (1931); **Tibet the Mysterious** Sir T. Holdich (1906); **An Account of Tibet** trans. I. Desideri (1937); "The Story of the Survey of India" G.F. Heaney, **Geographical Magazine** (1957); **Historical Records of the Survey of India 1830–43**, vol I G. Everest, ed. R.H. Phillimore (1958); **General Report on the Operations of the Great Trigonometrical Survey of India 1874–5** J.T. Walker (1876); **A Memoir on the Indian Surveys** C.R. Markham (1871); "Kishen Singh and the Indian Explorers" K. Mason, **Geographical Journal** (1923); **Travels in Tartary, Thibet and China Huc and Gabet** ed. P. Pelliot (1928); **The Tangut Country and the Solitudes of Northern Tibet** N. Przewalski, trans. E.D. Morgan (1876); **Travels in Central Asia** A. Vambery (1864); **Results of a Scientific Mission to India and High Asia** A., H. and R. Schlagintweit (1866); **Narrative of Various Journeys in Balochistan, Afghanistan, the Panjab and Kalat** C. Masson (1844); **The Gates of India** Sir H. Holdich (1910); **The Indian Borderland** Sir H. Holdich (1901); **The Russians in Central Asia** F. Von Hellwald, trans. T. Wirgman (1894); **Ney Elias** G. Morgan (1971); **The Russians on the Amur** E.G. Ravenstein (1861); **To the Arctic!** J. Mirsky (1949); **Maritime History of Russia** M. Mitchell (1949); **Further India** Sir H. Clifford (1905). **The Mystery Rivers of Tibet** F. Kingdon Ward (1923); **The Comparative Geography of Western Asia** J. Rennell (1831); **The Heart of a Continent** F. Younghusband (1896); **The Exploration of the Caucasus** D.W. Freshfield (1868); "Rennell and the Surveyors of India" G.F. Heaney, **Geographical Journal** (September 1968); **Bering's Voyages** ed. F.A. Golder (1922–5); **A History of Russia** B. Pares (1926); **An Historical Geography of Russia** W.H. Parker (1967).

NORTH AMERICA

A History of Geographical Discovery in the 17th and 18th Centuries E.A. Heawood (1912); **The Search for the Western Sea** L.J. Burpee (1908); **In Quest of the Western Ocean** N.M. Crouse (1928); **The First Exploration of the Trans-Allegheny Regions by the Virginians** C.W. Alvord and L. Bidgood (1912); **Early Western Travels** R.G. Thwaites (1904–7); **The Frontier in American History** F.J. Turner (1947); "The Spanish Occupation of Texas 1519–1690" **South-western Historical Quarterly**; **The Eyes of Discovery: The Pageant of N. America as seen by the First Explorers** J. Bakeless (1950); **The Founding of Spanish California** C.E. Chapman (1916); **Mackenzie of Canada** M.S. Wade (1927); **Mackenzie and his Voyageurs** A. Woollacott (1927); **Voyages from Montreal on the River St Lawrence through the Continent of North America to the Frozen and Pacific Oceans in the years 1789 and 1793** A. Mackenzie (1801); **David Thompson's Narrative of his Explorations in Western America** ed. J.B. Tyrrell (1916); **The North-west Passage by Land** W. Fitzwilliam and W.B. Cheadle (1865); **On the Old Athabaska Trail** L.J. Burpee (1926); **Handbook of Polar Discoveries** A.W. Greely (1910); **Canada, a Story of Challenge** J.M.S. Careless (1953); **Narrative of a Journey to the Shores of the Polar Sea in the years 1819–22** J. Franklin (1823); **Narrative of a Second Expedition to the Shores of the Polar Sea in the years 1825–7** J. Franklin (1828); **History of the Expedition under the command of Lewis and Clark** ed. E. Coues (1893); **Economic Beginnings of the Far West** K. Coman (1925); **The Expeditions of Zebulon M. Pike** E. Coues (1895); **Astoria; or, Enterprise beyond the Rocky Mountains** W. Irving (1839); **The Way to the West** E. Hough (1903); **History of the Early Western Fur Trade** H.M. Chittenden (1902); **The Ashley-Smith Explorations and the Discovery of a Central Route to the Pacific** H.C. Dale (1918); **Narrative Journal of Travels from Detroit North-West through the Great Chain of American Lakes to the Sources of the Mississippi River in the year 1820** H.R. Schoolcraft (1821); **Travels in the Central Portions of the Mississippi Valley** H.R. Schoolcraft (1825); **Narrative of an Expedition through the**

Upper Mississippi to Itaska Lake H.R. Schoolcraft (1834); **Memoir of the Life and Public Services of John Charles Frémont** J. Bigelow (1856); **Frémont, the World's Greatest Adventurer** A. Nevins (1928); **Exploration and Survey of the Valley of the Great Salt Lake of Utah** H. Stansbury (1852); **The Canyons of the Colorado** J.W. Powell (1895); **Exploration of the Colorado River of the West** J.W. Powell (1875); **The Penguin Book of the American West** D. Lavender (1965); **The American West** J.A. Hawgood (1967); **Westward Vision: the Story of the Oregon Trail** D. Lavender (1965); **The Far Western Frontier 1830–60** R.A. Billington (1956); **History of the American Frontier 1763–1893** F.L. Paxson (1924); **The California Trail** G.R. Stewart (1964); **Land of Many Frontiers: a History of the American Southwest** O.B. Faulk (1968); **Explorers of the New World** K. and J. Bakeless (1957); **The National Dream, the Great Railway** P. Berton (1971); **Canada, a Modern History** J.B. Brebner (1960); **Canada, a Story of Challenge** J.M.S. Careless (1959); **La Vérendrye, his Life and Times** M. Kavanagh (1967).

SOUTH AMERICA

Personal Narrative of Travels to the Equinoctial Regions of America A. von Humboldt, ed., trans. T. Ross (1851); **Humboldt and the Cosmos** D. Botting (1973); **The Voyage of the "Beagle"** C. Darwin (1906); **Darwin and the "Beagle"** A. Moorehead (1969); **Through the Brazilian Wilderness** T. Roosevelt (1914); **A History of Geographical Discovery in the 17th and 18th Centuries** A. Heawood (1912); **Journal of the Travels and Labours of Father Samuel Fritz in the River of the Amazons between 1686 and 1723** trans. G. Edmundson (1922); **The Naturalist on the Amazons** H.W. Bates (1863); **Henry Walter Bates, Naturalist of the Amazons** G. Woodcock (1969); **Tschiffely's Ride** A.F. Tschiffely (1933); **A Voyage to South America** G.J. and A. Ulloa (1760); **Narrative of Travels on the Amazon and Rio Negro** H.W. Bates (1905); **The Great Naturalists Explore South America** P.R. Cutright (1940); **The Explorers of South America** E.J. Goodman (1972); **Wanderings in South America** T. Waterton (1891); **Unknown Mexico** C. Lumholz (1903).

AFRICA

The Penetration of Africa to 1815 R. Hallett (1965); **Records of the Africa Association** R. Hallett (1964); **The Nile Quest** Sir H. Johnston (1903); **British Central Africa** Sir H. Johnston (1897); **A Short History of Africa** R. Oliver and J.D. Fage (1973); **African Discovery** ed. M. Perham and J. Simmons (1942); **The Travels of Ludovico di Varthema** trans. J.W. Jones, ed. G.P. Badger (1929); **The Niger Explored** E.W. Bovill (1968); **Travels in the Interior Districts of Africa** M. Park (1799); **Narratives of Travels and Discoveries in Northern and Central Africa** H. Clapperton and W. Oudney (1828); **Journal of A Second Expedition into the Interior of Africa** H. Clapperton (1829); **Journal of an Expedition to Explore the Course and Termination of the Niger** R. and J. Lander (1892); **Record of Captain Clapperton's Last Expedition to Africa** R. Lander (1830); **Travels in Western Africa** A. Laing (1825); **The Quest for Timbuctoo** B. Gardner (1968); **Travels and Discoveries in North and Central Africa** H. Barth (1857); **Travels Through Central Africa to Timbuctoo** R. Caillié (1830); **Travels in Nubia** J.L. Burckhardt (1819); **Travel Researches and Missionary Labours during an Eighteen Years' Residence in Eastern Africa** L. Krapf (1860); **The White Nile** A. Moorehead (1960); **The Blue Nile** A. Moorehead (1962); **The Albert N'Yanza, Great Basin of the Nile and Explorations of the Nile Sources** Sir S.W. Baker (1886); **The Nile Tributaries of Abyssinia** Sir S.W. Baker (1867); **The Lake Regions of Central Africa** Sir R. Burton (1860); **The Nile Basin** Sir R. Burton and J. M'Queen (1864); **Ten Years in Equatoria and the Return with Emin Pasha** C. Gaetano, trans. J.R. Clay (1891); **The Exploitation of East Africa, 1856–90** Sir R. Coupland (1939); **A Walk Across Africa** J.A. Grant (1864); **Missionary Travels and Researches in South Africa** D. Livingstone (1857); **Narratives of an Expedition to the Zambesi and Its Tributaries** D. Livingstone (1865); **Last Journals of David Livingstone in Central Africa, from 1865 to his Death** ed. H. Waller (1874); **The Rise of our East African Empire** F.D. Lugard (1893); **Travels to Discover the Source of the Nile** J. Bruce (1964); **History and Description of Africa** L. Africanus, ed. R. Brown (1896); **The Heart of Africa** G. Schweinfurth, trans. E.E. Frewer (1873); **What led to the Discovery of the Source of the Nile** J.H. Speke (1864); **Journal of the Discovery of the Source of the Nile** J.H. Speke (1863); **How I Found Livingstone** H.M. Stanley (1872); **Through the Dark Continent** H.M. Stanley (1878); **In Darkest Africa** H.M. Stanley (1890); **Travels in Africa, 1875–86** W. Junker, trans. A.H. Keane (1890–2); **Morning Star** ed. A. Baker (1972); **Joseph Thomson and the Exploration of Africa** R. Rotberg (1971); **To the Central African Lakes and Back** J. Thomson (1881); **Through Masai Land** J. Thomson (1887); **East and Central Africa to the Late 19th Century** B. Davidson (1962); **East African Explorers** C. Richards and J. Place (1960); **The Missionaries** G. Moorhouse (1973); **The Lunatic Express** C. Miller (1971); **The Man Eaters of Tsavo** J.H. Patterson (1914); **Brazza of the Congo** R. West (1972); **Explorations and Adventures in Equatorial Africa** P. du Chaillu (1861); **The Exploration Diaries of H.M. Stanley** ed. R. Stanley, A. Neame (1961); **George Grenfell and the Congo** Sir H. Johnston (1908); **The African Adventure** T. Severin (1973); **Africa and its Explorers** R. Rotberg (1970); **The Penetration of Arabia** D.G. Hogarth (1922); **Travels in Arabia** J.L. Burckhardt (1829); **Travels in the Arabian Desert** C.M. Doughty (1888); **Narrative of a Year's Journey through Central and Eastern Arabia in 1862–3** W. Palgrave (1865); **A Pilgrimage to Nejd** A.I.N. Blunt (1881); **The Seven Pillars of Wisdom** T.E. Lawrence (1935); **The Heart of Arabia** H.St J.B. Philby (1922); **Arabia Felix** B. Thomas (1932); **Arabian Sands** W. Thesiger (1959); **Description of Arabia** C. Niebuhr, trans. C.W.H. Sealy (1889); **The Fearful Void** G. Moorhouse (1974).

AUSTRALIA

The Discovery and Exploration of Australia E.H.J. Feeken, G.E.E. Feeken and O.H.K. Spate (1970); **The Discovery of Australia** A. Sharp (1963); **A Voyage of Discovery to the Southern Hemisphere . . . 1801–4** M.F. Péron (1809); **A Journal of Discovery across the Blue Mountains, N.S.W. in the year 1813** G. Blaxland; **Australia: History and Horizons** R. Cameron (1971); **Journals of Expeditions of Discovery into Central Australia and overland from Adelaide to King George's Sound** E.J. Eyre (1845); **A Voyage to Terra Australis** M. Flinders (1814); **The Voyage of the "Investigator" 1801–3** K.A. Austin (1958); **Alexander Forrest, His Life and Times** G.C. Boulton (1958); **Explorations in Australia** Sir J. Forrest (1875); **Realms and Islands; the World Voyage of Rose de Freycinet in the Corvette "Uranie", 1817–20** F.M. Bassett (1962); **Australia Twice Traversed: The Romance of Exploration** E. Giles (1889); **Journey of Discovery to Port Phillip, New South Wales, by Messrs W.H. Hovell and Hamilton Hume in 1924 and 1925** ed. W.H. Bland (1965); **Narrative of a Survey of the Intertropical and Western Coasts of Australia Performed Between the Years 1818 and 1822** P.P. King (1827); **The Letters of F.W.L. Leichhardt** ed. M. Aurousseau (1968); **Journal of an Overland Expedition in Australia from Moreton Bay to Port Essington** F.W.L. Leichhardt (1847); **Lachlan Macquarie—Governor of New South Wales—Journals of his Tours in New South Wales and Van Diemen's Land 1810–22** L. Macquarie (1956); **The History of Australian Exploration 1788–1888** E. Favenc (1908); **Three Expeditions into the Interior of Eastern Australia** Sir T.L. Mitchell (1839); **Journal of the Expedition into the Interior of Tropical Australia in search of a route from Sydney to the Gulf of Carpentaria** Sir T.L. Mitchell (1848); **Thomas Mitchell, Surveyor General and Explorer** J.H.L. Compston (1954); **Journals of two Expeditions into the Interior of New South Wales** J.J.W.M. Oxley (1820); **In the Steps of the Explorers** J. Carter (1970); **The Journals of John McDouall Stuart during the years 1858, 1859, 1860, 1861, and 1862** J. McDouall Stuart (1864); **John McDouall Stuart** M.S. Webster (1958); **Two Expeditions into the Interior of Southern Australia** C. Sturt (1833); **Journal of an Expedition into the Interior of Tropical Australia** Sir T.L. Mitchell (1848); **The Story of Australia** A.G.L. Shaw (1965); **Papers and Proceedings of the Royal Society of Tasmania** (1890); **Journal of the Central Australian Exploring Expedition 1889 under Command of W.H. Tietkens** W.H. Tietkens (1891); **Journey Across the Western Interior of Australia** P.E. Warburton (1875); **South Australian Exploration to 1856** G. Williams (1919); **Cooper's Creek** A. Moorehead (1963); **The Burke and Wills Exploring Expedition** (1861); **The Papers and Proceedings of the Royal Society of Tasmania** (1937); **Spinifex and Sand** D.W. Carnegie (1898); **Australian Discovery** ed. E. Scott (1929); **George William Evans, Explorer** G.W. Evans (1966).

ARCTIC

The Norwegian North Polar Expedition 1893–6 ed. F. Nansen (1900–6); **A Chronological History of Voyages in the Arctic Regions** Sir J. Barrow (1818); **Handbook of Polar Discoveries** A.W. Greeley (1910); **The Polar Regions in the 20th Century** A.W. Greeley (1929); **The Polar Regions; a physical and economic geography of the Arctic and Antarctic** R. Brown (1927); **Journal of a Voyage for the Discovery of the North-West Passage** J.H. Parry (1821); **Life of Sir John Franklin and the North-west Passage** Sir A. Markham (1891); **Life of Admiral Sir Leopold McClintock** Sir C. Markham (1909); **Ross's Voyages** Sir C. Markham (1919); **Lands of Silence** Sir C. Markham (1921); **To the Arctic!** J. Mirsky (1949); **The White Road** Sir L. Kirwan (1959); **Voyage of the "Terror"** G. Back (1838); **Sir John Franklin's Last Expedition** R.J. Cyriax (1939); **Schwatka's Search. Sledging in the Arctic in Quest of the Franklin Records** W.H. Gilder (1881); **Arctic Explorations** E.K. Kane (1856); **Farthest North** F. Nansen (1898); **Nearest the Pole** R.E. Peary (1907); **The North Pole** R.E. Peary (1910); **North-West Passage** R. Amundsen (1908); **Great Adventures and Explorations** V. Stefannsson (1947); **Portrait of an Ice-cap with Human Figures** J.M. Scott (1953); **Voyage of the "Vega" round Asia and Europe** N.A.E. Nordenskiöld, trans. A. Leslie (1885); **Maritime History of Russia** M. Mitchell (1949); **The Last of the Arctic Voyages** Sir E. Belcher (1855); "John King Davis and the Northwest Passage", E. Halladay **Geographical Magazine** (ix, 1961–2); **A Chronological History of Voyages in the Arctic Regions** Sir J. Barrow; **Quest for Franklin** N. Wright; **The Search for the North Pole** N.M. Crouse (1947); **The Conquest of the Arctic** L. Segal (1939); **Picture Atlas of the Arctic** R. Thoren (1969).

ANTARCTICA

Journals of Captain James Cook on his Voyages of Discovery Vol II, ed. J.C. Beaglehole (1961); **The Polar Regions in the 20th Century** A.W. Greely (1929); **The Polar Regions; a physical and economic geography of the Arctic and Antarctic** R. Brown (1927); **The White Road** Sir L. Kirwan (1959); **Lands of Silence** Sir C. Markham (1921); **Great Adventures and Explorations** V. Stefannsson (1947); **The Siege of the South Pole** H.R. Mill (1905); **Voyage to the Antarctic Seas** F.G. Bellingshausen (1945); **A Voyage towards the South Pole** J. Weddell (1825); **The Antarctic** H.G.R. King (1969); **Narrative of the U.S. Exploring Expedition, 1838–42** C. Wilkes (1845); **A Voyage of Discovery and Research in the Southern and Antarctic Regions, 1839–43** J.C. Ross (1847); **The Pacific-Russian Scientific Investigations** Academy of Science USSR (1926); **Geographical Journal** No. 16 (1900); **The Voyage of the "Discovery"** R.F. Scott (1905); **Heart of the Antarctic** E. Shackleton (1911); **The South Pole** R. Amundsen (1912); **Scott's Last Expedition** preface Sir C. Markham (1913); **The Worst Journey in the World, Antarctic 1910–13** A. Cherry-Garrard (1922); **The Home of the Blizzard; the story of the Australian Antarctic Expedition, 1911–14** Sir D. Mawson (1915); **South** E. Shackleton (1919); **A Continent for Science** R.S. Lewis (1965); **Antarctic Research—A Review of British Scientific Achievement** ed. Sir R. Priestley (1964); **The Geographical Magazine** (July 1974); **Antarctica** F. Debenham (1959); **Picture Atlas of the Arctic** R. Thoren (1969); **Man and the Conquest of the Poles** P.E-V. Victor (1964);

FINAL FRONTIERS

The World Atlas of Mountaineering W. Noyce and I. McMorrin (1969); **A Book of Modern Mountaineering** M. Milne (1968); **A Century of Mountaineering** Sir A. Lunn (1957); **The Cruise of HMS "Challenger"** W.J.J. Spry (1895); **Founders of Oceanography and their Work** W. Herdman (1923); **Report on the Scientific Results of the Voyage of HMS "Challenger" during the years 1873–6** (1880); **Oceans** G.E.R. Deacon (1968); **Space** P. Moore (1965); **Russians in Space** E. Riabchikov (1972); **History of Rocketry and Space Travel** W. von Braun and F.I. Ordway III (1969).

Index

Prepared by Brenda Hall, M.A., Registered Indexer of the Society of Indexers

A

Abalakov, 262
Abalus, 32
Abbai River, 205
Abd-al Wahhab, 200
'Abdul' Aziz, 200
Abdurrahman en-Nasir, 54
Aberdare Mountains, 214
Abnaki Indians, 103
Aborigines of Australia
adaptation to desert life, 230-1; cave paintings, 220, 227; observations of, relations with explorers, 126, 127, 139, 140, 219, 221, 222-3, 225, 226-7, 228, 231, 232, 233
Abreu, Antonio d', 81, 86
Abruzzi, Duke of, 224, 262
Absaroke Range, 176
Abu Hamed, 33
Abu Simbel temples, 200. 204
Abyssinia see Ethiopia
Academy of Science and Medicine, French, 145, 180
Acapulco, 96, 122, 123-4
Accault, 118
Acesines River, 28, 29
Acevedo, 191
Aconcagua, 262-3
Adahu, 64
Adam of Bremen, 42
Adamawa region, 196-7
Adams, Jameson Boyd, 255
Adams, William, 124
Addax, desert habitat, 203
Adelaide, 219, 231
Adélie Land, 249, 250-1, 260
Aden, 72, 74, 198-9, 200, 202, 206
Adirondack Mountains, 114
Admiralty Hydrographic Department, 221-2, 235
Admiralty Islands, 145
Adriatic Sea, 23
Advance (De Haven), 239
Adventure (Cook), 140, 142-3
Adventure Bay, 145
Aegean Sea, 20, 22, 24, 264
Aeolian (Lipari) Islands, 22
Aelius Gallus, 32, 33
Afghanistan, 43, 149
Afonso V, King of Portugal, 63, 69-70, 72
Africa
ancient cultures, 193; cannibalism in, 207, 212; Chinese links with. 58; Christian missions in, 204, 205, 208, 209, 210, 212, 213; see also *under individual missionaries;* early circumnavigation of, 22-3, 32, 33; Egyptian trade with interior, 21, 23; location of Equator, tropics of Cancer, Capricorn, 193; medieval gold trade, 62, 63, 69; physical realms, 193; Portuguese circumnavigation of, 72-3, 74; Roman expeditions to interior, 33; *stations civilisatrices,* 213; *see also* Africa, East; Africa, North; Africa, South; Africa, South-east; Africa, . South-west; Africa, West; South Africa, Union of
Africa, East
Arab, Chinese trade with, 12; botanical studies in, 207; expeditions to Nile from, 204-7; exploration, 72, 74, 214; railway, 214-15

Africa, North
French expansion in, 196; Roman penetration of, 33
Africa, South
British/Dutch conflict in, 216; Boer settlement, expansion in, 216-17
Africa, South-east
Natives' reception of da Gama, 76
Africa, South-west, missions to, 208
Africa, West
Columbus's voyages to, 83; dangers of coast, 63-4, 70; early maps of, 68, 196-7; native fishing fleets, 64; natives' reception of da Gama, 76
Agadèz, 70, 196
Agena 8, target satellite, 266
Agincourt, Battle of, 60
Aguado, Juan de, 84
Ahimann, H. W., 260
Ahutoru, 131
Aid (Frobisher), 106
Aidhab, 56
Air Mountains, 196-7
Ain (In) Salah, 70, 195
Aircraft, airships, in polar exploration, 245, 246-8, 256, 258, 260
Akbar, 154
Akiaki (Ile des Lanciers), 131
Al Bairouni, 55
Al Hadida, 203
Al Haj Abdullah see Burton
Al Luhayyah, 199
Al Maamoun, 55
Al Maqdisi, 54-5
Al Mas'udi, 55
Al Qatif, 202
Alabama, 18
Alamance, Battle of the, 173
Alan peoples, 54
Alascon, Pedro de, 102
Ala-Shan Desert, 153
Alaska
exploration, 144, 148-9, 169, 170, 235, 237; fur trade, 162, 166-7; Indians of, 164, 165; prehistoric union with Asia, 12, 16, 164, 168; Russian interests in, 162, 166-7; sale to United States, 149, 167; wildlife, 143
Albany (North America), 105, 108
Albany (Australia), 228-9, 230-1
Albemarle, Galápagos Islands, 188
Albuquerque, Afonso d', 58, 80, 81
Alcacovas, Treaty of, 70, 75
Aldan River, 147
Alemquer, Pero de, 75
Aleut peoples, 166
Aleutian Islands, 148-9, 166
Alexander (Parry), 235
Alexander I, Tsar, 249
Alexander VI, pope, 75
Alexander the Great, 13, 26-31, 42-3, 48
Alexander Archipelago, 148-9, 166-7
Alexander I Land, 249, 252, 253
Alexandria (Egypt), 24, 26, 28
Alexandria ad Caucasum, 27
Alexandria Eschate, 29
Alfa Station, 248
Algeria, French expansion in, 196
Algoa Bay, 73, 74
Algonquin Indians, 113, 115, 116, 117
Ali Bey al'Abbasi, 200
Alice Springs, 228-9
Al-Kemal, in Arab navigation, 57
Allahabad, 35

Allouex, Claude Jean, 117
Allumette Island, 115
Almagro, Diego de, 98, 99
Almalik (Kulja), 43
Almanach Perpetuum, Zacuto, 71
Almeida, Francisco de, 75, 80, 81
Almeida, Lourenço de, 80, 81
Almiranta (Quiros), 123, 124
Alps
Australian, 224, 228-9; European, 262-3
Altai Mountains, 152, 185
Altiplano, 99
Alto Acre River, 191-2
Alvarado, Pedro de, 95, 96
Amadi Fatouma, 194
Amazon River, region
exploration, 85, 100-1, 181, 182-5, 190-2; proroca (tidal bore), 101; watershed with Orinoco, 183-4; wildlife, 181, 183
Amazons, 100-1
Amber, trade in, 24, 32
Amboina Island, 81, 124, 145
Amercan Fur Company, 176-7
America, North
exploration, settlement of interior, 85, 101-2, 112-13, 114, 118-21, 162-3, 168, 171-80; land-bridge with Asia, 12, 16, 164, 168; legends surrounding early voyages to, 16-18; migration, distribution of Indian tribes, 94-5, 113, 117; rivalries on Pacific coast, 145, 166-7; 235; Viking voyages to, 39-42; wagon trails, 178-9
America, South
charting of coasts, 79, 92, 180, 186; Christian missions to, 182-5; early circumnavigations of, 86-7, 88-9, 90-1, 104, 124; exploration settlement, 79, 85, 180-5; geological link with Antarctic, 12, 253; impact of Conquistadors, 96-101; migration of Indian tribes, 94; wildlife, 186-90
American War of Independence, 163
Amoy (Zaiton), 50, 51, 53, 54, 56
Amsterdam (Houtman), 126
Amsterdam Company, 115
Amu Dar'ya (Oxus) River, region, 27, 29, 52, 149
Amundsen, Roald, 237, 239, 245, 246-8, 252, 253, 254, 255, 256-7, 261
Amundsen Sea, 143, 250
Amur River, region, 147, 149
An Nafud, 198-9
Anabasis, Xenophone, 26
Anadyr River, region, 146-7, 148
Anamis (Minab) River, 30
Anatolia, 24
Anau Island, 123
Andaman Islands, 50, 51, 53
Anderson, Vernon H., 261
Anderson, William, 144
Andes Mountains, 99-101, 184-5, 188-9
Andrade, Fernao Peres d', 81
Andrave, Father de, 155
Andrée, Salomon August, 245
Andrew, Master, of Bristol, 88
Andrew the Frank, 54
Andronicus, Emperor, 56
Anglican missions
to Africa, 208; to North American Indians, 165
Angmagssalik, Greenland, 38,

248
Angola, 209, 213
Angra do Pequena (Luderitz Bay), 73, 74
Angra dos Rivos, 64
Angra dos Vaqueiros (Cowherd's, Mossel Bay), 73, 76
Anjediva Island, 79
Anopheles mosquito, 196-7
Annapurna Range, 158-9, 262-3
Annedda *(Thuya occidentalis)* 114
Anoatok, Etah, 246
Anson, Admiral Lord, 130
Antarctic
aircraft in exploration of, 256, 258, 260; character, extent of ice-cap, 261; Cook's voyages, 137, 142, 143, 249; exploration of continental land mass, 249, 250-1, 261; geological link with South America, 12, 153; international rivalries, co-operation in, 260-1; overwintering in, 252, 253
Antarctic (Foyn), 252
Antarctic Circle, early crossings of, 249, 250-2
Antarctic Peninsula (Graham Land), 249, 250-1, 252, 253, 254, 260, 261
Antarctic Treaty, 261
Anticosti Island, 113
Antigua, 84
Antilles, 75, 84
Antimony, trade in, 21, 23
Antioch, 34, 35
Antioch, 34, 35
Anza, Juan Bautista de, 163
Aornos (Tashkurgan), 27
Apache Indians, 94, 163, 165
Apalachee Indians, 165
Apalachee Bay, 101, 102
Apollo spacecraft, 15, 266, 267
Apollonia, 265
Appalachian Mountains, 102, 118-19, 172-3
Apsley, 256
Apuré River, region, 193
Aqaba, 198-9
Aqualungs, 265
Arab peoples
influence in East Africa, 12, 76-7; learning, 54-6; revolt against Turks, 202, 203; ships, 66, 74; trade with Malabar Coast, 12, 49, 51, 52-3, 58, 72, 78
Arabia, 24, 28, 32, 33, 56, 198-203
Arabia Felix (Yemen), 198-9
Arabian Sands, Thesiger, 203
Arabian Sea, 28, 29
Aradus (Ruad), 22
Arachosia, 29, 30
Arafura Sea, 126, 127
Arago, Jacques, 221
Araguaia River, region, 190, 192
Arakan, 80
Aral Sea, 29, 52, 55, 149, 150-1
Arapaho Indians, 95
Aras (Araxes) River, region, 26, 29
Arawak peoples, 83-4
Arbuthnot Range, 224
Archaeology, undersea, 265
Archangel, 109
Archer, Colin, 242
Archipelago de las Perlas, 93
Arctic
Barents's map of, 111; international rivalries in, 235, 238; mythical continent, 111; Pytheas' voyages, 31-2; *see also*

Arctic Circle; Arctic Ocean; North Pole; Northeast Passage; Northwest Passage
Arctic Circle
delimited, 237, 247; early voyages into, 103, 105, 109, 144, 148; exploration in Canada, 171; voyage of *Nautilus,* 245, 248, 264; *see also* Northeast Passage; Northwest Passage
Arctic Ocean, currents, 242-3, 247
Arctic Pilot, 107, 110
Argentina
activity in Antarctic, 260-1; exploration, 180, 181, 190
Arghai, moutain sheep, 46, 47, 48, 153
Arghun, Ilkhan, 50
Arguin Island, 66, 70
Arikara Indians, 168, 176
Aristolochia, 182
Aristotle, 26, 30, 82
Arizona
Indians of, 164, 165; Spanish exploration, settlement, 102, 162, 164
Arkansas Indians, 118
Arkansas River, region, 102, 116, 117, 118, 175, 178
Armada, Spanish, 107, 124
Armaments, ships', 75
Armenia, 26, 43
Armitage, Lieutenant, 253
Armijo, Antonio, 178
Armilla tolemei, 104
Armstrong, Neil, 266, 267
Arnhem Bay, 219, 221
Arnhem Land, 126, 127, 129
Arrian, 28
Artaxerxes II, King of Persia, 24-6
Arthurian legends, 18
Aru Islands, 127
Arun Islands, 127
Ashley, William Henry, 177
Asia
ancient Roman voyages to, 33; caravan routes, 42, 55, 154; climate, vegetation, 150-1, 152, 153-4, 155-6; Cossack exploration of, 146-8; extreme eastern point, 148-9; landbridge with North America, 12, 16, 64, 168; mapping of, 159-60, 161; *see also* Asia, Central; Asia, South-east
Asia, Central
Alexander the Great's campaigns, 26-9; Mongol domination of, 43; spread of Islam, 54; trade routes, 42, 55, 154
Asia Minor, domination by Greeks, 23, 24
Asia, Southeast
acquisition of Portuguese Empire in, 80, 81; Dutch commercial interests, 126, 216; *see also individual islands*
Assam, 35
Assiniboine Indians, 164, 168
Assiniboine River, region, 168, 170
Association for Promoting the Discovery of the Interior Parts of Africa, 192, 194, 196-7, 200
Assyria, 22
Astin Tagh range, 154
Astor, John Jacob, 176-7
Astrolabe (D'Urville), 249, 250
Astrolabes, 55, 57, 77, 88, 104
Astronomy, Science of, Arab contribution to, 54-6, 57
Astrup, Eirund, 244
Aswan, 56, 204, 205

Ata Muhammad (the ''Mullah''), 160
Atabapo River, 184
Atacama Desert, 99
Atahualpa, 97, 98
Athabaska River, region, 170, 171
Athabaskan Indians 171
Atherton Tableland, 231
Atlantic Ocean
concept of Green Sea of Darkness, 16, 55; dangers off West Africa, 63-4, 70; search for strait linking with Pacific 96; undersea rift valley, 264-5; undersea telegraph, 264; winds, currents, 16, 56, 83
Atlantis, legends of, 192
Atlas Mountains, 32-3, 56, 214
Atlassov, Vladimir, 147, 148
Attock, 27, 29
Atures Cataract, Orinoco River, 183
Augustine, St, padroe named after, 71
Augustus, Emperor, 33
Auk, great, 143
Aurora (Mawson), 257-8
Australia
activity in Antarctic, 260-1; concept of inland sea, 225; concept of southern continent, 122-5; early landfalls, exploration, 125-9, 139-40, 218-21; exploration of interior, 13, 222-35; exploration of west, 130, 227; overland telegraph, 232, 233, 234; physical regions, characteristics, 222-3; sheep farming in, 227; wildlife, 143; *see also* Aborigines
Australia Felix, 227
Australia Twice Traversed, Giles, 233
Australian Alps, 224, 228-9
Austrialia del Espiritu Santo, 132, 140, 143
Austürhorn, 38, 42
Avacha Bay, 148, 149
Aveiro, Joao Afonso de, 72
Avienus, *Ora Maritima,* 23
Avila, Pedro Arias de, 93
Axayacatl Palace, 96
Axel Heiberg Glacier, 256
Axel Heiberg Island, 246
Axim, 196-7
Axum, 204
Ayas, 48
Ayer's Rock, 228-9, 234
Ayon Island, 241
Azara, Felix de, 181, 182
Azenegues, 64
Azores, 18, 63, 64, 84
Aztec Empire, 12, 93-6
Azurara, Gomez Eannes de, 62, 66, 69

278

282

Mount Hecla, 108
Mount Hope, 255
Mount Hopeless, 230, 232
Mount Kailas, 156
Mount Kenya, 204, 205, 214-15, 262-3
Mount Kilimanjaro, 204, 205, 214-15, 262-3
Mount Lofty Range, 226
Mount Logan, 262-3
Mount McKinley, 262-3
Mount Margaret Station, 232
Mount Markham, 257
Mount Olga, 233
Mount Raleigh, 107
Mount Sabine, 252
Mount Sarmiento, 188
Mount Shasta, 177
Mount Sinai, 198-9
Mount Terror, 252, 253
Mount Theches, 26
Mount York, 222
Mountain men, 176-8
Mountain sickness, 184, 185
Mountainous areas, mountains distribution, 193, 222-3, 262-3; history of exploration, 13, 262-3; *see also individual peaks ranges*
Moyano, Carlos, 191
Moyle, Le, Father, 116
Muchinga Mountains, 210
Mukalla, Hadhramaut, 202
Müller, 196
Multan, 56
Mumps, among North American Indians, 164
Murano, Fra, 72
Murat Bay, 221
Muraviev, Count N., 149
Murchison, Sir Roderick, 206
Murchison Falls, 204, 207
Murchison River, 233
Murex brandaris, source of Tyrian purple, 22-3, 24-5
Murman Coast, 110
Murmansk, 241
Murray, Mungo, 208
Murray, Sir George, 225
Murray Glacier, 252
Murray River, 224, 225-6, 227, 228-9, 231
Murrumbidgee River, region, 224, 225, 226, 227, 228-9
Muscat, 198-9, 202
Muscovy, 61, 146
Muscovy Company, 108, 109-10
Mussolini, Benito, 248
Mustagh-ata, 160
Musters, George Chatworth, 191
Mutesa, King of Buganda, 206
Mutinies, on voyages of exploration, 82, 88, 90, 108, 118, 123
Mutis, Father, 180-2, 184
Mylius-Erichsen Expedition, 248
Mylodon darwinii, 186
Myrrh, trade in, 21, 23
Mys Shmidta (Cape Irkaipij), 241
Mys Zelanija (Cape Mauritius), 110
"Mystery and Company of Merchant Venturers for the discovery of Regions, Dominions, Islands and places unkown" *see* Muscovy Company
Mythology, and exploration, 16-19

Nachtigal, Gustav, 198, 213
Naddod (Viking), 38
Nafud Desert, 202-3
Nagara (Nagarahara), 35
Nagurski, I., 246
Nai, Cornelis, 110
Nain Singh, 159-60
Namaqualand, 217
Namoi River, 224, 226
Nan Shan Mountains, 34, 154, 161
Nandi people, 214
Nanga Parbat, 262-3
Nanking, 53, 58-9, 150-1
Nansen, Fridtjof, 242-3, 247
Naos see Carracks
Napata, 33
Napo River, 99-100
Napoleon, 205, 220
Napoloen III, 202
Naqab al Hajar, 202
Nares, George, 244
Narrative of Travels and Discoveries in Northern and Central Africa, Denham, 194
Narvaez, Panfilo de, 95, 96, 101, 102
Nashville (French Lick), 172
Nasrulla, Emir, 149
Nassau Bay, 250
Nassau Strait (Yugorskiy Shar), 110
Natal, 74, 76, 216
Natchez Indians, 117, 165
National African Company, 214
National Antarctic Expeditions, 253
Natterer, Johann, 181, 190
Naturalist on the River Amazon, The, Wallace, 191
Naturaliste (Baudin), 220-1
Naucratis *see* Alexandria
Nautilus (United States Navy submarine), 245, 264
Nautilus (Wilkins), 248
Navajo Indians, 165
Navigation aids, techniques, 36-7, 57, 65, 69, 70, 73, 74, 75, 77, 82, 88, 103, 104, 106, 108, 118, 130, 132-3, 134, 136, 137, 138
Navigator's Islands, 145
Nearchus, 28-30
Nebraska, 174
Necho, Pharaoh, 21
Necho II, Pharaoh, 22
Nee, 182
Needham, Joseph, 58
Negro River, region, 1001-1, 180, 181, 184, 190, 191
Nejd, 198-9, 202-3
Nelson, Horatio, Lord, 235
Nelson River, 108, 120-1
Nepal, 156, 157
Nepean River, region, 222, 223
Nero, Emperor, 33
Netherlands
party to Antarctic Treaty, 261; war of independence, 124-5; *see also* Dutch, The
Nevada, 178
New, 214
New Albion *see* California
New Amsterdam, 108, 119
New Britain, 125, 126-7, 133
New Caledonia, 122, 145
New England, 120
New France *see* Canada; America, North
New Guinea, 122-4, 126-7, 129, 133, 136, 140
New Hampshire, 119
New Hebrides, 122, 123, 132, 137, 143
New Ireland, 126-7, 129

New Mexico, 102, 162, 164, 165
New Orleans, 162
New Siberian Islands, 240, 241, 247
New South Wales, 139
New York, 108, 162; *see also* Hudson River
New Zealand
activity in Antarctic, 260-1; Cook's visits, 136, 137, 138-9, 142, 144; Darwin's visit, 189; early Dutch voyages to, 126-7, 128-9, 130; scientific observations of wildlife, 143; *see also* Maori peoples
Newcastle Waters, 228-9, 232
Newfoundland
Beothuk Indians of, 103; early voyages to, 103, 105, 113, 114; fisheries, 112; Viking settlements, 42
Newnes, George, 252
Newnes Glacier, 252
Nez Percé Pass, 175
Ngawang Lohzang Gyatso, 156
Ng-nari Giongar Desert, 156
Niagara Falls, 116, 118
Niagara River, 116, 117
Niam-Niam people, 207
Nicobar Islands, 50, 51, 53
Nicolet, Jean, 116, 117
Nicusea, Diego de, 92
Niebuhr, Carsten, 199-200
Niger River, region, 55, 56, 63, 70, 192-8, 200, 212, 214
Nijni-Novgorod, 152
Nile River, region
Alexander the Great's view of, 28; ancient canal link with Red sea, 22; Canopic, 24; confluence of Blue, White, 204, 205; exploration, 26, 33, 56, 198-9, 200, 204-7, 209-12; importance to Ancient Egypt, 20-1
Nimrod (Shackleton), 254-5
Nina (Columbus), 82-3, 83-4, 103
Nineveh, 26, 29
Ninnis, B. E. S., 257-8
Nipissing Indians, 117
Niti Pass, 157
Niza, Marco de, 102
Nobel, Alfred, 245
Nobile, Umberto, 245, 246-8
Nolde, Edward, 203
Noli, Antonio da, 70
Nomi-Mansa, 69
Noort, Olivier van, 124-5
Nootka, Nootka Sound, 143, 144, 169
Nootka Convention, 169
Nordauslandet, 246
Nordenskiöld, Nils Adolf Eric, 239-41, 250-1, 253, 258
Nordenskjöld, Otto, 250-1, 253, 258
Nordquist, O., 239
Norfolk (Flinders), 218-19
Norfolk Island, 137, 143, 218
"Norge" (airship), 245, 246-8
Norsemen *see* Vikings
North Carolina, 85, 173
North Pole, search for, 15, 235, 237, 238, 239-41, 242-8, 252, 264; *see also* Magnetic Poles
North Sea, 37, 56, 110, 124
North Star (Davis), 107
North West Company of Montreal, 171, 174, 176
Northeast Passage, search for, 13, 103, 109-11, 112, 239-41
Northern Frigid Zone, 62
Northern Temperate Zone, 62
Northumbria (Esso Tanker), 90-1
Northwest Cape, 129
Northwest Passage, search for, 13, 103-8, 112, 119-20, 136, 143-4, 235-9
Norton Sound, 167

Norway
acquisition of Greenland, 39; activity in Antarctic, 260; support for Arctic exploration, 242, 245
Norwegian - British - Swedish Antarctic Expedition, 260
Novolazarevskaya Base, 261
Nova Scotia, 103, 105, 115
Novaya Zemlya, 109, 110, 240, 247
Novgorod, 36, 37, 61
Nubia, 33, 72, 205
Nubian Desert, 198-9, 200, 205
Nullarbor Plain, 222-3, 228-9, 230
Nundawar Range, 226
Nuristan (Kafiristan), 27, 149, 160
Nushki, 149
Nutmeg, trade in, 78, 80, 81
Nuyts, Pieter, 126-7, 128, 219
Nuyts Archipelago, 126-7, 219
Nyangwe, 210-11, 212
Niam-Niam people, 207

O'Sullivan, John L., 179
Oakover River, 228-9, 234
Oates, Lawrence, 256, 257
Oates Land, 250, 257, 260
Oaxaca, 96
Ob (Somor), 260-1
Ob River, region, 152, 240
Oberth, Hermann, 266
Obsidian, trade in, 22, 24
Octants, 106, 132-3
Odoric of Pordenone, 51-4
Ogadei, 43, 44
Ogané, king in West Africa, 72
Ogden, Peter Skene, 177-8
Ogowe River, region, 210-11, 213
Ohio River, 117, 172, 173
Ojeda, Alonzo de, 85, 92
Ojibwa Indians, 117
Okhotsk, 148-9
Oklahoma, 102
Oleg, prince in Kiev, 36
Olekma River, region, 147
Olenek River, region, 148
Olid, Cristobal de, 96
Olive oil, trade in, 24
Oman, 202
Omsk, 150-1
Oneida Indians, 115
Ontario, fur trading in, 168
Ophir, 22
Ora Maritima, Avienus, 23
Orange Islands, 110
Orange Free State, 217
Orange River, region, 216, 217
Ordos Desert, 154, 157, 161
Oregon, 144, 169, 170, 174-5, 178-9
Oregon Trail, 178-9
Orellana, Francisco de, 99-101
Origin of Species, Darwin, 185, 189, 190
Orinoco River, region
Columbus's expedition to, 84, 85; exploration, 181, 182-4, 190; source, 191; watershed with Amazon, 183-4
Orkney Islands, 38
Ornen (balloon), 245
Ortiz, Diogo, 72, 75
Orton, 191
Osage Indians, 95
Oscar, King of Norway, 242, 245
Oscar II Coast, 252
Oseberg Viking Ship, 38-9
Ostrova DeLonga (De Long Island), 242, 247
Ostrov Vrangelya (Wrangel Island), 240, 241
Oswego River, 116
Oswell, William, 208-9
Otaheite *see* Tahiti
Ottawa, 113
Ottawa Indians, 113, 117
Ottawa River, 113, 115, 116, 117
Otters (sea, inland), demand for pelts, 120, 144, 166, 167, 169
Ottoman Empire, 60-1
Ouadah, 196-7, 198
Oudney, Walter, 194, 196-7
Ovens, Major, 224, 228-9
Ovens River, 224
Overweg, Adolf, 196
Owens Valley, 177
Owzin, 146-7
Oxford University Arctic Expedition, 246
Oxley, John, 223-4, 225, 226, 227, 228-9
Oxus (Amu-Dar'ya) River, region, 27, 29, 151, 154, 160
Ozark Mountains, 102

Paccard, Michel, 263
Pacheco, Duarte, 73
Pacific Ocean
charting of south, 249; Drake's voyages in, 90-1; early Spanish enterprise in, 122-4; major exploration, 130-45; Russian exploration of north, 166-7; scale, characteristics of, 136-7; search for passage to, across Canada, 115, 116, 121; search for trail linking with Atlantic, 96; sighting, by Balboa's expedition, 92-3; winds, currents, 88-9, 122
Padroes, erection, 9, 65, 71, 73, 76, 79
Paesi novamente retrovati, 58
Paez, Pedro, 204
Paiute Indians, 94
Paiva, Afonso de, 72-3
Palander, Lieutenant, 239, 241
Palao Archipelago, 91
Palgrave, William, 202
Palinurus (survey ship), 201-2
Palmer, Nathaniel, 249
Palmer Archipelago, 252, 254, 256
Palmyra (Tadmur), 35, 200
Palo de Vaca (cow tree), 182
Palos, 82, *83*
Palomar, Telescope at, 266
Pamir mountain sheep, *see* Arghai
Pamir Mountains, Plateau, 34, 48, 52, 154-5, 160-1, 262-3
Pamlico Sound, 119
Panama, 92
Parramatta, Sydney, 222, 226
Panda, giant, 154-5
Pandora's Pass, 224
Panjim *see* Goa
Panjshir Valley, 27
Panuco River, 102
Papacy, Support for exploration, 43-4, 64, 68-9, 75, 79
Paraguay River, region, 182, 190-1
Parah, 29
Parallactic ruler, 55
Paramos areas, 184
Parana River, region, 181, 182
Paranatinga River, 192
Paris, Treaty of, **1763,** 163, 170
Park, Mungo, 192-4, 195, 196-7, 200
Park, Thomas, 194
Parkinson, Sydney, 134, 138, 139, 142-3
Paropamisus Mountains, 151
Parrots, trade in, *86*
Parry, Edward, 108, 235-7, 238, 252
Parsnip River, region, 171
Parthia *see* Persia
Pasitigris River, 30
Pasni, Baluchistan, 30
Pastaza River, region, 180
Patagonia
expeditions to interior, 187-8, 190, 191; exploration of coasts, 91, 180, 186, 187; guanaco of, 181; people, 130, 188; prehistoric creatures of, 186, 187
Patala, 28
Pataliputra (Patna), 35
Pathfinder ("Pathfollower"), 179
Patrick, St, 16
Paulet Island, 258
Pavon, 182
Pawnee Indians, 95
Pax Mongolica, 45
Payer, Julius, 240, 244
Peace River, region, 170, 171
Peacock (Wilkes), 250

Acknowledgments

Photographers, artists and agencies whose work appears in the book are listed as it appears on each page, in descending order left to right

1 Bodleian Library, Pictor, Pictor
2/3 Bodleian Library, Picturepoint, Spectrum, Scala, Hans Dossenbach, Daily Telegraph Colour Library
4/5 Spectrum, Western History Department, Denver Public Library, Popperfoto, By permission of the Royal Geographical Society, British Petroleum Co Ltd.
6/7 Pictor, Michael Holford, Picturepoint, Spectrum, Devon Commercial Photos, Picturepoint
8/9 Pictor
14/15 Loren McIntyre, Spectrum
18/19 Popperfoto, Minnesota Historical Society
20 Michael Holford
23 Werner Forman
25 C. M. Dixon, Clive Bubley
26 Barnabys
28 Mansell Collection/Alinari
30 Scala
33 Spink & Son
39 Knudsens Fotosenter
40/41 Royal Library of Copenhagen, Michael Holford
42/43 Picturepoint, Picturepoint, British Library Board
44 Pictor
47 Copyright of the Zoological Society of London
49 All Bodleian Library
52/53 Pictor, Bernard Hermann, John Hillelson Agency, Robert Harding Associates
55 Topkapi Museum
61 Scala
62 Mansell Collection
64 George Gerster/John Hillelson Agency
68 Mauro Pucciarelli
71 All John Gardey/Robert Harding Associates
72/73 Scala, Tony Stone Associates
75 Mark Edwards
78/79 Mark Edwards, Academia das Ciencias
80/81 Mauro Pucciarelli, Michael Holford
82 Picturepoint
88/89 Michael Holford, Scala, Cooper Bridgeman
92/93 Werner Forman, Ron Boardman
94 Mauro Pucciarelli, Spectrum, Pictor
96/97 Pictor, Loren McIntyre, Loren McIntyre
100/101 Picturepoint, Picturepoint, Douglas Botting, Picturepoint
102/103 Spectrum, Popperfoto
104 A. C. Waltham, Trustees of the British Museum
110 Nederlandsch Historisch Scheepvaart Museum
112 Mauro Pucciarelli, Robert Estall
114 Both Public Archives of Canada
116 Picturepoint, Canada Wide
118 Nederlandsch Historisch Scheepvaart Museum
120/121 Bruce Coleman, Canada Wide, Jen & Des Bartlett/Bruce Coleman, L. Lee Rue/Bruce Coleman, J. Van Wormer/Bruce Coleman
123 Michael Holford
124 Both Mansell Collection
126 Rex Nan Kivell collection in the National Library of Australia
130 National Portrait Gallery
132/133 All Michael Holford

136 Rex Nan Kivell collection in the National Library of Australia, Michael Holford
138 Australian Information Service
140 From the collection of the National Library of Australia
142/143 Michael Holford, Michael Holford, Michael Holford, National Publicity Studios of New Zealand, Michael Holford, Michael Holford, Michael Holford, Michael Holford, Ardea
145 Michael Holford
146 Douglas Botting
150/151 Bibliotheque Nationale, Douglas Botting, Douglas Botting
153 All Mansell Collection
159 Robert Harding Associates
161 Werner Forman
163 Spectrum, Pictor
164 Pictor, Popperfoto, British Columbia Government
166/167 Geoffrey Kinns/A.F.A., Fred Bruemmer, Jeff Foot/Bruce Coleman, Moira Burland/Bruce Coleman
169 By permission of the Royal Geographical Society
170 J. Kraulis/Canada Wide
172 Mansell Collection
174/175 Independence National Historical Park Collection Philadelphia, Mansell Collection
176 Mansell Collection
179 Western History Department, Denver Public Library
181 Both Francisco Erize
183 Douglas Botting
185 Popperfoto, Institut für Film und Bild
186 Popperfoto
189 Heather Angel, Adrian Warren/Ardea, Heather Angel
191 Popperfoto
192/193 Michael Freeman/Bruce Coleman, Pictor, Michael Holford, Picturepoint
194/195 Mansell Collection, Mansell Collection, Picturepoint
196/197 Picturepoint, National Portrait Gallery, By permission of the Royal Geographical Society
198 Mansell Collection
201 Anthony Howarth/Susan Griggs
203 P. Morris/Ardea
204/205 Barnabys, Picturepoint, Pictor, Michael Holford
208 Michael Holford
210/211 Popperfoto, Mansell Collection, Mansell Collection, Popperfoto
213 Hans Dossenbach
215 R. Campbell/Bruce Coleman, Picturepoint, Picturepoint, East African Railways
216/217 Mansell Collection, Hans Dossenbach, Popperfoto, Popperfoto
219 Mansell Collection, Australian Information Service
220 Picturepoint
222/223 Barnabys, Australian Information Service, Picturepoint, Australian Information Service, Picturepoint
226/227 Both Australian Information Service
228 National Portrait Gallery, Mansell Collection, Australian Information Service, Australian Information Service
230 S & K Breeden, Norman Chaffer, Australian Information Service, Bruce Coleman,

Australian Information Service, Australian Information Service
236 Scott Polar Institute
239 Charles Swithinbank
242/243 All Scott Polar Institute
250 By Permission of the Royal Geographical Society
253 Popperfoto
254 By Permission of the Royal Geographical Society
255 Scott Polar Institute, Scott Polar Institute, Popperfoto
259 Picturepoint
265 Both Michael Holford
266/267 Mary Evans, NASA, NASA
269 Novosti
270/271 James Tallon/NHPA, Douglas Botting
272/273 Barnabys, Picturepoint

Artists' Credits

17 Rodney Shackell (ACA)
25 Harold King
29 Studio Briggs Limited
32 Gerry Embleton (Linden Artists)
34 Norman Barber (Linden Artists)
36 Harold King
38/39 Harold King
49 Hussein Abo
50/51 Phil Green
56/57 Maurice Pledger, Melvin Raymond, Gerry Embleton (Linden Artists)
58/59 Harold King
63 Jill Platt
65 Gerry Embleton (Linden Artists) Rodney Shackell (ACA)
66 Brian and Constance Dear
67 Hussein Abo, Brian and Constance Dear
74 Jill Platt
77 Harold King, Gerry Embleton (Linden Artists)
80 Jill Platt
82/83 Brian and Constance Dear, Jill Platt
84 Gerry Embleton, Andrew Farmer
91 Brian and Constance Dear
99 Advent Graphics
106 Gerry Embleton
128 Advent Graphics
135 Harold King
140 David Watson
141 Hussein Abo
144 Harold King
149 Norman Barber
155 Richard Orr (Linden Artists)
179 John Thompson
183 Edward Wade, Charles Pickard
187 Charles Pickard
194/215 David Watson
233 Arka Graphics
242/243 David Watson
244/258 P. Endsleigh Castle
262/3 Sidney Woods
Black and White Retouching: D. N. Trevellyan, Michael Mann Studio and Studio Briggs Limited